W9-CAR-504

Numerical Methods with Fortran IV Case Studies

Numerical Methods with Fortran IV Case Studies

William S. Dorn
Daniel D. McCracken

John Wiley & Sons, Inc.
New York · London · Sydney · Toronto

Library of Congress Catalogue Card Number: 77-37365

ISBN 0-471-21918-5

Printed in the United States of America.

10 9 8 7 6 5 4 3 2 1

Preface

This textbook provides the student in engineering or science with a basic understanding of the numerical solution of problems on a modern electronic digital computer.

The emphasis is on carefully selected and highly practical methods for handling a variety of numerical problems encountered in modern computing. The methods presented here are not only of value in themselves but they also provide the student with insight into more sophisticated methods and prepare him to fully understand them. Just as a physicist finds it useful to have an intuitive grasp of the meaning of inertia before he can fully understand mechanics, so the user of a computer will find it beneficial to study numerical *methods* before he tackles numerical *analysis.* Our goal has thus been twofold: to provide tools for useful computation and to lay the groundwork for further study.

We assume that the reader either already knows the elements of Fortran programming or that he is learning them concurrently from other materials. Since most students in engineering or science today learn programming as freshmen or in high school, it seems unnecessary to include expository material on Fortran in a book on numerical methods. However, the programs in the case studies are all explained thoroughly, and the pace moves slowly in the early case studies to allow for a review of Fortran programming or for concurrent study. All of the programs have been run on a computer, and actual output is displayed for all programs.

The presentation in most of the chapters begins with an appeal to geometrical intuition to motivate the student's understanding. We then prove the central results analytically, and finally make the ideas concrete by applying them first to simple numerical examples and then to relatively more complex case studies. This approach, we believe, is the route to most rapid and thorough learning.

The selection of topics has been made after careful consideration of the needs of students for practical methods, the suitability of various methods for use on a computer, and the experience of students and instructors with our earlier book *Numerical Methods and FORTRAN Programming* (Wiley, 1964). Some of the topics in our earlier book that were found to be of limited interest have been deleted, and considerable new material has been added. In the present book we have increased emphasis on the practical problems caused by the finite precision of the computer representation of numbers, combined with roundoff errors, and the fact that—to the astonishment of many students—neither the associative law nor the distributive law is valid in computer arithmetic. These limitations are emphasized throughout, but especially in Chapter 3, which consists of four case studies demonstrating some of the problems and their solutions. Most of the material in Chapter 3 has received only limited dissemination prior to its appearance here.

The evolution of large computer storages, permitting economical storage of large quantities of data, has led to a renewed interest in interpolation. Treatment of this subject has accordingly been included in this book, although it did not appear in our 1964 text. At the same time, the condensed representation of information provided by least squares approximations is also now widely used, and has been given more thorough coverage than in our earlier book. Finally we note that although Fortran II was used in the earlier book, here we use Fortran IV (as specified by The American National Standards Institute).

In order to include this additional material on numerical instabilities, interpolation, least squares, and numerical differentiation, we have eliminated some of the topics that appeared in the earlier book. Specifically, Chebyshev polynomials, economization of powers series, rational approximations, and partial differential equations are not included here.

The sequence of study of topics is at the discretion of the student or instructor to a remarkable degree. Chapter 2 on errors needs to be studied before the succeeding chapters, but otherwise there is no implied sequence in the treatment. The choice can therefore be made on the grounds of interest, need, or convenience.

There are nearly 300 exercises, with answers to many of them at the end of the book. Some apply the techniques developed in the text to numerical examples; a number ask the student to prove or extend results in the text; many call for writing programs to apply the numerical methods presented in the text to practical situations. In the early chapters, in particular, there is a wide range of exercises requiring the writing of fairly extensive programs suitable for assignment as small term problems. Fewer exercises of this type have been included in later chapters, on the assumption that by that time students will ordinarily be working on problems related to their other courses.

It is a pleasure to acknowledge the contribution made by those who assisted us in the preparation of this book. Besides all the people mentioned in our earlier book, we wish to thank Mrs. Susan Jaedecke of the University of Denver, who checked most of the manuscript and provided other valuable assistance; Dean John A. Weese of the University of Denver, for suggesting a number of the case studies and exercises and for helping in their formulation and solution; Dean Ernest J. Henley of the University of Houston, also for suggesting a case study and a number of exercises; and Professor L. P. Huelsman of the University of Arizona, Professor Gene E. Smith of the University of Michigan, and Professor Jack Cohen of the University of Denver, all of whom suggested a number of exercises. Mrs. Phyllis Dennen typed the manuscript and assisted in many other important ways.

We especially wish to express our appreciation to Miss Carol Shanesy for her participation in the early stages of planning of this book, at a time when it was intended that she be a co-author. Changed circumstances on the part of the present authors altered that plan, and we regret not having had the opportunity to work with her.

We also gratefully acknowledge the assistance and cooperation of the following organizations that assisted in the running of programs presented or discussed in the book, and some of their personnel: Burroughs Corporation, Harold Atkins and Alan Steger; Computing Power Unlimited, Donald K. Williams; Control Data Corporation, Layton G. Kinney and Daniel B. Thalimer; McDonnell Douglas Automation, Ronald R. Rice; National CSS, Inc., Mrs. Ursula Connor and Douglas B. Kuhn; University of Nebraska, Omaha, Charles J. Gibbons and Jerry L. Ray.

Denver, Colorado   **William S. Dorn**
Ossining, New York   **Daniel D. McCracken**
January, 1972

Contents

Numerical Methods with Fortran IV Case Studies

1 Solution of Equations

We begin our study of numerical methods with the problem of finding a root of an equation. Given some equation, for example,

$$x \sin x + (x^2 + 4)\, e^x = \cos x$$

we say that x_0 is a *root* of this equation if

$$x_0 \sin x_0 + (x_0^2 + 4)\, e^{x_0} = \cos x_0$$

In more general terms, given the equation

$$F(x) = 0 \tag{1.1}$$

we say x_0 is a root of this equation if, when we replace x by the value x_0, the equation is true.

The simplest example is the linear equation

$$ax + b = 0$$

where a and b are given constants and $a \neq 0$. Then

$$x_0 = -b/a$$

is a root of this equation and the only root. The next most simple example is a quadratic equation

$$ax^2 + bx + c = 0$$

where again a, b, and c are given and $a \neq 0$. Then there are two roots

1

$$x_0 = \frac{-b + \sqrt{b^2 - 4ac}}{2a}$$

and

$$x_0 = \frac{-b - \sqrt{b^2 - 4ac}}{2a}$$

Of course, if $b^2 = 4ac$, then these two roots are identical.

For an arbitrary equation of the form given by (1.1), there may or may not be a root. If there is a root, there may be several. Generally we shall be concerned only with real roots. (The quadratic equation has no real roots if $b^2 < 4ac$.)

At any event, we ordinarily find it necessary to content ourselves with finding an *approximate root*. This is true even for the quadratic equation, since, unless $b^2 - 4ac$ is a perfect square, we cannot calculate the square root of $b^2 - 4ac$ exactly.

Therefore, it is necessary to discuss what we mean by an "approximate root" before we start to calculate one. In rough terms when we say "approximate root" we mean some value of x "near" a root. Now, if x_0 is a root of (1.1), then the graph of $F(x)$ crosses the x-axis at $x = x_0$ (see Figure 1.1). One way to define an approximate root, therefore, is to say it is some number $\bar{x}$ such that $|\bar{x} - x_0|$ is small where $F(x_0) = 0$. Another way is to say that an approximate root of $F(x) = 0$ is some number $\bar{x}$ such that $|F(\bar{x})|$ is small. That these two definitions of an approximate root are not equivalent is exhibited by Figure 1.2. In Figure 1.2a the value of $|\bar{x} - x_0|$ is indeed small, but $|F(\bar{x})|$ is not small. On the other hand, in Figure 1.2b, $|F(\bar{x})|$ is small, but $|\bar{x} - x_0|$ is not. Reflection will reveal that the first definition ($|\bar{x} - x_0|$ small) is not very satisfactory if the graph of $F(x)$ is "steep" near $x = x_0$. Similarly, the second definition is not really acceptable if the graph is "flat" near $x = x_0$.

In general we would like *both*

(i) that $|\bar{x} - x_0|$ be small where $F(x_0) = 0$ and
(ii) that $|F(\bar{x})|$ be small.

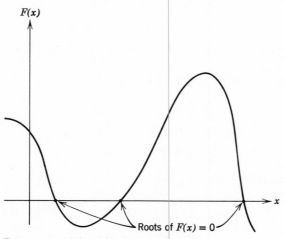

Figure 1.1. *The roots of an equation.*

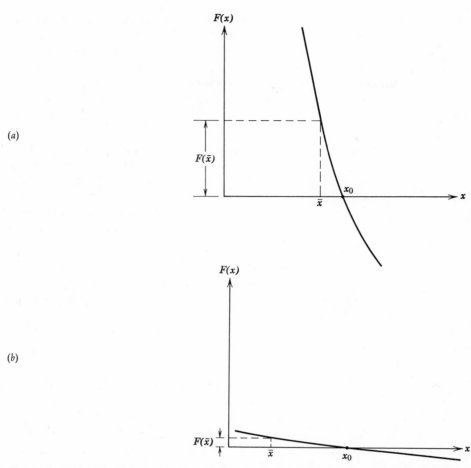

Figure 1.2. (a) An "approximate root" ($\overline{x}$) that is close to the exact root although $F(\overline{x})$ is not small. (b) An "approximate root" that is not close to the exact root although $F(\overline{x})$ is small.

We should realize, however, that it may not be possible to have both requirements satisfied simultaneously.

The algorithms that we shall develop will usually be aimed at satisfying *one* of these criteria. Clearly we must be aware of which of the criteria each algorithm uses. We must then choose an algorithm that satisfies a criterion commensurate with the aims of the particular problem at hand. Case Study 1, in the next section, uses criterion (i) above; at the end of the chapter we return to the question of choosing the criterion in Case Study 2.

1.2
Case Study 1: Finding Roots by Interval Halving

We begin our study of ways for finding roots of equations with a case study. As in all case studies in the book, a practical method for solving the numerical problem at hand is shown in the context of a complete computer program written in Fortran IV. The development and application of the numerical method are thus closely related to the development of the computer program, which is the realistic situation in working with computers.

In this book we do not attempt to teach the elements of Fortran programming; we assume either that the reader already knows the subject or that he is learning it concurrently from another text. In this first case study, however, we move at a slower pace than later, to allow time for some review of Fortran and of programming matters.

We consider a specific polynomial of the fourth degree:

$$x^4 - 9x^3 - 2x^2 + 120x - 130 \tag{1.2}$$

and we look for values of x that make this polynomial equal to zero. Such values of x are called *roots* of the polynomial equation. The procedure we use, called *interval-halving*, is applicable to more general polynomials. However, we leave the discussion of finding roots of a general polynomial of degree n until Section 1.10. There we shall also discuss additional and more efficient ways of finding the roots of polynomials and other functions.

If we let

$$f(x) = x^4 - 9x^3 - 2x^2 + 120x - 130 \tag{1.3}$$

then finding the roots of the polynomial is equivalent to finding solutions of the nonlinear equation

$$f(x) = 0$$

We shall be concerned only with *real roots*, i.e., values of x that do not involve complex numbers.

Let us first write a simple program that evaluates $f(x)$ for $x = -10$, $-9, \ldots, 9, 10$. The program and output are shown in Figure 1.3. In the program Y is the value of the polynomial. Thus we start with $X = -10$ and evaluate Y. We then print X and Y using 1P2E15.5 format (1P indicates one digit before the decimal point; the 5 indicates five digits after the decimal point). Next we check to see if we are finished, i.e., whether X has reached the value $+10$. The IF statement does that, since "if" X is greater than or equal to 10 the program stops. If X is less than 10, we increase X by 1 ($X = X + 1.0$) and return to statement 200 to calculate the value of the polynomial for this new value of x.

Now consider the output, which is also shown in Figure 1.3. Suppose we plot the data for $x = -4, -3, \ldots, 7, 8$. The graph is shown in Figure 1.4. Note that the graph crosses the x-axis four times. The value of x corresponding to each point where the graph crosses the x-axis is a root of the polynomial equation.

One of the roots, the smallest one, appears to be between $x = -4$ and $x = -3$. Actually, we could have deduced that there was a root within that range of x merely by examining the output of the program. Returning to Figure 1.3 we see that for $x = -4, y = 190$ and for $x = -3, y = -184$. The important thing to notice is not the values of y but their *signs*. Since y is positive for $x = -4$ and negative for $x = -3$, then somewhere between -4 and -3 the graph must cross the x-axis. Of course, the graph may cross the x-axis more than once, but it must cross it *at least* once. Thus, there is at least one root of the polynomial between $x = -4$ and $x = -3$.

Similarly, from Figure 1.3 we can deduce that the polynomial has at least one root between 1 and 2, one between 3 and 4, and one between

```
C CASE STUDY 1
C ROOT FINDING BY INTERVAL HALVING
C
C A PRELIMINARY PROGRAM TO COMPUTE VALUE OF POLYNOMIAL AT 19 POINTS
C
C SET X TO INITIAL VALUE
      X = -10.0
C COMPUTE THE VALUE OF THE POLYNOMIAL FOR THE CURRENT VALUE OF X
  200  Y = X**4 - 9.0*X**3 - 2.0*X**2 + 120.0*X - 130.0
C PRINT X AND VALUE OF POLYNOMIAL
        WRITE (6, 700) X, Y
  700  FORMAT (1P2E15.5)
C CHECK WHETHER LAST VALUE OF X HAS BEEN REACHED -- STOP IF SO
        IF (X .GE. 10.0) STOP
C INCREMENT X IF NOT FINISHED
        X = X + 1.0
C GO BACK AROUND THE LOOP
        GO TO 200
        END


     -1.00000E 01      1.74700E 04
     -9.00000E 00      1.17500E 04
     -8.00000E 00      7.48600E 03
     -7.00000E 00      4.42000E 03
     -6.00000E 00      2.31800E 03
     -5.00000E 00      9.70000E 02
     -4.00000E 00      1.90000E 02
     -3.00000E 00     -1.84000E 02
     -2.00000E 00     -2.90000E 02
     -1.00000E 00     -2.42000E 02
      0.0             -1.30000E 02
      1.00000E 00     -2.00000E 01
      2.00000E 00      4.60000E 01
      3.00000E 00      5.00000E 01
      4.00000E 00     -2.00000E 00
      5.00000E 00     -8.00000E 01
      6.00000E 00     -1.30000E 02
      7.00000E 00     -7.40000E 01
      8.00000E 00      1.90000E 02
      9.00000E 00      7.88000E 02
      1.00000E 01      1.87000E 03
```

Figure 1.3. *A program (and its output) to evaluate the polynomial* $x^4 - 9x^3 - 2x^2 + 120x - 130$ *at the* x *values* $-10, -9, \ldots, 9, 10$ *(Case Study 1).*

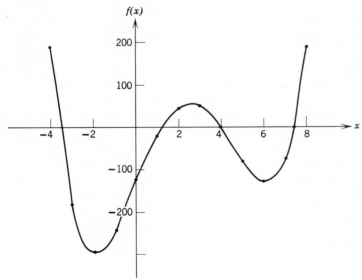

Figure 1.4. *Graph of the polynomial* $x^4 - 9x^3 - 2x^2 + 120x - 130$ *(Case Study 1).*

7 and 8. Since a fourth-degree polynomial has precisely four roots, then there must be precisely one root in each of the four intervals

$$-4 \text{ to } -3 \qquad\qquad (1.4)$$
$$1 \text{ to } 2$$
$$3 \text{ to } 4$$
$$7 \text{ to } 8$$

We emphasize that a change in sign of the polynomial over any x-interval does not always imply precisely *one* root in the interval. For example, consider the interval -4 to $+4$. At $x = -4$, the polynomial is positive. At $x = +4$, the polynomial is negative. Yet between -4 and $+4$ there are three roots, as we have seen. The only valid conclusion that can be drawn is: If a polynomial (or any reasonably well-behaved[1] function) has one sign at one end of an interval and a different sign at the other end of the interval, then the polynomial has an odd number of roots in the interval.

Let us return to the original polynomial given in (1.3). Now that we have isolated the four roots in the four intervals shown in (1.4), we seek a way of computing the values of the roots. Our strategy will be as follows:

(i)   Take a value of x midway in one of the intervals. For example, take $x = -3.5$, which is midway between -4 and -3.

(ii)   Evaluate the polynomial for this new value of x.

(iii)   Only three possibilities exist. (a) Either $y = 0$, in which case $x = -3.5$ is a root; or (b) $y > 0$, in which case a root lies between $x = -3.5$ and $x = -3$, since the polynomial is negative for $x = -3$; or (c) $y < 0$, in which case there is a root between $x = -4$ and $x = -3.5$, since the polynomial is positive for $x = -4$.

(iv)   In any case, we have either found a root or reduced the interval in which the root lies by a factor of one-half.

We then start over again and pick another value of x midway in this new smaller interval and repeat steps (i) to (iv) above. If we continue to repeat these steps, we continue to make the interval smaller and smaller. By repeating this process we can make the interval as small as we like. Therefore, we can compute the root as accurately as we like. For example, suppose we find that a root lies between $x = -3.6002$ and $x = -3.6001$. Then we know that to four digits the root is -3.600. (This is indeed the case in the present example.) Since our procedure involves successively dividing the interval in which the root lies by one-half, it is called the *method of interval-halving.*

Let us now try to describe our method more precisely. To do so we shall use *flow charts.* A flow chart is a sequence of boxes connected by arrows. We locate the box containing the word "Start." We follow the arrow from that box to another box (there will be only one arrow leaving the box). We do whatever the contents of the next box tells us to do and then follow the arrow leaving that box.

---

[1]Here by "well-behaved" we mean mathematically *continuous.*

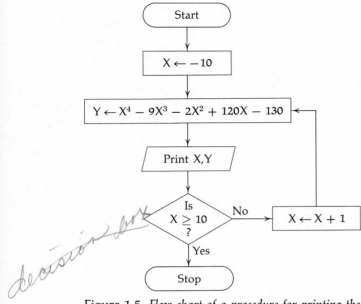

decision box

Figure 1.5. *Flow chart of a procedure for printing the values of a polynomial at 19 points. The program of Figure 1.3 follows this procedure (Case Study 1).*

Sometimes we encounter a box that asks a question such as "Is $X \geq 10$?". Then there will be two arrows leaving that box. One arrow is labeled "Yes" and one is labeled "No." We follow that arrow labeled with the correct answer to the question. A question-type box will be diamond-shaped and is called a *decision box*.

Eventually we shall encounter a box containing the word "Stop" and we do just that.

As an example, consider the flow chart corresponding to the program in Figure 1.3. The flow chart is shown in Figure 1.5. The left pointing arrow, which appears in three boxes, means: Compute the value of the expression at the tail of the arrow and assign that value to the variable at the head of the arrow. The Fortran equal sign in an assignment statement is equivalent to the left-pointing arrow in our flow charts.

Now that we have reviewed flow charts briefly, we return to our method of interval halving. First we must find an interval in which a root lies. To do this we start with $x = -10$ and evaluate the polynomial for that value of x and for $x + 1$. We then want to know if the two values of the polynomial thus obtained have opposite signs. An easy way to determine this is to multiply the two values of the polynomial. If the product is negative, then the two values have opposite signs. Otherwise they have the same sign.[2]

---

[2] We are ignoring for the moment the possibility that the polynomial may be zero for one of the values of x. For most polynomials, we will not encounter a value of x for which the polynomial is precisely zero. Thus we are not likely to make an error by neglecting the case where the polynomial is zero. Although it is unlikely, it can still occur. *Computer programs should take into account all possibilities.* However, we shall discuss this case later.

Case Study 1: Finding Roots by Interval Halving   7

A flow chart is shown in Figure 1.6. XL stands for the value of x at the *left* end of the interval. Similarly, XR stands for the value of x at the *right* end of the interval. The values of YL and YR are the polynomial values at the left and right ends respectively. The reader should study the flow chart to assure himself that it will stop after determining that there is a root between -4 and -3. Notice that the decision box that asks "Is XR $\geq$ 10?" serves as a check: If we inadvertently use a polynomial with no real roots, we do not want to search indefinitely for an interval containing a root. As it stands, the flow chart tests for x only between -10 and $+10$. It is good practice to put such checks into every flow chart and every program.

The flow chart in Figure 1.6 is very inefficient. For example, we first evaluate the polynomial for XL $= -10$ and XR $= -9$. We find that YL*YR is positive. We then evaluate the polynomial for XL $= -9$ and XR $= -8$. But we have already computed the value of the polynomial when X $= -9$. In fact, when we leave the decision box "Is YL*YR < 0?" on the "No" arrow, YR has the value of the polynomial when $x = -9$. Why bother to calculate that value of the polynomial again?

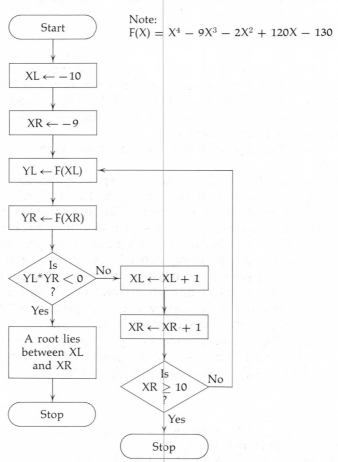

Figure 1.6. *Flow chart of a procedure for locating an interval that contains at least one root of a polynomial (Case Study 1).*

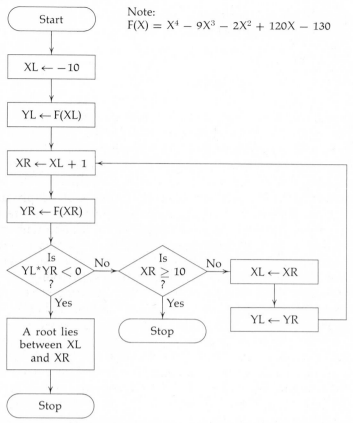

Note:
$F(X) = X^4 - 9X^3 - 2X^2 + 120X - 130$

Figure 1.7. *A more efficient version of the procedure flow charted in Figure 1.6 (Case Study 1).*

Whether we evaluate a polynomial twice for the same value of x may seem unimportant, especially since the computer will be doing all of the work. For large problems, however, reducing the amount of computation can result in a significant savings in computer time and, hence, in cost.

In any case, the flow chart in Figure 1.7 accomplishes the same task as the one in Figure 1.6. The reader should assure himself of two things. First, that Figure 1.7 is indeed equivalent to Figure 1.6 in terms of what its results are. Second, the reader should assure himself that, whereas Figure 1.6 requires that the fourth-degree polynomial be evaluated fourteen times, the flow chart in Figure 1.7 requires evaluation of that polynomial only eight times. If you try to evaluate the polynomial with paper and pencil or even a desk calculator, you will see that this is an appreciable savings.

The Fortran statements to accomplish the task described in Figure 1.7 are:

```
     F(X) = X**4 − 9.0*X**3 − 2.0*X**2 + 120.0*X − 130.0
     XL = −10.0
     YL = F(XL)
  10 XR = XL + 1.0
     YR = F(XR)
```

```
          IF (YL*YR .LT. 0.0) GO TO 20
          IF (XR .GE. 10.0) STOP
          XL = XR
          YL = YR
          GO TO 10
   20     . . .
```

The first statement in the program is the definition of an arithmetic statement function. With the definition established, we can later call for the evaluation of that function (which is our polynomial, of course) simply by writing the name of the function and enclosing in parentheses an expression giving the value for which we want it evaluated. The statement function definition *itself* is not executed, of course, but simply defines to the Fortran compiler what we shall mean later when we write F(XL) or F(XR) (or whatever) on the right-hand side of an assignment statement.

The three dots on line 20 indicate that more of the program is to follow. Indeed, when we reach statement 20 we have isolated a root in an interval of length one. We now wish to proceed to interval halving.

However, before doing so, we return to the case where YL or YR may be zero (see footnote 2). This, of course, implies that either XL or XR is a root. The flow chart to include this possibility is shown in Figure 1.8.

There is a new type of decision box in Figure 1.8. One of the diamond-shaped boxes contains "YL*YR:0" which is read "Compare YL*YR with 0." There are three arrows leading from that box. One arrow is for the case YL*YR < 0, one is for the case YL*YR = 0, and one is for the case YL*YR > 0. Notice that the symbols on the arrows are to replace the colon (:) that appears in the decision box. Thus, if YL*YR < 0, we take the left-directed arrow when leaving the decision box.

The FORTRAN statements corresponding to this flow chart follow.

```
          F(X) = X**4 − 9.0*X**3 − 2.0*X**2 + 120.0*X − 130.0
          XL = −10.0
          YL = F(XL)
   10     XR = XL + 1.0
          YR = F(XR)
          IF (YL*YR) 20, 30, 40
   40     IF (XR .GE. 10.0) STOP
          XL = XR
          YL = YR
          GO TO 10
   30     IF (YL .EQ. 0.0) GO TO 50
          WRITE (6,700) XR
          STOP
   50     WRITE (6,700) XL
  700     FORMAT (1PE15.5)
          STOP
   20     . . .
```

Decision boxes with two arrows leaving them correspond most naturally to Fortran *logical* IF statements. On the other hand, decision boxes with three arrows exiting correspond to *arithmetic* IF statements.

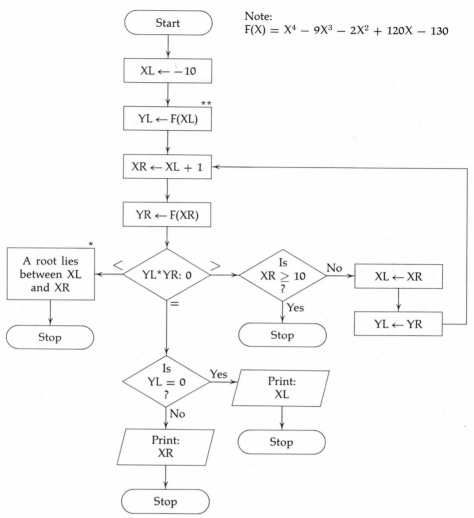

Note:
$$F(X) = X^4 - 9X^3 - 2X^2 + 120X - 130$$

Figure 1.8. *The procedure of Figure 1.7 extended to include the possibility that the polynomial is exactly zero for some value of* x *(Case Study 1).*

We now proceed to compute a root by interval halving. We assume that we have isolated a root between the values of XL and XR (see the box marked with * in Figure 1.8). Instead of stopping as indicated in Figure 1.8, we proceed to the "Start" box in Figure 1.9.

We first compute X as the point midway between XL and XR and then evaluate the polynomial for that value of X. Then we determine whether the desired root lies to the left, at, or to the right of X.

(a) If YL*Y < 0: The root lies between XL and X. In this case we replace XR by X and YR by Y, i.e., X becomes the right end of the interval.

(b) If YL*Y = 0: It is not possible that YL = 0 for if this were so we would have printed XL as a root in Figure 1.8. Thus, if YL*Y = 0, we print the value of X as a root.

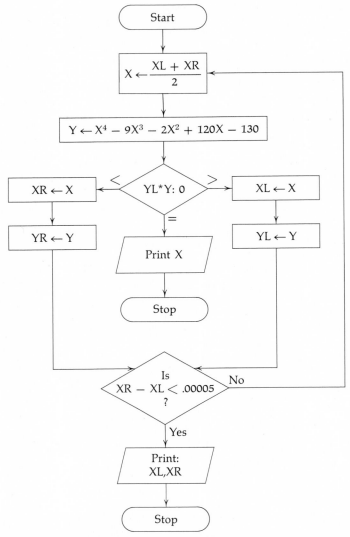

Figure 1.9. *Flow chart of a procedure to locate a root of a polynomial, given that a root lies between the values XL and XR. This flow chart is a continuation of that shown in Figure 1.8 (Case Study 1).*

(c) If $YL*Y > 0$: Then $Y*YR < 0$ since we already know that $YL*YR < 0$. In this case the root lies between X and XR. Therefore, we replace XL by X and YL by Y, i.e., X becomes the left end of the interval.

Once we have determined the new interval, which is one-half the length of the previous interval, we determine whether the new interval is small enough. In our case we want the interval to be less than 0.5×10^{-4}. If the interval is not that small, we calculate the value of X midway between the endpoints of the interval and repeat the process. If the interval is less than 0.5×10^{-4}, then we print the interval end points and stop.

The Fortran statements corresponding to Figure 1.9 are:

```
20    X = (XL + XR)/2.0
      Y = F(X)
      IF (YL*Y) 60,70,80
70    WRITE (6, 700) X
      STOP
60    XR = X
      YR = Y
      GO TO 90
80    XL = X
      YL = Y
90    IF (XR − XL .LT. 0.00005) GO TO 100
      GO TO 20
100   WRITE (6, 701) XL,XR
701   FORMAT (1P2E15.5)
      STOP
```

Notice that the first statement is labeled 20, which ties it together with the previous set of Fortran statements that ended with a 20 and an incomplete Fortran statement.

The above flow charts and Fortran statements find only one root (the one between −4 and −3). We shall now enlarge our program, with not much more work, to find all four roots.

When we leave Figure 1.8, we record the value of XR. After we have found one root, we shall use that value of XR for the left end of an interval and start again to search for an interval containing a root. Let us explore what additions to the flow charts of Figure 1.8 and 1.9 are necessary.

At the box marked "*" in Figure 1.8 we let XS ← XR before going to Figure 1.9 to "save" the value of the right end point. In Figure 1.9 the two "Stops" are replaced by XL ← XS followed by a test to see if XL ≥ 10. If XL is less than 10, the program transfers back to the box marked with ** in Figure 1.8. If XL ≥ 10, we stop.

Two of the "Stops" in Figure 1.8 must also be changed. After printing XL (when XL is a root), we go to the decision box containing "Is XR ≥ 10?"

On the other hand, after printing XR (when XR is a root), we do not want merely to go to that decision box mentioned in the previous paragraph. If we did so, we would let XL ← XR and find that we had reached the box that reads "Print: XL." Thus we would print the value of that root twice.

Therefore, after printing XR, we ask "Is XR ≥ 10?" If the answer is "Yes," we stop. If the answer is "No," we let XL ← XR + 1 and return to the box marked "**."

We are able to add 1.0 to the previous value of XR in giving XL its new value because one of the assumptions made in writing the flow chart and program is that no two roots are within 1.0 of each other. Of course, this is not true for all polynomials; we have taken essential advantage of what we know about the polynomial in writing the program. A more general routine must allow for closely spaced roots, among many other eventualities. We return to some of these considerations in Section 1.8.

The complete flow chart taking into account these additions and changes

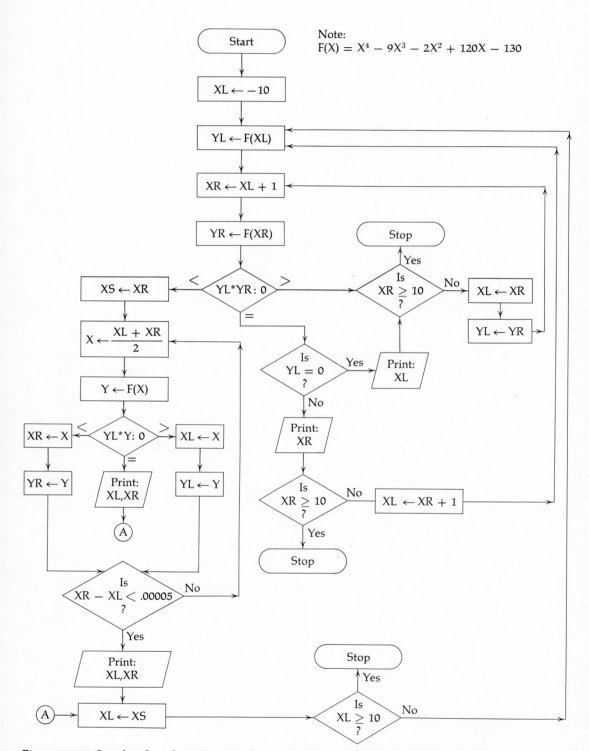

Figure 1.10. *Complete flow chart of a procedure to find the roots of a polynomial equation, corresponding to the program of Figure 1.11 (Case Study 1).*

is shown in Figure 1.10. The flow chart appears rather complicated, but it is really just a combination of the previous ones. Recall, furthermore, that it will determine all four roots to within an accuracy of 0.5×10^{-4}. Moreover, with minor changes it will find roots of other polynomials as well (see Exercises 21–24).

In this final flow chart we have introduced one more new device. In the lower left portion of the figure are two small circles containing the letter "A." These small circles are called *connectors*. They are used to avoid crossing lines in the flow chart. When leaving the box containing "Print: X" we encounter a connector, A. We then look for another A connector with an arrow leading away from it. We then follow the arrows as we did before. In this case we find a connector that leads to the box containing "XL ← XS."

We have made several significant assumptions in arriving at this flow chart. First, we have assumed that all the roots were in the interval -10 to $+10$. Secondly, we assumed that at most one root lay in any interval $K \leq X \leq K + 1$ where K is any integer from -10 to $+9$. Both of these assumptions are correct for the particular polynomial chosen. Of course, our flow chart provides a method of finding roots of other polynomials if we change the statement function where the polynomial is defined. Nevertheless, the two above assumptions are inherent in our flow chart. Of course, with a little extra effort we can relax either or both of the assumptions (see Exercises 21 and 22).

The process described by Figure 1.10 (or, for that matter, any flow chart similar to it) is called an *algorithm*; that is, it describes with no ambiguity a way to solve a certain problem.

In Figure 1.11 a Fortran program corresponding to the flow chart in Figure 1.10 is given. Notice that only one FORMAT statement is needed even though at times we print one number (statement 50) and at other times we print two numbers (statement 100). The FORMAT statement provides for two numbers to be printed on one line, but, if the list in the WRITE statement contains only one number, the second field specification in the FORMAT statement is ignored.

The output from running the program is shown in Figure 1.12. Notice that the first two lines and the last contain *two* numbers, indicating the left and right ends of the interval. The third line contains only one number, indicating that the polynomial is zero (to the accuracy of the computer[3]) at that value of x.

To four significant digits the roots of $x^4 - 9x^3 - 2x^2 + 120x - 130 = 0$ are -3.600, 1.229, 3.972, and 7.399. Notice that interval-halving produces two values of x, x_L, and x_R, such that for some value of x, say x_0,

$$x_L < x_0 < x_R$$

[3] The phrase "to the accuracy of the computer" suggests an issue to which we must return many times, beginning in earnest in Chapter 2—the question of the precision of computer representation of numbers. At this point we shall simply note that not every computer gives identical answers to this same Fortran program: When the program was run on one other computer, the result was that both the third *and* fourth lines contained only one number, indicating that for that computer both numbers were "exact" roots. In fact, of course, both roots are irrational numbers and thus cannot be represented "exactly" in *any* computer whatsoever.

```
C CASE STUDY 1
C ROOT FINDING BY INTERVAL HALVING
C THE COMPLETE PROGRAM
C
C THE FIRST STATEMENT IS A STATEMENT FUNCTION DEFINITION
C
      F(X) = X**4 - 9.0*X**3 - 2.0*X**2 +120.0*X - 130.0
C PROGRAM EXECUTION BEGINS HERE
      XL = -10.0
    5 YL = F(XL)
   10 XR = XL + 1.0
      YR = F(XR)
C TEST WHETHER XL AND XR BRACKET A ROOT
      IF (YL*YR) 20, 30, 40
C HERE IF XL AND XR DO NOT BRACKET A ROOT
   40 IF (XR .GE. 10.0) STOP
C PREPARE TO EXAMINE NEXT INTERVAL
      XL = XR
      YL = YR
      GO TO 10
C HERE IF XL OR XR IS A ROOT
   30 IF (YL .EQ. 0.0) GO TO 50
      WRITE (6, 700) XR
      IF (XR .GE. 10.0) STOP
      XL = XR +1.0
      GO TO 5
   50 WRITE (6, 700) XL
      GO TO 40
C HERE IF XL AND XR BRACKET A ROOT
   20 XS = XR
   25 X = (XL + XR)/2.0
      Y = F(X)
      IF (YL*Y) 60, 70, 80
C HERE IF XS IS A ROOT
   70 WRITE (6, 700) X
      GO TO 110
C HERE IF ROOT IS BETWEEN XL AND XS
   60 XR = X
      YR = Y
      GO TO 90
C HERE IF ROOT IS BETWEEN XS AND XR
   80 XL = X
      YL = Y
C TEST WHETHER APPROXIMATION IS CLOSE ENOUGH
   90 IF (XR-XL .GE. 0.00005) GO TO 25
C CLOSE ENOUGH - PRINT THE ROOT
  100 WRITE (6, 700) XL, XR
C GO ON TO EXAMINE NEXT INTERVAL
  110 XL = XS
      IF (XL .GE. 10.0) STOP
      GO TO 5
  700 FORMAT (1P2E15.5)
      END
```

Figure 1.11. *A program to find the roots of a certain polynomial. Note that this program contains unrealistic assumptions about the spacing of the roots of a more general polynomial: the reader is asked to remove these in Exercises 21 and 22 at the end of the chapter (Case Study 1).*

```
-3.60016E 00    -3.60013E 00
 1.22858E 00     1.22861E 00
 3.97208E 00
 7.39948E 00     7.39951E 00
```

Figure 1.12. *Output of the program of Figure 1.11, showing the bounds on the roots of the polynomial equation. Note that the third line contains only one number, indicating that the program found an "exact" root—but see text discussion (Case Study 1).*

it must be that
$$F(x_0) = 0$$
Since $x_R - x_L$ is small, it follows that $x_R - x_0$ is small, as is $x_0 - x_L$.
In the particular program in Figure 1.11, $x_R - x_L < 0.5 \times 10^{-4}$ so
$$x_R - x_0 < 0.5 \times 10^{-4}$$
and
$$x_0 - x_L < 0.5 \times 10^{-4}$$

Thus we have used criterion (i) noted on page 2, that is, we have found a number $\bar{x}$ such that $|\bar{x} - x_0|$ is small and $F(x_0) = 0$. For $\bar{x}$ we can use either x_L or x_R.

We can also test criterion (ii) simply by evaluating $F(x)$ at x_L and/or x_R. If $|F(x_L)|$ is small, then x_L satisfies both criteria. If not, we try $|F(x_R)|$. If neither of these is small, we must either continue the interval halving or be content with criterion (i) above.

No matter how long we continue reducing the interval by one-half, we may *never* be able to satisfy criterion (ii). This will happen if the graph is exceptionally steep near the root. One must keep in mind, therefore, that interval-halving uses criterion (i) to find an approximate root. When the algorithm terminates, criterion (ii) may or may not be satisfied.

Other algorithms developed later in this chapter will use criterion (ii) and will, therefore, be more appropriate in certain cases.

**1.3
Finding
Approxi-
mate Roots**

We now turn to general algorithms for finding approximations to the roots of a single equation in one variable. (In Section 1.13, we shall discuss several simultaneous equations in more than one variable.) Our strategy will be as follows.

(i) First, we shall try to obtain an initial "guess" at the root. This guess may at times be crude. In Case Study 1, for example, we found that there was a root of the polynomial equation $x^4 - 9x^3 - 2x^2 + 120x - 130 = 0$ between $x = -4$ and $x = -3$. We can take either of these values as our initial guess. In Section 1.14 we shall discuss different methods of finding such starting guesses.

(ii) Second, after obtaining an initial approximation—no matter how crude—we shall successively refine the approximation until it is near to a root of the equation. In Section 1.1 we discussed two ways of measuring nearness of an approximation. In the next sections we shall be concerned with improving an approximation to a root, that is, getting successively closer to it.

**1.4
Method of
Successive
Approxima-
tions**

We turn now to a simple, although rather inefficient, method for finding a real root of a general equation of the form
$$F(x) = 0 \qquad (1.5)$$
In Sections 1.6 and 1.7 we shall discuss variations of this method that will be more efficient. Suppose that (1.5) is rewritten in the form
$$x = f(x) \qquad (1.6)$$

This can usually be done in many different ways. For instance, if

$$F(x) = x^2 - c = 0$$

where $c \geq 0$, we may add x to both sides to get

$$x = x^2 + x - c \tag{1.7}$$

or we may divide by x to get

$$x = \frac{c}{x} \tag{1.8}$$

As a last example, we may rearrange the equation to get

$$x = x - \frac{x^2 - c}{2x} = \frac{1}{2}\left(x + \frac{c}{x}\right) \tag{1.9}$$

Obviously, the values of x that are solutions to these equations are $\pm\sqrt{c}$.

Let x_0 be an initial approximation to the solution of (1.6). Then, as the next approximation, take

$$x_1 = f(x_0)$$

As the next approximation take

$$x_2 = f(x_1)$$

Proceeding in this way, the nth approximation, or, as it is often called, the nth *iterate*, is

$$x_n = f(x_{n-1}) \tag{1.10}$$

The fundamental question is: Do the x_n converge to a solution of (1.6) as n increases?

We shall now develop *sufficient* conditions on $f(x)$ for this desired convergence, that is, conditions that will guarantee that x_n will get closer and closer to a solution of (1.6). These conditions are not *necessary*, however; there may be functions $f(x)$ that do not satisfy these conditions but for which the iteration method of (1.10) nevertheless produces a solution.

Let us first consider a geometrical representation of the process. The graph of the left-hand side of (1.6) is the line $y = x$. The graph of the right-hand side is some curve represented by $f(x)$. (See Figure 1.13.) A solution of (1.6) is represented by the value or values of x for which the two curves $y = x$ and $y = f(x)$ intersect. In Figure 1.13 $x = a$ is such a point and, therefore,

$$a = f(a) \tag{1.11}$$

Of course, we do not know the value of a at the outset. Indeed, the task set before us is to find the value of a.

Consider x_0 to be a guess or first approximation to a. To find $f(x_0)$ we raise a vertical line from x_0 on the x-axis until it intersects the graph of $f(x)$. In Figure 1.13, the length of the line segment OA is $f(x_0)$. The line

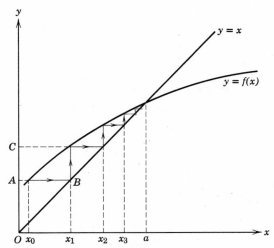

Figure 1.13. *Diagrammatic representation of the method of successive approximations for* $0 < f'(x) < 1$.

$y = x$ is at 45° to both the axes, so points on this line have equal x- and y-coordinates. If we move horizontally from point A [whose y-coordinate is $f(x_0)$], we keep the y-coordinate of the moving point fixed and equal to $f(x_0)$. When this moving point reaches point B, the x-coordinate will also be $f(x_0)$. This x-coordinate we call x_1 so that

$$x_1 = f(x_0)$$

This is the appropriate value as defined in the expression (1.10). Thus, in two steps the geometrical process produces the result indicated by the iterative formula (1.10). Point x_1 on the x-axis directly below B is the second approximation to a.

We continue in this way (i) raising a vertical line until it intersects the curve $y = f(x)$ and then (ii) drawing a horizontal line until it intersects $y = x$. Each double step of this type produces a new (and hopefully better) approximation to a. The arrows in Figure 1.13 indicate the steps in the process.

We seem, in this case, to be converging toward the solution $x = a$, since each successive approximation is closer to a. It is important to note that we took a curve $y = f(x)$ for which $0 < f'(x) < 1$.[4]

Consider now another shape for the curve $y = f(x)$, one in which the derivative is negative but less than 1 in absolute value. (See Figure 1.14.) Again the arrows indicate the pattern of the iterations, and again the approximations seem to converge to $x = a$. Now, however, each successive approximation is on the opposite side of $x = a$ from its predecessor, whereas in the first example of Figure 1.13 all the approximations were on the same side of $x = a$.

Finally, we consider approximation formulas for which the derivatives are greater than 1 (Figure 1.15) and less than -1 (Figure 1.16). In both cases the iterations do not converge. Each succeeding guess is farther from

[4]Prime denotes differentiation with respect to x.

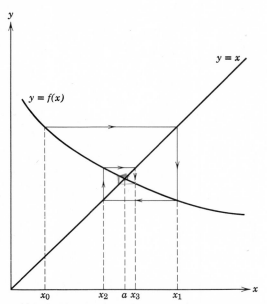

Figure 1.14. *Diagrammatic representation of the method of successive approximations for* $-1 < f'(x) < 0$.

$x = a$ than its predecessor. It seems, therefore, that if $f'(x)$ is less than 1 in absolute value, the iteration method described by (1.10) will converge. This is the case, as we can readily prove by an elementary argument. Note that from (1.11) and (1.10)

$$a = f(a)$$
$$x_n = f(x_{n-1})$$

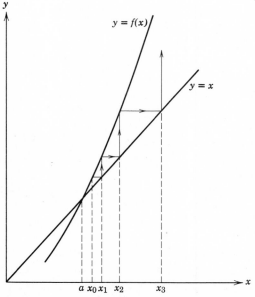

Figure 1.15. *Diagrammatic representation of the method of successive approximations for* $f'(x) > 1$.

20   Solution of Equations

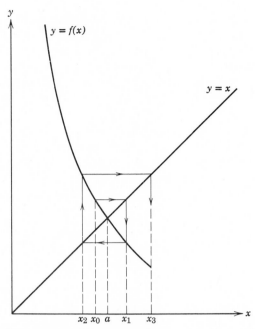

Figure 1.16. *Diagrammatic representation of the method of successive approximations for* f'(x) < −1.

so that

$$x_n - a = f(x_{n-1}) - f(a)$$

Multiplying on the right by $(x_{n-1} - a)/(x_{n-1} - a)$ and using the mean value theorem,[5] we have

$$x_n - a = f'(\xi)(x_{n-1} - a)$$

where ξ lies between x_{n-1} and a.

Now let m be the maximum absolute value of $f'(x)$ over the entire interval in question (the interval including $x_0, x_1, \ldots, x_n, a$). Then

$$|x_n - a| \leq m \, |x_{n-1} - a|$$

Similarly,

$$|x_{n-1} - a| \leq m \, |x_{n-2} - a|$$

so

$$|x_n - a| \leq m^2 \, |x_{n-2} - a|$$

Continuing in this way,

$$|x_n - a| \leq m^n \, |x_0 - a| \tag{1.12}$$

[5] The mean value theorem states that given two points a and b on a curve $y = f(x)$, where $f(x)$ has a continuous derivative, the slope of the chord between a and b

$$\frac{f(b) - f(a)}{b - a}$$

is equal to the slope of the tangent to the curve at some intermediate point.

If $m < 1$ over the entire interval, then, no matter what the choice of x_0, as n increases the right-hand member becomes small and x_n comes closer to a. On the other hand, for $|f'(x)| > 1$, $|x_n - a|$ becomes indefinitely large as n increases. The proof is left to the reader as an exercise. Thus, if $|f'(x)| < 1$, the process (1.10) converges. If $|f'(x)| > 1$, the process (1.10) diverges. Observe that the inequalities are assumed to hold at all the approximations $(x_0, x_1, \ldots, x_n)$.

What happens if at some points x_i the derivative $f'(x_i)$ is less than 1 in absolute value and at some other points x_j the derivative $f'(x_j)$ is greater than 1 in absolute value? The answer to this question is unresolved. The process sometimes converges and sometimes does not.

Let us return for a moment to our example of finding the square root of c. In (1.7)

$$f(x) = x^2 + x - c$$

so that

$$|f'(x)| < 1 \text{ if } -1 < x < 0$$

If we are searching for the square root of a number c that is less than 1, the process converges to the negative square root of c.

In (1.8), however,

$$f'(x) = \frac{-c}{x^2}$$

and, if x is close to $\sqrt{c}$ (as it must eventually be in order to converge to the square root of c), $f'(x) \simeq 1$ and indeed the process diverges.

Finally, using (1.9),

$$f'(x) = \frac{1}{2}\left(1 - \frac{c}{x^2}\right)$$

and again, if $x \simeq \sqrt{c}$, $f'(x) \simeq 0$ and the process converges (rapidly, as a matter of fact). Equation (1.9) is a special case that we shall encounter again in Section 1.7 on the Newton-Raphson method.

Although for any equation there is in general a wide choice of functions $f(x)$ for use in the method of successive approximations, a judicious choice is obviously necessary if convergence is to be obtained.

**1.5
The
Stopping
Criterion**

The method of successive approximations described in the previous section produces the values $x_1, x_2, \ldots, x_n, \ldots$. If the method converges, each successive approximation is closer to the root a than its predecessor. Eventually we must terminate the computations. How shall we know when to stop the iterations?

A typical stopping criterion is to note when two successive iterates differ by a small amount. That is to say, we choose a number ϵ and when

$$|x_n - x_{n-1}| < \epsilon$$

then we stop the iterations and take x_n to be the approximate root. However, this does *not* mean that x_n differs from the root a by less than ϵ. It tells us only that x_n differs from x_{n-1} by less than ϵ. Thus, we should compute

$$|f(x_n) - x_n|$$

If this is sufficiently small, then we may stop the iterations and take x_n to be an approximate root.

The method of successive approximations, therefore, uses criterion (ii) described in Section 1.1 in determining when a sufficiently good approximation has been achieved. By way of contrast, interval-halving as described in Case Study 1 uses criterion (i). We already have discussed how these criteria differ in the discussion in Section 1.1.

**1.6
A Modified
Method of
Successive
Approxima-
tions**

Consider Figure 1.13 again. Notice that although each iterate is closer to the solution than its predecessor, each falls short of the correct answer. It might be advantageous, therefore, to make a larger correction in each iteration. That is to say, instead of letting

$$x_{n+1} = x_n + \Delta x$$

where

$$\Delta x = f(x_n) - x_n$$

we might choose the next iterate after x_n to be

$$x_{n+1} = x_n + \alpha \, \Delta x$$

where $\alpha > 1$.

The situation is displayed in Figure 1.17, which is an enlargement of a small section of Figure 1.13. The best choice of α is the one shown, which would produce $x_{n+1} = a$. Let us try to determine the best value for α.

Notice that the distance between x_{n+1} and a is $(\alpha - 1) \Delta x$, and, since $y = x$ is a 45° line, the distance between $f(a)$ and $f(x_n)$ is also $(\alpha - 1) \Delta x$.

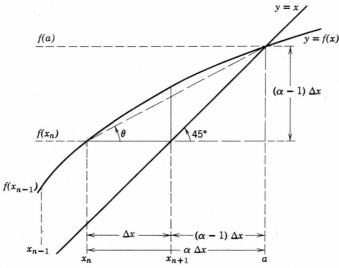

Figure 1.17. *Diagrammatic representation of the modified method of successive approximations for $0 < f'(x) < 1$.*

Therefore, the tangent of the angle θ is

$$\tan \theta = \frac{(\alpha - 1)\,\Delta x}{\alpha\,\Delta x} = \frac{\alpha - 1}{\alpha} \tag{1.13}$$

On the other hand,

$$\tan \theta = \frac{f(a) - f(x_n)}{a - x_n}$$

and, using the mean value theorem

$$\tan \theta = f'(\xi) \tag{1.14}$$

where $x_n \le \xi \le a$.

$$\alpha = \frac{1}{1 - f'(\xi)} \tag{1.15}$$

The value of ξ is unknown, of course, but we can approximate the value of $f'(\xi)$ by

$$f'(\xi) \simeq \frac{f(x_n) - f(x_{n-1})}{x_n - x_{n-1}} = \frac{f(x_n) - x_n}{x_n - x_{n-1}} \tag{1.16}$$

Geometrically, this amounts to drawing the chord between the points $(x_n, f(x_n))$ and $(x_{n-1}, f(x_{n-1}))$ and finding its intersection with the line $y = x$. The process is now

$$x_{n+1} = x_n + \alpha(f(x_n) - x_n) \tag{1.17}$$

where α is determined as in (1.15) and (1.16).

The question arises how convergence is affected by the modified method. Notice from (1.15) that, if $0 < f'(x) < 1$, then $1 < \alpha < \infty$. This is the case illustrated in Figure 1.13, in which the steps were too small; since $\alpha > 1$, the modified method will make them larger and therefore speed up convergence.

For $-1 < f'(x) < 0$, $1/2 < \alpha < 1$ from (1.15), which is the situation in Figure 1.14. There, each step was too large; the modified method decreases each step by a factor between $1/2$ and 1.

More important, perhaps, are the divergent cases. If $f'(x) > 1$, then $\alpha < 0$. As shown in Figure 1.15, each step is in the wrong direction; that is, the iterates are moving away from the solution. Since α for this case is negative, the modification reverses the direction as needed.

Finally, for $f'(x) < -1$, $0 < \alpha < 1/2$. Here, as seen in Figure 1.16, the steps were too large; the modification reduces them by a factor between zero and $1/2$. It is appropriate that the reduction should be greater in this case than in Figure 1.14, since it is divergent, whereas the other was convergent.

The process of extrapolation (overshooting) or interpolation (undershooting) is common in iterative methods.

A further slight modification of the method of successive approximations leads to one of the best-known numerical techniques, the Newton-Raphson method, for finding the roots of equations. Those already described, however, have a practical advantage over the Newton-Raphson method in certain cases. We shall return to this question after considering the Newton-Raphson method.

Recall that in (1.16) we approximated the derivative $f'(\xi)$ by a difference. Recall also that the optimum choice of ξ lay in the range $x_{n-1} \leq \xi \leq a$.

Suppose that for computational simplicity we choose $\xi = x_{n-1}$. Then we have

$$\alpha = \frac{1}{1 - f'(x_{n-1})} \qquad (1.18)$$

and

$$x_n = \frac{f(x_{n-1}) - x_{n-1}f'(x_{n-1})}{1 - f'(x_{n-1})} \qquad (1.19)$$

We note that (1.19) is equivalent to a method of successive approximations given by

$$x_n = g(x_{n-1})$$

where

$$g(x) = \frac{f(x) - xf'(x)}{1 - f'(x)}$$

Recall also that, if $|g'(x)| < 1$, then the method converges. Now

$$g'(x) = \frac{f''(x)[f(x) - x]}{(1 - f'(x))^2}$$

From (1.6), however, if x is sufficiently near a root, the term in square brackets is small. Therefore, the iteration method described in (1.19) converges, provided:

1. x_0 is sufficiently close to a root of $x = f(x)$,
2. $f''(x)$ does not become excessively large, and
3. $f'(x)$ is not too close to 1.

This is the celebrated Newton-Raphson method. It is usually written in the more familiar form

$$x_n = x_{n-1} - \frac{F(x_{n-1})}{F'(x_{n-1})} \qquad (1.20)$$

where

$$F(x) = f(x) - x = 0$$

That is to say, we have returned to the form given in (1.5).

The conditions for convergence now become

1. x_0 is sufficiently close to a root of $F(x) = 0$,
2. $F''(x)$ does not become excessively large, and
3. $F'(x)$ is not too close to zero.

The last condition means that no two roots are too close together. We shall return to a discussion of this problem in Section 1.8.

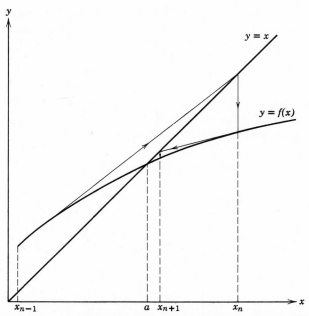

Figure 1.18. *Diagrammatic representation of the Newton-Raphson method for* f(x) = x.

Let us find a geometrical interpretation of the Newton-Raphson method. In (1.18) we choose the point ξ where the slope of $f(x)$ is computed to be at x_{n-1}. Thus, in Figure 1.17 the angle θ is chosen to be the slope of the tangent to $y = f(x)$ at x_{n-1}. The process then is to draw the tangent to the curve $y = f(x)$ at $x = x_{n-1}$ and find the intersection of the tangent with the line $y = x$. Doing so produces the new value x_n. A vertical line is drawn through x_n to the curve $y = f(x)$ and a new tangent is drawn. The path traced in Figure 1.18 is for the case in which $0 < f'(x) < 1$.

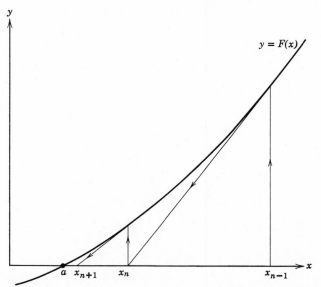

Figure 1.19. *Diagrammatic representation of the Newton-Raphson method for* F(x) = 0.

From the graphs in Figures 1.13 and 1.18 it appears as if the Newton-Raphson method converges much more rapidly than does the method of successive approximations. This is indeed the case. We shall discuss these rates of convergence in some detail in Section 1.9.

If the equation is put in the form of (1.5) and the iterative formula (1.20) is used, the geometric picture is that of Figure 1.19. We are now looking for the intersection of $y = F(x)$ and $y = 0$. Given a guess x_{n-1}, the tangent to $y = F(x)$ is drawn and its intersection with the x-axis produces the new value of $x = x_n$. It is easily determined that this is the x_n in (1.20): Find the equation of the line through the point x_{n-1}, $F(x_{n-1})$ with slope $F'(x_n)$ and then find the intersection of this line with the x-axis.

1.8 **Nearly** **Equal** **Roots**	We have already pointed out that difficulties may arise in the Newton-Raphson method if (1.5) or (1.6) has nearly equal roots. In that case, condition 3 for convergence is violated close to the nearly equal roots. The phenomenon is illustrated in Figure 1.20. (The scale is greatly enlarged.) Notice that the derivative of $f(x)$ is near 1 at the two roots a_1 and a_2. Moreover, from the mean value theorem the derivative is equal to 1 somewhere between a_1 and a_2.

Let us now examine what happens if we choose x_0 as an initial guess to the root a_1. The tangent constructed at C intersects $y = x$ at A and the new iterate is x_1. The tangent at B intersects $y = x$ at D, yielding x_0 again. The iteration, therefore, alternates between x_0 and x_1 indefinitely.

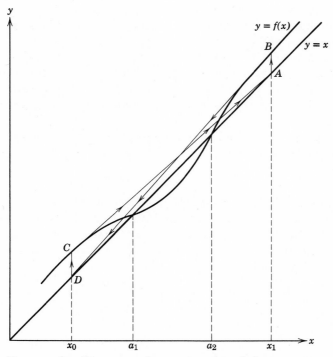

Figure 1.20. *Diagrammatic representation of the nonconvergence of the Newton-Raphson method for* $|f'(x)|$ *near 1.*

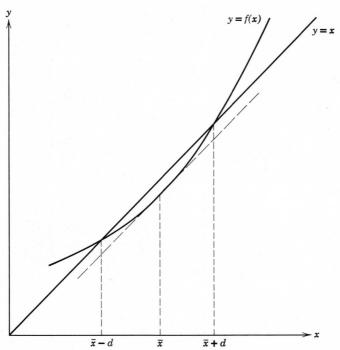

Figure 1.21. *Diagrammatic representation of the modified Newton-Raphson method for* $|f'(x)|$ *near 1.*

The process cannot resolve the two roots because they are too close together. Of course, we can say that it is condition 1 that is being violated and that x_0 was not sufficiently close to a_1.

Indeed, this is true. We should therefore explore a method by which a close first approximation may be found. Numerically, difficulties arise because the evaluation of the denominator in (1.19) requires the subtraction of two nearly equal numbers, which as we shall repeatedly see gives rise to inaccuracies.

Following Macon,[6] we shall first find the value of x where $f'(x) = 1$; that is, we solve the equation

$$x = x + f'(x) - 1$$

Let the solution be $x = \bar{x}$. This point lies between the two roots a_1 and a_2. In order to obtain a first approximation, we may assume that $\bar{x}$ lies midway between a_1 and a_2. (See Figure 1.21.) That is to say, we let $\bar{x} + d$ and $\bar{x} - d$ be the two roots. Expanding $f(x)$ in a Taylor series about $\bar{x}$ and noting that $f'(\bar{x}) = 1$, we have

$$f(x) = f(\bar{x}) + (x - \bar{x}) + \tfrac{1}{2}f''(\bar{x})(x - \bar{x})^2 + \cdots$$

We now terminate the series after three terms as shown and let $x = \bar{x} + d$,

[6]Nathaniel Macon, *Numerical Analysis* (New York: Wiley, 1963) pp. 34–36.

so that

$$f(\bar{x} + d) = f(\bar{x}) + d + \tfrac{1}{2}f''(\bar{x})d^2$$

But

$$f(\bar{x} + d) = \bar{x} + d$$

so, solving for d,

$$d = \sqrt{\frac{2(\bar{x} - f(\bar{x}))}{f''(\bar{x})}}$$

For the case in which we are solving the equation in the form

$$F(x) = 0$$

we get

$$d = \sqrt{\frac{-2F(\bar{x})}{F''(\bar{x})}}$$

noting that $F'(\bar{x}) = 0$. The reader should satisfy himself that the quantity under the square root sign is positive by referring to Figure 1.20.

A recapitulation is in order. Given an equation with two nearly equal roots and knowing at least approximately where they are, we solve the equation

$$x = x + f'(x) - 1$$

for a value $\bar{x}$, using any convenient method, such as Newton-Raphson. Using this value of $\bar{x}$, we solve for d with the expressions shown above. Finally, the values $\bar{x} - d$ and $\bar{x} + d$ are used as starting approximations for a Newton-Raphson solution for a_1 and a_2, respectively.

Of course, we may run into trouble if $f''(x)$ is near zero. This means that $f'(x) = 1$ has more than one root near $\bar{x}$. In this event we must first find a solution for $f''(x) = 0$. The details are not discussed here; the interested reader is referred to Macon's text.

1.9 Comparison of the Methods

We have already noted in Section 1.7 that the Newton-Raphson method appeared to converge more rapidly than did the method of successive approximations. This fact is somewhat surprising since as we have developed it the Newton-Raphson method is just a special case of successive approximations. As it turns out, the Newton-Raphson method is an *extremely* special case and does indeed converge quite rapidly. In this section we shall examine the rates of convergence of the most general method of successive approximations and of the special case (Newton-Raphson) and compare the methods from several points of view.

The method of successive approximations employed the iteration relation, stated before,

$$x_n = f(x_{n-1}) \tag{1.10}$$

where

$$a = f(a) \tag{1.11}$$

From Taylor's theorem,[7] if $f(x)$ has a continuous first derivative, then

$$f(x) = f(x_{n-1}) + (x - x_{n-1})f'(\xi)$$

where ξ lies in the closed interval bounded by x and x_{n-1}. If we let $x = a$, then using (1.10) and (1.11)

$$a = x_n + (a - x_{n-1})f'(\xi)$$

or

$$a - x_n = (a - x_{n-1})f'(\xi)$$

We define the *error*, ϵ_n, in the nth approximation, x_n, to be

$$\epsilon_n = a - x_n$$

so that

$$\epsilon_n = f'(\xi)\epsilon_{n-1} \tag{1.21}$$

where ξ is between x_{n-1} and x_n. Thus we see that in each iteration the error is reduced by a factor $f'(\xi)$. If the absolute value of the derivative of f is less than 1, then the error is reduced. The smaller the absolute value of the derivative, the greater the reduction in the error. As we might have expected, this analysis leads us to the same convergence criterion that we arrived at earlier in Section 1.4.

From (1.21) we see that the error in the nth iteration is directly proportional to the error in the $(n - 1)$st iteration. The constant of proportionality is $f'(\xi)$. In such a case, the convergence is said to be *linear* since the error is a linear function of the error in the previous approximation.

For the Newton-Raphson method, the iteration relationship is

$$x_n = \frac{f(x_{n-1}) - x_{n-1}f'(x_{n-1})}{1 - f'(x_{n-1})} \tag{1.19}$$

If the above argument is carried through with this iteration formula, we arrive at

$$\epsilon_n = f'(\xi)\epsilon_{n-1} - f'(x_{n-1})(x_n - x_{n-1}) \tag{1.22}$$

Assuming convergence, we note that for n sufficiently large $x_n - x_{n-1}$ should be close to ϵ_{n-1}. Similarly, since ξ should be "close" to x_{n-1}, then $f'(\xi)$ should be close to $f'(x_{n-1})$. Thus the two terms on the right side of (1.22) look as though they might very well cancel each other.

To examine this possible cancellation further we again use Taylor's theorem to obtain

$$f(x) = f(x_{n-1}) + (x - x_{n-1})f'(x_{n-1}) + \tfrac{1}{2}(x - x_{n-1})^2 f''(\eta)$$

where η is in the closed interval bounded by x and x_{n-1}. (This assumes

---

[7]Taylor's theorem states that if $F(x)$ has k continuous derivatives then

$$F(x) = F(x^*) + (x - x^*)F'(x^*) + \cdots + \frac{(x - x^*)^{k-1}}{(k - 1)!} F^{(k-1)}(x^*) + \frac{(x - x^*)^k}{k!} F^{(k)}(\xi)$$

where ξ lies in the closed interval bounded by x and x^*. For $k = 1$ this is merely a restatement of the mean value theorem (see footnote 5 on p. 21). For that reason Taylor's theorem is sometimes referred to as the "extended mean value theorem."

that $f(x)$ has a continuous second derivative.) Letting $x = a$,

$$f(a) = f(x_{n-1}) + (a - x_{n-1})f'(x_{n-1}) + \tfrac{1}{2}(a - x_{n-1})^2 f''(\eta)$$

Using (1.11) and (1.19) and assuming that $f'(x_n) \neq 1$, we arrive at

$$a = x_n + \frac{\tfrac{1}{2}(a - x_{n-1})^2 f''(\eta)}{1 - f'(x_{n-1})}$$

Thus

$$\epsilon_n = -\frac{1}{2} \frac{f''(\eta)}{1 - f'(x_{n-1})} \epsilon_{n-1}^2 \qquad (1.23)$$

where η is between x_{n-1} and x_n.

For the Newton-Raphson method the error in each iteration is proportional to the *square* of the error in the previous iteration. Such convergence is called *quadratic*.

From this we can see that the terms on the right side of (1.22) do not cancel each other exactly. However, these terms do cancel to the extent that only a term in ϵ_{n-1}^2 remains. (There is no term in ϵ_{n-1} itself.) Of course, if the derivative of f is close to 1, then the constant of proportionality in (1.23) becomes large and may in fact overwhelm the factor ϵ_{n-1}^2. The same thing is true if the second derivative is very large. This brings us back to conditions 2 and 3 in Section 1.7, which we already noted were necessary for convergence of the Newton-Raphson method.

To make the notion of quadratic convergence a little more concrete and to emphasize its importance, suppose that x_{n-1} is accurate to p digits after the decimal point. Then

$$|\epsilon_{n-1}| \leq \tfrac{1}{2} \cdot 10^{-p} \qquad (1.24)$$

For example, if p is 4, then the error ϵ_{n-1} does not exceed $0.00005 = \tfrac{1}{2} \times 10^{-4}$. Now we assume, albeit somewhat arbitrarily, that

$$|f''(x)| \leq 4|1 - f'(x_{n-1})|$$

for *all* values of x; that is to say, given x_{n-1}, the maximum value of the magnitude of the second derivative of f is

$$4|1 - f'(x_{n-1})|$$

This assumption can be relaxed considerably, as we shall discuss later. We make such an assumption for convenience and for simplification of the algebraic argument. At any rate, with this assumption (1.23) leads to

$$|\epsilon_n| \leq 2\epsilon_{n-1}^2$$

Taking logarithms to the base 10 of both sides (if $x \leq y$, then $\log_{10} x \leq \log_{10} y$),

$$\log_{10}|\epsilon_n| \leq (\log_{10} 2) + 2(\log_{10}|\epsilon_{n-1}|)$$

From (1.24)

$$\log_{10}|\epsilon_n| \leq -(\log_{10} 2) - 2p$$

Using each side of this last inequality as an exponent of 10 (if $x \le y$, then $10^x \le 10^y$),

$$|\epsilon_n| \le \tfrac{1}{2} \times 10^{-2p}$$

It follows that ϵ_n is accurate to at least $2p$ digits. Therefore, we double the number of accurate digits after the decimal point at each iteration. This, of course, assumes that

$$|f''(x)| < 4|1 - f'(x_n)|$$

for all values of x. Even if the last inequality is not satisfied, but the second derivative of $f(x)$ is at least bounded, we can still arrive at an analogous result—that is, the number of digits after the decimal point is doubled with each iteration.

Since the Newton-Raphson method converges much more rapidly than does the method of successive approximations, we might ask why the latter is ever used. The answer lies in the requirement, in Newton-Raphson, of the evaluation of both the function and its derivative at each iteration. These evaluations may be difficult, time-consuming, or impossible. For example, the function $f(x)$ may not be given by a formula at all but by a table of values. The derivative may not exist at all points. The method of successive approximations or its modification is often applied in such cases.

The choice of methods depends, in other words, on the particular function $f(x)$ or $F(x)$.

**1.10
Roots of
Polyno-
mials**

We now consider the very important special case in which $F(x)$ is a polynomial of degree m, that is,

$$F(x) = a_0 + a_1 x + a_2 x^2 + \cdots + a_m x^m \tag{1.25}$$

We will use the Newton-Raphson method in the form given by (1.20) to find a root of $F(x)$. Therefore, we shall need to evaluate the polynomial $F(x)$ and its derivative for several values of x, for example, $x_0, x_1, x_2, \ldots$.

Our first task is to develop an efficient algorithm for computing the numerical value of both a polynomial and its derivative. Suppose we divide $F(x)$ by $x - \bar{x}$ where $\bar{x}$ is some constant. (Think of $\bar{x}$ as one of the values for which we wish to evaluate $F(x)$ and $F'(x)$.) We shall get a quotient that is a polynomial of degree $m - 1$ and a remainder that is a constant, that is,

$$\frac{F(x)}{x - \bar{x}} = b_1 + b_2 x + \cdots + b_m x^{m-1} + \frac{b_0}{x - \bar{x}}$$

Multiplying this equation by $x - \bar{x}$,

$$F(x) = (x - \bar{x})(b_1 + b_2 x + \cdots + b_m x^{m-1}) + b_0 \tag{1.26}$$

Notice that $F(\bar{x}) = b_0$. Therefore, if we can find b_0, we shall have evaluated the polynomial $F(x)$ for $x = \bar{x}$.

To compute b_0, and indeed all b_j for $j = 0, 1, 2, \ldots, m$, we equate the coefficients of like powers of x on the right-hand sides of (1.25) and (1.26).

From the coefficients of x^m we get

$$a_m = b_m$$

From the coefficients of x^{m-1} then

$$a_{m-1} = b_{m-1} + \bar{x}b_m$$

In general, from equating the coefficients of x^{j-1} we get

$$a_{j-1} = b_{j-1} + \bar{x}b_j$$

for $j = m, m - 1, \ldots, 2, 1$. To compute the b_j we then "solve" these equations. First we compute

$$b_m = a_m \qquad (1.27)$$

then

$$b_{m-1} = a_{m-1} + \bar{x}b_m$$

and in general

$$b_j = a_j + \bar{x}\,b_{j+1} \qquad (1.28)$$

where $j = m - 1, m - 2, \ldots, 1, 0$. To calculate any b_j (except b_m) we need the value of b_{j+1}. Thus we must calculate the b_j successively, starting with b_m, in descending order, i.e., $b_m, b_{m-1}, b_{m-2}, \ldots, b_1, b_0$.

As an example for $m = 5$, the successive b's are

$$
\begin{aligned}
b_5 &= a_5 \\
b_4 &= a_4 + \bar{x}a_5 \\
b_3 &= a_3 + \bar{x}(a_4 + \bar{x}a_5) \\
b_2 &= a_2 + \bar{x}(a_3 + \bar{x}(a_4 + \bar{x}a_5)) \\
b_1 &= a_1 + \bar{x}(a_2 + \bar{x}(a_3 + \bar{x}(a_4 + \bar{x}a_5))) \\
b_0 &= a_0 + \bar{x}(a_1 + \bar{x}(a_2 + \bar{x}(a_3 + \bar{x}(a_4 + \bar{x}a_5))))
\end{aligned}
$$

This method of evaluating the polynomial $F(x)$ given in (1.25) is known as *Horner's method* and may be represented by

$$F(x) = a_0 + x(a_1 + x(a_2 + \cdots + x(a_{m-1} + x(a_m))\cdots)) \qquad (1.29)$$

Because of the appearance of the expression on the right of (1.29), Horner's method is often referred to as the *nesting procedure* (note the "nested" parentheses).

To evaluate a general polynomial of degree m by Horner's method requires m multiplications and m additions. There is no more efficient way (in the sense of requiring fewer arithmetic operations) to evaluate a general polynomial of mth degree. For special polynomials that are evaluated a large number of times for different arguments, methods have been devised that reduce the total number of operations considerably.[8]

We shall discuss the roundoff errors in Horner's method in Chapter 2 and compare the roundoff error with roundoff errors in other methods of evaluating a polynomial.

Now we turn to the problem of evaluating the derivative of $F(x)$. Taking

[8] See, for example, Donald E. Knuth, "Evaluation of Polynomials by Computer," *Communications of the Association for Computing Machinery*, Vol. 5, No. 12 (December 1962).

the derivative of $F(x)$ using (1.26) we get

$$F'(x) = (x - \bar{x})G'(x) + G(x)$$

where

$$G(x) = b_1 + b_2 x + \cdots + b_m x^{m-1}$$

Thus

$$F'(\bar{x}) = G(\bar{x})$$

But $G(x)$ is a polynomial of degree $m - 1$, so we can use Horner's method to evaluate $G(\bar{x})$ and thereby also evaluate $F'(\bar{x})$. Letting

$$c_m = b_m$$

$$c_j = b_j + \bar{x}c_{j+1} \qquad j = m - 1, \ldots, 1$$

It follows that

$$F'(\bar{x}) = G(\bar{x}) = c_1$$

From (1.20)

$$x_n = x_{n-1} - \frac{b_0}{c_1}$$

where b_0 and c_1 are calculated from

$$\left.\begin{array}{l} c_m = b_m = a_m \\ b_j = a_j + x_{n-1}b_{j+1} \text{ where } j = m - 1, \ldots, 0 \\ c_j = b_j + x_{n-1}c_{j+1} \text{ where } j = m - 1, \ldots, 1 \end{array}\right\} \qquad (1.30)$$

This entire procedure for polynomials is often called the *Birge-Vieta method*.

Example

As an example of the Birge-Vieta method we return to the polynomial

$$F(x) = x^4 - 9x^3 - 2x^2 + 120x - 130$$

already studied in Case Study 1, in which one root was calculated to be -3.6.

We start our calculations with an initial guess of $x_0 = -3$. The sequence of calculations using (1.30) is shown in Table 1.1.

The values of x_4 and x_5 agree to 7 figures. Moreover, because the value of the polynomial for $x = -3.600135$ is small (approximately 7×10^{-6}), we can stop the computations and take -3.600135 as an approximate root. In Case Study 1 we found that the root was between -3.60016 and -3.60013; thus this result agrees with our previous computations. Notice, however, that here we have no bounds on the root. Our criterion for stopping is that the value of the function is small.

If we had started with $x_0 = -4$, we would have arrived at the same result in one less iteration (see Exercise 25). However, it is not always true that the closer we start to the root, the fewer the number of iterations.

Table 1.1

i	a_i	b_i	c_i
4	1	1	1
3	−9	−12	−15
2	−2	34	79
1	120	18	−219
0	−130	−184	

$$x_1 = x_0 - \frac{b_0}{c_1} = -3 - \frac{-184}{-219} = -3.840183$$

i	a_i	b_i	c_i
4	1	1	1
3	−9	−12.84018	−16.68037
2	−2	47.30865	111.3643
1	120	−61.67384	−489.331
0	−130	106.8388	

$$x_2 = x_1 - \frac{b_0}{c_1} = -3.840183 - \frac{106.8388}{-489.3331} = -3.621847$$

i	a_i	b_i	c_i
4	1	1	1
3	−9	−12.62185	−16.24369
2	−2	43.7144	102.5466
1	120	−38.32687	−409.7349
0	−130	8.814062	

$$x_3 = \dot{x}_2 - \frac{b_0}{c_1} = -3.621847 - \frac{8.814062}{-409.7349} = -3.600335$$

i	a_i	b_i	c_i
4	1	1	1
3	−9	−12.60034	−16.20067
2	−2	43.36543	101.6933
1	120	−36.13011	−402.26
0	−130	0.080515	

$$x_4 = x_3 - \frac{b_0}{c_1} = -3.600335 - \frac{.080515}{-402.26} = -3.600135$$

i	a_i	b_i	c_i
4	1	1	1
3	−9	−12.60014	−16.20027
2	−2	43.36219	101.6854
1	120	−36.10976	−402.1908
0	−130	0.0000069	

$$x_5 = x_4 - \frac{b_0}{c_1} = -3.600135 - \frac{0.0000069}{-402.1908} = -3.600135$$

**1.11
Effect of
Uncertainty
in the Co-
efficients**

Often the coefficients a_i in the polynomial (1.25) are obtained from experimental equipment or as a result of prior calculations. In either case there is some uncertainty in the values of the coefficients. In this section we shall determine how errors in the coefficients affect the error in the computed root.

We shall assume that the roundoff error in the calculations is negligible. This is in fact often the case. For example, it is not uncommon to work with coefficients that are known to only a few percent (two or three digits) in a computer that carries six or more digits in each number. Except in unlikely circumstances, roundoff error will not matter in such a case.

Let the error in a_i be δ_i; that is, the *true* polynomial is

$$T(x) = (a_0 + \delta_0) + (a_1 + \delta_1)x + (a_2 + \delta_2)x^2 + \cdots + (a_m + \delta_m)x^m \quad (1.31)$$

The T stands for "true." Of course, we do not know the values of the δ_i. If we did know their values, we would find a root of the true polynomial $T(x)$ instead of a root of the approximate polynomial $F(x)$. However, we may know something about the δ_i without explicitly knowing their values. For example, if the coefficients a_i are experimental data, then we may know that the a_i are each accurate to a fixed number of decimal places, p. In this case

$$|\delta_i| \leq \tfrac{1}{2} \cdot 10^{-p} \quad (1.32)$$

We shall use these inequalities (1.32) to determine the error in a root of (1.25).

Suppose $\bar{x}$ is a root of the original polynomial (the approximate one)

$$F(x) = a_0 + a_1 x + a_2 x^2 + \cdots + a_m x^m$$

that is,

$$F(\bar{x}) = 0 \quad (1.33)$$

We let $\bar{\bar{x}}$ be a root of (1.31) so that

$$T(\bar{\bar{x}}) = 0 \quad (1.34)$$

Of course, we have no way of finding $\bar{\bar{x}}$, but we can compute $\bar{x}$ or at least an approximation to $\bar{x}$.

We define the error in $\bar{x}$ to be

$$\epsilon = \bar{\bar{x}} - \bar{x} \quad (1.35)$$

and proceed to estimate ϵ. We shall assume that $|\epsilon|$ is much less than $|\bar{x}|$. When we have estimated ϵ, we shall need to test this assumption. If indeed $|\epsilon|$ is small compared to $|\bar{x}|$, then the analysis that follows is valid. On the other hand, if the assumption is not valid, then the estimate of ϵ will not be valid either. In many cases the assumption is valid. In any case the assumption is easily tested *after*[9] ϵ has been estimated.

---

[9] It would, of course, be more satisfactory and more useful if we could test the assumption *before* ϵ is calculated. Unfortunately we cannot do so.

From (1.31), (1.34), and (1.35)

$$(a_0 + \delta_0) + (a_1 + \delta_1)(\overline{x} + \epsilon) + \cdots$$
$$+ (a_{m-1} + \delta_{m-1})(\overline{x} + \epsilon)^{m-1} + (a_m + \delta_m)(\overline{x} + \epsilon)^m = 0$$

Expanding each product of the form $(\overline{x} + \epsilon)^k$ and neglecting terms of second or higher powers of ϵ (recall the assumption that ϵ is small), we get

$$(a_0 + \delta_0) + (a_1 + \delta_1)(\overline{x} + \epsilon) + (a_2 + \delta_2)(\overline{x}^2 + 2\overline{x}\epsilon) + \cdots$$
$$+ (a_{m-1} + \delta_{m-1})(\overline{x}^{m-1} + (m-1)\overline{x}^{m-2}\epsilon) + (a_m + \delta_m)(\overline{x}^m + m\overline{x}^{m-1}\epsilon) = 0$$

We now remove the parentheses and neglect terms in $\delta_i \epsilon$ (recall that not only is ϵ small but the δ_i are also small). Using (1.33) we obtain

$$\delta_0 + \delta_1 \overline{x} + \cdots + \delta_{m-1}\overline{x}^{m-1} + \delta_m \overline{x}^m + \epsilon(a_1 + 2a_2\overline{x} + \cdots$$
$$+ (m-1)a_{m-1}\overline{x}^{m-2} + ma_m \overline{x}^{m-1}) = 0$$

Therefore

$$\sum_{i=0}^{m} \delta_i \overline{x}^i + \epsilon F'(\overline{x}) = 0$$

A bound for ϵ then is

$$|\epsilon| \leq \frac{\left| \sum_{i=0}^{m} \delta_i \overline{x}^i \right|}{|F'(\overline{x})|} \tag{1.36}$$

where again we need to require that the derivative of the polynomial does not vanish at $x = \overline{x}$.

For the case where the coefficients a_i are experimental data (accurate to a fixed number of decimals), the bound (1.36) takes on a particularly simple form. Using (1.32)

$$|\epsilon| \leq \frac{\frac{1}{2} \cdot 10^{-p}}{|F'(\overline{x})|} \left| \sum_{i=0}^{m} \overline{x}^i \right|$$

Now

$$\left| \sum_{i=0}^{m} \overline{x}^i \right| \leq \sum_{i=0}^{m} |\overline{x}|^i$$

by the triangle inequality. The right-hand member of this last inequality is a geometric series and is equal to

$$\frac{1 - |\overline{x}|^{m+1}}{1 - |\overline{x}|}$$

provided $|\overline{x}| \neq 1$. Using this

$$|\epsilon| \leq \frac{10^{-p}(1 - |\overline{x}|^{m+1})}{2|c_1|(1 - |\overline{x}|)} \tag{1.37}$$

where c_1 has replaced $F'(\overline{x})$ and is calculated from (1.30).

Example

Consider once more the polynomial of Case Study 1:

$$F(x) = x^4 - 9x^3 - 2x^2 + 120x - 130$$

An approximate root is $\bar{x} = -3.6$. Suppose the coefficients are accurate to two digits after the decimal point, for example,

$$a_1 = 120.00 \pm 0.005$$

Then $p = 2$, so from (1.37)

$$|\epsilon| \leq \frac{10^{-2}(1 - |3.6|^5)}{2 \cdot 402 \cdot (1 - 3.6)} = 0.289 \times 10^{-2}$$

The root then is

$$\bar{x} = -3.600 \pm 0.003$$

1.12
Complex
Roots

All the techniques described so far find the real roots of an equation. We shall now discuss briefly the solution of equations whose roots are complex numbers.

It should be clear that if the function is real-valued and if the initial guess x_0 is real, only real numbers will be produced. However, if x_0 is a complex number, then succeeding x_i may also be complex. Indeed, the methods described previously work equally well for complex numbers. Most Fortran systems have provisions for complex arithmetic; in these systems it is a minor problem to modify the program to make it find complex roots.

Finally, for polynomials with real coefficients, if $a + bi$ (where $i = \sqrt{-1}$) is a root, then $a - bi$ is also a root. Thus, if $P_m(x)$ is a polynomial of degree m, then the polynomial can be factored into the form

$$P_m(x) = (x - (a + bi)) \cdot (x - (a - bi)) \cdot P_{m-2}(x)$$

where $P_{m-2}(x)$ is a polynomial of degree $m - 2$, and $P_{m-2}(x)$ has real coefficients. Now

$$(x - (a + bi)) \cdot (x - (a - bi)) = x^2 - 2ax + (a^2 + b^2)$$

so

$$P_m(x) = (x^2 - 2ax + (a^2 + b^2)) \cdot P_{m-2}(x)$$

The term in parentheses is a quadratic factor and contains only real numbers. Consequently we may perform the same analysis as we did in Section 1.10 to find a and b using real arithmetic. The interested reader is referred to Chapter 10 of the text by Hildebrand for details.[10]

The use of the method of successive approximations in this way is usually referred to as Lin's method, and the Newton-Raphson method is known as Bairstow's method.

---

[10] F. B. Hildebrand, *Introduction to Numerical Analysis* New York, McGraw-Hill, 1956.

**1.13
Simul-
taneous
Equations**

Often we are faced with problems involving several unknowns and an equal number of equations. For example, we may wish to find x and y such that

$$x^2 + y = 3$$

and

$$y^2 + x = 5$$

In this case we may solve the first equation for y and substitute in the second to get

$$x^4 - 6x^2 + x + 4 = 0$$

Now we have a polynomial in x that can be solved by methods we know. One root is $x = 1$ and therefore $y = 2$.

Many times, however, it is difficult or impractical to reduce the problem in this way to the solution of one equation in one unknown. The most common situation occurs when the equations are linear; this special case is considered in detail in Chapter 4, since there are special methods for its solution. Here we shall develop iterative formulas for the solution of two simultaneous equations in two variables. These formulas are generalizations of the Newton-Raphson method. A generalization of the method of successive approximations to two equations in two unknowns is given in Exercise 40.

Let the equations be

$$\left.\begin{array}{c} F(x,y) = 0 \\ G(x,y) = 0 \end{array}\right\} \tag{1.38}$$

and let x_0, y_0 be an approximate solution. Now expanding $F(x,y)$ in a Taylor's series and neglecting terms except those linear in x and y

$$F(x,y) = F(x_0,y_0) + (x - x_0)\frac{\partial F}{\partial x} + (y - y_0)\frac{\partial F}{\partial y}$$

The partial derivatives are evaluated for $x = x_0$ and $y = y_0$.

Similarly

$$G(x,y) = G(x_0,y_0) + (x - x_0)\frac{\partial G}{\partial x} + (y - y_0)\frac{\partial G}{\partial y}$$

Using these two truncated series in (1.38) and rearranging terms

$$\frac{\partial F}{\partial x}x + \frac{\partial F}{\partial y}y = -F + \frac{\partial F}{\partial x}x_0 + \frac{\partial F}{\partial y}y_0 \tag{1.39}$$

$$\frac{\partial G}{\partial x}x + \frac{\partial G}{\partial y}y = -G + \frac{\partial G}{\partial x}x_0 + \frac{\partial G}{\partial y}y_0 \tag{1.40}$$

These are two linear equations for x and y. In Chapter 4 we shall discuss the solution of such linear systems of equations. However, for now we simply multiply (1.39) by $\partial G/\partial y$ and multiply (1.40) by $\partial F/\partial y$ and subtract the second of the resulting equations from the first. The terms involving y will cancel each other. The result of the subtraction is

$$\left(\frac{\partial G}{\partial y}\frac{\partial F}{\partial x} - \frac{\partial F}{\partial y}\frac{\partial G}{\partial x}\right)x = -\frac{\partial G}{\partial y}F + \frac{\partial G}{\partial y}\frac{\partial F}{\partial x}x_0 + \frac{\partial F}{\partial y}G - \frac{\partial F}{\partial y}\frac{\partial G}{\partial x}x_0$$

Now we define the *Jacobian* of the system (1.38) to be

$$J = \frac{\partial G}{\partial y} \frac{\partial F}{\partial x} - \frac{\partial F}{\partial y} \frac{\partial G}{\partial x}$$

Then, provided $J \neq 0$,

$$x = x_0 - \frac{F \dfrac{\partial G}{\partial y} - G \dfrac{\partial F}{\partial y}}{J} \tag{1.41}$$

Similarly, if we multiply (1.39) by $\partial G/\partial x$ and (1.40) by $\partial F/\partial x$ and subtract, the resulting equation will not have any term involving x. Solving that resulting equation for y,

$$y = y_0 + \frac{F \dfrac{\partial G}{\partial x} - G \dfrac{\partial F}{\partial x}}{J} \tag{1.42}$$

The values of x and y given by (1.41) and (1.42) are the new, and hopefully better, approximations to the solution of the system of (1.38). We call this new approximation x_1 and y_1 and then repeat the process with these values of x and y replacing x_0 and y_0. In this way we obtain still another approximation.

In general, given the $(n-1)$st approximation x_{n-1} and y_{n-1}, we calculate the nth approximation from

$$x_n = x_{n-1} - \frac{F \dfrac{\partial G}{\partial y} - G \dfrac{\partial F}{\partial y}}{J} \tag{1.43}$$

$$y_n = y_{n-1} + \frac{F \dfrac{\partial G}{\partial x} - G \dfrac{\partial F}{\partial x}}{J} \tag{1.44}$$

where

$$J = \frac{\partial F}{\partial x} \frac{\partial G}{\partial y} - \frac{\partial F}{\partial y} \frac{\partial G}{\partial x} \tag{1.45}$$

The functions F and G and the partial derivatives of these functions are all evaluated for $x = x_{n-1}$ and $y = y_{n-1}$. We also require that the Jacobian, J, is not zero. This is analogous to assuming that $F'(x_{n-1}) \neq 0$ in the single variable case.

The extension of these techniques to systems of three or more equations in an equal number of variables is straightforward. Derivation of the algorithm for m variables requires the solution of a system of m linear equations. The solution of such linear systems will be discussed in Chapter 4.

Numerical examples for two equations in two variables are given in Exercises 38 and 39.

1.14
Finding an
Initial Ap-
proximation

The method of successive approximations and the Newton-Raphson method both assume that we start with an initial approximation to the root of a function $F(x)$. In Case Study 1 (Section 1.2) we discussed one method of finding such an initial approximation. There we simply evaluated the function at a number of points until a change in the sign of $F(x)$ was found. Assuming $F(x)$ is continuous, a root lies between the values of x which produced values of $F(x)$ with opposite signs. More precisely, if

$$F(L) > 0$$

and

$$F(U) < 0$$

then the number of roots between L and U is 1 or greater than 1 by a multiple of 2.

As a first approximation to a root of $F(x)$, we may take

$$x_0 = \tfrac{1}{2}(L + U)$$

One way of determining L and U is to try to find a simpler equation whose roots are near those of the original equation. For example, suppose

$$F(x) = \frac{\sin x}{10} + x^3 - 1$$

For $0 \leq x \leq \pi/2$, the first term varies between 0 and 0.1. Because this is small compared with the other two terms, we consider the two extreme values for $(\sin x)/10$:

$$0 + x^3 - 1 = 0$$

and

$$\tfrac{1}{10} + x^3 - 1 = 0$$

Roots of each of these expressions are

$$L = +1$$
$$U = \sqrt[3]{0.9} = 0.965489$$

Now

$$F(L) = 0.084$$

and

$$F(U) = -0.18$$

Thus, as a first approximation we choose

$$x_0 = \tfrac{1}{2}(1 + 0.965489) = 0.982749$$

For polynomial equations special methods that are often of practical use exist. We shall discuss two of these here.

One easily applied method of isolating the real roots of a polynomial is:

Descartes' Rule of Signs. Let

$$F(x) = a_0 + a_1 x + \cdots + a_{m-1} x^{m-1} + a_m x^m$$

The number of *positive* roots of $F(x)$ is either equal to the number of changes in sign[11] in the coefficients $a_0, a_1, \ldots, a_m$ taken in that order or is less than that quantity by a multiple of 2.[12]

Example

$$F(x) = 1 + 3x - 3x^2 - 4x^3 + x^4 + x^5$$

The coefficients in order are $+1, +3, -3, -4, +1, +1$. There is one change in sign from $+3$ to -3 and a second from -4 to $+1$. Thus there are two sign changes and zero or two positive roots. In fact, there are two positive roots: One between 0 and 1 and one between 1 and 2.

We can use Descartes' Rule of Signs to gain some knowledge of the number of *negative* roots as well. We first note that a negative root of $F(x)$ is a positive root of $F(-x)$. Thus, if we count the number of sign changes in the coefficients of $F(-x)$, we shall know something about the number of negative roots of $F(x)$. Using the same example as above

$$F(-x) = 1 - 3x - 3x^2 + 4x^3 + x^4 - x^5$$

There are three sign changes and, therefore, one or three negative roots of $F(x)$. In fact there are three such roots: One each between -2 and -1.5, -1.5 and -1, and -1 and 0.

Descartes' rule tells us something about where to search for roots of $F(x)$, but it does not really isolate the roots. Its primary virtue lies in the ease with which it can be applied.

Another more powerful theorem is:

Budan's Theorem. Let $F^{(k)}(L)$ be the value of the kth derivative of $F(x)$ evaluated for $x = L$. Let V_L be the number of changes in sign in the sequence of numbers $F(L), F'(L), \ldots, F^{(m)}(L)$ taken in that order. The number of roots of $F(x)$ in the open interval $L < x < U$ is either equal to $|V_L - V_U|$ or is less than that quantity by a multiple of 2.[13]

We pause here to contrast this result with the simple function evaluation technique used in Case Study 1. There we evaluated only the function itself at various points. The number of roots between sign changes was 1 or *greater* than 1 by a multiple of 2. Here we evaluate not only the function but all of its derivatives at various points. However, here the number of roots is $|V_L - V_U|$ or *less* than that number by a multiple of 2. Therefore, Budan's theorem, although it is more work than simple function evaluation, provides us with more information about the roots.

---

[11]A zero coefficient is assumed to have the same sign as its predecessor.
[12]Proof of this result may be found in a number of algebra textbooks. Among them are *Theory of Equations* by J. V. Uspensky, McGraw-Hill, 1948, Section 10, Chapter VI, pp. 121–124; *Higher Algebra* by Ap. P. Mishina and I. V. Proskuryakov, translated by Ann Swinfen, Pergamon Press, 1965, pp. 193–195; and *Higher Algebra* by S. Bernard and J. M. Child, Macmillan, 1960, Section 9, Chapter 6.
[13]Proof of this theorem may be found in Section 8, Chapter 28 of *Higher Algebra* by S. Bernard and J. M. Child, Macmillan, 1960. Budan's theorem is also referred to in the literature as Fourier's theorem or, on occasions, as the Fourier-Budan theorem.

Example

$$F(x) = 1 + 3x - 3x^2 - 4x^3 + x^4 + x^5$$
$$F'(x) = 3 - 6x - 12x^2 + 4x^3 + 5x^4$$
$$F''(x) = -6 - 24x + 12x^2 + 20x^3$$
$$F'''(x) = -24 + 24x + 60x^2$$
$$F^{iv}(x) = 24 + 120x$$
$$F^v(x) = 120$$

The signs of these functions for $x = -2, -1, 0, 1, 2$ are shown in Table 1.2.

Thus, by Budan's theorem there are zero or two roots in $-2 < x < 1$; there is one root in each of $-1 < x < 0$, $0 < x < 1$, and $1 < x < 2$.

From the first column (evaluating $F(x)$ only) we can see that there is *at least* one root in $-1 < x < 0$, $0 < x < 1$ and $1 < x < 2$. Budan's theorem tells us there is *exactly* one root in each of those intervals.

Still more powerful theorems are available for isolating roots. However, as the power of the theorem increases so does the effort required to apply it. One such theorem is Sturm's theorem. We shall not present the theorem here but refer the interested reader to Section 4.2 of *Analysis of Numerical Methods* by Eugene Isaacson and Herbert B. Keller, Wiley, 1966; or, to pp. 138–145 of *Theory of Equations*, by J. V. Uspensky, McGraw-Hill, 1948.

Table 1.2

x	$F(x)$	$F'(x)$	$F''(x)$	$F'''(x)$	$F^{iv}(x)$	$F^v(x)$	V_x
-2	$-$	$+$	$-$	$+$	$-$	$+$	5
-1	$-$	$-$	$+$	$+$	$-$	$+$	3
0	$+$	$+$	$-$	$-$	$+$	$+$	2
1	$-$	$-$	$+$	$+$	$+$	$+$	1
2	$+$	$+$	$+$	$+$	$+$	$+$	0

1.15 Case Study 2: The Newton-Raphson Method in a Structures Problem

For an illustration of how some of the techniques presented in this chapter might be applied in the solution of a practical problem, we consider a realistic problem in structural design. As with all case studies, the illustration may hold somewhat more interest for the reader who is closely familiar with the subject matter, but understanding the discussion and the numerical techniques requires no background whatever in the specialized subject area.

For an eccentrically loaded, pinned-end column with allowable stress σ_0, the maximum permissable axial load, P, is the smallest positive root of the transcendental equation[14]

$$f(P) = \frac{P}{A} - \frac{\sigma_0}{1 + \dfrac{ec}{r^2}\sec\left[\dfrac{L}{2r}\sqrt{\dfrac{P}{EA}}\right]} = 0 \qquad (1.46)$$

[14]Higdon, A., Ohlsen, E., Stiles, S., and Weese, J., *Mechanics of Materials* (2nd ed.), New York, Wiley, 1967, pp. 430–432.

The length of the column is L; A, c and r (positive constants) are geometrical properties of the cross section; e (nonnegative) is the eccentricity of the loading (i.e., the initial misalignment between the loading and the column axis); and E is Young's modulus, a material parameter. From other considerations, it is known that, if the alignment is perfect ($e = 0$), then the maximum permissible load is found by equating the argument of the secant in (1.46) to $\pi/2$. This yields the so-called Euler buckling load

$$P_{cr} = \frac{\pi^2 EA}{(L/r)^2} \qquad (1.47)$$

which is an upper bound for P in (1.46).

To study the behavior of the solution of (1.46), we assume the values of A, c, and r to be unity, σ_0 to be 40,000, and E to be $30 \cdot 10^6$. The only remaining parameters in (1.46) are then P, e, and L.

Our task here is to find the smallest positive root of (1.46), given values of e and L. We shall use the Newton-Raphson method, starting the iteration with $P = P_{cr}/2$, since P_{cr} is an upper bound for physically meaningful values of P. A flow chart is shown in Figure 1.22. For clarity in reading the program that we shall write, the factors in the formulas that do not change in what we are doing (A, c, r, σ_0, and E) have been kept as variables, although the program might be slightly shorter and run slightly faster if the assumed values were used directly. These variables are given their values at the beginning of the program, after which we read values for e and L. The next step is to compute P_{cr} and give P its starting value. Since it is always poor practice to set up a iterative program without some mechanism for stopping it if for any reason—numerical difficulties, programming errors, or whatever—it should attempt to run indefinitely, we establish an *iteration counter*, named ITER, and give it its initial value.

Now we can enter the part of the program that carries out the iterative procedure. After getting the values of a few expressions that occur in the formulas for the function and the derivative, we proceed to compute those latter quantities themselves. Now we can compute the new approximation to P, which we call PNEW so that we can work for the moment with both the old and the new approximations. This is necessary because the immediate question is how close together the two values are, according to this convergence criterion: The process will be considered to have converged if the difference between two successive approximations is less than $\sigma_0 \cdot A \cdot 10^{-5}$. If so, we can print the input and output values (including P_{cr} for later reference) and go back to read more input. No provision is made for stopping the program; we shall let the operating system take care of that by detecting the end of the data cards. Or, in the time sharing environment in which the program shown below was actually run, we can signal our desire to stop program execution by pressing some appropriate key or keys.

If the process has not converged, we ask whether ITER exceeds 15, which we hope is far more iterations than the process ought to take if it is working correctly, and print a comment to the effect that the process has not converged if so. If we have not converged and ITER is not greater than 15, we set P equal to P_{new}, increment ITER, and go around again.

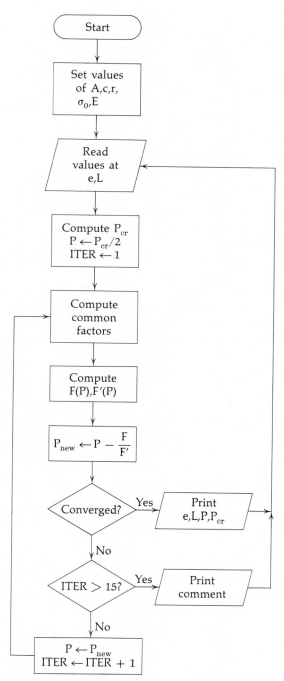

Figure 1.22. *Flow chart of a procedure for using the Newton-Raphson method to find a root of an equation in a structures problem.*

A program that follows the flow chart very closely is shown in Figure 1.23. Since Fortran accepts only upper case letters, separate variable names had to be used for e and E; EY was chosen for the latter (Y for Young's modulus). It seemed desirable to keep the variable name L for easy readability, requiring a REAL declaration to keep L from being interpreted

```
C CASE STUDY 2
C USING THE NEWTON-RAPHSON METHOD TO FIND THE ROOT OF A
C    STRUCTURES PROBLEM IN COLUMN BUCKLING
C
C SUGGESTED BY PROF. JOHN A. WEESE, DENVER UNIVERSITY
C
C SET THE VALUES OF THE UNCHANGING PARAMETERS
      REAL L
      A = 1.0
      C = 1.0
      R = 1.0
      SIGMA0 = 40000.0
      EY = 30E+6
C READ THE VALUES OF THE TWO PARAMETERS THAT CHANGE
C    IN THIS FORMULATION
   12 READ (5, 34) E, L
   34 FORMAT (2F10.0)
C COMPUTE THE MAXIMUM PERMISSIBLE LOAD, WHICH IS AN UPPER
C    BOUND FOR P
      PCR = 9.8696044 * EY * A / (L/R)**2
C START THE ITERATION WITH P = PCR/2
      P = PCR / 2.0
C INITIALIZE AN ITERATION COUNTER
      ITER = 1
C COMPUTE SOME COMMON FACTORS
   39 B = (L / (2.0 * R)) * SQRT(P / (EY * A))
      COSB = COS(B)
      SECB = 1.0 / COSB
      TANB = SIN(B) / COSB
C COMPUTE THE VALUE OF THE FUNCTION
      F = P/A - SIGMA0/(1.0 + E*C*SECB/R**2)
C COMPUTE THE VALUE OF THE DERIVATIVE
      FP = 1.0/A + (SIGMA0/(1.0 + E*C*SECB/R**2)**2) * (E*C/R**2)
     1   * (B/(2.0*P)) * SECB * TANB
C COMPUTE THE NEW APPROXIMATION TO THE ROOT
      PNEW = P - F/FP
C CHECK WHETHER LAST TWO APPROXIMATIONS ARE CLOSE ENOUGH
      IF (ABS(P - PNEW) .LT. SIGMA0*A*1.0E-5) GO TO 43
C CHECK WHETHER ITERATION COUNTER HAS BEEN EXCEEDED
      IF (ITER .GT. 15) GO TO 44
C NOT CONVERGED AND NOT TOO MANY ITERATIONS -- GO AROUND AGAIN
      P = PNEW
      ITER = ITER + 1
      GO TO 39
C WRITE OUT THE RESULT, ALONG WITH PCR FOR COMPARISON
   43 WRITE (6, 56) P, PCR
   56 FORMAT (1X, 2E15.6)
C GO BACK TO READ ANOTHER DATA POINT
      GO TO 12
C PRINT NON-CONVERGENCE COMMENT
   44 WRITE (6, 45)
   45 FORMAT (1X, 'PROCESS DID NOT CONVERGE IN 15 ITERATIONS')
      GO TO 12
      END
```

Figure 1.23. *A program corresponding to the flow chart of Figure 1.22 to find a root of a structures equation.*

as an integer variable. (This was of course forgotten in writing the initial version of the program!) The reader who wishes to review his calculus may verify that the formula for the derivative of $f(P)$ is correct. (Naturally, it could be written in other forms.)

Figure 1.24 shows the output of the program when it was run for several pairs of values for e and L. The first few lines present no problems, but when we get to the lines where e is small and L is large (long slender columns) something is obviously seriously amiss, because the computed values for P are greater than P_{cr}, which we said was an upper bound for P. What has happened?

```
0.3,50.0
   0.282355E 05     0.118435E 06
0.3,100.0
   0.196063E 05     0.296088E 05
0.3,150.0
   0.112597E 05     0.131595E 05
0.1,50.0
   0.347336E 05     0.118435E 06
0.1,100.0
   0.241327E 05     0.296088E 05
0.1,150.0
   0.446030E 05     0.131595E 05
0.05,50.0
   0.370925E 05     0.118435E 06
0.05,100.0
   0.261513E 05     0.296088E 05
0.05,150.0
   0.422302E 05     0.131595E 05
0.01,50.0
   0.393623E 05     0.118435E 06
0.01,100.0
   0.414598E 05     0.296088E 05
0.01,150.0
   0.404368E 05     0.131595E 05
0.01,180.0
   0.404094E 05     0.913852E 04
```

Figure 1.24. *The output of the program of Figure 1.24. The program was run on a time-sharing system; in each pair of lines the first is the input (e and L) and the second is the output (P and P_{cr}).*

To investigate the matter, we need to know more about $f(P)$; the problem statement was that we wanted the smallest positive root, and perhaps what we found was not the smallest. Toward this end a program was written (not shown) to compute the values of $f(P)$ for a number of values of P between 0 and 15 P_{cr}. The results are plotted in Figure 1.25, where we see fairly readily what has happened. We began the iterative process with $P = P_{cr}/2$. Since $f(P)$ is strongly negative at this point and the derivative is positive, the first application of the Newton-Raphson formula takes us far out beyond the smallest positive root—to about $3.6P_{cr}$, in fact—as

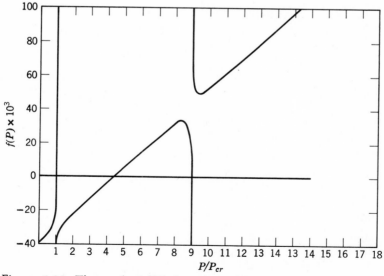

Figure 1.25. *The graph of f(P) for values of P ranging between 0 and 15 times P_{cr}.*

Case Study 2: The Newton-Raphson Method in a Structures Problem   47 we can determine by modifying the program of Figure 1.23 to print each successive approximation rather than just the final result. Now, roughly speaking, the process seeks the closest root to this point, which is the one at about $P = 4.4 \, P_{cr}$, and rapidly converges to it. But this root is of no interest to us.

Although it did not happen with any of the values shown in Figure 1.24, it could also turn out that the iteration formula would produce a

```
C CASE STUDY 2
C USING THE NEWTON-RAPHSON METHOD TO FIND THE ROOT OF A
C    STRUCTURES PROBLEM IN COLUMN BUCKLING
C
C SUGGESTED BY PROF. JOHN A. WEESE, DENVER UNIVERSITY
C
C MODIFIED VERSION - AVOIDS DISCONTINUITIES ON THE SECANT CURVE
C
C SET THE VALUES OF THE UNCHANGING PARAMETERS
      REAL L
      A = 1.0
      C = 1.0
      R = 1.0
      SIGMA0 = 40000.0
      EY = 30E+6
C READ THE VALUES OF THE TWO PARAMETERS THAT CHANGE
C    IN THIS FORMULATION
   12 READ (5, 34) E, L
   34 FORMAT (2F10.0)
C COMPUTE THE MAXIMUM PERMISSIBLE LOAD, WHICH IS AN UPPER
C    BOUND FOR P
      PCR = 9.8696044 * EY * A / (L/R)**2
C START THE ITERATION WITH P = PCR/2
      P = PCR / 2.0
C INITIALIZE AN ITERATION COUNTER
      ITER = 1
C COMPUTE SOME COMMON FACTORS
   39 B = (L / (2.0 * R)) * SQRT(P / (EY * A))
      COSB = COS(B)
      SECB = 1.0 / COSB
      TANB = SIN(B) / COSB
C COMPUTE THE VALUE OF THE FUNCTION
      F = P/A - SIGMA0/(1.0 + E*C*SECB/R**2)
C COMPUTE THE VALUE OF THE DERIVATIVE
      FP = 1.0/A + (SIGMA0/(1.0 + E*C*SECB/R**2)**2) * (E*C/R**2)
     1 * (B/(2.0*P)) * SECB * TANB
C COMPUTE THE NEW APPROXIMATION TO THE ROOT
      PNEW = P - F/FP
C CHECK WHETHER LAST TWO APPROXIMATIONS ARE CLOSE ENOUGH
      IF (ABS(P - PNEW) .LT. SIGMA0*A*1.0E-5) GO TO 43
C CHECK WHETHER ITERATION COUNTER HAS BEEN EXCEEDED
      IF (ITER .GT. 15) GO TO 44
C NOT CONVERGED AND NOT TOO MANY ITERATIONS -- GO AROUND AGAIN
C BUT FIRST CHECK IF P NEGATIVE OR GREATER THAN PCR
      IF (PNEW .LE. 0.0) P = P / 2.0
      IF (PNEW .GE. PCR) P = (P + PCR) / 2.0
      IF (PNEW .GT. 0.0 .AND. PNEW .LT. PCR) P = PNEW
      ITER = ITER + 1
      GO TO 39
C WRITE OUT THE RESULT, ALONG WITH PCR FOR COMPARISON
   43 WRITE (6, 56) P, PCR
   56 FORMAT (1X, 2E15.6)
C GO BACK TO READ ANOTHER DATA POINT
      GO TO 12
C PRINT NON-CONVERGENCE COMMENT
   44 WRITE (6, 45)
   45 FORMAT (1X, 'PROCESS DID NOT CONVERGE IN 15 ITERATIONS')
      GO TO 12
      END
```

Figure 1.26. *The program of Figure 1.23 modified to assure that it finds the smallest positive root.*

```
 0.3,50.0
     0.282355E 05     0.118435E 06
 0.3,100.0
     0.196063E 05     0.296088E 05
 0.3,150.0
     0.112597E 05     0.131595E 05
 0.1,50.0
     0.347336E 05     0.118435E 06
 0.1,100.0
     0.241327E 05     0.296088E 05
 0.1,150.0
     0.124162E 05     0.131595E 05
 0.05,50.0
     0.370925E 05     0.118435E 06
 0.05,100.0
     0.261513E 05     0.296088E 05
 0.05,150.0
     0.127697E 05     0.131595E 05
 0.01,50.0
     0.393623E 05     0.118435E 06
 0.01,100.0
     0.286634E 05     0.296088E 05
 0.01,150.0
     0.130782E 05     0.131595E 05
 0.01,180.0
     0.910428E 04     0.913852E 04
```

Figure 1.27. *The output of Figure 1.26, for the same sets of values of* e *and* L *as those used in Figure 1.24.*

negative value of P, which would cause the program to stop execution on attempting to take the square root of a negative number.

The solution to the problem is to inspect P_{new} after each iteration to see whether either of these problems has arisen. If P_{new} is negative, we might try half of the previous value of P (not P_{new}). If P_{new} is greater than P_{cr}, then since we know we are looking for a root between the old P and P_{cr}, we might try $P = (P + P_{cr})/2$.

These modifications are incorporated in the final program shown in Figure 1.26. Note carefully that after testing for P_{new} negative and greater than P_{cr} and taking appropriate action for each, we have placed a compound condition on the assignment of P_{new} to P if neither of the exceptional cases has occurred. What we want is for *exactly one* of the three formulas for giving P a new value to be applied. It would do little good if we were to set up the program so that after checking for P greater than P_{cr} and taking appropriate action, the program were to go on to give P the value P_{new} anyway. In other words, we want the assignment of P_{new} to P to happen *only if* neither of the other assignments has occurred. The IF statements shown do that.

The output in Figure 1.27 shows the same data points used in Figure 1.25, but now the value of P is always less than P_{cr}.

Bibliographic Notes

Interval halving is covered from a very elementary point of view by Barrodale et al. [1]. Hamming [6] warns of some numerical difficulties that may arise in interval halving in Sections 2.2, 2.3, and 2.4.

The method of successive approximations is also covered from an elementary point of view in Barrodale et al. [1]. Discussions following very closely the one in this text are given by Scarborough [17] in Section 70 and by Stark [3] in Sections 3.1 and 3.2. Scarborough also discusses the convergence of the method in Section 71 and discusses successive approximations for systems of equations in Sections 74 and 75. Stark [3] discusses convergence of the method in Section 3.4. The acceleration method is discussed by Ralston [19] in Section 8.7-1 and by Henrici [23] in Section 4.4.

Good discussions of the Newton-Raphson method are given by Scarborough [17] in Sections 66 and 67; by Henrici [23] in Sections 4.6 to 4.8; by Stark [3] in Section 3.5 and by Barrodale et al. [1] in Chapter 1. The last of these is the most elementary treatment. Scarborough and Henrici also discuss the quadratic convergence of the method. Hamming [6] in Section 2.8 recommends that the method be used with caution, if at all.

Multiple roots are discussed briefly by Hamming [6] in Section 2.9 and by Stark [3] in Section 3.15. Excellent discussions of finding roots of polynomials are contained in Ralston [19] in Section 8.11 and Hildebrand [18] in Section 10.9. Ralston also discusses the uncertainty in the roots because of uncertainty in the coefficients in Section 8.13, as does Redish [12] in Section 3.6.3.

Complex roots are discussed in much more detail than this present text does in several places. Among them are Ralston [19] in Sections 8.11 and 8.12; Hamming [6] in Sections 4.6 and 4.7; Hildebrand [18] in Sections 10.12 and 10.13; and Stark [3] in Sections 3.17, 3.18, and 4.9.

Roots of systems of equations are covered by Henrici [23] in Chapter 5 and Scarborough [17] in Section 73 and in Chapter 9 as well as in Sections 74 and 75 as noted above. Stark [3] also discusses systems of equations in Chapter 4.

Few books discuss finding a starting approximation. Stark [3] has a brief discussion in Sections 3.12 and 3.13. A more thorough discussion can be found in Ralston [19] in Section 8.9-1, or in Redish [12] in Section 3.1. In particular, Sturm sequences are discussed by Ralston.

A wide variety of algorithms (including successive approximations and Newton-Raphson) are covered by Carnahan et al. [20] in Chapter 3 where there are a wealth of flow charts, Fortran programs, and case studies. Systems of equations are covered by Carnahan et al. in Sections 5.8 and 5.9.

Two reference books, which are devoted exclusively to roots of equations are:

Iterative Methods for the Solution of Equations by J. F. Traub (Prentice-Hall, 1964)

Requires much more mathematical sophistication than present text. An extremely exhaustive study of iterative methods at a graduate level. Includes systems of nonlinear equations. Contains *no* flow charts or computer programs. An excellent and complete reference.

Constructive Aspects of the Fundamental Theorem of Algebra, ed. by Bruno Dejon and Peter Henrici (Wiley-Interscience, 1969)

A collection of scholarly and mathematically sophisticated papers on root finding techniques primarily for polynomials. One paper deals with systems of polynomials. Several papers contain flow charts and several others contain ALGOL programs. All of these papers represent the state-of-the-art of algorithms for finding roots of polynomials through 1969.

Exercises

The "computational" exercises in the following set (and in later chapters) have been devised so that they can be done with paper and pencil or a desk calculator if necessary. A number of them, however, are quite suitable for solution by computer, using routines that are described in other exercises. Applying the computer in this way may or may not save time, but it will force the reader to understand the methods in a way that working out the solutions without the computer may not.

*1 Find the negative square root of 0.5 to four decimals by writing $F(x) = x^2 - 0.5$ and solving $x = x^2 + x - 0.5$ by the method of successive approximations, with $x_0 = -0.6$. Could the positive square root be found by this method?

2 Find the negative square root of 0.25 by the method of Exercise 1, with $x_0 = -0.6$. Why does this converge faster?

3 Use the Newton-Raphson method to find to four decimals the square root of 4, with $x_0 = 1.5$. Repeat with $x_0 = 2.5$, $x_0 = -1.5$, $x_0 = 10.0$.

*4 Derive a Newton-Raphson iteration formula for finding the cube root of a positive number c.

5 Derive a Newton-Raphson iteration formula for finding arcsin A, given A.

6 Using the result of Exercise 5, find arcsin 0.5 to three decimal places.

*7 Find to three decimals the root of $0.1x^2 - x \log x = 0$ between 1 and 2.

8 Find to three decimals a root of $\cosh x + \cos x - 3 = 0$.

*9 Use the Newton-Raphson method to find to three decimals all roots of $x^3 - 1.473x^2 - 5.738x + 6.763 = 0$.

10 Use the Newton-Raphson method to find to three decimals the roots of $x^2 - x - 6 = 0$. Use $x_0 = 0$, then repeat with $x_0 = 4$. The iteration formula can be simplified considerably by algebraic manipulation.

11 The equation $4x^3 - 12.3x^2 - x + 16.2$ has two roots between 1 and 2. Find them to four decimals.

*12 Find to three significant figures the root between 2 and 3 of $x^3 - 0.39x^2 - 10.5x + 11.0 = 0$. If the coefficients contain errors of 2%, what is the bound on the error in this root?

13 Same as Exercise 12, but the error in the coefficients is 4%.

14 Show that, if the error in each of the coefficients in a polynomial equation is $P\%$, the bound on the error in any root is a linear function

---

* Answers to starred exercises appear at the back of the book.

of P as long as the assumptions in the derivation of the bound are valid.

15 The equation $2.0x^2 - 5.0x + 2.0 = 0$ has roots $x_1 = 0.5$, $x_2 = 2.0$. If the coefficients contain errors of 20%, the error bound for x_2 is 1.33. Yet the larger root of the equation $1.6x^2 - 6.0x + 1.6 = 0$, in which the coefficients are 20% different from the original equation, is 3.47 for an error of 1.47. Why is the actual error greater than the bound? On the other hand, the equation $1.6x^2 - 4.0x + 1.6 = 0$, in which the coefficients are also 20% different from the original, has a larger root of 1.79 for an error of only 0.21. Why is this error so much smaller than either the error in the other root or the bound?

16 Consider the equation

$$x^4 - 26x^3 + 131x^2 - 226x + 120 = 0$$

The roots are 1, 2, 3, and 20. Suppose first that there is a small error in the constant term and that the other coefficients are exact. Show that this error has more than twice as much effect on the error bound for the root near 2 as on the root near 1 and essentially no effect on the root near 20. Then suppose that there is a small error in the coefficient of x^3 and that the others are exact. Show that the error bound on the root near 1 is much less than the error in the coefficient but that the error bound on the root near 20 is larger than the error in the coefficient.

17 Apply the Newton-Raphson method to $x^3 - 2x^2 - 3x + 10 = 0$, with $x_0 = 1.9$. Can you explain the strange behavior of the successive iterates?

*18 Apply the Newton-Raphson method to $x^3 - 2x^2 - 3x + 10 = 0$, with $x_0 = 3 + i$, using complex arithmetic throughout.

19 The equation

$$x^4 - 7x^3 + 12x^2 + 4x - 16 = 0$$

has roots at -1 and $+2$. Yet, if we apply the Newton-Raphson method with $x_0 = -0.1$, we reach another root at $+4$. Explain.

20 Attempt to apply the Newton-Raphson method to the equation

$$x^5 + 8x^4 + 17x^3 - 8x^2 - 14x + 20 = 0$$

What happens?

21a Change the flow chart of Figure 1.10 so that the range of values searched is from A to B rather than from -10 to $+10$. Assume that A and B are read from cards.

b Change the program of Figure 1.11 accordingly. Have the program read the values of A and B.

22a Change the flow chart of Figure 1.10 so that the interval of search in the first pass is not 1.0 but D. Assume that the value of D is read from a card.

b Change the program of Figure 1.11 accordingly. Have the program read the value of D.

23 Change the flow chart of Figure 1.10 so that it reads the degree N of a polynomial and then reads the coefficients $a_N, a_{N-1}, \ldots, a_1, a_0$ of

$$a_N x^N + a_{N-1} x^{N-1} + \cdots + a_1 x + a_0$$

and isolates the roots for interval halving.

24 Integrate the changes in Exercises 21, 22, and 23 into the program of Figure 1.11. This produces a program which will take a general polynomial, a range (A,B) in which a root is expected, an interval D by which roots are separated and then proceed to find all roots in the range which are so separated. It will find the roots to within an accuracy of 0.5×10^{-4}.

25 Use the Newton-Raphson method to compute a root of

$$x^4 - 9x^3 - 2x^2 + 120x - 130$$

starting with $x_0 = -4$. Stop the iterations when the value of the polynomial is less than $\frac{1}{2} \times 10^{-3}$.

26a Write a FORTRAN program that (i) reads an integer M (the degree of the polynomial) from a card in a format I2, (ii) reads the M + 1 coefficients of the polynomial from a succession of cards in the format 5F10.0, (iii) reads an initial guess for a root from a card in a format F10.0, (iv) uses the Newton-Raphson method, (1.30), to compute an approximate root so that the value of the polynomial is less than $\frac{1}{2} \times 10^{-5}$, (v) prints the approximate root and the value of the polynomial. (*Notes:* Make sure that the process terminates, by placing a limit on the number of iterations. You should be able to compute the b_j and c_j in *one* loop.)

b Test your program using the polynomial $x^4 - 9x^3 - 2x^2 + 120x - 130$ and $x_0 = -3$. Print all values of b_j and c_j and compare them with the results given in Table 1.1 in the text.

27 Write a Fortran routine to find the square root of a variable A to which a value has previously been given; call the result SQRTA.

28 Show that if

$$x_{m+1} = x_m(2 - a x_m)$$

converges then it converges to $1/a$ as $m \to \infty$. This is an iterative method for doing division or finding inverses provided a reasonably good initial guess is available. (See Exercise 30.)

29 Consider the iterative formula given in Exercise 28. Find 1/12 to six decimals using:

a. $x_0 = 0.1$.

b. $x_0 = 1.0$.

c. Account for the strange behavior in **b**.

30 Consider the iterative formula given in Exercise 28. What bounds must x_0 satisfy to assure convergence?

31 Recall from Section 1.10 that if

$$F(x) = a_0 + a_1 x + \cdots + a_m x^m = (x - \bar{x})G(x) + b_0 \qquad \text{(a)}$$
$$G(x) = b_1 + b_2 x + \cdots + b_m x^{m-1} \qquad \text{(b)}$$

then

$$b_m = a_m \qquad \qquad (1.27)$$
$$b_j = a_j + \bar{x} b_{j+1} \qquad \text{where} \qquad j = m - 1, \ldots, 0 \qquad (1.28)$$

by equating coefficients of like powers of x in (a) and (b).

On the other hand,

$$F'(x) = (x - \bar{x})G'(x) + G(x)$$

so

$$F'(\bar{x}) = G(\bar{x}) = b_1 + b_2\bar{x} + \cdots + b_m\bar{x}^{m-1} \qquad \text{(c)}$$

If we differentiate (a) directly,

$$F'(x) = a_1 + 2a_2x + \cdots + ma_mx^{m-1}$$

so

$$F'(\bar{x}) = a_1 + 2a_2\bar{x} + \cdots + ma_m\bar{x}^{m-1} \qquad \text{(d)}$$

If we equate coefficients of like powers of $\bar{x}$ in (c) and (d), we obtain

$$b_j = ja_j \qquad j = m, \ldots, 1 \qquad \text{(e)}$$

How do you reconcile the paradox presented by (1.27) and (1.28) versus (e)?

32 Try to use the method of successive approximations to find the square root of c from the formula given in (1.8), i.e.,

$$x_{n+1} = \frac{c}{x_n}$$

a. Show that

$$x_{n+2} = x_n$$

b. Illustrate this oscillating process with a sketch.

33 Write a Fortran program to carry out the following iterative process:

a. Given a and x_0

b. $y_0 = a/x_0$

c. $x_{n+1} = \dfrac{x_n + y_n}{2}$ where $n = 0, 1, 2, \ldots$

$y_{n+1} = \dfrac{2}{\dfrac{1}{x_n} + \dfrac{1}{y_n}}$ where $n = 0, 1, 2, \ldots$

The values of y_n and x_n should converge to $\sqrt{a}$. For $n > 1$

$$x_n > \sqrt{a} > y_n$$

34a The Newton-Raphson method for $\sqrt{a}$ is

$$z_{n+1} = \frac{1}{2}\left(z_n + \frac{a}{z_n}\right) \qquad \text{where} \qquad n = 0, 1, 2, \ldots$$

Show that for the iteration procedure described in Exercise 33

$$x_n = z_n$$

b In view of the result in **a**, discuss the relative merits of the Newton-Raphson method as compared with the iteration method given in Exercise 33.

35 In the method of successive approximations let m^* be the minimum of $|f'(x)|$ for all x occurring in the iterations. Show that if $m^* > 1$ the process diverges.

36 Suppose that we have two values of x, x_0 and x_1, such that $F(x_0) < 0$ and $F(x_1) > 0$. Let x_2 be the point at which the x-axis intersects the straight line joining the points $(x_0, F(x_0))$ and $(x_1, F(x_1))$. Demonstrate geometrically that x_2 is a better approximation to a root of $F(x) = 0$ than either x_0 or x_1 and devise a computational procedure along the lines of that in Case Study 1—based on sign changes, that is—for finding the root.

This is called the method of *false position* or *regula falsi*.

37 Suppose we expand $F(x)$ in a Taylor series about $x = x_n$ and truncate after two terms:

$$F(x) = F(x_n) + (x - x_n)F'(x_n)$$

Show that this leads to the approximation formula

$$x = x_n - \frac{F(x_n)}{F'(x_n)}$$

What is this?

*38 Let

$$F(x,y) = x^2 + y^2 - 4$$
$$G(x,y) = xy - 1$$

Apply the method of Section 1.13 with $x_0 = 2$, $y_0 = 0$. Are there other solutions?

39 Let

$$F(x,y) = x^3 - x - 2x^2 - x + 2 - y$$
$$G(x,y) = x - y$$

Apply the method of Section 1.13 with $x_0 = y_0 = 0$. Explain the relationship between the two iteration formulas.

40 A generalization of the method of successive approximations to two equations

$$x = f(x,y)$$
$$y = g(x,y)$$

is given by

$$x_{n+1} = f(x_n, y_n)$$
$$y_{n+1} = g(x_n, y_n)$$

a. Show that sufficient conditions for convergence of this generalization are

$$\left| \frac{\partial f}{\partial x} \right| + \left| \frac{\partial g}{\partial x} \right| < 1$$

and

$$\left| \frac{\partial f}{\partial y} \right| + \left| \frac{\partial g}{\partial y} \right| < 1$$

(*Hint.* Consider bounds on the quantity $|x - x_n| + |y - y_n|$.)

b. Are the conditions in part (a) *necessary* for convergence?

c. Consider the linear equations

$$a_{11}x + a_{12}y = b_1$$
$$a_{21}x + a_{22}y = b_2$$

If $a_{11} \neq 0$ and $a_{22} \neq 0$, we may rewrite these equations as

$$x = \frac{1}{a_{11}}(b_1 - a_{12}y)$$

$$y = \frac{1}{a_{22}}(b_2 - a_{21}x)$$

What do the sufficient conditions for convergence given above become in this case? What do these conditions imply about the slopes of the lines represented by the original linear equations?

41 Consider the two simultaneous equations

$$x = 3 - 2y = -2y + 3$$

$$y = \frac{1}{4}(x + 3) = \frac{x + 3}{4}$$

a. Do they satisfy the conditions for convergence in part **a** of Exercise 40?

b. Show that

$$x_{n+1} = -2y_n + 3$$
$$y_{n+1} = \frac{x_n + 3}{4}$$

converges to the solution $x = y = 1$ from starting values $x_0 = y_0 = 0$.

c. Explain the discrepancy between the results in **a** and **b** above.

42 Consider the cubic equation

$$p_0(x) = x^3 + a_2x^2 + a_1x + a_0$$

a. If x_1, x_2, and x_3 are roots of $p_0(x) = 0$, show that

$$a_2 = -(x_1 + x_2 + x_3)$$
$$a_1 = x_1x_2 + x_1x_3 + x_2x_3$$
$$a_0 = -x_1x_2x_3$$

b. Show that if x_1, x_2, and x_3 are real and

$$|x_1| \gg |x_2| \gg |x_3|$$

then

$$x_1 \simeq -a_2$$

$$x_2 \simeq -\frac{a_1}{a_2}$$

$$x_3 \simeq -\frac{a_0}{a_1}$$

c. Show that the function

$$p_1(y) = -p_0(-x)p_0(x)$$
$$= y^3 + (-a_2^2 + 2a_1)y^2 + (a_1^2 - 2a_0a_2)y - a_0^2$$

where $y = x^2$.

d. Show that the roots of $p_1(y) = 0$ are

$$y_1 = x_1^2$$
$$y_2 = x_2^2$$
$$y_3 = x_3^2$$

e. Show that the roots of

$$p_2(z) = -p_1(-y)p_1(y)$$

are

$$z_1 = x_1^4$$
$$z_2 = x_2^4$$
$$z_3 = x_3^4$$

where $z = y^2 = x^4$.

f. What happens to the roots of the equations that result from iterating the process described by (c) and (e) above?

g. Describe how you would find an approximation to x_1, x_2, and x_3 after the iterations have been carried out enough times to separate the roots adequately.

This process is known as *Graeffe's root-squaring technique*. It can be generalized to higher order polynomial equations and to complex roots. See, for example, Section 10.11 of Hildebrand, *Introduction to Numerical Analysis* (New York: McGraw-Hill, 1956).

43 The following familiar puzzle problem leads to the solution of a quartic equation:

Two ladders, one 20-ft long and the other 30-ft long, lean against buildings across an alley, as shown in Figure 1.28. If the point at which the ladders cross is 8 ft above the ground, how wide is the alley?

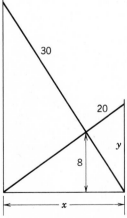

Figure 1.28. *The ladder problem of Exercise 43.*

Gruenberger and Jaffrey, in *Problems for Computer Solution* (New York: Wiley, 1964) show that this problem can be formulated to require solution of the following equation:

$$y^4 - 16y^3 + 500y^2 - 8000y + 32,000 = 0$$

Then $x = \sqrt{400 - y^2}$.

44 A man borrows A dollars from a bank, which adds on the total interest before computing the monthly payment. Thus, if the quoted annual interest rate (in percentage points) is q and the loan is for n months, the total amount that the borrower agrees to repay is

$$A + A\left(\frac{n}{12}\right)\left(\frac{q}{100}\right)$$

This is divided by n to give the amount of each payment, R:

$$R = A\left(\frac{1}{n} + \frac{q}{1200}\right) \qquad \text{(a)}$$

This is all perfectly legal and is widely done. (It is called an *add-on* loan.) But the true rate of interest that the borrower is paying is somewhat more than $q\%$, because he does not hold the amount of the loan for the full n months: He is paying it back as he goes along. The true rate of interest can be found by solving for a root t of the equation

$$F(t) = (At - R)(1 + t)^n + R = 0 \qquad \text{(b)}$$

This gives the rate of interest *per payment period*, which can be converted to an annual interest rate by multiplying by 12.

Write a program that accepts values for A, n, and q, and computes R from (a), solves for t in (b) using the Newton-Raphson method, then prints A, n, q, R, and the true annual interest rate in percentage points. For $A = \$5000$, $n = 60$, and $q = 7.5$, the correct result is $R = \$114.59$ and true interest $= 13.32\%$. Try your program first on shorter payment periods, however, because you will probably have severe accuracy problems to cope with on the values stated.

45 Write a program to find the positive root of

$$F(x) = \cosh x + \cos x - A$$

for $A = 4$, 3, 2, 1, using the Newton-Raphson method. Using a convergence criterion of 10^{-6}, the root found when $A = 2$ (if you do converge to a root) will be about 0.02, where the exact root, found by inspection of the equation, is zero. What happens? For $A < 2$ no real root exists; depending on the details of your computer, compiler, and operating system, you will probably eventually get an "approximation" in the range of $x = 600$. When you next try to find the exponential of such a large argument, you will encounter an error condition. Details of error handling vary widely among different systems, but it is altogether possible that the system will run indefinitely, "fixing up" each error with some standard procedure, such as substituting for the result of the impossible exponentiation the largest floating point number in the machine. If your system places no limit on the number of errors, the amount of computer time, or the amount of output, you will generate a boxful of 30 lb of output, all of which will consist of error messages. This should be avoided. *Programs for iterative processes should always contain iteration counters.*

46 There are several heat conduction problems whose solution for the temperature distribution requires the positive roots of the transcendental equation

$$\tan x = a/x$$

or

$$F(x) = x \tan x - a = 0 \tag{a}$$

where a is a constant with a positive or zero value and x is the desired root. The roots of this equation can be computed by the methods outlined in this chapter. Write a program that contains provisions to handle the periodic nature of the tangent function.

Plots of $y = \tan x$ and of $y = 1.0/x$ are shown in Figure 1.29. We see that the two curves cross in every vertical strip of width π; the x values where these intersections occur are the desired roots of (a). The program must accept as input both a value for a and a value for NMAX, the number of roots desired, starting with the one between zero and $\pi/2$.

If the Newton-Raphson method is used, it is likely that for some values of x, the method will produce a next approximation in a different vertical strip than the one in which a root is currently being sought. This possibility must be checked for and appropriate corrections applied. Alternatively, one might choose not to use the Newton-Raphson method, just because of this difficulty, or apply it

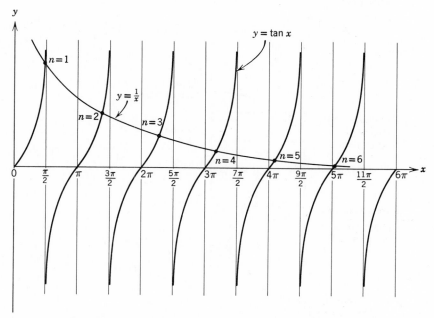

Figure 1.29. *Plots of the functions* y = *tan* x *and* y = 1/x *for Exercise 46.*

only after the root has already been found to moderate accuracy by some other method.

47 In analyzing the performance of reciprocating air compressors it is frequently necessary to obtain a graphical plot of pressure versus volume and pressure versus angular rotation of the compressor crankshaft during the compression stroke. Such data can be approximated analytically first by defining a model for the compressor and then by applying fundamentals of mechanisms and thermodynamics to the model. The basic components of the reciprocating compressor are shown in Figure 1.30, along with the geometrical parameters used in determining the volume enclosed within the piston and the cylinder. By applying the fundamentals of mechanisms, this volume can be expressed as

$$V = V_c + \frac{\pi d^2}{4}\left\{r(1 - \cos\theta) + l\left[1 - \sqrt{1 - \left(\frac{r}{l}\sin\theta\right)^2}\right]\right\} \quad \text{(a)}$$

where V_c = clearance volume (volume at top-dead-center)
r = radius of the crankshaft throw
d = diameter of cylinder
l = length of connecting rod
θ = degree of crankshaft rotation measured from top-dead-center

Let us now consider the compression stroke as the piston moves from bottom-dead-center ($\theta = 180°$) to top-dead-center ($\theta = 360°$). One model frequently used for this process assumes that the intake and exhaust valves remain closed and that there is no heat transfer to or from the air during the compression stroke. Applying thermodynamics to this model yields the following relationships between the pressure, volume, and temperature:

$$A \ln\left(\frac{T}{T_i}\right) + B(T - T_i) + \tfrac{1}{2}C\,(T^2 - T_i^2) + D \ln\left(\frac{V}{V_i}\right) = 0 \quad \text{(b)}$$

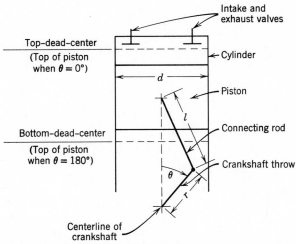

Figure 1.30. *Geometrical parameters of the reciprocating compressor of Exercise 47.*

60   Solution of Equations

$$P = P_i \left(\frac{V_i}{V} \right) \left(\frac{T}{T_i} \right) \qquad (c)$$

where P = pressure

V = volume

T = absolute temperature, °R

$A = 0.15787$

$B = 0.51001 \cdot 10^{-4}$

$C = -0.74171 \cdot 10^{-8}$

$D = 0.6855$

and the subscript i denotes the initial conditions at the beginning of the compression stroke, which are assumed to be known.

Equations (a), (b), and (c) can be used to determine P versus θ as desired. The procedure for obtaining such values is to select a value of θ between 180° and 360° in (a). The resulting value for V may then be used in (b), which is solved by the Newton-Raphson method to determine the temperature T. These values of T and V are then used in (c) to determine the value for P.

Write a program that accepts values for P_i, T_i, V_c, r, d, and l, then computes and prints P, V, and T for values of θ from 180° to 360° in steps of 5°. For $P_i = 14.7$, $T_i = 530°$, $\theta = 240°$, $V_c = 6.3$, $r = 2.0$, $d = 3.5$, and $l = 7.0$, the approximate results should be $P = 18.7$, $V = 37.3$, and $T = 568$.

48 It is desired to determine the effect of pressure upon the dew point temperature of the combustion products resulting from the complete combustion of a paraffin hydrocarbon with theoretical air. The dew point temperature is defined as the temperature at which water vapor will begin to condense from the products of combustion when the products are cooled at constant pressure. When the dew point temperature is reached, the partial pressure of the water vapor in the products will equal the vapor pressure of liquid water at the dew point temperature and this relationship can be used to determine the dew point temperature.

A paraffin hydrocarbon has the chemical formula C_nH_{2n+2} and the equation for complete combustion with theoretical air is written as

$$C_nH_{2n+2} + (2n + 1)O_2 + (2n + 1)3.76N_2 \rightarrow$$
$$nCO_2 + (n + 1)H_2O + (2n + 1)3.76N_2 \quad (a)$$

from which the mole fraction of water vapor in the products is

$$x_{H_2O} = \frac{n + 1}{n + (n + 1) + (2n + 1)3.76} = \frac{n + 1}{9.52n + 4.76} \qquad (b)$$

The partial pressure of the water vapor in the products is equal to the product of the mole fraction of water vapor and the pressure of the products of combustion. Thus

$$P_{H_2O} = x_{H_2O}P = \frac{(n + 1)P}{9.52n + 4.76} \qquad (c)$$

The relationship between the vapor pressure of liquid water and the temperature is

$$\ln P_v = 8.07284 - 2.3026\frac{x}{T}\left[\frac{a + bx + cx^3}{1 + dx}\right] \tag{d}$$

where P_v = vapor pressure, psi
T = temperature, $°R = °F + 459.69$
$x = 1165.09 - T$
$a = 3.2437814$
$b = 3.2601444 \cdot 10^{-3}$
$c = 2.0065808 \cdot 10^{-9}$
$d = 1.2154701 \cdot 10^{-3}$

Since the partial pressure and vapor pressure of water must be equal at the dew point, (b), (c), and (d) can be combined to give

$$\ln\left[\frac{(n + 1)P}{9.52n + 4.76}\right] = 8.07284 - 2.3026\frac{x}{T}\left[\frac{a + bx + cx^3}{1 + dx}\right] \tag{e}$$

which can be solved for T for given values of P and n. Since equation (e) is nonlinear, a method such as the Newton-Raphson technique must be used. For this purpose it is convenient to rewrite (e) as

$$F(T) = 2.3026\frac{x}{T}\left[\frac{a + bx + cx^3}{1 + dx}\right]$$

$$+ \ln\left[\frac{(n + 1)P}{9.52n + 4.76}\right] - 8.07284 = 0 \tag{f}$$

To use the Newton-Raphson method it is necessary to differentiate (f) with respect to T, which yields

$$\frac{dF}{dT} = 2.3026\left\{\left[\frac{a + bx + cx^3}{1 + dx}\right]\right.$$

$$\left.\times\left[\frac{xd}{T(1 + dx)} - \frac{1165.09}{T^2}\right] - \frac{x(b + 3cx^2)}{T(1 + dx)}\right\} \tag{g}$$

For ethane ($n = 2$) at one atmosphere ($P = 14.7$), the correct result is 582.97 °R = 123.28 °F.

49 A problem frequently encountered in designing electronic circuits is determining the dc operating point for the voltage and current variables of nonlinear circuit elements such as diodes and transistors. This is frequently referred to as the *biasing problem*. Such a determination involves the solution of a nonlinear equation (or set of equations); thus, it is readily treated by the root-solving techniques outlined in

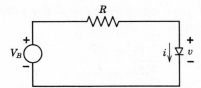

Figure 1.31. *The diode circuit of Exercise 49.*

this chapter. As an example of such a problem, consider a biasing circuit that consists of a battery with a voltage $V_B = 2.0$ V and a series 50-Ω resistor R connected to a solid-state semiconductor diode as shown in Figure 1.31. The operating characteristics over the normal operating range of such a diode are determined by the equation relating its terminal variables of voltage and current. If we let v and i be these variables and choose the relative reference directions shown, the equation relating these variables is

$$i = I_s(e^{qv/kT} - 1) \qquad \text{(a)}$$

where I_s = The magnitude of the reverse saturation current. This is the maximum current that flows when the diode is reverse biased, that is, when $v \ll 0$. It is a function of the material used in making the diode, the level of the doping, and the particular processing techniques. A typical value for a silicon diode at room temperature is 10^{-9} amp.

k = The Boltzman constant, which has the value $1.38047 \cdot 10^{-23}$ joules/°K.

T = The absolute temperature in °K at which the diode is operated.

q = The charge of the electron, which has the value $1.60203 \cdot 10^{-19}$ coulomb.

At normal room temperatures the value of the term q/Kt is approximately 40.

We may now proceed to solve the bias circuit, i.e., to find the values of v and i. To do this we apply Kirchhoff's voltage law to the circuit, thus obtaining

$$V_B = iR + v \qquad \text{(b)}$$

Inserting the values of V_B and R and using the relation given in (a), we can write this as

$$2.0 = 50\,I_s(e^{qv/kT} - 1) + v \qquad \text{(c)}$$

We now need to put this equation in a form such that the Newton-Raphson root-finding method may be easily applied, that is, the form $f(v) = 0$. We obtain

$$f(v) = 50\,I_s(e^{qv/kT} - 1) + v - 2.0 \qquad \text{(d)}$$

The derivative of this expression taken with respect to v is

$$\frac{df}{dv} = 50\,I_s\left(\frac{q}{kT}\right)(e^{qv/kT}) + 1 \qquad \text{(e)}$$

The relations given in (d) and (e) are readily programmed, so the Newton-Raphson algorithm may be applied to solve the biasing problem, i.e., to find the value of v, the voltage across the diode that occurs when $q/kT = 40$ and $I_s = 10^{-9}$. By applying the result of this computation in (a), the value of the bias current i is also readily obtained.

As an extension of this problem, we can determine the dynamic resistance of the diode at the operating point found above, that is, the change in the value of i caused by a change in the value of v. If we use r_d to indicate this resistance, on an incremental basis we may write

$$r_d = \frac{\Delta v}{\Delta i} \tag{f}$$

To compute the above quantities we need merely repeat the application of the Newton-Raphson algorithm given above using a value of battery voltage that has been changed by some small amount. For example, let $V_B = 2.01$ V. The new values of diode voltage v and current i found by again applying the Newton-Raphson algorithm may be used to compute Δv and Δi. Inserting these values in (f) we find the required dynamic resistance.

The approximate answers are: $v = 0.43$, $i = 0.031$, and $r_d = 0.8$.

50 The differential equation governing the mode shapes of the free lateral vibrations of a uniform beam are[15]

$$\frac{d^4 Y}{dx^4} = k^4 Y \tag{a}$$

where $k^4 = \omega^2 \rho A / EI$ is a constant. Here ω is proportional to the frequency of a mode of vibration and is unknown. ρ and E are material parameters and A and I are geometrical parameters. If the beam is built in at the left end ($x = 0$) and simply supported at the right ($x = L$), the boundary conditions are:

$$\begin{array}{l} \text{At } x = 0,\ Y = 0,\ dY/dx = 0 \\ \text{At } x = L,\ Y = 0,\ d^2Y/dx^2 = 0 \end{array} \tag{b}$$

(i) Verify that the solution of (a) is

$$Y = A \sin kx + B \cos kx + C \sinh kx + D \cosh kx$$

(ii) Show that for nontrivial solutions (that is, $Y \not\equiv 0$) the application of boundary conditions (b) requires $C = -A$, $D = -B$, and

$$\tan kL = \tanh kL \tag{c}$$

(iii) Write a program that uses the Newton-Raphson method to find the first five roots of the transcendental equation (c) other than the trivial one $k = 0$. For each root, use the definition of k^4 to compute ω. (For an aluminum beam $L = 30$ in. long, 1 in. wide, and 0.5 in. deep, the factor $k^4 = 1.243 \cdot 10^{-9}$.)

(iv) Each root of (c) corresponds to a particular mode of vibration of the beam. The shapes of these modes can be determined by finding the ratio A/B for a given root and plotting y as a function of x for suitably spaced values. The spacing required for plotting depends on the frequency.

[15] See S. P. Timoshenko, *Vibration Problems in Engineering* (3rd ed.), New York, McGraw-Hill, 1955, pp. 324–325 and p. 339.

2 Errors

Analysis of the error in a numerical result is fundamental to any intelligent computation, whether done manually or with a computer. Input values are seldom exact, since they are often based on experiments or estimates, and the numerical processes themselves introduce errors of various types. Before beginning our study of the subject of errors let us observe in a few examples how important it is.

Exercise 18 at the end of this chapter asks you to find one of the roots of the equation $x^2 + 0.4002x + 0.00008 = 0$, using four-digit floating point arithmetic. By employing the familiar formula

$$x = \frac{-b + \sqrt{b^2 - 4ac}}{2a}$$

we get an answer of -0.00015. This formula is usually presented in algebra courses without any qualification of its accuracy, yet errors are introduced by the four-digit floating point arithmetic that make the result wrong by 25%; the true root, found with eight-digit arithmetic, is -0.0002.

The culprit in this case was the four-digit arithmetic, but do not think that eight-digit floating point numbers solve all problems. Consider the Taylor series for the sine:

$$\sin x = x - \frac{x^3}{3!} + \frac{x^5}{5!} - \frac{x^7}{7!} + \cdots$$

This series is, in theory, valid for any finite angle, and the truncation error committed by stopping the summation after a finite number of terms is

65

less in absolute value than the first term neglected. These statements are true *if there were some way to keep an infinite number of digits in each arithmetic result*. In Case Study 3 in Chapter 3 we shall see that the series is, in fact, totally useless for large angles. Suppose, for instance, that we try to evaluate the sine of 1470° (= 25.7 rad, approximately), using six-digit floating point arithmetic and computing terms until we find one that is less than 10^{-8} in absolute value. The computed result will be 891.7993, which has the appearance of precision but is, of course, meaningless. Even if we use 16-digit floating point numbers, the sine of 2550° is computed as 158.

The difficulties in these examples were created by the finite representation of numbers. This is by no means the only problem. Consider the following two simultaneous equations:

$$5x - 331y = 3.5$$
$$6x - 397y = 5.2$$

An "exact" answer is readily found, with no problems of the type encountered above: $x = 331.7$, $y = 5.000$. These results have the appearance of containing four significant digits. Do they? Let us first see what happens to the answers if the constant in the second equation is changed to 5.1, a variation of about 2%. We now compute $x = 298.6$, $y = 4.5$. This is disturbing; a change of 2% in one data item changed the results by about 10%. Even more disturbing is that if we substitute $x = 358.173$, $y = 5.4$ into the equations the computed left-hand sides round off to exactly the same right-hand sides! We conclude that the computed values of x and y have at best one significant digit.

This was no fault of the arithmetic; all results were exact. The trouble lies in the nature of the data; the determinant of the system is small or, stated geometrically, the two lines represented by the equations are very nearly parallel.

For a final example, the integral

$$\int_{e-4}^{1} \frac{dx}{x}$$

is easily found to have the exact value 4. Yet integration with the familiar trapezoidal rule, using 10 intervals, gives a result of 5.3. Even using 40 intervals we get 4.13, off by 3%.

The difficulty this time is in the nature of the integrand, which is very large for small x, and in the numerical process. With exact data and exact calculations we still get a large error from the nature of the function and of the numerical technique employed.

Without multiplying the examples further, it should be clear that without an analysis of the errors in a calculation we really do not know very much about the results. It will sometimes happen, of course, that we can tell by a careful inspection of the calculations that no special problems will occur. This is distinctly *not* always true, however.

The material in this chapter should be interesting and useful in itself in analyzing the results of simple arithmetic computations. It is also fundamental to the development of the error analysis in the numerical procedures to be discussed in subsequent chapters.

**2.2
Relative
and Abso-
lute Errors**

The *error* is defined here to be the *true value* minus the *approximate value.*[1]

Of these three quantities only one, the approximate value, is usually known. However, we often know something about the error without knowing it precisely. For example, recall in Case Study 1 that one root of

$$x^4 - 9x^3 - 2x^2 + 120x - 130$$

was between -3.60016 and -3.60013 (see Figure 1.12). We can, therefore, say that this root is

$$-3.600145 \pm 0.000015$$

The approximate value is $\overline{x} = 3.600145$, which contains some error. Although we do not know the value of the error, we know that it does not exceed 1.5×10^{-5}.

We call this error the *absolute error,* to distinguish it from the relative error discussed below. One common notation is to write a bar over a symbol to indicate an approximation and to write an e with a subscript to stand for the error. Thus, if x is the true value, we would write

$$x = \overline{x} + e_x$$

Here e_x is the absolute error, which, to repeat, is defined as the difference between the true value and the approximation:

$$e_x = x - \overline{x}$$

The *relative error* is the absolute error divided by the approximation. It might seem more reasonable to define it as the absolute error divided by the *true* value, but as we noted earlier we usually do not know the true value. All we really know is the approximate value and an *estimate* of the error, or a *bound* on the maximum size of the error. If the error is small, the difference in definition has no sizable bearing on the numerical value of the relative error.

For numbers close to 1 the absolute error and the relative error are nearly equal. For numbers not close to 1 there can be a great difference. For example, if we have a true value of 0.00006 and an approximation of 0.00005, the absolute error is only 10^{-5} but the relative error is 0.2, or 20%. On the other hand, if we have a true value of 100,500 and an approximation of 100,000, the absolute error is 500 but the relative error is only 0.005, or 0.5%.

It obviously is essential to state in all cases whether we mean absolute or relative error, unless the meaning is clear from the notation or from the context.

**2.3
Inherent
Errors**

There are three basic types of errors in a numerical computation: inherent, truncation, and roundoff. Each of the three can be expressed in absolute or relative form.

---

[1] Other texts may define the error to be the approximate value minus the true value. Thus, the error would have the same magnitude as our error but would have the opposite sign. Since we will usually deal with the absolute value of the error, the sign is of little consequence *provided we are consistent.* The definition used here is by far the more prevalent one.

Inherent errors are errors in the values of data, caused by uncertainty in measurements, by outright blunders, or by the necessarily approximate nature of representing in some finite number of digits a number that cannot be represented exactly in the number of digits available.

A physical measurement, such as a distance, a voltage, or a time period, cannot be exact. If the measurement is given to many digits, such as a voltage of 6.4837569, we can be certain that at least some of the rightmost digits are not meaningful, since voltages cannot be measured to this accuracy. If the measurement is given to only a few digits, such as a time interval of 2.3 sec, we can be quite certain that there is some inherent error because only by accident would the time interval be exactly 2.3 sec.[2] In such cases we may know some reasonable limits on the inherent error, such as that the time is 2.3 within ±0.1 sec.

It is sometimes assumed that when a physical measurement is stated without any qualification on the significance of the digits it is accurate within a half a unit in the last place. Thus a distance stated as 5.63 cm. would be understood to be not less than 5.625 and not greater than 5.635. This convention is not universally observed, however. When the limits on accuracy are important, it is much better to state explicitly what they are, for example, by writing 5.63 ± 0.005.

Regardless of the number of digits used to represent a quantity, it may contain an outright mistake of some kind. These mistakes may range from simple blunders, such as miscopying data or misreading a scale, to "sophisticated" errors based on incomplete understanding of physical laws.

Many numbers cannot be represented exactly in a given number of decimal digits. If we need π in a calculation, we may write it as 3.14, 3.14159265, or 3.141592653589793. In any case, we have no *exact* representation of π, which is a transcendental number and therefore has no exact finite decimal representation. Similarly, $\sqrt{2}$ is an irrational number and so cannot be represented with a finite number of digits. Even a simple fraction in many cases has no exact decimal representation, such as $\frac{1}{3}$, which can be written only as a succession of 3's.

It also happens that many fractions that have terminating representations in one number base have no such representations in another base. The number $\frac{1}{10}$, for instance, obviously has the simple representation 0.1 in decimal, but the binary representation is 0.000110011001100 . . . , a nonterminating repeating binary number. Thus, forming the sum of 10 numbers, each of which is a binary approximation to decimal 0.1, will not give exactly 1.0. Beginners in work with binary computers have been known to become frustrated by their first encounter with this perversity of nature. The problem is unavoidable; its solution is not difficult once it is recognized, as we shall see in some of the case studies.

Note that transcendental and irrational numbers do not have a terminating representation in *any* number base. Rational numbers, however, may or may not have a terminating representation depending on the number base.

---

[2] As a matter of fact, it is not even meaningful to speak of an "exact" measurement; no workable definition of the term can be given.

2.4
Truncation
Errors

Inherent errors refer to errors in the data. The data may later be operated on by a computer using some numerical procedure. The other two types of errors, truncation and roundoff, refer to errors that are introduced by numerical procedures themselves.

The familiar infinite Taylor series

$$\sin x = x - \frac{x^3}{3!} + \frac{x^5}{5!} - \frac{x^7}{7!} + \cdots$$

may be used to calculate the sine of any angle x in radians. We cannot, of course, use all the terms in the series in a computation, since the series is infinite; we terminate after calculating some finite number of terms up to, say, x^7 or x^9. The terms omitted (which are infinite in number) introduce an error into calculated results. This error is called the *truncation error*, since it is caused by truncating an infinite mathematical process.

Many of the procedures used in numerical calculations are infinite,[3] so that this subject of truncation error assumes major importance. We shall discuss truncation errors in detail in later chapters in connection with the topics to which it applies.

We have already encountered truncation error without referring to it as such in Chapter 1. In particular, the method of successive approximations for approximating a root of an equation was used in the form

$$x_n = f(x_{n-1}) \tag{1.10}$$

(see Section 1.4). However, from Taylor's theorem

$$x_n = f(x_{n-1}) + (x_n - x_{n-1})f'(\xi)$$

where ξ lies in the closed interval bounded by x_n and x_{n-1}. Thus, in using (1.10) we have "truncated" the correct equation. The truncation error is

$$(x_n - x_{n-1})f'(\xi)$$

Although we cannot compute this truncation error precisely, we can estimate it after we have calculated x_n. Recall that, if the method of successive approximations converges, then the absolute value of $f'(x)$ is less than 1. Hence the truncation error cannot exceed $|x_n - x_{n-1}|$. As we get closer to a root of $x = f(x)$, the truncation error becomes smaller and smaller.

2.5
Floating
Point
Arithmetic

Before discussing the third source of error, roundoff error, we pause to describe in some detail floating point arithmetic. (In Fortran, when *real* quantities are involved, as distinguished from integer quantities, it is floating point arithmetic that is performed.) We shall find that a sound understanding of this type of arithmetic is essential in our discussion of roundoff error.

In floating point form, a number is represented as a *fraction*, also called the *mantissa*, and an integer, called the *exponent* or *characteristic*. The number

---

[3]Recall the procedures described in Chapter 1 for approximating roots of equations. All of these procedures were infinite in the sense that to obtain an exact root would require an infinite number of iterations.

so represented consists of the fraction multiplied by the number base of the computer raised to a power equal to the exponent. Thus, if we denote the number base by b, the fraction by f, and the exponent by e, a floating point number is of the form

$$f \cdot b^e$$

For instance, with a floating decimal system, the number 32.46 would be represented as $.3246 \cdot 10^2$. Other examples:

		Mantissa	Exponent
$7392 =$	$.7392 \cdot 10^4$	.7392	4
$.0001627 =$	$.1627 \cdot 10^{-3}$	.1627	-3
$-67.42 =$	$-.6742 \cdot 10^2$	$-.6742$	2

In many computers, there is only one sign position available for each number, which creates a problem since both the fraction and the exponent can be negative. The solution is to add a constant to the exponent in forming the number and take that constant into account in the various operations of arithmetic. For instance, in a decimal machine with a two-digit exponent, we would add 50 to all exponents, so that the exponents in the example above (4, -3, and 2) would actually be represented within the computer as 54, 47, and 52. In the IBM 360 and 370 lines, hexadecimal 40 is used.

The quantity added is usually called the *excess*, and we then speak of an excess-50 system, or excess-40 in hexadecimal or its decimal equivalent excess-64. The quantity added may also be called the *bias*, leading to the terminology biased-50 systems, and so forth.

This, of course, limits the minimum size (in absolute value) of the numbers that can be represented. An exponent of 00 in a two-digit floating decimal system represents 10^{-50}, and in a two-digit floating hexadecimal system 16^{-64}. The maximum (again, in absolute value) number that can be represented in two-digit floating decimal would be 99, corresponding to 10^{49}, and in two-digit floating hexadecimal would be 7F, corresponding to 16^{63}. (The first bit of the leading hexadecimal digit is not available to the exponent, since it carries the sign of the fraction.)

Such limits are adequate for the vast majority of applications and will suffice for all examples studied in this text. Representation of a wider range of values than provided by the normal hardware representation requires considerable additional effort.

A floating point number is said to be *normalized* if the leading digit of the mantissa is nonzero. It should be obvious that we can normalize any number except zero, but why should we want to do so? As our discussion of roundoff error will show, the answer is that we preserve maximum accuracy by normalizing all results.

With the symbols defined above, a number x is represented in floating decimal as $x = f \cdot 10^e$, and if it is normalized f cannot be less than $\frac{1}{10}$ since its leading digit in nonzero. Because, by assumption, f is a proper fraction, the absolute value of f cannot be as large as 1. In summary:

$$\tfrac{1}{10} \le |f| < 1 \tag{2.1}$$

Note the strict inequality on the right and the absence of this strictness on the left.

Now suppose we wish to add two floating point numbers. For example, consider

$$x_1 = 165.2 = .1652 \cdot 10^3$$

and

$$x_2 = 21.00 = .2100 \cdot 10^2$$

We cannot, of course, add the fractions as they stand because the decimal points of the numbers represented by the floating point numbers are not aligned. To align them we must "unnormalize" the number with the smaller exponent, shifting its fraction to the right the required number of places. "The required number of places" is just the difference in the two exponents. Thus if we change x_2 to

$$x_2 = .0210 \cdot 10^3$$

the fractions of both x_1 and x_2 are multiplied by 10 to the same power, and we may proceed to add:

$$\begin{aligned} x_1 + x_2 &= .1652 \cdot 10^3 + .0210 \cdot 10^3 \\ &= (.1652 + .0210) \cdot 10^3 \\ &= .1862 \cdot 10^3 \end{aligned}$$

For a further example of the operations performed in floating point addition, consider:

$$x_1 + x_2 = .1246 \cdot 10^1 + .3290 \cdot 10^{-1} \tag{2.2}$$

Again, we shift the fraction of the number having the smaller exponent, to the right, a number of places equal to the difference in the exponents:

$$\begin{aligned} x_1 + x_2 &= .1246 \cdot 10^1 + .003290 \cdot 10^1 \\ &= (.1246 + .003290) \cdot 10^1 \\ &= .1278 \cdot 10^1 \end{aligned}$$

Note that the digits of the fraction shifted out of the capacity of the system (four digits in these examples) have been lost. Furthermore, no rounding was performed when the digits were dropped. We shall consider this topic in considerably more detail in the next section; for now, note that, although a few Fortran systems do provide for rounding in this situation, it is uncommon. (This is not the result of caprice or laziness. Rounding is often quite expensive in computer time and not always of any advantage to the user. In situations where the rounding matters, the programmer can usually turn to extended precision, in which more digits are provided in the fraction.)

Let us now describe this procedure for adding two floating point numbers more precisely. Suppose we write

$$x_1 = f_1 \cdot 10^{e_1}$$

and

$$x_2 = f_2 \cdot 10^{e_2}$$

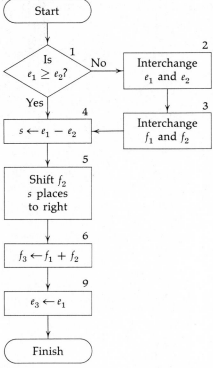

Figure 2.1. *Flow chart of some of the actions of floating point addition. The numbering of the boxes is chosen to correspond with Figure 2.2.*

and we wish to form $x_1 + x_2$, calling the sum

$$x_3 = f_3 \cdot 10^{e_3}$$

The flow chart in Figure 2.1 describes the process as we have outlined it. (The strange numbering of the boxes—7 and 8 have been omitted—is for convenience in extending the process later.)

We must begin by establishing which number has the larger exponent; there is obviously no guarantee that, as in both examples so far, the second number will have the smaller exponent (box 1). If the smaller exponent belongs to the first number, the two are exchanged (boxes 2 and 3). (This is not, of course, intended to be a literal description of exactly what happens in the registers of any specific machine. These functions have to be performed, but the details are different in different computers.) After interchanging if necessary, we establish what the difference of the exponents is and shift the fraction of the smaller number that many places to the right (boxes 4 and 5). Now the two fractions can be added (box 6) and, barring the eventualities considered below, the exponent of the result is simply the larger exponent (box 9).

Needless to say, things do not always work out so simply. First, when the two fractions are added, it may happen that the result is not a proper fraction and is therefore too large to fit in the space available. Again working through an example:

$$x_1 = .9964 \cdot 10^1$$
$$x_2 = .9803 \cdot 10^1 \tag{2.3}$$

Since the exponents are equal, no interchanging or shifting is needed, and we may proceed to add the fractions. The result, 1.9767, contains five digits and we are assuming for these examples that a floating point fraction has only four. The solution is to shift the sum fraction one place to the right (box 11 in Figure 2.2), adding 1 to the exponent to compensate for the shift (box 12). The result is then

$$x_3 = .1976 \cdot 10^2$$

The rightmost digit of the initial sum has been lost, and again we have shown the case of no rounding, which is the more common treatment.

Let us consider another possibility that must be allowed for—that of a result that is not normalized. Suppose we are adding

$$x_1 = .2631 \cdot 10^2$$
$$x_2 = -.1976 \cdot 10^2 \tag{2.4}$$

Again the exponents are equal, so we proceed to add, getting a fraction of .0655. Since this is not normalized we shift it left one position (box 15) and reduce the exponent by 1 (box 16), to get the result

$$x_3 = .6550 \cdot 10^1$$

Notice two things:

1. The last digit of this result has no significance whatever. The zero has been inserted in the shifting process since *something* has to be placed in that position in storage, but the zero does *not* reflect any information carried in the numbers that entered the operation. Nevertheless, all succeeding operations on this sum will act *as though* the zero were significant. This is a major source of error and one that we shall be investigating with great care many times in the rest of the book.
2. There can easily be more than one leading zero in the sum. For example, if we add $.3472 \cdot 10^5$ and $-.3471 \cdot 10^5$, we get an unnormalized result of $.0001 \cdot 10^5$, which becomes $.1000 \cdot 10^2$ after normalizing. The last three digits have no meaning.

In fact, the two numbers might be equal in magnitude but of opposite sign, leading to a sum of zero. There is no way to shift a fraction of zero until a nonzero digit appears in the leading digit position, of course, but we must decide what to do about the exponent of a zero fraction. It might be thought not to matter, since a zero fraction multiplied by *any* power of the number base is still zero. This is indeed true, but a problem arises if a number like $.0000 \cdot 10^4$ is added to something with a smaller exponent, such as $.1234 \cdot 10^2$. Following the rules, the fraction of the number with the smaller exponent would have to be shifted to the right two places before addition, in which process the last two digits would be lost. Even though the sum would be normalized after addition, those two lost digits would never come back. (But see below on the guard digit.) The solution to this problem, in virtually all machines, is that a floating point zero is

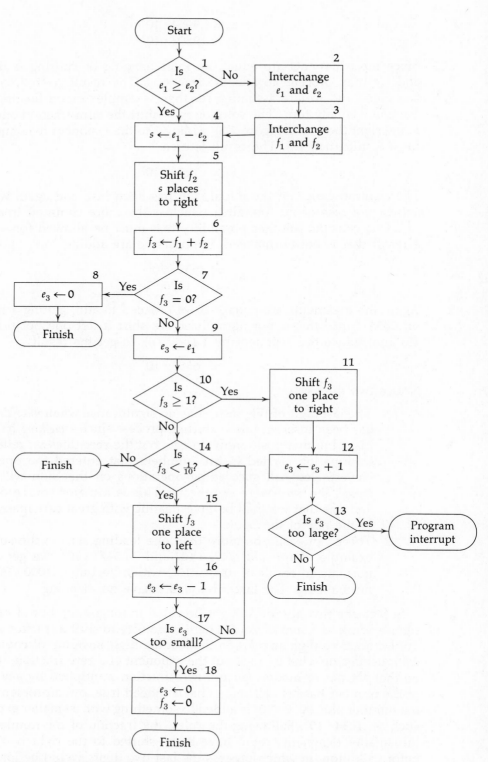

Figure 2.2. *Flow chart of the actions of floating point addition.*

always represented with the smallest exponent that is possible in the machine's representation of a floating point number. If, as usual, all exponents have an excess added to them, then the exponent is made to be zero (box 8). Thus, a decimal floating zero would stand for $.0000 \cdot 10^{-50}$. Such an exponent can obviously never be larger than that or any other number in the system.

In a number of machines, notably the IBM System/360 and 370, there is a *guard digit* position, which may be thought of as standing to the immediate right of the fraction of the number with the smaller exponent, into which digits are moved during the shifting process that takes place before addition when the exponents are not equal. Then, if the sum turns out not to be normalized, that one digit can be brought back in normalization. For an example, take

$$x_1 = .1064 \cdot 10^3$$
$$x_2 = -.3173 \cdot 10^2$$

The shifted fraction is $-.03173$ and, when this is subtracted from $.10640$ (note the extra digit position), we get $.07467$. In normalization the right-most 7 can be shifted back, giving a final result of $.7467 \cdot 10^2$. The guard digit can be utilized to make fairly simple provision for rounding, as well, but this is not usually done.

Finally, it is necessary to mention two other things that can happen. Suppose that we have two numbers that are nearly equal but are of opposite sign, and both have the same very small exponent—the smallest exponent that can be represented in the particular computer, in fact. What happens when we try to normalize? The exponent of the sum ought to be reduced by the number of places of left shift required, but such an exponent cannot be represented. This phenomenon is called *floating point underflow*. Different computers and compilers handle it differently, but one common approach is to set such a result equal to a floating point zero (box 18). If the programmer does not realize that this is happening, *very* strange results can be produced. Some truly colossal blunders have been attributable to this particular problem.

The corresponding problem on the other end of the number size range is *floating point overflow*. Suppose, for instance, that we add together two numbers, each of which is the largest possible in the machine's representation:

$$.9999 \cdot 10^{99} + .9999 \cdot 10^{99}$$

The sum is $1.9998 \cdot 10^{99}$, which needs to be adjusted to $.1999 \cdot 10^{100}$, but such an exponent is not representable in two digits. Most compilers are designed to interrupt program execution when this occurs, because no meaningful "fix" can be applied that corresponds to setting an underflow result equal to zero.

Figure 2.2 is an extension of the flow chart of Figure 2.1, modified to take all the possibilities into account.

Floating multiplication and division are actually somewhat simpler to perform and explain than addition. (Subtraction is performed by reversing the sign of the subtrahend and then proceeding exactly as in addition.) In multiplication the fractions are multiplied as they stand. If both factors were normalized to begin with, the product either already is normalized or has at most one leading zero, so that normalization of the result is easy. Rounding is not usually performed. The exponent of the result is simply the sum of the exponents of the factors, modified by normalization if performed. In systems that represent the exponent in an excess form, the excess has to be subtracted from the sum of the two exponents since the excess appears in both of the exponents that are added.

Floating division is closely related to multiplication. The quotient either already is normalized or has at most one leading zero, if we assume normalized dividend and divisor; the exponent of the quotient is the difference of the two exponents, with the excess added.

Either multiplication or division can produce both floating point underflow and floating point overflow. The extreme of floating point overflow on division occurs with any attempt to divide by zero, but such an attempt causes a program interruption in virtually all systems.

Most computers in widespread use carry out floating point operations in some base other than decimal, binary and hexadecimal being the only other bases of importance (octal is used very occasionally). The reason for such a choice is a combination of simplicity of machine design and operation, and greater efficiency of utilization of machine components, especially storage.

In a binary computer the representation is of the form

$$x = f \cdot 2^e$$

where

$$\tfrac{1}{2} \le |f| < 1$$

Hexadecimal machines lead to:

$$x = f \cdot 16^e$$

where

$$\tfrac{1}{16} \le |f| < 1$$

**2.6
Roundoff
Errors**

Suppose for the moment that we are using a computer with one or more guard digits. Suppose also that there are four digits in the mantissa. If we add two numbers such as those shown in (2.2), we get a sum of

$$x_3 = .12789 \times 10^1$$

We can express this as

$$x_3 = .1278 \times 10^1 + 0.9 \times 10^{-3}$$

Notice that the exponent of the second term is four less than the exponent of the first term. It will always be the case that the exponent of the second term is four less than the exponent of the first term, in our hypothetical four-digit examples.

We now turn to the more general case where there are t digits in the mantissa of a floating point number.

Any of the four arithmetic operations will produce a result that can be broken into two halves. In general, we denote the result (before rounding) by

$$\bar{y} = f_y \cdot 10^e + g_y \cdot 10^{e-t}$$

where f_y has t digits. The range of possible values of f_y, as we have seen, is

$$\frac{1}{10} \leq |f_y| < 1$$

For g_y it is different, since we cannot guarantee that g_y will be normalized; as a matter of fact, g_y can be zero. The range is $0 \leq |g_y| < 1$.

We now reach two questions of primary importance in this discussion: How is g_y to be taken into account in modifying f_y, and for each rule what is the maximum error in $\bar{y}$ as a result?

"Rounding" usually implies that something is done to f_y, depending on the value of g_y. Under a more general definition of rounding, however, we must include the approach of ignoring g_y entirely, which means that f_y is never modified. This usually is called *truncating* the result; we prefer to call it *chopping*—an accepted alternative—to avoid confusion with the truncation error in taking only a part of an infinite process, which is not the same thing at all.

A large number of Fortran compilers do in fact set up the object program to use chopping. If no guard digits are kept, it is the only alternative open. This kind of rounding introduces more error than the familiar rule, as we shall see. On the other hand, the use of a familiar rounding rule wastes computer time if it is used on *every* arithmetic operation, including the many places in a program in which it is not really essential. Many compiler designers have evidently made the economic decision that chopping does not cause enough trouble to justify the cost of a more sophisticated rule.

A bound on the maximum relative error in a chopped arithmetic result is easily found. The maximum relative error occurs when g_y is large and f_y is small. The maximum possible value of g_y is less than 1.0; the minimum value of f_y is 0.1. The absolute value of the relative error is therefore

$$\left| \frac{e_y}{\bar{y}} \right| = \left| \frac{g_y \cdot 10^{e-t}}{f_y \cdot 10^e} \right| \leq \frac{1 \cdot 10^{e-t}}{0.1 \cdot 10^e} = 10^{-t+1} \tag{2.5}$$

Remembering that t is the number of digits in the mantissa of *any* floating point number, we have an interesting and important result: The maximum relative rounding error in the result of a floating point arithmetic operation does not depend in any way on the sizes of the numbers. This fact gives us a firm hold on the relative error in floating point calculations.

The more familiar type of rounding, which is usually called *symmetric rounding*, can be expressed as follows: Given the two parts of a result, as before, let the rounded approximation to y be given by

$$|\bar{y}| = \begin{cases} |f_y| \cdot 10^e & \text{if } |g_y| < \frac{1}{2} \\ |f_y| \cdot 10^e + 10^{e-t} & \text{if } |g_y| \geq \frac{1}{2} \end{cases}$$

where $\bar{y}$ has the same sign as f_y. The addition of 10^{e-t} in the second line of the equation corresponds to adding 1 in the last digit retained if the first digit dropped is 5 or greater. The absolute value signs are written so that the same formulas apply to positive and negative numbers.

If $|g_y| < \frac{1}{2}$, the absolute error is

$$|e_y| = |g_y| \cdot 10^{e-t}$$

If $|g_y| \geq \frac{1}{2}$, the absolute error is

$$|e_y| = |1 - g_y| \cdot 10^{e-t}$$

In either case, we have 10^{e-t} multiplied by a factor whose absolute value is no greater than $\frac{1}{2}$. The absolute value of the absolute error, therefore, is

$$|e_y| \leq \frac{1}{2} \cdot 10^{e-t}$$

and the absolute value of the relative error is then

$$\left| \frac{e_y}{\overline{y}} \right| \leq \left| \frac{\frac{1}{2} \cdot 10^{e-t}}{f_y \cdot 10^e} \right| \leq \left| \frac{\frac{1}{2} \cdot 10^{e-t}}{0.1 \cdot 10^e} \right| = 5 \cdot 10^{-t} = \frac{1}{2} \cdot 10^{-t+1} \qquad (2.6)$$

Sometimes a slightly more refined rule is used to take into account the case in which $|g_y|$ is exactly $\frac{1}{2}$: f_y is left unchanged if its last digit is even and is rounded up if its last digit is odd. This complicates the design and operation of the computer.

We shall henceforth assume that the proper rule for rounding is the familiar one, with no special provision for $|g_y| = \frac{1}{2}$.

For an example of the difference between the two rounding rules, suppose that the result of some arithmetic operation is as follows:

$$y = 0.7324 \cdot 10^3 + 0.8261 \cdot 10^{-1}$$

For "chopping"

$$\overline{y} = 0.7324 \cdot 10^3$$

and

$$\left| \frac{e_y}{\overline{y}} \right| = \frac{0.8261 \cdot 10^{-1}}{0.7324 \cdot 10^3} \simeq 1.1 \cdot 10^{-4}$$

where $\simeq$ means "is approximately equal to."

For what we have called symmetric rounding

$$\overline{y} = 0.7325 \cdot 10^3$$
$$e_y = -0.1739 \cdot 10^{-1}$$

and

$$\left| \frac{e_y}{\overline{y}} \right| = \frac{0.1739 \cdot 10^{-1}}{0.7325 \cdot 10^3} \simeq 0.24 \cdot 10^{-4}$$

In this example the error from rounding is thus considerably less than the error from chopping. The rounding error never exceeds the chopping error and is less than the chopping error about half the time. Neither error is nearly so large as the corresponding bound, which is $10 \cdot 10^{-4}$ for chopping and $5 \cdot 10^{-4}$ for symmetric rounding. It can also happen, by good luck or by special circumstances, that the roundoff error will be zero. The typical situation is that we know a *bound* on the error in a calculation but not the *actual* error. To be completely safe, we shall always assume the worst; that is, that the error could be as large as the bound. A more satisfactory approach would be to take some kind of "average" error and use statistical techniques to find a most probable value for the total error in a computation. However, such techniques are beyond the scope of this book.

These results have been stated in terms of floating *decimal* numbers. A similar analysis can be given for binary (base 2), octal (base 8), or hexadecimal (base 16) numbers or, for that matter, for any number base. In all cases the bound on the relative roundoff error is independent of the size of the numbers. The bound depends only upon the number base, the number of digits in mantissa, and the method of rounding (chopping or symmetric).

For a binary computer with t binary digits (bits) in the mantissa, the bound on the relative roundoff error is 2^{-t} for symmetric rounding and $2 \cdot 2^{-t}$ for chopping. For a hexadecimal computer with t hexadecimal digits in the mantissa, symmetric rounding produces a bound of $8 \cdot 16^{-t}$ and chopping, $16 \cdot 16^{-t}$.

An interesting question arises when computers use a number base different from 10: How many significant decimal digits are contained in the mantissa of the floating point numbers?

A decimal computer is said to have a *precision* of t digits if there are t digits in the mantissa of a floating point number. Precision is related to significant figures but is really not synonymous with it.

In this section we found that the bound on the relative roundoff error is $0.5 \times 10^{-t+1}$ for symmetric rounding and 10^{-t+1} for chopping. Thus we shall "say" that a computer has t significant digits if, when numbers are chopped, the bound on the relative roundoff error is 10^{-t+1}.

Consider a binary computer that has 27 bits in the mantissa. The relative roundoff error in chopping does not exceed 2^{-26}. Thus it has p significant decimal digits where

$$2^{-26} = 10^{-p+1}$$

Taking logarithms to the base 10

$$p = 1 + 26 \log_{10} 2 \cong 8.8$$

Thus this computer has somewhat more than 8 significant digits but not 9. This *does not* mean that all 8-digit decimal fractions can be represented precisely in 27 bits, since not all decimal fractions have terminating binary representations. It *does* mean that all numbers in the binary computer are "correct" to 8 significant digits. Of course, the "correctness" is affected by errors (inherent, truncation, and roundoff) of previous calculations.

Consider next a hexadecimal computer with 6 hex-digits in the mantissa (for example, the IBM System 360 and 370). Then the relative roundoff error in chopping is 16^{-5}. This computer has p significant digits where

$$16^{-5} = 10^{-p+1}$$

Again taking logarithms

$$p = 1 + 20 \log_{10} 2 \cong 7$$

Once more we emphasize that by p significant digits we mean that the bound on the relative roundoff error does not exceed 10^{-p+1} when chopping is used. This is almost but not quite the same as saying that any p digit decimal number can be represented precisely.

In summary, the results given here for numbers of significant figures should be considered rules-of-thumb that give a rough indication of the number of correct decimal digits. We shall discuss floating point roundoff in later material entirely in terms of floating decimal, to stay with a familiar number system. However, the results will be slightly different in other number systems.

**2.7
Error Prop-
agation**

A major concern in numerical analysis is the question how an error at one point in a calculation *propagates,* that is, whether its effect becomes greater or smaller as subsequent operations are carried out. The subtraction of two nearly equal numbers is an extreme case: Even though the two numbers have small errors, the relative error in the difference may be quite large, as we shall show in Example 3 of Section 2.9. This large relative error will be propagated by any succeeding arithmetic operations.

Our first step in this very important study is to find expressions for the absolute and relative error in the result of each of the four arithmetic operations as functions of the operands and their errors. Then we shall develop in Section 2.8 a technique for finding a bound on the total error in a calculation containing any number of arithmetic operations.

Addition

We have two approximations, $\bar{x}$ and $\bar{y}$, to two true values, x and y, together with respective errors, e_x and e_y. Then we have

$$x + y = \bar{x} + e_x + \bar{y} + e_y = (\bar{x} + \bar{y}) + (e_x + e_y)$$

The error in the sum, which we shall denote by e_{x+y}, is therefore

$$e_{x+y} = e_x + e_y$$

Notice that we have neglected the roundoff error that arises in performing the addition of $\bar{x}$ and $\bar{y}$. This error then represents the error in the sum due to errors in the numbers to be added *and nothing else.* In the example at the close of this section and in the discussion in the next section we shall use these results, and at that time we shall take into account roundoff errors.

Subtraction

In a similar manner we get

$$e_{x-y} = e_x - e_y$$

Multiplication

In this case we have

$$x \cdot y = (\bar{x} + e_x) \cdot (\bar{y} + e_y)$$
$$= \bar{x}\bar{y} + \bar{x}e_y + \bar{y}e_x + e_x e_y$$

We assume that the errors are much smaller than the approximations and ignore the product of the errors. Thus

$$x \cdot y \simeq \overline{x} \cdot \overline{y} + \overline{x}e_y + \overline{y}e_x$$

and

$$e_{x \cdot y} \simeq \overline{x}e_y + \overline{y}e_x$$

Division

We have

$$\frac{x}{y} = \frac{\overline{x} + e_x}{\overline{y} + e_y}$$

Rearranging we get

$$\frac{x}{y} = \frac{\overline{x} + e_x}{\overline{y}} \left(\frac{1}{1 + e_y/\overline{y}} \right)$$

The factor in parentheses can be expanded in a series by long division:

$$\frac{x}{y} = \frac{\overline{x} + e_x}{\overline{y}} \cdot \left[1 - \frac{e_y}{\overline{y}} + \left(\frac{e_y}{\overline{y}} \right)^2 - \cdots \right]$$

Removing the outermost parentheses, multiplying, and dropping all terms that involve products or powers greater than 1 of e_x and e_y, we have

$$\frac{x}{y} \simeq \frac{\overline{x}}{\overline{y}} + \frac{e_x}{\overline{y}} - \frac{\overline{x}}{\overline{y}^2}e_y$$

Therefore

$$e_{x/y} \simeq \frac{1}{\overline{y}}e_x - \frac{\overline{x}}{\overline{y}^2}e_y$$

For a simple example of the meaning of these formulas, consider the addition of two four-place logarithms. Because we may assume that the logarithms are both correct to four places, we know that the error in each is no greater than 0.00005. The error in the sum can be no greater than 0.0001. Naturally, we do not know that it *is* that great but only that it *could* be that large.

It must be realized that we seldom know the sign of an error. It should not be inferred, for instance, that addition always increases the error and subtraction always decreases it just because the errors add in addition and subtract in subtraction. This is not true, of course, if the errors have different signs.

We now have formulas for the propagation of absolute errors in the four arithmetic operations, thus it is a simple matter to divide and get the relative errors. For addition and subtraction the results have been rearranged to display explicitly the effect of errors in the operands.

Addition

$$\frac{e_{x+y}}{\overline{x} + \overline{y}} = \frac{\overline{x}}{\overline{x} + \overline{y}} \left(\frac{e_x}{\overline{x}} \right) + \frac{\overline{y}}{\overline{x} + \overline{y}} \left(\frac{e_y}{\overline{y}} \right) \qquad (2.7)$$

Subtraction

$$\frac{e_{x-y}}{\overline{x} - \overline{y}} = \frac{\overline{x}}{\overline{x} - \overline{y}}\left(\frac{e_x}{\overline{x}}\right) - \frac{\overline{y}}{\overline{x} - \overline{y}}\left(\frac{e_y}{\overline{y}}\right) \qquad (2.8)$$

Multiplication

$$\frac{e_{x \cdot y}}{\overline{x} \cdot \overline{y}} = \frac{e_x}{\overline{x}} + \frac{e_y}{\overline{y}} \qquad (2.9)$$

Division

$$\frac{e_{x/y}}{\overline{x}/\overline{y}} = \frac{e_x}{\overline{x}} - \frac{e_y}{\overline{y}} \qquad (2.10)$$

It is important to understand clearly what these error propagation formulas mean. We start with two approximate values, $\overline{x}$ and $\overline{y}$, containing errors e_x and e_y. The errors may be of any type. The values of $\overline{x}$ and $\overline{y}$ may be experimental results containing inherent errors; they may be the results of some prior calculation by an infinite process and therefore may contain truncation errors; or they may be the results of prior arithmetic operations and therefore may contain roundoff errors. They may also easily be some combination of the three.

The formulas give the error in the result of each of the four arithmetic operations as functions of $\overline{x}$ and $\overline{y}$, e_x, and e_y, *assuming no roundoff error.* If, as is often the case, we want to know how the error in this result propagates in still other arithmetic operations, *we must add in the roundoff error explicitly.*

We often write x without the bar, even though to be completely precise the bar should be written. It will be clear from the context that an approximation is represented and not the true value.

The situation can be made much clearer with an example. Suppose we start a calculation with three numbers, x, y, and z, and to make matters simpler let us assume that they are exact, that is, that they have no errors of any kind. Suppose we calculate

$$u = (x + y) \cdot z$$

As the expression is written, the addition must be done first. Both operands are assumed to have no error, so that the error *propagated* by the addition is zero; however, a roundoff error is introduced in doing the addition. This roundoff error can be viewed as an inherent error in the sum as we now go on to do the multiplication. Let us agree to understand by e_{x+y} the total error in the sum, including any propagated error and roundoff. Then

$$\left| \frac{e_{x+y}}{x + y} \right| \leq 5 \cdot 10^{-t}$$

which is simply the bound on the roundoff error in any arithmetic operation, always assuming symmetric rounding. Here again we are assuming a computer in which a floating point number has a fractional part consisting of t decimal digits.

We know that the relative error in a product is the sum of the relative errors in the two factors, plus the rounding error in the multiplication.

Since the result of the multiplication is just $\bar{u}$, our approximation of u, we can write

$$\frac{e_u}{u} = \frac{e_{x+y}}{x+y} + \frac{e_z}{z} + r_m$$

where e_z/z is the relative error in z and r_m is the rounding error in the multiplication. But we have taken the error in z to be zero, and

$$\left|\frac{e_u}{u}\right| = \left|\frac{e_{x+y}}{x+y} + r_m\right| \leq \left|\frac{e_{x+y}}{x+y}\right| + |r_m|$$

(The last inequality is called the *triangle inequality*. The equality applies if $e_{x+y}/(x+y)$ and r_m have the same signs, and the inequality if they have different signs.) We thus have

$$\left|\frac{e_u}{\cdot u}\right| \leq 5 \cdot 10^{-t} + 5 \cdot 10^{-t}$$

Because we know $\bar{u}$ at the end of the calculation, we can easily get the bound on the absolute error:

$$|e_u| \leq |u| \cdot 10^{-t+1} \tag{2.11}$$

**2.8
Process
Graphs**

We now have expressions for the propagation of the errors in the operands of arithmetic operations, and we have seen in an example how to find the total error in a calculation. What we need is a more convenient way to handle the error propagation in a complete calculation.

A *process graph*[4] is a pictorial representation of the sequence in which the arithmetic operations in a calculation are carried out. We shall develop a scheme for labeling the arrows that appear in the graph so that the total error in the final result is more easily found. The method also makes it quite easy to determine the contribution of any one error, anywhere in the sequence, to the total error.

Figure 2.3 is the process graph for the example in Section 2.7,

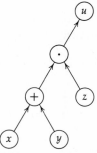

Figure 2.3. *Process graph of the operation* $u = (x + y) \cdot z$.

[4]Process graphs are a special kind of mathematical structure. The study of these structures comes under the heading of *graph theory*, a subject in which there is currently a great deal of interest and considerable research. The process graphs used here are referred to as "binary trees" in graph theory.

$u = (x + y) \cdot z$. A process graph is read from the bottom up, following the arrows. All operations at any one horizontal level are done first, then all operations at the next higher level, and so on. Figure 2.3 makes it explicit, for instance, that first x and y are added, and then the result is multiplied by z.

We call the circles in the process graph *nodes*. The arrows are called *branches*. This terminology is consistent with the terminology used in more general discussion of graph theory and is also quite convenient for us.

Imagine numbers moving along the branches in the direction of the arrows. In particular think of the number produced at a node as if it then moves along the branch that leaves the node. Returning to Figure 2.3, we imagine the value of the sum $x + y$ to be moving on the arrow leaving the node containing a $+$. Similarly, the value of u moves along the arrow leaving the node containing $\cdot$. The branch leaving the node containing y carries the value of y.

Next imagine that each branch carries a second number. This second number is the relative error in the first number. Again in Figure 2.3 the branch leaving the $+$ node carries the value of the sum $x + y$ and the value of the relative error in that sum. The branch leaving the y node carries the value of y and the relative error in y. We call the value of the number the *variable value* and the value of the relative error in that number the *error value*.

By using these devices the relative error in the final result is carried on the final branch as its error value. The analysis from the last section enables us to compute the relative errors on each branch of the graph.

We first note that the error in the result of any arithmetic operation is made up of two parts: (1) the error due to errors in the operands, and (2) roundoff error created in the operation. Thus the relative error on the branch leaving the $+$ node in Figure 2.3 is the sum of the relative errors on the branches entering the node (multiplied by the appropriate factors) and the relative roundoff error in the addition. The appropriate factors are $x/(x + y)$ and $y/(x + y)$ as we saw in the previous section.

If we label the branches entering the $+$ node with $x/(x + y)$ and $y/(x + y)$, then we can say that the relative error on the branch leaving the $+$ node is the sum of (1) the relative errors on the entering branches multiplied by the branch labels, and (2) the relative roundoff error created in the node. We can obviously make the same statement regarding any node provided we label[5] the branches correctly.

To this end we label all of the branches as follows:

Addition ($+$ node)

Let the branches leading into a $+$ node carry variable values a_1 and a_2. The branch whose variable value is a_1 is labeled $a_1/(a_1 + a_2)$. The branch whose variable value is a_2 is labeled $a_2/(a_1 + a_2)$.

Subtraction ($-$ node)

If the operation computes $a_1 - a_2$, the appropriate branches are labeled $a_1/(a_1 - a_2)$ and $-a_2/(a_1 - a_2)$.

[5] In many discussions of graph theory these labels are called "branch weights."

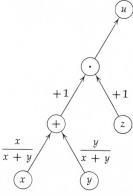

Figure 2.4. *Process graph of Figure 2.3, with the branches labeled to show the propagation of errors.*

Multiplication (· node)

The two branches leading into a · node are both labeled $+1$.

Division (/ node)

If the division is a_1/a_2, the branch with a value variable of a_1 is labeled $+1$, and the branch with a value variable of a_2 is labeled -1.

We have used these rules to produce Figure 2.4 from Figure 2.3.

We now can state a rule for computing the relative error on the branch leaving any node. *The relative error is the sum of three terms. Two of these terms are the error values on the branches entering the node each multiplied by the corresponding branch labels. The third term is the roundoff error created by the operation in the node itself.*

For example, if we wish to know the error value on the branch leaving the $+$ node in Figure 2.4, we compute

$$\left(\frac{e_x}{x}\right)\left(\frac{x}{x+y}\right)$$

the product of the relative error in x (error value on branch leaving x node) and the branch label,

$$\left(\frac{e_y}{y}\right)\left(\frac{y}{x+y}\right)$$

and

$$r_a$$

the relative error in performing the addition. Thus the error value on the branch leaving the $+$ node is

$$\left(\frac{e_x}{x}\right)\left(\frac{x}{x+y}\right)+\left(\frac{e_y}{y}\right)\left(\frac{y}{x+y}\right)+r_a \tag{2.12}$$

This is the relative error in $x+y$. We have omitted the bars from over the x and y, but it should be understood that these are approximations to the true values.

We now apply the rule to the branch leaving the · node. We multiply the error value on the leftmost branch by $+1$. That error value is given in (2.12). We then multiply (e_z/z) by $+1$. We add these terms and also add r_m, the relative roundoff error arising from the multiplication. The result is

$$\left(\frac{e_x}{x}\right)\left(\frac{x}{x+y}\right) + \left(\frac{e_y}{y}\right)\left(\frac{y}{x+y}\right) + r_a + \left(\frac{e_z}{z}\right) + r_m$$

which is the relative error in u, that is, e_u/u.

If all results are properly rounded (according to the agreed-upon rounding method), none of the roundoff errors will exceed $5 \cdot 10^{-t}$. Thus we have

$$\left|\frac{e_u}{u}\right| \leq \left(\left|\frac{x}{x+y}\right| + \left|\frac{y}{x+y}\right| + 3\right) \cdot 5 \cdot 10^{-t}$$

If x and y both have the same sign,

$$\left|\frac{x}{x+y}\right| + \left|\frac{y}{x+y}\right|$$

cannot exceed 1, and we finally have

$$\left|\frac{e_u}{u}\right| \leq 20 \cdot 10^{-t} = 2 \cdot 10^{-t+1}$$

This should be compared with the inequality (2.11). The discrepancy is due to the assumption in (2.11) that $e_x = e_y = e_z = 0$. Because we have assumed that x, y, and z were rounded symmetrically, the best we can safely say is

$$\left|\frac{e_x}{x}\right| \leq \tfrac{1}{2} \cdot 10^{-t}$$

and similarly for e_y and e_z.

We could have labeled the branches with the factors that multiply the *absolute* errors of the value variables. However, it should now be clear why we chose labels that were the proper factors by which to multiply the *relative* errors. In order to make this point once more, we make the following observations. At each node a roundoff error is added, and it must subsequently be multiplied by some factor. In floating point arithmetic we have bounds on the relative roundoff errors. Thus it is convenient that the factors later multiplying roundoff errors are the factors appropriate for relative errors.

**2.9
Examples**
Let us now apply the process graph technique to four examples, to see what error propagation means in terms of practical computations. The conclusions we draw will be directly usable in a number of situations in later chapters. These examples also nicely illustrate some of the special problems in working with a digital computer; the first two results, in particular, are not what our training in classical mathematics would lead us to expect.

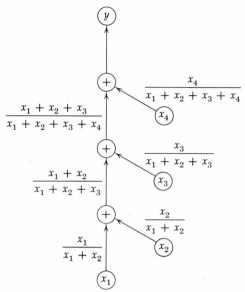

Figure 2.5. *Process graph for the addition* $y = x_1 + x_2 + x_3 + x_4$, *where* $0 < x_1 < x_2 < x_3 < x_4$.

Example 1

Addition of Positive Numbers That Are Sorted into Ascending Order
  Consider the problem of adding four positive numbers:

$$y = x_1 + x_2 + x_3 + x_4$$

where

$$0 < x_1 < x_2 < x_3 < x_4$$

A process graph is shown in Figure 2.5. Let us suppose that there are no inherent errors in the x_i, and let r_1, r_2, and r_3 be the relative roundoff errors, reading from the bottom. A systematic application of the rule for the total error in a process graph gives

$$\frac{e_y}{y} = r_1 \frac{x_1 + x_2}{x_1 + x_2 + x_3} \cdot \frac{x_1 + x_2 + x_3}{x_1 + x_2 + x_3 + x_4} + r_2 \frac{x_1 + x_2 + x_3}{x_1 + x_2 + x_3 + x_4} + r_3$$

Canceling the $x_1 + x_2 + x_3$ in the first term and multiplying through by $y = x_1 + x_2 + x_3 + x_4$ gives us

$$e_y = r_1(x_1 + x_2) + r_2(x_1 + x_2 + x_3) + r_3(x_1 + x_2 + x_3 + x_4)$$

Multiplying out and rearranging gives

$$|e_y| \leq (3x_1 + 3x_2 + 2x_3 + x_4) \cdot 5 \cdot 10^{-t}$$

The bound on the total error (absolute or relative) due to roundoff is obviously minimized by arranging the numbers so that the smallest numbers are added first. This result is somewhat on the surprising side, when one's whole mathematical training has been based on the assumption—often unstated—that addition is associative. The difference, if it is not obvious, is that we are not dealing with infinite precision, which is tacitly assumed in classical mathematics. Every result in a computer must be expressed in some finite number of digits, and this simple-appearing restriction completely changes many of the "standard" mathematical ideas.

The fact is that floating point addition is *not associative*.

For n numbers having no inherent errors the total error bound due to roundoff is

$$|e_y| \leq [(n-1)x_1 + (n-1)x_2 + (n-2)x_3 + \cdots + 2x_{n-1} + x_n] \cdot 5 \cdot 10^{-t}$$

For a numerical example suppose we must form the sums of the following numbers:

$$0.2897 \cdot 10^0$$
$$0.4976 \cdot 10^0$$
$$0.2488 \cdot 10^1$$
$$0.7259 \cdot 10^1$$
$$0.1638 \cdot 10^2$$
$$0.6249 \cdot 10^2$$
$$0.2162 \cdot 10^3$$
$$0.5233 \cdot 10^3$$
$$0.1403 \cdot 10^4$$
$$0.5291 \cdot 10^4$$

If we add in ascending order, with symmetric rounding, the successive partial sums are as follows. (The first partial sum is the sum of the first two numbers, the second partial sum is the sum of the first partial sum and the third number, and so forth.) Bear in mind that we are assuming a computer in which each mantissa is four digits; every partial sum that exceeds four digits must be rounded off. This fact, of course, is basic to the entire discussion, although six or eight digits are more typical of computer numbers.

$$0.7873 \cdot 10^0$$
$$0.3275 \cdot 10^1$$
$$0.1053 \cdot 10^2$$
$$0.2691 \cdot 10^2$$
$$0.8940 \cdot 10^2$$
$$0.3056 \cdot 10^3$$
$$0.8289 \cdot 10^3$$
$$0.2232 \cdot 10^4$$
$$0.7523 \cdot 10^4$$

If, on the other hand, we add the ten numbers in reverse order, from largest to smallest, the partial sums are

$$0.6694 \cdot 10^4$$
$$0.7217 \cdot 10^4$$
$$0.7433 \cdot 10^4$$
$$0.7495 \cdot 10^4$$
$$0.7511 \cdot 10^4$$
$$0.7518 \cdot 10^4$$
$$0.7520 \cdot 10^4$$
$$0.7520 \cdot 10^4$$
$$0.7520 \cdot 10^4$$

The correct sum to eight figures can be found by keeping all digits at each addition. It is $0.75229043 \cdot 10^4$. The error in the ascending sum is thus $-0.1 \cdot 10^0$, whereas the error in the descending sum is $2.9 \cdot 10^0$, about 30 times greater.

The bounds on the errors are about $5.5 \cdot 10^0$ for the ascending sum and $33 \cdot 10^0$ for the descending sum. In both cases the actual errors are considerably less than the maximum possible. The maximum error, as given by the bounds, occurs when rounding every partial sum requires dropping a less significant half that is nearly $\frac{1}{2}$, which is seldom the case.

Notice that, if the two smallest numbers are discarded, the ascending sum becomes $0.7522 \cdot 10^4$, which is slightly different, but the descending sum is unchanged at $0.7520 \cdot 10^4$. In the descending sum, the two smallest numbers are both too small to affect the last digit of the partial sum when they are added separately. In the ascending sum, on the other hand, they are added first, and their sum is large enough to have an effect on the last digit of the larger partial sums.

Example 2

Addition of Nearly Equal Positive Numbers

Suppose that we are adding four positive numbers, but now they are nearly equal. We may write

$$x_i = x_0 + \delta_i \qquad i = 1, 2, 3, 4$$

where

$$|\delta_i| \ll x_0$$

(The symbol $\ll$ means "is *much* less than.") A straightforward application of the result for adding four numbers gives

$$|e_y| \leq (9x_0 + 3|\delta_1| + 3|\delta_2| + 2|\delta_3| + |\delta_4|) \cdot 5 \cdot 10^{-t}$$

Since $|\delta_i|$ is small compared with x_0, we have approximately

$$|e_y| \leq 4.5 \cdot 10^{-t+1} \cdot x_0$$

This result is based on computing partial sums as expressed by the process graph of Figure 2.5. Consider an alternative way of forming the sum, as in the process graph of Figure 2.6. Here $y = (x_1 + x_2) + (x_3 + x_4)$, where

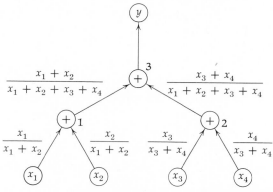

Figure 2.6. *A different process graph for adding four numbers. The numbers next to the addition circles give the sequence of the additions.*

the operations in parentheses are carried out first. If we call the relative roundoff errors in the three additions r_1, r_2, and r_3, with the subscripts corresponding to the order of the additions, we have

$$\frac{e_y}{y} = r_1 \cdot \frac{x_1 + x_2}{x_1 + x_2 + x_3 + x_4} + r_2 \cdot \frac{x_3 + x_4}{x_1 + x_2 + x_3 + x_4} + r_3$$

Rearranging, we get

$$|e_y| \leq (2x_1 + 2x_2 + 2x_3 + 2x_4) \cdot 5 \cdot 10^{-t}$$

Again setting $x_i = x_0 + \delta_i$ and neglecting terms in $|\delta_i|$ compared with x_0, we get finally

$$|e_y| \leq 4 \cdot 10^{-t+1} \cdot x_0$$

Compared with the error bound for the process graph of Figure 2.5, this arrangement of the additions yields a slightly lower bound, a result that is not intuitively obvious.

In general, if we wish to add n^2 positive numbers of approximately the same magnitude, the total roundoff error is reduced if they are added in n groups of n each and the n partial sums are added. For large n the bound on the error is only $1/n$ as large as it is for simple addition of all n^2 in a single "stream" (see Figure 2.5).

For a numerical example, consider these four numbers:

$$x_1 = 0.5243 \cdot 10^0$$
$$x_2 = 0.5262 \cdot 10^0$$
$$x_3 = 0.5226 \cdot 10^0$$
$$x_4 = 0.5278 \cdot 10^0$$

We can let $x_0 = 0.5200$ and $t = 4$ as usual. Adding them one after the other and rounding properly at each addition, we get $y = 0.2102 \cdot 10^1$. By forming $x_1 + x_2 = 0.1051 \cdot 10^1$ and $x_3 + x_4 = 0.1050 \cdot 10^1$, we get $y = 0.2101 \cdot 10^1$. The exact sum is $0.21009 \cdot 10^1$.

The inexperienced reader may wonder whether these small improvements are worth the trouble. He should always keep in mind that we are working with examples that need only a few operations. Later on we shall see processes that require hundreds or frequently even thousands of arithmetic operations; in these more realistic situations a small error can be greatly multiplied by the later operations. Our discussion of errors is definitely of practical importance.

Example 3

Subtraction of Two Nearly Equal Numbers
Suppose we have $z = x - y$. Then, from (2.8),

$$\frac{e_z}{z} = \frac{x}{x - y}\left(\frac{e_x}{x}\right) - \frac{y}{x - y}\left(\frac{e_y}{y}\right)$$

Suppose x and y are properly rounded positive numbers, so that

$$\left|\frac{e_x}{x}\right| \leq 5 \cdot 10^{-t} \quad \text{and} \quad \left|\frac{e_y}{y}\right| \leq 5 \cdot 10^{-t}$$

If $x - y$ is small, the relative error in z may be large, even though the absolute error is small. Because it is relative errors that are propagated in a floating point computation, this can have a drastic effect on the final results.

For a simple example suppose that we have

$$x = 0.5628 \cdot 10^4$$
$$y = 0.5631 \cdot 10^4$$

Then

$$z = -0.0003 \cdot 10^4$$

We know since $t = 4$ that

$$\left| \frac{e_x}{x} \right| \leq 0.5 \cdot 10^{-4} = 0.005\%$$

$$\left| \frac{e_y}{y} \right| \leq 0.5 \cdot 10^{-4} = 0.005\%$$

which are small relative errors. Yet

$$\left| \frac{e_z}{z} \right| \leq \left(\frac{.5628}{.0003} + \frac{.5631}{.0003} \right) \cdot 0.5 \cdot 10^{-4} \cong \frac{1}{6} \cong 17\%$$

which is large. This large relative error in $x - y$ is then propagated through all following computations. If the next operation were to multiply by $0.7259 \cdot 10^4$, the result, if we printed it, would be $0.2178 \cdot 10^5$, which has four digits of precision; the beginner is tempted to believe them. Yet there is only one digit that is significant.

This phenomenon where subtraction of two nearly equal numbers of the same sign gives rise to catastrophic error is known as *subtractive cancellation*. By far most of the serious errors in computer calculations are a result of subtractive cancellation. We shall encounter it again, among other places, in Case Study 4 of Chapter 3, where we shall discuss some techniques for avoiding it.

Example 4

Recall that in Chapter 1 (Section 1.10) we derived Horner's method of evaluation of a polynomial. There we noted that for a general polynomial Horner's method was the most economical method of polynomial evaluation in the sense that it requires fewer arithmetical operations than other methods.

Let us consider the simple case of a quadratic function and examine the roundoff error.

For an example, suppose we need to evaluate

$$p(x) = a + bx + cx^2$$

for some value x_0 where $|x_0| \leq 1$. The process graph for Horner's rule is shown in Figure 2.7.

Let m_1 and m_2 be the relative errors in the first and second multiplications, respectively. Similarly, let α_1 and α_2 be the relative roundoff errors in the two additions. Finally let Δ be the relative inherent error

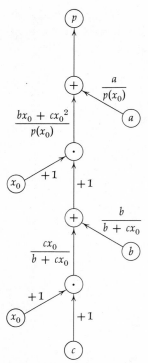

Figure 2.7. *Process graph for evaluating* $p(x) = a + bx + cx^2$ *by Horner's rule,*
$p(x) = a + x \cdot (b + x \cdot c)$.

in x_0 and let δ_a, δ_b, δ_c be the respective inherent relative errors in a, b, and c. Then

$$\frac{e_p}{p(x_0)} = \delta_c \frac{cx_0^2}{p(x_0)} + \delta_b \frac{bx_0}{p(x_0)} + \delta_a \frac{a}{p(x_0)} + \Delta\left(\frac{cx_0^2}{p(x_0)} + \frac{bx_0 + cx_0^2}{p(x_0)}\right)$$
$$+ m_1 \frac{cx_0^2}{p(x_0)} + m_2 \frac{bx_0 + cx_0^2}{p(x_0)} + \alpha_1 \frac{bx_0 + cx_0^2}{p(x_0)} + \alpha_2$$

The absolute error in $p(x_0)$ is

$$e_p = cx_0^2(\delta_c + 2\Delta + m_1 + m_2 + \alpha_1 + \alpha_2)$$
$$+ bx_0(\delta_b + \Delta + m_2 + \alpha_1 + \alpha_2) + a(\delta_a + \alpha_2)$$

For a computer with t decimal digits in the mantissa of each floating point number and since $|x_0| \le 1$ we have

$$|e_p| \le 5 \cdot 10^{-t}(7|c| + 5|b| + 2|a|) = E_H$$

Now consider another way of evaluating the polynomial, namely a straightforward evaluation of the polynomial as written. We can represent the sequence of operations by regrouping the terms as follows: Operations in parentheses are performed first, then the operation in brackets, and finally the operation in braces.

$$p(x_0) = \{[a + (b \cdot x_0)] + c \cdot (x_0 \cdot x_0)\}$$

The process graph is shown in Figure 2.8. Let α_1 and α_2 be the relative roundoff errors in the two additions as numbered, and let m_1, m_2, and m_3 be the relative roundoff errors in the three numbered multiplications. Then

$$e_p = cx_0^2(\delta_c + 2\Delta + m_2 + m_3 + \alpha_2)$$
$$+ bx_0(\delta_b + \Delta + m_1 + \alpha_1 + \alpha_2) + a(\delta_a + \alpha_1 + \alpha_2)$$

and again since $|x_0| \leq 1$

$$|e_p| \leq 5 \cdot 10^{-t}(6|c| + 5|b| + 3|a|) = E_*$$

Therefore

$$E_* - E_H = 5 \cdot 10^{-t}(|a| - |c|)$$

If $|a| \geq |c|$, Horner's rule produces a smaller bound for the effect of roundoff and inherent error. In many cases of interest this condition is satisfied. For example, suppose the polynomial is a truncated convergent series; then the coefficients become smaller for higher powers of x.

Thus here and in many other practical situations Horner's rule not only saves computing time by requiring fewer arithmetic operations but also produces a smaller absolute roundoff error.

For a general polynomial of degree n

$$p(x) = a_n x^n + a_{n-1} x^{n-1} + \cdots + a_2 x^2 + a_1 x + a_0$$

the error arising from Horner's rule is bounded by

$$\text{Error} \leq 5 \cdot 10^{-t} \left[\sum_{j=0}^{n} (3j + 2)|a_j| - |a_n| \right]$$

For convergent series the a_j decrease with j, and in the error-bound expression the larger coefficients are multiplied by the smaller numbers.

It is worth noting again that these are upper bounds to the roundoff and inherent error. The actual error is usually considerably smaller.

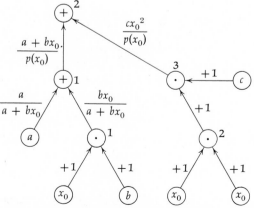

Figure 2.8. *Process graph for* $p(x) = \{[a + (b \cdot x_0)] + c \cdot (x_0 \cdot x_0)\}$.

2.10
An
Accuracy
Checklist

Some of the ideas presented in this chapter can be summarized in a short list of suggestions for practical computation. Some of the exercises that follow illustrate these points and are referenced accordingly.

1. When numbers are to be added and/or subtracted, work with the smallest numbers first (Exercise 13).
2. If possible, avoid subtraction of two nearly equal numbers. An expression containing such a subtraction can often be rewritten to avoid it (Exercises 12, 14, and 18).
3. An expression such as $a(b - c)$ can be rewritten as $ab - ac$, and $(a - b)/c$ can be rewritten as $a/c - b/c$. If there are nearly equal numbers, *do the subtraction before multiplying*. This will avoid compounding the problem with additional roundoff errors (Exercises 16 and 17).
4. When none of the above applies, minimize the number of arithmetic operations (Exercises 6 and 7).

Bibliographic Notes

Few books discuss roundoff errors in any depth. McCalla [8] in Section 2.4 develops error analysis in a manner quite similar to that used in this text. However, McCalla does not make use of process graphs and makes little use of his analysis in succeeding discussions. Sections 1.6 to 1.11 of Stark [3] also contain an introduction to the type of error analysis used here. Finally Pennington [10] has a brief discussion similar to the one in the present text including process graphs (called tree representations by Pennington) in Chapter 3. Roundoff error in polynomial evaluation is discussed by Pennington in Section 6.5.

Elementary discussions of probabilistic roundoff error analysis are contained in several texts. In particular Chapter 16 of Henrici [23] is an excellent treatment although it is the last chapter in the book and hence not used in the earlier discussions.

The classical reference on roundoff error analysis of the type described here is:
Rounding Errors in Algebraic Processes by J. H. Wilkinson (Prentice-Hall, 1963)

Requires considerably more mathematical sophistication than the present text. A classical treatise on roundoff error in the spirit of the analysis used in the present text. Examples are drawn from roots of polynomials and solution of systems of linear equations. Contains *no* flow charts or computer programs.

Exercises

*1 Current flows through a 10-ohm resistance that is accurate within 10%. The current is measured as 2.0 amp, within ± 0.1 amp. From Ohm's law, the voltage drop across the resistance is the product of the resistance and the current. What are the absolute and relative errors in the computed voltage? Neglect roundoff errors.

2 The average airline route distance from New York to San Francisco is 2700 mi, but it may be 200 mi shorter or longer because of route variations. The cruising speed of a certain airliner is 580 mph, but may vary as much as 60 mph either way because of winds. What are the bounds on the time of the flight?

3 The reactance of a capacitor is given by

$$X_c = \frac{1}{2\pi f C}$$

where X_c = capacitive reactance, Ω
f = frequency, hertz
C = capacitance, farads

What are the bounds on X_c for $f = 400 \pm 1$ hertz and $C = 10^{-7}$ farads $\pm$ 10%?

4 The position S of a body falling freely in a vacuum is given by

$$S = \tfrac{1}{2}gt^2$$

where g = acceleration of gravity, ft/sec^2
t = time since release, sec.
Assume that $g = 32.2$ ft/sec^2, exactly, but that t can be measured to only ± 0.1 sec. Show that, as t increases, the absolute error of the computed value of S increases but that the relative error decreases.

*5 Assume that a is a positive, properly rounded number, and that the number 2 can be represented in a computer exactly. Draw process graphs and derive bounds on maximum relative errors to show that the bounds are the same for $u = a + a$ and $v = 2a$.

*6 With the same assumptions as in Exercise 5, show that the bound on the maximum relative error for $u = a + a + a$ is greater than that for $v = 3a$. Illustrate with $a = 0.6992$, keeping only four digits after each arithmetic operation.

7 Assume that a and b are properly rounded positive numbers. Draw process graphs and derive error-bound expressions to show that the bound on the relative error of $u = 3(ab)$ is less than that for $v = (a + a + a)b$. Illustrate with $a = 0.4299$ and $b = 0.6824$.

*8 Assume that x is a properly rounded number. Draw process graphs and derive error-bound expressions to show that $u = x \cdot (x \cdot (x \cdot x))$ and $v = (x^2)^2$ have the same error bounds.

9 Assume that x is a properly rounded number. Draw process graphs and derive error-bound expressions to show that $u = x \cdot (x \cdot (x \cdot (x \cdot (x \cdot (x \cdot (x \cdot x))))))$ and $v = ((x^2)^2)^2$ have the same error bounds.

10 Show that in floating decimal $10./10. = 10.^*(1./10.)$ and $2./2. = 2.^*(1./2.)$, but $3./3. \neq 3.^*(1./3.)$.

*11 Assume that a, b, and x are positive and exact. Draw process graphs and derive error-bound expressions to show that the relative roundoff error bounds for $u = ax + bx^2$ and $v = x(a + bx)$ are the same. Use $a = 0.7625$, $b = 0.6947$, and $x = 0.4302$ to show that, although the bounds are the same, the actual errors, which are usually smaller than the bounds, need not be the same.

12 Assume that a and b are positive and exact and that $a > b$. Show that, although in infinite precision it is true that $a + b = (a^2 - b^2)/(a - b)$, roundoff errors may make the value of the right-hand expression considerably different from that of the left-hand. Show that the worst case occurs when the roundoff errors made in forming a^2 and b^2 are near the maximum but of opposite signs. Illustrate with $a = 0.3525$ and $b = 0.3411$, using four-digit floating point arithmetic.

13 Assume that a is a properly rounded positive number and that 1 can be represented exactly. Consider the expressions $u = (1 + a)^2$ and $v = 1 + (2a + a^2)$. Show that as a becomes very large the relative error bounds for u and v approach equality but that as a becomes very small the relative error bound for u approaches three times the relative error bound for v. Illustrate with $a = 0.2635$.

14 Draw a process graph and derive an expression for the bound on the relative error for $(a + b) - b$. Illustrate with $a = 0.8614 \cdot 10^{-2}$ and $b = 0.9949$ and with $a = 0.3204$ and $b = 0.5837$.

15 Consider the expression $5a + b$. Show that in the result the relative inherent error in a is weighted five times as heavily as the relative inherent error in b.

*16 Consider the expressions $u = (a - b)/c$ and $v = a/c - b/c$. Assume that a, b, and c are all positive and have no inherent errors and that $a \simeq b$. Show that the relative roundoff error in v can be much greater than the relative roundoff error in u. Illustrate with $a = 0.41$, $b = 0.36$, and $c = 0.70$, using two-digit floating point arithmetic.

17 Consider the expressions $u = a \cdot (b - c)$ and $v = ab - ac$, in which we assume that $a > 0$, $b > 0$, $c > 0$, $b > c$, and $b \simeq c$. Show that u has much better relative accuracy under the conditions stated. Show that, with $a = 0.9364$, $b = 0.6392$, and $c = 0.6375$, $u = 0.1592 \cdot 10^{-2}$, which is properly rounded from the exact answer, but $v = 0.1500 \cdot 10^{-2}$.

*18 In the quadratic equation $ax^2 + bx + c = 0$, assume that the coefficients are all positive and exact and that $b^2 \gg 4ac$. Show first that in infinite precision the smaller of the two roots is given either by

$$x_1 = \frac{-b + \sqrt{b^2 - 4ac}}{2a}$$

or

$$x_1' = \frac{-2c}{b + \sqrt{b^2 - 4ac}}$$

Show that for the conditions stated x_1' gives much better relative accuracy. Show that, with $a = 0.1000 \cdot 10^1$, $b = 0.4002 \cdot 10^0$, and $c = 0.8000 \cdot 10^{-4}$, $x_1 = -0.1500 \cdot 10^{-3}$ and $x_1' = -0.2000 \cdot 10^{-3}$. The last is the exact root. (You may show the square root operation in a process graph as a circle with only one operand leading to it. The inherent relative error in the operand appears in the square root multiplied by $\frac{1}{2}$, and the arrow leading from the operand to the square root circle may be so labeled. The square root contains an additional relative roundoff error that in most Fortran systems will not exceed 10^{-t+1}.)

19 Consider the simultaneous equations

$$ax + by = c$$
$$dx + ey = f$$

and the solution by Cramer's rule

$$x = \frac{ce - bf}{ae - bd}$$

$$y = \frac{af - cd}{ae - bd}$$

Show that if $ae - bd$ is small the accuracy of the solution may be poor, even if the coefficients have no inherent errors. Illustrate by showing that the solution of the system

$$0.2038x + 0.1218y = 0.2014$$
$$0.4071x + 0.2436y = 0.4038$$

obtained with four-digit floating point arithmetic is $x = -1.714$, $y = 4.286$, whereas the exact solution, which can be obtained with eight-digit floating point arithmetic, is $x = -2.000$, $y = 5.000$. If the coefficients themselves are inexact, as they almost always are, the "solution" of this system can be totally meaningless.

20 The following problem, suggested by Richard V. Andree, demonstrates effectively that roundoff is not the only problem in numerical computation. Consider the system

$$x + 5.0y = 17.0$$
$$1.5x + 7.501y = 25.503$$

Show that, if enough digits are carried to make all roundoff "errors" zero, the system will have a unique solution, $x = 2$, $y = 3$. Show that, if the constant term in the second equation is changed to 25.501, a modification of one part in about 12,000, a greatly different solution will be obtained.

If the coefficients and constant terms were experimental results, with a corresponding doubt about their exact values, the "solution" would be meaningless.

21 Show that with a computer having a number base of b, and t digits to the base b in the mantissa of its floating point number, the number of significant decimal digits is

$$p = t \log_{10} b + (1 - \log_{10} b)$$

22 One hexadecimal digit is equivalent to four binary digits in terms of hardware. Using this fact and the result of Exercise 21, show that a computer with any given number of binary digits is more accurate if treated as a binary computer than if treated as a hexadecimal computer.

23a The representation of one-tenth in the hexadecimal (base 16) system is

$$(0.199\ 999\ 999\ \ldots)_{16}$$

If we have a hexadecimal machine with six places in the fraction of a floating point number, show that adding ten one-tenths (*chopped* after six places) and subtracting the sum from one leaves a result of

$$6 \times 16^{-6} \cong 4 \times 10^{-7}$$

b Would the result be appreciably more accurate if the six-place representation were *rounded* instead of chopped? Why?

24a The representation of one-third in the decimal (base 10) system is

$$0.333\ 333\ \ldots$$

If we have a decimal machine with six places in the fraction of a floating point number, show that adding three one-thirds (chopped after six places) and subtracting the sum from one leaves a result of

$$1 \times 10^{-6}$$

b What is the representation of one-third in the hexadecimal system?

c What is the error in adding three one-thirds in a six-place hexadecimal machine?

25 Consider the quadratic function

$$p(x_0) = a + bx_0 + cx_0^2 = \{a + [(b \cdot x_0) + c \cdot (x_0 \cdot x_0)]\}$$

The last expression is evaluated as follows: operations in parentheses are evaluated first, then the operation in brackets, and finally the operation in braces.

a. Draw the process graph for this process.

b. Show that, if the relative inherent errors in a, b, c, and x and relative roundoff errors are bounded by $5 \cdot 10^{-t}$, then the absolute error, e_p, in $p(x_0)$ is bounded by

$$|e_p| \leq 5 \cdot 10^{-t}(7|c| + 5|b| + 2|a|)$$

c. Why is this the same as the bound E_H for Horner's rule whereas the bound for

$$p(x_0) = \{[a + (b \cdot x_0)] + c(x_0 \cdot x_0)\}$$

where only the square bracket has been moved is larger in the case $|a| > |c|$?

3 Numerical Instabilities and Their Cure

<table>
<tr><td>

**3.1
Introduc-
tion**

</td><td>

In the previous chapter we discussed a semigraphical method for analyzing the propagation of errors in a floating point calculation. In this chapter we shall continue our discussion of errors, concerning ourselves with more difficult and interesting problems than we encountered earlier.

The problems, although seemingly straightforward, produce completely nonsensical results when solved on a digital computer in what might seem to be the most obvious ways. We shall use the developments in Chapter 2 to analyze these problems.

Four quite specific problems will be discussed as case studies. However, the numerical difficulties that arise in these case studies are by no means unique and occur quite often in practice. Moreover, the solutions we shall devise to avoid the numerical problems have broad applicability.

We first discuss summation of a convergent series (Case Study 3). The numerical difficulty in the case we shall consider arises because the argument of the function is so large that many significant digits are lost before the convergence criterion is satisfied. One can partially alleviate the problem by increasing the precision used by the computer, that is, increasing the number of digits in the mantissa (fraction) of the floating point numbers. The best solution, however, is to make a change of variables to reduce the size of the argument.

The second problem (Case Study 4) involves a recursion formula for finding upper and lower bounds to the value of π. The results break down because of *subtractive cancellation* (see Example 3 in Chapter 2, p. 90). Once again increasing the precision used by the computer can partially alleviate

</td></tr>
</table>

99

the problem. A better solution to such problems, however, is to find which subtraction operation is causing the difficulty and to expand the two functions being subtracted in Taylor series.

The third problem (Case Study 5) again involves a recursion formula. The recursion determines the value of a definite integral that depends on a parameter n. The roundoff error grows as $n!$. This type of abnormal error growth results whenever the nth term in a recursion approaches zero. The solution, as we shall see, is to reverse the direction of the recursion.

Finally (Case Study 6) we study the computation of the mean and standard deviation of a set of numbers. Here we shall find that, if we use the most economical method for evaluating the standard deviation, then once again subtractive cancellation causes a great loss of accuracy. We can avoid the difficulty in this case by using a different algorithm. We shall thus see that what is the most "economical," in the sense of using the fewest number of arithmetic operations and the least memory, is not always the best way to proceed.

Although the material in this chapter is useful and interesting, we should note that the development in later chapters does not depend on it. The case studies here either could be studied at any other point in the book or could be omitted.

3.2
Case
Study 3:
Errors in
the Direct
Evaluation
of the Sine
Series

The Taylor series for the sine

$$\sin x = x - \frac{x^3}{3!} + \frac{x^5}{5!} - \frac{x^7}{7!} + \cdots$$

is, as we have noted, theoretically valid for all values of x. In actual fact it is almost useless for large values of x. It is instructive to investigate why this is so.

We shall write a program that evaluates the series directly, that is, starting with the first term and continuing to compute terms until finding one that is less in absolute value than, say, 10^{-8}. We know that the truncation error is then less than the first term neglected, so that it ought to be possible to compute the sine within 10^{-8} simply by taking enough terms. We shall see that it is not practically possible to do so because of extreme roundoff problems.

The program will require an interesting stratagem to avoid producing intermediate results too large for a floating point variable. The largest angle we shall consider will be about 50 rad; if we were to try to raise 50 to the large powers that will be required, we would greatly exceed the sizes permitted for floating point variables in all but a few Fortran systems. Therefore, we shall take another approach, that of computing each new term from the preceding term. The recursion relation is not complicated. Having the first term x, we can get the next term by multiplying by $-x^2$ and dividing by $2 \cdot 3$. Having the second term, we can get the third by multiplying by $-x^2$ and dividing by $4 \cdot 5$. In short, given the preceding term, we can get the next one by multiplying by $-x^2$ and dividing by the product of the next two integers.

A flow chart is shown in Figure 3.1. It is set up to read cards, each containing an angle in degrees, until it reaches a "sentinel card" with an

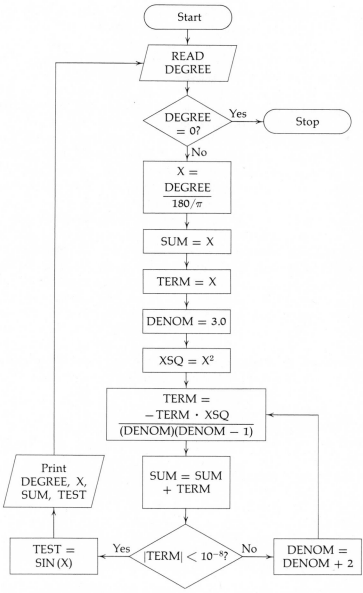

Figure 3.1. *Flow chart of a procedure for computing the sine of an angle by evaluating the power series.*

angle of zero. The angle in degrees is first converted to radians by dividing by $180/\pi$; the result is called X. Now we need to get the recursion process started. We shall continually be adding a new term to a sum that eventually becomes the sine when enough terms have been computed. To begin, we set this sum equal to X; the first term computed by the recursion method will be $-x^3/3!$. Thus the "preceding term" is also X. To get the successive integers, we start a variable named DENOM at 3. To save recomputing x^2 repeatedly, we compute it once before entering the loop and give it the name XSQ.

Getting a new term is now a simple matter of multiplying the preceding term by $-XSQ$ and dividing by the product of DENOM and DENOM $-$ 1.0. This new term replaces the preceding term and is added to the sum. We are now ready to find out whether enough terms have been computed. We ask if the absolute value of the term just computed is less than or equal to 10^{-8}. If it is, we are ready to print the result and to go back to read another card. If not, the value of DENOM must be increased by 2.0 before returning to compute another term.

Besides printing the value of the sine computed by this method, it might be interesting to use the sine function supplied with the Fortran system to compute it also, for comparison. This is done just before printing.

The program shown in Figure 3.2 follows the flow chart closely and involves no difficult programming concepts.

The results shown in Figure 3.3 are for 30° plus multiples of 360°. The result in every case should therefore be $\frac{1}{2}$. The entry for 30° is as close as we should reasonably expect in running the program on a machine in which floating point numbers have the equivalent of about seven decimal digits. The error builds with larger angles. For 390° the value is barely tolerable; at 750° the method is clearly falling apart; for 1110° and larger angles we get nonsensical results. The entries that consist of only asterisks indicate values too large to be contained in the space available.

Let us consider an entry in which the method fails completely, 1470°, to see if we can understand what is happening. By using a modified

```
C CASE STUDY 3
C COMPUTATION OF SINE BY SERIES EVALUATION
C FIRST VERSION - SINGLE PRECISION
C
C PRINT HEADINGS
      WRITE (6, 31)
   31 FORMAT (/' DEGREE',10X,'X',9X,'SERIES-SINE    FUNCTION-SINE'/)
C READ ANGLE
   62 READ (5, 100) DEGREE
  100 FORMAT (F10.0)
C CHECK FOR ZERO SENTINEL MARKING END OF INPUT
      IF (DEGREE .EQ. 0.0) STOP
C CONVERT TO RADIANS
      X = DEGREE / 57.2957795
C SET UP STARTING VALUES
      SUM = X
      TERM = X
      DENOM = 3.0
      XSQ = X * X
C COMPUTE NEXT TERM AND NEW SUM
   25 TERM = - TERM * XSQ / (DENOM * (DENOM - 1.0))
      SUM = SUM + TERM
C CHECK FOR CONVERGENCE
      IF (ABS(TERM) .LT. 1.0E-8) GO TO 16
C PREPARE TO GO AROUND AGAIN
      DENOM = DENOM + 2.0
      GO TO 25
C COMPUTE SINE BY BUILT-IN FORTRAN FUNCTION, PRINT RESULTS
   16 TEST = SIN(X)
      WRITE (6, 30) DEGREE, X, SUM, TEST
   30 FORMAT (F6.0, 3F16.7)
      GO TO 62
      END
```

Figure 3.2. *A program to compute a sine, following the method shown in the flow chart of Figure 3.1.*

DEGREE	X	SERIES-SINE	FUNCTION-SINE
30.	0.5235987	0.4999999	0.4999999
390.	6.8067837	0.5000133	0.4999996
750.	13.0899687	0.4998717	0.4999993
1110.	19.3731537	-11.2978935	0.4999991
1470.	25.6563263	891.7993164	0.4999881
1830.	31.9395142	639408.0000000	0.4999903
2190.	38.2227020	****************	0.4999925
2550.	44.5058899	****************	0.4999948
2910.	50.7890778	****************	0.4999970
-30.	-0.5235987	-0.4999999	-0.4999999
-390.	-6.8067837	-0.5000133	-0.4999996

Figure 3.3. *The output of the program of Figure 3.2. The rows of asterisks denote values that were too large to print in the space available.*

program, not shown, the values of the individual terms were printed. The first term is just the value of x, 25.65633 rad. The second term is -2814.700, to the seven equivalent decimal digits we are working with; when the first two terms are added, the last two digits of the first term are dropped.[1] Obviously these lost digits can never re-enter the computation later, when the sum should have been reduced to a number less than 1. The third term is 92638.31; in the addition to get a new sum of 89849.25, the last digit of the preceding sum is dropped. Thus three digits of the first terms are now lost. The fourth term is -1451878.0; the addition to get a new sum of -1362028.0 drops two digits of the preceding sum. The last *five* digits of the first terms have now been lost, which means the entire fractional part. This is clearly not good, when we hope eventually to arrive at a sum that is less than 1. The largest term in the series is $1094495 \cdot 10^4$; after adding it to the preceding sum *all* digits of the first term have left the scene, along with some of the digits of the other terms. In the next entry in Figure 3.3, that for 1830°, the largest term is about $-5 \cdot 10^{12}$; all but about one digit of the first *and* second terms are lost in adding them to a number this size.

One serious problem here, clearly, is that the additions are being done in a sequence that is far from ideal. We noted in Chapter 2 that it is much better to start with the smallest terms, or, more generally, to keep the partial sums as small as possible.

But this is not the only problem. This example was run on an IBM System/360 computer, where single-precision floating point numbers have six hexadecimal digits in their fractional parts. Consider a term such as 10944950272.0000000, which is the actual form in which the largest term in the computation of the sine of 1470° was printed. Because we know that six hexadecimal digits carry the equivalent of only about seven decimal digits of information, we can be sure that the digits 0272, at least,

---

[1]The conscientious reader who attempts to check the arithmetic here will have problems with the last digit, since we are dealing throughout with seven decimal-digit equivalents of six hexadecimal-digit floating point numbers. Since most hexadecimal fractions do not have exact seven-digit decimal equivalents and since the output routines round the results (even though arithmetic performed by the program is not rounded), there will sometimes be one-digit differences between arithmetic checked entirely in decimal and what the computer prints.

```
C CASE STUDY 3
C COMPUTATION OF SINE BY SERIES EVALUATION
C SECOND VERSION - DOUBLE PRECISION
C
C PRINT HEADINGS
      DOUBLE PRECISION X, SUM, TERM, XSQ, TEST
      WRITE (6, 31)
   31 FORMAT (/' DEGREE',14X,'X',16X,'SERIES-SINE',11X,'FUNCTION-SINE'/)
C READ ANGLE
   62 READ (5, 100) DEGREE
  100 FORMAT (F10.0)
C CHECK FOR ZERO SENTINEL MARKING END OF INPUT
      IF (DEGREE .EQ. 0.0) STOP
C CONVERT TO RADIANS
      X = DEGREE / 57.29577951308232
C SET UP STARTING VALUES
      SUM = X
      TERM = X
      DENOM = 3.0
      XSQ = X * X
C COMPUTE NEXT TERM AND NEW SUM
   25 TERM = - TERM * XSQ / (DENOM * (DENOM - 1.0))
      SUM = SUM + TERM
C CHECK FOR CONVERGENCE
      IF (DABS(TERM) .LT. 1.0D-16) GO TO 16
C PREPARE TO GO AROUND AGAIN
      DENOM = DENOM + 2.0
      GO TO 25
C COMPUTE SINE BY BUILT-IN FORTRAN FUNCTION, PRINT RESULTS
   16 TEST = DSIN(X)
      WRITE (6, 30) DEGREE, X, SUM, TEST
   30 FORMAT (F6.0, 3F23.14)
      GO TO 62
      END
```

Figure 3.4. *A double precision version of the program of Figure 3.2.*

are meaningless. In fact, the 5 is questionable also. What we can say with some degree of assurance is that the decimal equivalent of the hexadecimal number was between about 109449450000 and 109449550000, or, in other words, that there was an uncertainty in the representation of the number of about 50,000. In short, the number simply does not contain enough information for our purposes. It is an approximation to a quantity that we would need to know to about 18 decimal digits in order to retain what must be known about the fractional portion of the number to compute our sine. The procedure cannot possibly compute an accurate value for a sum that should eventually be less than 1.

We can demonstrate that this is the problem by re-running the program with double-precision variables in place of single-precision ones. Figure 3.4 shows the modified program and Figure 3.5 the results. We see that

DEGREE	X	SERIES-SINE	FUNCTION-SINE
30.	0.52359877559830	0.50000000000000	0.50000000000000
390.	6.80678408277789	0.50000000000000	0.50000000000000
750.	13.08996938995747	0.49999999999830	0.50000000000000
1110.	19.37315469713706	0.50000000016191	0.50000000000000
1470.	25.65634000431664	0.49999865780756	0.50000000000000
1830.	31.93952531149623	0.50012945598551	0.50000000000000
2190.	38.22271061867582	0.76348214126836	0.50000000000000
2550.	44.50589592585540	158.59741983818510	0.50000000000000
2910.	50.78908123303499	20217.91110845947000	0.50000000000000
-30.	-0.52359877559830	-0.50000000000000	-0.50000000000000
-390.	-6.80678408277789	-0.50000000000000	-0.50000000000000

Figure 3.5. *The output of the program of Figure 3.4.*

for the angle we examined above, 1470°, the result contains about five correct digits. Since we saw that we would have needed the equivalent of about 18 decimal digits to get seven-digit accuracy, whereas a System/360 double precision number contains about 16, this result is about what we might have expected. For larger angles, however, even double precision is not enough.

Of course, the precise values computed depend strongly on the amount of information contained in a word on the particular computer used. For instance, the program of Figure 3.4 was run on a Control Data CDC 6600, which, having been designed specifically for large-scale scientific calculation, has a somewhat longer word length than the IBM System/360 that we use in most examples in this book. A double precision word in the CDC 6600 contains the equivalent of about 24 decimal digits. The double precision sine routine gives a result for 2190° correct to about 12 digits, and the process does not break down completely until 3990°. These results go considerably beyond what we were able to achieve with the 360.

Double precision is highly useful in many practical situations, as we shall often see. It is not the intention of this case study to suggest, however, that it is a substitute for proper analysis; there is a much better way to compute the sines of large angles.

The proper solution to this problem is to reduce the size of the argument, making use of the periodicity of the sine function. One simple approach is to subtract multiples of 2π until the angle has been reduced to less than 2π (assuming a positive angle). For instance, in the program of Figure 3.2 we could insert the following statement immediately after the sentinal test, just before converting to radians: DEGREE = DEGREE − 360.0*(IFIX(DEGREE)/360)

IFIX is the name of a function that converts a number in real form to integer form, discarding any fractional part without rounding. When this result is divided by integer 360, the quotient gives the number of times 360 "goes into" DEGREE--again discarding any fractional part, without rounding. When *this* is multiplied by 360.0 and the product subtracted from DEGREE, the difference will be a number less than 360°. In other words, an integral multiple of 360 has been subtracted from DEGREE, reducing it to an angle less than 360. The reduction works correctly for negative angles, as well; the reader who satisfies himself of the truth of this assertion will have provided himself with a good review of the operation of Fortran integer arithmetic.

Figure 3.6 shows the results of running the revised program (single-precision version), where we see that the results are now as accurate as one should expect.

Even better results can be obtained by reducing the angle to something less than $\pi/2$, which requires some mechanism for keeping track of what quadrant the original angle was in so that the correct sign can be attached to the result. This reduction is what is commonly done in the sine routines supplied with a Fortran compiler, that is, what is done when one writes SIN(X).

We may note briefly how the sine function supplied with the system fared. In all cases there are at least five good digits. The decreased accu-

DEGREE	X (REDUCED)	SERIES-SINE	FUNCTION-SINE
30.	0.5235987	0.4999999	0.4999999
390.	0.5235987	0.4999999	0.4999999
750.	0.5235987	0.4999999	0.4999999
1110.	0.5235987	0.4999999	0.4999999
1470.	0.5235987	0.4999999	0.4999999
1830.	0.5235987	0.4999999	0.4999999
2190.	0.5235987	0.4999999	0.4999999
2550.	0.5235987	0.4999999	0.4999999
2910.	0.5235987	0.4999999	0.4999999
-30.	-0.5235987	-0.4999999	-0.4999999
-390.	-0.5235987	-0.4999999	-0.4999999

Figure 3.6. *The output of a program (not shown) to compute sines by series evaluation, but with a preliminary reduction of the angle to its equivalent less than 360°.*

racy for the larger angles is caused by a loss of significance in reducing the original angle to an angle less than $\pi/2$. For instance, when we convert 2190° to radians, we get 38.2227020. The computer has printed nine digits as the decimal equivalent of the floating hexadecimal value, but there simply cannot be more than seven meaningful digits there. When this seven-digit approximation is reduced to an angle less than $\pi/2$, we have in effect subtracted two nearly equal numbers, which we have seen before leads to reduced relative accuracy. In other words, we did not really compute the sine of 2190° but of some slightly different angle.

For large angles sines are literally never computed by the method of this case study, for obvious reasons. It is hoped that the reader has gained some appreciation of the problems that are faced in working with a computer, which inevitably involves approximations.

**3.3
Case
Study 4:
Subtractive
Cancella-
tion in a
Calculation
of π**

The number π, which appears in so many mathematical formulas, some having little to do with the geometry of circles, is of course defined as the ratio of the circumference of a circle to its diameter. From this definition Archimedes observed that one could find upper and lower bounds for π by finding the perimeter of circumscribed and inscribed polygons. Indeed, the perimeter of *any* polygon inscribed in a circle cannot exceed the circumference of the circle. On the other hand, the perimeter of any circumscribed polygon does exceed the circle's circumference. If we can make the two perimeters (inscribed and circumscribed) sufficiently close to each other, then we shall have a good estimate of π.

We start with a circle of radius 1 whose circumference, therefore, is 2π. An inscribed square has a side length of $\sqrt{2}$ (See Figure 3.7a). Thus a lower bound for 2π, found in this way, is $4\sqrt{2}$, the perimeter of the inscribed square. On the other hand, a circumscribed square has a side length of 2 (see Figure 3.7b), so an upper bound for 2π is $4 \cdot 2 = 8$.

Since we are interested in bounds on π itself, not 2π, we shall henceforth calculate one-half the perimeter. The inscribed and circumscribed squares thus lead to the bounds

$$2\sqrt{2} < \pi < 4$$

or

$$2.828 < \pi < 4$$

Now we could construct inscribed and circumscribed polygons of six, eight, and ten sides just as we did above for the case of four sides. As we increase the number of sides, we would expect the boundary of the polygons to approach the circle. Thus we expect that the lower bound (inscribed perimeter) should get larger while still remaining smaller than the circumference of the circle. Similarly the upper bound (circumscribed perimeter) should get smaller and yet always exceed the circle's circumference.

Rather than construct polygons with more and more sides, however, we instead derive a formula that computes the length of the side of an inscribed (or circumscribed) polygon with $2n$ sides, starting with the side length of an inscribed (or circumscribed) polygon with n sides. Since we already have the side length for a polygon with four sides, we can use the formula that we shall derive shortly to compute the side length of a polygon with eight sides (an octagon). Using this result we then apply the formula again to find the length of the side of a polygon with 16 sides. Continuing in this way we can find the side lengths of polygons with 32, 64, 128, ..., 2^n, ..., sides. Once we have the length of the side of any of these polygons we can obtain a bound for π by multiplying the side length by one-half the number of sides of the polygon.

We begin with inscribed polygons. Looking at Figure 3.8, we suppose s_n is the length of the side of a polygon with n sides (n arbitrary). If we want a polygon with $2n$ sides, then each side of the polygon with n sides must yield two sides of the new $2n$-gon. Thus we bisect the line segment BD, which has length s_n. The line segment OA is the desired bisector of BD. Thus the chord BA is a side of the polygon with $2n$ sides. We wish to find the length of BA. We call this length s_{2n}. Thus we wish to find s_{2n} in terms of s_n.

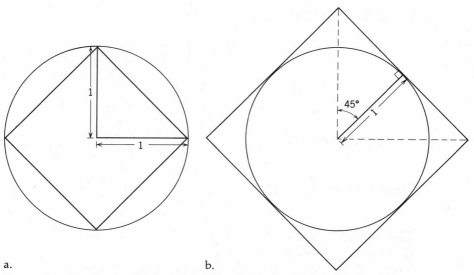

a.   b.

Figure 3.7. *Squares inscribed and circumscribed in a circle of radius 1.*

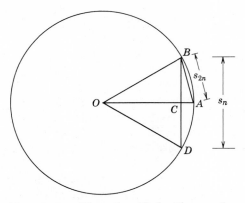

Figure 3.8. *Given the side length,* s_n, *of an inscribed* n-gon, *we wish to find the length,* s_{2n}, *of an inscribed* 2n-gon.

Now from the Pythagorean theorem

$$\overline{OC}^2 + \overline{BC}^2 = \overline{OB}^2 \tag{3.1}$$

and

$$\overline{AC}^2 + \overline{BC}^2 = \overline{BA}^2 \tag{3.2}$$

(The bar over the pair of letters indicates the length of the line segment joining the two points represented by the letters.)
Now

$$\overline{OB} = 1$$
$$\overline{BC} = s_n/2$$
$$BA = s_{2n}$$

and

$$\overline{AC} = 1 - \overline{OC}$$

Using these in (3.1) and (3.2) we get

$$\overline{OC}^2 + \left(\frac{s_n}{2}\right)^2 = 1 \tag{3.3}$$

and

$$(1 - \overline{OC})^2 + \left(\frac{s_n}{2}\right)^2 = s_{2n}^2 \tag{3.4}$$

Solving (3.3) for $\overline{OC}$

$$\overline{OC} = \tfrac{1}{2}\sqrt{4 - s_n^2} \tag{3.5}$$

Then substituting in (3.4)

$$s_{2n} = \sqrt{2 - \sqrt{4 - s_n^2}} \tag{3.6}$$

This is called a *recursion* or *iteration* formula, since it allows us to calculate the side length of various polygons recursively. That is, starting with the length of the side of any inscribed polygon, we use (3.6) to calculate the length of the side of a polygon with twice as many sides. We then use that result again in the same formula (which is what "recursively" means).

For example, with $n = 4$ we already found that $s_n = s_4 = \sqrt{2}$. Thus the length of the side of an inscribed octagon is, from (3.6) with $n = 4$,

$$s_{2n} = s_8 = \sqrt{2 - \sqrt{4 - 2}} = \sqrt{2 - \sqrt{2}}$$

We can use this value of s_8 in (3.6) and find the side length of a polygon with 16 sides. Setting $n = 8$ in (3.6) we get

$$s_{16} = \sqrt{2 - \sqrt{4 - s_8^2}} = \sqrt{2 - \sqrt{2 + \sqrt{2}}}$$

The lower bounds so far calculated for π are thus

$$2 \cdot s_4 = 2\sqrt{2} \qquad\qquad \cong 2.8285$$

$$4 \cdot s_8 = 4\sqrt{2 - \sqrt{2}} \qquad \cong 3.0615$$

$$8 \cdot s_{16} = 8\sqrt{2 - \sqrt{2 + \sqrt{2}}} \cong 3.1214$$

Before writing a Fortran program to carry out these calculations we first derive the formula for the length of the side of a circumscribed polygon with n sides. Having done so, we may write a program to get the upper and lower bounds at the same time.

Consider the diagram in Figure 3.9. Once again $\overline{BD}$ represents a side of an inscribed polygon with n sides. $\overline{EF}$ is the side of a circumscribed polygon with n sides. We wish to find $c_n = \overline{EF}$ in terms of $s_n = \overline{BD}$. OA bisects both BD and EF.

OCB and OAE are similar triangles. Therefore

$$\frac{\overline{OC}}{\overline{OA}} = \frac{\overline{BC}}{\overline{AE}} \tag{3.7}$$

From the Pythagorean theorem

$$\overline{OC}^2 + \overline{BC}^2 = \overline{OB}^2 \tag{3.8}$$

Again

$$\overline{OA} = 1$$

$$\overline{BC} = \frac{s_n}{2} \tag{3.9}$$

$$\overline{AE} = \frac{c_n}{2}$$

so from (3.7)

$$\overline{OC} = \frac{s_n}{c_n} \tag{3.10}$$

But, since $\overline{OB} = 1$, using (3.9) and (3.10) in (3.8) we get

$$c_n = \frac{2s_n}{\sqrt{4 - s_n^2}} \tag{3.11}$$

Again with $n = 4$ recall that $s_n = s_4 = 2$ so using (3.11) with $n = 4$

$$c_4 = \frac{2\sqrt{2}}{\sqrt{2}} = 2$$

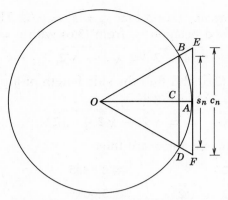

Figure 3.9. *Given the side length, s_n, of inscribed n-gon, we wish to find the length, c_n, of a circumscribed n-gon.*

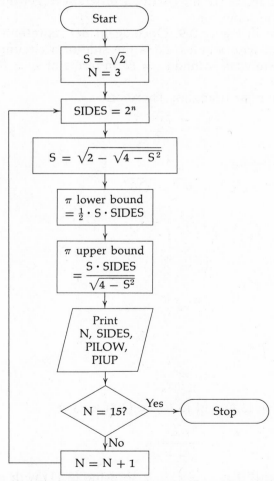

Figure 3.10. *Flow chart of a procedure for finding bounds on π by the method of inscribed and circumscribed polygons.*

Numerical Instabilities and Their Cure

This is the same result we got before, when we computed the length of the side of a circumscribed square, demonstrating the correctness of the formula.

We can now use (3.6) and (3.11) to find upper and lower bounds for π. The flow chart is shown in Figure 3.10. We start with s = the length of the side of an inscribed square. The index n keeps track of the number of sides, that is, the number of sides is 2^n. Each time through the loop we increase n by 1 and thus double the number of sides.

The first calculation of s computes the length of the side of an inscribed octagon using (3.6). We then calculate lower and upper bounds for π. The latter requires the use of (3.11). We print the results and stop if $n = 15$. Thus we use polygons with as many as $2^{15} = 32{,}768$ sides.

We can now write a Fortran program that follows the flow chart. The variable names are:

$$\text{SLNGTH} = \text{the side length, } s$$
$$\text{SIDES} = \text{number of sides}$$
$$\text{PILOW} = \text{lower bound for } \pi$$
$$\text{PIUP} = \text{upper bound for } \pi$$

The program is shown in Figure 3.11.

The results from running this program on an IBM System/360 are shown in Figure 3.12. Notice that up through $n = 7$ (a 128-sided polygon) the results are about what we might expect. The successive lower bounds get larger as the successive upper bounds get lower. For $n = 8$, however, a strange result appears. The lower bound, 3.142451, is *larger* than π, which we recall, is approximately 3.14159265359. As we go further, even stranger results appear. In fact, at $n = 12$ the upper bound no longer decreases

```
C CASE STUDY 4
C CALCULATION OF THE VALUE OF PI FROM THE PERIMETERS
C    OF INSCRIBED AND CIRCUMSCRIBED POLYGONS
C
C SINGLE PRECISION VERSION
C
C WRITE HEADINGS
      WRITE (6, 199)
  199 FORMAT (/1X, 'BOUNDS ON PI - SINGLE PRECISION VERSION'//
     1'   N     SIDES     SIDE LENGTH     PI - LOWER BOUND   PI - UPPER
     2BOUND'/)
C COMPUTE SIDE LENGTH OF INSCRIBED SQUARE
      SLNGTH = SQRT(2.0)
C GO NEXT TO OCTAGON
      N = 3
C PROGRAM REPEATS FROM HERE
    5 SIDES = 2.0**N
      SLNGTH = SQRT (2.0 - SQRT(4.0 - SLNGTH**2))
      PILOW = 0.5 * SIDES * SLNGTH
      PIUP = (SIDES * SLNGTH) / SQRT(4.0 - SLNGTH**2)
      WRITE (6, 200) N, SIDES, SLNGTH, PILOW, PIUP
  200 FORMAT (1X, I3, F9.0, F15.6, 2F19.6)
      IF (N .GE. 15) STOP
C PREPARE TO DOUBLE THE NUMBER OF SIDES, AND GO AROUND AGAIN
      N = N + 1
      GO TO 5
      END
```

Figure 3.11. *A program following the method of the flow chart of Figure 3.10 to find bounds on π.*

N	SIDES	SIDE LENGTH	PI - LOWER BOUND	PI - UPPER BOUND
3	8.	0.765366	3.061465	3.313705
4	16.	0.390180	3.121443	3.182595
5	32.	0.196034	3.136541	3.151717
6	64.	0.098134	3.140276	3.144062
7	128.	0.049081	3.141208	3.142154
8	256.	0.024550	3.142451	3.142688
9	512.	0.012275	3.142451	3.142510
10	1024.	0.006176	3.162277	3.162292
11	2048.	0.003088	3.162277	3.162282
12	4096.	0.001691	3.464102	3.464103
13	8192.	0.000977	4.000000	4.000000
14	16384.	0.0	0.0	0.0
15	32768.	0.0	0.0	0.0

Figure 3.12. *The output of the program of Figure 3.11. Observe that the method fails because of subtractive cancellation. The results would be different on different computers with different word lengths and rounding methods.*

but increases. At $n = 13$ both upper and lower bounds are 4. Thereafter both bounds are zero. Obviously there is some severe numerical problem.

To assure ourselves that the numerical problem is in some way connected with the finite number of digits in the computer, we re-run the problem using double precision on the IBM/360. This time we also allow n to be as large as 30 (a polygon with over a billion sides) and print 14 digits after the decimal point. The results are shown in Figure 3.13.

Notice that, roughly speaking, the number of digits to which π can be computed is one-half the number of digits in the mantissa of the computer's floating point numbers.

The numerical problem here is *subtractive cancellation*. To see this, we analyze (3.6). As n becomes large, s_n, the length of one side of the inscribed n-gon, becomes small. Its square, s_n^2, becomes even smaller. Therefore, for small n, $4 - s_n^2$ is close to 4. The square root of $4 - s_n^2$ is close to 2. Thus, when we subtract $\sqrt{4 - s_n^2}$ from 2, we are subtracting two positive numbers whose magnitudes are nearly equal. We have already seen that this can lead to very large errors (Example 3 of Chapter 2).

To observe this phenomenon of subtractive cancellation even more clearly we may follow through in detail the calculation for a hypothetical computer with *three* digits in the mantissa of a floating point number. No actual computer has so few digits, but the principle that will be exemplified is valid for any number of digits. The only difference between few digits and many, is that the trouble shows up sooner with few.

We shall assume further that our hypothetical computer *rounds symmetrically*. (See p. 77.) Moreover, we assume that given any three-digit number, the machine can find the square root of that number to three significant figures, symmetrically rounded. Not many actual computers satisfy these assumptions. The point is that even under such highly favorable conditions, completely useless "answers" are produced.

We start with $n = 2$ so $s = \sqrt{2} = 1.41$ to three digits. In our machine this is carried as $.141 \cdot 10^1$. We then compute

$$\sqrt{2 - \sqrt{4 - s^2}}$$

as follows.

$$s^2 = (.141 \cdot 10^1)^2 = .19881 \cdot 10^1$$

Since our hypothetical machine rounds symmetrically,

$$s^2 = .199 \cdot 10^1$$

We next compute

$$4 - s^2 = .400 \cdot 10^1 - .199 \cdot 10^1 = .201 \cdot 10^1$$

The square root of this result is

$$.142 \cdot 10^1$$

We now compute

$$2 - \sqrt{4 - s^2}$$

which in our computer is

$$.200 \cdot 10^1 - .142 \cdot 10^1 = .058 \cdot 10^1$$

When this result is normalized, we get

$$.580 \cdot 10^0$$

But the trailing zero has no significance at all. Actually, the correct result to three significant figures is .586, so that the zero as computed should have been a 6. The only way we can know this is to have carried out the calculations with more than three digits. Since that is impossible in a machine that carries only three digits, the fact that the computer inserts

BOUNDS ON PI - DOUBLE PRECISION VERSION

N	SIDES	SIDE LENGTH	PI - LOWER BOUND	PI - UPPER BOUND
3	8.	0.76536686473018	3.06146745892072	3.31370849898476
4	16.	0.39018064403226	3.12144515225805	3.18259787807453
5	32.	0.19603428065912	3.13654849054594	3.15172490742926
6	64.	0.09813534865484	3.14033115695474	3.14411838524589
7	128.	0.04908245704582	3.14127725093276	3.14222362994244
8	256.	0.02454307657144	3.14151380114415	3.14175036916881
9	512.	0.01227176929831	3.14157294036788	3.14163208070397
10	1024.	0.00613591352594	3.14158772527996	3.14160251025961
11	2048.	0.00306796037256	3.14159142150464	3.14159511774302
12	4096.	0.00153398063751	3.14159234561108	3.14159326967027
13	8192.	0.00076699037513	3.14159257654500	3.14159280755978
14	16384.	0.00038349519451	3.14159263346325	3.14159269121694
15	32768.	0.00019174759798	3.14159264532122	3.14159265975964
16	65536.	0.00009587379899	3.14159264532122	3.14159264893082
17	131072.	0.00004793689892	3.14159260737572	3.14159260827812
18	262144.	0.00002396845177	3.14159291093967	3.14159291116527
19	524288.	0.00001198422126	3.14159169668369	3.14159169674009
20	1048576.	0.00000599210136	3.14158683965504	3.14158683966914
21	2097152.	0.00000299605995	3.14159655370482	3.14159655370834
22	4194304.	0.00000149799292	3.14151884046555	3.14151884046643
23	8388608.	0.00000074892234	3.14120796828227	3.14120796828249
24	16777216.	0.00000037431290	3.13996417177012	3.13996417177017
25	33554432.	0.00000018730469	3.14245127249413	3.14245127249415
26	67108864.	0.00000009305772	3.12249899919920	3.12249899919920
27	134217728.	0.00000004712161	3.16227766016838	3.16227766016838
28	268435456.	0.00000002107342	2.82842712474619	2.82842712474619
29	536870912.	0.0	0.0	0.0
30	1073741824.	0.0	0.0	0.0

Figure 3.13. *The output of a double precision version (not shown) of the program of Figure 3.11. The results are better, but the method still fails, for large* n.

a zero at the right when normalizing a result tells us absolutely nothing about what the digit really should be.

This kind of thing is at the root of subtractive cancellation. We shift in zeros at the right of a number when we normalize it. The zeros are not significant, yet further operations will treat them as though they were. The consequences can be catastrophic, as we have seen and shall see again and again.

When we compute the square root of $.580 \cdot 10^0$, we get $.762 \cdot 10^0$. This is the value we will use for the side length of an inscribed octagon. The correct length, to three significant figures, is $.765 \cdot 10^0$. Notice that the error in s_8 is 3 in the third digit. This is smaller by a factor of one-half than the error created by the subtractive cancellation.

The lower bound, called PILOW in the program, and the upper bound, called PIUP, that result from our three-digit calculation are

$$PILOW = .305 \cdot 10^1$$
$$PIUP = .330 \cdot 10^1$$

Had we carried out the calculations with more precision and rounded only at the end, we would have computed

$$PILOW = .306 \cdot 10^1$$
$$PIUP = .331 \cdot 10^1$$

Thus our bounds for π are not too far from the correct ones.

Without going through all of the details, we now list the results of continuing the three-digit arithmetic along with the correct results to three digits. In each line marked * we have shifted an insignificant zero into the righthand part of the mantissa. Lines marked ** indicate that two trailing zeros have been introduced; both zeros are of course insignificant.

	Results of three-digit computation	Correct results to three digits
$n = 2$		
	$s_4 = .141 \cdot 10^1$	$s_4 = .141 \cdot 10^1$
$n = 3$		
	$s_8 = \sqrt{.200 \cdot 10^1 - \sqrt{4 - (.141 \cdot 10^1)^2}}$	
	$\quad = \sqrt{.200 \cdot 10^1 - .142 \cdot 10^1}$	
*	$\quad = \sqrt{.580 \cdot 10^0}$	$s_8 = \sqrt{.586 \cdot 10^0}$
	$\quad = .762 \cdot 10^0$	$\quad = .765 \cdot 10^0$
	$PILOW = .305 \cdot 10^1$	$PILOW = .306 \cdot 10^1$
	$PIUP = .330 \cdot 10^1$	$PIUP = .331 \cdot 10^1$
$n = 4$		
	$s_{16} = \sqrt{.200 \cdot 10^1 - \sqrt{.400 \cdot 10^1 - (.762 \cdot 10^0)^2}}$	
	$\quad = \sqrt{.200 \cdot 10^1 - .185 \cdot 10^1}$	
*	$\quad = \sqrt{.150 \cdot 10^0}$	$s_{16} = \sqrt{.152 \cdot 10^0}$
	$\quad = .387 \cdot 10^0$	$\quad = .390 \cdot 10^0$
	$PILOW = .310 \cdot 10^1$	$PILOW = .312 \cdot 10^1$
	$PIUP = .316 \cdot 10^1$	$PIUP = .318 \cdot 10^1$

Results of three-digit computation	Correct results to three digits
$n = 5$	

$$s_{32} = \sqrt{.200 \cdot 10^1 - \sqrt{.400 \cdot 10^1 - (.387 \cdot 10^0)^2}}$$
$$= \sqrt{.200 \cdot 10^1 - .196 \cdot 10^1}$$
** $$= \sqrt{.400 \cdot 10^{-1}}$$
$$= .200 \cdot 10^0$$
$$\text{PILOW} = .320 \cdot 10^1$$
$$\text{PIUP} = .322 \cdot 10^1$$

$$s_{32} = \sqrt{.384 \cdot 10^{-1}}$$
$$= .196 \cdot 10^0$$
$$\text{PILOW} = .314 \cdot 10^1$$
$$\text{PIUP} = .315 \cdot 10^1$$

Already we have run into serious trouble. Although the error in s_{32} is only 4 in the third place ($= .004$), to compute PILOW we multiply s_{32} by 16. Thus the error in PILOW is $16 \cdot .004 = .064 = .0064 \cdot 10^1$. This produces a "lower bound" that in fact *exceeds* π. If we did not already know the value of π, there would be no way to detect the error except to carry out the calculations to more than three digits.

Continuing the calculations:

Results of three-digit computation	Correct results to three digits
$n = 6$	

$$s_{64} = \sqrt{.200 \cdot 10^1 - \sqrt{.400 \cdot 10^1 - (.200 \cdot 10^0)^2}}$$
$$= \sqrt{.200 \cdot 10^1 - .199 \cdot 10^1}$$
** $$= \sqrt{.100 \cdot 10^{-1}}$$
$$= .100 \cdot 10^0$$
$$\text{PILOW} = .320 \cdot 10^1$$
$$\text{PIUP} = .320 \cdot 10^1$$

$$s_{64} = \sqrt{.963 \cdot 10^{-2}}$$
$$= .981 \cdot 10^{-1}$$
$$\text{PILOW} = .314 \cdot 10^1$$
$$\text{PIUP} = .314 \cdot 10^1$$

$n = 7$

$$s_{128} = \sqrt{.200 \cdot 10^1 - \sqrt{.400 \cdot 10^1 - (.100 \cdot 10^0)^2}}$$
$$= \sqrt{.200 \cdot 10^1 - .200 \cdot 10^1}$$
$$= \sqrt{0 \cdot 10^0}$$
$$= 0 \cdot 10^0$$
$$\text{PILOW} = 0 \cdot 10^0$$
$$\text{PIUP} = 0 \cdot 10^0$$

$$s_{128} = \sqrt{.241 \cdot 10^{-2}}$$
$$= .491 \cdot 10^{-1}$$
$$\text{PILOW} = .314 \cdot 10^1$$
$$\text{PIUP} = .314 \cdot 10^1$$

Notice that, henceforth, all values of s_n will be zero. This is what happens using both single and double precision on the IBM System/360. It also happens in both single and double precision on the CDC 6600, although not as soon because of the longer word length, in both single and double precision on the Burroughs B6700, and in normal and extended precision on the IBM 1130. On the National Cash Register NCR 315, the result was different. Because of the details of machine design and the particular square root routine used, the side length reached a value of 0.000032 after 16 iterations and did not change thereafter. The computed values for the perimeters accordingly increased without limit. Again we see that the details of numerical processes depend quite strongly on such things as word length, whether results are rounded, and floating-point normalization procedures.

We now ask: How could we calculate π more accurately using this method of inscribed and circumscribed polygons? Or, more generally, how could we avoid subtractive cancellation?

The answer lies in somehow avoiding the subtraction or subtractions that cause the problem. In some cases there may be more than one, but in this case just one subtraction is the source of all the trouble. In this particular case the calculation of $\sqrt{4 - s_n^2}$ is not the culprit, but rather the following operation, where we subtract that result from 2.

The guilty subtraction can be avoided altogether by the device of rewriting $\sqrt{4 - s_n^2}$ using the binomial theorem. Recall that the binomial theorem states that:

$$(a + b)^n = a^n + na^{n-1}b + \cdots$$
$$+ \frac{n!}{(n - k)!k!} a^{n-k}b^k$$
$$+ \frac{n!}{(n - (k + 1))!(k + 1)!} a^{n-(k+1)}b^{k+1}$$
$$+ \cdots$$

Generally we think of n as being an integer, so that the last term in the expression above is b^n. However, the expression is actually valid for *any* real value of n. We take $n = \frac{1}{2}$. There is now no last term, and what we have in fact written is the (infinite) Taylor series expansion for $\sqrt{a + b}$.

If we let t_k be the kth term, then

$$t_k = \frac{n!}{(n - k)!k!} a^{n-k}b^k$$

for $k = 0, 1, 2, \ldots$. Moreover,

$$t_{k+1} = \left(\frac{n - k}{k + 1} \cdot \frac{b}{a} \right) t_k$$

Letting $n = \frac{1}{2}$, $a = 4$ and $b = -s_n^2$, we get

$$(a + b)^n = \sqrt{4 - s_n^2} = 2 - d_1 - d_2 - \cdots - d_k - \cdots$$

where

$$d_{k+1} = \frac{2k - 1}{k + 1} \frac{s_n^2}{2^3} d_k \tag{3.12}$$

and

$$d_1 = \frac{s_n^2}{4} \tag{3.13}$$

Thus,

$$2 - \sqrt{4 - s_n^2} = d_1 + d_2 + d_3 + \cdots \tag{3.14}$$

Notice that if $s_n < 1$ then as k increases d_k gets small very rapidly, since each succeeding term is multiplied by s_n^2 and also by $\frac{1}{8}$. Therefore, we will calculate $2 - \sqrt{4 - s_n^2}$ by summing $d_1 + d_2 + \cdots + d_k + \cdots$. We

```
C CASE STUDY 4
C CALCULATION OF THE VALUE OF PI FROM THE PERIMETERS
C    OF INSCRIBED AND CIRCUMSCRIBED POLYGONS
C
C BINOMIAL THEOREM VERSION - AVOIDS SUBTRACTIONS
C
      REAL K
C WRITE HEADINGS
      WRITE (6, 198)
  198 FORMAT (/1X, 'BOUNDS ON PI - SINGLE PRECISION BINOMIAL THEOREM VER
     1SION'//'   N      SIDES      SIDE LENGTH      PI - LOWER BOUND   PI -
     2 UPPER BOUND'/)
C START WITH SQUARE
      SIDES = 4.0
C START SERIES SUM WITH D1 FOR SQUARE
      SUM = 2.0
C PREPARE TO GO TO OCTAGON
      N = 3
C DOUBLE THE NUMBER OF SIDES
    1 SIDES = 2.0 * SIDES
C SN SQUARED IS SAME AS PREVIOUS SUM
      SSQ = SUM
C START NEW SERIES
      SUM = 0.0
C COMPUTE STARTING TERM, D1
      TERM = 0.25 * SSQ
C SET UP RECURSION
      K = 1
C COMPUTE NEW SUM
    2 TEMP = TERM + SUM
C SEE IF TERM WAS TOO SMALL TO CHANGE PREVIOUS SUM
      IF (TEMP .LE. SUM) GO TO 4
C NO - MUST COMPUTE ANOTHER TERM
      SUM = TEMP
      FACT = (2.0 * K - 1.0) / (K + 1.0)
      TERM = FACT * SSQ * TERM / 8.0
      K = K + 1.0
      GO TO 2
C COMPUTE SIDE LENGTH AND BOUNDS
    4 SLNGTH = SQRT(SUM)
      PILOW = 0.5 * SIDES * SLNGTH
      PIUP = SIDES *  SLNGTH / (2.0 - SLNGTH)
      WRITE (6, 200) N, SIDES, SLNGTH, PILOW, PIUP
      IF (N .EQ. 15) STOP
      N = N + 1
      GO TO 1
  200 FORMAT (1X, I3, F9.0, F15.6, 2F19.6)
      END
```

Figure 3.14. *A program based of the use of the binomial theorem to rewrite the formula for the side length of the polygon so as to avoid subtractive cancellation.*

then calculate the square root of that sum to get s_{2n}. *Notice that no subtraction takes place.* The results, as we shall see, are very stable.

A Fortran program is shown in Figure 3.14. Each succeeding term, d_k, is called TERM, and the sum, as shown in (3.14), is called SUM. Notice that we start SUM at 2.0, because SUM is the square of the side length. With four sides, the side length is $\sqrt{2}$ so the beginning value of SUM = $(\sqrt{2})^2 = 2$. Each time we increase N by 1 (doubling the number of sides) we return to statement 1. There we double SIDE and set SSQ equal to the previous SUM, s_n^2. We then reset SUM = 0 to compute (3.14). The first term of the series, d_1, is computed from (3.13) as 0.25*SSQ. We then add that term into the sum and call the result TEMP. If the term just added is so small that TEMP and SUM are the same, we go to statement 4 to compute SNGTH, PILOW, and PIUP. If, however, TEMP is larger than SUM, we compute the next term and return to statement 2 to add this new term into the sum.

BOUNDS ON PI - SINGLE PRECISION BINOMIAL THEOREM VERSION

N	SIDES	SIDE LENGTH	PI - LOWER BOUND	PI - UPPER BOUND
3	8.	0.765367	3.061466	4.959311
4	16.	0.390180	3.121441	3.878001
5	32.	0.196034	3.136544	3.477387
6	64.	0.098135	3.140326	3.302365
7	128.	0.049082	3.141272	3.220302
8	256.	0.024543	3.141507	3.180538
9	512.	0.012272	3.141566	3.160961
10	1024.	0.006136	3.141581	3.151248
11	2048.	0.003068	3.141584	3.146411
12	4096.	0.001534	3.141584	3.143996
13	8192.	0.000767	3.141585	3.142791
14	16384.	0.000383	3.141584	3.142188
15	32768.	0.000192	3.141584	3.141886

Figure 3.15. *The output of the program of Figure 3.14.*

This method of summing a series computes the sum as accurately as the computer permits. That is, we add terms until the last term added is so small that it contributes nothing to the sum. This occurs because of the fixed and finite number of digits in the mantissa of a floating point number. Although no term is actually zero, they do eventually become so small that, in the process of lining up decimal points before adding, all the digits of the smaller number are shifted out of the picture. Thus, if we try to add $.499 \cdot 10^{-2}$ to $.100 \cdot 10^1$, the result is $.100 \cdot 10^1 + .000499 \cdot 10^1 = .100499 \cdot 10^1$. If the computer, as with our hypothetical machine a few pages back, has only three digits in the mantissa of a floating point number, the result will be $.100 \cdot 10^1$, whether the machine rounds *or* chops. The term $.499 \cdot 10^{-2}$ is so small that adding it to $.100 \cdot 10^1$ does not change the latter.

This method of summing should be used only on series that converge fairly rapidly, as the present one does. On more slowly converging series, such as

$$1 - \frac{1}{2} + \frac{1}{3} - \frac{1}{4} + \cdots + (-1)^{k-1}\frac{1}{k} + \cdots$$

different criteria should be used. See, for example, the approach taken in Case Study 3.

The results of running this program on an IBM 360 in single precision are shown in Figure 3.15. Notice that the results are stable and are accurate to five figures—almost to six. Since the computer in question carries only the equivalent of less than seven decimal digits, this is the best that should be expected.

If we run the same program using double precision, we get 12 digits of accuracy by letting n be as large as 30. (See Figure 3.16.) Compare these results with Figure 3.13, where subtractive cancellation destroyed all accuracy long before N became that large.

We now derive a general rule of thumb for handling subtractive cancellation.

1. Determine which subtraction is causing the difficulty. (This may not always be an easy matter.) Rewrite the expression as $f(x) - g(x)$, where the subtraction shown is the critical one.

2. Expand $f(x)$ and $g(x)$ in Taylor series about the value of x that causes the problem.
3. Subtract the corresponding terms of the two series. The constant terms, and perhaps some others as well, should cancel each other. (We say "should" because unless this is true it would be rare for subtractive cancellation to occur.)
4. Sum the resultant series.

In the example of this case study we determined that

$$f(x) = 2$$
$$g(x) = \sqrt{4 - s_n^2}$$

The expansion of $f(x)$ was, of course, trivial, since it consists of just the constant term. The expansion of $g(x)$ was achieved through the binomial theorem as

$$2 - d_1 - d_2 - \cdots - d_k - \cdots$$

where the d_i are given by (3.12) and (3.13).

As another example consider the evaluation of

$$F(x) = \sqrt[3]{1 + x} - \sqrt{1 - x} \tag{3.15}$$

For small x the two radicals will be nearly equal and subtractive cancellation will cause difficulties. Thus we let

$$f(x) = \sqrt[3]{1 + x}$$
$$g(x) = \sqrt{1 - x}$$

```
BOUNDS ON PI - DOUBLE PRECISION BINOMIAL THEOREM VERSION
```

N	SIDES	SIDE LENGTH	PI - LOWER BOUND	PI - UPPER BOUND
3	8.	0.76536686416123	3.06146745664491	4.95931522940221
4	16.	0.39018064372880	3.12144514983040	3.87800673121556
5	32.	0.19603428050516	3.13654848808260	3.47739256260471
6	64.	0.09813534857758	3.14033115448247	3.30237080975640
7	128.	0.04908245700716	3.14127724845826	3.22030755194228
8	256.	0.02454307655210	3.14151379866923	3.18054396568277
9	512.	0.01227176928864	3.14157293789188	3.16096827458911
10	1024.	0.00613591352110	3.14158772280191	3.15125563884332
11	2048.	0.00306796037015	3.14159141903594	3.14641796184338
12	4096.	0.00153398063628	3.14159234309486	3.14400376354168
13	8192.	0.00076699037454	3.14159257410961	3.14279782194889
14	16384.	0.00038349519432	3.14159263186330	3.14219514023125
15	32768.	0.00019174759804	3.14159264630172	3.14189387160331
16	65536.	0.00009587379913	3.14159264991133	3.14174325534202
17	131072.	0.00004793689958	3.14159265081373	3.14166795172429
18	262144.	0.00002396844979	3.14159265103933	3.14163030104340
19	524288.	0.00001198422490	3.14159265109573	3.14161147598496
20	1048576.	0.00000599211245	3.14159265110983	3.14160206352625
21	2097152.	0.00000299605622	3.14159265111336	3.14159735731451
22	4194304.	0.00000149802811	3.14159265111424	3.14159500421305
23	8388608.	0.00000074901406	3.14159265111446	3.14159382766343
24	16777216.	0.00000037450703	3.14159265111451	3.14159323938889
25	33554432.	0.00000018725351	3.14159265111453	3.14159294525169
26	67108864.	0.00000009362676	3.14159265111453	3.14159279818310
27	134217728.	0.00000004681338	3.14159265111453	3.14159272464882
28	268435456.	0.00000002340669	3.14159265111453	3.14159268788167
29	536870912.	0.00000001170334	3.14159265111453	3.14159266949810
30	1073741824.	0.00000000585167	3.14159265111453	3.14159266030632

Figure 3.16. *The output of a double precision version (not shown) of the program of Figure 3.14.*

Again using the binomial theorem we get

$$f(x) = a_0 + a_1 + a_2 + \cdots$$

where

$$a_0 = 1$$

$$a_{k+1} = -\frac{3k-1}{3(k+1)} \, a_k x$$

and

$$g(x) = b_0 + b_1 + b_2 + \cdots$$

where

$$b_0 = 1$$

$$b_{k+1} = \frac{2k-1}{2(k+1)} \, b_k x$$

Again the constant terms cancel if we subtract corresponding terms and we get

$$F(x) = c_1 + c_2 + \cdots$$

where

$$c_k = a_k - b_k \qquad k = 1, 2, \cdots \tag{3.16}$$

and

$$a_1 = \frac{x}{3} \tag{3.17}$$

$$a_{k+1} = \frac{3k-1}{-3(k+1)} a_k x \qquad k = 1, 2, \cdots \tag{3.18}$$

$$b_1 = -\frac{x}{2} \tag{3.19}$$

$$b_{k+1} = \frac{2k-1}{2(k+1)} b_k x \qquad k = 1, 2, \cdots \tag{3.20}$$

Exercise 5 asks you to write a program to evaluate (3.15) for small x.

**3.4
Case
Study 5:
Errors in
the
Recursive
Evaluation
of a
Definite
Integral**

Consider now the following definite integral:

$$\int_0^1 x^n e^{x-1} \, dx \qquad n = 1, 2, \ldots$$

In Chapter 5 we develop direct numerical methods for evaluating any definite integral. Here we shall integrate this particular integral by parts. Since the integral in question depends on a parameter, n, we may denote the value of the integral by I_n. That is,

$$I_n = \frac{1}{e} \int_0^1 x^n e^x \, dx \tag{3.21}$$

Recall that $\int u \, dv = uv - \int v \, du$. Letting $u = e^x$ and $dv = x^{n-1} \, dx$, then

$$du = e^x \, dx$$

$$v = \frac{x^n}{n}$$

so

$$\int_0^1 e^x x^{n-1} \, dx = e^x \frac{x^n}{n} \Big|_0^1 - \int_0^1 \frac{x^n}{n} e^x \, dx$$

$$= \frac{1}{n}\left(e - \int_0^1 x^n e^x \, dx \right)$$

Dividing both sides by e and noting the definition of I_n in (3.21), we have

$$I_{n-1} = \frac{1}{n}(1 - I_n)$$

or

$$I_n = 1 - nI_{n-1} \qquad n = 2, 3, \ldots \tag{3.22}$$

When $n = 1$,

$$I_1 = \frac{1}{e} \int_0^1 x e^x \, dx$$

so

$$I_1 = \frac{1}{e} \tag{3.23}$$

Equation (3.22) is a *recursion* or *iteration* formula for determining I_n. We start with (3.23) and use (3.22) with $n = 2$ to find

$$I_2 = 1 - \frac{2}{e}$$

Having calculated I_2 we use (3.22) again, this time with $n = 3$, to get

$$I_3 = 1 - 3I_2 = -2 + \frac{6}{e}$$

and so on.

We shall now use this recursion formula to evaluate I_n for $n = 2, 3, \ldots$. First, however, we note that the integrand in (3.21) is nonnegative, that is,

$$x^n e^x \geq 0$$

for $0 \leq x \leq 1$. Moreover, since the integral is not identically zero over the entire range of integration,

$$I_n > 0 \tag{3.24}$$

Consider now

$$I_n - I_{n-1} = \frac{1}{e} \int_0^1 (x - 1)x^{n-1} e^x \, dx$$

For $0 \leq x \leq 1$ it follows that

$$x - 1 \leq 0$$
$$x^{n-1} e^x \geq 0$$

so this integral is nonpositive. Again the integrand is not identically zero, so the integral is strictly negative. Thus

$$I_n - I_{n-1} < 0 \tag{3.25}$$

```
C CASE STUDY 5
C EVALUATING A DEFINITE INTEGRAL BY RECURSION
C
C FIRST VERSION - FORWARD RECURSION
C
      WRITE (6, 200)
  200 FORMAT (/1X, 'DEFINITE INTEGRAL BY FORWARD RECURSION'//
     1'    N         INTEGRAL'/)
      N = 1
C ASSIGN VALUE OF FIRST INTEGRAL TO 'VALUE'
      VALUE = 0.367879
    1 WRITE (6, 201) N, VALUE
  201 FORMAT (1X, I3, F17.8)
      IF (N. GE. 15) STOP
C PERFORM RECURSION
      N = N + 1
      XN = N
      VALUE = 1.0 - XN * VALUE
C GO AROUND AGAIN
      GO TO 1
      END
```

Figure 3.17. *A program to compute the value of a certain definite integral by a recursive method.*

By combining (3.24) and (3.25)

$$0 < I_n < I_{n-1} \qquad\qquad (3.26)$$

for all $n = 1, 2, 3, \ldots$.

Thus we know that each successive value calculated from the recursion (3.22) should be smaller than its predecessor and, furthermore, that each value of I_n should be positive.

A simple program to successively calculate I_n for $n = 1, 2, \ldots$ and print the results is shown in Figure 3.17. We let VALUE stand for the value of the integral, which for $n = 1$ is $1/e$. The results of running on an IBM 360 are shown in Figure 3.18.

Notice that when $n = 9$ the value of the integral becomes negative, contradicting (3.24). To analyze the problem we return to the process graphs of Chapter 2. Figure 3.19 is the process graph for the recursion formula (3.22). We assume that 1 and n have no inherent error, since they are small integers and therefore have exact floating point representations in the computer. (This assumption is usually valid in modern computers.) However, I_{n-1} does have some error. We let E_{n-1} be the *absolute* error

```
DEFINITE INTEGRAL BY FORWARD RECURSION

    N        INTEGRAL

    1        0.36787897
    2        0.26424205
    3        0.20727384
    4        0.17090464
    5        0.14547682
    6        0.12713909
    7        0.11002636
    8        0.11978912
    9       -0.07810211
   10        1.78102112
   11      -18.59123230
   12      224.09478760
   13    -2912.23217773
   14    40772.25000000
   15  -611582.75000000
```

Figure 3.18. *The output of the program of Figure 3.17.*

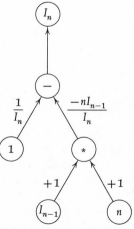

Figure 3.19. *Process graph for the recursive method used in the program of Figure 3.17.*

in I_{n-1}. Then

$$\frac{E_n}{I_n} = \left(\frac{-nI_{n-1}}{I_n}\right)\left(\frac{E_{n-1}}{I_{n-1}}\right) + \left(\frac{-nI_{n-1}}{I_n}\right)r_n + s_n$$

where r_n and s_n are the relative roundoff errors in the multiplication and subtraction, respectively. Thus

$$E_n = -nE_{n-1} - nI_{n-1}r_n + I_ns_n \tag{3.27}$$

But a similar analysis yields

$$E_{n-1} = -(n-1)E_{n-2} - (n-1)I_{n-2}r_{n-1} + I_{n-1}s_{n-1}$$

Using this in (3.27):

$$E_n = n(n-1)E_{n-2} - nI_{n-1}r_n + n(n-1)I_{n-2}r_{n-1} \\ + I_ns_n - nI_{n-1}s_{n-1}$$

We could now find E_{n-2}, E_{n-3}, and so on and substitute all of these to get finally

$$E_n = (-1)^{n+1}n!E_1 - \sum_{k=2}^{n}(-1)^{n+k}\frac{n!}{(k-1)!}I_{k-1}r_k$$

$$+ \sum_{k=2}^{n}(-1)^{n+k}\frac{n!}{k!}I_ks_k$$

Even supposing that there is no roundoff error, or, more realistically, that the roundoff errors cancel each other, then

$$E_n = (-1)^{n+1}n!E_1$$

and E_1 is the error in $1/e$. In our program we took $1/e = 0.367879$. Thus

$$E_1 = 0.441171 \cdot 10^{-6}$$

But

$$9! = 3.6288 \cdot 10^{6}$$

so

$$E_9 = 1.598$$

which is clearly larger than I_9 since $I_1 = 0.367879$.

The source of the difficulty here is the algorithm itself. Since we can never represent I_1 with complete numerical accuracy (since e is an irrational number), eventually for some n the value computed for I_n will have no significant digits at all.

This type of behavior is common to all recursion formulas in which the nth term tends toward zero. (We shall mention another example of such a recursion formula at the close of the case study.) The solution to the numerical difficulty that we have encountered is to *reverse the direction of the recursion*.

Although we have not proved it, the fact is that as n becomes large, I_n approaches zero. Suppose that we pick a large value of n, say N, and quite arbitrarily let

$$I_N = 0 \tag{3.28}$$

(Just *how* large N should be will be discussed shortly.) Now we rewrite (3.22) as

$$I_{n-1} = \frac{1}{n}(1 - I_n) \tag{3.29}$$

for $n = N - 1, \ldots, 2$. That is, we *recurse backward*.

At first glance, setting $I_N = 0$ seems to lead to meaningless results. After all, for any finite value of n we know that $I_n > 0$. The process outlined in (3.28) and (3.29) seems, therefore, to be a nonsensical one. Nevertheless, it does produce rather remarkable results, as we shall see.

For example, suppose we choose a relatively small value of N, say 10, and calculate with eight significant digits. Then the value of I_1 comes out to be 0.36787946, which is in error by only two units in the eighth place. It appears, therefore, that reversing the direction of the recursion, that is, using (3.28) and (3.29), offers a great deal of promise.

Of course, for any choice of N we can always check the accuracy of I_1 since we know what its value is. However, we started out to calculate I_n for $n = 2, 3, \ldots$. The question that we should ask ourselves is: How can we check the accuracy of $I_2, I_3, \ldots$, and so on?

To answer this question we choose another value of n different from N; let us call this other value M. Then we let

$$J_M = 0 \tag{3.30}$$

and calculate

$$J_{n-1} = \frac{1}{n}(1 - J_n) \text{ for } n = M, M - 1, M - 2, \ldots, 2$$

Since these formulas parallel (3.28) and (3.29), in principle the values calculated for J_n should coincide with those calculated for I_n. As a matter of fact, we shall compare the corresponding values of I_n and J_n. When they agree to any given number of digits, we shall accept that value as the value of I_n. A flow chart is shown in Figure 3.20.

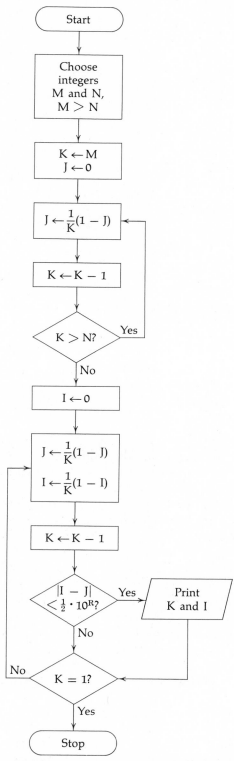

Figure 3.20. *Flow chart of a method for computing the value of the integral by backward recursion.*

```
C CASE STUDY 5
C EVALUATING A DEFINITE INTEGRAL BY RECURSION
C
C SECOND VERSION - BACKWARD RECURSION
C
      WRITE (6, 202)
  202 FORMAT (/1X, 'DEFINITE INTEGRAL BY BACKWARD RECURSION'//
     1'    K        INTEGRAL'/)
C CHOOSE VALUES OF M AND N
      M = 30
      N = 20
C START K
      K = M
C GIVE J AND K VALUES, IN REAL FORM
      XJ = 0.0
    1 XK = K
C PERFORM RECURSION ON J
      XJ = (1.0 - XJ) / XK
      K = K - 1
C HAVE WE DECREASED K TO VALUE OF N YET
      IF (K .GT. N) GO TO 1
C START I
      XI = 0.0
C COMPUTE I AND J
    2 XK = K
      XJ = (1.0 - XJ) / XK
      XI = (1.0 - XI) / XK
      K = K - 1
C ARE I AND J THE SAME TO WITHIN TOLERANCE
      IF (ABS(XI - XJ) .GE. 0.000005) GO TO 3
C CLOSE ENOUGH - PRINT
      WRITE (6, 201) K, XI
  201 FORMAT (1X, I3, F15.5)
    3 IF (K .EQ. 1) STOP
      GO TO 2
      END
```

Figure 3.21. *A program following the method of the flow chart of Figure 3.20.*

In this flow chart we first compute $J_{M-1}, J_{M-2}, \ldots, J_N$ noting that $M > N$. We then compute J_{N-1} and I_{N-1} and compare the values of these variables. If they differ by less than 5 in the $(R + 1)$st place, we print the value of I (we can just as well print J). We should use a FORMAT statement field specification of the form FX.R, since only R digits are significant. Here X is any integer that is large enough to contain the value.

We next recursively compute J_{N-2} and I_{N-2} and compare their values, and so on. Eventually we stop after having computed and compared J_1 and I_1. A Fortran program is shown in Figure 3.21. We have used M = 30, N = 20, and R = 5. Note that we use XJ and XI rather than J or I, since the values in question are Fortran real values rather than integers. Alternatively, we could have used J and I, but mentioned them in a REAL specification statement. As a final possibility, we might have left J and I in Fortran integer form, after checking that the mixed mode arithmetic that would have been involved would operate correctly. The method shown is perhaps the most straightforward. The output is shown in Figure 3.22.

The reader will find it instructive to change M, N, and R and observe the changes in the output.

This method of reversing the direction of recursion will always produce more accurate results if the nth term in the sequence tends toward zero. If it is a two-term recursion formula, that is, one containing only two different indices (n and $n - 1$ in this case), then we can choose a "large" value of the index, and set the variable equal to zero for that index value. By doing this twice and comparing the two sets of values we can determine the accuracy of the results.

Naturally, the recursion formula may contain more than two terms. For an example, a recursion formula for *Bessel functions of the first kind* is

$$J_{m+1}(x) = \frac{2m}{x} J_m(x) - J_{m-1}(x)$$

where $J_n(x)$ is the nth Bessel function of the first kind. For $m \gg (x/2)$ it turns out that $J_m(x) \cong (2m/x)^{-m}$ and as m becomes large, this approaches zero. Thus the same type of numerical problem arises. In fact the *absolute error*, E_{m+1}, in J_{m+1} exclusive of roundoff error is

$$E_{m+1} = m! \left(\frac{2}{x}\right)^m \left[E_1 + \sum_{k=1}^{m} \left(\frac{x}{2}\right)^{k-1} \left\{ \left(\frac{E_x}{x}\right) \frac{J_k(x)}{(k-1)!} - \left(\frac{x}{2}\right) \frac{E_k}{k!} \right\} \right]$$

where E_x is the absolute error in x.

The solution to this problem is, once again, to reverse the direction of the recursion, as follows:

$$J_{m-1}(x) = \frac{2m}{x} J_m(x) - J_{m+1}(x) \tag{3.32}$$

Now, however, we have a problem: There are *two different* functions, $J_m(x)$ and $J_{m+1}(x)$, on the right. If we set both of them equal to zero, then all succeeding value of $J_m(x)$ will also be zero.

To avoid this problem, we let

$$J_{M+1}^*(x) = 0 \tag{3.33}$$
$$J_M^*(x) = A \tag{3.34}$$

where A is any positive number. For our later convenience we assume that M is even. We then use (3.32) in the form

$$J_{m-1}^*(x) = \frac{2m}{x} J_m^*(x) - J_{m+1}^*(x) \tag{3.35}$$

DEFINITE INTEGRAL BY BACKWARD RECURSION

K	INTEGRAL
16	0.05572
15	0.05902
14	0.06273
13	0.06695
12	0.07177
11	0.07735
10	0.08388
9	0.09161
8	0.10093
7	0.11238
6	0.12680
5	0.14553
4	0.17089
3	0.20728
2	0.26424
1	0.36788

Figure 3.22. *The output of the program of Figure 3.21.*

Case Study 5: Errors in the Recursive Evaluation of a Definite Integral   127

to compute $J_{M-1}^*(x)$, $J_{M-2}^*(x)$, and so on until we have computed $J_0^*(x)$. Of course, since A was arbitrary, there is no reason to believe that we have actually computed the values of the Bessel functions. It is for that reason that we used $J_m^*(x)$ rather than $J_m(x)$.

However, there is an identity involving the sum of the Bessel functions that we may use:

$$J_0(x) + 2 \sum_{m=1}^{\infty} J_{2m}(x) = 1 \qquad (3.36)$$

We assume for computation purposes that $J_m(x) = 0$ for all $m > M$. Thus the sum in (3.36) need only extend to $M/2$, not ∞. (Here is where the assumption that M is even is convenient. If M were odd, we could still adjust the sum, but we have lost no generality by making the more convenient assumption.)

Suppose we compute the sum

$$J_0^*(x) + 2 \sum_{m=1}^{M/2} J_{2m}^*(x) = Q \qquad (3.37)$$

In general, $Q \neq 1$. But if we let

$$J_m(x) = \frac{J_m^*(x)}{Q} \qquad (3.37a)$$

for $m = 0, 1, \ldots, M$, then

$$J_0(x) + 2 \sum_{m=1}^{M/2} J_{2m}(x) = 1$$

and this is the identity (3.36) under the assumption that $J_m(x) = 0$ for $m > M$.

The procedure then is:

1. Choose an even integer M and a positive number A.
2. Use (3.33), (3.34), and (3.35) to compute successively $J_M^*(x)$, $J_{M-1}^*(x), \ldots, J_0^*(x)$.
3. Compute Q summing these results using (3.37).
4. Use (3.37a) to compute the actual values of the Bessel functions $J_0(x), \ldots, J_M(x)$.

Of course, the question of the accuracy of the results still remains. We solve this problem as we did before, that is, we repeat the entire four-step process described above with a different value of M. We then compare the results with the results obtained the first time the process was used.

In summary: If we have a three-term recursion formula for which the nth term approaches zero, we choose a "large" value of the index. We set the variable equal to zero for that index value and set the variable equal to an arbitrary value for an index value one less. We recurse backward and use one identity to normalize the results. To determine the accuracy we repeat the process with a different "large" value of the index and compare the results.

Recall that for a two-term recursion, we did not need any identity. For a three-term recursion, we needed one identity. In general, for an n-term recursion we shall need $n - 2$ identities.

3.5 Case Study 6: The Effect of Limited Precision in Calculating Means and Standard Deviations

In descriptive statistics two of the most commonly used measures of central tendency and dispersion are, respectively, the mean and the standard deviation. For a set of numbers $x_1, x_2, \ldots, x_n$ the arithmetic mean is defined to be

$$\mu = \frac{x_1 + x_2 + \cdots + x_n}{n} \tag{3.38}$$

The variance is then defined to be

$$v = \frac{(x_1 - \mu)^2 + (x_2 - \mu)^2 + \cdots + (x_n - \mu)^2}{n} \tag{3.39}$$

and the standard deviation is

$$\sigma = \sqrt{v} \tag{3.40}$$

Making use of (3.38) we can rewrite (3.39) as

$$v = \frac{x_1^2 + x_2^2 + \cdots + x_n^2}{n} - \mu^2 \tag{3.41}$$

A flow chart for a procedure that reads the values of $x_1, x_2, \ldots, x_n$ and computes μ, v, and σ from (3.38), (3.40), and (3.41) is shown in Figure 3.23. In that flow chart SUM is the sum of the numbers read at any given point and SUMSQ is the sum of the squares of the numbers read up to any point. The value of COUNT will be the number of cards (that is, values of x_i) read up to a given time. TEST is a special number called a "sentinel." It should be chosen so that no legitimate x_i will ever be equal to TEST. For example, if we are computing the mean and standard deviation of a set of positive numbers, we may choose TEST to be -1 or any other negative number. If the numbers whose mean and standard deviation we seek are between -100 and $+100$ then we can choose TEST $= 1000$ or TEST $= -10000$ and so on.

Box 4 in Figure 3.23 will discontinue the addition of terms to SUM, SUMSQ, and COUNT if X = TEST. Thus, if we place the data one number to a card, then we should follow this deck of cards with a card containing the number chosen for TEST. When this last card with a value of TEST is read, the values of SUM and SUMSQ are

$$\text{SUM} = x_1 + x_2 + \cdots + x_n \tag{3.42}$$
$$\text{SUMSQ} = x_1^2 + x_2^2 + \cdots + x_n^2 \tag{3.43}$$

and COUNT has the value of n. This technique of using a sentinel card to indicate the end of the data saves us the task of counting the cards before running the program. In effect the program counts the cards for us. Moreover, the program is useable for any number of items of data.

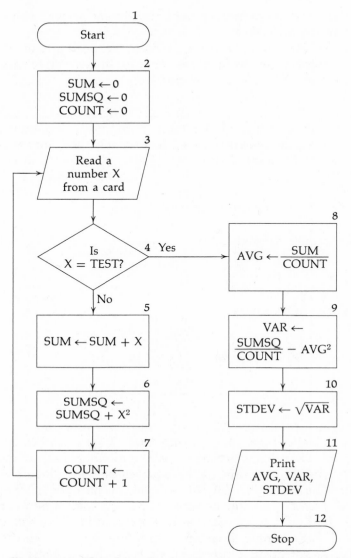

Figure 3.23. *Flow chart of a procedure for finding the mean and variance of a set of data points contained on cards.*

Boxes 8, 9, and 10 compute the mean from (3.38), the variance from (3.41), and the standard deviation from (3.40) in a straightforward way.

A computer program following the flow chart in Figure 3.23 is shown in Figure 3.24. Notice that no subscripted variables are used. Having initially zeroed SUM and SUMSQ, we read the value of x_1 and add it to SUM and add the value of x_1^2 to SUMSQ. Once we have done so we have no more need for the value of x_1. We call x_1 simply X. We then read the value of x_2 and call it X as well. We add X, which is now the same as x_2, to SUM and add x^2 to SUMSQ. Having done so we no longer have need for value of x_2. From SUM and SUMSQ as shown in (3.42) and (3.43) we can compute the mean, variance, and standard deviation without using the individual data.

If we choose to use (3.39) for the computation of the variance, things are not quite as simple. We must know the value of the mean, μ, before we can even start the computation of v. A flow chart doing this is shown in Figure 3.25. A program which follows this flow chart is shown in Figure 3.26. This program still counts the number of cards, but the number of cards cannot exceed 200. We could, of course, increase the maximum number of cards (items of data) by changing the DIMENSION statement. (Notice that the maximum value of the subscript for the one-dimensional array X must be one greater than the maximum number of items of data. This is to accommodate the sentinel card.)

Now clearly this second program requires more storage space (computer memory) than the first program since a memory location is required for each item of data. The second program also requires more arithmetic than the first program.

In the first program there are n multiplications (computations of x^2) and $2n$ additions (SUM and SUMSQ) in the loop. In boxes 8 and 9 of Figure 3.23 there are one more multiplication, one more addition, and two divisions. Thus the first method, using (3.41), requires

$$2n + 1 \text{ additions}$$
$$n + 1 \text{ multiplications}$$
$$2 \text{ divisions}$$

We have not included the additions necessary to count the number of cards.

The second program uses n additions in the first loop (boxes 4 through 8 of Figure 3.25). There are n multiplications [computation of

```
C CASE STUDY 6
C MEAN AND VARIANCE OF DATA ITEMS ON CARDS
C VERSION 1 - SUM ITEMS BEFORE SUBTRACTING MEAN
C
C 'TEST' IS THE VALUE FOR THE END-OF-DECK SENTINEL
C
      READ (5, 100) TEST
  100 FORMAT (F10.0)
C INITIALIZE
      SUM = 0.0
      SUMSQ = 0.0
      COUNT = 0.0
C READ A DATA CARD
    5 READ (5, 100) X
      IF (X .EQ. TEST) GO TO 10
C PROCESS THE DATA ITEM
      SUM = SUM + X
      SUMSQ = SUMSQ + X*X
      COUNT = COUNT + 1.0
      GO TO 5
C COMPUTE MEAN, VARIANCE, AND STANDARD DEVIATION
   10 AVG = SUM / COUNT
      VAR = SUMSQ/COUNT - AVG*AVG
      STDEV = SQRT(VAR)
      WRITE (6, 200) AVG, VAR, STDEV
  200 FORMAT (1X, 'MEAN = ', E14.6, ' VARIANCE = ', E14.6,
     1'  STANDARD DEVIATION = ', E14.6)
      STOP
      END
```

Figure 3.24. *A program corresponding to the flow chart of Figure 3.23 for finding the mean and variance of a set of numbers.*

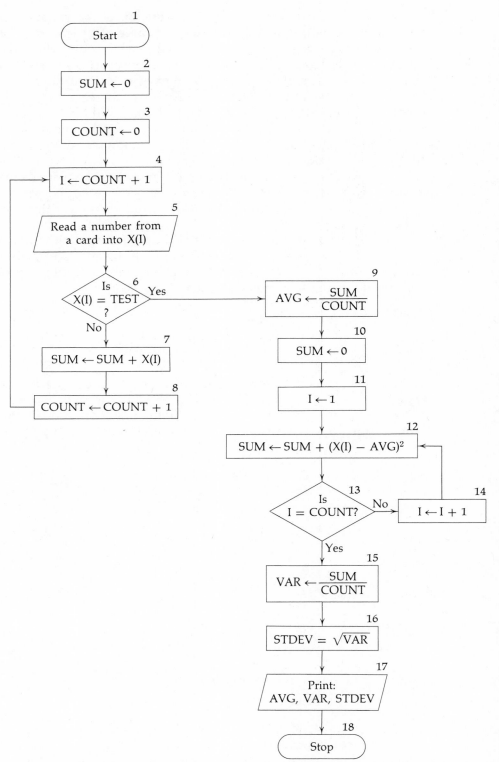

Figure 3.25. *Flow chart of a different procedure for finding the mean and variance of a set of numbers, which requires that the mean be available before computing the variance and therefore requires storage of the individual items.*

```
C CASE STUDY 6
C MEAN AND VARIANCE OF DATA ITEMS ON CARDS
C VERSION 2 -   SUBTRACT MEAN BEFORE FORMING SUM OF SQUARES
C
        DIMENSION X(201)
        READ (5, 100) TEST
100 FORMAT (F10.0)
C INITIALIZE
        SUM = 0.0
        COUNT = 0.0
C ADVANCE COUNTER ON EACH RETURN TO THIS POINT
      4 COUNT = COUNT + 1.0
        I = COUNT
C READ A DATA ITEM
        READ (5, 100) X(I)
C CHECK FOR END-OF-DECK SENTINEL
        IF (X(I) .EQ. TEST) GO TO 9
C PROCESS THE ITEM
        SUM = SUM + X(I)
        GO TO 4
C COMPUTE THE MEAN
      9 AVG = SUM / COUNT
C PREPARE TO COMPUTE SUM OF SQUARES
        SUM = 0.0
        LAST = COUNT
        DO 12 I = 1, LAST
     12 SUM = SUM + (X(I) - AVG)**2
C COMPUTE VARIANCE
        VAR = SUM / COUNT
C COMPUTE STANDARD DEVIATION
        STDEV = SQRT (VAR)
        WRITE (6, 200) AVG, VAR, STDEV
    200 FORMAT (1X, 'MEAN = ', E14.6, '  VARIANCE = ', E14.6,
       1'  STANDARD DEVIATION = ', E14.6)
        STOP
        END
```

Figure 3.26. *A program corresponding to the flow chart of Figure 3.25.*

$(X(I) - AVG)^2$] and $2n$ additions [computation of $X(I) - AVG$ and $SUM +$ squared term] in the second loop shown in boxes 12, 13, and 14. There are two divisions, one in box 9 and one in box 15. Thus the second method, using (3.39), requires

$3n$ additions

n multiplications

2 divisions

For large values of n, the second method requires 50% more additions and roughly the same number of multiplications and divisions. Had we counted the additions necessary to count as we go through the loops, the second method would be even more inefficient.

Why then does anyone ever use the second method? The answer lies in the relative accuracy of the two methods: The second method is more accurate, as we shall see.

To exhibit the numerical difficulties that can arise with the first method consider the following problem. There are 33 items of data equally spaced and at distance $\Delta x = (\frac{1}{16})^4$ from each other. The smallest is $1 - (\frac{1}{16})^3 = 0.999755859375$ and the largest is $1 + (\frac{1}{16})^3 = 1.000244140625$. The mean should be 1 since for each number smaller than 1 there is a corresponding number greater than 1, and the average of these two numbers is 1. The

```
C CASE STUDY 6
C MEAN AND VARIANCE
C
C A VERSION USING DATA GENERATED BY THE PROGRAM,
C   FOR WHICH EXACT THEORETICAL VALUES ARE COMPUTABLE
C
C INITIALIZE
      SUM = 0.0
      SUMSQ = 0.0
      COUNT = 1.0
      X = 1 - 1.0/16.0**3
      DEL = 1.0 / 16.0**4
C GENERATE THE DATA ITEMS, THEIR SUM, AND SUM OF SQUARES
    8 SUM = SUM + X
      SUMSQ = SUMSQ + X**2
      IF (COUNT .GE. 33.0) GO TO 5
      COUNT = COUNT + 1.0
      X = X + DEL
      GO TO 8
C COMPUTE MEAN, VARIANCE, AND STANDARD DEVIATION
    5 AVG = SUM / COUNT
      VAR = (SUMSQ - AVG * SUM) / COUNT
      STD = SQRT(VAR)
      WRITE (6, 200) AVG, VAR, STD
  200 FORMAT (1X, 'MEAN = ', E14.6, '  VARIANCE = ', E14.6,
     1'  STANDARD DEVIATION = ', E14.6)
      STOP
      END
```

Figure 3.27. *A program corresponding to the flow chart of Figure 3.25, except that the data points are generated by the program itself.*

variance is small. Indeed we can calculate the variance from (3.39) to be

$$v = \frac{2}{33}\left[\left(\frac{1}{16^4}\right)^2 + \left(\frac{2}{16^4}\right)^2 + \cdots + \left(\frac{15}{16^4}\right)^2 + \left(\frac{16}{16^4}\right)^2\right]$$

$$= \frac{17}{3 \cdot 16^7} = 2.110998 \cdot 10^{-8}$$

A program that essentially[2] follows the flow chart in Figure 3.25 and computes the mean, variance, and standard deviation for this set of 33 pieces of data is shown in Figure 3.27.

The results of running this program on an IBM System/360 are: MEAN = 0.1000000 E 01   VARIANCE = 0.0   STANDARD DEVIATION = 0.0. The mean is correct but the variance and standard deviation obviously are not.

If we rerun the program on an IBM System/360 in double precision with format specifications of D20.15 for the three results the program produces:

MEAN = .100000000000000D 01
VARIANCE = .211099783579508D-07
STANDARD DEVIATION = .145292724482715D-03

These results are extremely accurate.

[2]Data values are not read from cards but are generated by the program. (3.38), (3.40), and (3.41) are used in the computations.

Now we chose powers of $\frac{1}{16}$ in these calculations because such numbers can be represented as terminating fractions in a hexadecimal computer such as an IBM System/360. Thus there are no inherent errors in the data. The errors in the single precision result must come, therefore, from the calculations themselves.

To analyse this difficulty we return to our hypothetical decimal computer where we use powers of $\frac{1}{10}$ to avoid inherent errors in the data. We assume we have four decimal digits in the mantissa, and we use as data the following 21 numbers: .990, .001, ..., .999, 1., 1.001, 1.002, ..., 1.009, 1.010. Thus $\Delta x = (\frac{1}{10})^3$. The smallest number is $1 - (\frac{1}{10})^2$ and the largest is $1 + (\frac{1}{10})^2$. The mean is 1 and the variance is $0.36666 \ldots \cdot 10^{-5}$. The numbers with their partial sums are, in floating point:

x	Partial Sums
.990	$.9900 \cdot 10^0$
.991	$.1981 \cdot 10^1$
.992	$.2973 \cdot 10^1$
.993	$.3966 \cdot 10^1$
.994	$.4960 \cdot 10^1$
.995	$.5955 \cdot 10^1$
.996	$.6951 \cdot 10^1$
.997	$.7948 \cdot 10^1$
.998	$.8946 \cdot 10^1$
.999	$.9945 \cdot 10^1$
1.000	$.1095 \cdot 10^2$
1.001	$.1195 \cdot 10^2$
1.002	$.1295 \cdot 10^2$
1.003	$.1395 \cdot 10^2$
1.004	$.1495 \cdot 10^2$
1.005	$.1596 \cdot 10^2$
1.006	$.1697 \cdot 10^2$
1.007	$.1798 \cdot 10^2$
1.008	$.1899 \cdot 10^2$
1.009	$.2000 \cdot 10^2$
1.010	$.2101 \cdot 10^2$

We have rounded symmetrically. The sum of the 21 items of data is shown as 21.01 whereas the correct result is 21.00. This inaccuracy in the sum does not affect the mean, however, since

$$\mu = \frac{.2101 \cdot 10^2}{.2100 \cdot 10^2} = .1000 \cdot 10^1$$

rounded symmetrically.

We now sum squares of x_i. The results are:

x	x^2	Partial Sums
$.9900 \cdot 10^0$	$.9801 \cdot 10^0$	$.9801 \cdot 10^0$
$.9910 \cdot 10^0$	$.9821 \cdot 10^0$	$.1962 \cdot 10^1$
$.9920 \cdot 10^0$	$.9841 \cdot 10^0$	$.2946 \cdot 10^1$
$.9930 \cdot 10^0$	$.9860 \cdot 10^0$	$.3932 \cdot 10^1$
$.9940 \cdot 10^0$	$.9880 \cdot 10^0$	$.4920 \cdot 10^1$
$.9950 \cdot 10^0$	$.9900 \cdot 10^0$	$.5910 \cdot 10^1$
$.9960 \cdot 10^0$	$.9920 \cdot 10^0$	$.6902 \cdot 10^1$
$.9970 \cdot 10^0$	$.9940 \cdot 10^0$	$.7896 \cdot 10^1$
$.9980 \cdot 10^0$	$.9960 \cdot 10^0$	$.8892 \cdot 10^1$
$.9990 \cdot 10^0$	$.9980 \cdot 10^0$	$.9890 \cdot 10^1$
$.1000 \cdot 10^1$	$.1000 \cdot 10^1$	$.1089 \cdot 10^2$
$.1001 \cdot 10^1$	$.1002 \cdot 10^1$	$.1189 \cdot 10^2$
$.1002 \cdot 10^1$	$.1004 \cdot 10^1$	$.1289 \cdot 10^2$
$.1003 \cdot 10^1$	$.1006 \cdot 10^1$	$.1390 \cdot 10^2$
$.1004 \cdot 10^1$	$.1008 \cdot 10^1$	$.1491 \cdot 10^2$
$.1005 \cdot 10^1$	$.1010 \cdot 10^1$	$.1592 \cdot 10^2$
$.1006 \cdot 10^1$	$.1012 \cdot 10^1$	$.1693 \cdot 10^2$
$.1007 \cdot 10^1$	$.1014 \cdot 10^1$	$.1794 \cdot 10^2$
$.1008 \cdot 10^1$	$.1016 \cdot 10^1$	$.1896 \cdot 10^2$
$.1009 \cdot 10^1$	$.1018 \cdot 10^1$	$.1998 \cdot 10^2$
$.1010 \cdot 10^1$	$.1020 \cdot 10^1$	$.2100 \cdot 10^2$

The last number in the last column is the indicated sum of the squares of the data values. Using (3.41), then

$$v = \frac{.2100 \cdot 10^2}{.2100 \cdot 10^2} - (.1000 \cdot 10^1)^2$$

$$= 0$$

Thus we get a variance of zero just as our computer program did. This leads us to believe that if we can analyse the difficulty in our hypothetical computer we shall have an insight into the difficulty in the real computer.

Let us look at one particular item of data: $.997 = .9970 \cdot 10^0$. When we square this we get $.994009 \cdot 10^0$. However, in our four-digit mantissa this is represented as $.9940 \cdot 10^0$. The absolute roundoff error is $.9000 \cdot 10^{-5}$.

Suppose we were to use (3.39) to compute the variance instead of (3.41). Then, before we square the number $.9970 \cdot 10^0$, we subtract the mean. Thus we compute $(.9970 \cdot 10^0 - .1000 \cdot 10^1)^2 = (-.3000 \cdot 10^{-2})^2 = .9000 \cdot 10^{-5}$. It is this latter number that is added into the sum in (3.39). Notice that it is exactly equal to the roundoff error in the calculation of the square of $.9970 \cdot 10^0$.

Let us try another item of data. Consider $.1006 \cdot 10^1$. When we square this we get $.1012036 \cdot 10^1$. In our four-digit computer this is represented as $.1012 \cdot 10^1$ so the roundoff error is $.3600 \cdot 10^{-4}$. If we subtract the mean before squaring we get $(.1006 \cdot 10^1 - .1000 \cdot 10^1)^2 = (.6000 \cdot 10^{-2})^2 = .3600 \cdot 10^{-4}$, which again is precisely the roundoff error in squaring $.1006 \cdot 10^1$.

These examples lead us to believe that if we use (3.39) we should achieve more accurate results. The computation of the variance using (3.39) in a four-digit computer is as follows:

x	$x - \mu$	$(x - \mu)^2$	Partial Sums
$.9900 \cdot 10^0$	$-.1000 \cdot 10^{-1}$	$.1000 \cdot 10^{-3}$	$.1000 \cdot 10^{-3}$
$.9910 \cdot 10^0$	$-.9000 \cdot 10^{-2}$	$.8100 \cdot 10^{-4}$	$.1810 \cdot 10^{-3}$
$.9920 \cdot 10^0$	$-.8000 \cdot 10^{-2}$	$.6400 \cdot 10^{-4}$	$.2450 \cdot 10^{-3}$
$.9930 \cdot 10^0$	$-.7000 \cdot 10^{-2}$	$.4900 \cdot 10^{-4}$	$.2940 \cdot 10^{-3}$
$.9940 \cdot 10^0$	$-.6000 \cdot 10^{-2}$	$.3600 \cdot 10^{-4}$	$.3300 \cdot 10^{-3}$
$.9950 \cdot 10^0$	$-.5000 \cdot 10^{-2}$	$.2500 \cdot 10^{-4}$	$.3550 \cdot 10^{-3}$
$.9960 \cdot 10^0$	$-.4000 \cdot 10^{-2}$	$.1600 \cdot 10^{-4}$	$.3710 \cdot 10^{-3}$
$.9970 \cdot 10^0$	$-.3000 \cdot 10^{-2}$	$.9000 \cdot 10^{-5}$	$.3800 \cdot 10^{-3}$
$.9980 \cdot 10^0$	$-.2000 \cdot 10^{-2}$	$.4000 \cdot 10^{-5}$	$.3840 \cdot 10^{-3}$
$.9990 \cdot 10^0$	$-.1000 \cdot 10^{-2}$	$.1000 \cdot 10^{-5}$	$.3850 \cdot 10^{-3}$
$.1000 \cdot 10^1$	$.0000 \cdot 10^0$	$.0000 \cdot 10^0$	$.3850 \cdot 10^{-3}$
$.1001 \cdot 10^1$	$.1000 \cdot 10^{-2}$	$.1000 \cdot 10^{-5}$	$.3860 \cdot 10^{-3}$
$.1002 \cdot 10^1$	$.2000 \cdot 10^{-2}$	$.4000 \cdot 10^{-5}$	$.3900 \cdot 10^{-3}$
$.1003 \cdot 10^1$	$.3000 \cdot 10^{-2}$	$.9000 \cdot 10^{-5}$	$.3990 \cdot 10^{-3}$
$.1004 \cdot 10^1$	$.4000 \cdot 10^{-2}$	$.1600 \cdot 10^{-4}$	$.4150 \cdot 10^{-3}$
$.1005 \cdot 10^1$	$.5000 \cdot 10^{-2}$	$.2500 \cdot 10^{-4}$	$.4400 \cdot 10^{-3}$
$.1006 \cdot 10^1$	$.6000 \cdot 10^{-2}$	$.3600 \cdot 10^{-4}$	$.4760 \cdot 10^{-3}$
$.1007 \cdot 10^1$	$.7000 \cdot 10^{-2}$	$.4900 \cdot 10^{-4}$	$.5250 \cdot 10^{-3}$
$.1008 \cdot 10^1$	$.8000 \cdot 10^{-2}$	$.6400 \cdot 10^{-4}$	$.5890 \cdot 10^{-3}$
$.1009 \cdot 10^1$	$.9000 \cdot 10^{-2}$	$.8100 \cdot 10^{-4}$	$.6700 \cdot 10^{-3}$
$.1010 \cdot 10^1$	$.1000 \cdot 10^{-1}$	$.1000 \cdot 10^{-3}$	$.7700 \cdot 10^{-3}$

To compute the variance we use (3.39) and obtain

$$v = \frac{.7700 \cdot 10^{-3}}{.2100 \cdot 10^1} = .3667 \cdot 10^{-5}$$

This is the correct result, rounded symmetrically, to four significant digits.

In this case (3.39) produced much more accurate results than did (3.41). Will this always be the case? To answer this question we return to our process graphs and use them to analyse and compare the roundoff errors in the two methods.

Let us first consider (3.39). We shall look at the case $n = 4$ and then generalize the results for any value of n. We first compute $(x_1 - \mu)^2$ as indicated in Figure 3.28. The symbol adjacent to each operation node in that figure represents the relative roundoff error that occurs in that operation. For example r_{s_1} is the roundoff error in computing $x_1 - \mu$.

We assume there is *no error in* x_1 *or any of the* x_i. However, there will in general nevertheless be some error in μ. We let E_μ be the absolute error in μ. Then, if $E_{(x_1-\mu)^2}$ is the absolute error in $(x_1 - \mu)^2$,

$$\frac{E_{(x_1-\mu)^2}}{(x_1 - \mu)^2} = 2r_{s_1} + r_{m_1} + 2\left(\frac{E_\mu}{\mu}\right)\left(\frac{-\mu}{x_1 - \mu}\right)$$

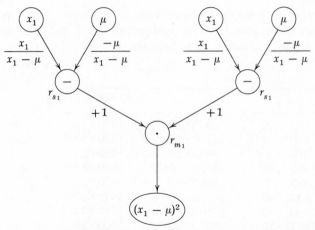

Figure 3.28. *Process graph for the operation of forming the squares in (3.39).*

We can obtain similar results for the errors in $(x_2 - \mu)^2$, $(x_3 - \mu)^2$, and $(x_4 - \mu)^2$ simply by replacing x_1 by x_2, x_3, or x_4. However, the roundoff errors r_{s_i} and r_{m_i} will be different in each of these. Thus

$$\frac{E_{(x_i - \mu)^2}}{(x_i - \mu)^2} = 2r_{s_i} + r_{m_i} + 2\left(\frac{E_\mu}{\mu}\right)\left(\frac{-\mu}{x_i - \mu}\right) \tag{3.44}$$

for $i = 1, 2, 3, 4$.

The process graph for summing these squares is shown in Figure 3.29. The result, called v_1, is the variance. The subscript "1" is used to indicate that this is the result of the "first" method for computing the variance. Using this process graph,

$$\frac{E_{v1}}{v_1} = \frac{(x_1 - \mu)^2}{(x_1 - \mu)^2 + (x_2 - \mu)^2 + (x_3 - \mu)^2 + (x_4 - \mu)^2}\left[\frac{E_{(x_1-\mu)^2}}{(x_1 - \mu)^2}\right]$$

$$+ \frac{(x_2 - \mu)^2}{(x_1 - \mu)^2 + (x_2 - \mu)^2 + (x_3 - \mu)^2 + (x_4 - \mu)^2}\left[\frac{E_{(x_2-\mu)^2}}{(x_2 - \mu)^2}\right]$$

$$+ \frac{(x_3 - \mu)^2}{(x_1 - \mu)^2 + (x_2 - \mu)^2 + (x_3 - \mu)^2 + (x_4 - \mu)^2}\left[\frac{E_{(x_3-\mu)^2}}{(x_3 - \mu)^2}\right]$$

$$+ \frac{(x_4 - \mu)^2}{(x_1 - \mu)^2 + (x_2 - \mu)^2 + (x_3 - \mu)^2 + (x_4 - \mu)^2}\left[\frac{E_{(x_4-\mu)^2}}{(x_4 - \mu)^2}\right]$$

$$+ r_{a1}\frac{(x_1 - \mu)^2 + (x_2 - \mu)^2}{(x_1 - \mu)^2 + (x_2 - \mu)^2 + (x_3 - \mu)^2 + (x_4 - \mu)^2}$$

$$+ r_{a2}\frac{(x_1 - \mu)^2 + (x_2 - \mu)^2 + (x_3 - \mu)^2}{(x_1 - \mu)^2 + (x_2 - \mu)^2 + (x_3 - \mu)^2 + (x_4 - \mu)^2}$$

$$+ r_{a3} + r_d \tag{3.45}$$

Now

$$v_1 = \frac{(x_1 - \mu)^2 + (x_2 - \mu)^2 + (x_3 - \mu)^2 + (x_4 - \mu)^2}{4} \qquad (3.46)$$

Using (3.44) and (3.46) in (3.45) we can obtain

$$E_{v_1} = \frac{1}{4} \sum_{i=1}^{4} (2r_{s_i} + r_{m_i})(x_i - \mu)^2$$

$$+ \frac{1}{4} \sum_{j=1}^{3} r_{a_j} \sum_{i=1}^{j+1} (x_i - \mu)^2$$

$$+ \frac{1}{4} r_d \sum_{i=1}^{4} (x_i - \mu)^2$$

Here we have made use of the fact that

$$\mu = \frac{1}{4} \sum_{i=1}^{4} x_i$$

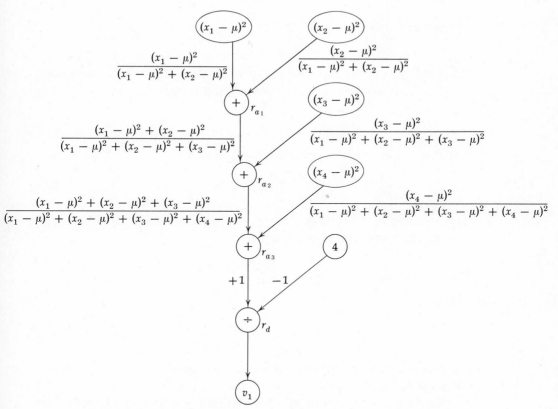

Figure 3.29. *Process graph for the operation of summing the squares in (3.39).*

In general for n items of data: $x_1, x_2, \ldots, x_n$ this becomes

$$E_{v_1} = \frac{1}{n} \sum_{i=1}^{n} (2r_{s_i} + r_{m_i})(x_i - \mu)^2$$

$$+ \frac{1}{n} \sum_{j=1}^{n-1} r_{a_j} \left(\sum_{i=1}^{j+1} (x_i - \mu)^2 \right) \qquad (3.47)$$

$$+ \frac{1}{n} r_d \sum_{i=1}^{n} (x_i - \mu)^2$$

Notice that the terms involving E_μ that appeared in (3.44) have vanished.

This leads to the following remarkable conclusion. *The error in the variance is independent of the error in the mean.* This does *not* mean that the error in the variance does not depend on the *value* of the mean. The mean itself does appear in (3.47). Moreover, if we change μ, we change the roundoff errors r_{a_j}, r_{m_i} and r_{a_j}. Nevertheless this is a significant observation that we shall return to later, and use it to our advantage.

All of the roundoff errors in (3.47) are relative errors and hence we can bound their values. In a decimal computer with t digits in its mantissa the relative roundoff errors are bounded by $\frac{1}{2} \cdot 10^{-t+1}$ for symmetric rounding and by 10^{-t+1} for chopping. In any case we denote the bound by δ.

Suppose also that

$$x_i = \mu + \Delta_i$$

and that the Δ_i are "small" compared to μ. This is certainly the case in the numerical examples we have encountered in this case study. We also let

$$\Delta = \max|\Delta_i|$$

Then using the triangle inequality (3.47) yields

$$|E_{v_1}| \leq \frac{\delta\Delta^2}{2n}(n^2 + 9n - 2) \qquad (3.48)$$

For large values of n the bound on E_{v_1} approaches $\delta\Delta^2 n^2/2n$. We say, in such cases, that the bound is *asymptotic* to

$$\frac{\delta\Delta^2 n}{2}$$

We write this as

$$|E_{v_1}| \leq \frac{\delta\Delta^2 n}{2} \qquad (3.49)$$

although strictly speaking this is not true. For large values of n, however, it is a good approximation.

We now turn to (3.41) and compute the variance using that expression. We first compute $(x_1^2 + x_2^2 + x_3^2 + x_4^2)/4$. We call this result s. The process graph is shown in Figure 3.30. We then subtract μ^2 from s and call the result v_2. This is shown in the process graph of Figure 3.31. Notice in the latter figure that we have not included the details of forming the sum $x_1 + x_2 + x_3 + x_4$. That process graph appeared earlier in Example 1 of Chapter 2 (Figure 2.3). For convenience we let

$$t = x_1 + x_2 + x_3 + x_4 \tag{3.50}$$

Notice that

$$t = 4 \cdot \mu \tag{3.51}$$

From the process graph in Figure 3.30, recalling that the x_i are assumed to have no inherent error,

$$
\begin{aligned}
\frac{E_s}{s} = {} & r_{m1} \frac{x_1^2}{x_1^2 + x_2^2 + x_3^2 + x_4^2} \\
& + r_{m2} \frac{x_2^2}{x_1^2 + x_2^2 + x_3^2 + x_4^2} \\
& + r_{m3} \frac{x_3^2}{x_1^2 + x_2^2 + x_3^2 + x_4^2} \\
& + r_{m4} \frac{x_4^2}{x_1^2 + x_2^2 + x_3^2 + x_4^2} \\
& + r_{a1} \frac{x_1^2 + x_2^2}{x_1^2 + x_2^2 + x_3^2 + x_4^2} \\
& + r_{a2} \frac{x_1^2 + x_2^2 + x_3^2}{x_1^2 + x_2^2 + x_3^2 + x_4^2} \\
& + r_{a3} + r_{d1}
\end{aligned}
\tag{3.52}
$$

Turning to the process graph in Figure 3.31 and using (3.50), we may write

$$
\begin{aligned}
\frac{E_{v2}}{v_2} = {} & 2\left(\frac{E_t}{t}\right)\left(\frac{-\mu^2}{v_2}\right) + 2 r_{d2}\left(\frac{-\mu^2}{v_2}\right) \\
& + r_{m5}\left(\frac{-\mu^2}{v_2}\right) + r_s + \left(\frac{E_s}{s}\right) \cdot \frac{s}{v_2}
\end{aligned}
\tag{3.53}
$$

In Chapter 2, Example 1, we found that

$$E_t = r_1(x_1 + x_2) + r_2(x_1 + x_2 + x_3) + r_3(x_1 + x_2 + x_3 + x_4) \tag{3.54}$$

Using (3.50), (3.51), (3.52), and (3.54) in (3.53) we can obtain

$$
\begin{aligned}
E_{v2} = {} & \frac{1}{4}\sum_{i=1}^{4} r_{mi} x_i^2 + \frac{1}{4}(r_{d1} + r_s)\sum_{i=1}^{4} x_i^2 \\
& + \frac{1}{4}\sum_{j=1}^{3} r_{aj}\left(\sum_{i=1}^{j+1} x_i^2\right) - \frac{2\mu}{4}\sum_{j=1}^{3} r_j\left(\sum_{i=1}^{j+1} x_i\right) \\
& - \mu^2(2 r_{d2} + r_{m5} + r_s)
\end{aligned}
$$

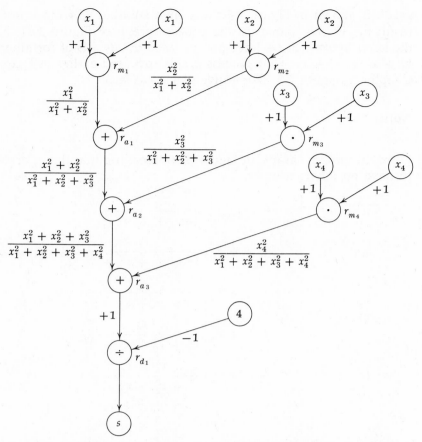

Figure 3.30. *Process graph for the operation of forming the sum of the squares and the division by* n, *in (3.41), for the special case of four data elements.*

where we have replaced v_2 by

$$v_2 = \frac{x_1^2 + x_2^2 + x_3^2 + x_4^2}{4} - \mu^2$$

For the more general case of n items of data: $x_1, x_2, \ldots, x_n$ the expression for the absolute error in v_2 becomes

$$E_{v_2} = \frac{1}{n} \sum_{i=1}^{n} r_{m_i} x_i^2 + \frac{1}{n}(r_{d_1} + r_s) \sum_{i=1}^{n} x_i^2$$
$$+ \frac{1}{n} \sum_{j=1}^{n-1} r_{a_j} \left(\sum_{i=1}^{j+1} x_i^2 \right) - \frac{2\mu}{n} \sum_{j=1}^{n-1} r_j \left(\sum_{i=1}^{j+1} x_i \right) \qquad (3.55)$$
$$- \mu^2 (2 r_{d_2} + r_{m_5} + r_s)$$

Compare this with (3.47) for E_{v_1}. The first two terms of the last equation above should be compared with the first term in (3.47). There are three relative roundoff errors in each case. However, the terms in (3.47) contain $(x_i - \mu)^2$ whereas the terms in (3.55) contain x_i^2. When we sum $(x_i - \mu)^2$ the result cannot exceed the sum of the x_i^2. Similarly the second term

142   Numerical Instabilities and Their Cure

in (3.47) appears to always be less than the third term in (3.55). There remains yet a third term in (3.47) and two more terms in (3.55). The comparison of these terms is not so clear-cut. However, intuitively it appears that (3.47) produces a smaller error than (3.55). We examine a special case and show that in this case this is indeed so.

We return to the case where

$$x_i = \mu + \Delta_i$$

and the

$$|\Delta_i| \ll |\mu|$$

That is to say, the Δ_i are small compared to μ. Again we let

$$\max |\Delta_i| = \Delta$$

and we let the bound on the relative roundoff errors be δ. Then from (3.55) we obtain

$$E_{v2} \leq \frac{\delta\mu^2}{2n}(3n^2 + 17n - 6) \tag{3.56}$$

For large values of n the term in n^2 dominates the other terms in parentheses. Therefore we write

$$|E_{v2}| \leq \frac{3\delta\mu^2 n}{2} \tag{3.57}$$

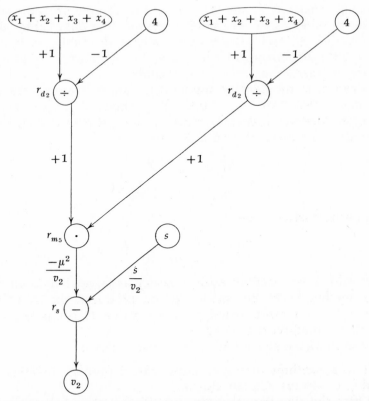

Figure 3.31. *Process graph for the subtraction of the square of the mean in (3.41), for the four-element case.*

Again we note that this is not a true bound but is approximately true for large values of n.

Let us now compare the bounds in (3.49) and (3.57). If we let B_1 be the bound on E_{v_1} and B_2 be the bound on E_{v_2}, then

$$\frac{B_1}{B_2} = \left(\frac{\Delta}{3\mu}\right)^2$$

But Δ is much smaller than μ, so B_1 is much smaller than B_2; that is, the first method, with its formula

$$v = \frac{\sum\limits_{i=1}^{n} (x_i - \mu)^2}{n}$$

has a much smaller error bound than does the second method, which was

$$v = \frac{\sum\limits_{i=1}^{n} x_1^2}{n} - \mu^2$$

Indeed we now have a measure of how much better the first method is compared to the second method. However, our result depends upon the data's being clustered about the mean. We cannot use our results to generalize to other cases. We note, however, that data values do often cluster together. In fact, clustering usually is desirable, as it indicates relatively little dispersion. In such cases the variance is small and our results are at least approximately applicable.

Let us return to the decimal numerical example where there were 21 items of data: $0.990, 0.991, \ldots, 1.009, 1.010$. Then $n = 21$, $\mu = 1$, $\Delta = .01$. Since we rounded symmetrically with a four-digit mantissa, $\delta = \frac{1}{2} \cdot 10^{-3}$. The bounds given in (3.49) and (3.57) are

$$|E_{v_1}| \le 5 \cdot 10^{-7}$$

and

$$|E_{v_2}| \le 15 \cdot 10^{-3}$$

The errors themselves were

$$E_{v_1} = 0$$
$$E_{v_2} = .3667 \cdot 10^{-5}$$

As we should expect, neither error is nearly as large as its bound. However, the method with the smaller bound produced the smaller error. Notice also that the error bound for method one, (3.39), is less than the error itself for method two, (3.41).

We close this case study with a few observations:

1. Two algorithms that apparently should produce identical results do not always actually do so.
2. Often the algorithm that requires the fewest arithmetic operations and least computer memory space is the least accurate. Thus there

144   Numerical Instabilities and Their Cure

is a tradeoff between "cost" of computing and the accuracy of the computation.

3. We do not need to know the exact value of the mean to use (3.39), the more accurate method, to compute the variance. If we have a "rough" value, say m, for μ, then we can let

$$y_i = x_i - m$$

and compute the variance of the y_i using (3.41). The variance of the y_i will be the same as the variance of the x_i; see Exercise 16. Recall that in using (3.39) the error in the mean μ did not appear explicitly in the error E_{v_1}; see (3.47). Hence an error in estimating μ by m rather than using the precise value of μ has little effect on E_{v_1}.

Bibliographic Notes

Problems of the type discussed in the case studies of this Chapter can be found in "Pitfalls of Computation" by Irene E. Stegun and Milton Abramowitz, *SIAM Journal* (December 1956). Hamming [6] also discusses problems of this nature in Sections 1.9 to 1.14. A brief discussion of subtractive cancellation may be found in Section 6.7 of Pennington [10]. Otherwise there are very few references in the published literature, although knowledge of these types of problems seems to be widespread and well-known to practicing numerical analysts.

Exercises

1a Develop an algorithm along the lines described in Case Study 4 for evaluating

$$f(x) = \cos x - \sin x$$

for x close to $45°$.

b Use trigonometric identities to find another way of evaluating $\cos x - \sin x$ for x near $45°$.

*2 Recall from the discussion in Case Study 4 (see Figure 3.2) that

$$\overline{OC} = \sqrt{1 - \left(\frac{s_n}{2}\right)^2}$$

$$\overline{AC} = 1 - \overline{OC}$$

$$s_{2n} = \sqrt{(\overline{AC})^2 + \left(\frac{s_n}{2}\right)^2}$$

Write a program that starts with $n = 4$ and $s_n = \sqrt{2}$ and computes $\overline{OC}$, $\overline{AC}$, and s_{2n} *in that order*. Repeat the process increasing n by 1 at each repetition.

Why is this more accurate than (3.6), which is merely the three equations above combined into one?

3a Derive an algorithm along the lines of Case Study 4 for evaluating

$$F(x) = \sqrt{1 + x} - \sqrt{1 - x}$$

for x near zero.

b Write a program to evaluate $F(x)$ for small values of x.

*4 Richard Andree has suggested (*Mathematics Teacher*, November 1968) that to evaluate

$$F(x) = \sqrt{1 + x} - \sqrt{1 - x}$$

for small x one should multiply and divide by $\sqrt{1 + x} + \sqrt{1 - x}$. This produces

$$F(x) = \frac{2x}{\sqrt{1 + x} + \sqrt{1 - x}}$$

Why does this increase accuracy?

Compare Andree's method, for both accuracy and ease of computing, with the method described in Case Study 4 and Exercise 3. Could Andree's technique be used to evaluate

$$\sqrt[3]{1 + x} - \sqrt{1 - x}$$

*5 Write a program to evaluate

$$y = \sqrt[3]{1 + x} - \sqrt{1 - x}$$

for small values of x. Evaluate this expression using

$$Y = (1. + X)**(1./3.) - SQRT (1. - X)$$

and a second time using (3.16) through (3.20) and summing the c_k. Compare the results.

6 Discuss the evaluation of

$$F(x) = \frac{1 - \cos x}{\sin x}$$

when x is small. (*Hints:* There are at least two possible approaches: (1) expand $\sin x$ and $\cos x$ in Taylor series about $x = 0$, or (2) multiply and divide by $1 + \cos x$.)

A discussion of this problem may be found in "Pitfalls of Computation" by Irene E. Stegun and Milton Abramowitz (*SIAM Journal*, December 1956).

7 Write a computer program to evaluate $F(x)$ as given in Exercise 6 using three different algorithms. One program should evaluate

$$y = (1 - \cos(x))/\sin(x)$$

The second should evaluate the function

$$\frac{x}{2} + \frac{x^3}{24}$$

The third should evaluate

$$\frac{\sin x}{1 + \cos x}$$

Compare the results for small values of x.

8 Following Stegun and Abramowitz (see reference in Exercise 6) we note that the square root of the complex number

$$z = x + iy$$

where $i = \sqrt{-1}$ can be computed as follows:

$$\sqrt{z} = \sqrt{\frac{r + x}{2}} + i\sqrt{\frac{r - x}{2}}$$

where

$$r = \sqrt{x^2 + y^2}$$

a. Discuss the accuracy of this algorithm for small values of y.
b. Notice that

$$\sqrt{\frac{r - x}{2}} = \sqrt{\frac{r - x}{2}}\sqrt{\frac{r + x}{r + x}} = \frac{y}{2}\sqrt{\frac{2}{r + x}}$$

How can this be used to increase the accuracy of $\sqrt{z}$ for small values of y?

9 Write a computer program that uses two different algorithms to compute the square root of

$$z = x + iy$$

The two algorithms are:
a.

$$r = \sqrt{x^2 + y^2}$$

$$\sqrt{z} = \sqrt{\frac{r + x}{2}} + i\sqrt{\frac{r - x}{2}}$$

b.

$$r = \sqrt{x^2 + y^2}$$

$$a = \sqrt{\frac{r + x}{2}}$$

$$\sqrt{z} = a + i\frac{y}{2a}$$

Compare the results of these algorithms when

$$z = 4.5 + .025i$$

10 The program in Case Study 5 (Figure 3.21) for evaluating

$$I_n = \int_0^1 x^n e^{x-1}\, dx$$

assumes that $M > N$. Change the program so that program will function even if $M \leq N$.

11 From (3.26) for large n the values of I_n and I_{n-1} are close together. Suppose then for $n = N$ we let $I_N = I_{N-1}$. From (3.22)

$$I_N = \frac{1}{N + 1}$$

Rewrite the program in Case Study 5 (Figure 3.21) so that I_N is set equal to $1/(N + 1)$ rather than zero. Compare the results with those shown in Figure 3.22.

*12 Show that if we let

$$I_m = 0$$

and compute

$$I_{n-1} = \frac{1}{n}(1 - I_n)$$

for $n = m, m - 1, \ldots, 2$, then the value of I_1 is the sum of the first $m + 1$ terms in the Taylor series for $1/e$.

13 Show that if we let

$$I_m = \frac{1}{m + 1}$$

as suggested in Exercise 11 and compute

$$I_{n-1} = \frac{1}{n}(1 - I_n)$$

for $n = m, m - 1, \ldots, 2$, then the value of I_1 is the sum of the first $m + 2$ terms in the Taylor series for $1/e$.

The authors are indebted to Professor Jack Cohen of the University of Denver for suggesting the refinements of Exercises 11 and 13.

14 Write a program to compute the Bessel functions of the first kind, $J_m(x)$, to two digits after the decimal point using the procedure described at the close of Case Study 5.

15 Write a Fortran program that reads in order: a "rough" estimate of the mean of the data, then the data followed by a sentinel card. The program should compute the mean, variance, and standard deviation of the given data without using a subscripted variable. The program should produce the most accurate results possible under these restrictions. (See Exercise 16.)

*16 Given a set of data $x_1, x_2, \ldots, x_n$. Let

$$y_i = x_i - m$$

where m is any arbitrary constant. Show that the variance of the y_i as defined by (3.39) is the same as the variance of the x_i.

17 Show that the variance as defined in (3.39) can be expressed as shown in (3.41) by making use of (3.38).

18 Derive (3.55) for the error in the variance using

$$v = \frac{\displaystyle\sum_{i=1}^{n} x_i^2}{n} - \mu^2$$

from (3.38) and (3.51)–(3.54).

19 Derive (3.47) for the error in the variance using

$$v = \frac{\displaystyle\sum_{i=1}^{n} (x_i - \mu)^2}{4}$$

from (3.38) and (3.44)–(3.46).

20 Show that the variance of

$$1 - \left(\frac{1}{16}\right)^3, \; 1 - \left(\frac{1}{16}\right)^3 + \left(\frac{1}{16}\right)^4, \; 1 - \left(\frac{1}{16}\right)^3 + 2\left(\frac{1}{16}\right)^4$$

$$+ \cdots + 1 - \left(\frac{1}{16}\right)^4, \; 1, \; 1 + \left(\frac{1}{16}\right)^4, \; 1 + 2\left(\frac{1}{16}\right)^4$$

$$+ \cdots + 1 + \left(\frac{1}{16}\right)^v$$

is

$$v = 2.110998 \cdot 10^{-8}$$

Hint: Use the identity

$$\sum_{k=1}^{n} k^2 = \frac{n(n + 1)(2n + 1)}{6}$$

21 Use the triangle inequality to derive the bound (3.48) on the error in the variance from (3.47). Recall that

$$x_i = \mu + \Delta_i$$
$$\Delta = \max |\Delta_i|$$
$$\Delta \ll |\mu|$$

and δ is the relative roundoff error in any arithmetic operation.

22 Use the triangle inequality to derive the bound (3.59) on the error in the variance from (3.55). Use the relationship in Exercise 21 above.

4 Simultaneous
Linear Algebraic Equations

**4.1
Introduc-
tion**

In Section 1.13 we discussed a system of two simultaneous equations. There we developed an algorithm for finding an approximate solution to such a system. We also pointed out that the algorithm, the Newton-Raphson method, could be extended to a system of three or more equations.

There were several shortcomings to the algorithm of Section 1.13. First, the algorithm required that we have some initial "guess" at the solution and that this guess be not too far from the solution. Second, the algorithm was infinite; that is, to find the exact solution required an infinite number of iterations. Of course, it is not possible to iterate an infinite number of times so we contented ourselves with a finite number of iterations and, as a result, an approximate solution.

In defense of the Newton-Raphson method we should point out that it is applicable to any arbitrary equations provided we can compute all of the partial derivatives of the functions that appear in the equations.

If we are willing to sacrifice some loss in generality, we can obtain much more efficient algorithms. For example, if we restrict ourselves to linear equations, then we do not need an initial guess and, moreover, we can develop finite algorithms. We proceed to that now. First, however, we note that an introduction to one algorithm for systems of linear equations was discussed in Exercise 40 of Chapter 1. The reader is well advised to review that exercise before proceeding with this chapter.

150

4.2
Existence,
Unique-
ness, and
Ill-Condi-
tioning

Before developing some specific algorithms, we shall discuss what we mean by a solution and the conditions under which a solution exists. (After all, there is little use in attempting to compute a solution if there is none.)

An equation is *linear* if each term contains no more than one variable and each variable appears to the first power.

For example

$$2x + y - 6z = 4$$

is linear but

$$2xy + y - 7 = 2$$

is not (first term contains two variables) nor is

$$x^2 + y + z = 0$$

(first term contains a variable squared).

We shall consider n linear equations in n variables (unknowns) and shall refer to these equations as a system of n linear equations. A *solution* to this system of equations consists of values for the n variables such that when these values are substituted into the equations, all of the n equations are satisfied simultaneously.

For example, the system of three linear equations

$$\begin{aligned} x + y + z &= 4 \\ 2x + 3y + z &= 9 \\ x - y - z &= -2 \end{aligned}$$

has the solution $x = 1$, $y = 2$, and $z = 1$. The reader can verify this by substituting these values for the variables and checking the validity of the three equations.

Given an arbitrary system of equations, we cannot say without investigation that there *is* a solution or, if there is one, that it is unique. There are three and only three possibilities.

1. The system has a unique solution. For example,

$$\left. \begin{aligned} 2x + y &= 4 \\ x - y &= -1 \end{aligned} \right\} \tag{4.1}$$

The solution is $x = 1$ and $y = 2$; no other pair of values of x and y satisfies both equations. This type of system, which will, of course, be our primary concern, is represented geometrically for the two-dimensional case in Figure 4.1. Any point on line L_1 has coordinates that satisfy the first of the equations in (4.1). Similarly, all points on L_2 satisfy the second equation of (4.2). The points that satisfy both equations must lie on both lines. There is only one such point. The coordinates of this point are the solution we seek. Such a system has a unique solution.

2. The system has no solution. For example,

$$\left. \begin{aligned} 4x + 6y &= 10 \\ 2x + 3y &= 6 \end{aligned} \right\} \tag{4.2}$$

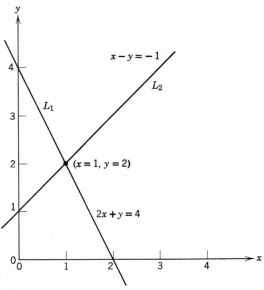

Figure 4.1. *Geometrical representation of a system of two simultaneous equations having a unique solution; the lines are distinct and intersect.*

Figure 4.2 shows the graphs of these two lines. They are parallel; since they never meet, there is no solution.

3. The system has an infinite number of solutions. For example,

$$4x + 6y = 12$$
$$2x + 3y = 6$$

These are actually alternative forms of the equation of the same line, as we see in Figure 4.3. Any point on the line is a solution, such as $x = 0$, $y = 2$; $x = 1$, $y = \frac{4}{3}$; or $x = 3$, $y = 0$, etc.

A system of type 2 or 3 is said to be *singular*. Sometimes we know from the formulation of a problem that the system cannot be singular.

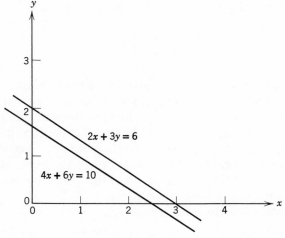

Figure 4.2. *Geometrical representation of a system of two simultaneous equations having no solution; the lines are parallel.*

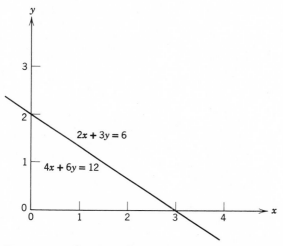

Figure 4.3. *Geometrical representation of a system of two simultaneous equations having infinitely many solutions; the lines are identical.*

If this information is lacking, as it often is, we must either depend on the method of solution to signal singularity or make an explicit test for the possibility. We shall see in Section 4.3 that Gaussian elimination does give immediate information about singularity. A direct test is to compute the determinant of the system of coefficients; a zero value indicates singularity. Unfortunately, evaluating the determinant is as much work as solving the system.

From the standpoint of infinite precision arithmetic, a system is either singular or it is not. From the standpoint of practical computation, a system can be *almost* singular, leading to a "solution" that has little reliability. Consider the equations

$$\left.\begin{array}{r} 5x + 7y = 12 \\ 7x + 10y = 17 \end{array}\right\} \tag{4.3}$$

These have the unique solution $x = 1$, $y = 1$. But consider the pair of values $x = 2.415$, $y = 0$. Then

$$\left.\begin{array}{r} 5x + 7y = 12.075 \\ 7x + 10y = 16.905 \end{array}\right\} \tag{4.4}$$

When rounded to two digits, these right-hand sides agree with the right-hand sides of the original equations. Since the original values were given to only two figures, the solution (4.4) should be accepted as being as good as the "unique" one.

The problem is that the two lines are *nearly* parallel, as shown in Figure 4.4. The point given by (4.4), although it does not lie on either line, is very close to both.

Equations such as (4.3) are called *ill-conditioned*. Whenever two lines (or planes or hyperplanes) are almost parallel, the equations will be ill-conditioned. It is then difficult to find a numerical solution, and, as we have just seen, it will be of doubtful accuracy. In three or more dimensions there are ways that a system of equations can be singular or nearly

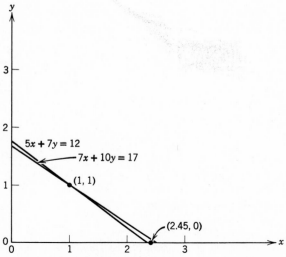

Figure 4.4. *Geometrical representation of a system of two simultaneous equations that is almost singular; the lines are almost identical.*

singular without any planes' being parallel or nearly parallel.[1] Regardless of what the geometrical "mechanism" is, however, Gaussian elimination or an explicit test will detect it.

Before delving into the details of the methods of solution, we shall preview briefly the main avenues of approach.

In general, there are two types of numerical techniques for solving simultaneous equations: *direct* methods, which are finite (Section 4.3), and *indirect* methods, which are infinite (Section 4.10). Naturally, no practical technique can actually be infinite. What we mean is that the direct methods will in principle (neglecting roundoff errors, that is) produce an exact solution, if there is one, in a finite number of arithmetic operations. An indirect method, on the other hand, would in principle require an infinite number of arithmetic operations to produce an exact solution. Stated otherwise, an indirect method has a truncation error, whereas a direct method has not.

The "in principle" in the last paragraph is crucial; however, there *are* roundoff errors. We shall have to consider this question most carefully. In a large ill-conditioned system the roundoff errors in a direct method may make the "solution" meaningless. Despite its theoretical truncation error, an indirect method may be much more desirable because in such a method the roundoff errors do not accumulate.

After studying the most common examples of both methods and their errors, we shall briefly compare them. We shall see that both are useful; both have advantages and limitations.

[1] Visualize three parallel lines passing through the corners of a triangle and perpendicular to the plane of the triangle. Now pass a plane through each pair of lines: The three planes are not parallel, but they meet nowhere at one point. If one of the planes is tilted slightly, they will meet in a point, but the system of equations representing the planes is ill-conditioned.

We now turn to the method of Gaussian elimination, one of the oldest and most widely used finite techniques for the solution of simultaneous linear equations.

To illustrate the method, we shall first consider the case of three equations in three variables.

$$a_{11}x_1 + a_{12}x_2 + a_{13}x_3 = b_1 \qquad (4.5)$$
$$a_{21}x_1 + a_{22}x_2 + a_{23}x_3 = b_2 \qquad (4.6)$$
$$a_{31}x_1 + a_{32}x_2 + a_{33}x_3 = b_3 \qquad (4.7)$$

At least one of a_{11}, a_{21}, and a_{31} is not zero; otherwise, only two variables would appear in the three equations. If a_{11} is zero, we reorder the equations so that the coefficient of x_1 in the first equation is not zero. Interchanging two rows in the system of equations, of course, leaves the solution of the system unchanged.

Next define a multiplier

$$m_2 = \frac{a_{21}}{a_{11}}$$

We multiply the first equation (4.5) by m_2 and subtract from the second equation (4.6). ("First" and "second" refer to the equations *as reordered*, if necessary.) The result is

$$(a_{21} - m_2 a_{11})x_1 + (a_{22} - m_2 a_{12})x_2 + (a_{23} - m_2 a_{13})x_3 = b_2 - m_2 b_1 \qquad (4.8)$$

But

$$a_{21} - m_2 a_{11} = a_{21} - \frac{a_{21}}{a_{11}} a_{11} = 0$$

so x_1 has been *eliminated* from the second equation. (This result is, of course, the reason for the choice of m_2.) If we now define

$$a'_{22} = a_{22} - m_2 a_{12}$$
$$a'_{23} = a_{23} - m_2 a_{13}$$
$$b'_2 = b_2 - m_2 b_1$$

then (4.8) becomes

$$a'_{22}x_2 + a'_{23}x_3 = b'_2 \qquad (4.9)$$

We replace the second of the original equations (4.6) by (4.9). Notice that the solution of this "new" system comprised of (4.5), (4.9), and (4.7) is identical with the solution of the original system.

Similarly, we define a multiplier for the third equation:

$$m_3 = \frac{a_{31}}{a_{11}}$$

We multiply the first equation by this multiplier and subtract from the third. Again the coefficient of x_1 vanishes and the result is

$$a'_{32}x_2 + a'_{33}x_3 = b'_3 \qquad (4.10)$$

where

$$a'_{32} = a_{32} - m_3 a_{12}$$
$$a'_{33} = a_{33} - m_3 a_{13}$$
$$b'_3 = b_3 - m_3 b_1$$

If we now use (4.10) to replace (4.7), the resulting three equations in three variables are

$$a_{11}x_1 + a_{12}x_2 + a_{13}x_3 = b_1 \tag{4.5}$$
$$a'_{22}x_2 + a'_{23}x_3 = b'_2 \tag{4.9}$$
$$a'_{32}x_2 + a'_{33}x_3 = b'_3 \tag{4.10}$$

These are completely equivalent to the original equations, with the added advantage that x_1 appears only in the first of them. The last two are two equations in two variables. If we can solve these last two for x_2 and x_3, the results can be substituted into the first to get x_1. The problem, therefore, has been reduced from that of solving three equations in three variables to that of solving two equations in two variables.

We can now proceed to eliminate x_2 from one of the last two equations. Again, if $a'_{22} = 0$, we interchange the last two equations. (If it should happen that $a'_{22} = 0$ *and* $a'_{32} = 0$, the equations are singular and have either no solution or an infinite number of solutions.)

We define a new multiplier m'_3:

$$m'_3 = \frac{a'_{32}}{a'_{22}}$$

We multiply (4.9) by m'_3 and subtract from (4.10). The result is

$$(a'_{32} - m'_3 a'_{22})x_2 + (a'_{33} - m'_3 a'_{23})x_3 = b'_3 - m'_3 b'_2$$

Again,

$$a'_{32} - m'_3 a'_{22} = 0$$

and letting

$$a''_{33} = a'_{33} - m'_3 a'_{23}$$
$$b''_3 = b'_3 - m'_3 b'_2$$

we get

$$a''_{33}x_3 = b''_3 \tag{4.11}$$

This replaces (4.10), so that the final set of equations is

$$a_{11}x_1 + a_{12}x_2 + a_{13}x_3 = b_1 \tag{4.5}$$
$$a'_{22}x_2 + a'_{23}x_3 = b'_2 \tag{4.9}$$
$$a''_{33}x_3 = b''_3 \tag{4.11}$$

Such a system of equations is called *triangular* from its appearance.

It is now a straightforward process to solve (4.11) for x_3, to substitute that result in (4.9) to find x_2, and finally to substitute into (4.5) to get x_1. This process, called *back substitution*, is given by

$$x_3 = \frac{b''_3}{a''_{33}}$$

$$x_2 = \frac{(b_2' - a_{23}'x_3)}{a_{22}'}$$

$$x_1 = \frac{(b_1 - a_{12}x_2 - a_{13}x_3)}{a_{11}}$$

We recall that $a_{11} \neq 0$, $a_{22}' \neq 0$. If $a_{33}'' = 0$, once again it means that the original system is singular.

Consider an example.

$$\left. \begin{array}{r} x + y + z = 4 \\ 2x + 3y + z = 9 \\ x - y - z = -2 \end{array} \right\} \qquad (4.12)$$

It is easy to verify that the multiplier for the second equation is 2 and that for the third is 1. After eliminating x from the second and third equations, the new multiplier for eliminating y from the third equation is -2. The triangular system is

$$\begin{array}{r} x + y + z = 4 \\ y - z = 1 \\ -4z = -4 \end{array}$$

From the last equation, $z = 1$; from the second, $y = 2$; from the first, $x = 1$. These results may be substituted into the original equations (4.12), which are thereby exactly satisfied. We have therefore found an exact solution in a finite number of arithmetic operations. In this case there were no roundoff errors.

The reader will find it instructive to solve (4.1) by elimination and to attempt to solve the singular system (4.2).

Before proceeding to the more general case of a system of n equations in n variables, we pause to make some observations that will simplify the developments that follow. First, consider once more (4.9). Suppose in that equation we "rename" the coefficients as follows:

$$\begin{array}{ll} a_{22}' & \text{is renamed} \quad a_{22} \\ a_{23}' & \text{is renamed} \quad a_{23} \\ b_2' & \text{is renamed} \quad b_2 \end{array}$$

Then (4.9) becomes

$$a_{22}x_2 + a_{23}x_3 = b_2$$

In doing so we no longer can identify the names a_{22}, a_{23}, and b_2 with the coefficients in (4.6). However, *we never again use* (4.6). In fact, (4.6) is replaced by (4.9) and the former never reappears in the discussion. Thus our renaming will not lead to any difficulties.

The renaming has an important advantage, however, in terms of writing a computer program. The programming equivalent of working with primes, double primes, etc., as we did above, is to require new variables with different names, and, usually, additional computer storage. By renaming coefficients in the manner indicated, we need only set up a single subscripted variable with a name like $A(I, J)$ to describe all the coefficients, before and after the operations involved in elimination.

The second observation we make is that we used three basic operations, none of which changed the solution of the system of equations. The operations are:

(i) Multiplication of an equation by a constant. (The constant may be zero.)
(ii) Subtraction of one equation from another and replacement of the second equation by the result of the subtraction.
(iii) Reordering the equations.

We shall continue to use these operations in the remaining discussion with the assurance that thereby we shall derive a new system whose solution is identical with the solution of the original system.

We may now generalize the procedure to the case of n simultaneous linear equations in n variables. After an "algebraic" description, we shall present a flow chart that not only makes the process more graphic but also provides a direct guide to writing a program.

Let the n variables be $x_1, x_2, \ldots, x_n$ and let the equations be

$$\left.\begin{aligned}
a_{11}x_1 + a_{12}x_2 + \cdots + a_{1j}x_j + \cdots + a_{1n}x_n &= b_1 \\
a_{21}x_1 + a_{22}x_2 + \cdots + a_{2j}x_j + \cdots + a_{2n}x_n &= b_2 \\
\cdots\cdots\cdots\cdots\cdots\cdots\cdots\cdots\cdots\cdots\cdots\cdots\cdots \\
a_{i1}x_1 + a_{i2}x_2 + \cdots + a_{ij}x_j + \cdots + a_{in}x_n &= b_i \\
\cdots\cdots\cdots\cdots\cdots\cdots\cdots\cdots\cdots\cdots\cdots\cdots\cdots \\
a_{n1}x_1 + a_{n2}x_2 + \cdots + a_{nj}x_j + \cdots + a_{nn}x_n &= b_n
\end{aligned}\right\} \tag{4.13}$$

We assume that the equations have been so ordered that $a_{11} \neq 0$. Define $n - 1$ multipliers:

$$m_i = \frac{a_{i1}}{a_{11}}, \ i = 2, 3, \ldots, n$$

and subtract m_i times the first equation from the ith equation. If we define

$$\begin{aligned}
a'_{ij} &= a_{ij} - m_i a_{1j}, & i &= 2, \ldots, n \\
b'_i &= b_i - m_i b_1, & j &= 1, \ldots, n
\end{aligned}$$

it is easy to see that

$$a'_{i1} = 0, \quad i = 2, \ldots, n$$

The transformed equations are

$$\begin{aligned}
a_{11}x_1 + a_{12}x_2 + \cdots + a_{1j}x_j + \cdots + a_{1n}x_n &= b_1 \\
0 + a_{22}x_2 + \cdots + a_{2j}x_j + \cdots + a_{2n}x_n &= b_2 \\
\cdots\cdots\cdots\cdots\cdots\cdots\cdots\cdots\cdots\cdots\cdots \\
0 + a_{i2}x_2 + \cdots + a_{ij}x_j + \cdots + a_{in}x_n &= b_i \\
\cdots\cdots\cdots\cdots\cdots\cdots\cdots\cdots\cdots\cdots\cdots \\
0 + a_{n2}x_2 + \cdots + a_{nj}x_j + \cdots + a_{nn}x_n &= b_n
\end{aligned}$$

Here we have once again "renamed" the a'_{ij} and b'_i to be a_{ij} and b_i. We re-emphasize that these a_{ij} and b_i are not the same coefficients appearing in (4.13). We also re-emphasize that this last system of equations has the same solution as does (4.13).

We continue in this way. At the kth stage we eliminate x_k by defining multipliers

$$m_i = \frac{a_{ik}}{a_{kk}}, \quad i = k + 1, \ldots, n \tag{4.14}$$

where $a_{kk} \neq 0$. Then

$$a_{ij} = a_{ij} - m_i a_{kj} \tag{4.15}$$
$$b_i = b_i - m_i b_k \tag{4.16}$$

for $i = k + 1, \ldots, n$ and for $j = k, \ldots, n$. The index k takes on consecutive integer values from 1 through and including $n - 1$. At the point where $k = n - 1$ we are eliminating x_{n-1} from the last equation.

The final triangular set of equations is given by

$$
\left.
\begin{aligned}
a_{11}x_1 + a_{12}x_2 + \cdots + a_{1j}x_j + \cdots + a_{1n}x_n &= b_1 \\
a_{22}x_2 + \cdots + a_{2j}x_j + \cdots + a_{2n}x_n &= b_2 \\
\cdots \cdots \cdots \cdots \cdots \cdots \cdots \cdots \cdots \cdots \cdots \cdots \\
a_{jj}x_j + \cdots + a_{jn}x_n &= b_j \\
\cdots \cdots \cdots \cdots \cdots \cdots \cdots \\
a_{nn}x_n &= b_n
\end{aligned}
\right\} \tag{4.17}
$$

Back-substitution then produces the solution as follows:

$$
\left.
\begin{aligned}
x_n &= \frac{b_n}{a_{nn}} \\
&\vdots \\
x_j &= \frac{b_j - (a_{j,j+1}x_{j+1} + \cdots + a_{jn}x_n)}{a_{jj}} \\
&\vdots \\
x_1 &= \frac{b_1 - (a_{12}x_2 + \cdots + a_{1n}x_n)}{a_{11}}
\end{aligned}
\right\} \tag{4.18}
$$

**4.4
Matrix
Formula-
tion**

It should be clear from the foregoing that we are merely manipulating the a_{ij} and the b_i. The names of the variables, x_i, are immaterial. Therefore, we should somehow be able to write down the a_{ij} and b_i without explicitly writing down the x_i and thereby simplify the bookkeeping. We can, and the answer lies in the use of matrices.

Suppose we define A to be the $n \times n$ matrix

$$
A = \begin{pmatrix}
a_{11} & a_{12} & \cdots & a_{1j} & \cdots & a_{1n} \\
a_{21} & a_{22} & \cdots & a_{2j} & \cdots & a_{2n} \\
\vdots & \vdots & & \vdots & & \vdots \\
a_{i1} & a_{i2} & \cdots & a_{ij} & \cdots & a_{in} \\
\vdots & \vdots & & \vdots & & \vdots \\
a_{n1} & a_{n2} & \cdots & a_{nj} & \cdots & a_{nn}
\end{pmatrix}
$$

We also define X and B to be n-component column vectors as follows

$$X = \begin{pmatrix} x_1 \\ x_2 \\ \vdots \\ x_j \\ \vdots \\ x_n \end{pmatrix} \qquad B = \begin{pmatrix} b_1 \\ b_2 \\ \vdots \\ b_i \\ \vdots \\ b_n \end{pmatrix}$$

Then the system of n equations, (4.13) may be written as the single matrix equation

$$AX = B \qquad\qquad (4.19)$$

As noted earlier, we need only deal with A and B in Gaussian elimination. To simplify the notation even further we form the _augmented matrix._ This is the matrix A with the vector B appended to A as the $(n + 1)$st column. The augmented matrix, A^*, then is

$$A^* = \begin{pmatrix} a_{11} & a_{12} & \cdots & a_{1j} & \cdots & a_{1n} & b_1 \\ \vdots & & & & & & \\ a_{i1} & a_{i2} & \cdots & a_{ij} & \cdots & a_{in} & b_i \\ \vdots & & & & & & \\ a_{n1} & a_{n2} & \cdots & a_{nj} & \cdots & a_{nn} & b_n \end{pmatrix}$$

In Gaussian elimination we perform operations with the rows of this augmented matrix.

The operations are:

(i) Multiplication of a row by a constant.
(ii) Subtraction of one row from another and replacement of the second row by the result of the subtraction.
(iii) Reordering the rows.

Note the correspondence between these operations and the previous section's three rules for operations on equations.

Before we proceed to re-examine Gaussian elimination, we make one further change to simplify our work. We rename the b_i to be $a_{i,n+1}$; that is, we assign the values of the b_i in (4.13) to the coefficients $a_{i,n+1}$. The augmented matrix then is

$$A^* = \begin{pmatrix} a_{11} & a_{12} & \cdots & a_{1n} & a_{1,n+1} \\ \vdots & & & & \\ a_{i1} & a_{i2} & \cdots & a_{in} & a_{i,n+1} \\ \vdots & & & & \\ a_{n1} & a_{n2} & \cdots & a_{nn} & a_{n,n+1} \end{pmatrix} \qquad (4.20)$$

The advantage of this renaming is that we now have only one $n \times (n + 1)$ matrix with which to deal rather than a matrix A and a vector B. We must remember, however, to use the constant terms on the right-hand side of (4.13) for the $(n + 1)$st column of the matrix.

The result of triangularization produces an augmented matrix that looks like

$$A^* = \begin{pmatrix} a_{11} & a_{12} & \cdots & & a_{1i} & \cdots & & a_{1n} & a_{1,n+1} \\ 0 & a_{22} & \cdots & & a_{2i} & \cdots & & a_{2n} & a_{2,n+1} \\ \vdots & & & & & & & & \\ 0 & 0 & \cdots & 0 & a_{ii} & \cdots & & a_{in} & a_{i,n+1} \\ \vdots & & & & & & & & \\ 0 & 0 & \cdots & 0 & 0 & \cdots & a_{n-1,n-1} & a_{n-1,n} & a_{n-1,n+1} \\ 0 & 0 & \cdots & 0 & 0 & \cdots & 0 & a_{nn} & a_{n,n+1} \end{pmatrix}$$

We now make an observation that reduces the number of arithmetic operations we shall have to perform. When we multiply a row by a constant and subtract the result from another row, we do not need to work with the entire row. Indeed, if the kth row is the one multiplied by the constant, this implies that the variable x_k is being eliminated. Therefore the matrix entries in the first $k - 1$ columns and in all rows $k, k + 1, \ldots, n$ are zero. We can, therefore, ignore the first $k - 1$ columns. We can also ignore the kth column since the multiplier has been chosen to produce a zero there in the subtraction process. This accounts for starting the index i at the value $k + 1$ in the flow chart in Figure 4.5 of the next section.

We now re-examine back-substitution from the point of view of matrices. We take the last row of the triangularized matrix and multiply that row by $1/a_{nn}$ producing

$$\left(0, 0, \ldots, 0, 1, \frac{a_{n,n+1}}{a_{nn}}\right)$$

We rename the last entry $a_{n,n+1}$ so that we have

$$(0, 0, \ldots, 0, 1, a_{n,n+1})$$

This last entry is the value of x_n.

We multiply this new last row by $a_{n-1,n}$ and subtract the result from the next-to-last row. This yields

$$(0, 0, \ldots, a_{n-1,n-1}, 0, a_{n-1,n+1} - a_{n-1,n} \cdot a_{n,n+1})$$

Multiplying this row by $1/a_{n-1,n-1}$ produces the value of x_{n-1} in the $(n + 1)$st column. We rename this last entry $a_{n-1,n+1}$.

Proceeding in this way, we determine the values of $x_n, x_{n-1}, x_{n-2}, \ldots, x_2, x_1$ in that order. The final augmented matrix is

$$A^* = \begin{pmatrix} 1 & 0 & \cdots & & 0 & a_{1,n+1} \\ 0 & 1 & \cdots & & 0 & a_{2,n+1} \\ \vdots & & & & & \\ 0 & 0 & \cdots & 1 & 0 & a_{n-1,n+1} \\ 0 & 0 & \cdots & 0 & 1 & a_{n,n+1} \end{pmatrix}$$

We once again observe that we need not compute the 1's along the diagonal nor do we need to compute the 0's. The multipliers have been chosen to produce them automatically. All we need compute are the entries in the last column. Equations (4.18) produce those if b_j is replaced by $a_{j,n+1}$.

4.5
Flow
Charts for
Gaussian
Elimination

The flow chart for the elimination process is shown in Figure 4.5. It follows the description just given fairly closely, with two exceptions. The box marked * that contains "arrange rows so $a_{kk} \neq 0$" refers to a process that we shall consider after discussing roundoff errors in Section 4.6. We shall see that the roundoff errors in the values of the variables can be substantially reduced by a judicious choice of rows to interchange.

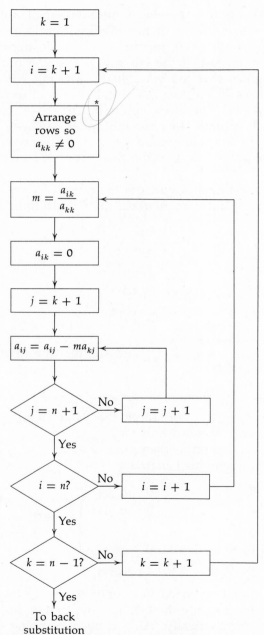

Figure 4.5. *Flow chart of the method of Gaussian elimination.*

A second difference between the flow chart and the description above is that we have used one symbol, m, for all multipliers in the flow chart, for if the operations are suitably arranged we shall never need more than one multiplier at a time.

In reading this flow chart, it may help to note the meanings assigned to the subscripts i, j, and k:

k refers to the number of the row being subtracted from other rows; it is also the number of the variable being eliminated from the last $n - k$ rows.

i refers to the number of the row from which a variable is currently being eliminated.

j refers to the number of a column.

A careful study of this flow chart is worth the effort. It not only helps to make clear the method of Gaussian elimination, but also exhibits many standard techniques in flow charting, particularly the handling of subscript notation.

It is worth noting that the elimination process does not change the value of the determinant of A, although each row interchange does reverse the sign. After the elimination process is complete, the value of the determinant is just the product of the main diagonal elements, with the sign of the product reversed if there has been an odd number of row interchanges. In fact, when a determinant is to be evaluated, elimination is a good way to proceed.

The flow chart for back-substitution shown in Figure 4.6 is relatively straightforward. We can diagram the method more simply if we compute the value of x_n in a separate step at the beginning. It is possible to draw a more compact flow chart without this separate step, but it would pointlessly complicate the testing in the formation of the sum of the terms after the main diagonal term: The first "sum" would be zero, which would force us to test before accumulating. Notice that, although in Figure 4.5 all subscripts *increased*, here in Figure 4.6 one of them (i) decreases.

**4.6
Roundoff
Errors**

We now turn to a discussion of roundoff errors when the elimination process is carried out in floating point arithmetic. Contrary to our usual approach, the goal this time will not be to obtain bounds on the errors— although this could certainly be done. Instead we shall seek a rule that will hold the roundoff error as small as possible, which is the first practical concern. The second concern—knowing the size of the errors—is discussed in Section 4.8 in connection with a method that makes it possible to use the computer itself, not only to estimate the error but also to correct for the effects of roundoff.

Recall that we may have to rearrange rows at each stage of the elimination process in order to avoid division by zero. There are, in general, several such arrangements. We shall show how to choose one that reduces roundoff errors. We shall also see that rearrangement is usually desirable even if the diagonal term is *not* zero.

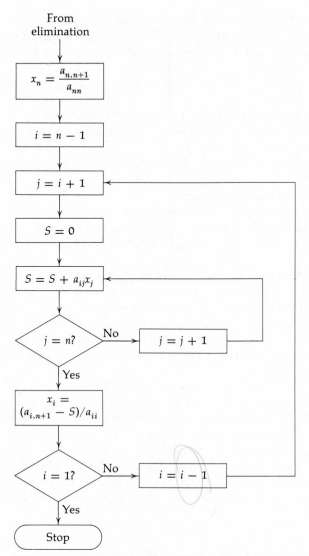

Figure 4.6. *Flow chart of the back substitution in Gaussian elimination.*

Let us suppose we are about to eliminate x_k. The augmented matrix will be

$$
\begin{pmatrix}
a_{11} & a_{12} & \cdots & & a_{1k} & \cdots & a_{1j} & \cdots & a_{1n} & a_{1,n+1} \\
0 & a_{22} & \cdots & & a_{2k} & \cdots & a_{2j} & \cdots & a_{2n} & a_{2,n+1} \\
\vdots & & & & & & & & & \\
0 & 0 & \cdots & 0 & a_{kk} & \cdots & a_{kj} & \cdots & a_{kn} & a_{k,n+1} \\
\vdots & & & & & & & & & \\
0 & 0 & \cdots & 0 & a_{ik} & \cdots & a_{ij} & \cdots & a_{in} & a_{i,n+1} \\
\vdots & & & & & & & & & \\
0 & 0 & \cdots & 0 & a_{nk} & \cdots & a_{nj} & \cdots & a_{nn} & a_{n,n+1}
\end{pmatrix}
$$

To eliminate x_k from the ith row we compute

$$m_i = \frac{a_{ik}}{a_{kk}}$$

We then compute for $j = k + 1, \ldots, n + 1$

$$a_{ij} - m_i a_{kj}$$

This is the new value of a_{ij}. The process graph is shown in Figure 4.7. In the process graph, a_{ij} represents the old value of a_{ij}, and $\overline{a}_{ij}$ represents the new value to be computed.

We now compute the relative roundoff error in the new value of $\overline{a}_{ij}$. Let α_{ij} be the relative roundoff error in the old value of a_{ij} and let δ, μ, and σ be the relative roundoff errors in the division, multiplication, and subtraction, respectively. Then, if e_{ij} is the absolute error in the new value of $\overline{a}_{ij}$,

$$\frac{e_{ij}}{\overline{a}_{ij}} = -\frac{m_i a_{kj}}{\overline{a}_{ij}}(\alpha_{ik} - \alpha_{kk} + \alpha_{kj} + \delta + \mu) + \frac{a_{ij}}{\overline{a}_{ij}} \cdot \alpha_{ij} + \sigma$$

If δ, μ, and σ are bounded by $5 \cdot 10^{-t}$ and the α_{ij} are bounded by $K \cdot 10^{-t}$, where $K \geq 5$, we have

$$|e_{ij}| \leq \{3 \cdot (K + 5) \cdot |a_{kj}| \cdot |m_i| + (K + 5)|a_{ij}|\} \cdot 10^{-t}$$

Consider now a fixed j (a given column). The dominant term is in general the first one in the braces, which is small if $|m_i|$ is small. Thus we wish to make $|m_i|$ as small as possible. To make $|m_i|$ small requires that $|a_{kk}|$ be as large as possible. In other words, we wish to choose the row that is to become the kth row so that

$$|a_{kk}| \geq |a_{ik}| \qquad i = k + 1, \ldots, n$$

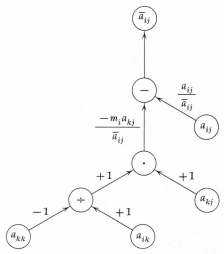

Figure 4.7. *Process graph for Gaussian elimination.*

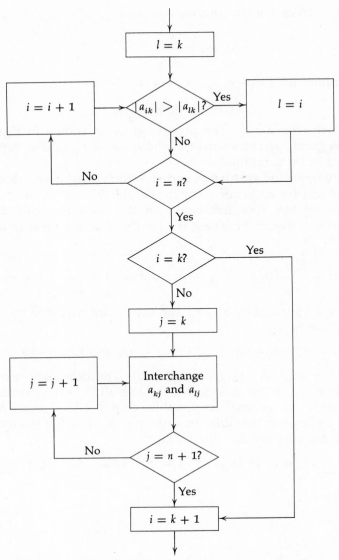

Figure 4.8. *Flow chart of the process of choosing the kth row and performing a row interchange if necessary to get the element that is largest in absolute value into the main diagonal position. All of the flow chart replaces the box marked * in Figure 4.5.*

because then

$$|m_i| \leq 1$$

If the kth row is not so chosen, at least one of the multipliers will be greater than 1 in absolute value.

Our rule then is to rearrange the last $n - k + 1$ rows so that the largest—in absolute value—of the coefficients in the kth column is in the kth row. This operation is sometimes referred to as *partial pivotal condensation*.

Hamming has shown[2] that in some cases it is better not to rearrange the rows so that the largest coefficient in the kth column is also in the kith row. However, such cases seldom arise in practice and there is substantial empirical evidence to indicate that pivotal condensation does reduce roundoff errors in problems that are likely to arise in any real environment.

A flow chart of the testing and (if necessary) the interchanging is shown in Figure 4.8. It should be thought of as replacing the box marked * in Figure 4.5. In studying Figure 4.8, recall from Figure 4.5 that as we enter this phase k has some value and i has just been set to $k + 1$. We begin by setting an auxiliary subscript l, equal to k. The first comparison is between a_{ik}, the element just below the diagonal term a_{kk}, and a_{lk}, which is a_{kk}. If a_{ik} is found to be larger in absolute value, we set $l = i$. The subscript l therefore always represents the row number of the element in the kth column that is so far the largest one tested. The subscript i runs through all values from $k + 1$ to n, inclusive. Thus, at the end of this loop l identifies the largest element, the one we want for a_{kk} after interchanging, if necessary.

Of course, the original a_{kk} could already be the largest. We therefore immediately test for this possibility and omit the interchanging if it is so. Before returning to the main elimination process, however, it is necessary to set i back to the value it had before we used it as a subscript in the testing loop. This is easily done: In the main flow chart the value of i had just been made $k + 1$, which we repeat here.

The actual interchanging is done on pairs of values, one from row k and one from row l, whatever l may be. The interchange of each pair of values requires a three-step process. For example, to interchange a_{kj} and a_{lj} we write

$$\text{TEMP} = A(K,J)$$
$$A(K,J) = A(L,J)$$
$$A(L,J) = \text{TEMP}$$

This operation must be done on all pairs in the two rows, and is carried out by a loop using j as a subscript.

The roundoff error can be further reduced by testing and interchanging columns as well as rows. In other words, we search all remaining coefficients for the largest element rather than restricting the range to those in the kth column. This does in fact reduce the roundoff error even further, but at the expense of an additional complication: An interchange in columns implies renaming the variables or keeping some record of the interchanges. This can certainly be done, but it is not usually worth the programming effort or the slight extra machine time in running the program. Exercise 26 in this chapter sketches the programming technique by which the renaming of the variables may be done.

[2]See Section 5.5 of *Introduction to Applied Numerical Methods* by Richard W. Hamming (McGraw-Hill, 1971).

To indicate the practical value of row rearrangement, consider the following set of equations:

$$3.241 \cdot 10^0 x_1 + 1.600 \cdot 10^2 x_2 = 1.632 \cdot 10^2$$
$$1.020 \cdot 10^4 x_1 + 1.540 \cdot 10^3 x_2 = 1.174 \cdot 10^4$$

$$(4.21)$$

The exact solution is

$$x_1 = 1.000 \cdot 10^0$$
$$x_2 = 1.000 \cdot 10^0$$

Let us solve these equations by elimination, in the order shown, using floating point arithmetic with four-digit mantissas.

The first and only multiplier is

$$m = \frac{1.020 \cdot 10^4}{3.241 \cdot 10^0} = 3.147 \cdot 10^3$$

The new second equation is

$$5.730 \cdot 10^{-1} x_1 - 5.020 \cdot 10^5 x_2 = -5.019 \cdot 10^5$$

Naturally, the new coefficient of x_1 should be zero, but roundoff error has prevented our getting the exact result. This coefficient, however, never enters the subsequent calculations, and we proceed with the back substitution.

$$x_2 = \frac{-5.019 \cdot 10^5}{-5.020 \cdot 10^5} = 9.998 \cdot 10^{-1}$$

From the first equation, then,

$$x_1 = 9.873 \cdot 10^{-1}$$

Now let us reverse the order of the equations, which is what the row rearrangement amounts to in this case. The multiplier now is

$$m = \frac{3.241 \cdot 10^0}{1.020 \cdot 10^4} = 3.177 \cdot 10^{-4}$$

The new second equation is

so that

$$0.000 x_1 + 1.595 \cdot 10^2 x_2 = 1.595 \cdot 10^2$$

$$x_2 = 1.000 \cdot 10^0$$

and

$$x_1 = 1.000 \cdot 10^0$$

This example has coefficients that vary widely in size; usually the variation is not so wide. However, when there are many equations (a system of 10 equations is commonplace, and 100 is not unusual), the effects of roundoff errors accumulate. What happens in the first elimination has a profound effect on later accuracy. It is easy to construct examples of relatively small systems in which *all* accuracy is lost without rearrangement; that is, the answers will have *no* significant figures. Any practical program for computer solution of simultaneous linear algebraic equations by Gaussian elimination *must* include row interchange, except possibly in the case of very specialized systems in which a great deal is known about the coefficients.

**4.7
Case
Study 7:
Solving the
Simultane-
ous Equa-
tions of a
Chemical
Process by
Gaussian
Elimination**

Figure 4.9 depicts a hypothetical continuous-process chemical plant. It accepts a *feed*, or input, designated as stream 1, that consists of 40 lb/hr of a compound called *A*, 40 lb/hr of *B*, and 20 lb/hr of *C*. The function of the plant is to convert some of the *A* and some of the *B* into *C*, and to partially separate the components so that the product consists mostly of *C*. The situation is obviously idealized, but it is indicative of processes that are used in the chemical industry and provides a good example of how systems of simultaneous equations arise in practical industrial design work.

The separation of the three components is based on differences in their boiling points: *C* has a lower boiling point than has either *A* or *B*. When a mixture of the three is boiled, the vapor contains a higher proportion of *C* than the liquid does. Similarly, when a vessel containing the three components in both liquid and vapor phases is cooled, the liquid has a higher fraction of *A* and *B* than does the vapor.

With this background we can describe the operation of the plant and write the equations that govern it.

Unit 1 is a *mixer-heater*. The heating is required to get the mixture up to the operating point of the reactor into which it will go next. The mixing involves the input stream, which we know, and the material being returned, or *recycled*, from Unit 5. If we describe the lb/hr of *A* in stream 2 by S2A, the lb/hr of *B* in stream 2 by S2B, etc., we can write three equations that describe the output of Unit 1. For each component leaving the unit, we know that it is simply the sum of the two inputs. The feed stream is known, and the three components of stream 9 are three of the variables that we wish to determine. Thus we have our first three equations:

$$S2A = S9A + 40$$
$$S2B = S9B + 40$$
$$S2C = S9C + 20$$

Unit 2 is a *reactor*. Its function is to convert some of the entering *A* into *C* and some of the entering *B* into *C*. Numerically, it converts half of the entering *B* into *C*, and 35/90 of the entering *A* into *C*. In both cases, the material that is not converted into *C* simply leaves the unit

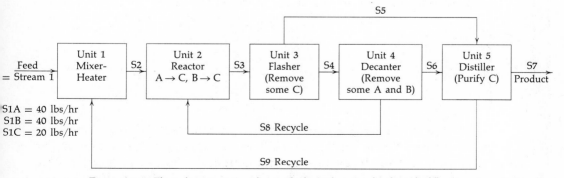

Figure 4.9. *Flow diagram of a chemical plant that can be described by a system of simultaneous equations* (*Case Study 7*).

unchanged. Since the input in this unit consists of the sum of streams 2 and 8, we can write the equations for stream 3 as follows:

$$S3A = 55/90(S2A + S8A)$$
$$S3B = 0.5(S2B + S8B)$$
$$S3C = 0.5(S2B + S8B) + 35/90(S2A + S8A) + S2C + S8C$$

Unit 3 is called a *flasher*. Heat is added, causing some of the mixture in the unit to be vaporized; the vapor will be relatively "rich" in C since its boiling point is lower than that of A or B. This C-rich portion is sent ahead to Unit 5. This time the numerical data is in the form of ratios, or splits, one for each component, of the concentrations of the three components in the two output streams:

$$S5A/S4A = 0.1$$
$$S5B/S4B = 1/6$$
$$S5C/S4C = 6/5$$

We know that the sum of streams 4 and 5 must be equal to stream 3, that is, $S3A = S4A + S5A$, and so forth. Combining this fact with the ratios given, we arrive at three equations for stream 4 and three for stream 5:

$$S4A = 10/11 \ S3A$$
$$S4B = 6/7 \ S3B$$
$$S4C = 5/11 \ S3C$$
$$S5A = 1/11 \ S3A$$
$$S5B = 1/7 \ S3B$$
$$S5C = 6/11 \ S3C$$

Unit 4 is called a *decanter*. "Decant" means "to pour off": the input mixture is cooled, leading to a liquid phase that has a high proportion of A and B. Some of this A- and B-rich liquid is sent back ("recycled") to Unit 2. The process in Unit 4 is thus somewhat similar to that in Unit 3, but with different splits:

$$S6A/S8A = 1.5$$
$$S6B/S8B = 2$$
$$S6C/S8C = 4$$

Combining these ratios with the fact that the sum of streams 6 and 8 is equal to stream 4, we arrive at six more equations:

$$S6A = 3/5 \ S4A$$
$$S6B = 2/3 \ S4B$$
$$S6C = 4/5 \ S4C$$
$$S8A = 2/5 \ S4A$$
$$S8B = 1/3 \ S4B$$
$$S8C = 1/5 \ S4C$$

Unit 5 is a *distiller*. For our purposes we can think of its operation as being similar to the flasher in Unit 3: A process of vaporization and condensation leads to an output that contains a higher proportion of C than its input does. This C-rich fraction, stream 7, is the product; the rest is recycled back to Unit 1. The splits are:

$$S7A/S9A = 1/6$$
$$S7B/S9B = 1/4$$
$$S7C/S9C = 9$$

Combining these ratios with the fact that $S7A + S9A = S5A + S6A$, and so forth, we arrive at a final six equations:

$$S7A = 1/7 \ (S5A + S6A)$$
$$S7B = 1/5 \ (S5B + S6B)$$
$$S7C = 9/10 \ (S5C + S6C)$$
$$S9A = 6/7 \ (S5A + S6A)$$
$$S9B = 4/5 \ (S5B + S6B)$$
$$S9C = 1/10 \ (S5C + S6C)$$

We have now arrived at 24 equations in 24 variables, one variable for each of the three components in each of the eight streams other than the input. We take it that the process has been in operation long enough to have reached *steady-state*, that is, the rate of flow of each component of each stream does not change with time. Our task is now to find the values of the variables by solving the system.

So far in this discussion we have used variable names that relate closely to the description of the process, to simplify the explanation. For computer solution we will use a routine that calls them $X(1)$ to $X(24)$, of course. If we wish, we can write a simple routine to accept the descriptive names of the variables and label the output accordingly. This has not been done in what follows, but something similar has been done in Case Study 8 at the end of this chapter.

To enter the coefficients into the machine, however, we must somehow associate them with the indexing system used by the program. This, too, could be done in terms of names like S2B and S7C, by writing an appropriate program to make the conversions, but it seemed more reasonable in this case to set up a matrix of coefficients in which the elements are numbered the same way the Gaussian elimination subroutine numbers them, and use those row and column numbers to identify the input. Figure 4.10 shows the matrix that we get when this is done, with blanks for zeros.

Because most of the elements in the matrix are zero, it makes sense to enter only the nonzero elements. Furthermore, because of the way the equations have been written, all the diagonal terms are 1.0, so the program may as well make those assignments as well.

The main program in Figure 4.11 does these operations in a straightforward way. The only feature that might not be familiar to some readers is the passing of the dimensions of the arrays to the subroutine in the CALL statement. This is permitted in order to make it possible to write subroutines that can be used with many different sizes of systems. Readers wishing to use this feature in their programs will do well to read the rules governing its use carefully, since not everything that one might think of doing is permissible.

The subroutine shown in Figure 4.12 follows the flow charts of Figures 4.5, 4.6, and 4.8 so closely that we hardly need describe it. The multiplier

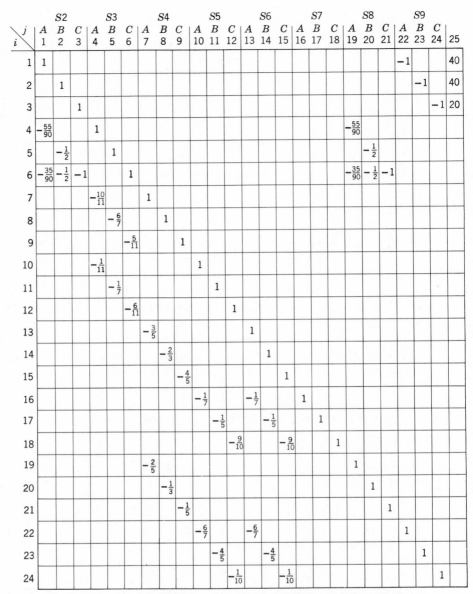

i \ j	S2 A 1	B 2	C 3	S3 A 4	B 5	C 6	S4 A 7	B 8	C 9	S5 A 10	B 11	C 12	S6 A 13	B 14	C 15	S7 A 16	B 17	C 18	S8 A 19	B 20	C 21	S9 A 22	B 23	C 24	25
1	1																					-1			40
2		1																					-1		40
3			1																					-1	20
4	$-\frac{55}{90}$			1															$-\frac{55}{90}$						
5		$-\frac12$			1															$-\frac12$					
6	$-\frac{35}{90}$	$-\frac12$	-1				1												$-\frac{35}{90}$	$-\frac12$	-1				
7				$-\frac{10}{11}$			1																		
8					$-\frac67$			1																	
9						$-\frac{5}{11}$			1																
10				$-\frac{1}{11}$						1															
11					$-\frac17$						1														
12						$-\frac{6}{11}$						1													
13							$-\frac35$						1												
14								$-\frac23$						1											
15									$-\frac45$						1										
16										$-\frac17$			$-\frac17$			1									
17											$-\frac15$			$-\frac15$			1								
18												$-\frac{9}{10}$			$-\frac{9}{10}$			1							
19							$-\frac25$												1						
20								$-\frac13$												1					
21									$-\frac15$												1				
22										$-\frac67$			$-\frac67$									1			
23											$-\frac45$			$-\frac45$									1		
24												$-\frac{1}{10}$			$-\frac{1}{10}$									1	

Figure 4.10. *The matrix of coefficients for the chemical plant of Case Study 7.*

has been called FACTOR instead of M, a trivial change to avoid having to declare M as a real variable. Both N and N + 1 are passed to the subroutine by the main program, which is required by the rules for handling of variable-dimension arrays; since both numbers are available and both are needed in the subroutine, we use them freely.

Figure 4.13 presents the output when the programs of Figure 4.11 and 4.12 were run with the data indicated in Figure 4.10. We see that the 100 lb/hr of input, consisting of 40 lb/hr of A, 40 lb/hr of B, and 20 lb/hr of C, has been converted into 100 lb/hr of output in stream 7 (which obviously must be true if the equations were correct), but the amounts of A, B, and C are now 5, 5, and 90, respectively. The results, which should be integer-valued in all cases if exact, are fully accurate enough for the purposes of this kind of design study, but nevertheless do contain errors resulting from roundoff. Bearing in mind that a real chemical plant would ordinarily involve a great many more processes and components, leading to systems of perhaps hundreds of equations in as many variables, we can readily imagine that roundoff would be a serious problem. In such a case the methods presented in the remainder of the chapter might well come into play, possibly in combination with Gaussian elimination.

As one indication of the kind of study that can be carried out once a program like this is available, we ask what the difference in operation of the system would be if one of the units were to operate differently. Suppose, for a concrete example, that a modification of the flasher is being contemplated that would make it cheaper to operate but reduce the ratio S5C/S4C from 1.2 to 1.0. What would this do to the purity of the output and to the amounts of material being recycled? Figure 4.14 shows the output for this case, which indicates that the product is barely different, although the amounts of C in the internal streams do change. Given adequate information about the increased operating costs of the other units caused by these changes, an engineer could decide whether the change was advantageous.

```
C CASE STUDY 7
C SOLUTION OF THE EQUATIONS DESCRIBING A HYPOTHETICAL CHEMICAL PLANT
C    BY THE METHOD OF GAUSSIAN ELIMINATION
C
C SUGGESTED BY PROF. ERNEST J. HENLEY, UNIVERSITY OF HOUSTON
C    REFERENCE: ERNEST J. HENLEY AND EDWARD M. ROSEN, 'MATERIAL
C    AND ENERGY BALANCE COMPUTATIONS,' (NEW YORK, WILEY, 1969)
C
C THIS MAIN PROGRAM CALLS FOR THE INPUT TO A GAUSSIAN ELIMINATION
C    SUBROUTINE, WHERE THE MAIN DIAGONAL ELEMENTS ARE ALL 1.0
C    AND MOST OFF-DIAGONAL ELEMENTS ARE ZERO, SO THAT ONLY
C    THE OFF-DIAGONAL NON-ZERO ELEMENTS NEED BE ENTERED.
C THE PROGRAM THEN CALLS THE SUBROUTINE AND PRINTS THE RESULTS.
C
        DIMENSION A(24, 25), S(24)
C ZERO THE ARRAY
        DO 78 I = 1, 24
        DO 78 J = 1, 25
     78 A(I, J) = 0.0
C SET DIAGONAL ELEMENTS TO 1.0
        DO 79 I = 1, 24
     79 A(I, I) = 1.0
C CALL FOR NON-ZERO ELEMENTS, WITH A ZERO 'ELEMENT' FOR SENTINEL
     80 READ (5, 81)  I, J, A(I, J)
        IF (A(I, J) .NE. 0.0) GO TO 80
     81 FORMAT (2I2, F10.0)
C CALL THE SUBROUTINE
      9 CALL GAUSS (A, S, 24, 25)
C PRINT THE RESULTS
        WRITE (6, 83) S
     83 FORMAT (8(1X/3F9.4))
        STOP
        END
```

Figure 4.11. *A program to read the coefficients of the matrix of Figure 4.10 that are nonzero and are off the main diagonal. It then calls the subroutine of Figure 4.12 to solve the system of equations by Gaussian elimination.*

```
C CASE STUDY 7
C THE METHOD OF GAUSSIAN ELIMINATION
C     FOR SOLVING SIMULTANEOUS LINEAR ALGEBRAIC EQUATIONS
C
C THE PROGRAM IS WRITTEN AS A SUBROUTINE TO PERMIT GREATER
C     FLEXIBILITY IN THE METHOD OF ENTERING THE COEFFICIENTS
C
C PARTIAL PIVOTAL CONDENSATION IS USED, THAT IS, A SEARCH IS
C     MADE IN EACH COLUMN FOR THE LARGEST ELEMENT BELOW THE
C     DIAGONAL, BUT OTHER COLUMNS ARE NOT SEARCHED
C
      SUBROUTINE GAUSS (A, X, N, NP1)
C THE SUBROUTINE ACCEPTS THE DIMENSIONS OF THE MATRIX AS VARIABLES
      DIMENSION A(N, NP1), X(N)
C BEGIN THE PARTIAL PIVOTAL CONDENSATION
C K NAMES THE PIVOTAL ROW
      NM1 = N - 1
      DO 600 K = 1, NM1
      KP1 = K + 1
      L = K
C FIND TERM IN COLUMN K, ON OR BELOW MAIN DIAGONAL, THAT IS LARGEST
C     IN ABSOLUTE VALUE.  AFTER THE SEARCH, L IS THE ROW NUMBER OF
C     THE LARGEST ELEMENT.
      DO 400 I = KP1, N
  400 IF (ABS(A(I, K)) .GT. ABS(A(L, K))) L = I
C CHECK WHETHER L = K, WHICH MEANS THAT THE LARGEST ELEMENT IN
C     COLUMN K WAS ALREADY THE DIAGONAL TERM, MAKING ROW INTERCHANGE
C     UNNECESSARY
      IF (L .EQ. K) GO TO 500
C INTERCHANGE ROWS L AND K, FROM DIAGONAL RIGHT
      DO 410 J = K, NP1
      TEMP = A(K, J)
      A(K, J) = A(L, J)
  410 A(L, J) = TEMP
C ELIMINATE ALL ELEMENTS IN COLUMN K BELOW MAIN DIAGONAL
C ELEMENTS 'ELIMINATED' ARE NOT ACTUALLY CHANGED - SEE TEXT
  500 DO 600 I = KP1, N
      FACTOR = A(I, K) / A(K, K)
      DO 600 J = KP1, NP1
  600 A(I, J) = A(I, J) - FACTOR * A(K, J)
C BACK SOLUTION
      X(N) = A(N, NP1) / A(N, N)
      I = NM1
  710 IP1 = I + 1
      SUM = 0.0
      DO 700 J = IP1, N
  700 SUM = SUM + A(I, J) * X(J)
      X(I) = (A(I, NP1) - SUM) / A(I, I)
      I = I - 1
      IF (I .GE. 1) GO TO 710
      RETURN
      END
```

Figure 4.12. *A subroutine to solve a system of simultaneous equations by Gaussian elimination. This subroutine is called by the main program of Figure 4.11 to solve the system of equations describing a hypothetical chemical plant.*

```
70.0003   60.0000   30.0000
55.0002   35.0000  110.0001
50.0002   30.0000   50.0000
 5.0000    5.0000   60.0000
30.0001   20.0000   40.0000
 4.9998    5.0000   90.0000
20.0001   10.0000   10.0000
30.0003   20.0000   10.0000
```

Figure 4.13. *The output of the programs of Figure 4.11 and 4.12, run with the data shown in Figure 4.10.*

```
70.0003   60.0000   30.0000
55.0002   35.0000  111.1112
50.0002   30.0000   55.5556
 5.0000    5.0000   55.5556
30.0001   20.0000   44.4445
 4.9998    5.0000   90.0000
20.0001   10.0000   11.1111
30.0003   20.0000   10.0000
```

Figure 4.14. *The output of the programs of Figures 4.11 and 4.12, run with the data of Figure 4.10 modified to represent a different operation of one of the chemical processes.*

4.8 Refinement of the Solution

Whether we interchange rows or not, roundoff errors do ordinarily have some effect on the results. We now turn to a method of refining the solution once it has been found. This technique will ordinarily reduce the roundoff errors in the solution and may permit a reasonable solution of some ill-conditioned systems.

Let $x_1^{(0)}$, $x_2^{(0)}$, ..., $x_n^{(0)}$ be an approximate solution of (4.13) found by Gaussian elimination or any other method. If we substitute this solution in the left-hand sides of (4.13), we get

$$\left. \begin{aligned} a_{11}x_1^{(0)} + a_{12}x_2^{(0)} + \cdots + a_{1n}x_n^{(0)} &= b_1^{(0)} \\ a_{21}x_1^{(0)} + a_{22}x_2^{(0)} + \cdots + a_{2n}x_n^{(0)} &= b_2^{(0)} \\ \cdots\cdots\cdots\cdots\cdots\cdots\cdots\cdots\cdots\cdots\cdots \\ a_{n1}x_1^{(0)} + a_{n2}x_2^{(0)} + \cdots + a_{nn}x_n^{(0)} &= b_n^{(0)} \end{aligned} \right\} \quad (4.22)$$

If the $b_i^{(0)}$ differ from the b_i by a great deal, the $x_i^{(0)}$ are not a good approximation to the solution of (4.13). On the other hand, even if all the $b_i^{(0)}$ and b_i are very close to one another, the $x_i^{(0)}$ may still not be a good approximation to the solution. [Recall (4.3) in Section 4.2.]

If we subtract each equation in (4.22) from the corresponding equation in (4.13) and let

$$\epsilon_i^{(0)} = x_i - x_i^{(0)} \qquad i = 1, \ldots, n \quad (4.23)$$
$$\beta_i^{(0)} = b_i - b_i^{(0)} \qquad i = 1, \ldots, n \quad (4.24)$$

then

$$\left. \begin{aligned} a_{11}\epsilon_1^{(0)} + a_{12}\epsilon_2^{(0)} + \cdots + a_{1n}\epsilon_n^{(0)} &= \beta_1^{(0)} \\ a_{21}\epsilon_1^{(0)} + a_{22}\epsilon_2^{(0)} + \cdots + a_{2n}\epsilon_n^{(0)} &= \beta_2^{(0)} \\ \cdots\cdots\cdots\cdots\cdots\cdots\cdots\cdots\cdots\cdots\cdots \\ a_{n1}\epsilon_1^{(0)} + a_{n2}\epsilon_2^{(0)} + \cdots + a_{nn}\epsilon_n^{(0)} &= \beta_n^{(0)} \end{aligned} \right\} \quad (4.25)$$

The $\beta_i^{(0)}$ are readily calculated and the $\epsilon_i^{(0)}$ may be calculated from (4.25) by Gaussian elimination. A new approximation to the solution of (4.13) is then

$$x_i^{(1)} = x_i^{(0)} + \epsilon_i^{(0)} \qquad i = 1, \ldots, n$$

Again the $x_i^{(1)}$ may be substituted into the left-hand sides of (4.13) and the resulting right-hand sides called $b_i^{(1)}$. A new correction to the x_i is then obtained by solving

$$
\left.
\begin{aligned}
a_{11}\epsilon_1^{(1)} + a_{12}\epsilon_2^{(1)} + \cdots + a_{1n}\epsilon_n^{(1)} &= \beta_1^{(1)} \\
a_{21}\epsilon_1^{(1)} + a_{22}\epsilon_2^{(1)} + \cdots + a_{2n}\epsilon_n^{(1)} &= \beta_2^{(1)} \\
\cdots\cdots\cdots\cdots\cdots\cdots\cdots\cdots\cdots \\
a_{n1}\epsilon_1^{(1)} + a_{n2}\epsilon_2^{(1)} + \cdots + a_{nn}\epsilon_n^{(1)} &= \beta_n^{(1)}
\end{aligned}
\right\}
\qquad (4.26)
$$

where

$$
\beta_i^{(1)} = b_i - b_i^{(1)}, \qquad i = 1, \ldots, n
$$

The new approximation is given by

$$
x_i^{(2)} = x_i^{(1)} + \epsilon_i^{(1)} \qquad i = 1, \ldots, n
$$

This process can, of course, be continued until all the ϵ_i are small. It is important that the iterations not be stopped simply because the β_i are small: We again point to the example in (4.3) to emphasize that small β_i do not necessarily imply an accurate solution.

As an example, consider the two equations (4.21) solved without interchange. The solution obtained was

$$
x_1^{(0)} = 9.873 \cdot 10^{-1}
$$
$$
x_2^{(0)} = 9.998 \cdot 10^{-1}
$$

Substituting these values in (4.21) and using floating point calculations with four-digit mantissas, we get

$$
\begin{aligned}
b_1^{(0)} &= (3.241 \cdot 10^0)(9.873 \cdot 10^{-1}) + (1.600 \cdot 10^2)(0.998 \cdot 10^{-1}) \\
&= 1.632 \cdot 10^2 \\
b_2^{(0)} &= (1.020 \cdot 10^4)(9.873 \cdot 10^{-1}) + (1.540 \cdot 10^3)(9.998 \cdot 10^{-1}) \\
&= 1.161 \cdot 10^4
\end{aligned}
$$

So

$$
\begin{aligned}
\beta_1^{(0)} &= b_1 - b_1^{(0)} = 0 \\
\beta_2^{(0)} &= b_2 - b_2^{(0)} = 1.300 \cdot 10^2
\end{aligned}
$$

We now solve (4.21) with the right-hand sides given by $\beta_1^{(0)}$ and $\beta_2^{(0)}$, that is, we solve

$$
3.241 \cdot 10^0 \epsilon_1^{(0)} + 1.600 \cdot 10^2 \epsilon_2^{(0)} = 0
$$
$$
1.020 \cdot 10^4 \epsilon_1^{(0)} + 1.540 \cdot 10^3 \epsilon_2^{(0)} = 1.300 \cdot 10^2
$$

Again by not using row interchange, the solution is

$$
\epsilon_1^{(1)} = 1.284 \cdot 10^{-2}
$$
$$
\epsilon_2^{(1)} = -2.600 \cdot 10^{-4}
$$

so the new approximation is

$$
x_1^{(1)} = x_1^{(0)} + \epsilon_1^{(0)} = 1.000 \cdot 10^0
$$
$$
x_2^{(1)} = x_2^{(0)} + \epsilon_2^{(0)} = 9.995 \cdot 10^{-1}
$$

Substituting these in (4.21), we find

$$\beta_1^{(1)} = b_1 - b_1^{(1)} = 1.000 \cdot 10^{-1}$$
$$\beta_2^{(1)} = b_2 - b_2^{(1)} = 0$$

so

$$\epsilon_1^{(1)} = -9.256 \cdot 10^{-5}$$
$$\epsilon_2^{(1)} = 6.268 \cdot 10^{-4}$$

The next approximation is

$$x_1^{(2)} = x_1^{(1)} + \epsilon_1^{(1)} = 1.000 \cdot 10^0$$
$$x_2^{(2)} = x_2^{(1)} + \epsilon_2^{(1)} = 1.000 \cdot 10^0$$

In three iterations, therefore, without row interchanges, a solution has been found that is accurate to four significant figures. (Recall that with row interchanges only one iteration was required.)

The important point, however, is that the solution was improved even though the method used produced large roundoff error. Naturally, in practice we *do* use row interchanges. The real interest in the technique of refining a solution lies in its application to a solution obtained *with* row interchanges that nevertheless contains accumulated roundoff error.

**4.9
Effect of
Uncertainty
in the Coef-
ficients:
Attainable
Accuracy**

We now ask ourselves this question: If the a_{ij} and/or the b_i are the results of an experiment or are computed values, what effect will errors in these numbers have on the solution x_i?

To answer this important question, we proceed as we did in Section 1.11. Let the true coefficients be $a_{ij} + \alpha_{ij}$ and $b_i + \beta_i$, where α_{ij} and β_i are small compared with a_{ij} and b_i; that is to say, we really want the solution of

$$\left.\begin{aligned}
(a_{11} + \alpha_{11})x_1 + (a_{12} + \alpha_{12})x_2 + \cdots + (a_{1n} + \alpha_{1n})x_n &= b_1 + \beta_1 \\
\cdots\cdots\cdots\cdots\cdots\cdots\cdots\cdots\cdots\cdots\cdots\cdots\cdots\cdots\cdots\cdots \\
(a_{i1} + \alpha_{i1})x_1 + (a_{i2} + \alpha_{i2})x_2 + \cdots + (a_{in} + \alpha_{in})x_n &= b_i + \beta_i \\
\cdots\cdots\cdots\cdots\cdots\cdots\cdots\cdots\cdots\cdots\cdots\cdots\cdots\cdots\cdots\cdots \\
(a_{n1} + \alpha_{n1})x_1 + (a_{n2} + \alpha_{n2})x_2 + \cdots + (a_{nn} + \alpha_{nn})x_n &= b_n + \beta_n
\end{aligned}\right\} \quad (4.27)$$

Of course, if we knew the values of the α_{ij} and β_i, we would simply solve those equations instead of the original ones. Usually, all we know is some bound on the α_{ij} and β_i. For example, if the a_{ij} and b_i are experimental results given to d decimal places, then

$$|\alpha_{ij}| \le \tfrac{1}{2} \cdot 10^{-d}$$
$$|\beta_i| \le \tfrac{1}{2} \cdot 10^{-d}$$

We let $x_1, x_2, \ldots, x_n$ be the solution of the original (4.13) and let

$$x_i + \delta_i$$

be the solution of (4.27). We will assume that

$$|\delta_i| \ll |x_i| \qquad i = 1, \ldots, n$$

By substituting $x_i + \delta_i$ into (4.27) and using (4.13), it follows that

$$(a_{11}\delta_1 + \cdots + a_{1n}\delta_n) + (\alpha_{11}x_1 + \cdots + \alpha_{1n}x_n) = \beta_1$$

$$\cdots\cdots\cdots\cdots\cdots\cdots\cdots\cdots\cdots\cdots\cdots\cdots\cdots\cdots\cdots\cdots\cdots$$

$$(a_{i1}\delta_1 + \cdots + a_{in}\delta_n) + (\alpha_{i1}x_1 + \cdots + \alpha_{in}x_n) = \beta_i$$

$$\cdots\cdots\cdots\cdots\cdots\cdots\cdots\cdots\cdots\cdots\cdots\cdots\cdots\cdots\cdots\cdots\cdots$$

$$(a_{n1}\delta_1 + \cdots + a_{nn}\delta_n) + (\alpha_{n1}x_1 + \cdots + \alpha_{nn}x_n) = \beta_n$$

where terms involving the products of the α_{ij} and δ_i are neglected. Thus the δ_i are the solution of

$$\left.\begin{aligned}
&a_{11}\delta_1 + \cdots + a_{ij}\delta_j + \cdots + a_{1n}\delta_n = \beta_1 - (\alpha_{11}x_1 + \cdots + \alpha_{1n}x_n) \\
&\cdots\cdots\cdots\cdots\cdots\cdots\cdots\cdots\cdots\cdots\cdots\cdots\cdots\cdots\cdots \\
&a_{i1}\delta_1 + \cdots + a_{ij}\delta_j + \cdots + a_{in}\delta_n = \beta_i - (\alpha_{i1}x_1 + \cdots + \alpha_{in}x_n) \\
&\cdots\cdots\cdots\cdots\cdots\cdots\cdots\cdots\cdots\cdots\cdots\cdots\cdots\cdots\cdots \\
&a_{n1}\delta_1 + \cdots + a_{nj}\delta_j + \cdots + a_{nn}\delta_n = \beta_n - (\alpha_{n1}x_1 + \cdots + \alpha_{nn}x_n)
\end{aligned}\right\} \quad (4.28)$$

We now consider separately four possible cases:

1. The a_{ij} are precise but the b_i are given to d decimal places; that is,

$$\alpha_{ij} = 0$$
$$|\beta_i| \leq \tfrac{1}{2} \cdot 10^{-d}$$

Then it follows from (4.28) that

$$\left.\begin{aligned}
&|a_{11}\delta_1 + \cdots + a_{1j}\delta_j + \cdots + a_{1n}\delta_n| \leq \tfrac{1}{2} \cdot 10^{-d} \\
&\cdots\cdots\cdots\cdots\cdots\cdots\cdots\cdots\cdots\cdots\cdots\cdots\cdots\cdots\cdots \\
&|a_{i1}\delta_1 + \cdots + a_{ij}\delta_j + \cdots + a_{in}\delta_n| \leq \tfrac{1}{2} \cdot 10^{-d} \\
&\cdots\cdots\cdots\cdots\cdots\cdots\cdots\cdots\cdots\cdots\cdots\cdots\cdots\cdots\cdots \\
&|a_{n1}\delta_1 + \cdots + a_{nj}\delta_j + \cdots + a_{nn}\delta_n| \leq \tfrac{1}{2} \cdot 10^{-d}
\end{aligned}\right\} \quad (4.29)$$

These inequalities can be "solved" (we shall see how to do this shortly) at the same time as the original (4.13) are solved, leading directly to an estimate of the effect of the uncertainty in the right-hand sides on the solution. Notice first that, if $\Delta_i(i = 1, \ldots, n)$ is called the solution when all of the right-hand sides of (4.29) are $+1$, then

$$\delta_i = (\tfrac{1}{2} \cdot 10^{-d})\Delta_i \qquad i = 1, \ldots, n \tag{4.30}$$

In solving the original system we carry along an extra column initially set with all elements equal to $+1$. Thus we augment the matrix A once more so that it now is

$$A^{**} = \begin{pmatrix}
a_{11} & a_{12} & \cdots & a_{1n} & b_1 & +1 \\
a_{21} & a_{22} & \cdots & a_{2n} & b_2 & +1 \\
\vdots & & & & & \\
a_{i1} & a_{i2} & \cdots & a_{in} & b_i & +1 \\
\vdots & & & & & \\
a_{n1} & a_{n2} & \cdots & a_{nn} & b_n & +1
\end{pmatrix} \tag{4.31}$$

This is an $n \times (n + 2)$ matrix, that is, n rows and $n + 2$ columns. We refer to A^{**} as a doubly augmented matrix. We once again let

$$a_{i,n+1} = b_i \qquad i = 1, \ldots, n \tag{4.32}$$

and we also let

$$a_{i,n+2} = +1 \qquad i = 1, \ldots, n \tag{4.33}$$

We proceed as we did in Gaussian elimination except that the $(n + 2)$ column is treated in a different way. Since (4.29) are inequalities, we never subtract when operating on the $(n + 2)$nd column. Rather we add and, moreover, add absolute values.

An example is in order. Consider the equations given in (4.12). Suppose the right-hand sides are given to two decimal places; that is,

$$|\beta_i| \leq \tfrac{1}{2} \cdot 10^{-2} \tag{4.34}$$

The doubly augmented matrix is

$$A^{**} = \begin{pmatrix} 1 & 1 & 1 & 4 & 1 \\ 2 & 3 & 1 & 9 & 1 \\ 1 & -1 & -1 & -2 & 1 \end{pmatrix}$$

The first multiplier is 2 so we multiply the first row by 2 producing

$$(2, 2, 2, 8, 2)$$

We then subtract this from the second row of A^{**} with one exception: The last entry (5th column) is added. Thus we obtain

$$A^{**} = \begin{pmatrix} 1 & 1 & 1 & 4 & 1 \\ 0 & 1 & -1 & 1 & 3 \\ 1 & -1 & -1 & -2 & 1 \end{pmatrix}$$

Similarly we multiply the first row by $+1$ and subtract the result from the third row (in the last column we add). This produces

$$A^{**} = \begin{pmatrix} 1 & 1 & 1 & 4 & 1 \\ 0 & 1 & -1 & 1 & 3 \\ 0 & -2 & -2 & -6 & 2 \end{pmatrix}$$

The final triangular matrix is

$$A^{**} = \begin{pmatrix} 1 & 1 & 1 & 4 & 1 \\ 0 & 1 & -1 & 1 & 3 \\ 0 & 0 & -4 & -4 & 8 \end{pmatrix}$$

In back-substitution we continue to add absolute values in the last column. We multiply the last row by -4 to get

$$(0, 0, 1, 1, 2)$$

Notice that the last entry is $+2$, not $8/-4 = -2$. Multiply this row by

-1 and subtract the result from row 2:

$$A^{**} = \begin{pmatrix} 1 & 1 & 1 & 4 & 1 \\ 0 & 1 & 0 & 2 & 5 \\ 0 & 0 & 1 & 1 & 2 \end{pmatrix}$$

Again we add in the last column.
Continuing the back-substitution:

$$A^{**} = \begin{pmatrix} 1 & 0 & 0 & 1 & 8 \\ 0 & 1 & 0 & 2 & 5 \\ 0 & 0 & 1 & 1 & 2 \end{pmatrix}$$

The next-to-last column contains the solution

$$x = 1; \; y = 2; \; z = 1$$

The last column contains Δ_i

$$\Delta_x = 8; \; \Delta_y = 5; \; \Delta_z = 2 \tag{4.35}$$

Using (4.30) and (4.34),

$$|\delta_x| \leq 4 \cdot 10^{-2}$$
$$|\delta_y| \leq 2.5 \cdot 10^{-2}$$
$$|\delta_z| \leq 1 \cdot 10^{-2}$$

or

$$x = 1 \pm .04$$
$$y = 2 \pm .025$$
$$z = 1 \pm .01$$

We remind the reader that not all of the matrix operations need be carried out, as we pointed out in Section 4.4. In the triangularization the zeroes below the diagonal need not be computed. In backsubstitution the ones along the diagonal and the zeroes above the diagonal are not computed.

We turn now to a second case.

2. The b_i are precise, but the a_{ij} are given only to d decimal places; that is,

$$|\alpha_{ij}| \leq \tfrac{1}{2} \cdot 10^{-d}$$
$$\beta_i = 0$$

Then, from (4.28) and the triangle inequality,

$$|a_{11}\delta_1 + \cdots + a_{1j}\delta_j + \cdots + a_{1n}\delta_n| \leq \tfrac{1}{2} \cdot 10^{-d}(|x_1| + \cdots + |x_n|)$$

$$\cdots \cdots \cdots \cdots \cdots \cdots \cdots \cdots \cdots \cdots \cdots \cdots \cdots \cdots \cdots$$

$$|a_{i1}\delta_1 + \cdots + a_{ij}\delta_j + \cdots + a_{in}\delta_n| \leq \tfrac{1}{2} \cdot 10^{-d}(|x_1| + \cdots + |x_n|)$$

$$\cdots \cdots \cdots \cdots \cdots \cdots \cdots \cdots \cdots \cdots \cdots \cdots \cdots \cdots \cdots$$

$$|a_{n1}\delta_1 + \cdots + a_{nj}\delta_j + \cdots + a_{nn}\delta_n| \leq \tfrac{1}{2} \cdot 10^{-d}(|x_1| + \cdots + |x_n|)$$

Again, if Δ_i is the solution when the right-hand sides are $+1$, then

$$\delta_i = \tfrac{1}{2} \cdot 10^{-d}(|x_1| + \cdots + |x_n|)\Delta_i$$

As an example, consider (4.12) again and suppose that the coefficients on the left are given to two decimal places. Then, since

$$|x| + |y| + |z| = 4$$

it follows from (4.35) that

$$|\delta_x| \le 1.6 \cdot 10^{-1}$$
$$|\delta_y| \le 1 \cdot 10^{-1}$$
$$|\delta_z| \le 4 \cdot 10^{-2}$$

3. Suppose now that both the a_{ij} and the b_i are given to d decimal places. A similar argument produces the result that

$$\delta_i = \tfrac{1}{2} \cdot 10^{-d}(1 + |x_1| + \cdots + |x_n|)\Delta_i$$

In the example of (4.12), if all coefficients and right-hand sides are given to two decimal places,

$$|\delta_x| \le 2 \cdot 10^{-1}$$
$$|\delta_y| \le 1.25 \cdot 10^{-1}$$
$$|\delta_z| \le 0.5 \cdot 10^{-1}$$

4. The final case we shall consider is the one in which the a_{ij} and the b_i are both calculated results given to t significant figures. Then

$$\left|\frac{\alpha_{ij}}{a_{ij}}\right| \le 5 \cdot 10^{-t}$$

and

$$\left|\frac{\beta_i}{b_i}\right| \le 5 \cdot 10^{-t}$$

The analysis leads to

$$\delta_i = k \cdot \Delta_i \cdot 5 \cdot 10^{-t}$$

where

$$k = \max \left(|b_i| + |a_{i1}x_1| + |a_{i2}x_2| + \cdots + |a_{in}x_n|\right)$$

and the maximum is taken over all i.

Let us turn again to our example (4.12), and suppose that the coefficients and right-hand sides are given to four significant digits; that is, $t = 4$. Then

$$|b_1| + |a_{11}x| + |a_{12}y| + |a_{13}z| = 4 + 1 + 2 + 1 = 8$$
$$|b_2| + |a_{21}x| + |a_{22}y| + |a_{23}z| = 9 + 2 + 6 + 1 = 18$$
$$|b_3| + |a_{31}x| + |a_{32}y| + |a_{33}z| = 2 + 1 + 2 + 1 = 6$$

Thus $k = 18$, so that

$$\delta_x \le 7.2 \cdot 10^{-2}$$
$$\delta_y \le 4.5 \cdot 10^{-2}$$
$$\delta_z \le 1.8 \cdot 10^{-2}$$

All of these bounds are in general extremely conservative; that is, the actual δ_i are usually much smaller than predicted by these bounds. Better bounds—in the sense that they are usually smaller—can be obtained, but finding them involves matrix inversion techniques that are beyond the scope of this book.[3]

The reader should consider what changes he would make in the flow charts of Figures 4.5 and 4.6 in order to compute error estimates for any or all of the four cases discussed in this section.

**4.10
Iterative
Methods of
Solution**

In Section 4.3 we discussed Gaussian elimination, a finite method of solving a system of simultaneous linear algebraic equations. Then, in Section 4.8 we found how to improve the solution by repeatedly using Gaussian elimination. This method of improvement was actually an iterative technique. We saw, in examples, the common contradictions between theory and practice: Because of roundoff, the "finite" and "exact" method actually produces a solution that can contain serious errors; the solution can then be significantly improved by an iterative method.

We shall now discuss another and more common iterative technique. It is marked by its simplicity and the ease with which it may be programmed for a computer. Like the iterative techniques discussed in Chapter 1, the roundoff error is small, but the method converges (produces a solution) only under certain conditions that we shall develop.

Consider now three equations in three unknowns (4.5), (4.6), and (4.7). We suppose that $a_{11} \neq 0$, $a_{22} \neq 0$, and $a_{33} \neq 0$ and rewrite the equations as

$$x_1 = \frac{1}{a_{11}}(b_1 - a_{12}x_2 - a_{13}x_3) \tag{4.36}$$

$$x_2 = \frac{1}{a_{22}}(b_2 - a_{21}x_1 - a_{23}x_3) \tag{4.37}$$

$$x_3 = \frac{1}{a_{33}}(b_3 - a_{31}x_1 - a_{32}x_2) \tag{4.38}$$

We now take any first approximation to the solution; call it $x_1^{(0)}$, $x_2^{(0)}$, and $x_3^{(0)}$. We solve (4.36) for a new approximation to x_1:

$$x_1^{(1)} = \frac{1}{a_{11}}(b_1 - a_{12}x_2^{(0)} - a_{13}x_3^{(0)})$$

Using the new value of x_1, together with $x_3^{(0)}$, we solve (4.37) for x_2:

$$x_2^{(1)} = \frac{1}{a_{22}}(b_2 - a_{21}x_1^{(1)} - a_{23}x_3^{(0)})$$

Finally we use the newly computed values of x_1 and x_2 in (4.34) to find a new value of x_3:

$$x_3^{(1)} = \frac{1}{a_{33}}(b_2 - a_{31}x_1^{(1)} - a_{32}x_2^{(1)})$$

This completes one iteration. We can start all over by replacing $x_1^{(0)}$, $x_2^{(0)}$, and $x_3^{(0)}$ by $x_1^{(1)}$, $x_2^{(1)}$, and $x_3^{(1)}$ and find another approximation. In general,

---

[3]See, for instance, F. B. Hildebrand, *Introduction to Numerical Analysis*, McGraw-Hill, 1956, pp. 436–437.

the kth approximation is given by

$$x_1^{(k)} = \frac{1}{a_{11}}(b_1 - a_{12}x_2^{(k-1)} - a_{13}x_3^{(k-1)})$$

$$x_2^{(k)} = \frac{1}{a_{22}}(b_2 - a_{21}x_1^{(k)} - a_{23}x_3^{(k-1)}) \qquad (4.39)$$

$$x_3^{(k)} = \frac{1}{a_{33}}(b_3 - a_{31}x_1^{(k)} - a_{32}x_2^{(k)})$$

Notice that the most recently computed values for each x_i are always used and that we cannot calculate $x_2^{(k)}$ until $x_1^{(k)}$ has been computed. Similarly, the calculation of $x_3^{(k)}$ requires the prior calculation of $x_1^{(k)}$ and $x_2^{(k)}$.

The technique we have illustrated here is known as the *Gauss-Seidel iteration method*. It is extremely well adapted for use on a digital computer. Before discussing the general case of n equations in n unknowns and investigating the convergence properties, we shall consider a simple numerical example.

$$4x_1 - x_2 + x_3 = 4$$
$$x_1 + 6x_2 + 2x_3 = 9$$
$$-x_1 - 2x_2 + 5x_3 = 2$$

One can easily verify that $x_1 = x_2 = x_3 = 1$ is the exact solution. Let $x_1^{(0)} = x_2^{(0)} = x_3^{(0)} = 0$, which is a usual first approximation. Then, since

$$x_1 = \tfrac{1}{4}(4 + x_2 - x_3)$$
$$x_2 = \tfrac{1}{6}(9 - x_1 - 2x_3)$$
$$x_3 = \tfrac{1}{5}(2 + x_1 + 2x_2)$$

it follows that

$$x_1^{(1)} = \tfrac{1}{4}(4 + 0 + 0) = 1$$
$$x_2^{(1)} = \tfrac{1}{6}(9 - 1 - 0) = \tfrac{4}{3}$$
$$x_3^{(1)} = \tfrac{1}{5}(2 + 1 + \tfrac{8}{3}) = \tfrac{17}{15}$$

The successive solutions, using four-place floating point arithmetic, are shown in Table 4.1.

It is interesting to note that eight-place floating point arithmetic still requires five iterations to obtain four significant figures. After another four iterations, however, the eight-place arithmetic reaches a solution accurate to eight places.

Consider now n equations in n unknowns (4.13). Again we assume that

Table 4.1

Iteration	x_1	x_2	x_3
0	0	0	0
1	$0.1000 \cdot 10^1$	$0.1333 \cdot 10^1$	$0.1133 \cdot 10^1$
2	$0.1050 \cdot 10^1$	$0.9473 \cdot 10^0$	$0.9889 \cdot 10^0$
3	$0.9896 \cdot 10^0$	$0.1005 \cdot 10^1$	$0.9999 \cdot 10^0$
4	$0.1001 \cdot 10^1$	$0.9999 \cdot 10^0$	$0.1000 \cdot 10^1$
5	$0.1000 \cdot 10^1$	$0.1000 \cdot 10^1$	$0.1000 \cdot 10^1$

$a_{ii} \neq 0$ for all i. The kth approximation to x_i is

$$x_i^{(k)} = \frac{1}{a_{ii}}[b_i - a_{i1}x_1^{(k)} - \cdots - a_{i,i-1}x_{i-1}^{(k)} - a_{i,i+1}x_{i+1}^{(k-1)} - \cdots - a_{in}x_n^{(k-1)}]$$

$$i = 1, \ldots, n$$

The process is iterated until all $x_i^{(k)}$ are sufficiently close to $x_i^{(k-1)}$. A typical way of determining closeness is to let

$$M^{(k)} = \max |x_i^{(k)} - x_i^{(k-1)}|$$

where the maximum is taken over all i. Then if

$$M^{(k)} < \epsilon$$

where ϵ is some small positive number, the iteration process is stopped. Alternatively, the relative difference may be tested, using the test

$$M^{(k)} = \max \left| \frac{x_i^{(k)} - x_i^{(k-1)}}{x_i^{(k)}} \right|$$

A flow chart describing the Gauss-Seidel iteration method is given in Figure 4.15. It is not nearly so complicated as it might appear at first glance. It should be remembered that Gaussian elimination was diagrammed in three separate places (Figures 4.5, 4.6, and 4.8).

The boxes at the left are used to read the data and initialize the starting approximations to zero and start the counter of the number of iterations, ITER, at 1. They are never repeated. At the end of this set is a connector, indicating that the diagram continues at the correspondingly numbered connector at the top of the middle group.

The variable BIG is used to determine the maximum value of $|x_i^{(k)} - x_i^{(k-1)}|$. It is initially set to zero; then every difference is tested against it and any that is larger is placed in it. After computing all the new x_i, BIG will contain the largest difference.

Now comes the part that develops the sum of all terms in one row of the system, excluding the diagonal term. Basically, we shall compute and sum all terms in the row before the diagonal and then add in all terms after the diagonal. Separate tests are necessary to handle the fact that there is no term before the diagonal in the first equation and no term after it in the last. The logic is not complex otherwise.

The group of boxes at the right begins by completing the computation of $x_i^{(k)}$, checks the maximum difference, and then stores the new $x_i^{(k)}$. If this is not the last equation, we increment i and return to compute the next $x_i^{(k)}$. If it is the last, we check $M_i^{(k)}$ (=BIG) against ϵ and print the results if the process has converged. If it has not, we do something that is not part of the numerical analysis but rather is a matter of good programming practice. It is not wise to assume that a process that *should* converge always *will*. Many strange things, from programming errors to bad data, can invalidate such an assumption. We therefore have arranged to read a fixed point number MAX that specifies the maximum number of iterations to be permitted. This number would ordinarily be chosen to be somewhat larger than the analyst expects would ever be necessary. (A typical value would be 50 iterations for 50 equations.) Then, if for

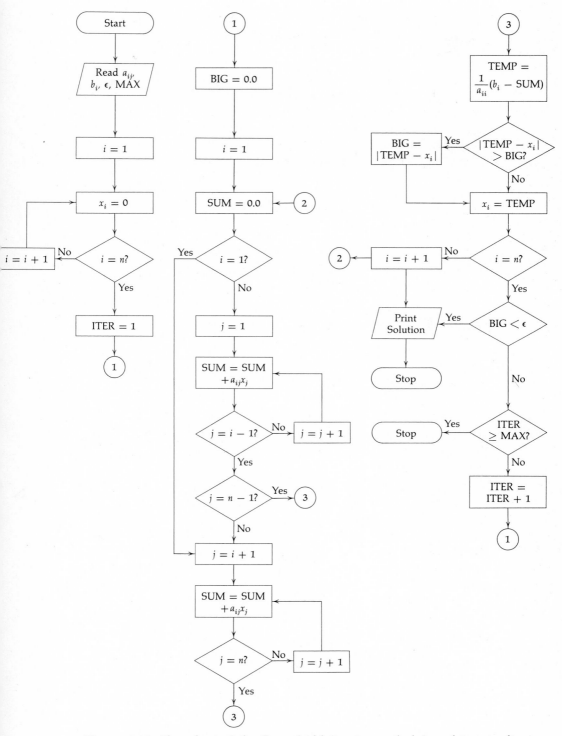

Figure 4.15. *Flow chart of the Gauss-Seidel iteration method for solving simultaneous equations.*

any reason the process does not converge, the computer will not run indefinitely. Such a counter is a good idea in the program for any iterative method.

We have shown the data being read and the results printed; in other words, this block diagram assumes that a program to do all this would operate by itself. In actual practice often the data would have been generated by a preceding program and/or utilized by a following one. We shall see these ideas applied in Case Study 8 at the end of the chapter.

We now turn to the question of the convergence of the method. Before stating the criteria for the general case of n equations, we shall investigate a simpler case in considerable detail.

Let $n = 2$. Then

$$a_{11}x + a_{12}y = b_1 \tag{4.40}$$
$$a_{21}x + a_{22}y = b_2 \tag{4.41}$$

so that

$$x^{(k)} = \frac{1}{a_{11}}[b_1 - a_{12}y^{(k-1)}] \tag{4.42}$$

$$y^{(k)} = \frac{1}{a_{22}}[b_2 - a_{21}x^{(k)}] \tag{4.43}$$

If we define

$$\Delta x^{(k)} = x - x^{(k)}$$
$$\Delta y^{(k)} = y - y^{(k)}$$

then from (4.40) and (4.42)

$$\Delta x^{(k)} = -\frac{a_{12}}{a_{11}}\Delta y^{(k-1)}$$

and from (4.41) and (4.43)

$$\Delta y^{(k)} = -\frac{a_{21}}{a_{22}}\Delta x^{(k)}$$

Combining these last two equations

$$\Delta x^{(k)} = \frac{a_{12}a_{21}}{a_{11}a_{22}}\Delta x^{(k-1)}$$

Similarly,

$$\Delta x^{(k-1)} = \frac{a_{12}a_{21}}{a_{11}a_{22}}\Delta x^{(k-2)}$$

so

$$\Delta x^{(k)} = \left(\frac{a_{12}a_{21}}{a_{11}a_{22}}\right)^2\Delta x^{(k-2)}$$

Proceeding in this way

$$\Delta x^{(k)} = \left(\frac{a_{12}a_{21}}{a_{11}a_{22}}\right)^k\Delta x^{(0)}$$

Similarly,

$$\Delta y^{(k)} = \left(\frac{a_{12}a_{21}}{a_{11}a_{22}}\right)^k\Delta y^{(0)}$$

Thus, if

$$\left|\frac{a_{12}a_{21}}{a_{11}a_{22}}\right| < 1 \qquad (4.44)$$

the process converges to a solution of (4.40) and (4.41).

The observant reader will see the analogy between this argument and the one used in discussing the convergence of the method of successive approximations in Section 1.4.

We can satisfy (4.44) if

$$\left.\begin{array}{l} |a_{11}| > |a_{12}| \\ |a_{22}| \geq |a_{21}| \end{array}\right\} \qquad (4.45)$$

or if

$$\left.\begin{array}{l} |a_{11}| \geq |a_{12}| \\ |a_{22}| > |a_{21}| \end{array}\right\} \qquad (4.46)$$

This says that the diagonal terms a_{11} and a_{22} must be *dominant*; that is, they must be at least as large as the off-diagonal terms and actually larger in at least one case.

Consider a simple example

$$2x + y = 2$$
$$x - 2y = -2$$

The exact solution is $x = \frac{2}{5}$, $y = \frac{6}{5}$. The results of the iterations are

Iteration	x	y
0	0	0
1	1	3/2
2	1/4	9/8
3	7/16	39/32

A geometrical interpretation of the process will be instructive, as shown in Figure 4.16. We start at the origin (0,0). Since y is kept fixed in solving for x, we move along a horizontal line until we reach the line represented by the first equation ($2x + y = 2$). Then, keeping x fixed, we move along a vertical line until we reach the line represented by the second equation ($x - 2y = -2$). In Figure 4.16 we trace the path OAB. This completes one iteration.

We continue horizontally and vertically as shown by the arrows. Notice that the process is converging to a solution. Notice also the similarity between this situation and that described by Figure 1.14 in Chapter 1.

Let us now see what happens if we reverse the order of the equations, so that

$$x^{(k)} = -2 + 2y^{(k-1)}$$
$$y^{(k)} = 2 - 2x^{(k)}$$

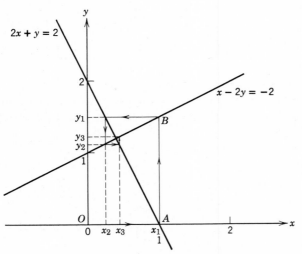

$2x + y = 2$

$x - 2y = -2$

y_1

B

y_3

y_2

O

x_2 x_3

x_1

A

2

Figure 4.16. *Geometrical representation of the method of Gauss-Seidel iteration in a convergent case.*

The results are

Iteration	x	y
0	0	0
1	−2	6
2	10	−18
3	−38	78

The geometric interpretation is shown in Figure 4.17. Again, note the similarity to Figure 1.16. The difficulty is that the slope of the first equation is smaller than 1. Thus Δx tends to be large. Similarly, the large slope of the second line tends to make Δy large. In short, the process diverges.

Obviously, then, for the process to converge, the first equation should have a slope greater than 1 and the second equation should have a slope less than 1. That is precisely what (4.45) and (4.46) tell us.

Remember, however, that the actual condition we needed to satisfy was (4.44), which is not so rigid as either (4.45) or (4.46). We might ask this question: Is it possible for the first equation to have a slope less than 1 and for the second equation to have such a small slope that it nevertheless forces convergence? Or, in other words, even though Δx may be large, if Δy is small enough can it overcome the effect of the large Δx? The answer is yes.

Consider the following example:

$$x + 2y = 3$$
$$x - 4y = -3$$

The slope of both equations is less than 1. Thus

$$|a_{11}| < |a_{12}|$$

188   Simultaneous Linear Algebraic Equations

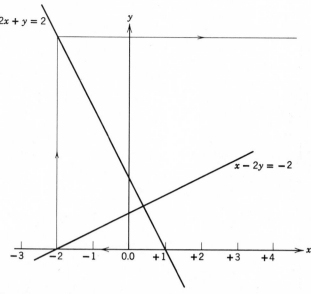

2x + y = 2

x − 2y = −2

Figure 4.17. *Geometrical representation of the method of Gauss-Seidel iteration in a divergent case.*

violating both (4.45) and (4.46). Notice, however, that (4.44) is satisfied. The geometric picture is shown in Figure 4.18. The numerical results are

Iteration	x	y
0	0	0
1	3	3/2
2	0	3/4
3	3/2	9/8
4	3/4	15/16

The solution is $x = y = 1$.

Thus the conditions (4.45) or (4.46) are *sufficient* conditions for convergence, but they are not *necessary;* that is to say, if either of them is satisfied, convergence is guaranteed, but there are systems that violate them that nevertheless converge.

We have seen an example in which the slope of the first line is less than -1 and the slope of the second line is positive but less than $+1$:

$$s_1 < -1$$
$$0 < s_2 < +1$$

This produced convergence of an oscillating nature, as we saw in Figure 4.16.

We have also seen an example in which

$$0 < s_1 < 1$$
$$s_2 < -1$$

This produced divergence of an oscillating nature, as in Figure 4.17.

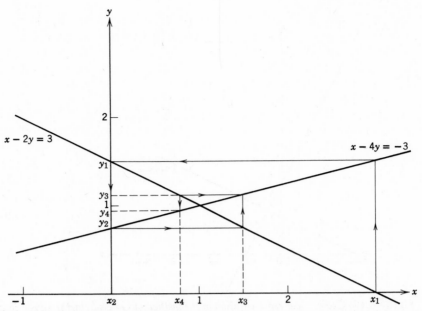

Figure 4.18. *Geometrical representation of the method of Gauss-Seidel iteration in a case that is convergent, although it does not satisfy the sufficient conditions for convergence.*

It can easily be verified that if $|s_1| \geq 1$, $|s_2| \leq 1$, and at least one of the two is a strict inequality, then the following will hold:

1. If s_1 and s_2 have the same sign, the convergence is from one side.
2. If s_1 and s_2 have opposite signs, the convergence is oscillatory.

We may now proceed to a statement of sufficient conditions for the convergence of the Gauss-Seidel iteration method for n equations.

If the equations are irreducible[4] and

$$|a_{ii}| \geq |a_{i1}| + \cdots + |a_{i,i-1}| + |a_{i,i+1}| + \cdots + |a_{in}| \quad (4.47)$$

for all i, and if for at least one i

$$|a_{ii}| > |a_{i1}| + \cdots + |a_{i,i-1}| + |a_{i,i+1}| + \cdots + |a_{in}| \quad (4.48)$$

then the Gauss-Seidel method converges to a solution of (4.13).

These conditions guarantee convergence. We emphasize that they are by no means necessary. They are a proper generalization of (4.45) and (4.46).

The reader may wonder whether these rather stringent conditions leave any practical applicability for the Gauss-Seidel method. As a matter of fact, they do. Systems of equations occur in a number of different areas in which the method of generation of the coefficients automatically guarantees that these conditions will be met.

---

[4]This means that they cannot be rearranged so that some of the variables can be solved for by solving less than n equations. (See Exercise 24.)

Figures 4.16 and 4.17 should remind the reader of the diagrams in Section 1.4 where the method of successive approximations for finding roots of nonlinear equations was discussed. In particular Figure 4.16 looks very much like Figure 1.14. For both figures the corresponding algorithm converges but oscillates from one side of the solution to the other. On the other hand, Figure 4.17 resembles Figure 1.16. The algorithms corresponding to these latter figures diverge and oscillate. As noted at the close of the previous section, the Gauss-Seidel method can also converge from one side if the slopes of the two lines have the same sign. Divergence to one side is also possible. These last two cases would produce diagrams resembling Figures 1.13 and 1.15, respectively. Thus, for each case discussed in Section 1.4, there is a corresponding case in the Gauss-Seidel method.

Recall that in Section 1.6 we found that we could modify the method of successive approximations to speed up the convergence of the algorithm. Moreover, we could actually turn some divergent cases into convergent ones. From the similarity between the geometry of the Gauss-Seidel method and the geometry of the method of successive approximations, we might suspect that we could somehow use similar modifications to accelerate the convergence of the Gauss-Seidel method. This is in fact the case, and we now proceed to a discussion of the modifications to the algorithm that will accomplish this acceleration.

We rewrite (4.39) for the Gauss-Seidel method for a system of three equations as

$$\begin{aligned}
x_1^{(k)} &= x_1^{(k-1)} + \Delta x_1 \\
x_2^{(k)} &= x_2^{(k-1)} + \Delta x_2 \\
x_3^{(k)} &= x_3^{(k-1)} + \Delta x_3
\end{aligned} \tag{4.49}$$

where

$$\Delta x_1 = \frac{1}{a_{11}}(b_1 - a_{12}x_2^{(k-1)} - a_{13}x_3^{(k-1)}) - x_1^{(k-1)}$$

$$\Delta x_2 = \frac{1}{a_{22}}(b_2 - a_{21}x_1^{(k)} - a_{23}x_3^{(k-1)}) - x_2^{(k-1)} \tag{4.50}$$

$$\Delta x_3 = \frac{1}{a_{33}}(b_3 - a_{31}x_1^{(k)} - a_{32}x_2^{(k)}) - x_3^{(k-1)}$$

Thus Δx_1, Δx_2, and Δx_3 are "corrections" to $x_1^{(k-1)}$, $x_2^{(k-1)}$, and $x_3^{(k-1)}$. The corrections yield $x_1^{(k)}$, $x_2^{(k)}$ and $x_3^{(k)}$. Sometimes these corrections are too large (see Figure 4.16); sometimes they are too small. Therefore, we would expect that, depending upon which case arises, if we undercorrect or overcorrect we might achieve a better correction. Here better means that $x_1^{(k)}$, $x_2^{(k)}$, and $x_3^{(k)}$ would be closer to the solution than they would be using the corrections as given in (4.50).

Thus we replace (4.49) by

$$\begin{aligned}
x_1^{(k)} &= x_1^{(k-1)} + \omega \Delta x_1 \\
x_2^{(k)} &= x_2^{(k-1)} + \omega \Delta x_2 \\
x_3^{(k)} &= x_3^{(k-1)} + \omega \Delta x_3
\end{aligned} \tag{4.51}$$

where ω is some real number. If $0 < \omega < 1$, we undercorrect, which is what we wish to do in the case exhibited in Figure 4.16. If $\omega > 1$, then we will overcorrect. This is what we wish to do if the convergence is from one side (see Exercise 36). Of course, we could in principle choose $\omega < 0$. This would be an appropriate choice only if the Gauss-Seidel method were diverging in a nonoscillatory way.

Before generalizing these results to a system of n equations let us turn to a numerical example. We shall use only two equations in two variables in order to simplify the numerical work. Consider the system of equations

$$x + 2y = 3$$
$$x - 4y = -3$$

We have already considered this system as the last example in the previous section where the convergence was oscillatory to $x = y = 1$.

Now following the argument above we let

$$x^{(k)} = x^{(k-1)} + \omega \Delta x$$
$$y^{(k)} = y^{(k-1)} + \omega \Delta y$$

where

$$\Delta x = (3 - 2y^{(k-1)}) - x^{(k-1)}$$
$$\Delta y = \tfrac{1}{4}(3 + x^{(k)}) - y^{(k-1)}$$

If $\omega = 1$, we get the results shown earlier. If we use the convergence criterion

$$\text{Max}\,|x_i^{(k)} - x_i^{(k-1)}| < \epsilon$$

then in this case we require that *both*

$$|\Delta x| < \epsilon$$

and

$$|\Delta y| < \epsilon$$

Using $\epsilon = 10^{-6}$, then with $\omega = 1$ it turns out that the process converges after 23 iterations. A computer program (not shown) to verify this assertion produced the following results for $x^{(k)}$ and $y^{(k)}$

Iteration No.	x	y
0	0	0
1	3	1.5
2	0	0.75
3	1.5	1.125
4	0.75	0.9375
5	1.125	1.03125
6	0.9375	0.984375
7	1.03125	1.007813
8	0.984375	0.9960938
9	1.007813	1.001953
10	0.9960938	0.9990234
11	1.001953	1.000488
12	0.9990234	0.9997559
13	1.000488	1.000122

Iteration No.	x	y
14	0.9997559	0.999939
15	1.000122	1.000031
16	0.999939	0.9999847
17	1.000031	1.000008
18	0.9999847	0.9999962
19	1.000008	1.000002
20	0.9999962	0.999999
21	1.000002	1.
22	0.999999	0.9999998
23	1.	1.

By virtue of the oscillatory nature of the solution we are lead to try a value of $\omega < 1$. Let us try $\omega = 0.9$. The algorithm then converges in only 9 iterations. The values for the successive values of $x^{(k)}$ and $y^{(k)}$ are:

Iteration No.	x	y
0	0	0
1	2.7	1.2825
2	0.6615	0.9520875
3	1.052393	1.006997
4	0.9926445	0.9990447
5	1.000984	1.000126
6	0.9998718	0.9999838
7	1.000016	1.000002
8	0.9999979	0.9999997
9	1.	1.

This is a considerable saving in effort. Indeed, we have reduced the number of iterations by a factor between 2 and 3. What happens if we undercorrect even more? Suppose we try $\omega = 0.8$. The results then are

Iteration No.	x	y
0	0	0
1	2.4	1.08
2	1.152	1.0464
3	0.95616	1.000512
4	0.9904128	0.998185
5	1.000987	0.9998343
6	1.000462	1.000059
7	0.9999975	1.000011
8	0.9999813	0.9999985
9	0.9999986	0.9999994
10	1.000001	1.

Thus we have increased the number of iterations from 9 to 10. What is the value of ω which produces the fewest number of iterations?

Again using a computer program not shown we find the required number of iterations for successive values of Δx and Δy to be less than 10^{-6} in absolute value.

ω	No. of Iterations
.3	38
.5	20
.6	15
.7	13
.8	10
.85	9
.88	8
.9	9
.91	10
.95	15
1.	23
1.1	67

These results are plotted in Figure 4.19. It appears from this plot that the number of iterations decreases as ω increases until $\omega = .88$ after which

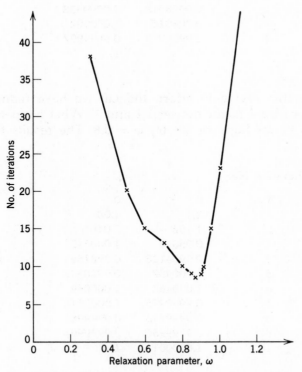

Figure 4.19. *Plot of the number of iterations required to solve a certain system of equations by the modified Gauss-Seidel method, as a function of the relaxation parameter ω. For other systems the plot would naturally be different, but the shape is representative.*

the number of iterations increases. Actually closer examination of the process near $\omega = .88$ shows that for $\omega = .881$ the number of iterations is 7, and 7 is indeed the minimum number of iterations possible.

Unfortunately there is no way to determine the "best" value of ω á priori. Here the best value for ω is .881. For a different system of equations it will be some other value (see Exercises 34, 36, and 37). In all cases, however, the plot of ω versus the number of iterations will have the same general shape as the curve in Figure 4.19; that is to say, the number of iterations will decrease in a somewhat jerky fashion until the "best" value of ω is reached and will increase thereafter. Of course, the best value may not be unique—there may be several best values of ω. There will be only one minimum value for the number of iterations.

In the more general case of n equations, the modified Gauss-Seidel method is given by

$$x_i^{(k)} = x_i^{(k-1)} + \omega \Delta x_i$$

where

$$\Delta x_i = \bar{x}_i - x_i^{(k-1)}$$

and

$$\bar{x}_i = \frac{1}{a_{ii}} [b_i - a_{i1}x_1^{(k)} - \cdots - a_{i,i-1}x_{i-1}^{(k)} - a_{i,i+1}x_{i+1}^{(k-1)} - \cdots - a_{in}x_n^{(k-1)}]$$

for $i = 1, 2, \ldots, n$. For $\omega = 1$ this is the standard Gauss-Seidel method.

We close this section with an important observation. In Section 4.9 we stated, without proof, that the Gauss-Seidel method converges if the equations are irreducible and if the matrix of coefficients is *diagonally dominant*, that is, if (4.47) and (4.48) are valid. The modified method ($\omega \neq 1$) may or may not converge under these same circumstances. Thus if we use a value of ω different from 1 we cannot even guarantee convergence. On the other hand, there is a good chance that we can speed up the convergence if we alter ω. Indeed, in some cases we can change a divergent process, which does not satisfy (4.47) and (4.48), into a convergent one (see Exercise 35). Just when this trick of changing ω will work is an unanswered question except in a few special cases.

The fact is, convergence is assured only when (4.47) and (4.48) are satisfied and $\omega = 1$. The reader is therefore advised to use the modified Gauss-Seidel method with caution. In particular a counter that limits the number of iterations to some reasonable value should *always* be placed in the loop. Nevertheless, the modification is frequently an extremely valuable one. In most cases there is some value of ω that will speed up the convergence. In practice it is wise to experiment a little searching for a good choice of ω. The time and effort spent in such experimentation is usually repaid in a decrease in the number of iterations in solving related systems.

4.12 Comparison of the Methods

We have discussed two methods for solving a system of simultaneous linear algebraic equations. There are many others. However, all methods are either direct, as is Gaussian elimination, or indirect, as is the Gauss-Seidel iteration method. In this section we shall compare the two methods that we have discussed. Although our specific results apply only to these specific methods, the general conclusions can be applied to other algorithms as well.

Gaussian elimination has the advantage that it is finite and works—in theory—for any nonsingular system of equations. The Gauss-Seidel iteration method converges only for special systems of equation. For some systems elimination is the only course available.[5]

On the other hand, many systems of equations arising in practice are *sparse,* that is, they contain a high proportion of zeros. In these cases iteration—if it works—is highly preferable, since elimination usually produces a triangular system that is no longer sparse.[6] In computer terms a sparse system is desirable because we can test the coefficients and not multiply at all when they are zero.

Gaussian elimination requires $(4n^3 + 9n^2 - 7n)/6$ arithmetic operations (addition, subtraction, multiplication, and/or division). The Gauss-Seidel method requires $2n^2 - n$ arithmetic operations *per iteration.* For large values of n, the number of arithmetic operations are approximately

Gaussian elimination: $2n^3/3$
Gauss-Seidel: $2n^2$ per iteration

Thus, if the number of iterations in the Gauss-Seidel method is less than or equal to $n/3$, then the iteration method requires fewer arithmetic operations.

As a specific example, consider a system of 100 equations. Elimination requires 681,550 operations whereas iteration requires 19,900 operations per iteration. For 34 or fewer iterations, Gauss-Seidel requires less arithmetic than elimination. For 35 or more iterations, the opposite is true.

In addition to the amount of arithmetic, Gaussian elimination requires more bookkeeping. For example, it is virtually certain that several row interchanges will take place. This is quite time consuming in all cases and in modern paging computers can be extremely costly. Iterative processes suffer much less from this movement of data and are, in fact, well suited to a paging environment. Thus, even if the number of iterations exceeds $n/3$, iteration may require less computer time.

Iterative techniques have less roundoff error than elimination techniques, since only the roundoff errors committed in the final iteration have any effect. As we mentioned in Chapter 1, the values of the variables at the start of any iteration may be considered to be a "guess" at the solution. This "guess" contains no roundoff error since it might well have been a set of values provided by the program's user. Elimination, on the other hand, has roundoff errors propagated throughout its n^3 operations. The smaller roundoff error in Gauss-Seidel is often important enough to justify its use even when the total amount of computation exceeds that of Gaussian elimination.

---

[5] Actually, iterative methods exist for solving *any* nonsingular system, but they are usually impractical. See, for instance, W. E. Milne, *Numerical Solution of Differential Equations,* Wiley, 1953, Section 76.

[6] Some special sparse systems do remain sparse when reduced to triangular form by Gauss elimination. (See Exercise 10.)

4.13
Case
Study 8:
Solving the
Simultane-
ous Equa-
tions of a
Cost
Accounting
Problem by
Gauss-
Seidel
Iteration

Corporations comprised of several divisions are faced with the problem of determining the net operating costs of each of the divisions. The costs that are directly available usually are the direct costs. For example, the Development Division may have an operating budget of $3,000,000. However, the Development Division may provide services to other divisions. Again, by way of example, 20% of the Development Division's effort may be for the direct benefit of the Production Division through temporary assignment of personnel, design of pilot plants, etc. Similarly, the Development Division may spend 20% of its effort in assisting the Research Division. Thus only 60% of the Development Division's effort is expended on development activities per se. It is tempting in such a case to say that the cost of development is 60% of $3,000,000 or $1,800,000. However, the Research Division and Production Division provide some service to the Development Division and that should be added to the development cost. But then part of this added cost of development should be assigned back to the Research and Production Divisions.

The dilemma may be resolved by the following analysis:[7]

Let D_i be the total direct cost of the ith division. This number is usually known. Let P_{ij} be the fraction of its direct cost that division i charges to division j. These numbers we assume to be given as well.

We let T_i be the total cost of operation of division i, and let N_i be the net cost of division i. These numbers are unknown and must be computed.

Suppose there are n divisions. Then the total cost of the first division is its direct cost, D_1, plus what is apportioned to it from the *total* cost of the other divisions; that is to say,

$$T_1 = D_1 + P_{21}T_2 + P_{31}T_3 + \cdots + P_{n1}T_n$$

We still cannot compute T_1 since we do not know the values of $T_2, \ldots, T_n$. However, we can write similar equations for each of the divisions. The resulting system of n equations is

$$T_k = D_k + \sum_{\substack{j=1 \\ j \neq k}}^{n} P_{jk}T_j \qquad k = 1, 2, \ldots, n \qquad (4.52)$$

This is a system of n linear equations in n variables: $T_1, T_2, \ldots, T_n$. We rewrite them as

$$T_k - \sum_{\substack{j=1 \\ j \neq k}}^{n} P_{jk}T_j = D_k \qquad k = 1, 2, \ldots, n \qquad (4.53)$$

In matrix notation these are

$$AT = D$$

[7]This type of analysis may be found in many modern accounting textbooks and is in use in most present day accounting departments. Precomputer cost accounting handbooks usually dismiss these methods as impractical. An excellent reference is *Bank Cost Accounting and Profitability Analysis*, an IBM Data Processing Application publication.

where

$$A = \begin{pmatrix} 1 & -P_{21} & -P_{31} & \cdots & -P_{n1} \\ -P_{12} & 1 & -P_{32} & \cdots & -P_{n2} \\ \vdots & & & & \vdots \\ -P_{1n} & -P_{2n} & -P_{3n} & \cdots & 1 \end{pmatrix}$$

$$T = \begin{pmatrix} T_1 \\ T_2 \\ \vdots \\ T_n \end{pmatrix} \qquad D = \begin{pmatrix} D_1 \\ D_2 \\ \vdots \\ D_n \end{pmatrix}$$

These equations can be solved using Gaussian elimination. They may also be solved by the Gauss-Seidel iteration method. In most cases they will satisfy the convergence conditions (4.47) and (4.48) since it is unlikely that more than 100% of various other divisions' costs will be charged to any one division. Thus usually

$$\sum_{\substack{j=1 \\ j \neq k}}^{n} |P_{jk}| \leq 1 \tag{4.54}$$

and in at least one case strict inequality holds. The equations are also irreducible if the divisions are all interdependent. If they are not, they should be separated into two or more sets of divisions in such a way that the divisions in each set are interrelated.

Even if (4.54) is not satisfied for all k, there generally will be a sufficient number of strict inequalities to guarantee convergence of the Gauss-Seidel method. We shall not discuss such convergence here. We content ourselves with referring the reader to Figure 4.18 where the sufficient conditions (4.47) and (4.48) were not satisfied, yet the Gauss-Seidel method converged. Notice that (4.52) are in the precise form needed for use of the Gauss-Seidel method.

Once we have solved the system (4.53) either in that form or in the form (4.52), then the net costs are

$$N_k = P_{kk} T_k \qquad k = 1, \ldots, n \tag{4.55}$$

Let us take a specific example. Suppose a corporation has five divisions: Research, Development, Production, Accounting, and Computation. We number them from 1 to 5 in the order shown.

Table 4.2 shows the fractions of direct costs charged by each division and the divisions to which the charges are made. For example, the Research Division charges 40% of its cost to other divisions—20% to Development, 10% to Production, and 10% to Computation. Notice that the Computation Division is strictly a service operation—all of its costs are charged to other divisions.

The total direct costs are

Research: $D_1 = \$2,000,000$
Development: $D_2 = \$3,000,000$
Production: $D_3 = \$6,000,000$
Accounting: $D_4 = \$500,000$
Computation: $D_5 = \$300,000$

Table 4.2

| | Charged by (i) | | | | |
Charged to (j)	Research (1)	Development (2)	Production (3)	Accounting (4)	Computation (5)
Research (1)	.60	.20	0	.10	.30
Development (2)	.20	.60	.20	.20	.20
Production (3)	.10	.20	.80	.50	.20
Accounting (4)	0	0	0	.10	.30
Computation (5)	.10	0	0	.10	0

If we use \$1 million as the unit of money then (4.52) becomes

$$\left. \begin{array}{l} T_1 = 2 + .2T_2 + .1T_4 + .3T_5 \\ T_2 = 3 + .2T_1 + .2T_3 + .2T_4 + .2T_5 \\ T_3 = 6 + .1T_1 + .2T_2 + .5T_4 + .2T_5 \\ T_4 = .5 + .3T_5 \\ T_5 = .3 + .1T_1 + .1T_4 \end{array} \right\} \qquad (4.56)$$

Equations (4.55) are

$$\left. \begin{array}{l} N_1 = .6T_1 \\ N_2 = .6T_2 \\ N_3 = .8T_3 \\ N_4 = .1T_4 \\ N_5 = 0 \end{array} \right\} \qquad (4.57)$$

Figures 4.20, 4.21, and 4.22 present a main program and two subroutines that solve this problem using the Gauss-Seidel method. The Gauss-Seidel subroutine is the last of these, and, once again, follows the flow chart so closely that we shall hardly need to pause over it. It will be easier to follow the logic, however, if we begin with the main program in Figure 4.20.

It is desirable to set up a program of this sort so that it will work with any number of divisions up to some reasonable maximum, here chosen

```
C CASE STUDY 8
C A COST ACCOUNTING APPLICATION OF THE GAUSS-SEIDEL METHOD
C
C READ THE NUMBER OF DIVISIONS - THIS WILL BE USED IN CALLING
C    A SUBROUTINE THAT MAKES IT POSSIBLE TO USE OBJECT-TIME
C    DIMENSIONS
C
      DIMENSION A(10, 10), T(10), D(10), P(10), N(10), NAMES(10,4)
      REAL N
      READ (5, 100) NODIV
 100 FORMAT (I2)
C CALL THE SUBROUTINE THAT WILL READ THE DATA AND CALL THE
C    GAUSS-SEIDEL SUBROUTINE
      CALL CS8SUB(A, T, D, P, N, NAMES, NODIV)
      STOP
      END
```

Figure 4.20. *A main program for a cost-accounting application of the Gauss-Seidel method for solving simultaneous equations. The only function of the program is to establish the maximum sizes of the arrays and read a number giving the actual sizes (Case Study 8).*

```
C CASE STUDY 8
C A COST ACCOUNTING APPLICATION OF THE GAUSS-SEIDEL METHOD
C THE SUBROUTINE THAT DOES THE WORK
C SET UP THIS WAY SO DIMENSIONS OF ARRAYS CAN BE DETERMINED
C    WHEN THE PROGRAM IS RUN
C
      SUBROUTINE CS8SUB(A, T, D, P, N, NAMES, NODIV)
      DIMENSION A(NODIV, NODIV), T(NODIV), D(NODIV), P(NODIV), N(NODIV),
     1 NAMES(NODIV, 4)
      REAL N
C READ DIVISION NAMES
      DO 200 I = 1, NODIV
  200 READ (5, 101) (NAMES(I, J), J = 1, 4)
  101 FORMAT (4A4)
C READ OPERATING COSTS, IN $MILLIONS, FOR EACH DIVISION
      READ (5, 102) (D(I), I = 1, NODIV)
  102 FORMAT (10F8.0)
C ZERO THE ARRAY OF COEFFICIENTS
      DO 201 I = 1, NODIV
      DO 201 J = 1, NODIV
  201 A(I, J) = 0.0
C READ COST ALLOCATIONS, LOOKING FOR ZERO SENTINEL
C NOTE SUBSCRIPT MEANING - P(I, J) IS THE CHARGE BY DIVISION I
C    TO DIVISION J.  THIS GOES INTO COEFFICIENT POSITION A(J, I)
  202 READ (5, 103) I, J, X
  103 FORMAT (2I2, F10.0)
      IF (X .EQ. 0.0) GO TO 203
      A(J, I) = -X
      GO TO 202
C CHECK THAT SUM OF ALLOCATIONS FOR EACH DIVISION IS 1.0
  203 DO 205 J = 1, NODIV
      SUM = 0.0
      DO 204 I = 1, NODIV
  204 SUM = SUM + A(I, J)
      IF (ABS(1.0 + SUM) .GT. 0.0001) WRITE (6, 104) J
  104 FORMAT (1X, 'SUM OF ALLOCATIONS NOT 1.0 FOR DIVISION', I5)
  205 CONTINUE
C MOVE DIAGONAL ELEMENTS TO VECTOR P AND PUT 1.0'S ON DIAGONAL
      DO 206 I = 1, NODIV
      P(I) = -A(I, I)
  206 A(I, I) = 1.0
C PUT ZEROS IN VARIABLE VECTOR FOR STARTING GUESSES
      DO 207 I = 1, NODIV
  207 T(I) = 0.0
C CALL GAUSS-SEIDEL SUBROUTINE
      CALL GSEID (A, D, T, NODIV, 0.00001, 20, .TRUE., &211)
C COMPUTE NET COSTS
      DO 208 I = 1, NODIV
  208 N(I) = P(I) * T(I)
C CHECK THAT COMPUTED NET COSTS ARE CONSISTENT WITH DIRECT COSTS
      SUMNET = 0.0
      SUMDCT = 0.0
      DO 209 I = 1, NODIV
      SUMNET = SUMNET + N(I)
  209 SUMDCT = SUMDCT + D(I)
      IF (ABS(SUMNET - SUMDCT) .GT. 0.0001) WRITE (6, 105)
  105 FORMAT (1X, 'SUM OF DIRECT COSTS NOT EQUAL TO SUM OF NET COSTS')
C WRITE RESULTS
      DO 210 I = 1, NODIV
  210 WRITE (6, 106) (NAMES(I, J), J = 1, 4), N(I)
  106 FORMAT (1X, 4A4, F12.4)
      STOP
C THE NON-STANDARD RETURN IN CASE OF NO CONVERGENCE
  211 WRITE (6, 107)
  107 FORMAT (1X, 'DID NOT CONVERGE IN 20 ITERATIONS')
      STOP
      END
```

Figure 4.21. *A subroutine that reads data, makes various checks, calls a Gauss-Seidel subroutine, and writes the results, in a cost-accounting application.*

```
C CASE STUDY 8
C THE GAUSS-SEIDEL METHOD
C    FOR SOLVING SIMULTANEOUS LINEAR ALGEBRAIC EQUATIONS
C
      SUBROUTINE GSEID (A, B, X, N, EPS, MAX, PRINT, *)
      DIMENSION A(N, N), B(N), X(N)
      LOGICAL PRINT
C X IS BOTH INPUT AND OUTPUT, CONTAINING THE STARTING
C   APPROXIMATIONS TO BEGIN WITH AND THE FINAL RESULTS ON EXIT
C 'PRINT' IS A LOGICAL VARIABLE THAT DETERMINES WHETHER TO
C    PRINT THE SUCCESSIVE APPROXIMATIONS
C THE NON-STANDARD RETURN IS TAKEN IF THE PROCESS DOES NOT
C   CONVERGE IN 'MAX' ITERATIONS
C   (THIS IS NOT A FEATURE OF ANSI FORTRAN)
C
C BEGIN THE ITERATION SCHEME
      ITER = 1
C STATEMENT 99 IS EXECUTED ONCE PER SWEEP
   99 BIG = 0.0
C INDEX I SELECTS A ROW
      DO 100 I = 1, N
C STATEMENT 102 IS EXECUTED ONCE PER ROW
  102 SUM = 0.0
C THE SEGMENT FROM HERE THROUGH STATEMENT 107 FORMS THE SUM OF
C    THE TERMS IN A ROW, EXCLUDING THE MAIN DIAGONAL TERM
      IF (I .EQ. 1) GO TO 105
      LAST = I - 1
      DO 106 J = 1, LAST
  106 SUM = SUM + A(I,J)*X(J)
      IF (I .EQ. N) GO TO 103
  105 INITL = I + 1
      DO 107 J = INITL, N
  107 SUM = SUM + A(I,J)*X(J)
C COMPUTE THE NEW VALUE OF A VARIABLE
  103 TEMP = (B(I) - SUM) / A(I, I)
      RESID = ABS(TEMP - X(I))
C AT END OF SWEEP, THE NEXT STATEMENT WILL HAVE PUT LARGEST RESIDUAL IN
C    BIG
      IF (RESID .GT. BIG) BIG = RESID
  100 X(I) = TEMP
C ONE SWEEP HAS NOW BEEN COMPLETED - PRINT VARIABLES IF REQUESTED
      IF (PRINT) WRITE (6, 200) X
  200 FORMAT (1X, 8F10.3)
C IF LARGEST RESIDUAL IS LESS THAN EPS, PROCESS HAS CONVERGED
      IF (BIG .LT. EPS) RETURN
C IF ITERATION COUNTER EXCEEDS MAXIMUM ALLOWABLE, GIVE UP
      IF (ITER .GT. MAX) RETURN 1
C OTHERWISE GO AROUND AGAIN FOR ANOTHER SWEEP
      ITER = ITER + 1
      GO TO 99
      END
```

Figure 4.22. *A subroutine to solve a system of simultaneous equations by the Gauss-Seidel method.*

to be 10. All the arrays that we used are declared in the main program, with integer constants for the dimensions. We then read one data card that gives the number of divisions. Using this information we immediately call a subroutine; the main program has no other function than to obtain the number that establishes the sizes of the arrays. The call of the subroutine, named CS8SUB, lists all the arrays and the variable that gives the dimensioning information; both the names and the size must appear in the call. (And the size must not be greater than the absolute size specified in the main program.)

The subroutine that "does the work," other than the work of actually solving the system, is shown in Figure 4.21. It begins by reading as many data records as there are divisions, which is given by the value of the variable NODIV, so that the output can be identified. Next a single data record is read that contains the operating costs of the divisions, in the same order as the names were just read. Since we assume that many of the coefficients will be zero, we zero the array and require that only the nonzero elements be entered. Now we read the elements, in any order, since each record contains the row and column number associated with the value, according to the layout of Table 4.1. Because the indexing is backward from the way the equations are laid out in (4.53), the program reverses the indices in placing the elements in the matrix of coefficients. The signs are reversed to fit the convention established.

After a zero element has signaled the end of the input, we check that the sum of elements in each column is suitably close to 1.0, as the theory requires. If not, we write a warning comment but proceed. Next the diagonal elements are moved to a separate array for later use in computing the net costs, restoring their original signs, and 1's are placed on the main diagonal. After putting all zeros in the vector of starting guesses, we call the Gauss-Seidel subroutine, named here GSEID.

This subroutine has been set up to accept the matrix of coefficients without the constant terms, contrary to what we did in Case Study 7. Thus it requires, in order, the name of the array of coefficients, the name of the vector of constant terms, the name of the vector of starting guesses (which become the answers), and the name of the variable giving the sizes of these arrays. Next come EPS, the tolerance, and MAX, the maximum number of iterations to be allowed. Finally there are two items not explicitly introduced in the flow chart of the method: a logical variable that informs the subroutine whether or not we want to see the successive approximations, and a statement number for a nonstandard return in case the method does not converge in MAX iterations. (This last feature is available in most Fortran systems, but it is not specified in the Fortran standard of the American National Standards Institute.)

When the results have been returned by GSEID, we compute the net costs of the divisions from (4.55), which is the only output of the program (besides the division names) as written. But as one final check we sum the direct costs and the net costs and see whether they are the same to

```
              2.000      3.400      6.880      0.500      0.550
              2.895      5.165      7.682      0.665      0.656
              3.296      5.460      7.885      0.697      0.699
              3.371      5.531      7.932      0.710      0.708
              3.390      5.548      7.945      0.712      0.710
              3.394      5.552      7.948      0.713      0.711
              3.395      5.553      7.949      0.713      0.711
              3.395      5.554      7.949      0.713      0.711
              3.395      5.554      7.949      0.713      0.711
              3.395      5.554      7.949      0.713      0.711
              3.395      5.554      7.949      0.713      0.711
RESEARCH                 2.0372
DEVELOPMENT              3.3322
PRODUCTION               6.3593
ACCOUNTING              0.0713
COMPUTATION             0.0
```

Figure 4.23. *The output of the three programs of Case Study 8, when run with the data given in the text. The eleven sets of five numbers are the successive iterates to the* T_i.

within a tolerance of 0.0001 (= \$100). Finally, the results are written. The nonstandard return simply takes us to a WRITE statement to issue a warning.

Figure 4.23 shows the output when these programs were run with the data contained in the text. We see that the iterative process converged to a solution, within the tolerance of 0.00001 specified in the CALL, in 11 iterations. (These are the T's, the total costs of [4.52] or [4.56].) We see that the net costs of research, development, and production are somewhat higher than their direct costs, as we might expect, since part of the cost of accounting and all of the cost of computation have been allocated to the others.

Figure 4.24 shows the output when P_{21} was changed to 0.1, and the programs re-run.

```
SUM OF ALLOCATIONS NOT 1.0 FOR DIVISION    1
        2.000      4.200      7.040      0.500      0.550
        3.055      6.451      7.956      0.665      0.672
        3.558      6.994      8.221      0.702      0.726
        3.687      7.142      8.293      0.718      0.740
        3.722      7.184      8.316      0.722      0.744
        3.732      7.196      8.322      0.723      0.746
        3.735      7.199      8.324      0.724      0.746
        3.736      7.200      8.325      0.724      0.746
        3.736      7.201      8.325      0.724      0.746
        3.736      7.201      8.325      0.724      0.746
        3.736      7.201      8.325      0.724      0.746
        3.736      7.201      8.325      0.724      0.746
SUM OF DIRECT COSTS NOT EQUAL TO SUM OF NET COSTS
RESEARCH               2.2418
DEVELOPMENT            4.3204
PRODUCTION             6.6599
ACCOUNTING             0.0724
COMPUTATION            0.0
```

Figure 4.24. *The output of the programs of Case Study 8 when run with erroneous data.*

Bibliographic Notes

Gaussian elimination is covered very briefly and in an elementary way in Barrodale et al. [1] in Chapter 3, Section 3. A flow chart is included there. In Sections 5.10 and 5.11 Stark [3] has a slightly more detailed explanation and includes an 1130 Fortran program. Other discussions of Gaussian elimination about the same level as that of the present text may be found in Hamming [6], Section 5.1; Scarborough [17], Section 157; and Hildebrand [18], Section 10.3. Discussions that are slightly more difficult reading are found in Ralston [19] Section 9.3–1 where a count of the number of arithmetic operations is given, and Carnahan et al. [20] in Section 5.3 where the discussion is in terms of elementary matrices and operations with them.

Refinement of the solution (as described in Section 4.8 of the present text) is also discussed briefly by Hildebrand [18] in Section 10.4. Ill-conditioning is covered by Stark [3] in Section 5.12; Ralston [19] in

Sections 9.2 and 9.5; Hamming [6] in Sections 5.7 and 5.9; and Carnahan et al. [20] at the close of Section 5.4.

Pivotal condensation is discussed by Scarborough [17] in Section 157; Ralston [19] in Section 9.3–2; and Hamming [6] in Sections 5.2, 5.4, and 5.10. Hamming also points out in Section 5.7 that pivotal condensation is not always the best strategy to be used.

The effect of uncertainty in the coefficients of the system of equations is discussed in Section 10.6 of Hildebrand [18] and Section 2.3.1 of Redish [12] in a way quite similar to the presentation in the present text. More general results can also be found in that same section of Hildebrand and also in Ralston [19] in Section 9.4–2. These more general results require the use of inverse matrices and in some cases also matrix norms.

The Gauss-Seidel method is covered in many texts. The most elementary discussion is in Barrodale et al. [1], Chapter 3, where a word description equivalent to a flow chart is also found. Other discussions are to be found in Stark [3], Sections 5.13 and 5.14; Hildebrand [18], Section 10.7; Scarborough [17], Section 164, where convergence is discussed in terms of nonlinear equations; Ralston [19], Section 9.7–2; and Carnahan et al. [20], where a Fortran program and example are included. Ralston [19] also discusses the roundoff error in Gauss-Seidel in Section 9.7–3.

Acceleration of the Gauss-Seidel process is discussed by Ralston [19] in Section 9.7–5. An excellent discussion of this acceleration process is also to be found in Fox (see below), Section 15 of Chapter 8. The latter, however, involves the notion of eigenvalues.

Three reference and text books that are concerned solely with the solution of systems of linear equations and related problems are:

An Introduction to Numerical Linear Algebra by L. Fox (New York: Oxford University Press, 1964).

> Requires much more mathematical sophistication than present text. Does *not* contain flow charts or computer programs except for a brief introductory chapter. Extremely thorough discussion of several direct methods (Gauss, Gauss-Jordan, Doolittle, Crout, Cholesky) and a comparison of the effort required by each. Also discusses iterative methods (Gauss-Seidel and Jacobi). Detailed discussion of ill-conditioning. Covers eigenvalues and eigenvectors including Jacobi, Givens, Householder, and Lanczos methods.

Computer Solution of Linear Algebraic Systems George Forsythe and Cleve B. Moler (Englewood, N.J.: Prentice-Hall, 1967).

> Requires much more mathematical sophistication than present text. Graduate-level material that contains programs in PL/I, Fortran, and ALGOL; no flow charts. Discusses both direct and iterative methods with careful error analysis. An extremely thorough and accurate treatment.

A Handbook of Numerical Matrix Inversion and Solution of Linear Equations Joan R. Westlake (New York: Wiley, 1968).

> An encyclopedia of algorithms both direct and iterative. Requires more mathematical maturity than present text. Does *not* include flow charts or computer programs. Compares various methods from different points of view. A brief (five-page) discussion of errors.

Exercises

*1 Solve the following system of simultaneous equations by the method of Gaussian elimination. No row interchanges will be necessary.

$$x - y + z = -4$$
$$5x - 4y + 3z = -12$$
$$2x + y + z = 11$$

2 Solve the following system of simultaneous equations by the method of Gaussian elimination. No row interchanges will be necessary.

$$w + x + y + z = 10$$
$$2w + 3x + y + 5z = 31$$
$$-w + x - 5y + 3z = -2$$
$$3w + x + 7y - 2z = 18$$

*3 Solve the following system by Gaussian elimination, using four-digit floating point arithmetic and row interchanges.

$$2x + 6y - z = -12$$
$$5x - y + 2z = 29$$
$$-3x - 4y + z = 5$$

4 Attempt to solve the following system by Gaussian elimination. What happens and what causes the trouble?

$$x + y + z = 2$$
$$2x - 3y + z = 11$$
$$4x - y + 3z = 10$$

5 Attempt to solve the following system by Gaussian elimination. What happens and what causes the trouble?

$$2x - 3y + 4z = 8$$
$$4x + 2y - 3z = -1$$
$$6x + 7y - 10z = -10$$

*6 Solve the following system by Gaussian elimination, using complex arithmetic throughout.

$$(2 + 3i)x + (2 - i)y = 2 + i$$
$$(4 + 6i)x + (3 - 6i)y = -2 - 5i$$

7 In the system of Exercise 6 write $x = x_r + ix_i$, $y = y_r + iy_i$. Multiply out and equate the real and imaginary parts of each equation separately. Show that the result is a system of four equations in four unknowns, the solution of which gives the real and imaginary parts of the solution of Exercise 6.

*8 Solve the following system by Gaussian elimination, first without row interchanges and then with row interchanges, using four-digit floating point arithmetic.

$$x + 592y = 437$$
$$592x + 4308y = 2251$$

9 Recall that in solving (4.5), (4.6), and (4.7) by Gaussian elimination we first eliminated x_1 and obtained

$$a_{11}x_1 + a_{12}x_2 + a_{13}x_3 = b_1 \tag{4.5}$$
$$a_{22}'x_2 + a_{23}'x_3 = b_2' \tag{4.9}$$
$$a_{32}'x_2 + a_{33}'x_3 = b_3' \tag{4.10}$$

We then defined a multiplier

$$m_3' = \frac{a_{32}'}{a_{22}'}$$

and subtracted m_3' times (4.9) from (4.10) to obtain

$$a_{33}''x_3 = b_3'' \tag{4.11}$$

Show that if we define

$$m_1' = \frac{a_{12}}{a_{22}'}$$

and subtract m_1' times (4.9) from (4.5) we obtain

$$a_{11}'x_1 + a_{13}'x_3 = b_1' \tag{a}$$

Find expressions for a_{11}', a_{13}', and b_1'.

Now define multipliers

$$m_1'' = \frac{a_{13}'}{a_{33}''}$$

$$m_2'' = \frac{a_{23}'}{a_{33}''}$$

Show that, if we subtract m_1'' times (4.11) from the equation marked (a) and m_2'' times (4.11) from (4.9), the resulting three equations are of the form

$$a_{11}''x_1 = b_1''$$
$$a_{22}''x_2 = b_2''$$
$$a_{33}''x_3 = b_3''$$

Find expressions for a_{11}'', a_{22}'', and a_{33}''.

Notice that these three equations may be solved *without* back-substitution. This method of elimination is called the *Gauss-Jordan method*.

10 Consider the following "sparse" set of equations.

$$
\begin{aligned}
2x_1 - x_2 &&&&&&= 1 \\
-x_1 + 2x_2 - x_3 &&&&&= 1 \\
- x_2 + 2x_3 - x_4 &&&&= 1 \\
- x_3 + 2x_4 - x_5 &&&= 1 \\
- x_4 + 2x_5 - x_6 &= 1 \\
- x_5 + 2x_6 &= 1
\end{aligned}
$$

Show that the system remains sparse when reduced to triangular form by Gaussian elimination. A system like the original set is called *tridiagonal* because of the arrangement of the coefficients. Such systems appear frequently in the solution of partial differential equations.

11 Suppose you wish to solve two sets of simultaneous linear equations that are identical except for their right-hand sides. If Gaussian elimination is used, would the triangular sets of equations for the two sets differ on the left-hand sides? On the right-hand sides?

Describe an addition to the Gaussian elimination method as stated in the text that will find the solutions to both sets of equations with only one elimination process.

12 The method suggested in Exercise 11 applies as well to three different right-hand sides. Using the technique, solve the following three sets of equations.

$$x - y = 1$$
$$x + y + z = 0$$
$$y - z = 0$$

$$x - y = 0$$
$$x + y + z = 1$$
$$y - z = 0$$

$$x - y = 0$$
$$x + y + z = 0$$
$$y - z = 1$$

Let x_1, y_1, z_1 be the solution to the first set, x_2, y_2, z_2 the solution to the second set, and x_3, y_3, z_3 the solution to the third set. Show that the solution to the system

$$x - y = b_1$$
$$x + y + z = b_2$$
$$y - z = b_3$$

is given by

$$x = b_1 x_1 + b_2 x_2 + b_3 x_3$$
$$y = b_1 y_1 + b_2 y_2 + b_3 y_3$$
$$z = b_1 z_1 + b_2 z_2 + b_3 z_3$$

What conclusion can you draw from this example regarding the number of sets of equations that must be solved in order to be able to obtain the solution for *any* right-hand side in a straightforward manner? The matrix having x_1, x_2, and x_3 as its first row, y_1, y_2, and y_3 as its second row, and z_1, z_2, and z_3 as its third row, is called the *inverse* of the original matrix of the system.

13 Using the method of Section 4.8, refine the solution to the system in Exercise 8 that you found *without* row interchanges.

*14 The following system has the approximate solution $x_1 = 2$, $x_2 = 3$, $x_3 = 4$. Refine it by using the method in Section 4.8.

$$1.781x_1 + 3.008x_2 - 4.880x_3 = -7.704$$
$$4.632x_1 - 1.064x_2 - 2.274x_3 = -6.359$$
$$-3.387x_1 + 9.814x_2 - 4.779x_3 = 3.946$$

15 The following system has the approximate solution $x = 10$,

$y = -3.99$. Refine it, first using four-digit floating point arithmetic, then six-digit floating point arithmetic.

$$234x + 546y = 156$$
$$158x + 371y = 103$$

16 In the system of Exercise 15 change the 371 to 371.2 and resolve. Compare the percentage change in the coefficient with the resulting percentage change in y.

*17 In the following system assume that the a_{ij} are exact but that the b_i are given to two decimal places. Find the bounds on the errors in the solution. Do this first with the equations as written, then repeat with the equations reversed.

$$x + y = 2$$
$$x + 2y = 3$$

*18 Consider the following system.

$$x - y + 4z = 6$$
$$2x + 3y - z = 18$$
$$3x + y + z = 19$$

Solve the system without row interchanges (which, as we have seen in Exercise 17, would change the error bounds) and find the bounds on the errors in the solution under the following assumptions:
a. The a_{ij} are precise; the b_i are given to two decimals.
b. The b_i are precise; the a_{ij} are given to two decimals.
c. The a_{ij} and b_i are both given to two decimals.
d. The a_{ij} and b_i both have two significant figures.

19 Same as Exercise 18, with the following system:

$$2x + y + z = 7$$
$$2x + 2y + 3z = 10$$
$$-4x + 4y + 5z = 14$$

*20 Solve the following system by the method of Gauss-Seidel iteration, continuing the iterative process until the maximum difference between successive values of x, y, or z is less than 0.02. Does this mean that the approximate solution is within 0.02 of the exact solution?

$$10x + 2y + 6z = 28$$
$$x + 10y + 9z = 7$$
$$2x - 7y - 10z = -17$$

21 Solve the following system by the method of Gauss-Seidel iteration, continuing the iterative process until the maximum difference between successive values of x, y, or z is less than 0.02. Compare the convergence rate with that in Exercise 20. Why the difference?

$$20x + 2y + 6z = 38$$
$$x + 20y + 9z = -23$$
$$2x - 7y - 20z = -57$$

22 Consider two simultaneous equations

$$a_1 x + b_1 y = c_1$$
$$a_2 x + b_2 y = c_2$$

Let s_1 be the slope of the first equation and let s_2 be the slope of the second. Show the following:

a. If $s_1 > 1$ and $-1 < s_2 < 0$, the convergence by Gauss-Seidel iteration is oscillatory.

b. If $s_1 > 1$ and $0 < s_2 < 1$, the convergence by Gauss-Seidel iteration is from one side.

c. If $s_1 < -1$ and $-1 < s_2 < 0$, the convergence by Gauss-Seidel iteration is from one side.

23 Consider the two linear equations

$$a_{11} x_1 + a_{12} x_2 = b_1$$
$$a_{21} x_1 + a_{22} x_2 = b_2$$

Suppose we use the following iteration procedure to solve these two equations:

$$x_1^{(k)} = \frac{1}{a_{11}} (b_1 - a_{12} x_2^{(k-1)})$$

$$x_2^{(k)} = \frac{1}{a_{22}} (b_2 - a_{21} x_1^{(k-1)})$$

a. Show that a necessary and sufficient condition for convergence of the iteration procedure is

$$\left| \frac{a_{12} a_{21}}{a_{11} a_{22}} \right| < 1$$

Compare this with the condition for the Gauss-Seidel method.

b. Show that the Gauss-Seidel method converges twice as fast as this method.

c. Verify the relative rates of convergence stated in (b) by carrying out four iterations on

$$2x + y = 2$$
$$x - 2y = -2$$

and by comparing with the results for the Gauss-Seidel method shown on p. 187.

d. Give a geometric interpretation of this iterative method. See also Exercise 39.

24 Which of the following systems of equations are *reducible*? (See footnote on p. 190.)

a.
$$-x_1 \qquad\; + 3x_3 + \; x_4 = 3$$
$$3x_1 + 2x_2 + \; x_3 - 2x_4 = 4$$
$$2x_1 \qquad\qquad\qquad + 4x_4 = 6$$
$$\qquad\qquad\quad x_3 - \; x_4 = 0$$

b.
$$\begin{aligned}
-x_1 \quad\quad\quad + 3x_3 + x_4 &= 3 \\
3x_1 + 2x_2 + x_3 - 2x_4 &= 4 \\
2x_2 \quad\quad\quad + 4x_4 &= 6 \\
x_3 - x_4 &= 0
\end{aligned}$$

c.
$$\begin{aligned}
x_2 + x_3 &= 2 \\
x_1 \quad\quad - x_3 &= 0 \\
2x_1 + x_2 \quad\quad &= 3
\end{aligned}$$

d.
$$\begin{aligned}
x_1 + 2x_2 \quad\quad &= 3 \\
x_1 + x_2 + x_3 &= 3 \\
2x_1 + x_2 \quad\quad &= 3
\end{aligned}$$

25 Solve the following four equations by the Gauss-Seidel method:

$$\begin{aligned}
x_1 \quad\quad\quad\quad + x_4 &= 2 \\
x_1 + 4x_2 \quad\quad - x_4 &= 4 \\
x_1 \quad\quad + x_3 \quad\quad &= 2 \\
x_3 + x_4 &= 2
\end{aligned}$$

Do the coefficients in these equations satisfy the inequalities required for convergence? Why does the process diverge? What is the solution of these equations?

26 Referring to the program of Figure 4.12 in Case Study 7, suppose we had an array named NROW. It is one-dimensional with N elements; at the beginning of the program each element is loaded with its element number, so that $NROW(I) = I$. Let us pretend that a variable in a Fortran subscript expression can itself be subscripted, and consider a modification of the program as follows.

i When the pivotal condensation search has established that rows L and K should be interchanged, interchange NROW(L) and NROW(K) but leave the actual coefficients unchanged.

ii Whenever a subscript, say I, refers to a row number, write NROW(I) in place of I. For instance, statement 600 would become

```
600 A(NROW(I),J) = A(NROW(I),J) - FACTOR*A(NROW(K),J)
```

Devise a small example to show that if Fortran permitted such subscripts the Gaussian elimination process would be carried out properly without ever actually performing any row interchanges.

Fortran of course does not permit variables in subscript expressions to be subscripted, as some languages do. However, we can program the same thing by preceding each statement in which a row number appears as a subscript, with one or more statements that accomplish the same result. Indicate with an example how this can be done.

Write a program to do row *and* *column* pivotal condensation without any actual interchanges, following these ideas. Demonstrate with an example that the problem of variable identification in column interchanges is properly handled.

27a For a system of *three* simultaneous equations check that Gaussian elimination requires $(4n^3 + 9n^2 - 7n)/6$ arithmetic operations whereas Gauss-Seidel iteration requires $2n^2 - n$ arithmetic operations per iteration. Be careful not to count the arithmetic operations that produce the zeroes in elimination. (As an aid to you we point out that elimination should require 11 multiplications, 11 additions, and 6 divisions; iteration requires 6 multiplications, 6 additions, and 3 divisions for each iteration.)

b In this case, two iterations of Gauss-Seidel requires more arithmetic than does Gaussian elimination. But $n/3 = 1$, not 2. Explain.

28 Devise a system of simultaneous equations having an infinite number of solutions, for instance by making every equation after the first a nonzero multiple of the first. The system will not, of course, satisfy the sufficient condition for the convergence of the Gauss-Seidel method, but try it anyway. What conclusion can you draw from the results?

29 In the system of equations you devised for Exercise 28 change one of the righthand sides. Now the system has no solution. Try the Gauss-Seidel method again.

30 Write a program to solve a system of six simultaneous equations by Gauss-Jordan elimination (see Exercise 9), assuming that the co-efficients and constant terms are given.

31 Modify the program in Figure 4.12 so that if D is a one-dimensional array containing a second right-hand side both systems will be solved in one elimination process.

32 Modify the program in Exercise 31 so that the elements of D are initially set to $+1$ and all operations on D involve addition of absolute values. The back-solution, again adding absolute values and ignoring any minus signs in division, will produce the Δ_i of Section 4.9.

33 Write a program to evaluate an Nth-order determinant. Use Gaussian elimination to form a triangular system, then form the product of the main diagonal elements; this product is the determinant. If row interchanges are used, and they should be, set up a variable to count the number of row interchanges; if this count is odd, the sign of the product of the main diagonal elements must be reversed.

*34 Use the modified Gauss-Seidel method of Section 4.11 to solve

$$2x + y = 2$$
$$x - 2y = -2$$

Use as a convergence criterion that

$$|\Delta x| < 10^{-6}$$

and

$$|\Delta y| < 10^{-6}$$

Find a value of ω for which only 6 iterations are required.

35 The Gauss-Seidel method applied to

$$x - 2y = -2$$
$$2x + y = 2$$

diverges. (Reordering the equations would produce a convergent system.) Use the modified Gauss-Seidel method of Section 4.11 with the equations in the order shown to produce a convergent algorithm. (*Hint:* Use a value of ω between 0 and $\frac{1}{2}$.)

36 Use the modified Gauss-Seidel method of Section 4.11 to solve

$$2x - y = 1$$
$$-x + 2y = 4$$

Use a convergence criterion of

$$|\Delta x| < 10^{-6}$$

and

$$|\Delta y| < 10^{-6}$$

a. Show numerically that for $\omega = 1$, there are 12 iterations required for convergence.
b. Show numerically that for $\omega = 1.1$, there are 8 iterations required.
c. Show numerically that for $\omega = 1.2$, there are 10 iterations required.
d. Find a value of ω that requires only 7 iterations.

37 Find the value of ω that requires the fewest number of iterations in the modified Gauss-Seidel method applied to

$$
\begin{aligned}
4x_1 - x_2 - x_3 &= -1 \\
-x_1 + 4x_2 - x_3 - x_4 &= 2 \\
-x_1 - x_2 + 4x_3 - x_4 - x_5 &= 6 \\
- x_2 - x_3 + 4x_4 - x_5 &= 2 \\
- x_3 - x_4 + 4x_5 &= -1
\end{aligned}
$$

38 Change the flow chart in Figure 4.10 so that it uses the modified Gauss-Seidel method as outlined in Section 4.11.

39 Some large modern computers have extensive facilities for parallel operation of multiple arithmetic units. A machine might have, say, 64 separate arithmetic units, all operating simultaneously. Various architectures are possible, but we shall assume for this exercise that all of them operate on data contained in the same high-speed data storage.

Such machines are ideally suited for solving systems of simultaneous equations by the Gauss-Seidel method. Indeed, the primary motivation for building such machines has often been the need to solve huge systems of equations arising out of the solution of the partial differential equations of various physical systems, such as weather prediction or thermonuclear reactions.

It must be considered, however, that if a set of parallel processing elements are working at the same time, each one will be working entirely with *old* values for the variables, whereas our analysis assumed that, as soon as a new value had been computed from one equation, that new value would immediately be used in the next equation to get a new estimate for the next variable. We must expect, therefore, that convergence would require more iterations, although naturally each iteration would be carried out a great deal more rapidly than in a serial processor of the same basic speed.

Revise the program of Figure 4.22 to simulate the operation of a machine with at least as many parallel processing elements as there are equations. You will need another vector for the variables, so that in effect you keep separate the new and old values; the iteration scheme is carried out always using old values. After each iteration, the "new" values are transferred to the "old" vector before going around again. Try the program out on a variety of systems and compare the number of iterations required for convergence with the number required by the program as shown in the text. See also Exercise 23.

40 The chemical plant shown in Figure 4.25 is somewhat simpler than the one used in Case Study 7. It consists of a mixer, where the feed stream and one recycle stream are mixed, and two reactors. There are three components in the system, named A, B, and C; the feed consists of 40 lb/hr of A, 20 lb/hr of B, and 40 lb/hr of C. Reactor I separates the incoming mixture of A, B, and C into two parts. The "top" fraction consists solely of A and B and is the product. The amount of A in the product is 25% of the weight of the total stream $(A + B + C)$ entering Reactor I, and the amount of B in the product is 20% of this reactor input stream. The "bottom" fraction of Reactor I consists of C only and is therefore 55% of the weight of the input stream to Reactor I. Reactor II converts the C that enters it into 10% A, 20% B, and the rest C. This output is recycled back to the mixer.

Write nine equations in nine variables that describe this system, and solve them. The nine variables will be the weights of: A, B, and C in the stream leaving the mixer, the A and B leaving the top of Reactor I, the C leaving the bottom of Reactor I, and the A, B, and C leaving Reactor II. Solve the system by Gauss-Seidel iteration, which will work even though the system does not meet the sufficient conditions stated in the text.

41 A frequently encountered application of the techniques for the solution of sets of linear algebraic equations given in this chapter is the analysis of electronic circuits consisting of frequency-invariant elements. An example is the network consisting of independent voltage sources and lumped resistors shown in Figure 4.26. The complete analysis of such a network requires the determination of the values of the mesh currents i_k indicated in the figure for the specified values of the voltage sources and the resistors. To perform such an analysis it is necessary first to formulate a set of simultaneous equations with the quantities i_k as unknowns. Each of the equations of such a simul-

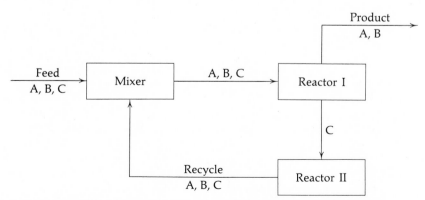

Figure 4.25. *Flow sheet for the hypothetical chemical plant in Exercise 40.*

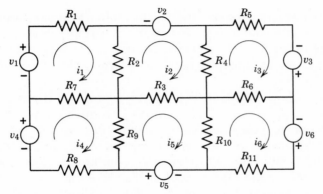

Figure 4.26. *Resistance network discussed in Exercise 41.*

taneous set is determined by applying Kirchhoff's voltage law around one of the meshes. For example, for the mesh defined by the current i_1, we have

$$v_1 = R_1 i_1 + R_2(i_1 - i_2) + R_7(i_1 - i_4)$$

This may be written in the form

$$v_1 = r_{11} i_1 + r_{12} i_2 + r_{14} i_4$$

where

$$r_{11} = R_1 + R_2 \qquad r_{12} = -R_2 \qquad r_{14} = -R_7$$

We may note the following properties of the quantities r_{ij} defined above:

a. The coefficient r_{11} multiplying i_1 is the sum of the values of the resistors that are in the first mesh.

b. The coefficient r_{12} multiplying i_2 is the negative of the value of the resistor that is common to both the first and the second meshes.

c. The coefficient r_{14} multiplying i_4 is the negative of the value of the resistor that is common to both the first and fourth meshes.

Making a similar evaluation for the other meshes we obtain the following set of simultaneous equations.

$$
\begin{aligned}
v_1 &= r_{11} i_1 + r_{12} i_2 + 0\, i_3 + r_{14} i_4 + 0\, i_5 + 0\, i_6 \\
v_2 &= r_{21} i_1 + r_{22} i_2 + r_{23} i_3 + 0\, i_4 + r_{25} i_5 + 0\, i_6 \\
v_3 &= 0\, i_1 + r_{32} i_2 + r_{33} i_3 + 0\, i_4 + 0\, i_5 + r_{36} i_6 \\
v_4 &= r_{41} i_1 + 0\, i_2 + 0\, i_3 + r_{44} i_4 + r_{45} i_5 + 0\, i_6 \\
v_5 &= 0\, i_1 + r_{52} i_2 + 0\, i_3 + r_{54} i_4 + r_{55} i_5 + r_{56} i_6 \\
v_6 &= 0\, i_1 + 0\, i_2 + r_{63} i_3 + 0\, i_4 + r_{65} i_5 + r_{66} i_6
\end{aligned}
$$

where, in general, the coefficients r_{ij} are defined as follows:

r_{ii} — The total resistance that is present in the ith mesh
$r_{ij}(i \neq j)$ — The negative of the resistance that is common to both the ith and the jth meshes

Considering the above relations we see that the effect of any single resistor R_k that is located only in the ith mesh is to add R_k to the coefficient r_{ii}. On the other hand, a resistor R_k that is common to both the ith and jth meshes affects four of the coefficients r_{ij} as follows:

a. It adds R_k to r_{ii}.

b. It subtracts R_k from r_{ij} and r_{ji}.

c. It adds R_k to r_{jj}.

These effects are readily implemented in a program to compute the coefficients r_{ij} and to solve the set of simultaneous equations. The inputs required for such a program are: n, the number of meshes; V_i ($i = 1, 2, \ldots, n$), the value of the voltage source in the ith mesh; n_r, the number of resistors; R_i, the values of the resistors; and m_{1i} and m_{2i}, the numbers identifying the meshes in which the ith resistance is found. If the ith resistor is located in only a single mesh, then the quantity m_{2i} should be set to zero.

Write a program following this scheme and use it to solve the system shown. The correct results are $i_1 = 0.0151a$, $i_2 = 0.0129a$, $i_3 = -0.0002a$, $i_4 = 0.0158a$, $i_5 = 0.0125a$, and $i_6 = 0.0020a$.

42 Another frequently encountered problem in electrical engineering is the analysis of a network under conditions of sinusoidal steady-state excitation. In such an application the transient effects are ignored and only steady-state conditions are considered. This means that all the voltage and current variables in the network will have a sinusoidal form. The frequency of these sinusoids is the same as the one used to provide the excitation. Since the frequency of oscillation is the same throughout the entire network, all the variables can be represented by a complex number giving the magnitude and phase of the associated sinusoid. Thus, in general, we may write

$$A_0 \cos(\omega t + \alpha) \rightarrow A_0 e^{j\alpha} = A_0 \cos \alpha + j A_0 \sin \alpha \qquad (a)$$

where the arrow should be read "is represented by." Such a representation, that is, a complex number that is used to represent a sinusoidally varying quantity, is called a *phasor*. Phasor quantities can be used to directly characterize network elements. For example, let $V_0 e^{j\alpha}$ be a voltage phasor and $I_0 e^{j\beta}$ be a current phasor. If these phasors represent the terminal variables associated with a two-terminal resistor, then we may write

$$V_0 e^{j\alpha} = R I_0 e^{j\beta}$$

In the above relation, since R is real, α must equal β, that is, as is well known, there is no phase shift observed between the sinusoidal voltage and current variables associated with a resistor. For an inductor, the terminal voltage and current phasors are related as follows

$$V_0 e^{j\alpha} = j\omega L I_0 e^{j\beta} = \omega L e^{j\pi/2} I_0 e^{j\beta}$$

where the quantity $j\omega L$ is called the complex impedance of the inductor at the frequency ω. If we equate the phase in both members of the above equation, we see that $\omega = \beta + \pi/2$. Thus, the phase of the voltage phasor is 90 degrees ($\pi/2$ rad) greater than that of the current phasor. This means, of course, that the voltage sinusoid *leads* the current sinusoid by 90 degrees in an inductor. Finally, for a

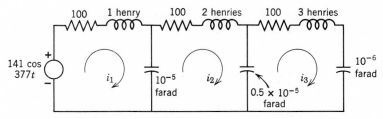

Figure 4.27. *Network in Exercise 42.*

capacitor, the terminal voltage and current phasors are related by the expression

$$V_0 e^{j\alpha} = \frac{1}{j\omega C} I_0 e^{j\beta} = \frac{1}{\omega C} e^{-j\pi/2} I_0 e^{j\beta}$$

where the quantity $1/j\omega C$ is the complex impedance of the capacitor at the frequency ω. In this case, we see that the voltage sinusoid *lags* the current sinusoid by 90 degrees. Since Kirchhoff's voltage and current laws apply equally well to phasors as they do to time-varying quantities, network analysis in terms of complex impedances and phasors is readily performed. As an example, consider the network shown in Figure 4.27. This is redrawn in Figure 4.28 to indicate the impedance of the network elements and the phasor representation for the voltage source. Applying Kirchhoff's voltage law around each of the three meshes we obtain

$$141 e^{j0} = \left(100 + 377 + \frac{10^5}{j377}\right) I_1 - \frac{10^5}{j377} I_2$$

$$0 = \frac{10^5}{j377} I_1 + \left(100 + j754 + \frac{10^5}{j377} + \frac{10^5}{j188.5}\right) I_2 - \frac{10^5}{j188.5} I_3$$

$$0 = -\frac{10^5}{j188.5} I_2 + \left(\frac{10^5}{j188.5} + 100 + j1131 + \frac{10^6}{j377}\right) I_3$$

where the quantities I_i are the phasor representations for the sinusoidal steady-state mesh currents. The relations given above may be treated as a set of simultaneous equations with complex coefficients. The techniques given in this chapter are readily employed to solve such a set of equations simply by replacing the real variables with complex variables. The resulting solution will give the complex phasor values for quantities I_i. These may readily be converted to the sinusoidal steady-state time domain mesh currents i_i by using the relation given in (a).

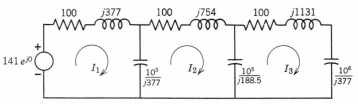

Figure 4.28. *The network of Figure 4.27, with quantities represented in phasor form.*

*43 Suppose a university is comprised of three colleges: Arts and Sciences, Engineering, and Business. The annual budgets for these colleges are \$16 million, \$5 million, and \$8 million, respectively. The full-time enrollments are 4000 in Arts and Sciences, 1000 in Engineering, and 2000 in Business. The enrollment in Arts and Sciences courses consists of 70% from Arts and Sciences, 20% from Engineering and 10% from Business. (For example, all English courses are taught by Arts and Sciences.) Similarly Engineering and Business courses contain some students from other colleges. The distribution is as follows:

| | Courses taught by | | |
Students from	Arts and Sciences	Engineering	Business
Arts and Sciences	70%	10%	15%
Engineering	20%	90%	10%
Business	10%	0	75%

Following the development in Case Study 8 (Section 4.11), determine to the nearest cent the annual cost of educating a student in each of the three colleges.

44 Propane (C_3H_8) is to be burned with 25% more air than the amount required for full combustion. The chemical reaction can be written:

$$C_3H_8 + 5O_2 + (\text{Excess air}) \rightarrow 3CO_2 + 4H_2O + (\text{Excess air}) \quad (a)$$

What is called "excess air" in this equation consists of the additional oxygen beyond that needed for full combustion, plus the nitrogen, which does not enter the reaction. The mixture of gases on the right is called the *flue gas*, that is, the combination of combustion products, unused oxygen, and nitrogen, that goes up the flue.

We ask the question: For each 100 moles of flue gas, how much air is required? (A *mole* of a compound is its molecular weight expressed in some convenient weight unit. Since the molecular weight of water is about 18, for instance, a gram-mole of water would be 18 grams, a pound-mole 18 pounds, etc. Since this problem in effect calls only for ratios, the weight units are not important and have not been included.)

The problem can be approached by writing a series of equations that express known relationships among various components of the reaction. We shall use the following symbols:

P = moles of propane entering combustion chamber (Molecular weight = 44)

A = moles of air entering combustion chamber (Average mol wt = 28.84)

C = moles of CO_2 in flue gas (mol wt = 44)

W = moles of H_2O in flue gas (mol wt = 18)

N = moles of N_2 in flue gas (mol wt = 28)

ϕ = moles of O_2 in flue gas, other than that contained in H_2O or CO_2 (mol wt = 32)

We first write four equations expressing the fact that there must be as much of each element entering the reaction as leaving it:

Carbon balance:	$3P = C$	(b)
Hydrogen balance:	$4P = W$	(c)
Oxygen balance:	$0.21A = \phi + W/2 + C$	(d)

(This assumes that air is 21% oxygen, 79% nitrogen)

Nitrogen balance:	$0.79A = N$	(e)

Next, from the definition of the variables and the fact that we are asking what is required to produce 100 moles of flue gas:

$$N + \phi + C + W = 100 \tag{f}$$

Next we have the specification of 25% excess air. This means that $25/125 = 0.2$ of the entering oxygen must leave as uncombined oxygen:

$$(0.21A)(0.2) = \phi \tag{g}$$

Now we have two relationships giving the ratios between reactants. Since five oxygen molecules are required for each propane molecule, plus an excess of oxygen, we get

$$0.21A = (1.25)(5P) \tag{h}$$

And, since CO_2 and H_2O must occur in a fixed ratio,

$$4C = 3W \tag{i}$$

Now we can write an equation giving the overall mass balance:

$$44P + 28.84A = 44C + 18W + 32\phi + 28N \tag{j}$$

Lastly we have an equation stating what happens to the air that enters the reaction:

$$A = C + W/2 + N + \phi \tag{k}$$

Now we have a problem: We have written down eleven equations in the six variables P, A, C, W, N, and ϕ. See what happens if you try to pick out sets of six equations that contain all the variables and solve them, ignoring the others. Try (b) through (g) as one set, (f) through (k) as another, and (d) through (i). Write out the matrix of the full eleven equations in six variables and see if you can give an explanation of the redundancy, that is, how some equations are linear combinations of others. Is there any set of six equations, as written, that contains all the information of the full set?

The correct answer is 93.70 moles of air.

5 Numerical
Differentiation and Integration

The application of mathematics to the physical and social sciences often requires finding the derivative or the integral of some function. Sometimes it is possible to find the derivative or integral in *closed form*; that is, for some functions we can write down a formula for the derivative or the integral. For example, if the function is

$$f(x) = \sin x$$

then the derivative is

$$\frac{df}{dx} = \cos x$$

and the indefinite integral is

$$\int f(x)\, dx = -\cos x + C$$

where C is an arbitrary constant.

In many practical cases, however, either (1) no closed form solution can be found, (2) the closed form solution is difficult to find, or (3) the closed form solution is of little practical value. Difficulties of this kind arise more frequently in integration than in differentiation. The indefinite integral of the simple function

$$f(x) = \frac{e^x - e^{-x}}{x}$$

cannot be expressed in closed form. The derivative, of course, may be computed in a straightforward way. Similarly the integral of

$$f(x) = \frac{1}{2 + \cos x}$$

can be determined to be

$$\frac{2}{\sqrt{3}} \log \left(\frac{\sqrt{3} \tan \left(\frac{x}{2}\right) + 3}{\sqrt{3} \tan \left(\frac{x}{2}\right) - 3} \right) + C$$

but only after considerable algebraic manipulation.

Even when a closed form solution exists and can be found, it may not be practical to use such a solution for calculations. The last example above is one case in point. Another example is

$$\int_0^\pi \cos (4x) \cos (3 \sin (x)) \, dx = \pi J_4(3) \tag{5.1}$$

where J_4 is the fourth-order Bessel function of the first kind. If we wish to evaluate the definite integral on the left of (5.1), then we could evaluate $J_4(3)$, but this is at best a difficult computation to perform. It would be just as easy and, as we shall see, more straightforward to evaluate the integral itself numerically.

Finally we point out that we may wish to find the derivative or integral of a function that is not given by a formula at all. Suppose, for example, that we have measured the velocity (in ft/sec) of an object at various points in time (in seconds). We might write these measurements in tabular form as follows:

Table 5.1

Time	Velocity
0.1	10.443
0.2	9.984
0.4	9.432
0.5	9.375
0.6	9.488
0.8	10.296
0.9	11.027
1.1	13.233
1.2	14.744
1.4	18.672
1.5	21.125
1.6	23.928
1.8	30.656
1.9	34.617

The velocity of this object is a function of time, and the function is defined by the table of entries. Since acceleration is the rate of change of velocity, the acceleration is the derivative of the velocity with respect to time. If we wish to compute the acceleration, then we must somehow find the derivative of the function specified by the table. We are forced to use numerical methods in such a case.[1]

Similarly, the distance traveled by the object is the integral of the velocity. Thus, if we wish to compute the distance traveled, then we must integrate the velocity function specified by the table. Once again we have no choice except to use numerical methods.

In this chapter we study numerical techniques for differentiating and integrating functions. We shall find that it is relatively easy to perform numerical integration. On the other hand, numerical differentiation is fraught with difficulties and hazards. This is exactly the opposite of analytical techniques where differentiation is usually easy but integration is difficult. It is curious, and at the same time fortunate, that what is difficult analytically is easy numerically and vice versa.

In this section we shall discuss the simplest, most straightforward algorithms for the numerical computation of first and second derivatives. After discussing the truncation error and the numerical errors that arise from subtractive cancellation, we shall return in Section 5.5 to the derivation of more general algorithms for numerical differentiation.

The derivative of a function $f(x)$ at $x = x_0$ is defined as

$$f'(x_0) = \lim_{\Delta x \to 0} \frac{f(x_0 + \Delta x) - f(x_0)}{\Delta x}$$

provided the limit exists. Therefore, if we compute the ratio

$$\frac{f(x_0 + \Delta x) - f(x_0)}{\Delta x} \tag{5.2}$$

for a small value of Δx, we should have a fairly good approximation for $f'(x_0)$. Of course, Δx may be positive or negative. Thus, if we think of Δx as being a positive number, then

$$\frac{f(x_0 - \Delta x) - f(x_0)}{-\Delta x} \tag{5.3}$$

is another approximation for $f'(x_0)$.

In Figure 5.1 the line $L+$ has a slope equal to (5.2) and the line $L-$ has a slope equal to (5.3). The derivative $f'(x_0)$ is equal to the slope of the tangent to the curve at x_0. It is intuitively obvious that as $\Delta x \to 0$, the lines $L+$ and $L-$ both approach the tangent line at x_0. From the figure, however, we might suspect that if we drew the chord from P to Q the slope of this new line would provide a better approximation for $f'(x_0)$ than would either (5.2) or (5.3). This is indeed true (see Exercise 1).

---

[1] Such methods are discussed in this chapter. We will also discuss methods of computing such derivatives in Chapter 7 on least squares approximations.

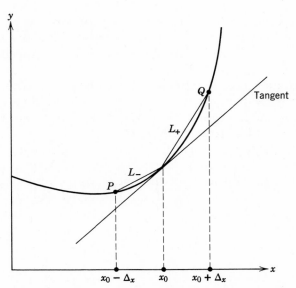

Figure 5.1. *Geometrical representation of two possible approximations to the derivative of a function.*

The slope of the line passing through P and Q is

$$\frac{f(x_0 + \Delta x) - f(x_0 - \Delta x)}{2\Delta x} \tag{5.4}$$

Notice that this is the average of the two ratios (5.2) and (5.3). For convenience we let $h = 2\Delta x$ and obtain from (5.4)

$$f'(x_0) \cong \frac{f\left(x_0 + \dfrac{h}{2}\right) - f\left(x_0 - \dfrac{h}{2}\right)}{h} \tag{5.5}$$

We use this as an approximation for $f'(x_0)$. In the next section we discuss the truncation error in (5.5).

Now suppose we wish to compute the second derivative of $f(x)$ at $x = x_0$. From (5.5) with $f(x)$ replaced by $f'(x)$

$$f''(x_0) \cong \frac{f'\left(x_0 + \dfrac{h}{2}\right) - f'\left(x_0 - \dfrac{h}{2}\right)}{h} \tag{5.6}$$

But again using (5.5)

$$f'\left(x_0 + \frac{h}{2}\right) \cong \frac{f(x_0 + h) - f(x_0)}{h}$$

and

$$f'\left(x_0 - \frac{h}{2}\right) \cong \frac{f(x_0) - f(x_0 - h)}{h}$$

Using both of these in (5.6)

$$f''(x_0) \cong \frac{f(x_0 + h) - 2f(x_0) + f(x_0 - h)}{h^2} \tag{5.7}$$

We could, of course, continue in this way to obtain approximations to third-, fourth-, and higher-order derivatives. We defer doing this, however, until Section 5.5. (See also Exercise 2.)

We turn now to a discussion of the truncation error in using the approximations (5.5) and (5.7). In the next section we shall discuss other numerical errors that arise in the use of these approximations.

From Taylor's theorem

$$f(x) = f(x_0) + (x - x_0)f'(x_0) + \frac{(x - x_0)^2}{2}f''(x_0) + \frac{(x - x_0)^3}{6}f'''(\xi)$$

where ξ lies in the closed interval bounded by x and x_0. Replacing x by $x_0 + h/2$

$$f\left(x_0 + \frac{h}{2}\right) = f(x_0) + \frac{h}{2}f'(x_0) + \frac{h^2}{8}f''(x_0) + \frac{h^3}{48}f'''(\xi_1) \tag{5.8}$$

where

$$x_0 \le \xi_1 \le x_0 + \frac{h}{2}$$

Similarly, using $x = x_0 - h/2$

$$f\left(x_0 - \frac{h}{2}\right) = f(x_0) - \frac{h}{2}f'(x_0) + \frac{h^2}{8}f''(x_0) - \frac{h^3}{48}f'''(\xi_2) \tag{5.9}$$

where

$$x_0 - \frac{h}{2} \le \xi_2 \le x_0$$

Subtracting (5.9) from (5.8) and rearranging

$$f'(x_0) = \frac{f\left(x_0 + \frac{h}{2}\right) - f\left(x_0 - \frac{h}{2}\right)}{h} - \frac{h^2}{24}\left(\frac{f'''(\xi_1) + f'''(\xi_2)}{2}\right)$$

If $f'''(x)$ is continuous, then by the Intermediate Value Theorem[2] there is some value ξ such that $\xi_2 \le \xi \le \xi_1$ and

$$\frac{f'''(\xi_1) + f'''(\xi_2)}{2} = f'''(\xi)$$

---

[2] The *Intermediate Value Theorem* states that if $F(x)$ is continuous, then for $F(a) \le M \le F(b)$ there exists at least one number c such that $F(c) = M$ and c lies in the closed interval bounded by a and b. In the above argument we choose $F = f'''$, $a = \xi_1$, $b = \xi_2$, and $M =$ the average of $f'''(\xi_1)$ and $f'''(\xi_2)$. We rename c to be ξ so that $\xi_1 \le \xi \le \xi_2$.

Thus

$$f'(x_0) = \frac{f\left(x_0 + \frac{h}{2}\right) - f\left(x_0 - \frac{h}{2}\right)}{h} - \frac{h^2}{24}f'''(\xi) \qquad (5.10)$$

where

$$x_0 - \frac{h}{2} \le \xi \le x_0 + \frac{h}{2}$$

By comparing this with (5.5), the truncation error (true value—approximate value) is

$$e_t = \frac{h^2}{24}f'''(\xi) \qquad (5.11)$$

Thus, if we decrease the interval by a factor of two (replace h by $h/2$), we decrease the truncation error by a factor of four; provided, of course, that the third derivative does not fluctuate too much. In principle, then, as h becomes small, the approximation (5.5) becomes better and better. As we shall see in the next section, however, the "in principle" is once again important and matters are not quite so simple as our discussion thus far would lead us to believe.

A similar analysis (see Exercise 3) leads to a truncation error in (5.7) for the second derivative.

$$e_t = -\frac{h^2}{12}f^{iv}(\xi) \qquad (5.12)$$

Note that this truncation error is also proportional to h^2. It depends upon the fourth derivative rather than the third derivative as did (5.11).

5.4
Total Error

Consider the simple function

$$f(x) = e^x$$

so that

$$f''(x) = f'(x) = f(x) = e^x$$

Suppose we wish to compute $f'(1)$ using (5.5) from five-place tables of e^x. Using $h = .01$, we compute

$$f'(1) \cong \frac{2.7319 - 2.7047}{0.01} = 2.7200$$

Then, using $h = 0.001$

$$f'(1) \cong \frac{2.7196 - 2.7169}{0.001} = 2.7000$$

This leads us to the alarming conclusion that decreasing h from $\frac{1}{100}$ to $\frac{1}{1000}$ actually produces a less accurate result. The same unhappy phenomenon also appears in the second derivative using (5.7). (See Exercise 4.)

A Fortran program that starts with $h = \frac{1}{32}$ and successively reduces h by a factor of one-half is shown in Figure 5.2. The program prints h, $f'(x)$, and $f''(x)$ using (5.5) and (5.7). The results of running that program for $x = 1$ are also shown in Figure 5.2. Notice that for small values of h, both the first and second derivative approximations deteriorate.

The difficulty arises because of "subtractive cancellation" (see Example 3 of Section 2.9 and Case Study 4 in Chapter 3). When we compute $f[x_0 + (h/2)]$ and $f[x_0 - (h/2)]$, we obtain two numbers whose values are nearly equal. If we subtract one of these values from the other, the relative error is quite large. Dividing by h amounts to multiplying by a large number and hence aggravates the error. Thus to increase the accuracy of $f'(x_0)$ and $f''(x_0)$ we need not only to decrease h but also to increase the number of significant digits in $f(x)$ itself. We can also increase the accuracy by using other approximations some of which are discussed in the next section.

```
C FIGURE 5.2
C A PROGRAM TO COMPUTE FIRST AND SECOND DERIVATIVES
C    OF THE EXPONENTIAL OF 1.0, FOR DIFFERENT VALUES OF H,
C    TO DEMONSTRATE EFFECT OF SUBTRACTIVE CANCELLATION
C
      H = 1.0/32.0
      DO 400 I = 1, 25
      FPRIME = (EXP(1.0+H/2.0) - EXP(1.0-H/2.0)) / H
      FDPRIM = (EXP(1.0+H) - 2.0*EXP(1.0) + EXP(1.0-H)) / H**2
      WRITE (6, 500) H, FPRIME, FDPRIM
  500 FORMAT (1X, 1P3E14.6)
  400 H = H / 2.0
      STOP
      END


15.40.25  RUN DERIV
EXECUTION:
   3.125000E-02   2.718384E 00   2.718750E 00
   1.562500E-02   2.718262E 00   2.718750E 00
   7.812500E-03   2.718262E 00   2.718750E 00
   3.906250E-03   2.718506E 00   2.750000E 00
   1.953125E-03   2.718262E 00   2.750000E 00
   9.765625E-04   2.717773E 00   3.000000E 00
   4.882813E-04   2.718750E 00   4.000000E 00
   2.441406E-04   2.718750E 00   0.0
   1.220703E-04   2.718750E 00   0.0
   6.103516E-05   2.718750E 00   0.0
   3.051758E-05   2.718750E 00   0.0
   1.525879E-05   2.750000E 00   4.096000E 03
   7.629395E-06   2.750000E 00   0.0
   3.814697E-06   2.750000E 00   0.0
   1.907349E-06   3.000000E 00   2.621440E 05
   9.536743E-07   1.000000E 00   0.0
   4.768372E-07   2.000000E 00  -4.194304E 06
   2.384186E-07   0.0           -1.677722E 07
   1.192093E-07   0.0            0.0
   5.960464E-08   0.0            0.0
   2.980232E-08   0.0            0.0
   1.490116E-08   0.0            0.0
   7.450581E-09   0.0            0.0
   3.725290E-09   0.0            0.0
   1.862645E-09   0.0            0.0
```

Figure 5.2. *A program, with its output, to illustrate the problem of subtractive cancellation in evaluating derivatives numerically. In theory, every entry in the second and third columns should be* e $\cong$ 2.7182818.

5.5 Generalized Numerical Differentiation

In this section we shall develop general formulas for first, second, third, and fourth derivatives. In particular recall that (5.5) for the first derivative required the value of $f(x)$ at two points: $x_0 + h/2$ and $x_0 - h/2$. We shall develop three- and five-point formulas here. We shall see that the greater the number of points used in the approximation for $f'(x_0)$, the smaller the truncation error. This will enable us to reduce the truncation error without decreasing h. As we saw in the previous section, decreasing h can lead to disastrous results.

We look then for an approximation for $f'(x_0)$ that involves the value of f at three points. We label the points x_{-1}, x_0, x_1 where

$$x_{-1} < x_0 < x_1$$

We let

$$x_{-1} = x_0 - h_1$$
$$x_1 = x_0 + h_2$$

where $h_1 > 0$ and $h_2 > 0$. We then write

$$f'(x_0) \cong p_{-1}f(x_{-1}) + p_0 f(x_0) + p_1 f(x_1) \tag{5.13}$$

or

$$f'(x_0) \cong p_{-1}f(x_0 - h_1) + p_0 f(x_0) + p_1 f(x_1 + h_2) \tag{5.14}$$

We wish to find the constants p_{-1}, p_0, and p_1.

Consider first the case where $f(x)$ is a constant. We certainly want (5.14) to be accurate for this simple case. Thus we let

$$f(x) = 1$$

Then

$$f'(x) = 0$$

Therefore, from (5.14)

$$0 = p_{-1} + p_0 + p_1 \tag{5.15}$$

The three constants must satisfy this equation if (5.14) is to be valid when $f(x)$ is a constant.

Next we consider $f(x)$ to be a linear function. In particular we let

$$f(x) = x - x_0$$

so that

$$f'(x) = 1$$

From (5.14)

$$1 = -h_1 p_{-1} + h_2 p_1 \tag{5.16}$$

Finally we let $f(x)$ be a quadratic function

$$f(x) = (x - x_0)^2$$

so

$$f'(x) = 2(x - x_0)$$

Again from (5.14)

$$0 = h_1^2 p_{-1} + h_2^2 p_1 \tag{5.17}$$

The constants p_{-1}, p_0, and p_1 must satisfy the system of three equations (5.15), (5.16), and (5.17). In the previous chapter we discussed algorithms for determining the solution of such systems numerically. In this case, a little algebra produces the following solution:

$$p_{-1} = -\frac{h_2}{h_1(h_1 + h_2)}$$

$$p_0 = \frac{h_2^2 - h_1^2}{h_1 h_2 (h_1 + h_2)}$$

$$p_1 = \frac{h_1}{h_2(h_1 + h_2)}$$

Notice that, since $h_1 > 0$ and $h_2 > 0$, this solution always exists. Thus (5.14) becomes

$$f'(x_0) = \frac{h_1^2 f(x_0 + h_2) + (h_2^2 - h_1^2)f(x_0) - h_2^2 f(x_0 - h_1)}{h_1 h_2 (h_1 + h_2)} \qquad (5.18)$$

This approximation has been derived from three particular functions: 1, $x - x_0$, and $(x - x_0)^2$. Exercise 5 will show, however, that (5.18) produces the correct value for the derivative of *any* quadratic function; that is to say, there is no truncation error if $f(x)$ is a quadratic, linear, or constant function. For a more general function, however, there will be a truncation error. We shall investigate that truncation error shortly. First, however, we note that if

$$h_1 = h_2 = h/2$$

then (5.18) is identical with (5.5) as we should expect.

Thus (5.18) is a generalization of (5.5). It allows us to use data points that are not equally spaced in x. Table 5.1 is an example of such data. If we wish to compute the derivative of the velocity at a time of $x = 1.1$ sec, we shall have difficulty using (5.5), since if we choose $h/2 = .1$ then we do not know $f(x - h/2) = f(1)$. If we choose $h/2 = .2$ then we do not know $f(x + h/2) = f(1.3)$. Not until we use $h/2 = .3$ can we use (5.5). Thus if we use (5.5) we are ignoring the data close to 1.1 which should intuitively seem to be a bad practice. On the other hand, we can use (5.18) by letting $h_1 = .2$ and $h_2 = .1$. Indeed (5.18) then becomes

$$f'(1.1) = \frac{(.2)^2 f(1.2) + (.1^2 - .2^2)f(1.1) - (.1)^2 f(.9)}{(.2)(.1)(.3)}$$

$$f'(1.1) = 13.75 \qquad (5.19)$$

This is an approximation for the acceleration (in ft/sec²) of the object at a time of 1.1 sec. This differs from the result obtained by using (5.5) and $h/2 = .3$ (see Exercise 6).

We now turn to our discussion of the truncation error in (5.18). Our discussion will follow the argument of Section 5.3 quite closely.

Again we start with Taylor's Theorem

$$f(x) = f(x_0) + (x - x_0)f'(x_0) + \frac{(x - x_0)^2}{2}f''(x_0) + \frac{(x - x_0)^3}{6}f'''(\xi)$$

Then letting $x = x_0 + h_2$ and multiplying by h_1^2

$$h_1^2 f(x_0 + h_2) = h_1^2 f(x_0) + h_1^2 h_2 f'(x_0) + \frac{h_1^2 h_2^2}{2}f''(x_0) + \frac{h_1^2 h_2^3}{6}f'''(\xi_1)$$

where $x_0 \leq \xi_1 \leq x_0 + h_2$. Next we let $x = x_0 - h_1$ and multiply by h_2^2 so that

$$h_2^2 f(x_0 - h_1) = h_2^2 f(x_0) - h_1 h_2^2 f'(x_0) + \frac{h_1^2 h_2^2}{2} f''(x_0) - \frac{h_1^3 h_2^2}{6} f'''(\xi_2)$$

Subtracting the second of these from the first and rearranging terms

$$f'(x_0) = \frac{h_1^2 f(x_0 + h_2) + (h_2^2 - h_1^2) f(x_0) - h_2^2 f(x_0 - h_1)}{h_1 h_2 (h_1 + h_2)}$$

$$- \frac{h_1 h_2}{6(h_1 + h_2)} [h_2 f'''(\xi_1) + h_1 f'''(\xi_2)]$$

Therefore the truncation error in (5.18) is

$$e_t = -\frac{h_1 h_2}{6(h_1 + h_2)} [h_2 f'''(\xi_1) + h_1 f'''(\xi_2)] \qquad (5.20)$$

If $h_1 = h_2 = h/2$ this reduces to (5.11) if we once again invoke the Intermediate Value Theorem. Finally we note that, if the third derivative of $f(x)$ is bounded for $x_0 - h_1 \leq x \leq x_0 + h_2$, then there exists a number M such that

$$|f'''(x)| \leq M$$

From (5.20) then

$$|e_t| \leq \frac{h_1 h_2}{6} M \qquad (5.21)$$

Equation (5.18) is no more accurate than (5.5) even though the former uses three points while the latter uses two points. The advantage (5.19) provides us is that we do not need to have equal spacing between the points. As we have seen, if the function is defined by a table of values such as Table 5.1, then the ability to use unequally spaced points is a distinct advantage.

If the function is specified by a formula, however, (5.5) is just as accurate as (5.18) and considerably easier to apply. Therefore, we shall confine our succeeding discussions to equally spaced points concentrating on increasing the accuracy (decreasing the truncation error) of our approximations. If we have need for differentiating from tables with unequally spaced points, we shall use (5.18).

Consider then a five-point formula. We take the five points to be $x_0 - 2h$, $x_0 - h$, x_0, $x_0 + h$, and $x_0 + 2h$. We shall use the value of $f(x)$ at these five points to approximate the value of $f'(x_0)$. Thus we write

$$f'(x_0) \cong p_{-2} f(x_0 - 2h) + p_{-1} f(x_0 - h) + p_0 f(x_0) + p_1 f(x_0 + h)$$
$$+ p_2 f(x_0 + 2h) \qquad (5.22)$$

and we seek the values of p_{-2}, p_{-1}, p_0, p_1, and p_2.

We proceed as before and let $f(x) = 1$ so that $f'(x) = 0$. Using these in (5.22)

$$0 = p_{-2} + p_{-1} + p_0 + p_1 + p_2 \qquad (5.23)$$

Next we let $f(x) = x - x_0$ so $f'(x) = 1$. Again from (5.22)

$$1 = -2hp_{-2} - hp_{-1} + hp_1 + 2hp_2 \tag{5.24}$$

Letting $f(x) = (x - x_0)^2$ we get

$$0 = 4h^2 p_{-2} + h^2 p_{-1} + h^2 p_1 + 4h^2 p_2 \tag{5.25}$$

Letting $f(x) = (x - x_0)^3$ then

$$0 = -8h^3 p_{-2} - h^3 p_{-1} + h^3 p_1 + 8h^3 p_2 \tag{5.26}$$

Finally letting $f(x) = (x - x_0)^4$

$$0 = 16h^4 p_{-2} + h^4 p_{-1} + h^4 p_1 + 16h^4 p_2 \tag{5.27}$$

Equations (5.23) through (5.27) are a system of five linear equations[3] in the five variables: p_{-2}, p_{-1}, p_0, p_1, p_2. The solution is

$$p_{-2} = \frac{1}{12h} \qquad p_2 = -\frac{1}{12h}$$

$$p_{-1} = -\frac{8}{12h} \qquad p_1 = \frac{8}{12h}$$

$$p_0 = 0$$

Thus (5.22) becomes

$$f'(x_0) \cong \frac{1}{12h}[f(x_0 - 2h) - 8f(x_0 - h) + 8f(x_0 + h) - f(x_0 + 2h)] \tag{5.28}$$

This approximation is exact (no truncation error) for *any* polynomial of degree four or less.

The analysis of the truncation error proceeds as before using Taylor's Theorem with a remainder term involving the fifth derivative of $f(x)$. The truncation error resulting from such an analysis is

$$e_t = \frac{24}{5} h^4 f^v(\xi) \tag{5.29}$$

where $x_0 - 2h \leq \xi \leq x_0 + 2h$. This is much smaller than (5.11) provided $f^v(x)$ does not become too large. In particular (5.29) is proportional to h^4 which, for small h, is much smaller than h^2.

We now have an alternative to decreasing the value of h in (5.5). Although in principle (5.5) could be used to estimate $f'(x_0)$ as accurately as we wished by decreasing h, we found that in practice there were severe limitations because of subtractive cancellation. We can decrease the truncation error without decreasing h if we use (5.28) rather than (5.5). The price we pay, of course, is additional computation and the necessity of having more points available.

We can also find formulas for higher order derivatives. The five-point formulas using equally spaced points are

$$f''(x_0) \cong \frac{1}{12h^2}[-f(x_0 - 2h) + 16f(x_0 - h) - 30f(x_0) + 16f(x_0 + h) - f(x_0 + 2h)] \tag{5.30}$$

---

[3] Actually, (5.24) through (5.27) is a system of four equations in the four variables: p_{-2}, p_{-1}, p_1, p_2. The value of p_0 is then given by (5.23). This refers to the question of reducibility; see Footnote 4 and Exercise 24 in Chapter 4.

$$f'''(x_0) \cong \frac{1}{2h^3}[-f(x_0 - 2h) + 2f(x_0 - h) - 2f(x_0 + h) + f(x_0 + 2h)]$$

$$(5.31)$$

$$f^{\prime v}(x_0) \cong \frac{1}{h^4}[f(x_0 - 2h) - 4f(x_0 - h) + 6f(x_0) - 4f(x_0 + h) + f(x_0 + 2h)]$$

$$(5.32)$$

We could also derive formulas for more than five points and continue to reduce the truncation error. The derivations are quite straightforward and each requires the solution of a linear system of equations. The number of equations in the system is equal to the number of points in the formula.

We close this section by pointing out that the sum of the coefficients in all of the approximations—(5.5), (5.28), (5.30), (5.31), (5.32)—is always zero. Thus, as we let h get small, we shall always have difficulty with subtractive cancellation. It is important to notice that increasing the number of points in the approximation delays the onset of the subtractive cancellation problems but does not erase it. All numerical differentiation formulas are subject to subtractive cancellation for h sufficiently small. No matter how many points we use in a formula, it is dangerous to let h approach zero without some checks and balances.

5.6 Some Dangers in Differentiation

We have already discussed some of the numerical difficulties that arise in numerical differentiation. In this section we discuss a serious error that may occur even if we use an infinite amount of precision in the calculations.

Consider the function

$$f(x) = \begin{cases} x^2 \sin\left(\dfrac{792\pi}{100x}\right) & x \neq 0 \\ 0 & x = 0 \end{cases} \qquad (5.33)$$

The derivative of this function is well defined and is given by

$$f'(x) = \begin{cases} 2x \sin\left(\dfrac{792\pi}{100x}\right) - \dfrac{792\pi}{100}\left[\cos\left(\dfrac{792\pi}{100x}\right)\right] & x \neq 0 \\ 0 & x = 0 \end{cases} \qquad (5.34)$$

Notice that the second derivative, $f''(x)$, does not exist at $x = 0$. We now compute $f'(0.1)$ using (5.28) and $h = 0.01$.

$$\begin{aligned} f(x_0 + 2h) &= f(0.12) = 0.0144 \sin(66\pi) = 0 \\ f(x_0 + h) &= f(0.11) = 0.0121 \sin(72\pi) = 0 \\ f(x_0 - h) &= f(0.09) = 0.0081 \sin(88\pi) = 0 \\ f(x_0 - 2h) &= f(0.08) = 0.0064 \sin(99\pi) = 0 \end{aligned}$$

so (5.28) produces
$$f'(0.1) = 0$$

On the other hand, from (5.34)

$$f'(0.1) = 0.2 \sin(792\pi) - (7.92\pi)\cos(792\pi) = -7.92\pi$$

Thus, although (5.28) predicted a derivative of zero, the derivative is far

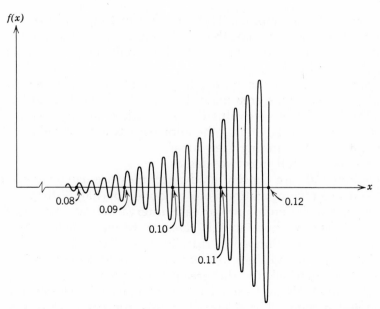

Figure 5.3. *A function used in the text to illustrate another pitfall in numerical differentiation.*

from zero. Notice that this difficulty did not arise from subtractive cancellation, roundoff error, or any other phenomenon associated with floating point arithmetic. The graph of this function is shown in Figure 5.3. At $x = 0.08, 0.09, 0.11$, and 0.12 the function has a root. Indeed there are many roots between 0.08 and 0.12 (33 including the end points). The function oscillates rapidly in the interval $0.08 \le x \le 0.12$ but our approximation, (5.28), only examines the value at four points. At those four points $f(x) = 0$.

In general the problem we must face in numerical differentiation is this: Any approximation formula uses the value of the function at discrete points. Such a formula can in no way anticipate the behavior of the function between the points.

**5.7
Numerical
Integration**

We now turn our attention to numerical integration. Whereas in numerical differentiation disaster lurked around every corner, numerical integration is by comparison well behaved and stable. Thus we shall find our analysis in the remainder of this chapter to be much less tricky.

We shall confine ourselves to evaluation of definite integrals with a finite range of integration, that is,

$$I = \int_a^b f(x)\,dx \tag{5.35}$$

where a and b are finite and $f(x)$ is a continuous function of x for $a \le x \le b$.

Cases in which either or both of the limits of integration are infinite are sometimes of interest, as is the integration of functions having singularities [points where $f(x)$ becomes infinite] within the range of integration or perhaps at the endpoints. These cases can frequently be reduced to the form (5.35), which may then be integrated by the methods to be discussed. We shall consider these cases only in the exercises.[4] (See Exercises 33 and 35.)

We may characterize the approach we shall take as follows. The definite integral I represents the area under the curve $y = f(x)$ between $x = a$ and $x = b$. We can therefore evaluate I by dividing the interval a to b into many smaller intervals, finding the approximate area of each of the strips thus formed, and summing their areas.

The techniques fall into two classes:

1. The intervals are chosen in advance; they are usually selected to be equal, and if the computation is to be done "by hand" they are usually selected so that the endpoints of each interval fall at easily computable values of x. The methods in this category to be discussed here are the trapezoidal rule and Simpson's rule (Sections 5.8 and 5.12).

2. The intervals and their location are dictated by the analysis, in the sense that we first ask for the greatest accuracy possible with a given number of intervals and then let the intervals fall wherever this prior requirement dictates. The example of this approach is Gaussian quadrature (Section 5.14).

There are naturally many other integration rules of both types. The ones we shall consider adequately demonstrate the general approach to numerical evaluation of integrals and to error estimation. In fact, the methods presented here are suitable for actual computation in a large majority of practical applications.

**5.8
The Trap-
ezoidal
Rule**

Consider the integral in (5.35), which represents the shaded area in Figure 5.4. We shall break the interval into n equal intervals, each of size $h = (b - a)/n$. Consider now one of those intervals, as in Figure 5.5, in which the scale along the x-axis has been greatly expanded. The area under the curve $y = f(x)$ between x_i and x_{i+1} is

$$I_i = \int_{x_i}^{x_{i+1}} f(x)\, dx$$

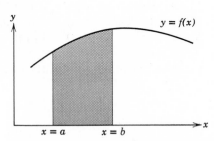

Figure 5.4. *Geometrical interpretation of the problem of numerical integration.*

---

[4]The interested reader is referred to pp. 203–205 of Franz Alt, *Electronic Digital Computers,* Academic Press, New York, 1958, and to pp. 370–386 of Z. Kopal, *Numerical Analysis,* Wiley, New York, 1961.

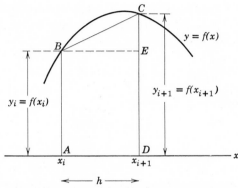

Figure 5.5. *One interval from the shaded area of Figure 5.4, with the scale along the x-axis expanded.*

But, if h is small enough, then I_i can be approximated fairly well by the area of the trapezoid $ABCD$. If we write $y_i = f(x_i)$, the area of the rectangle $ABED$ is $y_i h$ and the area of the triangle BEC is $\frac{1}{2}(y_{i+1} - y_i)h$, so that

$$I_i \simeq \tfrac{1}{2}h(y_i + y_{i+1})$$

Since

$$\int_a^b f(x)\,dx = \int_a^c f(x)\,dx + \int_c^b f(x)\,dx \tag{5.36}$$

then

$$I = \sum_{i=0}^{n-1} I_i \tag{5.37}$$

where $x_0 = a$ and $x_n = b$. Then from (5.36) and (5.37) we have

$$I \simeq I_h = \frac{h}{2}(y_0 + 2y_1 + 2y_2 + \cdots + 2y_{n-2} + 2y_{n-1} + y_n) \tag{5.38}$$

This is the well-known *trapezoidal rule,* so-called because it approximates the integral (5.35) by the sum of n trapezoids. It is one of the simplest formulas for numerical integration. The truncation error, which we investigate in the following section, is greater than for most other methods, but the very simplicity of the technique sometimes makes it attractive. The method is important in any case because it demonstrates the basic idea of integration formulas in which the interval size is fixed in advance. In essence, the technique is to divide the total interval into small intervals and approximate the curve $y = f(x)$ in several small intervals by some simpler curve whose integral can be calculated analytically.

**5.9
Truncation
Error in the
Trapezoidal
Rule**

The truncation error committed by using (5.38) is the sum of the areas between the curve $y = f(x)$ and the chords between y_i and y_{i+1} (BC in Figure 5.5). We approach the estimation of this error by obtaining a Taylor series expansion of the function $y = f(x)$ at the end points of the intervals in order to get the equation of the true curve into a form that will permit a comparison with the approximation (5.38).

Consider the Taylor series expansion of $y = f(x)$ about the point $x = x_i$. We assume that $f(x)$ has as many continuous derivatives as may be required.

$$y = y_i + (x - x_i)y'_i + \frac{(x - x_i)^2}{2}y''_i + \cdots \qquad (5.39)$$

Similarly, the expansion about $x = x_{i+1}$ is

$$y = y_{i+1} + (x - x_i - h)y'_{i+1} + \frac{(x - x_i - h)^2}{2}y''_{i+1} \cdots \qquad (5.40)$$

Equations (5.39) and (5.40) are, of course, both valid; neither one alone, however, leads to the result we want. Our goal can be reached by taking the average of the two.

$$y = \frac{y_{i+1} + y_i}{2} + \frac{x - x_i}{2}(y'_{i+1} + y'_i) - \frac{h}{2}y'_{i+1}$$

$$+ \frac{(x - x_i)^2}{4}(y''_{i+1} + y''_i) - \frac{(x - x_i)h}{2}y''_{i+1} + \frac{h^2}{4}y''_{i+1} + \cdots$$

Integrating $y\,dx$ from x_i to x_{i+1},

$$\int_{x_i}^{x_{i+1}} y\,dx = \frac{h}{2}(y_{i+1} + y_i) + \frac{h^2}{4}(y'_{i+1} + y'_i) - \frac{h^2}{2}y'_{i+1}$$

$$+ \frac{h^3}{12}(y''_{i+1} + y''_i) - \frac{h^3}{4}y''_{i+1} + \frac{h^3}{4}y''_{i+1} + \cdots \qquad (5.41)$$

$$= \frac{h}{2}(y_{i+1} + y_i) - \frac{h^2}{4}(y'_{i+1} - y'_i) - \frac{h^3}{6}(y''_{i+1} - 2y''_i) + \cdots$$

This equation gives an estimate of the true value of the integral. We can make the estimate as accurate as we wish by taking enough terms of the Taylor series expansion. The trapezoidal rule is obtained by dropping all terms containing h^2 and higher powers of h. The truncation error in using the trapezoidal rule is therefore

$$E_{T_i} = -\frac{h^2}{4}(y'_{i+1} - y'_i) - \frac{h^3}{6}(y''_{i+1} - 2y''_i) + \cdots \qquad (5.42)$$

For small h the first term is the dominant one, so that we might be tempted to take the approximate error to be given by just the first term of (5.42). Notice, however, that if we expand $y' = df/dx$ and multiply by h^2 we have

$$y'_{i+1}h^2 = y'_i h^2 + y''_i h^3 + \cdots$$

so that terms in $y''_i h^3$ do contribute to the first term in E_{T_i} in (5.42). And, as a matter of fact, *all* higher terms in (5.42) contribute to the first term to some degree.

Let us *assume* that the error in the trapezoidal rule is of the form

$$E_{T_i} \simeq Kh^2(y'_{i+1} - y'_i) \qquad (5.43)$$

where K is a constant to be determined. This will, of course, be only an approximation based on the assumption that K is a constant. This assumption is true only to the extent that y'' and higher derivatives do not vary much between x_i and x_{i+1}.

Now we have the problem of determining K. To do this, observe that (5.41) *is true for any function whatsoever*. We can, therefore, choose *any* convenient function for which there is a truncation error and the result will be valid for all functions.

One simple function would be $y = x$, but the reader can readily verify that the truncation error would turn out to be zero, which means simply that the trapezoidal rule is exact in integrating linear functions. The next most likely candidate is $y = x^2$. In this case

$$I_i = \int_{x_i}^{x_{i+1}} x^2 \, dx = x_i^2 h + x_i h^2 + \frac{h^3}{3} \qquad \text{exactly} \qquad (5.44)$$

But from (5.41) and (5.42), using $y_i = x_i^2$ and $y_{i+1} = (x_i + h)^2$, we have

$$I_i = x_i^2 h + x_i h^2 + \frac{h^3}{2} + E_{T_i} \qquad (5.45)$$

Equations (5.44) and (5.45) produce

$$E_{T_i} = -\frac{h^3}{6}$$

But, since $y' = 2x$, we have from (5.43)

$$E_{T_i} = 2Kh^2(x_i + h - x_i) = 2Kh^3$$

It follows, therefore, that

$$K = \frac{-1}{12}$$

and

$$E_{T_i} \simeq -\frac{h^2}{12}(y'_{i+1} - y'_i) \qquad (5.46)$$

The total truncation error is estimated by

$$e_T = \sum_{i=0}^{n-1} E_{T_i} = -\frac{h^2}{12}(y'_b - y'_a) \qquad (5.47)$$

where y'_b is the value of df/dx at $x = b$ and y'_a is the value of df/dx at $x = a$.

(The reader will find it instructive to carry out the evaluation of K for the function $y = x^3$ and thus perhaps satisfy himself that the result is not dependent on the particular choice of a function. Of course, K should be determined only from the term in h^3 because of the assumption that y'' is constant.)

Another form of the error formula is perhaps more frequently encountered. We recall from the mean value theorem that

$$y'_b - y'_a = (b - a)y''(\xi)$$

where $a < \xi < b$, so that

$$e_T \simeq -\frac{h^2}{12}(b - a)y''(\xi) \tag{5.48}$$

Moreover, it can be shown[5] that if

$$M = \max |y''(\xi)|$$

for $a \leq \xi \leq b$, then

$$|e_t| \leq \frac{h^2}{12}(b - a)M \tag{5.49}$$

It is important to note that (5.47) provides an approximation to the truncation error, not an upper bound. However, it is an important approximation. Notice that (5.47) only requires knowledge of the first derivative at two points—the end points of the range of integration. On the other hand, (5.48) and (5.49) require knowledge of the second derivative *everywhere* in the range of integration.

To see the advantage of (5.47) more clearly we examine a particular case

$$I = \int_{-2}^{2} e^{-x^2/2} \, dx \tag{5.50}$$

We shall examine this integral in detail in Section 5.15. Now

$$f(x) = e^{-x^2/2}$$

so

$$f'(x) = -xe^{-x^2/2}$$

and

$$f''(x) = (x^2 - 1)e^{-x^2/2}$$

Using (5.47) we find

$$e_T \cong \frac{1}{3}\frac{h^2}{e^2}$$

For $h = 0.5$,

$$e_T \cong 0.01128 \tag{5.51}$$

We shall see in Section 5.15 that this is quite accurate.

On the other hand, to make use of (5.48) or (5.49) we need to know the maximum value of $|f''(x)|$. After considerable labor we can find that the maximum value of $|(x^2 - 1)e^{-x^2/2}|$ in the interval $-2 \leq x \leq 2$ occurs at $x = 0$. Moreover, the maximum value is 1. Equation (5.49) tells us

$$|e_T| \leq \frac{h^2}{3}$$

and (5.48) tells us that e_T is negative. Thus, for $h = 0.5$ we arrive at

$$e_T \cong -0.08333$$

This is eight times as large as (5.51) and is overly conservative.

---

[5] See Exercise 6 at the close of Chapter 6.

.10
Roundoff
Errors in
the Trap-
ezoidal
Rule

The process graph for the trapezoidal rule is shown in Figure 5.6, in which it is assumed that the terms to be multiplied by 2 are all added together first and their sum is multiplied by 2. (This not only saves the time of multiplying each term separately by 2 and then adding but also reduces the roundoff error.)

Let $\delta_i (i = 0, 1, \ldots, n)$ be the relative inherent error in y_i. Let $\alpha_i (i = 0, 1, \ldots, n)$ be the relative roundoff errors in the $n + 1$ additions. The additions are numbered according to the small numerals adjacent to the

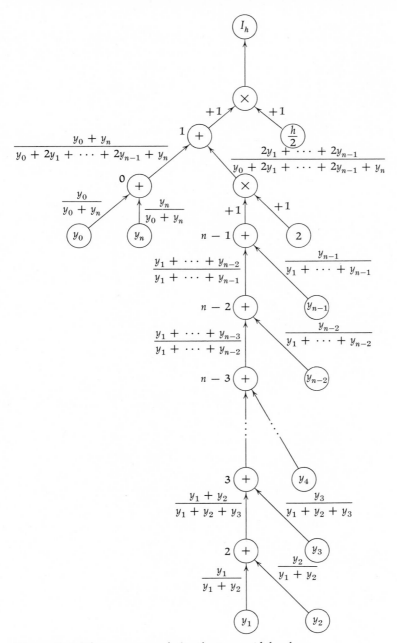

Figure 5.6. *The process graph for the trapezoidal rule.*

circles with the plus signs. For example, α_2 is the relative roundoff error in performing

$$2 \oplus$$

Finally, let μ_1 be the relative roundoff error in performing the first multiplication, that of $(y_1 + \cdots + y_{n-1})$ by 2, and μ_2 be the relative roundoff error in the second multiplication, that of $h/2$ by $(y_0 + 2y_1 + \cdots + 2y_{n-1} + y_n)$. The relative roundoff error in I_h is

$$
\frac{e_R}{I_h} = \mu_2 + \alpha_1 + \alpha_0 \frac{y_0 + y_n}{y_0 + 2y_1 + \cdots + 2y_{n-1} + y_n}
$$

$$
+ \delta_0 \frac{y_0}{y_0 + 2y_1 + \cdots + 2y_{n-1} + y_n}
$$

$$
+ \delta_n \frac{y_n}{y_0 + 2y_1 + \cdots + 2y_{n-1} + y_n}
$$

$$
+ \mu_1 \frac{2y_1 + \cdots + 2y_{n-1}}{y_0 + 2y_1 + \cdots + 2y_{n-1} + y_n}
$$

$$
+ \alpha_{n-1} \frac{2y_1 + \cdots + 2y_{n-1}}{y_0 + 2y_1 + \cdots + 2y_{n-1} + y_n}
$$

$$
+ \alpha_{n-2} \frac{2(y_1 + \cdots + y_{n-2})}{y_0 + 2y_1 + \cdots + 2y_{n-1} + y_n}
$$

$$
+ \delta_{n-1} \frac{2y_{n-1}}{y_0 + 2y_1 + \cdots + 2y_{n-1} + y_n}
$$

$$
+ \alpha_{n-3} \frac{2(y_1 + \cdots + y_{n-3})}{y_0 + 2y_1 + \cdots + 2y_{n-1} + y_n}
$$

$$
+ \delta_{n-2} \frac{2y_{n-2}}{y_0 + 2y_1 + \cdots + 2y_{n-1} + y_n}
$$

$$
+ \cdots + \alpha_2 \frac{2(y_1 + y_2)}{y_0 + 2y_1 + \cdots + 2y_{n-1} + y_n}
$$

$$
+ \delta_3 \frac{2y_3}{y_0 + 2y_1 + \cdots + 2y_{n-1} + y_n}
$$

$$
+ \delta_2 \frac{2y_2}{y_0 + 2y_1 + \cdots + 2y_{n-1} + y_n}
$$

$$
+ \delta_1 \frac{2y_1}{y_0 + 2y_1 + \cdots + 2y_{n-1} + y_n}
$$

The absolute error is

$$
e_R = h\left(\delta_0 \frac{y_0}{2} + \delta_1 y_1 + \cdots + \delta_{n-1} y_{n-1} + \delta_n \frac{y_n}{2}\right)
$$

$$
+ h[\alpha_2(y_1 + y_2) + \alpha_3(y_1 + y_2 + y_3) + \cdots
$$

$$
+ \alpha_{n-2}(y_1 + \cdots + y_{n-2}) + \alpha_{n-1}(y_1 + \cdots + y_{n-1})]
$$

$$+ \frac{h}{2}[\alpha_0(y_0 + y_n) + \alpha_1(y_0 + 2y_1 + \cdots + 2y_{n-1} + y_n)$$

$$+ \mu_1(2y_1 + \cdots + 2y_{n-1}) + \mu_2(y_0 + 2y_1 + \cdots + 2y_{n-1} + y_n)]$$

Now suppose that $y_i = \bar{y} + \theta_i$, where $\bar{y}$ is the average of the y_i and $|\theta_i| \ll |\bar{y}|$, so that terms in $\theta_i \alpha_i$, $\theta_i \mu_i$, and $\theta_i \delta_i$ may be neglected. Further suppose that

$$|\alpha_i| \leq \epsilon$$
$$|\mu_i| \leq \epsilon$$
$$|\delta_i| \leq \phi\epsilon$$

where ϵ is the relative roundoff error in an arithmetic operation, which we have generally written as $5 \cdot 10^{-t}$ previously, and ϕ is some fixed constant that gives the relative size of the inherent and roundoff errors. Then

$$|e_R| \leq h|\bar{y}|\epsilon\phi n + h|\bar{y}|\epsilon \sum_{j=2}^{n-1} j + h|\bar{y}|\epsilon(3n)$$

Recalling that

$$\sum_{j=1}^{m} j = \frac{m(m+1)}{2}$$

then

$$|e_R| \leq \frac{h|\bar{y}|\epsilon}{2}[n^2 + (5 + 2\phi)n - 2]$$

But

$$n = \frac{b-a}{h}$$

so

$$|e_R| \leq \frac{|\bar{y}|\epsilon}{2}\left[\frac{(b-a)^2}{h} + (5 + 2\phi)(b-a) - 2h\right]$$

For small h the first term in the brackets dominates the other two, and we may approximate the bound on e_R by

$$|e_R| \leq \frac{|\bar{y}|\epsilon(b-a)^2}{2}\left(\frac{1}{h}\right) \tag{5.52}$$

We thus have the interesting result that the bound on the roundoff error increases as $1/h$, soon dominating the truncation error, which is proportional to h^2. Actually, the roundoff error itself does not grow as h^{-1} but as h^{-p}, where $0 < p < 1$, and still overtakes the truncation error if we decrease h sufficiently.

We have also found another discrepancy between theoretical and practical computing. In theory we can make I_h as close to I as we wish by taking h sufficiently small. In practice, however, the roundoff error prevents this arbitrarily close approach to I.

As an example consider the integral

$$I = \int_0^{\pi} \sin x \, dx = 2$$

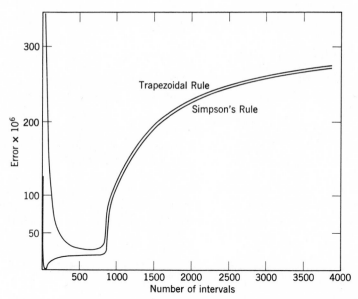

Figure 5.7. *Plots of the total error (truncation and roundoff) in integrating a simple function by the trapezoidal rule and by Simpson's rule.*

A plot of the total error E_I versus n, the number of intervals, is given in Figure 5.7, which also shows the error for Simpson's rule, to be considered in Section 5.12. Notice that as n increases the total error, which is the sum of the truncation error and the roundoff error, decreases until $n = 775$. Thereafter the roundoff error dominates; further increases in the number of intervals *increase* the total error.

Finally, notice that the δ_i, the μ_i, α_0, and α_1 do not contribute to the $1/h$ term in e_I. It is the computation of

$$y_1 + \cdots + y_{n-1}$$

and the roundoff errors in these additions that affect the $1/h$ term. Thus increasing the accuracy of the computation of the y_i does not help matters.

The error may be decreased by performing the additions in double precision, whereas all other operations are done in single precision. This technique is referred to as *partial double precision*.

**5.11
The
Deferred
Approach
to the Limit**

A relatively simple modification of the trapezoidal rule can be used to find a better approximation to the value of an integral.

Recall from (5.48) that for an interval of size h

$$e_T = Ch^2$$

where

$$C = -\frac{b-a}{12}y''(\xi) \qquad a < \xi < b$$

If the second derivative of y is reasonably constant, C may also be taken to be a constant.

Suppose now that we take a different step size $k = (b - a)/m$ where $m \neq n$. Then

$$e_T = Ck^2$$

Let I_h be the result from the trapezoidal rule using step size h in (5.38) and let I_k be the result using a step size of k. Then

$$I = I_h + Ch^2 \qquad (5.53)$$
$$I = I_k + Ck^2$$

If we subtract these two equations, it follows that

$$C = \frac{I_h - I_k}{k^2 - h^2} \qquad (5.54)$$

Using (5.54) to replace C in (5.53), we have

$$I = I_h + \frac{I_h - I_k}{\dfrac{k^2}{h^2} - 1} \qquad (5.55)$$

This produces a better approximation to I than I_h or I_k. If, in fact, the second derivative $y''(x)$ is actually a constant for $a \leq x \leq b$, the truncation error in (5.55) is zero.

The method is called *Richardson's deferred approach to the limit*.[6]

**.12
.impson's
.ule**

We now apply the results of the previous section to derive one of the most widely used techniques in numerical integration, Simpson's rule. The development we shall use can be extended to derive the Romberg integration formulas, although we shall not carry out these extensions.

Simpson's rule is similar to the trapezoidal rule in that both require that the range of integration be divided into several small intervals and that the integrand be evaluated at the endpoints of all of these small intervals. The difference occurs in the manner in which the area under the curve is approximated. In the trapezoidal rule we used areas of trapezoids to approximate the area in one small interval. In Simpson's rule we use the area under a parabola to approximate the area of two adjacent intervals. From this we would expect that whereas the trapezoidal rule is exact for first-degree polynomials Simpson's rule would be exact for second-degree or lower. Actually, it turns out somewhat surprisingly that Simpson's rule is exact for third-degree polynomials or polynomials of lower degree. It is, therefore, a rather accurate method for the effort required, and the formula is not significantly more complex than that for the trapezoidal rule. These characteristics account for the wide usage of Simpson's rule.

We turn now to the derivation of Simpson's rule based on the trape-

---

[6]L. F. Richardson and J. A. Gaunt, "The Deferred Approach to the Limit," *Trans. Roy. Soc. London*, 226A, 300 (1927).

zoidal rule and the deferred approach to the limit. Recall that the number of intervals n in the trapezoidal rule was given by

$$n = \frac{b - a}{h}$$

Suppose that n is even and let

$$k = 2h \tag{5.56}$$

Then

$$I_h = \frac{h}{2}(y_0 + 2y_1 + 2y_2 + \cdots + 2y_{n-2} + 2y_{n-1} + y_n) \tag{5.57}$$

$$I_k = h(y_0 \qquad + 2y_2 + \cdots + 2y_{n-2} \qquad + y_n) \tag{5.58}$$

Equations (5.56), (5.57), and (5.58) can be substituted into (5.55), as follows:

$$I = I_h + \frac{I_h - I_k}{\dfrac{k^2}{h^2} - 1}$$

$$
\begin{aligned}
&= h(\quad \tfrac{1}{2}y_0 + y_1 + y_2 + \cdots + y_{n-2} + y_{n-1} + \tfrac{1}{2}y_n)\\
&+ h(\quad \tfrac{1}{6}y_0 + \tfrac{1}{3}y_1 + \tfrac{1}{3}y_2 + \cdots + \tfrac{1}{3}y_{n-2} + \tfrac{1}{3}y_{n-1} + \tfrac{1}{6}y_n)\\
&+ h(-\tfrac{1}{3}y_0 \qquad - \tfrac{2}{3}y_2 - \cdots - \tfrac{2}{3}y_{n-2} \qquad - \tfrac{1}{3}y_n)\\
&= h(\quad \tfrac{1}{3}y_0 + \tfrac{4}{3}y_1 + \tfrac{2}{3}y_2 + \cdots + \tfrac{2}{3}y_{n-2} + \tfrac{4}{3}y_{n-1} + \tfrac{1}{6}y_n)
\end{aligned}
$$

So

$$I = \frac{h}{3}(y_0 + 4y_1 + 2y_2 + 4y_3 + 2y_4 + \cdots$$

$$+ 2y_{n-4} + 4y_{n-3} + 2y_{n-2} + 4y_{n-1} + y_n) \tag{5.59}$$

The result (5.59) is called Simpson's rule. At the expense of considerably more effort we could have arrived at this formula by (1) finding the equation of the parabola that passes through the three ordinates of two adjacent intervals, (2) computing the area under each parabola, and (3) summing the areas under all of the parabolas. We shall not carry out this exercise. It is mentioned to show how Simpson's rule compares geometrically with the trapezoidal rule.

Neither shall we go through the manipulations to find the truncation error, which can be computed by methods similar to those in Section 5.9. The result is

$$e_T \simeq -\frac{h^4}{180}(b - a)f^{iv}(\xi) \qquad a < \xi < b \tag{5.60}$$

The important thing to notice is that the error here is proportional to h^4, whereas the error for the trapezoidal rule is proportional to h^2. This reflects the fact that Simpson's rule happens to correspond to the first *three* terms of the Taylor expansion, whereas we might expect it to agree with only the first two terms. The method is therefore exact for a polynomial of degree no higher than third.

We shall return to this somewhat perplexing but pleasant problem—that Simpson's rule is more accurate than we expect—after we have examined Gaussian quadrature. (See next-to-last paragraph in Section 5.14.)

If we assume that the fourth derivative is reasonably constant, we can once again use the deferred approach to the limit to improve on Simpson's rule. In fact, it is entirely possible to derive formulas akin to (5.59) of higher and higher accuracy. The results are called *Romberg integration formulas*.[7]

We note finally, again without displaying the derivation, that the bound on the roundoff error for Simpson's rule is proportional to $1/h$ for small h, the same as with the trapezoidal rule.

Figure 5.7 also shows the results of integrating $\sin x$ from 0 to π, using Simpson's rule. Notice that the error diminishes much more rapidly than when the trapezoidal rule is used (h^4 versus h^2). Since the roundoff errors are approximately equal, however, they become dominant more rapidly and the total error increases when $n > 40$.

Whether we use the trapezoidal rule, Simpson's rule, or any other similar rule; we are faced with the problem of checking the accuracy of the computation. The truncation errors in (5.47) or (5.48) and in (5.60) provide some estimate of the error. However, the derivatives in those formulas are not always easy to compute and, moreover, the formulas neglect roundoff error. Another check on accuracy that is rather straightforward but requires considerable numerical computation is given here.

Suppose we have an integration formula in which the truncation error is proportional to h^q (for the trapezoidal rule $q = 2$ and for Simpson's rule $q = 4$). Then

$$I = I_h + Ch^q \tag{5.61}$$

where I_h is the result of using the particular integration rule in question.

Suppose we use the rule three times: once with an interval of k, once with $2k$, and once with $4k$. Then following (5.61)

$$I = I_k + C(k)^q$$
$$I = I_{2k} + C(2k)^q$$
$$I = I_{4k} + C(4k)^q$$

Subtracting the first of these from the second and the second from the third produces two equations neither of which contains I. If we eliminate C from these two resulting equations, we obtain

$$\frac{I_{4k} - I_{2k}}{I_{2k} - I_k} = 2^q$$

Therefore, suppose we compute

$$p = \frac{I_{4k} - I_{2k}}{I_{2k} - I_k} \tag{5.62}$$

If $p = 2^q$ (or is nearly equal to 2^q), then the error term was of the form

---

[7]See, for example, Section 8.4 of Thomas Richard McCalla *Introduction to Numerical Methods and Fortran Programming*, New York, Wiley, 1967.

Ch^q as shown in (5.61). Suppose, however, that

$$p \ll 2^q$$

Then the error in (5.61) is Ch^m where $m < q$. Thus the integration rule is not as accurate as we expected. It follows that some of the assumptions made in deriving the rule were not valid for the particular situation tested. For example, appropriate derivatives may not be constant or may not even exist.

Finally suppose that

$$p \gg 2q$$

Then the error in (5.61) is Ch^n where $n > q$, and the integration rule is more accurate than we expected.

Yet another way of looking at this accuracy check is to compute p as given in (5.62). Then if we let

$$q = \log_2 p$$

the truncation error is Ch^q.

It is this type of argument that is used to develop the Romberg integration formulas. The interested reader is referred to the previous footnote.

5.14
Gaussian
Quadrature[8] So far we have discussed integration methods in which the analyst is free to choose the interval. We have, in fact, always chosen equal intervals. We now ask, could we achieve a smaller truncation error for a given number of intervals if we were willing to let the endpoints of the intervals fall wherever a desire for higher accuracy might demand? From a philosophical standpoint, we might expect improvement: Since we are giving up the freedom to choose the intervals, we might expect to get something in return, namely, higher accuracy. The answer to the question is an emphatic "yes."

Recall that with two ordinates (trapezoidal rule) the best we could do before was to obtain the exact value for a linear function (first-degree polynomial). We shall now show that by choosing the location of the two points properly we can obtain an exact formula for the integral of a cubic (third-degree polynomial). Although we shall not prove the fact in complete generality, it is perhaps intuitively obvious that if an integration method gives an exact result for a higher degree polynomial it is *in general* more accurate.

We first change the limits of integration from a to b to -1 to $+1$, in order to simplify the analysis. Define a new variable

$$u = \frac{2x - (b + a)}{b - a}$$

so that

$$x = \tfrac{1}{2}(b - a)u + \tfrac{1}{2}(b + a)$$

---

[8]"Quadrature" is alternative terminology for "numerical integration." The common usage "Simpson's rule" rather than "Simpson quadrature," and so forth, is a matter of convention.

The integral (5.35) thus becomes

$$I = \int_{-1}^{+1} \phi(u) \, du \tag{5.63}$$

where

$$\phi(u) = \tfrac{1}{2}(b - a) \cdot f[\tfrac{1}{2}(b - a)u + \tfrac{1}{2}(b + a)]$$

This means that the change of variable reduces all integrations to the form (5.63) ("all" integrations within the restrictions assumed, that is, finite limits and a continuous integrand).

We are still trying to see what we can do with only two ordinates, which means that the approximating curve will be a line. In other words, we hope to find a linear function

$$y = \alpha_0 + \alpha_1 u$$

such that

$$\int_{-1}^{1} (\alpha_0 + \alpha_1 u) \, du = \int_{-1}^{1} \phi(u) \, du \tag{5.64}$$

The integral on the left is the area of the trapezoid shown in Figure 5.8. This area will be identical with the area under the curve $y = \phi(u)$ if the vertically striped areas (those between -1 and u_0 and between u_1 and $+1$) are precisely equal to the shaded area (that between u_0 and u_1). We wish to choose the line so that this cancellation is achieved.

To this end, let

$$I_G = A_0 \phi(u_0) + A_1 \phi(u_1) \tag{5.65}$$

where A_0, A_1, u_0, and u_1 are to be chosen. Since there are four parameters, it is reasonable to expect that they can be chosen to give an exact formula for a cubic integrand:

$$\phi(u) = a_0 + a_1 u + a_2 u^2 + a_3 u^3$$

We rewrite this as

$$\phi(u) = \alpha_0 + \alpha_1 u + (u - u_0)(u - u_1)(\beta_0 + \beta_1 u)$$

If α_0 and α_1 are to satisfy (5.64), then u_0 and u_1 must be chosen so that

$$\int_{-1}^{+1} (u - u_0)(u - u_1)(\beta_0 + \beta_1 u) \, du = 0$$

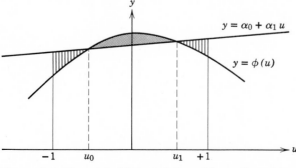

Figure 5.8. *Geometrical interpretation of the method of Gaussian quadrature with two points.*

Since this must be true for *any* choice of β_0 and β_1, it follows that we must require that

$$\int_{-1}^{1} (u - u_0)(u - u_1) \, du = 0$$

$$\int_{-1}^{1} u(u - u_0)(u - u_1) \, du = 0$$

After integration these become

$$\tfrac{2}{3} + 2u_0 u_1 = 0$$
$$u_0 + u_1 = 0$$

from which it follows that

$$u_1 = -u_0 = \frac{1}{\sqrt{3}} \tag{5.66}$$

We now need only to find A_0 and A_1 in (5.65). Note that

$$\int_{-1}^{1} \phi(u) \, du = \int_{-1}^{1} (\alpha_0 + \alpha_1 u) \, du = 2\alpha_0 \tag{5.67}$$

and from (5.65) and (5.66)

$$I_G = A_0(\alpha_0 + \alpha_1 u_0) + A_1(\alpha_0 + \alpha_1 u_1)$$

$$= \alpha_0(A_0 + A_1) - \frac{\alpha_1}{\sqrt{3}}(A_0 - A_1)$$

Since this must be equal to the integral (5.67) for all α_0 and α_1,

$$A_0 + A_1 = 2$$
$$A_0 - A_1 = 0$$

Thus

$$A_0 = A_1 = 1 \tag{5.68}$$

Equation (5.65) becomes

$$I_G = \phi\left(-\frac{1}{\sqrt{3}}\right) + \phi\left(\frac{1}{\sqrt{3}}\right)$$

This is the Gaussian quadrature formula for two points. The truncation error in integrating a polynomial of degree 3 or lower is zero. For polynomials of higher degree and for other functions the truncation error can be expected to be of the form

$$e_T = K\phi^{iv}(\xi) \qquad -1 < \xi < 1$$

where

$$\int_{-1}^{1} \phi(u) \, du = I_G + e_T = \phi\left(-\frac{1}{\sqrt{3}}\right) + \phi\left(\frac{1}{\sqrt{3}}\right) + e_T \tag{5.69}$$

To find K, let

$$\phi(u) = u^4$$

then

$$\phi^{iv}(u) = 24$$

so

$$e_T = 24K \tag{5.70}$$

Now

$$\int_{-1}^{1} \phi(u)\, du = \int_{-1}^{1} u^4\, du = \tfrac{2}{5}$$

But, on the other hand, from (5.69) and (5.70)

$$\int_{-1}^{1} \phi(u)\, du = \left(-\frac{1}{\sqrt{3}}\right)^4 + \left(\frac{1}{\sqrt{3}}\right)^4 + 24K$$

Therefore

$$K = \frac{1}{135}$$

and

$$e_T = \frac{\phi^{iv}(\xi)}{135} \qquad -1 < \xi < 1$$

Higher order Gaussian quadrature formulas can be found by using more points and, in general, different *weights* (the A_i):

$$\int_{-1}^{1} \phi(u)\, du = \sum_{i=0}^{n-1} A_i \phi(u_i) \tag{5.71}$$

In general, with n points (as shown above), we get an exact formula for a polynomial of degree $2n - 1$.

It turns out that the u_i in (5.71) are the roots of the Legendre polynomial of degree n. For this reason the method described above is often referred to as *Legendre-Gauss quadrature*. The Legendre polynomials $P_n(u)$ may be defined recursively by

$$\left.\begin{aligned}
P_0(u) &= 1 \\
P_1(u) &= u \\
P_m(u) &= \frac{1}{m}[(2m - 1)\, u\, P_{m-1}(u) - (m - 1)P_{m-2}(u)]
\end{aligned}\right\} \tag{5.72}$$

For example, letting $m = 2$,

$$P_2(u) = \tfrac{1}{2}(3u \cdot u - 1 \cdot 1) = \frac{3u^2}{2} - \frac{1}{2}$$

Notice that the roots of $P_2(u)$ are $\pm 1/\sqrt{3}$ as we found earlier.

The weights in (5.71) are given by

$$A_i = \frac{2}{(1 - u_i^2)[P_n'(u_i)]^2}$$

As an example consider $n = 2$, so that $u_0 = -1/\sqrt{3}$, $u_1 = 1/\sqrt{3}$, and $P_2' = 3u$. Then

$$A_0 = \frac{2}{(1 - \tfrac{1}{3}) \cdot 3} = 1$$

and likewise $A_1 = 1$ as before.

In the general case the truncation error is given by

$$e_T = \frac{\phi^{(2n)}(\xi)}{(2n)!} \left(\frac{2}{2n+1} - \sum_{i=0}^{n} A_i u_i^{2n} \right)$$

where $-1 < \xi < 1$.

Another form for this truncation error is

$$e_T = \frac{2^{2n+1}(n!)^4}{(2n+1)[(2n)!]^3} \phi^{(2n)}(\xi)$$

where again $-1 < \xi < 1$.

Table 5.2 gives the u_i and A_i for $n = 2, \ldots, 6$. Note that the u_i are symmetric about the origin and that the coefficient A_k for u_k is the same as that for $-u_k$. A more complete 16-place table for n up to 50 is given in *Nodes and Weights of Quadrature Formulas* by Aleksandr Semenovich Kronrod (Consultants Bureau Enterprises, Inc., 1965).

We now make an important and rather interesting observation. For $n = 3$, one of the points at which the integrand is evaluated is the midpoint of the interval $a \leq x \leq b$ corresponding to $u = 0$. In Simpson's rule (Section 5.12) we had an even number of intervals. If we consider these intervals in pairs and think of two adjacent intervals as one double interval, then in Simpson's rule we are evaluating the integrand at three points in the double interval. If we use a three-point Gaussian quadrature on this double interval, we also evaluate the integrand at three points, one of which is the midpoint. Thus, in Simpson's rule, one of the points at which the integrand is evaluated coincides with one of the points used in Gaussian quadrature. This coincidence of points lies behind the unexpected extra accuracy obtained in Simpson's rule. (Recall that Simpson's rule has no truncation error for a cubic equation, whereas we had only expected it to be exact for quadratic equations.)

In summary, Gaussian quadrature gives more accuracy than does Simpson's rule for the same number of ordinates at the expense of a

Table 5.2. Gaussian quadrature abscissas and coefficients

	u	A
$n = 2$	±0.57735 02692	1.00000 00000
$n = 3$	±0.77459 66692	0.55555 55556
	0.00000 00000	0.88888 88889
$n = 4$	±0.86113 63116	0.34785 48451
	±0.33998 10436	0.65214 51549
$n = 5$	±0.90617 98459	0.23692 68851
	±0.53846 93101	0.47862 86705
	0.00000 00000	0.56888 88889
$n = 6$	±0.93246 95142	0.17132 44924
	±0.66120 93865	0.36076 15730
	±0.23861 91861	0.46791 39346

complete lack of choice of locating the points. As in so many other cases, we have an economic choice, this time between the simplicity of Simpson's rule and the potential time savings of Gaussian quadrature. In practice, Simpson's rule is more commonly used.

.15
Numerical
Examples
and Com-
parison of
Methods

To illustrate the three methods we have discussed and to see how they compare in accuracy, consider the integral

$$I = \int_{-2}^{2} e^{-x^2/2} \, dx$$

which was previously discussed in Section 5.9 [see (5.50)]. The exact value to four decimals is 2.3925.

Let us first apply the trapezoidal rule with the rather broad spacing of $h = 1.0$. Then

$$I_T = \frac{1.0}{2}(e^{-(-2)^2/2} + 2e^{-(-1)^2/2} + 2e^{-(0)^2/2} + 2e^{-(1)^2/2} + e^{-(2)^2/2})$$

$$= 0.5(0.13534 + 2 \cdot 0.60653 + 2 \cdot 1.00000 + 2 \cdot 0.60653 + 0.13534)$$
$$= 2.3484$$
$$\epsilon = 0.0441$$

Simpson's rule with $h = 1.0$ leads to

$$I_S = \frac{1.0}{3}(e^{-(-2)^2/2} + 4e^{-(-1)^2/2} + 2e^{-(0)^2/2} + 4e^{-(1)^2/2} + e^{-(2)^2/2})$$

$$= 0.33333(0.13534 + 4 \cdot 0.60653 + 2 \cdot 1.00000 + 4 \cdot 0.60653 + 0.13534)$$
$$= 2.3743$$
$$\epsilon = 0.0182$$

Gaussian quadrature with two points requires evaluation of

$$I_G = A_0 \phi(u_0) + A_1 \phi(u_1)$$

where

$$\phi(u) = \frac{b-a}{2} f\left(\frac{b-a}{2} u + \frac{b+a}{2}\right)$$

$$= 2 \cdot e^{-(2u)^2/2}$$

So we have

$$I_G = 2\left\{\exp\frac{[-(-2 \cdot 0.57735)^2]}{2} + \exp\frac{[-(2 \cdot 0.57735)^2]}{2}\right\}$$

$$= 2.0536$$
$$\epsilon = 0.3389$$

Repeating these calculations for $h = 0.5$ and $h = 0.25$, and with three, four, five, and six points in the Gaussian method, we get the results shown in Table 5.3.

Valid general conclusions cannot be drawn from one small example,

Table 5.3

Trapezoidal Rule		
h	I_T	ϵ
1.0	2.3484	0.0441
0.5	2.3813	0.0112
0.25	2.3898	0.0027

Simpson's Rule		
h	I_S	ϵ
1.0	2.3743	0.0182
0.5	2.3923	0.0002
0.25	2.3926	−0.0001

Gaussian Quadrature		
Number of points	I_G	ϵ
2	2.0536	0.3389
3	2.4471	−0.0546
4	2.3859	0.0066
5	2.3931	−0.0006
6	2.3925	0.0000

but it happens that the following observations about these results have fairly wide applicability.

1. Simpson's rule with n points provides the same general order of accuracy as does the trapezoidal rule with $2n$ points.
2. Gaussian quadrature with n points provides the same general order of accuracy as Simpson's rule with $2n$ points.

Although neither of these statements is *exactly* true, there is, in fact, some mathematical basis for accepting them as *approximately* true.

3. For the same accuracy, Simpson's rule requires about half as much effort as the trapezoidal rule, since there are half as many ordinates to evaluate.
4. For the same accuracy, Gaussian quadrature requires about half as much effort as does Simpson's rule, since there are about half as many ordinates to evaluate.

For "hand" calculation, (4) is somewhat offset by the fact that the abscissas are prescribed and occur—for the most part—at values that are awkward to work with. (In our example it is easier to look up $e^{-0.5}$ than $e^{-0.16667}$.) In a computer, however, this consideration is of no consequence.

The savings in Gaussian quadrature are partly offset by the fact that if the integral is to be re-evaluated with more points the preceding ordinates cannot be reused, since they are at the wrong locations. (This is not so with Simpson's rule; see Exercise 22.)

For integrating experimental data, Gaussian quadrature can be used only if the abscissas are properly chosen in advance; this is seldom the case. Simpson's rule can be applied as long as adjacent pairs of intervals are equal. If the abscissas are randomly spaced, the only one of these methods that can be used is the trapezoidal.

In view of the quite acceptable accuracy for the number of ordinates required, the simplicity of the formula, and the case of modifying the interval and re-evaluating, it should not be surprising that Simpson's rule is widely used in practical computations.

One popular and extremely accurate method involves a combination of the trapezoidal-type rule and Gaussian quadrature. Suppose we divide the interval of integration into n equal subintervals as we would if we were about to apply the trapezoidal rule. In each of these subintervals we apply a three-point Gaussian quadrature. That is, we perform Gaussian quadrature n times, each time on a different subinterval. We sum the n results so obtained. This will produce a quite accurate and usually far-preferable result compared with the one obtained by even a $3n$-point Gaussian quadrature.

The difficulty of the method lies in the complexity of the programming. Each subinterval must be transformed into the interval $-1 \leq u \leq 1$ before the Gaussian quadrature formulas can be applied. The transformations, although straightforward, are rather complicated. We close this discussion by noting that we could also use a two-point Gaussian quadrature in each of the subintervals. It usually does not pay to use more than the three-point formula.

We make one final observation. Notice that the error, ϵ, in the trapezoidal rule using $h = 0.5$ is 0.0112 from Table 5.2. In Section 5.9 we used (5.47) to estimate the error to be 0.01128. Thus (5.47) provides an extremely good error estimate in this case. Our other error estimate, (5.49), produced a value eight times as large and hence of little value.

<table>
<tr><td>

.16
Case
Study 9:
Using
Simpson's
Rule in
Computing
Luminous
Efficiency

</td><td>

The following case study will give us an opportunity to apply some of the ideas presented in this chapter.

A blackbody (perfect radiator) emits energy at a rate proportional to the fourth power of its absolute temperature, according to the Stefan-Boltzmann equation,

$$E = 36.9 \cdot 10^{-12} T^4$$

where E = emissive power, watts/cm^2
$\qquad T$ = temperature, °K

We are interested in the fraction of this total energy contained in the visible spectrum, which is taken here to be $4 \cdot 10^{-5}$ to $7 \cdot 10^{-5}$ cm. We can get the visible part by integrating Planck's equation between these limits:

$$E_{\text{visible}} = \int_{4 \cdot 10^{-5}}^{7 \cdot 10^{-5}} \frac{2.39 \cdot 10^{-11} \, dx}{x^5(e^{1.432/Tx} - 1)}$$

where x = wavelength, cm; E and T as before.

The *luminous efficiency* is defined as the ratio of the energy in the visible spectrum to the total energy. If we multiply by 100 to get the efficiency

</td></tr>
</table>

in percent and combine the constants, the problem becomes that of evaluating

$$EFF = \frac{64.77 \int_{4 \cdot 10^{-5}}^{7 \cdot 10^{-5}} \dfrac{dx}{x^5(e^{1.432/Tx} - 1)}}{T^4}$$

We wish to write a program that computes *EFF* for a number of temperatures, ranging from an initial value of TEMP1 to a maximum value of TEMP2, in increments of TMPINC. We shall also read in values of the limits of the visible spectrum, A to B, so that these slightly indefinite numbers can be varied if desired. A fixed point number N will be read to give the number of intervals to be used in the numerical integration. We shall return to the question of what N should be to give sufficient accuracy.

A flow chart for the procedure to be used is shown in Figure 5.9. We begin by reading the six input values and then carry out two steps that will never be repeated: computing H, the interval size, and setting T equal to the initial temperature in the range. Now we are ready to start into the numerical integration routine. We establish two summing locations, SUM4 and SUM2, to hold the sum of the ordinates to be multiplied by 4 and 2, respectively, in Simpson's rule. We shall shortly be computing a value for the integrand at the first interior point A + H (added to SUM4) and at the second interior point (added to SUM2), so we give X the suitable starting value.

Now comes a problem. We want to set up a loop to run through the values of X at all the interior points and then stop. If we test for the completion of this loop by comparing X with B − H, the last interior point, we are in trouble on two scores. First, there is one more point to be multiplied by 4 than to be multiplied by 2; we must stop short in the loop and take care of the last interior point after getting out of the loop. Second, if we start X at A + H and repeatedly add 2H to it, roundoff errors will accumulate, so that we will in general never arrive at a value of X that is *exactly* equal to B − 3H.

One solution to this impasse is to count the number of interior points computed with a fixed-point variable. We accordingly set I equal to 1 before going into the summation loop. (A quick sketch will help to clarify the question of the proper value of I at which to stop.)

Now we compute the next two interior points, add them to the appropriate sums, and ask whether we are finished with this loop. If not, we increment I and X and go around again. If so, we are ready to compute EFF. SUM4 contains all the ordinates to be multiplied by 4, except the one for B − H, which must accordingly be computed. SUM2 contains all the ordinates to be multiplied by 2. This leaves out the ordinates for A and B. At this point, therefore, we write a statement to get the three ordinates not found by the loop, using a function defined earlier, and do the multiplications by 4 and 2. This statement also handles the factor of H/3 from Simpson's rule, and the $64.77/T^4$ from the formula.

After printing the result, T is incremented and then tested. If the incremented value is less than TEMP2, the input value that gives the largest temperature to be considered, we go back to do the entire integra-

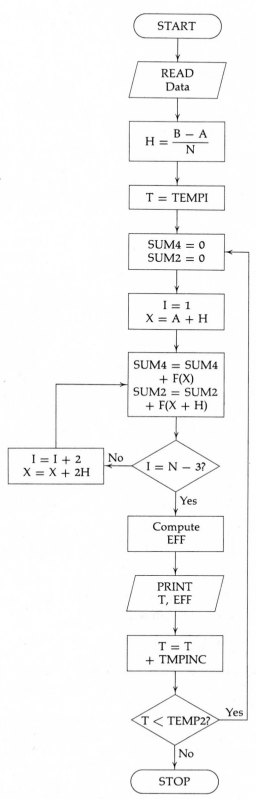

Figure 5.9. *Flow chart of the method of computing luminous efficiency, using Simpson's rule for the integration (Case Study 9).*

```
C CASE STUDY 9
C NUMERICAL INTEGRATION BY SIMPSON'S RULE
C    TO COMPUTE THE LUMINOUS EFFICIENCY OF A
C    BLACKBODY RADIATOR
C
C DEFINE A FUNCTION FOR THE INTEGRAND
      F(Y) = 1.0/(Y**5 * (EXP(1.432/(T*Y)) - 1.0))
C
C READ PARAMETERS
      READ (5, 60) TEMP1, TEMP2, TMPINC, A, B, N
   60 FORMAT (5F10.0, I4)
C SET UP INTEGRATION PARAMETERS
      FN = N
      H = (B - A) / FN
      TWOH = H + H
      T = TEMP1
C SET UP SUMMING VARIABLES
  100 SUM4 = 0.0
      SUM2 = 0.0
C GIVE X ITS STARTING VALUE FOR LOOP
      X = A + H
C INITIALIZE LOOP COUNTER
      I = 1
C THE SUMMING LOOP
   12 SUM4 = SUM4 + F(X)
      SUM2 = SUM2 + F(X + H)
      IF (I .GE. N - 3) GO TO 32
      I = I + 2
      X = X + TWOH
      GO TO 12
C COMPUTE AND PRINT EFFICIENCY
   32 EFF = 64.77 * H/3.0 * (4.0*SUM4 + 2.0*SUM2
     1    + F(A) + 4.0*F(B - H) + F(B)) / T**4
      WRITE (6, 61) T, EFF
   61 FORMAT (1X, 1P2E15.6)
C INCREMENT AND TEST TEMPERATURE
      T = T + TMPINC
      IF (T .LE. TEMP2) GO TO 100
      STOP
      END
```

Figure 5.10. *A program corresponding to the flow chart of Figure 5.9, for computing luminous efficiency.*

tion section again. If the luminous efficiency has been calculated for the largest temperature specified, we are finished.

The program is shown in Figure 5.10. The reader may wish to check it carefully to determine that it actually does the processing described more graphically in the flow chart.

Estimating the truncation error from the error bound is possible, but in practical terms it is more trouble than it is worth in this case. First we would have to find the fourth derivative of

$$\frac{1}{x^5(e^{1.432/Tx} - 1)}$$

which is considerable work although it can, of course, be done. Then we would need to have some idea of where in the interval the fourth derivative was largest.

A much more practical approach is to let the computer help us. A formula for the deferred approach to the limit for Simpson's rule, similar to (5.55) for the trapezoidal rule, is easily derived.

$$I = I_h + \frac{I_h - I_k}{1 - k^4/h^4}$$

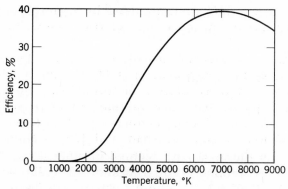

Figure 5.11. *Luminous efficiency as a function of the temperature (°K) of the radiating blackbody.*

This means, for instance, that if we run the program for, say, N = 10 and then for N = 20 we have a way of estimating the true integral. From the size of the difference between the two computed values we also have a fairly good idea of how many intervals to use routinely.

This was done for this program, with T = 3500°K. For 10 intervals the computed value was 14.51275% and for 20 it was 14.51269%. The difference is so much less than any practical use of the results could possibly demand that we immediately drop any further worry about accuracy.

Although it is not a question of numerical analysis, it is interesting to plot the variation of efficiency with temperature, as shown in Figure 5.11. We see that the visible fraction of the total energy is negligible below approximately 2000°C (≃2300°K); that at the melting point of tungsten, about 3600°K, only about 15% of the radiated energy is visible; and that the curve has a broad peak around 7000°K. Such considerations as these set limits on the efficiency of an incandescent light bulb.

Bibliographic Notes

Numerical differentiation is discussed in a way quite analogous to the development in the present text in Section 6.1 of Stiefel [9]. Hildebrand [18] develops differentiation formulas based on difference operators in Section 5.3. Discussions based on interpolation may be found in Section 43 of Scarborough [17]; Chapter 12 of Henrici [23]; and Section 2.11 of Carnahan et al. [20]. In Sections 4.1 and 4.2 Ralston [19] covers numerical differentiation and includes a discussion of truncation and roundoff errors.

The trapezoidal rule is covered in every text on numerical methods. An elementary discussion is found in Section 2, Chapter 2, of Barrodale et al. [1]. Stark [3] discusses the trapezoidal rule in Section 6.2 and gives a Fortran program for that rule in Section 6.3. Other good references for the trapezoidal rule are Hildebrand [18], Section 3.5; Hamming [6], Section 7.2; Ralston [19], Section 4.12; and Carnahan et al. [20], Section 2.3. Most of these are based on interpolation formulas.

The deferred approach to the limit is discussed by Stiefel [9] in Sections 6.22 and 6.23. Ralston [19] also discusses the deferred approach in Section 4.12–1.

Simpson's rule also is covered in virtually every text. The most elementary discussion is again in Barrodale et al. [1], Section 3, Chapter 2. Stark [3] in Sections 6.5 and 6.6 derives Simpson's rule by passing a parabola through three points. Stark also presents a Fortran program for Simpson's rule in Section 6.7. Other references for Simpson's rule are Scarborough [17], Section 46, and Carnahan et al. [20], Section 2.3.

Roundoff error is, for the most part, ignored in other texts. However, Stark [3] produces curves of roundoff and truncation errors similar to those given in this text in Sections 6.3, 6.4, and 6.7 where both the trapezoidal and Simpson's rule are discussed.

Gaussian quadratures are developed much as they are in this text in Section 7.10 of Hamming [6] and Section 6.11 of Stark [3]; that is to say, both Hamming and Stark develop the two-point formula in detail as is done in this text. Stark also has a Fortran program for Gaussian quadrature in Section 6.12. More general discussions with extensions to infinite integrals are to be found in Hildebrand [18] Chapter 8; Ralston [19], Section 4.5; and Carnahan [20], Section 2.10.

Ralston [19] gives some comparisons of the relative strengths and weaknesses of the trapezoidal and Simpson rules versus Gaussian quadratures in Section 4.13.

Exercises

1a Show that the truncation error in

$$f'(x_0) \cong \frac{f(x_0 + h) - f(x_0)}{h}$$

is

$$E_T = \frac{h}{2} f''(\xi)$$

where $x_0 \leq \xi \leq x_0 + h$

b Compare this error with the truncation error in (5.5) and discuss the relative accuracy of (5.5) and the above approximation.

2 By using (5.5) and (5.7) derive the following approximation for the third derivative

$$f'''(x) \cong \frac{f\left(x_0 + \frac{3h}{2}\right) - 3f\left(x_0 + \frac{h}{2}\right) + 3f\left(x_0 - \frac{h}{2}\right) - f\left(x_0 - \frac{3h}{2}\right)}{h^3}$$

3 Using Taylor's Theorem with a remainder term that involves the fourth derivative, show that the truncation error in (5.7) is that given in (5.12).

*4 Using five-place tables of e^x estimate the second derivative of $f(x) = e^x$ at $x = 1$ from (5.7). Use $h = 0.1$ and 0.01.

    Compare these results with those in Section 5.4 for the first derivative. Explain why the loss of accuracy occurs for larger h in the case of the second derivative than in the first derivative.

5 Show that (5.18) produces the correct value of the derivative for the most general quadratic function

$$f(x) = Ax^2 + Bx + C$$

6 Using Table 5.1 and (5.5) approximate the derivative of the velocity at a time of 1.1 sec using $h = .6$. Compare the result with (5.19) given in Section 5.5. Which result do you think is the most accurate? Why?

*7 Suppose that for the velocity function in Table 5.1 the third derivative is known to be bounded as follows:

$$|f'''(x)| \leq 18$$

    a. Estimate the truncation error if (5.5) is used with $h = 0.6$. This truncation error is given by (5.11).

    b. Estimate the truncation error if (5.18) is used with $h_1 = 0.2$ and $h_2 = 0.1$. This truncation error is given by (5.20) or (5.21).

8 Consider the function

$$f(x) = x^4 + 3x^3 + 4x + 10$$

Use (5.5) to approximate the derivative at $x = 1000$. Write a Fortran program that lets $h = 2^{-5}, 2^{-6}, \ldots, 2^{-30}$.

    a. What do the numerical results tell you about $f'(1000)$?

    b. How might you improve your results?

9 Compute the exact value of the integral $I = \int_0^2 f(x)\,dx$, the approximation from the trapezoidal rule, with $h = 1$, and the approximation from Simpson's rule, with $h = 1$, for each of the following integrands.

    a. $f(x) = 1 + x$

    b. $f(x) = 1 + x^2$

    c. $f(x) = 1 + x^3$

    d. $f(x) = 1 + x^4$

10 Demonstrate geometrically and prove analytically that if $f''(x) > 0$ and $a \leq x \leq b$, the approximation to $\int_a^b f(x)\,dx$ given by the trapezoidal rule will always be greater than the true value of the integral. (Such functions are called *convex*.)

11 Consider the integral $\int_{-1}^1 (1 + x + x^2 + x^3)\,dx$. Show that Simpson's rule with $h = 1$ and Gauss's method with two points both give exact results, even though Gauss's method requires one less ordinate.

12 Consider the integral $\int_0^1 \sin x\,dx = 0.45970$. Show that the result obtained by Simpson's rule with $h = 0.5$ is surprisingly close to the exact result (within about one part in 3000). Explain "qualitatively" why the close agreement is obtained.

13 In contrast with Exercise 12, consider the simple-appearing integral $\int_{0.1}^1 dx/x = 2.30259$. The approximations given by Simpson's rule for three different interval sizes, together with the errors, are listed.

n	h	I_S	Error
2	0.45	3.3500	−1.0474
4	0.225	2.4079	−0.1053
8	0.1125	2.3206	−0.0180

Explain the difference between the results of this exercise and the preceding one.

14 Use the deferred approach to the limit with the last two lines in the list above to arrive at a better estimate for the value of the integral $\int_{0.1}^{1} dx/x$. Equation 5.55 seems to imply that the result should be exact. Why is it not?

15 The complete elliptic integral of the first kind is

$$K(\theta) = \int_0^{\pi/2} \frac{d\phi}{\sqrt{1 - \sin^2 \theta \sin^2 \phi}}$$

Compute $K(30°)$, using Simpson's rule with four intervals. The exact result to four decimals is 1.6858. Evaluate $K(85°)$ with Simpson's rule and four intervals; the exact result to three decimals is 3.832. Why is this result so badly in error, whereas the other (that for $\theta = 30°$) was accurate?

16 Consider the following integral, suggested by Scarborough.[9]

$$\int_{-1}^{1} \frac{x^7 \sqrt{1 - x^2}\, dx}{(2 - x)^{13/2}}$$

Write a program to evaluate this integral, using Simpson's rule; arrange the program to read in a value of h, the interval size. Run with $h = 0.25$, then with $h = 0.1$, 0.05, 0.02, and 0.01. Explain the perhaps unexpected behavior of the result as h is decreased. (It might help if the program were set up to print the values of the ordinates at each point.)

*17 Consider the integral

$$I = \int_0^{10} e^{-x}\, dx = 0.999955$$

Evaluate by
a. Gaussian quadrature with 6 points.
b. The trapezoidal rule with 10 intervals.
c. Simpson's rule with 10 intervals.
d. The rectangular rule of Exercise 26 with 10 intervals. Compare the results. Is it better to integrate forward or backward? Why?

*18 Write programs to carry out the evaluations in Exercise 17.

19 Generalize your program for Simpson's rule so that it reads a data

[9]J. B. Scarborough, *Numerical Mathematical Analysis*, Baltimore, Md., The Johns Hopkins Press, 1950.

card containing values for a, b, and n and computes the required value for h.

20 Add to your program for Exercise 19 a test to determine whether n is even and stop the program without doing the integration if it is not. (*Hint.* Fortran integer division truncates. If N is odd, $(N/2)*2$ will not be equal to N.)

*21 Modify the program in Figure 5.10 so that it computes and prints the efficiency as computed by the trapezoidal rule and by Simpson's rule, without evaluating any ordinate more than once.

22 Suppose that the computation of the program of Figure 5.10 has just been completed and that we wish to recompute the integral with twice as many points. All the points previously computed and summed in SUM2 and SUM4 would be needed in the new computation; together they would be the ordinates to be multiplied by 2. In addition, we would need new ordinates at points midway between all the preceding ones. Modify the program so that after computing the integral with an interval size dictated by A, B, and N it recomputes with twice as many points but without ever recomputing any ordinates. With the two approximations to the integral, use the deferred approach to the limit to compute a more accurate value.

23 Write a program that reads values of a_0, a_1, a_2, a_3, a_4, a_5, and a_6 (one card) and also values of a, b, and n (another card), then evaluates and prints the value of

$$I = \int_a^b (a_0 + a_1 x + a_2 x^2 + a_3 x^3 + a_4 x^5 + a_5 x^5 + a_6 x^6)\, dx$$

Use Simpson's rule with n intervals.

24 Modify the program of Figure 5.10 so that it identifies the approximate maximum efficiency, if a maximum is found in the range of temperatures called for. If three temperatures T_1, T_2, and T_3 are found such that $Eff(T_1) < Eff(T_2) > Eff(T_3)$, print the three temperatures and the three efficiencies. If three such numbers are not found in the range from TEMP1 to TEMP2, print zeros for all six numbers.

25 Given three values of $x = -h$, 0, h and three corresponding values of $y = y_0$, y_1, y_2, substitute the three pairs of values of x and y into the general equation of a parabola, $y = a + bx + cx^2$, to get three equations in the three unknowns a, b, and c. Using these values of a, b, and c, integrate the equation of the parabola between the limits $-h$ and h to get

$$\int_{-h}^h (a + bx + cx^2)\, dx = \frac{h}{3}(y_0 + 4y_1 + y_2)$$

which is, of course, Simpson's rule for three adjacent points. Simpson's rule is thus shown to be equivalent to approximating the given function by a series of segments of parabolas, as stated in the text.

26 Derive an integration formula for

$$I = \int_a^b f(x)\, dx$$

by dividing the interval into n equal intervals of width

$$h = \frac{b - a}{n}$$

Approximate the integral for each interval by the area of the rectangle whose height is the value of $f(x)$ at the *left* end (see sketch).

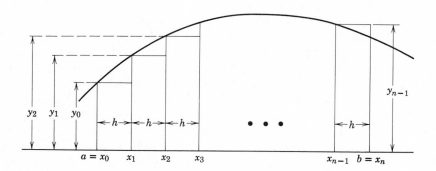

27 Show that the truncation error in the formula derived in Exercise 26 is

$$E_T = \left[\frac{b - a}{2} y'(\xi) \right] h$$

where $a < \xi < b$.

28 Use the deferred approach to the limit on the formula derived in Exercise 26, together with the truncation error in Exercise 27, assuming that $y'(x)$ is constant, to obtain a new integration formula

$$\int_a^b y(x)\,dx \simeq h(y_{1/2} + y_{3/2} + \cdots + y_{n-1/2})$$

where

$$y_{1/2} = y\left(x + \frac{h}{2} \right)$$

$$y_{3/2} = y\left(x + \frac{3h}{2} \right)$$

$$y_{i+1/2} = y[x + (i + \tfrac{1}{2})h], \qquad i = 0, \ldots, n - 1$$

Interpret the formula geometrically.

29 The truncation error in the formula of Exercise 28 is

$$E_T = \left[\frac{(b - a)y''(\xi)}{24} \right] h^2, \qquad a < \xi < b$$

Compare this with the truncation error in the trapezoidal rule. Can you explain why these truncation errors should be expected to be of the same order?

30 Show that the Gaussian quadrature formula that exactly integrates a linear function and no more is

$$\int_{-1}^{1} \phi(u) \, du = 2\phi(0)$$

31 Consider the trapezoidal rule with $n = 3m$; that is, the number of steps is a multiple of 3. Write down the trapezoidal rule for a step size $k = 3h$ and use the deferred approach to the limit to obtain the integration formula

$$I = \frac{3h}{8}(y_0 + 3y_1 + 3y_2 + 2y_3 + 3y_4 + 3y_5 + 2y_6 + 3y_7 + \cdots$$

$$+ \, 3y_{n-4} + 2y_{n-3} + 3y_{n-2} + 3y_{n-1} + y_n)$$

This is usually called the *three-eighths rule*. It is equivalent to passing a cubic equation through four successive ordinates and using the integral of the cubic to approximate the integral of the function over the three intervals.

The truncation error is

$$E_T = -\frac{(b-a)y^{iv}(\xi)}{80}h^4 \qquad a < \xi < b$$

Compare with the truncation error for Simpson's rule. What does this imply with regard to the advantage of this four-point formula over the three-point formula given by Simpson's rule?

32 Consider Simpson's rule with $n = 4m$ intervals. Write down Simpson's rule with $k = 2h$ and use the deferred approach to the limit to obtain the formula

$$I = \frac{2h}{45}(7y_0 + 32y_1 + 12y_2 + 32y_3 + 14y_4 + 32y_5 + \cdots$$

$$+ \, 14y_{n-4} + 32y_{n-3} + 12y_{n-2} + 32y_{n-1} + 7y_n)$$

This is the *fourth Newton-Cotes formula* (the trapezoidal rule, Simpson's rule, and the three-eighths rule are the first three). The truncation error is

$$E_T \simeq Kh^6$$

33 Consider the semi-infinite integral

$$I = \int_{0}^{\infty} f(x) \, dx$$

where $f(x)$ can be written as

$$f(x) = e^{-x}\phi(x)$$

a. Show that, if $\phi(x)$ is a polynomial of degree 3 or less, I can be calculated from

$$I = A_0\phi(x_0) + A_1\phi(x_1)$$

where $x_0 = 2 - \sqrt{2}$
$x_1 = 2 + \sqrt{2}$
$A_0 = (2 + \sqrt{2})/4$
$A_1 = (2 - \sqrt{2})/4$

b. Show that the truncation error is

$$e_T = \frac{\phi^{iv}(\xi)}{6} \qquad 0 < \xi < \infty$$

This is the *Laguerre-Gauss quadrature* formula of order 2. The name is derived from the fact that x_0 and x_1 are the roots of the Laguerre polynomial of second degree.

For a general development and a tabulation of the abscissas and weights for higher order Laguerre-Gauss formulas see Section 8.6 of Hildebrand, *Introduction to Numerical Analysis,* or Section 7.5 and Appendix C of Krylov, *Approximate Calculation of Integrals.*

34 Show that if $f(x)$ is a polynomial of degree 3 or less

$$\int_{-2}^{\infty} e^{-x} f(x)\, dx = \frac{e^2}{4}[(2 + \sqrt{2})f(-\sqrt{2}) + (2 - \sqrt{2})f(\sqrt{2})]$$

Hint. Reduce the problem by a change of variables to the form given in Exercise 33.

35 Consider the infinite integral

$$I = \int_{-\infty}^{\infty} f(x)\, dx$$

where $f(x)$ can be written

$$f(x) = e^{-x^2} \phi(x)$$

Show that, if $\phi(x)$ is a polynomial of degree 3 or less,

$$I = \frac{\sqrt{\pi}}{2}\left[\phi\left(-\frac{\sqrt{2}}{2}\right) + \phi\left(\frac{\sqrt{2}}{2}\right)\right]$$

is exact.

This is the *Hermite-Gauss quadrature* formula of order 2. The name is derived from the fact that the points at which ϕ is evaluated are the roots of the Hermite polynomial of second degree.

For further information see the references listed in Exercise 33.
Hint. Recall that

$$\int_{0}^{\infty} e^{-x^2}\, dx = \frac{\sqrt{\pi}}{2}$$

36 Use the trapezoidal rule twice to obtain the formula

$$\int_{x_0}^{x_n} \int_{y_0}^{y_m} f(x,y)\, dx\, dy$$

$$= \frac{hk}{4}[f_{0,0} + f_{n,0} + f_{0,m} + f_{n,m}$$

$$+ 2(f_{1,0} + f_{2,0} + \cdots + f_{n-1,0} + f_{0,1} + \cdots + f_{0,m-1}$$
$$+ f_{n,1} + f_{n,2} + \cdots + f_{n,m-1} + f_{1,m} + f_{2,m} + \cdots + f_{n-1,m})$$
$$+ 4(f_{1,1} + f_{2,1} + \cdots + f_{n-1,1}$$
$$+ f_{1,2} + f_{2,2} + \cdots + f_{n-1,2}$$
$$\cdots\cdots\cdots\cdots\cdots$$
$$+ f_{1,m-1} + f_{2,m-2} + \cdots + f_{n-1,m-1})]$$

where $f_{i,j} = f(x_i, y_j)$
$$h = x_i - x_{i-1}$$
$$k = y_j - y_{j-1}$$

Such integration formulas over a rectangle are called *cubature formulas* for numerical integration of double integrals. Other formulas may be obtained by a double application of other quadrature formulas, such as Simpson's rule.

*37 An engineer wishes to obtain the "best" average reading of a certain meter in a plant over the span of one hour. How many minutes after the start of the hour should the readings be taken if
 a. Only two readings can be made.
 b. Three readings can be made.
 c. Four readings can be made.
 The answers should be computed to the nearest minute.

38 Given the following experimental data, where y is assumed to be some (unknown) function of x, find the area under the curve represented approximately by y by the following methods:
 a. Using the trapezoidal rule.
 b. Using Simpson's rule over the interval from 1.0 to 3.0.
 c. Using the trapezoidal rule for the interval from 1.0 to 1.2 and for the interval from 2.8 to 3.0 and Simpson's rule for the interval from 1.2 to 2.8.
 Without knowing more about the data, can you say which of the three answers is "best"?

x	y
1.0	1.00
1.2	1.82
1.4	2.08
1.6	3.18
1.8	3.52
2.0	4.70
2.2	5.12
2.4	6.38
2.6	6.98
2.8	8.22
3.0	9.00

39 Show that for the case $n = 2$ the truncation error given in page 248 for Legendre-Gauss quadrature reduces to the previously computed value

$$e_t = \frac{\phi^{iv}(\xi)}{135} \qquad -1 < \xi < 1$$

40 Given the experimental data shown on the next page, where y is assumed to be some (unknown) function of x, find the area under the curve represented approximately by y, using the trapezoidal rule.

x	y
20	0.21
25	0.30
30	0.37
40	0.45
50	0.49
60	0.50
70	0.49
80	0.47
90	0.45
100	0.43
120	0.37
140	0.33
160	0.29
180	0.25
200	0.19
250	0.13
300	0.08
400	0.04

41 In Case Study 5 (Section 3.4) a recursion formula was given for

$$I_n = \int_0^1 x^n e^{x-1} \, dx$$

a. Evaluate this integral using the trapezoidal rule, Simpson's rule, and Gaussian quadrature.

Choose the number of points so that you can compute I_{10} to four significant digits ($=0.08388$).

b. Compare the work necessary in any one of the three methods in part (a) with the work required in backward recursion (see Case Study 5).

42a Use the trapezoidal rule with $h = 0.25$ to evaluate

$$\int_0^1 (1 - 3x^2 + 2x^3) \, dx = \frac{1}{2}$$

b Equation (5.47) produces an error estimate of zero. Explain.

43 In Case Study 5 we developed a recursion formula

$$I_n = 1 - n\,I_{n-1}$$

for the integral

$$I_n = \int_0^1 x^n e^{x-1} \, dx \qquad n = 1, 2, \ldots$$

a. Use Simpson's rule to evaluate I_8. Determine the subintervals necessary to obtain five significant figures in the result. The correct result is 0.10093 as shown in Figure 3.22.

b. Use Gaussian quadrature to evaluate I_8. Determine the number of points necessary to obtain five significant figures.

44 The formulation of Case Study 9 does not take into account that light of different wave lengths does not produce the same sensation of brightness in the human eye. Light at $5 \cdot 10^{-5}$ cm, for example, seems to be only about a third as bright as light at $5.55 \cdot 10^{-5}$ cm, the wave length to which the eye is most sensitive. The following table, called the Standard Luminosity Function, has been adopted by the International Commission on Illumination as an average response to light at fairly high levels of illumination. (The response is somewhat different at low levels.) The table gives the wave length, λ, in milli-microns (mμ); 1 mμ = 10^{-7} cm. The function $\bar{y}\,(\lambda)$ gives the relative response of the eye, as a fraction of the maximum response at 555 mμ.

Modify the formulation and the program of the case study to include this factor, that is, to multiply each value of the integrand by the appropriate value from the table. The result will be to include in the efficiency calculation the actual response of the human eye.

It will be necessary either to accept the nearest value in the table to value of x being used, or to interpolate in the table (see chapter 6).

λ in mμ	$\bar{y}(\lambda)$	λ in mμ	$\bar{y}(\lambda)$	λ in mμ	$\bar{y}(\lambda)$	λ in mμ	$\bar{y}(\lambda)$
380	0.0000	480	0.139	580	0.870	680	0.0170
390	.0001	490	.208	590	.757	690	.0082
400	.0004	500	.323	600	.631	700	.0041
410	.0012	510	.503	610	.503	710	.0021
420	.0040	520	.710	620	.381	720	.0010
430	.0116	530	.862	630	.265	730	.0005
440	.0230	540	.954	640	.175	740	.0003
450	.0380	550	.995	650	.107	750	.0001
460	.0600	560	.995	660	.061	760	.0001
470	.0910	570	.952	670	.032		

45 The Debye function is encountered in statistical thermodynamics when evaluating the constant-volume specific heat of certain substances. The function is expressed as

$$D(x) = 3x^{-3} \int_0^x \frac{y^3}{e^y - 1}\, dy$$

Write a program to evaluate this integral for x = 0.5, 10.0, 50.0, and 100.0, using Simpson's rule. Write another program using Gaussian integration. For x = 0.5, the correct answer is about 0.4899.

46 The Clapeyron equation encountered in the study of thermodynamic property relations can be expressed as

$$\frac{d \ln P}{dT} = \frac{\Delta H_v}{RT^2} \tag{a}$$

where P = vapor pressure
T = absolute temperature
ΔH_v = enthalpy of vaporization
R = gas constant

This equation, which is valid for a limited range of pressure and temperature, can be used to determine the vapor pressure at any temperature by rewriting (a) and integrating from some known pressure and temperature P_0, T_0. Thus

$$\int_{P_0}^{P} d \ln P = \int_{T_0}^{T} \frac{\Delta H_v}{RT^2} dT$$

or

$$\ln \frac{P}{P_0} = \int_{T_0}^{T} \frac{\Delta H_v}{RT^2} dT \qquad \text{(b)}$$

Solution of (b) requires the evaluation of the indicated integral. However, in many cases ΔH_v cannot be expressed by a convenient analytical expression and the integral must be evaluated by a method such as Simpson's rule.

Consider a substance for which the following data are known:

T, °R	ΔH_v, Btu/lb
330	81.577
340	80.617
350	79.663
360	78.714
370	77.764
380	76.812
390	75.853
400	74.885
410	73.906
420	72.913
430	71.903

$R = 0.01614$ Btu/lb-°R
$P_0 = 0.41224$ lb/in² at $T_0 = 330$°R

It is desired to determine the vapor pressure at a temperature of 430°R. Write a program to integrate (b) by Simpson's rule. With the value of the integral determined, a final exponentiation yields the desired pressure. The correct result is 12.00 lb/in.².

6 Interpolation

Before the advent of computers if we wished to compute the square root or sine of some number, say x, we went to a table of such functions and looked up the appropriate value. If the number, x, whose square root (or sine) we wanted did not appear in the table, we found two other numbers, one greater than x and one smaller than x, and "interpolated" to find the function of x. For example, suppose we wanted the square root of 2.155 and had a table that listed the square roots of 2.150 and 2.160 but not of 2.155. Part of the table might read

n	$\sqrt{n}$
—	—
—	—
2.14	1.46287
2.15	1.46629
2.16	1.46969
2.17	1.47309
—	—
—	—

The difference between the square roots of 2.15 and 2.16 is 0.00340. Since 2.155, the number whose square root we seek, is halfway between 2.15

267

and 2.16, we could assume that the difference between $\sqrt{2.155}$ and $\sqrt{2.15}$ is one-half the difference between $\sqrt{2.15}$ and $\sqrt{2.16}$. So we take one-half of 0.00340 and add it to $\sqrt{2.15}$ producing

$$\sqrt{2.155} = 1.46799$$

Had we sought $\sqrt{2.153}$, we would have added $\frac{3}{10}$ths of 0.00340 to $\sqrt{2.15}$. This is the process of *interpolation* or to be more precise, *linear interpolation*.

Early digital computers had insufficient memory to contain the extensive tables needed to carry out evaluation of functions by these methods. However, computers did have the ability to carry out iterative calculations rapidly and economically. Therefore, evaluation of a function, such as the square root or the sine, generally was carried out on a computer through a program that performed some iterative process. For example, the square root of A can be computed using the Newton-Raphson method where successive approximations x_n are given by

$$x_n = \frac{1}{2}\left(x_{n-1} + \frac{A}{x_{n-1}}\right)$$

as we saw in Chapter 1. The sine can be computed using a Taylor series

$$\sin A = A - \frac{A^3}{3!} + \frac{A^5}{5!} + \cdots$$

if A is sufficiently small (see Case Study 3 in Chapter 3).

Thus with digital computers the process of interpolation became in many cases uneconomical. Interpolation, however, was still of practical value when a function was not defined through a formula, but instead was defined by a table. The table might, for example, be the results of some experiment. Moreover, interpolation was a powerful theoretical tool and many textbooks on numerical methods started with the theory of interpolation and built other developments, such as numerical integration, upon that theory. In the exercises at the close of this chapter we shall reexamine some topics, for example, numerical integration and differentiation, in light of the theory of interpolation.

As computer memories became larger and less expensive, interpolation again became a more practical device since extensive tables could be contained within the computer. With this in mind we turn now to a discussion of interpolation. We discuss first linear interpolation, which is the process we used in computing the square root of 2.155, and then go on to two other types, Lagrangian and repeated linear interpolation.

**6.2
Linear
Interpola-
tion**

Suppose that we have a set of m numbers $x_1, x_2, \ldots, x_m$, and that corresponding to each x_i there is another number y_i. The y_i are to be considered to define a function over the x_i. If we are given a value that is exactly equal to one of the x_i we can readily enough locate the corresponding y_i, but what if we are given a value $\bar{x}$ that falls between two values of x, say x_k and x_{k+1}? If the x and y values were derived from some experimental procedure, we may not have any accurate idea of what the functional relationship between them might be, in terms of an analytical expression; we may have little choice but to try to find the value of y corresponding to $\bar{x}$ by some approximate process. Even if we know perfectly well what the analytical relationship is, such as a square root or a sine, especially if that relationship is complicated to compute, we may choose to interpolate because it is simpler, faster, or cheaper.

In doing so, of course, we are assuming that *some* functional relationship (such as a line or a parabola, perhaps, depending on the type of interpolation) does hold in between the x values contained in the given set. It will be our responsibility to assure that this is a valid assumption. If, for a rather extreme example, we are working with a table of values derived from $y = 1/(x - 1.25)$, for x values 1.0, 1.1, 1.2, 1.3, and so forth, and we ask for the value of y corresponding to $x = 1.25$, the interpolation method will give us a finite value rather than returning the information that the function is unbounded at that point. If we have used linear interpolation, which means assuming that the relationship between x and y in the interval of $x = 1.2$ to 1.3 is a line, there is no way the interpolation method can tell us that we made a bad assumption.

In general, however, we assume that given any x the corresponding value of y exists, and we shall proceed to calculate the value of y. Let us first plot the corresponding values of x_i and y_i for $i = 1, 2, \ldots, m$ as shown for hypothetical values in Figure 6.1. The ith point in that figure has coordinates (x_i, y_i). We suppose that the x_i and y_i are given and that they are ordered so that $x_1 \leq x_2 \leq \cdots x_{m-1} \leq x_m$. Of course, the values of the y_i will not in general be in order as we can see from Figure 6.1.

Suppose we are given a value of x, say $\bar{x}$, such that

$$x_k \leq \bar{x} \leq x_{k+1}$$

and we wish to calculate the value of y corresponding to that $\bar{x}$. To do so, we draw a line segment joining the points (x_k, y_k) and (x_{k+1}, y_{k+1}). We then find the point on that line at a distance $\bar{x}$ from the y-axis. Figure 6.2 shows the line segment, L, joining (x_k, y_k) and (x_{k+1}, y_{k+1}). The value of $\bar{x}$ is shown along the x-axis. The point on L directly above $\bar{x}$ is the

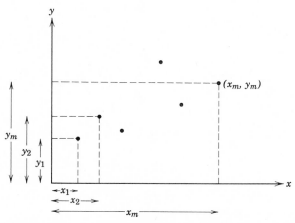

Figure 6.1. *A set of data points for interpolation. The location of the points is intended to suggest the generality of the problem, rather than to correspond to any realistic situation.*

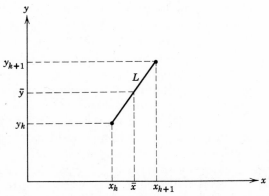

Figure 6.2. *A line segment, L, joining two points between which we wish to interpolate.*

point $(\bar{x}, \bar{y})$, and $\bar{y}$ is then taken to be the value of y corresponding to $x = \bar{x}$. Because we use a *line* rather than some other curve, this type of interpolation is called *linear interpolation*.

We now proceed to derive an algebraic expression for the calculation of $\bar{y}$ in terms of $\bar{x}$ and the values of x_k, y_k and x_{k+1}, y_{k+1}. The equation of the line through (x_k, y_k) and (x_{k+1}, y_{k+1}) is

$$y = y_k + \left(\frac{x - x_k}{x_{k+1} - x_k} \right)(y_{k+1} - y_k) \tag{6.1}$$

so

$$\bar{y} = y_k + \left(\frac{\bar{x} - x_k}{x_{k+1} - x_k} \right)(y_{k+1} - y_k) \tag{6.2}$$

Before analyzing the error involved in linear interpolation we consider a simple example. Suppose we have tabulated the values of $y = x^2$ for all integer values of x. We use this table to estimate the values of x^2 for noninteger values of x. To take a specific case we calculate the value of the square of 6.5. Thus

$$\begin{aligned} x_k &= 6 & y_k &= 36 \\ x_{k+1} &= 7 & y_{k+1} &= 49 \end{aligned}$$

and

$$\bar{x} = 6.5$$

Using (6.2)

$$\bar{y} = 36 + \frac{0.5}{1}(49 - 36) = 42.5$$

Since the correct value of $y = (6.5)^2 = 42.25$, the error (true value minus the calculated value) is

$$E_T = -0.25$$

This is a truncation error (thus the subscript T) since it results from truncating a nonlinear process by a linear one.

To analyze this error we subtract the approximate value of $\bar{y}$ given by the right-hand side of (6.2) from the true value, $\bar{x}^2$.

$$E_T = \bar{x}^2 - y_k - \left(\frac{\bar{x} - x_k}{x_{k+1} - x_k}\right)(y_{k+1} - y_k)$$

Now $y_k = x_k^2$ and $y_{k+1} = x_{k+1}^2$ so

$$E_T = \bar{x}^2 - x_k^2 - \left(\frac{\bar{x} - x_k}{x_{k+1} - x_k}\right)(x_{k+1}^2 - x_k^2)$$

$$= (\bar{x} - x_k)(\bar{x} + x_k) - \left(\frac{\bar{x} - x_k}{x_{k+1} - x_k}\right)(x_{k+1} - x_k)(x_{k+1} + x_k)$$

Finally,

$$E_T = (\bar{x} - x_k)(\bar{x} - x_{k+1}) \tag{6.3}$$

Again using $\bar{x} = 6.5$, $x_k = 6$, and $x_{k+1} = 7$,

$$E_T = (6.5 - 6)(6.5 - 7) = -0.25$$

which agrees with the previously computed value of the error.

In general, of course, y represents a more general function than x^2, and we cannot replace y_k and y_{k+1} by expressions such as x_k^2 and x_{k+1}^2 as we did above. However, it is still possible to carry through an analysis of the truncation error in much the same way as we did above. We proceed to that analysis now.

We suppose the true value of y is given by $f(x)$, which possesses a continuous second derivative. The approximate value of y is given by the right-hand side of (6.1), so the truncation error is

$$E_T = f(x) - y_k - \frac{x - x_k}{x_{k+1} - x_k}(y_{k+1} - y_k)$$

This truncation error obviously depends upon the particular value of x, although we have assumed that x lies between x_k and x_{k+1}. Thus E_T is a function of x. We designate this function by $F(x)$, that is,

$$F(x) = f(x) - y_k - \frac{x - x_k}{x_{k+1} - x_k}(y_{k+1} - y_k) \tag{6.4}$$

Now we arbitrarily define a function $G(x)$ to be

$$G(x) = (x - x_k)(x - x_{k+1}) \tag{6.5}$$

and form

$$H(t) = F(x)G(t) - F(t)G(x) \tag{6.6}$$

where x is considered to be a parameter. (For example, if we write $g(t) = at + b$ we usually consider a and b to be parameters and t to be the independent variable.) From (6.6)

$$H(x) = 0$$

Since $y_k = f(x_k)$, (6.4) produces

$$F(x_k) = 0$$

Moreover, from (6.5)

$$G(x_k) = 0$$

Therefore

$$H(x_k) = F(x)G(x_k) - F(x_k)G(x) = 0$$

Similarly, we find that

$$H(x_{k+1}) = 0$$

Since $H(x)$ vanishes at x_k, x, and x_{k+1}, by the Mean Value Theorem there exist numbers ξ_1 and ξ_2 such that

$$x_k \leq \xi_1 \leq x \leq \xi_2 \leq x_{k+1}$$

and

$$H'(\xi_1) = H'(\xi_2) = 0$$

By again applying the Mean Value Theorem to the function $H'(x)$, there exists a number ξ such that

$$H''(\xi) = 0$$

where

$$\xi_1 \leq \xi \leq \xi_2$$

Thus

$$x_k \leq \xi \leq x_{k+1}$$

By differentiating (6.6) twice and substituting ξ for t

$$H''(\xi) = F(x)G''(\xi) - F''(\xi)G(x)$$

Since this vanishes it follows that

$$\frac{F(x)}{G(x)} = \frac{F''(\xi)}{G''(\xi)} \tag{6.7}$$

But differentiating (6.4) twice and substituting ξ for x yields

$$F''(\xi) = f''(\xi)$$

Similarly, differentiation of (6.5) produces

$$G''(\xi) = 2$$

Using these results and (6.5) in (6.7) we get finally

$$F(x) = \frac{f''(\xi)}{2}(x - x_k)(x - x_{k+1}) \tag{6.8}$$

But $F(x)$ is the truncation error, E_T. For the case where $f(x) = x^2$ it follows that $f''(\xi) = 2$ and (6.8) reduces to (6.3) as expected.

As another example consider the case where

$$f(x) = \log_e x$$

Then

$$f''(x) = -1/x^2$$

and from (6.8)

$$E_T = -\frac{1}{2\xi^2}(x - x_k)(x - x_{k+1})$$

Thus, when linear interpolation is used on a table of logarithms, the truncation error is largest for small x and decreases as x gets larger and larger. We can see this intuitively from Figure 6.3, where a graph of log x is shown. Notice that the chord joining two points where x is small (line L_1) is more distant from the curve than is the chord joining two points where x is large (line L_2).

As a numerical example we consider

$$f(x) = \log_{10}x = \log_{10}e \, \log_e x$$

so

$$f''(x) = -\frac{\log_{10}e}{x^2}$$

and

$$E_T = -\frac{\log_{10}e}{2}(x - x_k)(x - x_{k+1})\frac{1}{\xi^2} \tag{6.9}$$

Suppose we are given the logarithms of 1.500 and 1.600 and use linear interpolation to calculate the log 1.530. Using four-digit floating point arithmetic

$$x_k = .1500 \times 10^1 \qquad y_k = .1761 \times 10^0$$
$$x_{k+1} = .1600 \times 10^1 \qquad y_{k+1} = .2041 \times 10^0$$
$$x = .1530 \times 10^1$$

so

$$x - x_k = .3000 \times 10^{-1} \qquad x_{k+1} - x_k = .1000 \times 10^0$$

$$\frac{x - x_k}{x_{k+1} - x_k} = .3000 \times 10^0$$

$$y_{k+1} - y_k = .2800 \times 10^{-1}$$

and from (6.1)

$$y = .1845 \times 10^0$$

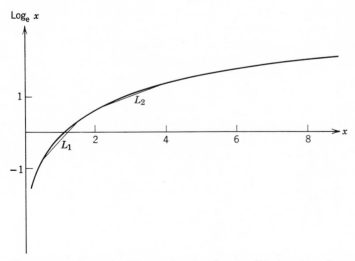

Figure 6.3. *A graph of log* x, *showing that for this function, the truncation error is greater for small* x.

The correct result is

$$y = .1847 \times 10^0$$

so the truncation error is

$$E_T = .2000 \times 10^{-3}$$

Using this in (6.9) and noting that

$$\log_{10}e = .4343 \times 10^0$$
$$x - x_k = .3000 \times 10^{-1}$$
$$x - x_{k+1} = -.7000 \times 10^{-1}$$

it follows that

$$\xi^2 = 2.28$$

Thus

$$\xi = 1.51$$

which verifies the result that

$$1.5 = x_k \leq \xi \leq x_{k+1} = 1.6$$

The value of ξ is usually not of much interest and sheds little light on the problem. We have computed it here only to indicate that in this one case, at least, ξ does lie in the interval $x_k \leq x \leq x_{k+1}$. Notice that the computation of ξ requires that we know the value of the truncation error E_T. It is this latter quantity that is of real interest to us and whose value is usually not known.

6.4 Roundoff Error in Linear Interpolation

We turn now to the analysis of the roundoff error in linear interpolation, which we shall later compare with the truncation error.

The process graph is shown in Figure 6.4, where the six operations are numbered from 1 to 6. We assume that there is *no error* in the values of the independent variable: x, x_k, and x_{k+1}. In many cases this is a reasonable assumption since if we are constructing a table we can pick the values of the independent variable. For example, a table of sines of x_i for $x_i = 0^0, 1^0, \ldots, 45^0$ may be constructed, and there is no error in x_i. In addition we usually know precisely the value of x for which we wish to evaluate the function.

On the other hand, there will in general be errors in the dependent variable. We let E_i be the *absolute* error in y_i. In addition we let $r_j(j = 1, 2, \ldots, 6)$ be the *relative* roundoff error arising from the jth operation. Finally we let E_y be the *absolute* error in the interpolated value y. (*Note:* Capital letters here will refer to absolute errors and small letters will refer to relative errors.)

From the process graph we can determine the relative error in y to be

$$\frac{E_y}{y} = \left(\frac{x - x_k}{x_{k+1} - x_k} \right) \frac{E_{k+1}}{y} - \left(\frac{x - x_{k+1}}{x_{k+1} - x_k} \right) \frac{E_k}{y}$$
$$+ \left(\frac{x - x_k}{x_{k+1} - x_k} \right) \left(\frac{y_{k+1} - y_k}{y} \right) (r_1 - r_2 + r_3 + r_4 + r_5) + r_6$$

(6.10)

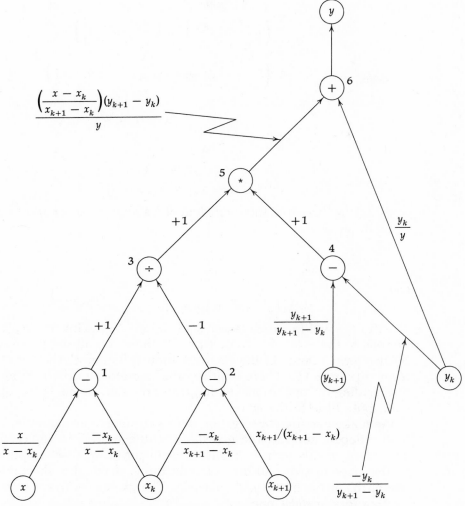

Figure 6.4. *The process graph for the roundoff error in linear interpolation.*

To find an upper bound for E_y we multiply by y. We take absolute values and use the triangle inequality. Thus

$$|E_y| \leq \left| \frac{x - x_k}{x_{k+1} - x_k} \right| |E_{k+1}|$$

$$+ \left| \frac{x - x_{k+1}}{x_{k+1} - x_k} \right| |E_k| + \left| \frac{x - x_k}{x_{k+1} - x_k} \right| |y_{k+1} - y_k|$$

$$\times (|r_1| + |r_2| + |r_3| + |r_4| + |r_5|) + |y| \, |r_6|$$

We now let E be the maximum absolute error in any of the y_k so that

$$|E_i| \leq E$$

for all i. Similarly, r is the maximum relative roundoff error so

$$|r_i| \leq r$$

Thus

$$|E_y| \leq \left(\left| \frac{x - x_k}{x_{k+1} - x_k} \right| + \left| \frac{x - x_{k+1}}{x_{k+1} - x_k} \right| \right) E$$

$$+ \left(5 \left| \frac{x - x_k}{x_{k+1} - x_k} \right| |y_{k+1} - y_k| + |y| \right) r$$

Now

$$x_k \leq x \leq x_{k+1}$$

so

$$|x - x_k| = x - x_k$$
$$|x - x_{k+1}| = -x + x_{k+1}$$
$$|x_{k+1} - x_k| = x_{k+1} - x_k$$

Substituting these into the coefficient of E above, we see that the coefficient is 1. Moreover,

$$\left| \frac{x - x_k}{x_{k+1} - x_k} \right| \leq 1$$

so

$$|E_y| \leq E + (5|y_{k+1} - y_k| + |y|)r \qquad (6.11)$$

Usually $|y|$ will be much larger than $|y_{k+1} - y_k|$. Thus the major contributions to the error, E_y, come from (1) the errors in the y_k as evidenced by the term E and (2) the final addition (number 6) that produces the term $|y|r$ in (6.11). There is little value therefore in performing the first five arithmetic operations with great precision since these operations contribute little to the error.

We make one final observation before turning to an example. The error in the dependent variable gives rise to the term E in (6.11). Since the coefficient of this term is 1, the error in the data is *not* amplified. That is, the error in y due to the errors in the y_k is roughly the same as any one of the errors in the y_k themselves. The process of linear interpolation is, therefore, a *stable* one.

**6.5
Numerical
Example**

As an example we consider a three-digit table of values of x^2 where x is taken in increments of one tenth. Part of the table reads:

x	x^2
$\vdots$	$\vdots$
5.9	34.8
6.0	36.0
6.1	37.2
6.2	38.4
$\vdots$	$\vdots$

Suppose we wish to use this table to interpolate for the square of 6.09. Then for x_k we choose 6.0 and for x_{k+1} we choose 6.1. Using three-digit floating point arithmetic

$$x_k = .600 \times 10^1 \qquad x_{k+1} = .610 \times 10^1$$
$$y_k = .360 \times 10^2 \qquad y_{k+1} = .372 \times 10^2$$
$$E_k = 0 \qquad\qquad E_{k+1} = .100 \times 10^{-1}$$

Since $x = .609 \times 10^1$ we calculate

$$x - x_k = .900 \times 10^{-1}$$

and $r_1 = 0$. Then we calculate

$$x_{k+1} - x_k = .100 \times 10^0$$

and $r_2 = 0$. Next we find

$$\frac{x - x_k}{x_{k+1} - x_k} = .900 \times 10^0$$

and again $r_3 = 0$. The fourth operation is

$$y_{k+1} - y_k = .120 \times 10^1$$

so $r_4 = 0$. Then

$$\left(\frac{x - x_k}{x_{k+1} - x_k}\right)(y_{k+1} - y_k) = .108 \times 10^1$$

and $r_5 = 0$. Finally we calculate y to be

$$y = .3708 \times 10^2$$

and rounding symmetrically

$$y = .371 \times 10^2 \tag{6.12}$$

so

$$r_6 = \frac{-.200 \times 10^{-1}}{.371 \times 10^2}$$

Using equation (6.10)

$$E_y = (.900 \times 10^0)(.100 \times 10^{-1}) + \left(\frac{-.200 \times 10^{-1}}{.371 \times 10^2}\right)(.371 \times 10^2)$$

$$E_y = -.110 \times 10^{-1}$$

From (6.3) the truncation error is

$$E_T = (x - x_k)(x - x_{k+1})$$
$$= -0.900 \times 10^{-3}$$

so the total error, e, is

$$e = E_y + E_T = -0.119 \times 10^{-1}$$

If we add this to the value calculated for y in (6.12) we get

$$y = .371 \times 10^2 - .119 \times 10^{-1}$$
$$= .370881 \times 10^2$$

which is indeed $(6.09)^2$ to six digits. Here we computed all of the roundoff errors precisely. In general we cannot do so.

Notice that in this case the truncation error is much smaller than the roundoff error and, moreover, the major contribution to the roundoff error results from the final addition, that is, from r_6.

To examine the bound on the roundoff error for this example we return to (6.11) and note that in this case

$$E = 0.5 \times 10^{-1}$$

and since we are assuming symmetric rounding

$$r = 0.5 \times 10^{-2}$$

(Actually the only nonzero roundoff error was smaller than r by a factor of 10, but this is the best *a priori* bound we can assume.) Thus from (6.11)

$$|E_y| \leq 0.5 \times 10^{-1} + (5 \times 1.2 + 37.1)(0.5 \times 10^{-2}) = 0.2655 \times 10^0$$

which is larger than the actual roundoff error (-0.011) by a factor of over 25. As usual, therefore, the bound as given in (6.11) is extremely conservative, because of the fact that both E and r are extremely conservative and assume the worst cases, which in practice do not usually arise.

6.6 Quadratic Interpolation

In many cases linear interpolation is unsatisfactory since the function being interpolated deviates by a considerable amount from a linear function. In such cases we can use other polynomials, second or higher degree, to approximate the function. For linear interpolation we chose two points (x_k, y_k) and (x_{k+1}, y_{k+1}) and drew a line through those two points. We found the equation of that line and used it to evaluate the function for any x such that $x_k < x < x_{k+1}$.

We could take n points and pass an $(n-1)$st-degree polynomial through those n points and then use that polynomial to evaluate the function. Of course, the question arises: Is there more than one polynomial of degree $n-1$ that can be passed through a given n points? The answer is no, which we shall confirm in Section 6.7. This allows us to speak of *the* interpolating polynomial, and we shall do so when referring to various interpolating schemes in what follows. For any given set of n points, there will be one and only one interpolating polynomial.

In preparation for this more general discussion we first choose three points and pass a second-degree polynomial through these three points. We shall show that there is only one such polynomial possible and shall derive an expression for that polynomial. In the next section we shall consider the case of n points.

Suppose, therefore, that we wish to use a second-degree polynomial to approximate the function and that we wish to evaluate the function for a value of x such that

$$x_k < x < x_{k+1}$$

We then choose the three points (x_{k-1}, y_{k-1}), (x_k, y_k), and (x_{k+1}, y_{k+1}) and pass a curve through them (see Figure 6.5). In this case there is one point

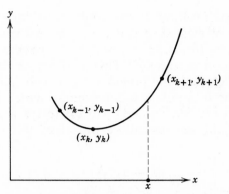

Figure 6.5. *Geometrical representation of quadratic interpolation.*

to the right of x and are two points to the left of x. We could just as well have chosen two points to the right and one point to the left. In the latter case we would have used (x_k, y_k), (x_{k+1}, y_{k+1}), and (x_{k+2}, y_{k+2}). The choice is somewhat arbitrary except that x should be greater than the value of x_i with the smallest subscript and also be less than the value of x_i with the largest subscript. Here we choose

$$x_{k-1} < x_k < x < x_{k+1}$$

as indicated previously.

The most general second-degree polynomial in x may be written

$$P(x) = a_2 x^2 + a_1 x + a_0 \qquad (6.13)$$

We are seeking a second-degree polynomial that passes through the three points (x_{k-1}, y_{k-1}), (x_k, y_k), and (x_{k+1}, y_{k+1}). Thus when $x = x_{k-1}$ in (6.13) the value of the polynomial should be y_{k-1}, that is,

$$y_{k-1} = a_2 x_{k-1}^2 + a_1 x_{k-1} + a_0 \qquad (6.14)$$

Similarly

$$y_k = a_2 x_k^2 + a_2 x_k + a_0 \qquad (6.15)$$
$$y_{k+1} = a_2 x_{k+1}^2 + a_2 x_{k+1} + a_0 \qquad (6.16)$$

Equations (6.14), (6.15), and (6.16) are three linear equations for the three variables a_2, a_1, and a_0. The questions that arise are: "Does a solution a_2, a_1, a_0 exist?" and "If a solution exists, is it unique?"

To answer these question we consider the corresponding homogeneous equations

$$\begin{aligned}
a_2 x_{k-1}^2 + a_1 x_{k-1} + a_0 &= 0 \\
a_2 x_k^2 + a_1 x_k + a_0 &= 0 \\
a_2 x_{k+1}^2 + a_1 x_{k+1} + a_0 &= 0
\end{aligned} \qquad (6.17)$$

If a solution exists for these homogeneous equations for which at least one of the coefficients a_i is not zero, then that solution substituted into (6.13) produces a second-degree polynomial with three roots: one at x_{k-1}, one at x_k, and one at x_{k+1}. Since a second-degree polynomial has precisely two roots or is identically zero, it follows that a nontrivial solution to the homogeneous equations cannot exist. We can conclude, therefore, that the nonhomogeneous equations (6.14), (6.15), and (6.16) have a unique solution, that is, the system is nonsingular.[1] This answers affirmatively the questions we posed at the close of the previous paragraph. Therefore, we may speak of *the* quadratic interpolating polynomial, which is given by (6.13) where the coefficients are determined by (6.14), (6.15), and (6.16).

In order to solve (6.14), (6.15), and (6.16) we introduce three special functions as follows:

$$\begin{aligned}
\Pi_{k-1}(x) &= (x - x_k)(x - x_{k+1}) \\
\Pi_k(x) &= (x - x_{k-1})(x - x_{k+1}) \\
\Pi_{k+1}(x) &= (x - x_{k-1})(x - x_k)
\end{aligned} \tag{6.18}$$

All of these are second-degree polynomials in x. Since we have assumed that the x_i are distinct, it follows from these definitions that

$$\begin{aligned}
\Pi_{k-1}(x_{k-1}) &\neq 0 \\
\Pi_k(x_k) &\neq 0 \\
\Pi_{k+1}(x_{k+1}) &\neq 0
\end{aligned} \tag{6.19}$$

On the other hand,

$$\begin{aligned}
\Pi_{k-1}(x_k) &= \Pi_{k-1}(x_{k+1}) = 0 \\
\Pi_k(x_{k-1}) &= \Pi_k(x_{k+1}) = 0 \\
\Pi_{k+1}(x_{k-1}) &= \Pi_{k+1}(x_k) = 0
\end{aligned} \tag{6.20}$$

We now rewrite $P(x)$ as a linear combination of the functions Π_{k-1}, Π_k, and Π_{k+1}.

$$P(x) = b_{k-1}\Pi_{k-1}(x) + b_k\Pi_k(x) + b_{k+1}\Pi_{k+1}(x) \tag{6.21}$$

This again is a general second-degree polynomial since each of the Π_i is a second-degree polynomial, and there are three arbitrary parameters: b_{k-1}, b_k, and b_{k+1}.

Substituting $x = x_{k-1}$ in (6.21) and using (6.19) and (6.20)

$$y_{k-1} = b_{k-1}\Pi_{k-1}(x_{k-1})$$

Similarly using $x = x_k$ and $x = x_{k+1}$

$$\begin{aligned}
y_k &= b_k\Pi_k(x_k) \\
y_{k+1} &= b_{k+1}\Pi_{k+1}(x_{k+1})
\end{aligned}$$

By virtue of (6.19), these equations can be solved for the b_i; substituting these values for b_i in (6.21) we get

$$P(x) = y_{k-1}\frac{\Pi_{k-1}(x)}{\Pi_{k-1}(x_{k-1})} + y_k\frac{\Pi_k(x)}{\Pi_k(x_k)} + y_{k+1}\frac{\Pi_{k+1}(x)}{\Pi_{k+1}(x_{k+1})} \tag{6.22}$$

---

[1] See, for example, Murray H. Protter and Charles B. Morrey, Jr., *Modern Mathematical Analysis*, Boston, Addison-Wesley, 1900, Theorem 15 and its corollary in Chapter 6.

or using (6.18)

$$
\begin{aligned}
P(x) = {} & \frac{y_{k-1}(x - x_k)(x - x_{k+1})}{(x_{k-1} - x_k)(x_{k-1} - x_{k+1})} \\
& + \frac{y_k(x - x_{k-1})(x - x_{k+1})}{(x_k - x_{k-1})(x_k - x_{k+1})} \\
& + \frac{y_{k+1}(x - x_{k-1})(x - x_k)}{(x_{k+1} - x_{k-1})(x_{k+1} - x_k)}
\end{aligned}
\tag{6.23}
$$

We shall not discuss the truncation and roundoff error since we shall do that later for the more general case of an $(n - 1)$st-degree polynomial passing through n points. However, we shall consider a simple example before going on to the more general case.

Consider the following values of x and y:

x	y
0	1
2	5
4	17

We take these to be the $(k - 1)$st, kth, and $(k + 1)$st points, respectively. Then

$$
\begin{aligned}
\Pi_{k-1}(x) &= (x - 2)(x - 4) \\
\Pi_k(x) &= (x - 0)(x - 4) \\
\Pi_{k+1}(x) &= (x - 0)(x - 2)
\end{aligned}
$$

and

$$
b_{k-1} = \frac{y_{k-1}}{\Pi_{k-1}(x_{k-1})} = \frac{1}{(0 - 2)(0 - 4)} = \frac{1}{8}
$$

$$
b_k = \frac{y_k}{\Pi_k(x_k)} = \frac{5}{(2 - 0)(2 - 4)} = -\frac{5}{4}
$$

$$
b_{k+1} = \frac{y_{k+1}}{\Pi_{k+1}(x_{k+1})} = \frac{17}{(4 - 0)(4 - 2)} = \frac{17}{8}
$$

so

$$
P(x) = \frac{1}{8}(x - 2)(x - 4) - \frac{5}{4}x(x - 4) + \frac{17}{8}x(x - 2)
$$

Collecting terms

$$
P(x) = x^2 + 1
$$

which can easily be verified to produce the three points given at the beginning of this example.

**6.7
Lagrangian
Interpola-
tion**

In Section 6.2 we used two points and passed a first-degree (linear) polynomial through the two points. In Section 6.6 we used three points and passed a second-degree (quadratic) polynomial through the three points. In this section we shall use n points and pass an $(n - 1)$st degree polynomial through the n points. The entire development in this section will parallel that of the previous section (Section 6.6).

If we wish to interpolate for the value of y corresponding to some value of x, we choose from our table the x_i whose values "straddle" the value of x. In the linear case (Section 6.2) we found x_k and x_{k+1} such that

$$x_k < x < x_{k+1}$$

In the quadratic case we found x_{k-1}, x_k, and x_{k+1} such that

$$x_{k-1} < x_k < x < x_{k+1}$$

In general we choose n values of x_i so that close to one-half of these x_i are less than x and one-half are greater than x. We hasten to point out however that we need not do so. All we need do is make sure that x is greater than the smallest x_i and less than the largest x_i. Different sets of x_i will produce different interpolated values. For example consider the six points shown in Figure 6.6. If we use the first four points we get the curve shown in the upper diagram. Use of the last four points results in the curve in the lower diagram. In the lower diagram the upper curve is reproduced as a dashed curve. If $x_3 < x < x_4$, then the two choices result in a substantial difference in the interpolated value of y. These different results are labeled y_u (for y from the upper diagram) and y_l (for y from the lower diagram).

Once the choice of the n points has been made, however, we call these points (x_1, y_1), (x_2, y_2), . . . , (x_n, y_n). To go back to our linear case, we would rename the point (x_k, y_k) as (x_1, y_1), and the point (x_{k+1}, y_{k+1}) would be renamed (x_2, y_2). This renaming is merely a convenience for us and avoids some complications with the subscripts.

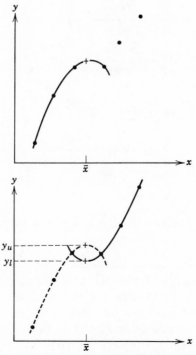

Figure 6.6. *Sketch showing, in exaggerated form, that the choice of points in higher-order interpolation affects the interpolated value.*

A general $(n - 1)$st-degree polynomial can be written

$$P(x) = a_{n-1}x^{n-1} + a_{n-2}x^{n-2} + \cdots + a_1 x + a_0 \tag{6.24}$$

If it is to pass through these n points, then

$$
\begin{aligned}
y_1 &= a_{n-1}x_1^{n-1} + a_{n-2}x_1^{n-2} + \cdots + a_1 x_1 + a_0 \\
y_2 &= a_{n-1}x_2^{n-1} + a_{n-2}x_2^{n-2} + \cdots + a_1 x_2 + a_0 \\
&\vdots \\
y_i &= a_{n-1}x_i^{n-1} + a_{n-2}x_i^{n-2} + \cdots + a_1 x_i + a_0 \\
&\vdots \\
y_n &= a_{n-1}x_n^{n-1} + a_{n-2}x_n^{n-2} + \cdots + a_1 x_n + a_0
\end{aligned}
\tag{6.25}
$$

These are n equations in n variables $a_0, a_1, \ldots, a_{n-1}$. We proceed to show that they have a unique solution.

Consider first the corresponding homogeneous equations

$$
\begin{aligned}
0 &= a_{n-1}x_1^{n-1} + a_{n-2}x_1^{n-2} + \cdots + a_1 x_1 + a_0 \\
0 &= a_{n-1}x_2^{n-1} + a_{n-2}x_2^{n-2} + \cdots + a_1 x_2 + a_0 \\
&\vdots \\
0 &= a_{n-1}x_n^{n-1} + a_{n-2}x_n^{n-2} + \cdots + a_1 x_n + a_0
\end{aligned}
$$

Assume that this latter homogeneous system has a nontrivial solution, that is, a solution for which not all of the $a_i = 0$. Then the polynomial (6.24) has n roots, and those roots are $x_1, x_2, \ldots, x_n$. However, an $(n - 1)$st-degree polynomial with n roots must be identically zero hence

$$a_{n-1} = a_{n-2} = \cdots = a_1 = a_0 = 0$$

so that the only solution is a trivial one. This contradicts the assumption that a nontrivial solution existed. Since no nontrivial solution to the homogeneous system exists, it follows that the inhomogeneous system (6.25) has a unique solution.[2] Of course, if all of the $y_i = 0$ ($i = 1$, $2, \ldots, n$), then the unique solution is $P(x) \equiv 0$. This should not surprise us since then all n points lie on the x-axis. If at least one $y_i \neq 0$, then $P(x)$ is not identically zero.

In order to solve (6.25) we introduce n new functions all of which are $(n - 1)$st-degree polynomials.

$$
\begin{aligned}
\Pi_1(x) &= (x - x_2)(x - x_3) \cdots (x - x_n) \\
\Pi_2(x) &= (x - x_1)(x - x_3) \cdots (x - x_n) \\
&\vdots \\
\Pi_k(x) &= (x - x_1) \cdots (x - x_{k-1})(x - x_{k+1}) \cdots (x - x_n) \\
&\vdots \\
\Pi_n(x) &= (x - x_1)(x - x_2) \cdots (x - x_{n-1})
\end{aligned}
$$

or more concisely

$$\Pi_i(x) = \prod_{\substack{j=1 \\ j \neq i}}^{n} (x - x_j) \qquad i = 1, 2, \ldots, n \tag{6.26}$$

where the Π on the right indicates, as usual, repeated multiplication.

[2] See previous footnote.

Now notice that

$$\Pi_i(x_i) \neq 0 \qquad (6.27)$$

if all x_i are distinct, as we have assumed, and moreover

$$\Pi_i(x_j) = 0 \qquad \text{for } i \neq j \qquad (6.28)$$

We now rewrite $P(x)$ as a linear combination of $\Pi_1, \Pi_2, \ldots, \Pi_n$

$$P(x) = b_1\Pi_1(x) + b_2\Pi_2(x) + \cdots + b_n\Pi_n(x)$$

or again more concisely

$$P(x) = \sum_{i=1}^{n} b_i\Pi_i(x) \qquad (6.29)$$

This is a general $(n - 1)$st-degree polynomial since each Π_i is an $(n - 1)$st-degree polynomial and there are n arbitrary parameters $b_1, b_2, \ldots, b_n$.

Substituting x_k in (6.29) and using (6.27) and (6.28), we see that

$$P(x_k) = b_k\Pi_k(x_k)$$

since all terms in the sum in (6.29) except for the kth will vanish. But

$$y_k = P(x_k)$$

so

$$b_k = \frac{y_k}{\Pi_k(x_k)}$$

and this is valid for $k = 1, 2, \ldots, n$.

Therefore, (6.29) becomes

$$P(x) = \sum_{i=1}^{n} y_i \frac{\Pi_i(x)}{\Pi_i(x_i)} \qquad (6.30)$$

Alternatively we could use (6.26) to rewrite this as

$$P(x) = \sum_{i=1}^{n} y_i \frac{\displaystyle\prod_{\substack{j=1 \\ j\neq i}}^{n} (x - x_j)}{\displaystyle\prod_{\substack{j=1 \\ j\neq i}}^{n} (x_i - x_j)}$$

or

$$P(x) = \sum_{i=1}^{n} y_i \prod_{\substack{j=1 \\ j\neq i}}^{n} \left(\frac{x - x_j}{x_i - x_j}\right) \qquad (6.31)$$

Equation (6.30) corresponds to (6.21) of the previous section. Similarly, (6.31) corresponds to (6.23) in the previous section. Either (6.30) together with (6.26), or (6.31) alone, is called *Lagrange's Interpolation Formula*, and the process of using this formula is called *Lagrangian Interpolation*.

Of course, we should expect that for the case $n = 2$ this formula will reduce to the linear interpolation formula (6.1). This is left as an exercise for the reader.

6.8 Truncation Error in Lagrangian Interpolation

We now discuss the truncation error in using Lagrangian interpolation. Our development here will closely parallel the derivation in Section 6.3 of the truncation error for linear interpolation.

We assume that the function $f(x)$ being interpolated possesses n continuous derivatives throughout the range of interpolation, that is, for $x_1 \leq x \leq x_n$. Now $P(x)$ in (6.31) is the approximation to $f(x)$ given by the nth-order Lagrangian interpolation. The truncation error E_T is a function of x, that is,

$$E_T = F(x) = f(x) - P(x) \tag{6.32}$$

We define a function $G(x)$ to be

$$G(x) = \prod_{j=1}^{n} (x - x_j) = (x - x_1)(x - x_2) \cdots (x - x_n) \tag{6.33}$$

and form

$$H(t) = F(x)G(t) - F(t)G(x) \tag{6.34}$$

where again x is considered to be a parameter. From (6.33)

$$G(x_j) = 0 \qquad j = 1, 2, \ldots, n$$

By virtue of (6.31)

$$P(x_j) = y_j \qquad j = 1, 2, \ldots, n$$

and since $f(x)$ is the function being interpolated it must also pass through the n points (x_1, y_1), (x_2, y_2), $\ldots$, (x_n, y_n) so

$$f(x_j) = y_j \qquad j = 1, 2, \ldots, n$$

Therefore, from (6.32)

$$F(x_j) = 0 \qquad j = 1, 2, \ldots, n$$

Letting $t = x_j$ in (6.34) then

$$H(x_j) = 0 \qquad j = 1, 2, \ldots, n$$

Moreover, letting $t = x$ in (6.34)

$$H(x) = 0$$

Thus the function $H(t)$ has $n + 1$ roots at the points $x, x_1, x_2, \ldots, x_n$. By the Mean Value Theorem it follows that $H'(t)$ has a root between each of these $n + 1$ roots of $H(t)$. Thus $H'(t)$ has n roots that we shall label $\xi_1, \xi_2, \ldots, \xi_{n-1}, \xi_n$. In other words

$$H'(\xi_1) = H'(\xi_2) = \cdots = H'(\xi_n) = 0$$

Notice that all ξ_i lie between x_1 and x_n.

We now apply the Mean Value Theorem to the function $H'(t)$. Since this function has n roots, its derivative $H''(t)$ must have $n - 1$ roots, one each between the roots ξ_i of $H'(t)$. These $n - 1$ roots of $H''(t)$ we call

$$\xi_1^{(1)}, \xi_2^{(1)}, \ldots, \xi_{n-1}^{(1)}$$

so that

$$H''(\xi_1^{(1)}) = H''(\xi_2^{(1)}) = \cdots = H''(\xi_{n-1}^{(1)}) = 0$$

where
$$x_1 \leq \xi_i^{(1)} \leq x_n \qquad i = 1, 2, \ldots, n-1$$

Continuing in this way the function $H'''(t)$ will have $n-2$ roots, the function $H^{iv}(t)$ will have $n-3$ roots, and so on until the nth derivative of $H(t)$ has one root, which we call ξ, that is to say,

$$H^{(n)}(\xi) = 0 \qquad (6.35)$$

where $x_1 \leq \xi \leq x_n$.

From the definition (6.34) of $H(t)$ it follows that

$$H^{(n)}(t) = F(x)G^{(n)}(t) - F^{(n)}(t)G(x) \qquad (6.36)$$

but from (6.33) we see that

$$G(t) = t^n + \text{terms in } t^{n-1}, t^{n-2}, \ldots, t$$

so

$$G^{(n)}(t) = n! \qquad (6.37)$$

Moreover, $P(x)$ is a polynomial of degree $n-1$ so

$$P^{(n)}(t) = 0$$

From (6.32)

$$F^{(n)}(t) = f^{(n)}(t) \qquad (6.38)$$

Therefore, substituting (6.37) and (6.38) into (6.36) we get

$$H^{(n)}(t) = n!F(x) - f^{(n)}(t)G(x)$$

Letting $t = \xi$ and using (6.35)

$$F(x) = \frac{f^{(n)}(\xi)}{n!} G(x)$$

Thus from (6.32) and (6.33) the truncation error is

$$E_T = \frac{f^{(n)}(\xi)}{n!}(x - x_1)(x - x_2) \cdots (x - x_n)$$

or more concisely

$$E_T = \frac{f^{(n)}(\xi)}{n!} \prod_{j=1}^{n} (x - x_j) \qquad (6.39)$$

where

$$x_1 \leq \xi \leq x_n$$

Notice that as n increases the truncation error decreases as $n!$ *provided the nth derivative of $f(x)$ does not vary too much.* As we shall see, the roundoff error increases with increasing n but not as rapidly as the truncation error decreases. Therefore, in general, the total error will decrease with an increase in n.

This does not mean that if we increase n we are guaranteed that the truncation error decreases. For example, if

$$|f^{(k)}(t)| > \frac{k}{|x - x_k|} |f^{(k-1)}(t)|$$

for all t such that $x_1 \leq t \leq x_k$, then the truncation error for interpolation using k points is greater than the truncation error using $k-1$ points.

Fortunately, because the last inequality above does not hold in most cases, increasing the degree of the interpolation will ordinarily decrease the truncation error.

6.9 Roundoff Error in Lagrangian Interpolation

We turn to a discussion of the roundoff error in Lagrangian interpolation with n points. As we should expect, as n increases, the roundoff error also increases.

We first draw a flow chart, shown in Figure 6.7, describing the opera-

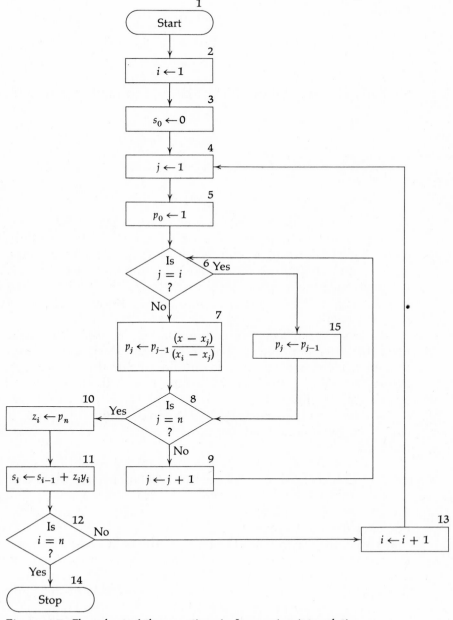

Figure 6.7. *Flow chart of the operations in Lagrangian interpolation.*

tions in equation (6.31). Before describing the flow chart we rewrite (6.31) as follows.

For a fixed value of i let $p_k^{(i)}$ be a partial product of the first k terms in the n-term product in (6.31), for example,

$$p_k^{(i)} = \prod_{\substack{j=1 \\ j \neq i}}^{k} \left(\frac{x - x_j}{x_i - x_j} \right) \tag{6.40}$$

Note that if we let

$$z_i = p_n^{(i)} \tag{6.41}$$

then

$$P(x) = \sum_{i=1}^{n} y_i z_i$$

Similarly we let s_k be the kth partial sum in the last equation above

$$s_k = \sum_{i=1}^{k} y_i z_i \tag{6.42}$$

so that

$$P(x) = s_n \tag{6.43}$$

We now proceed to discuss the flow chart in Figure 6.7. The outer loop starting at box 4 computes s_n. More precisely, the first time through the outer loop we compute s_1, the second time s_2, and so on. Each successive term is computed in box 11 and added to the previous partial sum. Since we go through the loop n times ($i = 1, \ldots, n$), the last time when we leave box 12 with a "Yes" we have computed s_n. Recall that $s_n = P(x)$ and is the final result.

Of course, each time we compute an s_k, we see from (6.42) that we need the corresponding z_k. The second loop starting at box 6 computes z_k, which from (6.41) is $p_n^{(k)}$. In the flow chart the superscript does not appear with the p_j. We start by setting $p_0 = 1$ (box 5) then in box 7 we successively multiply by $(x - x_j)/(x_i - x_j)$ as $j = 1, 2, \ldots, n$. Box 6 is used to omit the term $(x - x_i)/(x_i - x_i)$. When $p_n^{(i)}$ (called simply p_n in the flow chart) has been computed, we go to box 10 and set $z_i = p_n$ as indicated in (6.41).

Of course, if we were writing a program we would not save all of the partial products p_k since only the most recent, p_{k-1}, is needed to compute p_k, and once we have computed p_k we no longer need p_{k-1} nor any of the previous p_i. Similarly, we would not save all of the partial sums s_k but only the most recent one.

We shall use the individual partial products and partial sums to evaluate the roundoff error and that is why they appear in the flow chart. Let us first look at the error in the jth partial products, p_j. The process graph from box 7 is shown in Figure 6.8, where the dotted line indicates that p_j replaces p_{j-1} in the next calculations.

As before we assume that x, x_i, and x_j have no error. We let $r_{k,j}$ be

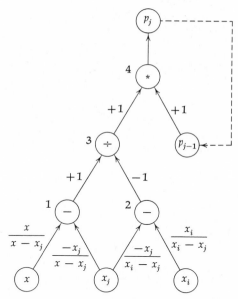

Figure 6.8. *Process graph of one operation (box 7 in the flow chart of Figure 6.7) in Lagrangian interpolation.*

the *relative* roundoff error in the kth operation ($k = 1, 2, 3, 4$) in computing p_j. We also let ξ_j be the *relative* error in p_j.

Because $p_0 = 1$, $\xi_0 = 0$ and thus

$$\xi_1 = r_{1,1} - r_{2,1} + r_{3,1} + r_{4,1}$$

and

$$\xi_2 = r_{1,2} - r_{2,2} + r_{3,2} + r_{4,2} + \xi_1$$

and so on, so that

$$\xi_{i-1} = r_{1,i-1} - r_{2,i-1} + r_{3,i-1} + r_{4,i-1} + \xi_{i-2}$$

From box 15 of Figure 6.7,

$$\xi_i = \xi_{i-1}$$

and then

$$\xi_{i+1} = r_{1,i+1} - r_{2,i+1} + r_{3,i+1} + r_{4,i+1} + \xi_i$$
$$\vdots$$
$$\xi_n = r_{1,n} - r_{2,n} + r_{3,n} + r_{4,n} + \xi_{n-1}$$

Therefore, the relative error ζ_i in z_i is

$$\zeta_i = \sum_{\substack{j=1 \\ j \neq i}}^{n} (r_{1,j} - r_{2,j} + r_{3,j} + r_{4,j})$$

If, for $k = 1, 2, 3, 4$ and all $j = 1, 2, \ldots n$,

$$|r_{k,j}| \leq r \tag{6.44}$$

then

$$|\zeta_i| \le 4(n-1)r \qquad (6.45)$$

We turn now to the outer loop of the flow chart. The process graph is shown in Figure 6.9, where again the dotted line indicates that s_i replaces s_{i-1} in the next calculation.

Again $r_{k,i}$ is the relative roundoff error in the kth operation ($k = 5, 6$) in computing s_i. Recall that ζ_i is the relative error in z_i. We let e_i be the relative error in y_i. We shall compute the relative error, σ_i, in s_i.

Now $s_0 = 0$, so $\sigma_0 = 0$. Thus from Figure 6.9

$$\sigma_1 = (\zeta_1 + e_1 + r_{5,1})\frac{z_1 y_1}{s_1} + r_{6,1}$$

$$\sigma_2 = (\zeta_2 + e_2 + r_{5,2})\frac{z_2 y_2}{s_2} + \sigma_1\frac{s_1}{s_2} + r_{6,2}$$

$$\vdots$$

$$\sigma_{n-1} = (\zeta_{n-1} + e_{n-1} + r_{s,n-1})\frac{z_{n-1} y_{n-1}}{s_{n-1}} + \sigma_{n-2}\frac{s_{n-2}}{s_{n-1}} + r_{6,n-1}$$

$$\sigma_n = (\zeta_n + e_n + r_{5,n})\frac{z_n y_n}{s_n} + \sigma_{n-1}\frac{s_{n-1}}{s_n} + r_{6,n}$$

Replacing σ_{n-1} in the last equation by its value from the next-to-last equation we get

$$\sigma_n = (\zeta_n + e_n + r_{5,n})\frac{z_n y_n}{s_n} + (\zeta_{n-1} + e_{n-1} + r_{5,n-1})\frac{z_{n-1} y_{n-1}}{s_n}$$

$$+ r_{6,n} + r_{6,n-1}\frac{s_{n-1}}{s_n} + \sigma_{n-2}\frac{s_{n-2}}{s_n}$$

Continuing in this way by replacing σ_{n-2}, then σ_{n-3}, we arrive finally at

$$\sigma_n = \sum_{i=1}^{n} (\zeta_i + e_i + r_{5,i})\frac{z_i y_i}{s_n} + \sum_{i=1}^{n} r_{6,i}\frac{s_i}{s_n} \qquad (6.46)$$

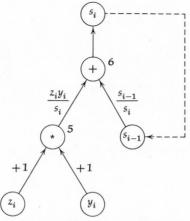

Figure 6.9. *Process graph of the outer loop of Lagrangian interpolation, flow charted in Figure 6.7.*

From (6.45)

$$|\check{\zeta}_i| \leq 4(n-1)r$$

and we assume again that for $k = 5, 6$ and $i = 1, 2, \ldots, n$

$$|r_{k,j}| \leq r$$

and also that for $i = 1, 2, \ldots n$

$$|e_i| \leq e$$

From (6.43), $s_n = P(x)$ so the absolute error, Σ_n, in $P(x)$ is

$$\Sigma_n = \sigma_n s_n$$

It is bounded by

$$|\Sigma_n| \leq [(4n-3)r + e] \sum_{i=1}^{n} |z_i y_i| + r \sum_{i=1}^{n} |s_i| \qquad (6.47)$$

Since $z_i y_i$ is computed in box 11 of the flow chart (Figure 6.7) and s_i is computed in box 11 of the same flow chart, it would be a simple matter to amend the flow chart to compute the sums of the absolute values of those quantities. Once the sums of the absolute values are computed, then the bound in (6.47) is easily computed.

In order to get some qualitative feeling for the roundoff error, however, we make the assumption that "on the average" the partial sums s_i are each approximately equal in absolute value to s_n—that is, although some partial sums may exceed s_n, others will be less than s_n—and that on the average the absolute values of the partial sums are equal to or less than absolute value of s_n. (Note that if all terms in the sum have the same sign then each s_i is always less than or equal to s_n in absolute value. Thus our assumption is certainly true in this case.) Similarly we assume that "on the average" the partial products $z_i y_i$ are less than or equal to s_n in absolute value. Then we may approximate the value of σ_n by

$$|\sigma_n| \cong 2r(2n^2 - n) + en$$

and the relative error in $P(x)$ grows as n^2. The inherent errors in the y_i give rise to the term en. If n is large the error is dominated by the other term, which implies that the roundoff error overshadows the errors introduced by errors in y_i. Moreover, the error due to the errors in the y_i grows only linearly with n, the number of points used in the interpolation. Thus, as with linear interpolation, the Lagrangian formula is stable.

Finally we compare this roundoff error, which grows as n^2, with the truncation error, which decreases as $n!$. We conclude that the truncation error decreases more rapidly than the roundoff error increases as n gets larger. We point out, however, that we have assumed (1) that the nth derivative of the function being interpolated is well behaved and (2) that the absolute values of the partial sums and partial products "on the average" do not exceed the absolute value of the final sum. In any given case, one or both of these assumptions may be violated thus voiding the conclusion drawn in this paragraph.

We turn now to one final form of interpolation. We shall take three points (x_k, y_k), (x_{k+1}, y_{k+1}), and (x_{k+2}, y_{k+2}) where $x_k < x < x_{k+1} < x_{k+2}$. We shall use linear interpolation twice—once using the first two points and then a second time using the last two points—which will in general produce two different results for the interpolated value of y. We shall use these two interpolated values of y along with two values of x, in particular x_k and x_{k+2}, and interpolate linearly once more. As we shall see, this is equivalent to quadratic interpolation using the three initial points.

Figure 6.10 shows the three points and also the two lines representing the first two linear interpolations. In particular line L_1 is the line that interpolates linearly using (x_k, y_k) and (x_{k+1}, y_{k+1}). The equation of that line from (6.1) is

$$y = y_k + \left(\frac{x - x_k}{x_{k+1} - x_k} \right) (y_{k+1} - y_k)$$

The value of y on that line corresponding to any x we call $y_k^{(1)}$ since it represents the first linear interpolation (thus the superscript 1) and uses the kth point as the first point of the two points in the interpolation. So

$$y_k^{(1)} = y_k + \left(\frac{x - x_k}{x_{k+1} - x_k} \right) (y_{k+1} - y_k) \tag{6.48}$$

This is a linear function of x. Similarly L_2 represents the line obtained by interpolating using (x_{k+1}, y_{k+1}) and (x_{k+2}, y_{k+2}). We call the value of y on line L_2 corresponding to any value of x

$$y_{k+1}^{(1)} = y_{k+1} + \left(\frac{x - x_{k+1}}{x_{k+2} - x_{k+1}} \right) (y_{k+2} - y_{k+1}) \tag{6.49}$$

since it represents a first-linear interpolation and uses the $(k + 1)$st point as the first point. Equation (6.49) is also a linear function of x.

We interpolate once more using $(x_k, y_k^{(1)})$ and $(x_{k+2}, y_{k+1}^{(1)})$ as points. (Note that the subscripts on x are different from the subscripts on y in the second of these two points.) The result of that interpolation is shown by line L_3 in Figure 6.11, in which P_k is the point $(x_k, y_k^{(1)})$ and P_{k+2} is the point

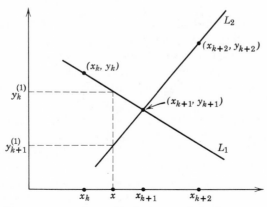

Figure 6.10. *Geometrical picture of the first stage of repeated linear interpolation.*

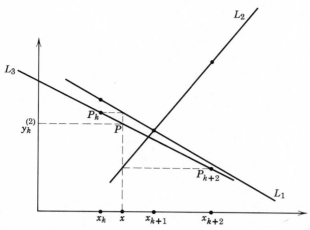

Figure 6.11. *The second stage (line L_3) of the process of repeated linear interpolation, with the two lines (L_1 and L_2) of the first stage also shown.*

$(x_{k+2}, y_{k+1}^{(1)})$. The lines L_1 and L_2 from Figure 6.10 are also shown in Figure 6.11 for ease of reference.

The point P on L_3 directly above x is the result of this final interpolation. The y-coordinate of P we call $y_k^{(2)}$ since it is the result of a second stage in the interpolation and uses the x_k as the first x-coordinate. The value of $y_k^{(2)}$ from (6.11) is

$$y_k^{(2)} = y_k^{(1)} + \left(\frac{x - x_k}{x_{k+2} - x_k} \right) [y_{k+1}^{(1)} - y_k^{(1)}] \tag{6.50}$$

Notice that (6.50) is *not* a linear function of x although it appears as a line in Figure 6.11. To see this we note that if we change x we get a different line from the line L_3. Another way to observe this nonlinearity is to use (6.48) and (6.49) to replace $y_k^{(1)}$ and $y_{k+1}^{(1)}$ in (6.50). The result is a quadratic function of x.

We now examine the value of $y_k^{(2)}$ when $x = x_k$, x_{k+1}, and x_{k+2}. First from (6.50) when $x = x_k$

$$y_k^{(2)} = y_k^{(1)}$$

Then from (6.48) we see that

$$y_k^{(1)} = y_k$$

Thus

$$y_k^{(2)} = y_k \qquad \text{when} \qquad x = x_k \tag{6.51}$$

Returning once more to (6.50) and letting $x = x_{k+1}$

$$y_k^{(2)} = y_k^{(1)} + \left(\frac{x_{k+1} - x_k}{x_{k+2} - x_k} \right) (y_{k+1}^{(1)} - y_k^{(1)}) \tag{6.52}$$

Letting $x = x_{k+1}$ in (6.48) and (6.49) we get

$$y_k^{(1)} = y_{k+1}$$

and

$$y_{k+1}^{(1)} = y_{k+1}$$

Substituting these in (6.52) then

$$y_k^{(2)} = y_{k+1} \qquad \text{when} \qquad x = x_{k+1} \tag{6.53}$$

Finally, letting $x = x_{k+2}$ in (6.50) we get

$$y_k^{(2)} = y_{k+1}^{(1)}$$

But from (6.49) when $x = x_{k+2}$

$$y_{k+1}^{(1)} = y_{k+2}$$

so

$$y_k^{(2)} = y_{k+2} \qquad \text{when} \qquad x = x_{k+2} \tag{6.54}$$

From (6.51), (6.53), and (6.54) we see that the "curve" represented by (6.50) passes through the three points (x_k, y_k), (x_{k+1}, y_{k+1}), and (x_{k+2}, y_{k+2}). Moreover, as we noted earlier, if we substitute $y_k^{(1)}$ and $y_{k+1}^{(1)}$ from (6.48) and (6.49) into (6.50), we see that $y_k^{(2)}$ is quadratic in x. Therefore, $y_k^{(2)}$ is *the* quadratic interpolating polynomial that passes through the three points (x_k, y_k), (x_{k+1}, y_{k+1}), and (x_{k+2}, y_{k+2}).

Had we started with the points (x_{k-1}, y_{k-1}), (x_k, y_k), and (x_{k+1}, y_{k+1}), we would have arrived at the quadratic interpolating polynomial through those points given by

$$y_{k-1}^{(2)} = y_{k-1}^{(1)} + \left(\frac{x - x_{k-1}}{x_{k+1} - x_{k-1}} \right) (y_k^{(1)} - y_{k-1}^{(1)}) \tag{6.55}$$

where

$$y_{k-1}^{(1)} = y_{k-1} + \left(\frac{x - x_{k-1}}{x_k - x_{k-1}} \right) (y_k - y_{k-1}) \tag{6.56}$$

and

$$y_k^{(1)} = y_k + \left(\frac{x - x_k}{x_{k+1} - x_k} \right) (y_{k+1} - y_k) \tag{6.48}$$

Notice that the last equation is (6.48) and that it was also used in computing $y_k^{(2)}$ earlier.

The derivation of (6.55) and the verification that it passes through the points (x_{k-1}, y_{k-1}), (x_k, y_k), and (x_{k+1}, y_{k+1}) is left as an exercise for the reader.

The natural question that now arises is: What would we get if we were to interpolate again linearly, using $[x_{k-1}, y_{k-1}^{(2)}]$ and $[x_{k+2}, y_k^{(2)}]$, where the y values are given by (6.50) and (6.55)?

As one might expect, the result is the cubic interpolating polynomial that passes through the four points (x_{k-1}, y_{k-1}), (x_k, y_k), (x_{k+1}, y_{k+1}), and (x_{k+2}, y_{k+2}). We shall not carry out the computations. We note, however, that we could continue adding points and repeating linear interpolation. This leads to what is known as *Aitken-Neville interpolation*. It does not produce results that are different from Lagrangian interpolation since we have already proved that there is only one interpolating polynomial with a given degree.

Aitken-Neville (repeated linear) interpolation does, however, have some computational advantages and disadvantages when compared with Lagrangian interpolation. We shall discuss some of these in the next section.

We close this section by noting the analogy between repeated linear interpolation as discussed here and the deferred approach to the limit applied to numerical integration in Chapter 5. The deferred approach to the limit was, in a sense, repeated use of the trapezoidal rule. It produced Simpson's rule. Had we continued applying the trapezoidal rule, we would have arrived at the Romberg integration formulas. Similarly, if we continued linear interpolation here, we would arrive at Aitken-Neville interpolation.

We close our presentation of interpolation methods with a discussion of the relative merits of the Lagrangian algorithm for quadratic interpolation as described in Section 6.7 and repeated linear interpolation as described in Section 6.10. We must realize that these comments apply to a comparison of the general Lagrangian algorithm and Aitken-Neville algorithm. The latter, as pointed out earlier, is an extension of repeated linear interpolation.

Consider first the number of arithmetic operations required by each algorithm. Recall that repeated linear interpolation required three linear interpolations: one to calculate $y_k^{(1)}$, one to calculate $y_{k+1}^{(1)}$, and one to calculate $y_k^{(2)}$. Each linear interpolation requires 4 additions, 1 multiplication, and 1 division. Thus repeated linear interpolation to obtain the quadratic interpolation result requires 12 addition, 3 multiplications, and 3 divisions or a total of 18 arithmetic operations.

If we use Lagrangian interpolation in the form (6.31)

$$P(x) = \sum_{i=1}^{3} y_i \prod_{\substack{j=1 \\ j \neq i}}^{3} \left(\frac{x - x_j}{x_i - x_j} \right)$$

computation of each product requires 4 additions, 2 divisions, and 1 multiplication. There are three such products. The sum requires another 3 multiplications and 2 additions. Therefore, the entire computation requires 14 additions, 6 multiplications, and 6 divisions or a total of 26 arithmetic operations.[3] Using (6.30)

$$P(x) = \sum_{i=1}^{3} y_k \frac{\displaystyle\prod_{\substack{j=1 \\ j \neq i}}^{3} (x - x_j)}{\displaystyle\prod_{\substack{j=1 \\ j \neq i}}^{3} (x_i - x_j)} \tag{6.57}$$

requires 14 additions, 9 multiplications, and 3 divisions for, again, a total of 26 arithmetic operations. The form (6.30) then merely exchanges some

---

[3] Actually the number of additions could be reduced to 6 since only $x - x_1, x - x_2, x - x_3,$ $x_1 - x_2, x_1 - x_3,$ and $x_2 - x_3$ are needed. However, the bookkeeping necessary to take advantage of this fact is usually not worth the trouble and may not result in saving any time.

multiplications for some divisions and does not change the total number of operations.

In any case, repeated linear interpolation results in fewer computations provided we wish to interpolate for one value of x. For higher degree interpolation, repeated linear interpolation has an increasingly greater advantage in terms of the number of arithmetic operations.

Suppose, however, we wish to interpolate for several values of x all lying in the interval $x_k < x < x_{k+1}$. Using repeated linear interpolation we must compute $y_k^{(1)}$, $y_{k+1}^{(1)}$, and $y_k^{(2)}$ for each value of x. On the other hand, using the Lagrangian formula in the form (6.57), the denominators may be computed once and used in all interpolations. Thus, if there are sufficiently many values of x for which interpolations are to be carried out, it is more efficient to compute and save the denominators in (6.57) and use the Lagrangian formula rather than repeated linear interpolation.

Still another advantage of the Lagrangian method arises if several functions are tabulated for the same set of x values, $x_1, x_2, \ldots, x_m$. In this case both numerator and denominator of (6.57) may be computed for a given x and the evaluation of each function then requires only formation of the sum. Of course, with repeated linear interpolation each function must be treated independently.

Finally we note that the bound on the roundoff error in repeated linear interpolation is less than the corresponding bound for Lagrangian interpolation.

6.12 Extrapolation

The discussion thus far has been confined to estimating a value of a function $f(x)$ for $x = \bar{x}$ where $\bar{x}$ lies within the range of values for which $f(x)$ is tabulated; that is to say, we have always required that

$$x_k \leq \bar{x} \leq x_{k+1}$$

for some k where the values of $f(x_1), f(x_2), \ldots, f(x_m)$ are given. We shall continue to use this requirement in Case Study 10 in the next section.

However, a natural question is: What can be done if

$$\bar{x} < x_1$$

or

$$\bar{x} > x_m?$$

Our discussion thus far has not addressed this question.

Consider first linear interpolation. If $\bar{x} < x_1$ then we could use (6.2) with $k = 1$, that is,

$$\bar{y} = y_1 + \left(\frac{\bar{x} - x_1}{x_2 - x_1} \right)(y_2 - y_1)$$

If $\bar{x} > x_m$ then let $k = m - 1$ or

$$\bar{y} = y_{m-1} + \left(\frac{\bar{x} - x_{m-1}}{x_m - x_{m-1}} \right)(y_m - y_{m-1})$$

Since the value of $\bar{x}$ lies outside the range $x_1 \leq x \leq x_n$, we call such a process as the one just outlined *extrapolation*. (If $\bar{x}$ lies *interior* to the range, we use the word "interpolation." If $\bar{x}$ is *exterior* to the range, we use "extrapolation.")

The truncation error is still given by (6.8), that is, for $\bar{x} < x_1$

$$E_T = \frac{f''(\xi)}{2}(\bar{x} - x_1)(\bar{x} - x_2)$$

where $\bar{x} \le \xi \le x_2$.

Notice now, however, that $\bar{x} - x_2$ may be quite large. Using interpolation neither term in parentheses could exceed $|x_{k+1} - x_k|$. The bound (6.11) on the roundoff error also becomes much larger. Thus the error in extrapolation is much more severe than the error in interpolation [see Exercise 10(b)].

Of course, we can use extrapolation with the Lagrangian formula (6.31) as well. If $\bar{x} < x_1$ then we use the first n points. If $\bar{x} > x_m$ we use the last n points. Again the truncation error is still given by (6.39). The roundoff error is still bounded by (6.47); however, the assumptions leading to the approximation at the close of Section 6.9 are usually not valid for extrapolation.

Care must be used, therefore, in using extrapolation. In the next chapter we shall discuss least squares approximations. The latter are generally more useful in extrapolation than are the interpolation methods described in this chapter.

13
Case Study 10: Two-Dimensional Interpolation in a Wind Chill Factor Table

Heat loss from the surface of the human body is affected not only by the surrounding temperature but also by the wind velocity. For example, the heat loss at 0° Fahrenheit accompanied by a 20-mph wind is equivalent to the heat loss at $-40°$ F in still air.

Given the temperature and the wind velocity, it is possible to compute the temperature that, in still air, has the equivalent cooling effect. The results of such computations are given in a *wind chill table* prepared by the Environmental Science Services Administration (ESSA) of the United States Department of Commerce. A portion of such a table is shown in Table 6.1. To find the equivalent still air temperature from this table we locate the actual temperature in a column heading and the wind velocity in a row heading. The entry in that column and row is the still air equivalent. For example, at 10° F with a wind velocity of 20 mph, the equivalent still air temperature is $-24°$ F.

Table 6.1   Wind Chill Table

		Temperature, °F						
		-30	-20	-10	0	10	20	30
	0	-30	-20	-10	0	10	20	30
Wind	10	-58	-45	-31	-22	-9	2	16
Velocity	20	-81	-68	-52	-40	-24	-9	3
(mph)	30	-94	-78	-63	-49	-33	-18	-2
	40	-101	-87	-69	-54	-36	-22	-4
	50	-103	-88	-70	-56	-38	-24	-7

Now suppose we wish to know the still air temperature for 5° F and a 15-mph wind. How can this result be obtained from the table?

An obvious response is to interpolate, but now we have two variables (temperature and wind velocity) on which we must interpolate. There are several ways to approach this problem. We shall take the most straightforward and easiest one. Later we shall write a computer program to carry out the interpolation.

First we shall restrict ourselves to linear interpolation. (Exercise 13 asks you to extend the results to quadratic interpolation.) Secondly, we shall interpolate initially on the wind velocity for temperatures given in the table. This produces the equivalent still air temperature for (1) a wind velocity of 15 mph and an actual air temperature of 0° F and (2) a wind velocity of 15 mph and an actual air temperature of 10° F. We shall use these values and interpolate once more; this time the wind velocity will be constant (15 mph), and we shall interpolate on the temperature. A numerical example is in order.

If we wish the equivalent still air temperature for 5° and 15 mph, we first find the two temperatures that straddle 5°, namely 0° and 10°. For each of these we interpolate to find the still air temperature at 15 mph wind velocity. In the 0° column we then find two velocities that straddle 15 mph—10 and 20. Since 15 is precisely midway between 10 and 20, the result for 0° and 15 mph is

$$\frac{(-40) + (-22)}{2} = -31°$$

Next for 10° we also find that 10 mph and 20 mph straddle 15 mph. The result of linear interpolation for 10° and 15 mph is

$$\frac{(-24) + (-9)}{2} = -16.5°$$

We have at this point computed two entries in what could be a 15-mph row, corresponding to 0° and 10°. Since 0° and 10° straddle 5°, we can interpolate again. Once more 5 is midway between 0° and 10° so the final result is

$$\frac{(-16.5) + (-31)}{2} = -23.75°$$

This is the still air temperature corresponding to 5° and 15 mph if we use linear interpolation. The correct value is −25°. Thus, if we need a result more accurate than 1° or so, the table in Figure 6.1 together with linear interpolation is inadequate. At this point we have two choices if we desire more accuracy: Use a higher-order interpolation formula or use a larger and more densely filled-in table.

Assuming this accuracy is sufficient, we now proceed to formalize the use of linear interpolation in two variables.

Suppose we have a function $f(x,y)$ of two variables x and y. Suppose further that the values of the function are tabulated for m values of x; for each of these x values, the function is tabulated for n values of y. We then have $m \times n$ values of f. In Table 6.1 if we let x be the temperature and y be the wind velocity, then $m = 7$ and $n = 6$ and we see that there are 42 temperatures recorded in the table. The values of x for which $f(x,y)$ are tabulated we label $x_1, x_2, \ldots, x_m$. Similarly the values of y are labeled $y_1, y_2, \ldots, y_n$.

If we wish to compute the value of the function f for $x = \bar{x}$ and $y = \bar{y}$, we first find values of x_j and y_i that straddle $\bar{x}$ and $\bar{y}$, that is, we find

$$\left. \begin{array}{c} x_{j-1} \leq \bar{x} \leq x_j \\ y_{i-1} \leq \bar{y} \leq y_i \end{array} \right\} \tag{6.58}$$

and record the values of the subscripts j and i. For $x = x_{j-1}$, the function $f(x_{j-1}, y)$ is a function of one variable, y. We interpolate linearly to estimate $f(x_{j-1}, \bar{y})$. Using (6.2)

$$f(x_{j-1}, \bar{y}) = f(x_{j-1}, y_{i-1}) + \frac{\bar{y} - y_{i-1}}{y_i - y_{i-1}} [f(x_{j-1}, y_i) - f(x_{j-1}, y_{i-1})] \tag{6.59}$$

Similarly for $x = x_j$ we interpolate and obtain

$$f(x_j, \bar{y}) = f(x_j, y_{i-1}) + \frac{\bar{y} - y_{i-1}}{y_i - y_{i-1}} [f(x_j, y_i) - f(x_j, y_{i-1})] \tag{6.60}$$

If we now consider $y = \bar{y}$, then $f(x, \bar{y})$ is a function of one variable: x. Since x_{j-1} and x_j straddle $\bar{x}$, we can interpolate $f(x, \bar{y})$ to estimate $f(\bar{x}, \bar{y})$. Again, by using (6.2) this results in

$$f(\bar{x}, \bar{y}) = f(x_{j-1}, \bar{y}) + \frac{\bar{x} - x_{j-1}}{x_j - x_{j-1}} [f(x_j, \bar{y}) - f(x_{j-1}, \bar{y})] \tag{6.61}$$

Notice that the values of $f(x_{j-1}, \bar{y})$ and $f(x_j, \bar{y})$ needed on the right side of (6.61) are given by (6.59) and (6.60). The reader unsure of this discussion would do well to use the wind chill table and (6.59), (6.60), and (6.61) to estimate the still air temperature equivalent to 5° and 15 mph. The result should be $-23.75°$ as pointed out earlier.

Figure 6.12 is a flow chart of this method, which is quite straightforward and relatively easy to follow. The first part of the program shown later, corresponding to this flow chart, will begin by setting up the table in storage. We establish a maximum size for the table in the DIMENSION statement, then read from cards the actual size. With the table properly set up, we read $\bar{x}$ and $\bar{y}$, called XBAR and YBAR in the program and proceed to determine which values of x and y from the table bracket the input values. In the course of this search it is a simple matter to check whether XBAR and YBAR are within the limits of the table values and skip program execution if so. Once the bracketing values corresponding to (6.58) have been located, we can use (6.59), (6.60), and (6.61) to interpolate for the table value corresponding to XBAR and YBAR.

In the Fortran program shown in Figure 6.13 we have followed this flow chart so closely that little further explanation should be needed. When we are ready to interpolate we first compute FACTOR, to avoid computing a common factor twice in the statements that follow. The basic method is, of course, valid for any two-dimensional table, but in the program here we have particularized the output to the wind chill example.

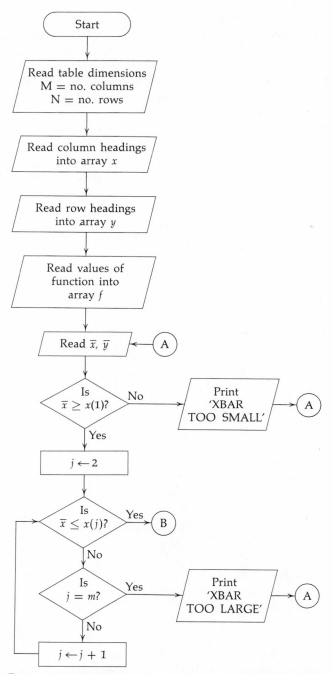

Figure 6.12. *Flow chart of a procedure for two-dimensional interpolation. Note the validity checking of the input.*

This program was set up to run on a time-sharing system utilizing a Xerox Data Systems Sigma 7. In this system the default options for input and output from the terminal are 105 and 108 rather than the 5 and 6 that appear in other programs in this book. The change is of no consequence. The more common defaults of 5 and 6 are by no means universal,

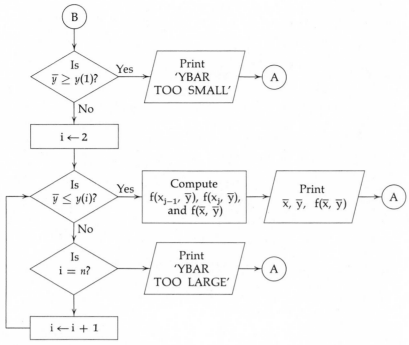

Figure 6.12. (*Cont.*)

and in any case it is a simple matter to assign input and output unit numbers in a way that is convenient to the programmer. In a time-sharing system this assignment might be done with a system command having a name like "filedef." An operating system might require the inclusion of a "data definition" card or something of that sort.

Suppose now that we use this program to compute values of the equivalent still air temperature using the wind chill table in Table 6.1. The result using 5° F and 15 mph is

```
TEMP =      5.00    WIND VEL =      15.00
STILL AIR EQUIVALENT =    -23.75
```

which agrees with our hand calculations. Next we try a value that appears in the table: 20° and 20 mph. The output is

```
TEMP =     20.00    WIND VEL =      20.00
STILL AIR EQUIVALENT =     -9.00
```

It is good programming practice to check the correctness of a program by trying cases for which the result is known and also extreme cases (both $\bar{x}$ and $\bar{y}$ are tabulated). Another good type of check is to choose a $\bar{y}$ that is in the table and see if interpolation on x alone works. Thus we try 15° and 20 mph. The output is

```
TEMP =     15.00    WIND VEL =      20.00
STILL AIR EQUIVALENT =    -16.50
```

This also agrees with our previous hand calculations. We should also check that the program gives correct results if $\bar{x}$ is one of the x_j but $\bar{y}$

```
C CASE STUDY 10
C A PROGRAM TO PERFORM DOUBLE INTERPOLATION
C
C THE ARRAY X(J) CONTAINS M VALUES OF X
C THE ARRAY Y(I) CONTAINS N VALUES OF Y
C (MAXIMUM OF 30 FOR BOTH)
C THE VALUE OF THE ENTRY FOR X = X(J) AND Y = Y(I) IS F(J,I)
C
C THE PROGRAM READS VALUES FOR X = XBAR AND Y = YBAR
C AND INTERPOLATES TO FIND THE CORRESPONDING VALUE OF F
C
C
      DIMENSION X(30), Y(30), F(30, 30)
C READ DIMENSIONS OF ARRAYS (M COLUMNS AND N ROWS)
      READ (105, 100) M, N
 100  FORMAT (2I3)
      IF (M .LE. 30) GO TO 1
      WRITE (108, 101)
 101  FORMAT  (1X, 'NO. OF COLS. EXCEEDS 30')
      STOP
   1  IF (N .LE. 30) GO TO 2
      WRITE (108, 102)
 102  FORMAT (1X, 'NO. OF ROWS EXCEEDS 30')
      STOP
C READ ARRAY X (COLUMN HEADINGS), ONE TO A CARD
   2  DO 3 J = 1, M
   3  READ (105, 103) X(J)
C READ ARRAY Y (ROW HEADINGS), ONE TO A CARD
      DO 4 I = 1, N
   4  READ (105, 103) Y(I)
 103  FORMAT (F10.0)
C READ TABLE ENTRIES INTO ARRAY F, ROW-BY-ROW, ONE PER CARD
      DO 5 I = 1, N
      DO 5 J = 1, M
   5  READ (105, 103) F(J, I)
C READ VALUES OF XBAR AND YBAR
C    FOR WHICH TABLE VALUE IS TO BE INTERPOLATED
C    BOTH ARE PUNCHED ON ONE CARD
  99  READ (105, 104) XBAR, YBAR
 104  FORMAT (2F10.0)
C CHECK FOR XBAR OUT OF RANGE WHILE LOCATING COLUMNS
C    THAT STRADDLE XBAR
      IF (XBAR .GE. X(1)) GO TO 6
      WRITE (108, 105)
 105  FORMAT (1X, 'XBAR IS TOO SMALL')
      GO TO 99
   6  DO 7 J = 2, M
      IF (XBAR .LE. X(J)) GO TO 8
   7  CONTINUE
      WRITE (108, 106)
 106  FORMAT (1X, 'XBAR IS TOO LARGE')
      GO TO 99
C XBAR IS BETWEEN X(J-1) and X(J)
```

Figure 6.13. *A program for two-dimensional interpolation, following the method flow charted in Figure 6.12. In the time-sharing system used here, the default unit numbers for input and output are 105 and 108 rather than 5 and 6 as in most other programs in the book.*

is not one of the y_i. We have not done so but have left this as an exercise for the reader (Exercise 18).

Finally, we may try a data point that is outside the range of the table, to be sure that the program correctly identifies an error:

```
?32.0,10.0,
 XBAR IS TOO LARGE
```

We close this case study by pointing out that there is no reason why

```
C NEXT CHECK FOR YBAR OUT OF RANGE WHILE LOCATING ROWS
C    THAT STRADDLE YBAR
   8 IF (YBAR .GE. Y(1)) GO TO 9
     WRITE (108, 107)
 107 FORMAT (1X, 'YBAR IS TOO SMALL')
     GO TO 99
   9 DO 10 I = 2, N
     IF (YBAR .LE. Y(I)) GO TO 11
  10 CONTINUE
     WRITE (108, 108)
 108 FORMAT (1X, 'YBAR IS TOO LARGE')
     GO TO 99
C INTERPOLATE ON X (COLUMNS) USING ROWS I-1 and I
  11 FACTOR = (YBAR - Y(I-1))/(Y(I) - Y(I-1))
     XJ1 = F(J-1,I-1) + FACTOR*(F(J-1,I) - F(J-1,I-1))
     XJ  = F(J,  I-1) + FACTOR*(F(J,  I) - F(J,  I-1))
C INTERPOLATE ON Y (ROWS) USING ROW ENTRIES JUST COMPUTED
     ANSWER = XJ1 + ((XBAR - X(J-1))/(X(J) - X(J-1)))
   1     * (XJ - XJ1)
C PRINT RESULTS
     WRITE (108, 109) XBAR, YBAR, ANSWER
 109 FORMAT (1X,'TEMP = ',F8.2,'    WIND VEL =    ',F8.2/
   1     1X,'STILL AIR EQUIVALENT = ',F8.2//)
C GO BACK FOR MORE VALUES OF XBAR AND YBAR
     GO TO 99
     END
```

Figure 6.13. (*Cont.*)

we should interpolate first on y and then on x as we did. We could just as well have interpolated first on x and then on y, that is, reversed the order. If we did so, we would still find i and j satisfying (6.58) and then would compute

$$f(\overline{x},y_{i-1}) = f(x_{j-1},y_{i-1}) + \frac{\overline{x} - x_{j-1}}{x_j - x_{j-1}}[f(x_j,y_{i-1}) - f(x_{j-1},y_{i-1})] \quad (6.62)$$

$$f(\overline{x},y_i) = f(x_{j-1},y_i) + \frac{\overline{x} - x_{j-1}}{x_j - x_{j-1}}[f(x_j,y_i) - f(x_{j-1},y_i)] \quad (6.63)$$

$$f(\overline{x},\overline{y}) = f(\overline{x},y_{i-1}) + \frac{\overline{y} - y_{i-1}}{y_i - y_{i-1}}[f(\overline{x},y_i) - f(\overline{x},y_{i-1})] \quad (6.64)$$

We might suspect that reversing the order of interpolation, as these last three equations do, would produce different results—but it does not! Whether we use (6.59), (6.60), and (6.61) or whether we use (6.62), (6.63), and (6.64); the results are identical (see Exercises 19 and 20.)

Finally we point out that the ideas in this section can easily be extended to function of 3, 4, or more variables.

Bibliographic Notes

Many texts include linear interpolation merely as a special case of Lagrangian interpolation. However, several books discuss linear interpolation separately. One of the most readable of these is Stark [3], Section 8.2. Other references to linear interpolation are Hamming [6], Section 6.1, and Hildebrand [18], Section 2.2.

Lagrangian interpolation is discussed in most textbooks. Stark [3] discusses this topic in Sections 8.5 and 8.7. Stark also has a Fortran program for Lagrangian interpolation in Section 8.6. Carnahan *et al.* [20] discusses Lagrangian interpolation and also has a flow chart and Fortran program in Section 1.7. Other references to Lagrangian interpolation are Ralston [19], Section 3.2; Hildebrand [18], Section 3.2; and Scarborough [17], Section 26.

Truncation error in Lagrangian interpolation is discussed in Section 8.9 of Stark [3]; Section 3.2 of Ralston [19]; Section 1.6 of Carnahan *et al.* [20]; and Section 32 of Scarborough [17]. Roundoff error does not seem to be discussed in any of the texts listed in the bibliography, although Jennings [15] does discuss roundoff in linear interpolation in Section 3.5.

Aitken-Neville interpolation (which is a generalization of repeated linear interpolation discussed in this text) is covered by Stark [3] in Section 8.8; Ralston [19] in Section 3.6 and Hildebrand [18] in Section 2.7. Extrapolation is discussed by Ralston [19] in Section 3.10 and Hamming [6] in Section 6.9.

Few textbooks discuss double interpolation (see Case Study 10). One exception, however, is Scarborough [17] where double interpolation is covered in Section 39 using difference tables.

Exercises

*1   In (6.23) let $x_k = x_0$, $x_{k-1} = x_0 - h_1$, and $x_{k+1} = x_0 + h_2$. Then

$$y_{k-1} = f(x_0 - h_1)$$
$$y_k = f(x_0)$$
$$y_{k+1} = f(x_0 + h_2)$$

   a. Differentiate (6.23) and let $x = x_0$. Show that the resulting expression is the right-hand side of (5.18).
   b. Differentiate a second time to obtain an approximation for the second derivative of $f(x)$ at $x = x_0$. This produces a differentiation formula for the second derivative with unequally spaced points. Show that for $h_1 = h_2 = h$ the resulting approximation reduces to (5.7).

2   In (6.31) let $n = 5$ and let $x_1 = x_0 - 2h$, $x_2 = x_0 - h$, $x_3 = x_0$, $x_4 = x_0 + h$, and $x_5 = x_0 + 2h$.
   a. Differentiate the resulting expression. Let $x = x_0$. Show that the resulting approximation for the derivative at $x = x_0$ is (5.28).
   b. Differentiate a second time and again let $x = x_0$. Show that the resulting approximation for the second derivative is (5.30).

3   Equation (6.39) with $n = 3$ represents the truncation error in quadratic interpolation. Use (6.39) and $n = 3$ with $x_1 = x_0 - h_1$, $x_2 = x_0$, and $x_3 = x_0 + h_2$ to show that the truncation error in (5.18) is

$$E_T = -\frac{h_1 h_2}{6} f'''(\xi)$$

   where $x_0 - h_1 \leq \xi \leq x_0 + h_2$.

304   Interpolation

4 In (6.39) let $n = 5$ and let $x_1 = x_0 - 2h$, $x_2 = x_0 - h$, $x_3 = x_0$, $x_4 = x_0 + h$, and $x_5 = x_0 + 2h$. Show that the truncation error in (5.28) is

$$E_T = \frac{24}{5} h^4 f^{iv}(\xi)$$

where $x_0 - 2h \leq \xi \leq x_0 + 2h$.

*5 Integrate the linear interpolating polynomial (6.1) from x_k to x_{k+1}. Show that the result is the trapezoidal rule for integration.

*6 Using the truncation error (6.8) for linear interpolation and assuming the results for Exercise 5, show that the truncation error in the trapezoidal rule is bounded by

$$|e_t| \leq \frac{h^2}{12}(b - a)M$$

where

$$M = \max |y''(\xi)|$$

for $a \leq \xi \leq b$ [see (5.49)].
(Hint: Use the *first mean value theorem for integrals*, which says: If $F(x)$ and $G(x)$ are continuous for $a \leq x \leq b$ and if $F(x)$ does not change sign for $a < x < b$, then

$$\int_a^b F(x)G(x)\, dx = G(\xi) \int_a^b F(x)\, dx$$

for $a \leq \xi \leq b$.)

7 Show that when $n = 2$ the Lagrangian interpolation formula (6.31) reduces to the linear interpolation formula (6.1).

8 Show that (6.48), (6.55), and (6.56) produce a value for $y_{k-1}^{(2)}$ equal to the value obtained using the quadratic interpolating polynomial (6.23) that passes through the points (x_{k-1}, y_{k-1}), (x_k, y_k), and (x_{k+1}, y_{k+1}).

9 Use a table of sines accurate to five digits. Write a Fortran program to:

a. Read the sines of $0°$, $1°$, ..., $45°$ into a one-dimensional array.
b. Read any real number (positive or negative) that represents an angle in degrees.
c. Reduce the angle read in (b) to an equivalent angle between $0°$ and $45°$.
d. Compute the sine of the angle using linear interpolation.
e. Compare the results of (d) with the output of the SIN function.

*10a Given a table of the squares of the 32 integers 1, 2, ..., 32, what is the largest truncation error that occurs if linear interpolation is used to approximate x^2 for $1 \leq x \leq 32$?

b What is the largest truncation error in extrapolating for $32 < x < 40$?

11 Write a Fortran program that reads an integer, $M \leq 40$, and then reads two one-dimensional arrays X and Y each with M entries. Follow this with a program to read a value XBAR and N, the number of points to be used in Lagrangian interpolation (following the flow chart in Figure 6.7) to compute the value of YBAR.

12a Modify the flow chart in Figure 6.7 so that the error bound in (6.47) is computed concurrently with interpolation.

b Write a program following the directions in Exercise 11 and compute the bound (6.47) as well.

13 Modify the program in Case Study 10, Section 6.13, so that quadratic rather than linear interpolation is used. Compare the results of running this new program with the results of the case study.

a. Use the Lagrangian formula (6.23).

b. Use repeated linear interpolation given in (6.48), (6.55), and (6.56).

c. Both (a) and (b) should produce the same results. Discuss the programming effort in the two methods. Which method do you prefer?

*14 In Section 6.10 it was shown that repeated linear interpolation is equivalent to quadratic interpolation. Consider the table

k	x	y
1	0.5	0.125
2	1.0	1.0
3	2.0	8.0
4	2.5	15.625
5	3.0	27.0
6	5.0	125.0
7	6.5	268.125

Using (6.23) to interpolate at $\bar{x} = 4$ produces $\bar{y} = 65.5$. On the other hand using (6.48), (6.49), and (6.50) produces $\bar{y} = 62.74$. Explain this paradox.

15 Let

$$y_{k-1}^{(3)} = y_{k-1}^{(2)} + \frac{x - x_{k-1}}{x_{k+2} - x_{k-1}}(y_k^{(2)} - y_{k-1}^{(2)})$$

where $y_k^{(2)}$ is given by (6.50) and $y_{k-1}^{(2)}$ is given by (6.55). Of course (6.48), (6.49), and (6.56) are also needed to compute $y_k^{(2)}$ and $y_{k-1}^{(2)}$.

a. Show that $y_{k-1}^{(3)}$ is a cubic function of x.

b. Show that $y_{k-1}^{(3)}$ is *the* cubic interpolating polynomial that passes through (x_{k-1}, y_{k-1}), (x_k, y_k), (x_{k+1}, y_{k+1}), and (x_{k+2}, y_{k+2}).

c. How many linear interpolations are required to compute $y_{k-1}^{(3)}$?

d. Compare the number of arithmetic operations required to find $y_{k-1}^{(3)}$ with the number of operations required for (6.31) with $n = 4$.

*16 Show that Lagrangian interpolation using (6.31) requires a total of $(4n + 1)(n - 1)$ arithmetic operations.

17 Show that Lagrangian interpolation using (6.30) and (6.26) requires a total of $(4n + 1)(n - 1)$ arithmetic operations.

*18a For the wind chill table shown in Table 6.1 compute the still air temperature equivalent to $-20°$ F and 24 mph.

b Use $\bar{x} = -20$ and $\bar{y} = 24$ in the program in Figure 6.13 and the results of part (a) to verify the correctness of the program.

*19a Use (6.59), (6.60), and (6.61) and Table 6.1 to estimate the still air temperature for a temperature of $-4°$ F and a wind velocity of 18 mph.

  b Use (6.62), (6.63), and (6.64) and Table 6.1 to estimate the still air temperature for a temperature of $-4°$ F and a wind velocity of 18 mph.

20 Show that (6.59), (6.60), and (6.61) produce identical results to (6.62), (6.63), and (6.64) for *any* table.

21 The elliptic integral of the first kind is defined to be

$$F(\theta,\phi) = \int_0^\phi \frac{d\phi}{\sqrt{1 - \sin^2 \theta \sin^2 \phi}}$$

A partial table of the value of this function is:

ϕ \ θ	50°	60°	70°	80°	90°
50°	0.9401	0.9647	0.9876	1.0044	1.0107
55°	1.0500	1.0848	1.1186	1.1444	1.1542
60°	1.1643	1.2125	1.2619	1.3014	1.3170
65°	1.2833	1.3489	1.4199	1.4810	1.5065
70°	1.4068	1.4944	1.5959	1.6918	1.7354
75°	1.5345	1.6492	1.7927	1.9468	2.0276
80°	1.6660	1.8125	2.0119	2.2653	2.4362

(See, for example, *Chemical Rubber Publishing Co. Standard Mathematical Tables*, 12th ed., Chemical Rubber Publishing Co., 1959, p. 265.)

  a. Use double linear interpolation to estimate $F(55°,53°)$. The correct result to five figures is 1.0205.

  b. Use double quadratic interpolation to estimate $F(55°,53°)$. Compare your result with the result of part (a).

22 Lumber with a large percentage of knots is not as strong as knot-free lumber. Standards have been established to determine the strength ratio of a knotted wood beam to a knot-free beam. For example, for beams or stringers the knots are measured on the narrow face of the beam. The percentage strength ratio depends upon the face width and the knot size. A partial table of these strength ratios is:

Knot Size (in.) \ Face Width (in.)	3	4	5	6
$\frac{1}{2}$	86	90	91	93
1	72	78	82	85
$1\frac{1}{2}$	57	67	73	77
2	35	55	64	70
$2\frac{1}{2}$	18	47	56	61

(See, for example, *1971 Annual Book of ASTM Standards,* Part 16 New York, American Society for Testing Materials, 1971, p. 156.)

a. Use double linear interpolation to determine the strength ratio for a knot size of $1\frac{7}{8}$-in. with a face width of $3\frac{3}{4}$-in. The correct result is 55%.

b. Use double quadratic interpolation to solve the problem in part (a). Compare the two results.

23 The equilibrium constant for ammonia reacting in hydrogen and nitrogen gases depends upon the hydrogen–nitrogen mole ratio, the pressure, and the temperature. For a 3-to-1 hydrogen–nitrogen mole ratio the equilibrium constant for a range of pressures and temperatures is given by:

°C	Equilibrium Constant, K_p (pressure, atm)				
	100	200	300	400	500
400	0.014145	0.015897	0.018060	0.020742	0.024065
450	0.007222	0.008023	0.008985	0.010134	0.011492
500	0.004013	0.004409	0.004873	0.005408	0.006013
550	0.002389	0.002598	0.002836	0.003102	0.003392
600	0.001506	0.001622	0.001751	0.001890	0.002036

(See, for example, *Encyclopedia of Chemical Technology,* Vol. 2, 2nd ed., New York, Wiley, 1963, p. 269.)

Use double linear interpolation to estimate the equilibrium constant for 473° C and 217 atm pressure.

24 The mole percentage of ammonia at equilibrium with no inerts present is given, in part, by:

Mole Percentage of Ammonia at Equilibrium

°C	Pressure (atm)			
	200	300	400	500
400	38.74	47.85	54.87	60.61
450	27.44	35.93	42.91	48.84
500	18.86	26.00	32.25	37.79
550	12.82	18.40	23.55	28.31
600	8.77	12.93	16.94	20.76

(See, for example, *Encyclopedia of Chemical Technology,* Vol. 2, 2nd ed., New York, Wiley, 1963, p. 270.)

Use double linear interpolation to estimate the mole percentage of ammonia at 512° C and 401 atm.

25 The specific heat of water as a function of temperature, in terms of the 15° cal, is

Temperature, °C	Specific Heat
20	0.99907
25	0.99852
30	0.99826
35	0.99818
40	0.99828
45	0.99849
50	0.99878

a. Use linear interpolation to estimate the specific heat at 37° C.
b. Use quadratic interpolation to estimate the specific heat at 37° C. (Note: We return to this example in Chapter 7 during our discussion of least squares.)

26 Using three points

$$P_1: (x_{k-1}, y_{k-1})$$
$$P_2: (x_k, y_k)$$
$$P_3: (x_{k+1}, y_{k+1})$$

Interpolate linearly between P_1 and P_2. Let $y_{k-1}^{(1)}$ be the value of y corresponding to any value of x in that interpolation. Interpolate between P_2 and P_3, and let $y_k^{(1)}$ be the value of y on this second line. Interpolate linearly once more between $(x_{k-1}, y_{k-1}^{(1)})$ and $(x_{k-1}, y_k^{(1)})$. Show that the result is (6.55) and is *the* quadratic interpolating polynomial through P_1, P_2, and P_3.

27 Write a program that performs quadratic interpolation using the Lagrangian formula (6.57) but requires only 6 additions and a total of 18 arithmetic operations.

28 Consider $y = x^2$ when $x_i = 6$ and $x_{i+1} = 7$. Use linear interpolation to compute the value of x^2 at $x = 6.9$ using two-digit floating point arithmetic.

Show that it is multiplication (operation 5 in process graph of Figure 6.4) that contributes to roundoff error and not addition (operation 6) as expected. Explain.

29 For linear interpolation we use $n = 2$ in the Lagrangian formula.
The error bound is

$$|\psi_2| \leq 12r + 2e$$

So the absolute error is bounded by

$$E_y \leq (12r + 2e)|y|$$

The bound found earlier was

$$E_y \leq r|y| + 5r|\Delta y| + ey_m$$

Discuss why the Lagrangian error appears to be larger than the other one.

7 Least Squares Approximations

7.1
Introduc-
tion

In Chapter 6 we discussed one way—interpolation—of handling a function that is defined by a table of values. If, however, the table is a result of some physical experiment, the table entries may contain inherent errors. Moreover, these inherent errors usually will not be predictable with any degree of certainty; that is to say, the inherent errors are distributed according to some statistical pattern, and there is a reasonable probability that some of the errors are quite large. Suppose, for instance, that we have run some sort of experiment and have obtained a table of x and y values that can be plotted as shown in Figure 7.1.[1] One would guess that the two points labeled with asterisks (*) have a substantial error in their y values since they do not follow the pattern of the other points. Interpolation where either of these asterisked points is used would, therefore, produce results that also had substantial errors. Before we can use such data we must "smooth" the data to wash out the statistical errors as much as possible.

In Section 6.12 we also pointed out some of the hazards in extrapolation (going beyond the range of the data) using interpolation formulas. However, in many cases the extrapolated values are the ones of most interest. This is particularly true of economic data. By way of example, we may know the water consumption in the United States for 1900, 1910, . . . , 1970

---

[1]We will return to the experiment represented by the data in Figure 7.1 later, in Case Study 11.

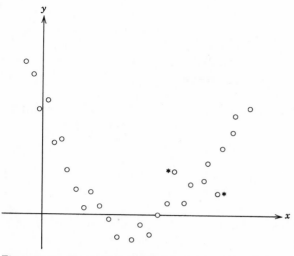

Figure 7.1. *Illustrative experimental data for which an approximate functional relationship is sought.*

and may wish to predict water consumption in 1980, 1990, and so on for planning purposes (see Exercise 36). Thus we wish to extrapolate to future years. This is an example of a *time series*, so called because the independent variable is time. We shall return to time series and predictions, using them in Section 7.3 and in the exercises.

All of these considerations lead us to seek a method for using the data in a table of experimental data to produce a formula relating y and x. Hopefully the formula will be a simple one. The first issue facing us is: How shall we decide when a formula is a good approximation to the data in a table? In graphical terms this question translates to: How shall we decide if a curve is a good "fit" to the plotted points?

We turn to a discussion of these questions now. We shall, however, not answer them satisfactorily until the next section.

Suppose we have a formula relating y to x, that is,

$$\bar{y} = f(x)$$

where the bar over the y indicates, as usual, that this is an approximate value of y. The "true" value of y is found in the table. We define the deviation (error) to be the true value less the approximate value, that is, $y - \bar{y}$. Now y is actually known only at the tabulated values, hence the deviation is only known for those values. Suppose that there are m entries in the table $x_1, x_2, \ldots, x_m$, and corresponding to each x_i there is a y value: $y_1, y_2, \ldots, y_m$. Then there are m deviations

$$\left.\begin{array}{l} d_1 = y_1 - \bar{y}_1 = y_1 - f(x_1) \\ d_2 = y_2 - \bar{y}_2 = y_2 - f(x_2) \\ \vdots \\ d_m = y_m - \bar{y}_m = y_m - f(x_m) \end{array}\right\} \tag{7.1}$$

Of course, because at this stage we do not know how to specify the function f, we cannot calculate $f(x_1), f(x_2), \ldots,$ and so on. Indeed our objective is to find some way of specifying this function. We shall find that we need to specify the *form* of $f(x)$ in advance from some observation. For example, in Figure 7.1 it would be natural to assume $f(x)$ is a parabola from the pattern of the data as plotted. It still remains to determine *which* parabola. Once we have determined what the function $f(x)$ is, then the deviations are readily calculated from (7.1).

Clearly we want to choose $f(x)$ so that the deviations are, in some sense, small. It is tempting to try simply to make the sum of the deviations small, that is, to ask that

$$\sum_{i=1}^{m} (y_i - \bar{y}_i) \tag{7.2}$$

be a minimum. This certainly has the attractiveness of simplicity. Suppose, however, that we have only two points ($m = 2$) with coordinates (x_1, y_1) and (x_2, y_2) (see Figure 7.2). If we think of $f(x)$ as a line

$$y = a + bx$$

then clearly the "best" line is the one that passes through both points because for that line (7.2) is zero. However, for the dashed line L shown in Figure 7.2 the sum of the deviations is also zero since $y_1 - \bar{y}_1$ is negative, $y_2 - \bar{y}_2$ is positive, and both have the same magnitude. Indeed there are infinitely many lines for which the sum of the deviations (7.2) is zero (see Exercise 1).

Since it is clearly the signs that are causing the trouble in (7.2), the next logical step is to minimize the sum of the absolute values of the deviations

$$\sum_{i=1}^{m} |d_i| = \sum_{i=1}^{m} |y_i - \bar{y}_i| \tag{7.3}$$

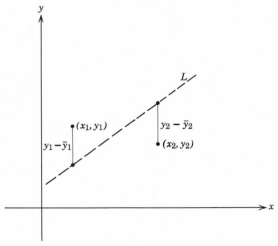

Figure 7.2. *Example showing that minimizing the sum of the deviations is not a satisfactory criterion of goodness of fit.*

This viable approach produces useful results; it is, however, a difficult numerical problem, in part because the derivative of the absolute value function does not exist at the origin. Nevertheless, algorithms have been developed for minimizing (7.3). These algorithms are beyond the scope of our discussion and, as we shall see in the next section, there are statistical reasons for rejecting (7.3) if the data contain statistical errors.

Even if we use (7.3) some of the deviations may be extremely large. In fact, in order to get most of the deviations to be small, we may be *forced* to allow some of the deviations to be large. Returning to Figure 7.1 we may have to allow the deviations of the two asterisked points to become quite large. It is sometimes desirable to keep all of the deviations within some bound. In those cases, minimizing (7.3) is inappropriate. Therefore, we might as an alternative try to minimize the maximum error; that is to say, we try to minimize d where

$$|d_i| \leq d \tag{7.4}$$

for $i = 1, 2, \ldots, m$. This is sometimes called a *Chebyshev approximation*. Algorithms can be constructed to find $f(x)$ so that d is a minimum subject to (7.4).

However, a few large deviations are not necessarily bad if the data values contain statistical errors. Moreover, the algorithms for finding the Chebyshev approximation are rather complex. Thus we turn to still another variation, the sum of the squares of the deviations.

In order to overcome the difficulty of opposite signs posed by (7.2), we try to minimize the sum of the squares of the deviations,

$$\sum_{i=1}^{m} d_i^2 = \sum_{i=1}^{m} (y_i - \bar{y}_i)^2 \tag{7.5}$$

This will produce results different from any of the three previous methods: (7.2), (7.3), or (7.4). From a practical point of view (7.5) is handled much more readily. For example, suppose from observing the general trend of the data we choose $\bar{y}$ to be a linear function

$$\bar{y} = a + bx$$

Then (7.5) becomes

$$\sum_{i=1}^{m} d_i^2 = \sum_{i=1}^{m} (y_i - a - bx_i)^2$$

This is a quadratic function of the parameters a and b. The methods of the calculus enable us to find the values of a and b that minimize this expression. We return to the details of accomplishing this in Section 7.3.

There are also statistical reasons for using (7.5). If the experimentally measured values of y follow a normal distribution (bell-shaped curve), then the function of $f(x)$ that results from minimizing (7.5) can be shown to be the most probable one.[2] Indeed, if the statistical errors in the y_i follow *any* distribution with constant variance, then (7.5) produces the most probable solution.

We cannot make these statements regarding the most probable solution for any of the other methods: (7.2), (7.3), or (7.4); that is, none of these other methods will produce the most probable equation for any reasonable assumption regarding the statistical distribution of the inherent errors in the data.

For all of these reasons we choose to minimize (7.5). The remainder of this chapter is concerned with techniques for doing so. Because we are making the square of the deviations small, (7.5) is called the *Principle of Least Squares*. It is also sometimes called *Gauss' Principle*.

**7.3
Linear
Regression**

Consider Table 7.1, which we assume has resulted from some experiment.

Table 7.1

x	y
1	1
3	2
4	4
6	4
8	5
9	7
11	8
14	9

If we plot the data we obtain the graph shown in Figure 7.3. Taking into account experimental errors of a statistical nature, the graph in Figure 7.3 appears to resemble a line. Thus we assume that the relationship between x and y is linear,

$$ax + by = 1 \tag{7.6}$$

We are faced with the problem of determining the "best" values for the coefficients a and b. We interpret "best" to be the ones that minimize the sum of the squares of the deviations, for the reasons outlined in Sections 7.1 and 7.2.

We now face another problem. Which deviations do we mean: the deviations of the tabulated y values from those y values given by (7.6), or the deviations in the x values?

In fact, we discuss both cases, and we shall see that they produce different results. In any given case, however, we must decide ahead of

---

[2]See, for example, Section 8.19 of Brice Carnahan, H. A. Luther, and James O. Wilkes, *Applied Numerical Methods*, New York, Wiley, 1969; or footnote on p. 165 of Bruce W. Arden and Kenneth N. Astill, *Numerical Algorithms: Origins and Applications*, Addison-Wesley, 1970.

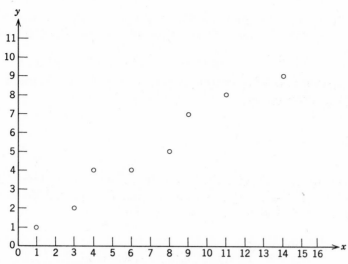

Figure 7.3. *Illustrative experimental data points.*

time which variable contains the statistical errors. If the y values have inherent statistical errors, then we should deal with the y deviations,

$$\sum_{i=1}^{m} (y_i - \bar{y}_i)^2 \qquad (7.7)$$

where $\bar{y}_i$ is obtained from (7.6) as

$$ax_i + b\bar{y}_i = 1 \qquad i = 1, \ldots, m \qquad (7.8)$$

On the other hand, if the x values possess inherent errors that follow a normal distribution, we should attempt to minimize

$$\sum_{i=1}^{m} (x_i - \bar{x}_i)^2 \qquad (7.9)$$

where

$$a\bar{x}_i + by_i = 1 \qquad i = 1, \ldots, m \qquad (7.10)$$

Recall that the x_i and y_i are the actual values in the table.

We shall deal with each of these cases. Of course, it is possible that both the x and y values have statistical errors. Techniques for this last case exist but will not be included in our discussion, except in the exercises. If a statistical error occurs—and we shall treat examples where it does—when we wish to estimate y for a given x, we treat y as the variable with statistical errors and minimize (7.7). Similarly, if we wish to estimate x for a given value of y, we treat x as the variable with statistical errors and minimize (7.9).

As noted above, it is possible to consider the case where x and y both have statistical errors. To do so we minimize the sums of the squares of the *distances* of the data points from the line (7.6). Here distance is measured perpendicular to the line. The algorithms, however, are considerably more complicated (see Exercise 39) and are not very widely used.

Suppose that the tabulated values of y include statistical errors that follow a normal distribution. Then we wish to minimize (7.7) where

$$\bar{y}_i = a_1 x_i + a_0 \qquad i = 1, \ldots, m \tag{7.11}$$

This last equation is (7.8) rewritten. Notice that $a_1 = -a/b$ and $a_0 = 1/b$. Using (7.11) in (7.7) we get

$$S = \sum_{i=1}^{m} (y_i - a_1 x_i - a_0)^2 \tag{7.12}$$

We wish to minimize S. Notice that there are only two unknown quantities in S: a_0 and a_1. If S is to be a minimum, the first partial derivatives of S with respect to a_0 and a_1 must be zero. Thus

$$\frac{\partial S}{\partial a_0} = \sum_{i=1}^{m} 2(y_i - a_1 x_i - a_0)(-1) = 0$$

$$\frac{\partial S}{\partial a_1} = \sum_{i=1}^{m} 2(y_i - a_1 x_i - a_0)(-x_i) = 0$$

Rearranging terms we get[3]

$$m\, a_0 + \left(\sum x_i\right) a_1 = \sum y_i \tag{7.13}$$

$$\left(\sum x_i\right) a_0 + \left(\sum x_i^2\right) a_1 = \sum x_i y_i \tag{7.14}$$

These are two linear equations in two variables: a_0 and a_1. They can be solved using the techniques described in Chapter 4. In particular it is easily verified that a_0 and a_1 are given by

[3] Readers not comfortable with operations on summations may rely on the following simple identities, in which a is any constant and x_i and y_i are any variables.

$$\sum_{i=1}^{m} (x_i + y_i) = \sum_{i=1}^{m} x_i + \sum_{i=1}^{m} y_i \tag{1}$$

$$\sum_{i=1}^{m} (a x_i) = a \sum_{i=1}^{m} x_i \tag{2}$$

$$\frac{d}{dx} \sum_{i=1}^{m} f(x_i) = \sum_{i=1}^{m} \left[\frac{d}{dx} f(x_i) \right] \tag{3}$$

$$\sum_{i=1}^{m} a = ma \tag{4}$$

Henceforth we shall assume that the summations extend over all the data points, that is, the symbol $\sum$ should be understood to mean $\sum_{i=1}^{m}$ unless specifically stated otherwise.

$$a_0 = \frac{\sum y_i \sum x_i^2 - \sum x_i \sum x_i y_i}{m \sum x_i^2 - \left(\sum x_i\right)^2} \tag{7.15}$$

$$a_1 = \frac{m \sum x_i y_i - \sum x_i \sum y_i}{m \sum x_i^2 - \left(\sum x_i\right)^2} \tag{7.16}$$

Moreover, the denominator in these last expressions vanishes only if all of the x_i are identical (see Exercise 3). Therefore, as long as two or more values of x are tabulated, the solution (7.15) and (7.16) exists and is unique.

Equations (7.13) and (7.14) are called *normal equations*. Their solution (7.15) and (7.16) when used in

$$y = a_1 x + a_0 \tag{7.17}$$

produces the *linear least squares* curve fit. The latter is also called the *linear regression of y on x*. We say that we have "regressed on x" since the x_i are assumed to contain no errors. We shall later follow a similar development to regress on y. First, however, we turn to a numerical example.

Recall Table 7.1, which listed eight values of x and y. To evaluate (7.15) and (7.16) we need the sum of the x_i, the sum of the y_i, the sum of x_i^2, and the sum of the products $x_i y_i$. They are shown in Table 7.2. Using these results in (7.15) and (7.16)

$$a_0 = \frac{40 \times 524 - 56 \times 364}{8 \times 524 - (56)^2} = \frac{6}{11}$$

$$a_1 = \frac{8 \times 364 - 56 \times 40}{8 \times 524 - (56)^2} = \frac{7}{11}$$

The equation of the least squares line (the linear regression of y on x) is

$$y = \frac{7}{11}x + \frac{6}{11} \tag{7.18}$$

or

$$11y - 7x = 6 \tag{7.19}$$

Table 7.2

x	y	x^2	xy
1	1	1	1
3	2	9	6
4	4	16	16
6	4	36	24
8	5	64	40
9	7	81	63
11	8	121	88
14	9	196	126
SUMS = 56	40	524	364

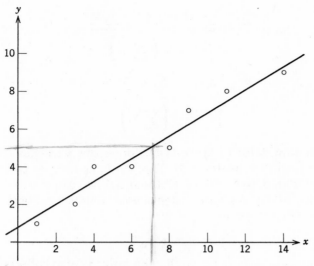

Figure 7.4. *The linear regression of* y *on* x *for the data points of Figure 7.3.*

Figure 7.4 shows a graph of this line together with the data points. Notice that the mean or average value of the x_i is $\frac{56}{8} = 7$ and the mean of the $y_i = \frac{40}{8} = 5$. The line (7.18) passes through this point (7,5). Indeed the linear regression of y on x will always pass through the point whose coordinates are the mean values of the x_i and the y_i (see Exercise 5).

We turn next to the case where the tabulated values of x are the ones with statistical errors and the y values are assumed to be exact. In this case we wish to minimize (7.9) where

$$\bar{x}_i = b_1 y_i + b_0 \qquad i = 1, \ldots, m \tag{7.20}$$

This is (7.10) rewritten. Using (7.20) in (7.9) we get

$$T = \sum (x_i - b_1 y_i - b_0)^2$$

and we wish T to be a minimum. Accordingly, we set the partial derivatives of T with respect to b_0 and b_1 equal to zero. Doing so produces the normal equations

$$m\,b_0 + \left(\sum y_i\right) b_1 = \sum x_i \tag{7.21}$$

$$\left(\sum y_i\right) b_0 + \left(\sum y_i^2\right) b_1 = \sum x_i y_i \tag{7.22}$$

Notice that (7.21) and (7.22) are (7.13) and (7.14) with b_0 and b_1 replacing a_0 and a_1 and with the roles of the x_i and y_i interchanged. The solution of these equations is

$$b_0 = \frac{\sum x_i \sum y_i^2 - \sum y_i \sum x_i y_i}{m \sum y_i^2 - \left(\sum y_i\right)^2} \tag{7.23}$$

$$b_1 = \frac{m \sum x_i y_i - \sum x_i \sum y_i}{m \sum y_i^2 - \left(\sum y_i \right)^2} \tag{7.24}$$

Using these values for b_0 and b_1 in

$$x = b_1 y + b_0 \tag{7.25}$$

produces the *linear regression of x on y*. We say in this case that we have "regressed on y" since the y_i are assumed to have no errors.

Let us return to the example given in Table 7.1 to find the linear regression of x on y. In addition to the data given in Table 7.2 we need the sum of the y_i^2. Without going through the details this sum is

$$\sum_{i=1}^{8} y_i^2 = 256$$

Thus (7.23) and (7.24) are

$$b_0 = \frac{56 \times 256 - 40 \times 364}{8 \times 256 - (40)^2} = -\frac{1}{2}$$

$$b_1 = \frac{8 \times 364 - 56 \times 40}{8 \times 256 - (40)^2} = \frac{3}{2}$$

The equation of the least squares line (the linear regression of x on y) is then

$$x = \frac{3}{2}y - \frac{1}{2} \tag{7.26}$$

or

$$2x - 3y = -1 \tag{7.27}$$

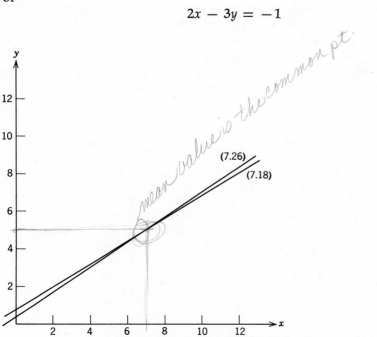

Figure 7.5. *The linear regression of* y *on* x *and of* x *on* y, *for the data points of Figure 7.3.*

Notice that this equation is *not* the same as (7.19), although the lines are very nearly the same. The two lines are shown together in Figure 7.5. They intersect at the point (7,5) whose coordinates are the mean of the x_i and y_i respectively. This will always be the case as we can infer from Exercises 5 and 6.

Before going on to curves more complex than lines and to a discussion of numerical problems, we discuss two examples of the use of linear regression.

Example 1

In Table 7.3 the heights and weights of nine men between the ages of 25 and 29 are shown. A graph of these points is shown in Figure 7.6. From an observation of this graph it would seem that there is a linear relationship between the height and weight.

If we wish to estimate the weight of an individual given his height, we should regress on height, that is, assume no errors in height. On the other hand, if we want to estimate the height of individuals with a given weight, we should regress on weight. The data for both types of regression are also given in Table 7.3. The resulting regression equations are

$$w = -39.2617 + 2.8902h \qquad (7.28)$$

and

$$h = 22.7630 + 0.2881w \qquad (7.29)$$

The first is the regression of weight on height and is obtained from (7.15), (7.16), and (7.17) where the weight (w_i) replaces y_i and the height (h_i) replaces x_i. The second, (7.29), is obtained from (7.23), (7.24), and (7.25) with the same replacements.

Suppose we wish to estimate the weight of an individual whose height is 70 in. From (7.28) we get 163.05. This is slightly different from the result, 163.96, which we would obtain using (7.29). The former result, 163.05, is generally accepted as more accurate.

Similarly, if we wish to estimate the height of a person whose weight is 175 lb, we use (7.29). The result is 73.18.

Table 7.3

	h_i	w_i	h_i^2	w_i^2	$h_i w_i$
	72	174	5184	30276	12528
	68	152	4624	23104	10336
	66	154	4356	23716	10164
	74	180	5476	32400	13320
	62	135	3844	18225	8370
	70	161	4900	25921	11270
	64	140	4096	19600	8960
	76	174	5776	30276	13224
	64	157	4096	24649	10048
SUM	616	1427	42352	228167	98220

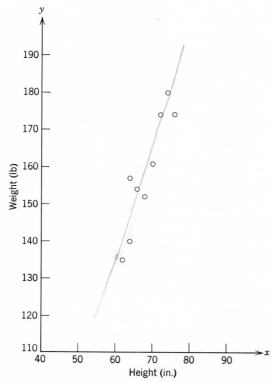

Figure 7.6. *A plot of the height and weight of nine men, ages 25–29.*

Example 2[4]

As a second example suppose we take a rod of high-strength steel with a cylindrical cross section. The rod has a length, L_0, and a diameter, d_0. If we suspend the rod and hang a slowly increasing weight onto it, the rod will stretch and at the same time its diameter will decrease. For a given weight (or load) of P measured in kips,[5] we measure the length, L, and the diameter, d, both in inches. We can then compute the stress, σ, from

$$\sigma = \frac{4P}{\pi d^2} \qquad (7.30)$$

and the strain, ϵ, from

$$\epsilon = \frac{L - L_0}{L_0} \qquad (7.31)$$

The stress, σ, is in kips per square inch (ksi) and the strain, ϵ, is dimensionless. The results of using 14 different loads are shown in Table 7.4. Notice that the stress is in units of kips per square inch and the strain

[4]The authors are indebted to Dr. John Weese, Dean of the Engineering College at the University of Denver, for the material in this example and in Case Study 12 (Section 7.9).
[5]A kip is 1000 lb.

Table 7.4

Stress, σ_i (in ksi)	Strain, ϵ_i ($\times 10^3$)	σ_i^2	ϵ_i^2	$\sigma_i \epsilon_i$
8.37	0.15	70.0569	0.0225	1.2555
17.9	0.52	320.41	0.2704	9.308
27.8	0.76	772.84	0.5776	21.128
34.2	1.01	1169.64	1.0201	34.542
38.8	1.12	1505.44	1.2544	43.456
44.8	1.42	2007.04	2.0164	63.616
51.3	1.52	2631.69	2.3104	77.976
55.5	1.66	3080.25	2.7556	92.13
61.3	1.86	3757.69	3.4596	114.018
67.5	2.08	4556.25	4.3264	140.4
72.1	2.27	5198.41	5.1529	163.667
76.9	2.56	5913.61	6.5536	196.864
83.5	2.86	6972.25	8.1796	238.81
88.9	3.19	7903.21	10.1761	283.591
728.87	22.98	45858.7869	48.0756	1480.7615

has been multiplied by 1000; that is, the first strain entry of 0.15 is in actuality 0.00015. A graph is shown in Figure 7.7. Again this appears to be a linear relationship.

We shall compute both the linear regression of stress on strain and of strain on stress. The first will be useful if we wish to estimate the stress for a given strain. The latter will be used when we want to compute the strain that a given stress will produce. All of the data for these calculations are included in Table 7.4.

First we wish to compute E and σ_0 such that

$$\sigma = E\epsilon + \sigma_0 \tag{7.32}$$

that is, we assume that strains are accurate and regress on them. Using (7.15) and (7.16) and replacing x_i by ϵ_i, y_i by σ_i, a_1 by E, and a_0 by σ_0, we obtain

$$\sigma_0 = \frac{\sum \sigma_i \sum \epsilon_i^2 - \sum \epsilon_i \sum \epsilon_i \sigma_i}{14 \sum \epsilon_i^2 - \left(\sum \epsilon_i\right)^2}$$

$$E = \frac{14 \sum \epsilon_i \sigma_i - \sum \epsilon_i \sum \sigma_i}{14 \sum \epsilon_i^2 - \left(\sum \epsilon_i\right)^2}$$

where the sums extend from 1 to 14. From Table 7.4 then

$$\sigma_0 = \frac{(728.87)(48.0756) - (22.98)(1480.7615)}{(14.)(48.0756) - (22.98)^2}$$

$$\sigma_0 = \frac{1012.963302}{144.978} = 6.9870139 \tag{7.33}$$

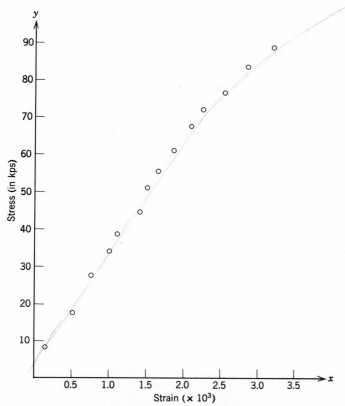

Figure 7.7. *A plot of the stress-strain relationship for a certain material, obtained experimentally.*

and

$$E = \frac{(14.)(1480.7615) - (22.98)(728.87)}{(14.)(48.0756) - (22.98)^2}$$

$$E = \frac{3981.2284}{144.978} = 27.460914 \qquad (7.34)$$

These parameters, σ_0 and E, have a physical interpretation. The value of σ_0 is the prestress in ksi, which arises because in this test the rod was subjected to an initial load before any strain measurements were taken. This was done to assure that no slack existed in the testing apparatus. The parameter E is called *Young's modulus.* We must remember, however, that the strain, ϵ, was multiplied by 10^3. Thus Young's modulus in ksi is the value of E multiplied by 10^3. Therefore, for this material it is 27.46×10^3 ksi.

Given a value of the strain, the stress can be calculated from

$$\sigma = (27.46 \times 10^3)\epsilon + 6.987$$

where now ϵ is the true strain and σ is in ksi.

Suppose we assume that the stress is precise, but that the stress measurements are in error. We replace (7.32) by

$$\epsilon = \left(\frac{1}{E}\right)\sigma + \epsilon_0 \qquad (7.35)$$

This leads to

$$\epsilon_0 = \frac{\sum \epsilon_i \sum \sigma_i^2 - \sum \sigma_i \sum \sigma_i \epsilon_i}{14 \sum \sigma_i^2 - \left(\sum \sigma_i\right)^2}$$

$$\frac{1}{E} = \frac{14 \sum \sigma_i \epsilon_i - \sum \sigma_i \sum \epsilon_i}{14 \sum \sigma_i^2 - \left(\sum \sigma_i\right)^2}$$

Using Table 7.4 again

$$\epsilon_0 = -0.00022973$$

$$\frac{1}{E} = 0.03594$$

From this we find

$$E = 27.8241$$

This agrees reasonably well with (7.34), although the two estimates for Young's modulus do differ by more than 1%.

Given a value of the stress, the strain is calculated from

$$\epsilon = (0.03594\sigma - 0.22973) \times 10^{-3}$$

where we have again introduced the true strain by using the factor 10^{-3}.

If the stress is increased beyond 90 ksi, then the stress-strain curve ceases to be linear, because the material instead of being *elastic* becomes *plastic*. We shall return to this example and extend our results to the plastic range in Case Study 12 (Section 7.9).

**7.4
Polynomial
Regression**

Linear regression is often unsatisfactory. If we look back at the experimental data plotted in Figure 7.1 it is obvious that a line cannot "fit" the data very well. However, it appears that a quadratic or cubic equation might fit the data nicely. This is indeed the case, and we shall return to this set of data and a cubic equation that fits it quite well in the next section (Case Study 11).

We can easily imagine data for which neither a quadratic nor a cubic equation is suitable. In this section we broaden our discussion of least squares approximations to polynomials of degree n. When $n = 1$, the polynomial is a linear function. We have already discussed this case quite thoroughly in the preceding section. For $n = 2$ the polynomial is a quadratic function, and for $n = 3$ it is a cubic polynomial.

Suppose that we are given a table of values $x_1, x_2, \ldots, x_m$ and corresponding to each of these there is another value $y_1, y_2, \ldots, y_m$. We further suppose that after examining the data we conclude that y appears to be a polynomial of degree n in x. Notice that *the degree n must be chosen before the least squares process is started*. In the preceding section the data values were such that we chose $n = 1$. We also assume that the y values contain statistical errors, so we regress on x. It should be clear that by reversing the roles of x and y we could regress on y if we so chose. However, in the latter case we would have to assume that x was a polynomial of degree n in y. This is not the same as assuming y is a polynomial of degree n in x except for the case $n = 1$.

In any case analogous to (7.17) we write

$$y = a_n x^n + a_{n-1} x^{n-1} + \cdots + a_1 x + a_0 \tag{7.36}$$

When $x = x_i$ we call the value of the right-hand side $\bar{y}_i$ so that

$$\bar{y}_i = a_n x_i^n + a_{n-1} x_i^{n-1} + \cdots + a_1 x_i + a_0$$

We still wish to minimize the sum of the square of the y deviations (7.7), which becomes

$$S = \sum (y_i - a_n x_i^n - a_{n-1} x_i^{n-1} - \cdots - a_p x_i^p - \cdots - a_1 x_i - a_0)^2$$

Differentiating S with respect to $a_0, a_1, \ldots, a_p, \ldots, a_n$, respectively, and setting each of these derivatives equal to zero, we get

$$
\left.
\begin{aligned}
ma_0 + &\left(\sum x_i \right) a_1 + \cdots + \left(\sum x_i^k \right) a_k + \cdots + \left(\sum x_i^n \right) a_n \\
&= \sum y_i \\[2ex]
\left(\sum x_i \right) a_0 + &\left(\sum x_i^2 \right) a_1 + \cdots + \left(\sum x_i^{k+1} \right) a_k \\
&+ \cdots + \left(\sum x_i^{n+1} \right) a_n = \sum x_i y_i \\[1ex]
\vdots \\
\left(\sum x_i^p \right) a_0 + &\left(\sum x_i^{p+1} \right) a_1 + \cdots + \left(\sum x_i^{k+p} \right) a_k \\
&+ \cdots + \left(\sum x_i^{n+p} \right) a_n = \sum x_i^p y_i \\[1ex]
\vdots \\
\left(\sum x_i^n \right) a_0 + &\left(\sum x_i^{n+1} \right) a_1 + \cdots + \left(\sum x_i^{k+n} \right) a_k \\
&+ \cdots + \left(\sum x_i^{2n} \right) a_n = \sum x_i^n y_i
\end{aligned}
\right\} \tag{7.37}
$$

These equations are $n + 1$ linear equations in the $n + 1$ unknown quantities $a_0, a_1, \ldots, a_n$. They are called the normal equations for the polynomial regression of degree n, which may be solved by Gaussian elimination as described in Chapter 4. However, severe numerical problems may arise. We return to a discussion of the numerical problems in Section 7.8. In principle, however, the values of $a_0, a_1, \ldots, a_n$ may be computed in a straightforward way. Once we have solved the normal equations, we use these values in (7.36) and thereby obtain the *polynomial regression of degree n of y on x*, which is sometimes referred to as the least squares curve fit of a polynomial of degree *n*.

The reader might wonder what happens if the data values are such that *no* polynomial of reasonable degree seems to fit the data. In such cases we resort to exponential or trigonometric functions. A discussion of the use of these functions is taken up in Section 7.6. In the next section we discuss a case study where a polynomial of degree 3 fits the experimental data quite well.

7.5 Case Study 11: Specific Heat of Water

The information shown in Figure 7.1 was derived from a table of values of the specific heat of water as a function of temperature in terms of the 15°C cal.[6] The tabular values are shown in Table 7.5. The plot suggests that a cubic might fit the data fairly well, and we shall proceed to find the best cubic fit by least squares. Fitting a quadratic and comparing the fits are left as Exercise 9.

Before proceeding to write a program it is helpful to write out the normal equations. From (7.37) with $m = 21$ (21 data points) and $n = 3$ (a cubic):

$$21a_0 + \left(\sum x_i\right)a_1 + \left(\sum x_i^2\right)a_2 + \left(\sum x_i^3\right)a_3 = \sum y_i$$

$$\left(\sum x_i\right)a_0 + \left(\sum x_i^2\right)a_1 + \left(\sum x_i^3\right)a_2 + \left(\sum x_i^4\right)a_3 = \sum x_i y_i$$

$$\left(\sum x_i^2\right)a_0 + \left(\sum x_i^3\right)a_1 + \left(\sum x_i^4\right)a_2 + \left(\sum x_i^5\right)a_3 = \sum x_i^2 y_i$$

$$\left(\sum x_i^3\right)a_0 + \left(\sum x_i^4\right)a_1 + \left(\sum x_i^5\right)a_2 + \left(\sum x_i^6\right)a_3 = \sum x_i^3 y_i$$

Table 7.5

T, °C	c_p	T, °C	c_p
0	1.00762	55	0.99919
5	1.00392	60	0.99967
10	1.00153	65	1.00024
15	1.00000	70	1.00091
20	0.99907	75	1.00167
25	0.99852	80	1.00253
30	0.99826	85	1.00351
35	0.99818	90	1.00461
40	0.99828	95	1.00586
45	0.99849	100	1.00721
50	0.99878		

---

[6] See Archie G. Worthing and Joseph Geffner *Treatment of Experimental Data*, New York, Wiley, 1943, p. 268. The original source is a paper by N. S. Osborne, H. F. Stimson, and D. C. Jennings that appeared in *J. Res. Nat. Bur. Standards*, 23 (1939), 197.

We now make an observation that will simplify the program somewhat. Once we have computed the various sums in these equations, we have no further need for the x_i and y_i. Thus we read a pair of values of temperature (y_i) and specific heat (x_i) from one card, add the appropriate term into each sum, and then discard the values of temperature and specific heat. The sums we need are

$$\text{SUM (1)} = \sum x_i$$

$$\text{SUM (2)} = \sum x_i^2$$

$$\text{SUM (3)} = \sum x_i^3$$

$$\text{SUM (4)} = \sum x_i^4$$

$$\text{SUM (5)} = \sum x_i^5$$

$$\text{SUM (6)} = \sum x_i^6$$

For the right-hand sides we need

$$\text{RIGHT (1)} = \sum y_i$$

$$\text{RIGHT (2)} = \sum x_i y_i$$

$$\text{RIGHT (3)} = \sum x_i^2 y_i$$

$$\text{RIGHT (4)} = \sum x_i^3 y_i$$

In our case, x corresponds to temperature and y to specific heat.

A program to carry out the calculations of this least squares fit is shown in Figure 7.8. We have chosen, in the interest of easy readability, to set up the summations using variables named SUM and RIGHT, as shown above, and then place the appropriate summations in a matrix of coefficients called MATRIX. Furthermore, the program is written specifically to handle this particular problem (that is, a cubic fit to 21 points), rather than being a more general routine. Again, the goal is understandability.

The program begins by clearing the summing locations, then moves immediately to a loop that reads the 21 data points in succession. For each data point, the ten sums that we need are formed, utilizing the index of a DO loop in the exponent of an arithmetic expression. This is all perfectly legal, including raising a number to a zero power—so long as the number being exponentiated is not zero. In our case we do have such a data point, which was changed to 0.0000001 when the program was run. This avoids a diagnostic error message and does not change the results. In a more general program, however, it would not be wise to set things up this way. If speed of execution is of any importance, the program can be written to run much more rapidly than this one does.

After all the summations have been formed, two nested DO loops quickly place the proper sum in each coefficient position. Note the handling of subscripts to do this in a simple way. [In most Fortran systems, it would be permissible to write MATRIX(I,J) = SUM(I+J−2), but this

```
C CASE STUDY 11
C LEAST SQUARES CURVE FITTING APPLIED TO THE
C SPECIFIC HEAT OF WATER AS A FUNCTION OF TEMPERATURE
C
C THIS PROGRAM SETS UP THE MATRIX, THEN CALLS THE GAUSSIAN
C   ELIMINATION SUBROUTINE OF CASE STUDY 7
C
C THE PROGRAM IS SET UP FOR THE SPECIFICS OF THIS CASE STUDY
C
        DIMENSION MATRIX(4,5), A(4), SUM(6), RIGHT(4)
        REAL MATRIX
C CLEAR THE VARIABLES THAT ARE USED TO ACCUMULATE THE SUMS
        DO 10 I = 1, 6
10      SUM(I) = 0.0
        DO 11 I = 1, 4
11      RIGHT(I) = 0.0
C READ THE DATA POINTS AND FORM THE VARIOUS SUMS
        DO 40 J = 1, 21
        READ (5, 1000) T, C
1000    FORMAT (2F10.0)
        DO 30 I = 1, 6
30      SUM(I) = SUM(I) + T**I
        DO 40 I = 1, 4
40      RIGHT(I) = RIGHT(I) + C*(T**(I-1))
C SET UP MATRIX OF COEFFICIENTS
        MATRIX(1, 1) = 21.0
        DO 50 I = 1, 4
        MATRIX(I, 5) = RIGHT(I)
        DO 50 J = 1, 4
        K = I + J
        IF (K .NE. 2) MATRIX(I, J) = SUM(K - 2)
50      CONTINUE
C CALL THE GAUSSIAN ELIMINATION SUBROUTINE
        CALL GAUSS (MATRIX, A, 4, 5)
C PRINT THE RESULTS
        WRITE (6, 2000) A
2000    FORMAT (1X, 1P4E14.6)
        STOP
        END
```

Figure 7.8. *A main program for least squares curve fitting of a cubic to experimental data. The normal equations are solved by calling the Gaussian elimination subroutine of Figure 4.12.*

feature is not a part of USA Standard Fortran. Hence, we have inserted the statement $K = I + J$.]

With the MATRIX properly loaded with the summations, it is a simple matter to call the subroutine named GAUSS that we wrote in Case Study 7, which appears in Figure 4.12. It is necessary, of course, somehow to combine the program in Figure 7.8 with the subroutine, which can be done in many ways depending on the way the computer is being utilized. It might involve combining the main program with an object deck for the subroutine from the user's private library of programs, or telling the time-sharing system to do the same thing. In many installations it would be a simple matter to use a preprogrammed Gaussian elimination subroutine provided by the manufacturer or a user's organization, without ever having to write it ourselves at all. In the latter case, naturally the CALL statement would almost certainly be different, along with the way the matrix or matrices would need to be set up. All such information would be provided in a program description accompanying the subroutine library.

When the program was run the results were:

```
1.006525E 00 -5.082556E-04  8.685488E-06 -3.601298E-08
```

We note, of course, that Fortran does not permit zero subscripts, so that what has printed as A(1) is our a_0, etc., so that the functional relation we sought is:

$$c_p = 1.006525 - 0.0005082556T + 0.000008685488T^2$$
$$- 0.00000003601298T^3$$

Figure 7.9 shows a plot of the fitted curve with the experimental values (small circles). We see that the positive and negative deviations are more or less balanced, as we would expect. A comparison of the computed values with the experimental values shows a maximum deviation of 0.001 at 0 °C, with most deviations being considerably less.

If errors of this size are acceptable, we can now use the fitted cubic in any calculation that requires the specific heat of water as a function of temperature. If these errors are not acceptable, we can look into a higher-order polynomial, or possibly investigate a high-order interpolation formula.

The entire program was rerun in double precision as a check on the possibility of roundoff trouble, giving these results:

```
1.006438D 00 -4.975807D-04  8.429216D-06 -3.437429D-08
```

At first glance we might think we are in very serious trouble indeed, having achieved only one significant figure in one case. But remember that what we want is a good fit, not any particular values of the coefficients. One particular coefficient might not have a large effect on the deviations, or the changes in the other coefficients might compensate. This is in fact the case. The largest deviation from the double precision fit is actually a very small amount *larger* than the largest deviation from the single

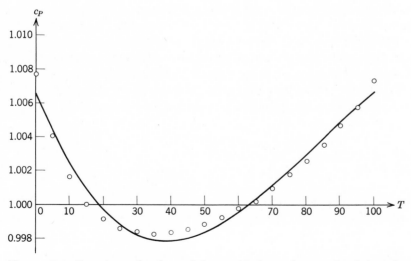

Figure 7.9. *Experimental values of the specific heat of water (circles) and a fitted cubic.*

precision fit. And the sum of the squares of the deviations from the single precision fit (0.00000482) is only an insignificant amount larger than the sum of the squares of the deviations from the double precision fit (0.00000480).

We shall see in Section 7.8, however, that things do not by any means always work out so smoothly.

7.6 Exponential, Geometric, and Trigonometric Regression

As we have implied earlier, polynomial regression is sometimes inadequate. Many cases arise when the data when plotted resembles a *hyperbola*.

$$y = \frac{1}{a_0 + a_1 x} \tag{7.38}$$

or an *exponential curve*.

$$y = a(b^x) \tag{7.39}$$

or a *geometric curve*.

$$y = ax^b \tag{7.40}$$

or a *trigonometric curve*.[7]

$$y = a_0 + a_1 \cos \omega x \tag{7.41}$$

where ω is given, or more generally

$$y = a_0 + \sum_{k=1}^{n} a_k \cos (k\omega x) + \sum_{k=1}^{n} b_k \sin (k\omega x) \tag{7.42}$$

where again ω is given.

If the data when log y is plotted against x appear to be linear, then (7.39) is usually appropriate. Semilog graph paper is helpful in this case. On the other hand, if the plot of log y vs log x appears to be linear, then (7.40) should be used. Log-log graph paper permits ease of plotting in the latter case. Finally, if the data oscillate and appear to be periodic in x (repeat themselves), then (7.41) or (7.42) may be useful.

In this section we shall discuss how the least squares principle may be applied to each of these cases. At the close of the section we shall point out the difficulties that arise in even slight variations of these cases.

Consider first the hyperbolic curve (7.38). If we let

$$z = \frac{1}{y}$$

then

$$z = a_0 + a_1 x \tag{7.43}$$

This is a linear equation in x and z. We assume that y, hence z, contains statistical errors and minimizes the sum of the squares of the deviations

---

[7]In most texts the constant term is written $a_0/2$ rather than a_0 as we have done here.

in z. That is to say, we minimize

$$\sum (z_i - \bar{z}_i)^2$$

where $\bar{z}_i$ are calculated from (7.43) with $x = x_i$ and the z_i are the recipro-cals of the y_i. Thus the sum of the deviations becomes

$$\sum \left(\frac{1}{y_i} - a_0 - a_1 x_i \right)^2$$

The normal equations are

$$m\, a_0 + \left(\sum x_i \right) a_1 = \sum \frac{1}{y_i} \Bigg\}$$

$$\left(\sum x_i \right) a_0 + \left(\sum x_i^2 \right) a_1 = \sum \frac{x_i}{y_i} \Bigg\} \qquad (7.44)$$

We hasten to point out that the values of a_0 and a_1 obtained from (7.44) do *not* minimize the sum of the y deviations. Rather they minimize the sum of the deviations of the reciprocal of y. Thus the statistical basis on which the previous discussion rested (see Section 7.2) is not valid in this case. Nevertheless we proceed since the process does lead to an easily computable solution and one that fits the data reasonably well (see Exercise 12a).

We next turn to the exponential curve (7.39). Taking logarithms to the base $e\ (= 2.718\ldots)$ we get

$$\log y = \log a + x \log b$$

Now let

$$z = \log y$$
$$A = \log a$$
$$B = \log b$$

so

$$z = A + Bx$$

This is again linear in x and z and we minimize the sum of the squares of the deviations in z. We emphasize that this amounts to minimizing the sum of the squares of the deviations in the *logarithms of* y.

In any case we minimize

$$\sum (\log y_i - A - Bx_i)^2$$

The normal equations become

$$m\, A + \left(\sum x_i \right) B = \sum \log y_i$$

$$\left(\sum x_i \right) A + \left(\sum x_i^2 \right) B = \sum x_i \log y_i$$

Solving these and replacing A by $\log a$ and B by $\log b$, we obtain finally

$$a = \exp\left\{\left[\sum \log y_i \sum x_i^2 - \sum x_i \sum x_i \log y_i\right]\middle/\left[m \sum x_i^2 - \left(\sum x_i\right)^2\right]\right\}$$

$$b = \exp\left\{\left[m \sum x_i \log y_i - \sum x_i \sum \log y_i\right]\middle/\left[m \sum x_i^2 - \left(\sum x_i\right)^2\right]\right\}$$

(7.45)

where "exp" indicates "e" to be raised to the power in braces (see Exercises 12b and 13).

Next we turn to the geometric curve (7.40). Again taking logarithms to the base e,

$$\log y = \log a + b \log x \qquad (7.46)$$

Now we let

$$z = \log y$$
$$A = \log a$$
$$t = \log x$$

so (7.46) becomes

$$z = A + bt$$

which is linear in z and t. The normal equations are

$$m A + \left(\sum \log x_i\right) b = \sum \log y_i$$

$$\left(\sum \log x_i\right) A + \left(\sum (\log x_i)^2\right) b = \sum (\log x_i \log y_i)$$

Solving these for A and b and replacing A by $\log a$

$$a = \exp\left\{\left[\sum \log y_i \sum (\log x_i)^2\right.\right.$$

$$\left.\left. - \sum \log x_i \sum (\log x_i \log y_i)\right]\middle/\left[m \sum (\log x_i)^2 - \left(\sum \log x_i\right)^2\right]\right\}$$

$$b = \left\{\left[m \sum (\log x_i \log y_i)\right.\right.$$

$$\left.\left. - \sum \log x_i \sum \log y_i\right]\middle/\left[m \sum (\log x_i^2) - \left(\sum \log x_i\right)^2\right]\right\}$$

(7.47)

(see Exercise 14).

Finally we turn to the trigonometric curves (7.41) and (7.42). Using (7.41) first we let

$$t = \cos \omega x$$

so that we get a linear equation. (Recall that ω is assumed to be known.) The normal equations are

332   Least Squares Approximations

$$m \, a_0 + \left[\sum \cos(\omega x_i) \right] a_1 = \sum y_i$$

$$\left[\sum \cos(\omega x_i) \right] a_0 + \left\{ \sum [\cos(\omega x_i)]^2 \right\} a_1 = \sum y_i \cos \omega x_i$$

The coefficients a_0 and a_1 are

$$\left. \begin{array}{l} a_0 = \dfrac{\sum y_i \sum [\cos(\omega x_i)]^2 - \sum \cos(\omega x_i) \sum [y_i \cos(\omega x_i)]}{m \sum [\cos(\omega x_i)]^2 - \left[\sum \cos(\omega x_i) \right]^2} \\[3em] a_1 = \dfrac{m \sum [y_i \cos(\omega x_i)] - \sum \cos(\omega x_i) \sum y_i}{m \sum [\cos(\omega x_i)]^2 - \left[\sum \cos(\omega x_i) \right]^2} \end{array} \right\} \quad (7.48)$$

Notice that, in contrast to the other cases discussed in this section, for the trigonometric function *we are minimizing the sum of the squares of the deviations in y*. Thus the statistical discussion of Section 7.2 does apply to this case and the following one as well. For the more general trigonometric function (7.42) we use a different approach. We shall carry out the derivation for the case $n = 2$ but the generalization to other values of n will be straightforward. Thus instead of (7.42) we write

$$y = a_0 + a_1 \cos(\omega x) + a_2 \cos(2\omega x) + b_1 \sin(\omega x) + b_2 \sin(2\omega x) \quad (7.49)$$

We wish to minimize

$$S = \sum [y_i - a_0 - a_1 \cos(\omega x_i) - a_2 \cos(2\omega x_i) \\ - b_1 \sin(\omega x_i) - b_2 \sin(2\omega x_i)]^2$$

Differentiating with respect to a_0, a_1, a_2, b_1, and b_2 and setting each of these derivatives equal to zero, we get the following five normal equations.

$$\left. \begin{array}{l} m \, a_0 + \left[\sum \cos(\omega x_i) \right] a_1 + \left[\sum \cos(2\omega x_i) \right] a_2 \\[1em] \quad + \left[\sum \sin(\omega x_i) \right] b_1 \\[1em] \quad + \left[\sum \sin(2\omega x_i) \right] b_2 = \sum y_i \\[1.5em] \left[\sum \cos(\omega x_i) \right] a_0 + \left[\sum \cos^2(\omega x_i) \right] a_1 \\[1em] \quad + \left[\sum \cos(\omega x_i) \cos(2\omega x_i) \right] a_2 \\[1em] \quad + \left[\sum \cos(\omega x_i) \sin(\omega x_i) \right] b_1 \\[1em] \quad + \left[\sum \cos(\omega x_i) \sin(2\omega x_i) \right] b_2 = \sum y_i \cos(\omega x_i) \end{array} \right\} \quad (7.50)$$

$$\left[\sum \cos(2\omega x_i)\right]a_0 + \left[\sum \cos(2\omega x_i)\cos(\omega x_i)\right]a_1$$

$$+ \left[\sum \cos^2(2\omega x_i)\right]a_2$$

$$+ \left[\sum \cos(2\omega x_i)\sin(\omega x_i)\right]b_1$$

$$+ \left[\sum \cos(2\omega x_i)\sin(2\omega x_i)\right]b_2 = \sum y_i \cos(2\omega x_i)$$

$$\left[\sum \sin(\omega x_i)\right]a_0 + \left[\sum \sin(\omega x_i)\cos(\omega x_i)\right]a_1$$

$$+ \left[\sum \sin(\omega x_i)\cos(2\omega x_i)\right]a_2$$

$$+ \sum [\sin^2(\omega x_i)]b_1$$

$$+ \left[\sum \sin(\omega x_i)\sin(2\omega x_i)\right]b_2 = \sum y_i \sin(\omega x_i)$$

$$\left[\sum \sin(2\omega x_i)\right]a_0 + \left[\sum \sin(2\omega x_i)\cos(\omega x_i)\right]a_1$$

$$+ \left[\sum \sin(2\omega x_i)\cos(2\omega x_i)\right]a_2$$

$$+ \sum [\sin(2\omega x_i)\sin(\omega x_i)]b_1$$

$$+ \sum [\sin^2(2\omega x_i)]b_2 = \sum y_i \sin(2\omega x_i)$$

$$(7.50)$$

These five equations may be solved by Gaussian elimination for the five coefficients a_0, a_1, a_2, b_1, and b_2. For (7.42) we would obtain a system of $2n + 1$ equations.

This derivation of the coefficients for what we have called trigonometric curves is usually called *discrete harmonic analysis* or *discrete Fourier analysis*. A complete discussion may be found in Kaj L. Nielsen, *Methods of Numerical Analysis*, 2nd ed., New York: Macmillan, 1965, pp. 313–320; or Bruce W. Arden and Kenneth N. Astill, *Numerical Algorithms: Origins and Applications*, Addison-Wesley, 1970, pp. 188–195; as well as in several other places.

We close this section by pointing out that not all functions can be so easily translated into a linear form. In fact some functions that frequently arise cannot be so transformed.

For example, suppose we add a constant term to the right sides of (7.39) and (7.40) to produce

$$y = ab^x + c$$

and

$$y = ax^b + c \qquad (7.51)$$

Neither of these can be linearized. Of course, if we know the value of

c we can introduce a new variable $r = y - c$ and proceed as we did earlier to linearize the equation.

It turns out that the stress-strain curve in Case Study 12 has the form of (7.51). We shall find that there are some "tricks" we can use in that case study to predict the value of c. However, these tricks are very much dependent upon the particular form of the data. Therefore, we cannot give any straightforward description of how to handle equations of the form (7.51).

Recall also that we needed to know the value of ω to use (7.42). If ω is unknown, there is no easy way to handle (7.42) either.

There are other types of equations that can be linearized. They are relegated to the exercises since they do not appear with the frequency that (7.38) to (7.42) do (see Exercises 17 to 20).

7
Multiple
Regression

There are often cases when experimental data involve more than two variables. Consider for example the equilibrium constant for ammonia reacting in hydrogen and nitrogen gases with a given hydrogen–nitrogen mole ratio. As we noted in Exercise 23 at the close of Chapter 6, the equilibrium constant, K_p, depends upon the temperature, T, and the pressure, p. Thus there are three variables involved: K_p, T, and p. We can think of any one of them as being determined by the other two. In this case it is usual to think of T and p as given and K_p to be computed, that is,

$$K_p = f(T,p)$$

(see Exercise 23).

In general we think of three variables x, y, and z and suppose that

$$z = f(x,y) \tag{7.52}$$

where the function f is not completely determined. Suppose we have a table that lists corresponding values for the three variables, that is, (x_1,y_1,z_1), (x_2,y_2,z_2), ..., and (x_m,y_m,z_m). If we assume that the tabulated values of z_i contain statistical errors that follow a normal distribution, then the most probable function f is the one obtained by regressing on both x and y.

In this section we discuss only linear regression although other forms such as polynomial, exponential, geometric, and trigonometric can be handled in analogous ways. Thus we assume the function f is linear in both x and y, and (7.52) can be replaced by

$$z = A + Bx + Cy \tag{7.53}$$

Instead of the least squares line we now think of the least squares plane, that is to say, we think of the plane represented by (7.53) as being chosen so that the sum of the squares of the deviations of the tabulated z_i from the values of z produced by (7.53) is as small as possible. We then wish to minimize

$$S = \sum (z_i - A - Bx_i - Cy_i)^2$$

Differentiating S with respect to A, B, and C and setting each partial derivative equal to zero, we arrive at the three normal equations for A, B, and C.

$$m A + \left(\sum x_i\right) B + \left(\sum y_i\right) C = \sum z_i$$

$$\left(\sum x_i\right) A + \left(\sum x_i^2\right) B + \left(\sum x_i y_i\right) C = \sum x_i z_i \qquad (7.54)$$

$$\left(\sum y_i\right) A + \left(\sum x_i y_i\right) B + \left(\sum y_i^2\right) C = \sum y_i z_i$$

The solution, A, B, and C of these equations when used in (7.53) produces the linear regression of z on y and x. We could, of course, compute the linear regression of y on z and x and so on. If we change the variables that we regress on, we shall in general obtain a different plane.

Needless to say we could perform regressions on more than two variables. In general, if the table lists v variables then we choose one variable as the one with statistical errors and regress on the remaining $v - 1$ variables. If all of the variables contain statistical errors, we choose the variable whose value we wish to estimate later and regress on the others.

7.8
Numerical
Problems

In many problems in numerical analysis algorithms that on the surface are straightforward are fraught with numerical difficulties, sometimes quite obscure. As we have seen repeatedly, some of these difficulties arise because of the way in which the arithmetic is carried out and some arise because the problem itself possesses instabilities (see Section 2.1). Least squares (or regression) is no exception.

Let us first look at the solution to the linear regression problem of Section 7.3. We found that the coefficients a_0 and a_1 for $y = a_0 + a_1 x$ were given by (7.15) and (7.16). The denominators of both of these equations are identical and are

$$m \sum x_i^2 - \left(\sum x_i\right)^2 \qquad (7.55)$$

Recall now the second form we used for computing the variance of x_1, $x_2, \ldots, x_m$. From (3.41) in Case Study 6 the variance is

$$v = \frac{\sum x_i^2}{m} - \mu^2$$

which can be rewritten

$$v = \frac{\sum x_i^2 - \dfrac{\left(\sum x_i\right)^2}{m}}{m}$$

since

$$\mu = \frac{\sum x_i}{m}$$

As we saw in that case study, this form of computing the variance produces a much larger error than does

$$v = \frac{\sum (x_i - \mu)^2}{m}$$

We should expect therefore that (7.55) is equally error prone. To circumvent this numerical problem we note that

$$m \sum (x_i - \mu)^2 = m \sum x_i^2 - \left(\sum x_i\right)^2 \qquad (7.56)$$

and use the left side of (7.56) as the denominator in (7.15) and (7.16).

But our troubles are not yet ended. The numerators of (7.15) and (7.16) will also be inaccurate in many cases. We can improve the accuracy of the numerators by noting that

$$m \sum y_i(x_i - \mu) = m \sum x_i y_i - \sum x_i \sum y_i \qquad (7.57)$$

and also that

$$m \sum y_i \sum (x_i - \mu)^2 - m \sum x_i \sum [y_i(x_i - \mu)]$$

$$= m \sum y_i \sum x_i^2 - m \sum x_i \sum x_i y_i \qquad (7.58)$$

We use (7.57) to replace the numerator in (7.16) and (7.58) to replace the numerator in (7.15). We use (7.56) to replace both denominators. The result of all this is

$$a_0 = \frac{\sum y_i \sum (x_i - \mu)^2 - \sum x_i \sum [y_i(x_i - \mu)]}{m^2 \sum (x_i - \mu)^2} \qquad (7.59)$$

$$a_1 = \frac{\sum y_i(x_i - \mu)}{\sum (x_i - \mu)^2} \qquad (7.60)$$

where, of course,

$$\mu = \frac{\sum x_i}{m}$$

It turns out that (7.59) and (7.60) are more accurate than (7.15) and (7.16). The above equations, (7.59) and (7.60), require considerably more computation than do (7.15) and (7.16). They also require more computer storage. Hence (7.59) and (7.60) should only be used when accuracy may be a problem. Accuracy may be a problem if the x_i are closely clustered. Otherwise, the simpler equations (7.15) and (7.16) should be used.

Even under the best conditions if the degree of the polynomial used in a polynomial regression becomes even reasonably large (say $n = 7$), numerical problems arise. Suppose, for example, that the x_i are not clustered but are evenly spaced. (Recall that clustering of the x_i was the problem earlier in this section. Even spacing of the data is the opposite of clustering.) In order to tie down a specific case, suppose the x_i are all between 0 and 1 and evenly spaced. Thus

$$x_i = i/m$$

for $i = 1, 2, \ldots, m$. We can then compute the coefficients in the normal equations (7.37) for $n = 5$ (see Exercises 24 and 25). The matrix (*not* augmented) for $m = 100$ is

$$
\begin{pmatrix}
100 & 50.5 & 33.8 & 25.5 & 20.5 & 17.2 \\
50.5 & 33.8 & 25.5 & 20.5 & 17.2 & 14.8 \\
33.8 & 25.5 & 20.5 & 17.2 & 14.8 & 13.0 \\
25.5 & 20.5 & 17.2 & 14.8 & 13.0 & 11.6 \\
20.5 & 17.2 & 14.8 & 13.0 & 11.6 & 10.5 \\
17.2 & 14.8 & 13.0 & 11.6 & 10.5 & 9.6
\end{pmatrix}
$$

The ratio of the largest term (100) to the smallest (9.6) is about 10. That large a ratio usually portends numerical difficulties in solving the equations. For $n = 10$ the ratio is about 20. As n gets large, the ratio of the largest term to the smallest term also gets larger. It can be shown[8] that for large m (number of points) the nonaugmented matrix approaches the so-called Hilbert matrix, which is notoriously ill-conditioned.

The way out of this dilemma is either to confine ourselves to polynomials of low degree[9] or to use *orthogonal functions*. A discussion of the latter is beyond the scope of this text. The interested reader is referred to Section 8.22 (pp. 574–575), Brice Carnahan, H. A. Luther, and James D. Wilkes *Applied Numerical Methods*, New York, Wiley, 1969.

For a numerical illustration of what can happen, consider the problem of fitting a sixth-degree polynomial to the data in the table at the top of the next page. As a matter of fact, the y values were generated from the polynomial

$$y = 40 + 10x + 5x^2 + 3x^3 + 2x^4 + x^5 + x^6$$

but we cannot reasonably ask that the least squares method give us back the coefficients with great accuracy; all we require, actually, is that the

[8] See, for example, Bruce W. Arden and Kenneth N. Astill, *Numerical Algorithms: Origins and Applications*, Reading, Mass.: Addison-Wesley, 1970.
[9] Actually, taking into consideration functions other than polynomials (Section 7.6), we *should* confine ourselves to functions with few unknown parameters (see also Exercise 26).

x	y
1	62
2	232
3	1330
4	5984
5	20590
6	57952
7	140642
8	305080
9	606334
10	1123640
11	1966642
12	3282352
13	5262830
14	8153584

deviations at the data points be as small as possible. However, with evenly spaced x values and a very wide range of y values, we are in fact going to get into trouble very quickly. The smallest coefficient in the normal equations is 14 and the largest nearly 10^{14}, making it impossible to get much accuracy. In single precision on an IBM 360, the fitted curve was:

$$y = 7434.164 - 10135.40x + 4422.734x^2 - 856.6970x^3$$
$$+ 85.02283x^4 - 2.888804x^5 + 1.070349x^6$$

This is, of course, very different from the polynomial used to generate the data points. If the values of x at the 14 points used in fitting the curve are substituted into the polynomial just given, the deviations range from 48 to 886, which is clearly unacceptable in almost all applications.

The double precision fit was:

$$y = 47.12713 + 8.562260x + 5.066897x^2 + 3.005381x^3$$
$$+ 1.999317x^4 + 1.000023x^5 + 1.000000x^6$$

Some of these coefficients are surely not very close to the polynomial that generated the data either, but at least they are a lot closer than the single-precision results, and the deviations from the y values range from zero to a maximum of 5.7. For some applications this also might not be acceptable, but the fit is clearly a great deal better in double precision, suggesting that the problem was indeed the range of sizes of the elements in the matrix of the normal equations.

Once again our only recourse, if we wish to use polynomials of high degree (six in this case), is to use orthogonal polynomials.

In summary, regression is subject to severe numerical errors. However, if we use functions with relatively few parameters serious problems usually do not arise. Even then we have ways of improving accuracy—see, for example, (7.59) and (7.60). Of course, we must be sure that the data points are such that the chosen function actually is a reasonable approximation to the data. There is little use, for example, in trying to fit the data in Figure 7.1 with a linear function. The point is that we cannot arbitrarily decide to use a function with few parameters just to avoid numerical problems. If serious numerical problems arise, orthogonal polynomials are the only way around them.

It is also necessary to be assured that there really is some relationship between the variables being fitted. One might be able to fit a good quadratic to the relation between the frequency of power breakdowns in New York and the consumption of Coca Cola in Atlanta, but if the good fit is only a coincidence, the quadratic is of no predictive value. Likewise, if two physical variables have no inherent dependence on each other, the fact that a smooth curve can be fitted to selected data points is of no interest or value.

7.9 Case Study 12: Curve Fitting of a Stress-Strain Law

In Example 2 of Section 7.3 we discussed a cylindrical rod of high-strength steel subjected to a uniaxial load, P. As P increased, the rod lengthened and concurrently its diameter diminished. For a given load P (measured in units of 1000 pounds $= 1$ kip), the length, L, and diameter, d, were measured, both in inches. From the data we calculated the stress

$$\sigma = \frac{4P}{\pi d^2}$$

in ksi (kips per square inch) and the strain

$$\epsilon = \frac{L - L_0}{L}$$

where L_0 is the original length. L_0 is not the unstressed length, however: to avoid the possibility of slack in the experimental apparatus, a small load is applied at the outset and the length under that condition is denoted as L_0. One of the quantities that we shall develop in our subsequent analysis is the corresponding initial strain, ϵ_0.

In Table 7.4 we listed 14 data items, consisting of gradually increasing stresses and strains, corresponding to increasing loads. For those data (plotted in Figure 7.7) we obtained a linear least squares fit. When we regressed on the strain, ϵ, we obtained

$$\sigma = E\epsilon + \sigma_0 \qquad (7.61)$$

where

$$E = 27.46 \cdot 10^3 \text{ ksi} \qquad (7.62)$$
$$\sigma_0 = 6.987 \text{ ksi} \qquad (7.63)$$

When we regressed on the stress, σ, on the other hand,

$$\epsilon = \left(\frac{1}{E}\right)\sigma + \epsilon_0$$

where

$$E = 27.82 \cdot 10^3 \text{ ksi}$$
$$\epsilon_0 = -0.00023$$

If we continue to increase the load beyond the values shown so far, the stress-strain relationship ceases to be linear. The first 14 data points lie in the region of the stress-strain curve where this material behaves *elastically.* In such an elastic region, when the stress is removed, the rod returns to its initial length. In other words, it "springs back," without any residual effects of having been stressed. (We are ignoring fatigue.) However, there comes a point beyond which the material cannot recover its initial length when the stress is removed: It has been permanently stretched. This behavior is called *plastic.* Figure 7.10 shows the complete stress-strain curve for our experiment, where we see that after the first 14 or 15 points the form of the curve changes dramatically. After a transition region where the relationship is an actual curve, we reach another region that is approximately linear, but with a very different slope. The positive slope in the plastic region indicates that strain hardening is taking place.

(This curve is shown in the form that is customary in mechanics. In what follows we shall be regressing on stress as the independent variable, in which case we would ordinarily plot the curve the other way. The analysis is the same, of course.)

Stress-strain curves such as the one indicated by Figure 7.10 may be described by a Romberg-Osgood law,[10] which may be written

$$\epsilon = \frac{\sigma}{E}\left[1 + A\left(\frac{\sigma}{\sigma_y}\right)^{n-1}\right] + \epsilon_0 \qquad (7.64)$$

where, in general, A, n, E, σ_y, and ϵ_0 are constants to be determined.

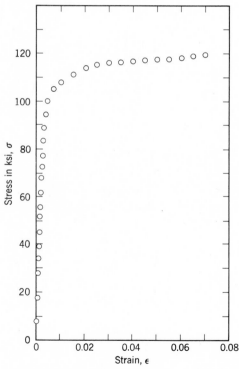

Figure 7.10. *A plot of the experimental results of a stress-strain test for a certain high-strength steel, to which a curve is to be fitted.*

[10]See, for example, Archie Higdon, Edward H. Ohlsen, William B. Stiles, and John A. Weese, *Mechanics of Materials,* 2d ed., Wiley, 1967, p. 63.

Now (7.64) is of the form

$$y = ax^b + cx + d$$

This is somewhat more complicated than the form given in (7.51) at the close of Section 7.6. We noted there that there was no standard way to perform a regression with such an equation. However, there are some "tricks" we can employ here to handle this problem.

To begin, E in (7.64) is Young's modulus. We have already estimated the value of E by performing a linear regression of σ on ϵ for the first 14 data points. The value of E is given in (7.62).

Next notice that $\epsilon = \epsilon_0$ when the stress is zero in (7.64). From our linear regression of stress on strain we can estimate ϵ_0. In particular, setting $\sigma = 0$ in (7.61) and using (7.62) and (7.63)

$$\epsilon_0 = -\frac{\sigma_0}{E} = -0.254 \cdot 10^{-3}$$

Now suppose we perform another linear regression of σ on ϵ, this time using the last 11 data points. These points appear to behave quite linearly. The intersection of the two lines obtained from the two linear regressions is an estimate of the *yield stress*, represented by the parameter σ_y in (7.64).

Thus from two linear regressions we can obtain estimates of E, ϵ_0, and σ_y. Now we rewrite (7.64) as

$$\left(\epsilon - \epsilon_0 - \frac{\sigma}{E}\right)\frac{E}{\sigma_y} = A\left(\frac{\sigma}{\sigma_y}\right)^n$$

and let

$$q = \left(\epsilon - \epsilon_0 - \frac{\sigma}{E}\right)\frac{E}{\sigma_y} \tag{7.65}$$

Then the Romberg-Osgood law is

$$q = A\left(\frac{\sigma}{\sigma_y}\right)^n \tag{7.66}$$

Equation (7.66) is a geometric curve of the type shown in (7.40) of Section 7.6. There we took logarithms of both sides to linearize the equation. We follow that strategy here, so that

$$\log q = \log A + n \log\left(\frac{\sigma}{\sigma_y}\right)$$

The only unknown quantities now are $\log A$ and n.

From (7.15) and (7.16) we can, after a little algebra, arrive at the following expressions for $\log A$ and n

$$\log A = \frac{\sum[\log(q_i)]\sum\left[\log\left(\frac{\sigma_i}{\sigma_y}\right)\right]^2 - \sum\left[\log\left(\frac{\sigma_i}{\sigma_y}\right)\right]\sum\left[\log(q_i)\log\left(\frac{\sigma_i}{\sigma_y}\right)\right]}{m\sum\left[\log\left(\frac{\sigma_i}{\sigma_y}\right)\right]^2 - \left[\sum\log\left(\frac{\sigma_i}{\sigma_y}\right)\right]^2}$$

$$\tag{7.67}$$

$$n = \frac{m \sum \left[\log(q_i) \log \left(\frac{\sigma_i}{\sigma_y} \right) \right] - \sum \left[\log \left(\frac{\sigma_i}{\sigma_y} \right) \right] \sum [\log(q_i)]}{m \sum \left[\log \left(\frac{\sigma_i}{\sigma_y} \right) \right]^2 - \left[\sum \log \left(\frac{\sigma_i}{\sigma_y} \right) \right]^2} \qquad (7.68)$$

where

$$q_i = \left(\epsilon_i - \epsilon_0 - \frac{\sigma_i}{E} \right) \frac{E}{\sigma_y} \qquad (7.69)$$

We can, finally, compute A itself from

$$A = e^{\log A} \qquad (7.70)$$

However, we must use some care in selecting the points to be used in the nonlinear regression. First we notice that by taking logarithms we are biasing the results in favor of points with small values of ϵ and σ. Thus it would seem wise to eliminate some or all of the points with small stresses and strains. Secondly, we notice that some of the points used for the first linear regression (the first 14 points) will produce negative values for q_i in (7.69). In particular, points that lie above the regression line will produce $q_i < 0$. When we try to compute $\log(q_i)$ as required in (7.67) and (7.68), we run into problems.

In addition to these numerical problems there are physical reasons for avoiding points with small stresses and strains. We shall not go into the details of these reasons but shall merely point out that the linear regression given by (7.61) through (7.63) is usually preferable to the nonlinear least squares solution when the material is in the elastic region.

All of these considerations lead us to ignore the points used in the elastic linear regression (first 14 points) in the computations in (7.67) through (7.69). Thus we start with point 15 and use the last 16 points in the computation. (Exercise 27 will ask you to redo the calculation using the last 15 and the last 17 points and compare the results.) The sums, therefore, extend from 15 to 30 and $m = 16$.

In summary, then, we have a four-stage strategy:

1. Using the first 14 points, perform a least squares linear curve fit regression on ϵ. This produces E and σ_0 in (7.61)

$$\sigma = E\epsilon + \sigma_0$$

and ϵ_0 from

$$\epsilon_0 = -\frac{\sigma_0}{E} \qquad (7.71)$$

2. Using the last 11 points, perform a least squares linear curve fit regressing on ϵ. This produces

$$\sigma = E_p \epsilon + \sigma_p \qquad (7.72)$$

The subscript p denotes the plastic region.

3. Determine the value of σ at which (7.61) and (7.72) intersect. This is the yield stress, σ_y, which is given by

$$\sigma_y = \frac{E\sigma_p + E_p\sigma_0}{E - E_p} \tag{7.73}$$

4. Using E, σ_y, and ϵ_0 and the last 16 points evaluate A and n from (7.67) through (7.70).

The data points are given in Table 7.6.

The values of A, n, E, σ_y, and ϵ_0 found by this four-stage process may now be used in (7.64) to compute the strain, given the stress. It turns out that we get a reasonably good fit for the *entire* curve, not just the last 16 points used in the fourth step. This good fortune is the result of the form of (7.64) and the fact that n turns out to be a fairly large number, about 22 in our case. That being true, the term

$$A\left(\frac{\sigma}{\sigma_y}\right)^{n-1}$$

in (7.64) is negligible for values of σ appreciably less than σ_y, in which case the formula becomes simply

$$\epsilon = \frac{\sigma}{E} + \epsilon_0$$

which is just Hooke's law, describing the elastic region in terms of E and ϵ_0.

A program to carry out Step 4 is shown in Figure 7.11. We omit reproducing the minor changes to the program of Case Study 11 that were used to get the linear fits and to evaluate the formula of step three. The program is entirely straightforward, consisting mostly of summations to get the quantities required in (7.67) and (7.68).

Table 7.6

Data Point	Stress, ksi	Strain $\times 10^3$	Data Point	Stress, ksi	Strain $\times 10^3$
1	8.37	0.15	19	111.4	15.40
2	17.9	0.52	20	114.0	20.30
3	27.8	0.76	21	115.4	25.00
4	34.2	1.01	22	116.0	30.00
5	38.8	1.12	23	116.3	35.00
6	44.8	1.42	24	117.0	40.00
7	51.3	1.52	25	117.2	45.00
8	55.5	1.66	26	117.4	50.00
9	61.3	1.86	27	117.7	55.00
10	67.5	2.08	28	118.0	60.00
11	72.1	2.27	29	119.1	65.00
12	76.9	2.56	30	119.5	70.00
13	83.5	2.86			
14	88.9	3.19			
15	94.2	3.74			
16	100.0	4.55			
17	105.3	7.27			
18	108.3	10.10			

```
C CASE STUDY 12
C LEAST SQUARES CURVE FIT OF STRESS-STRAIN DATA
C
C THIS PROGRAM FITS THE ROMBERG-OSGOOD LAW AFTER
C   THE LINEAR PORTIONS HAVE BEEN FITTED USING
C   A MODIFIED VERSION OF THE PROGRAM OF CASE STUDY 11
C
C SUGGESTED BY PROF. JOHN A. WEESE, DENVER UNIVERSITY
C
      REAL M, N
C CLEAR THE SUMMING VARIABLES
      SUM1 = 0.0
      SUM2 = 0.0
      SUM3 = 0.0
      SUM4 = 0.0
C READ THE VALUE OF YOUNG'S MODULUS, EY, THE YIELD STRESS, SY,
C   AND THE INITIAL STRAIN, E0
      READ (5, 89) EY, SY, E0
89    FORMAT (3F10.0)
C SET TO COUNT DATA POINTS, FOR INPUT FLEXIBILITY
      M = 0.0
C INPUT LOOP
12    READ (5, 89, END=123) S, E
C FORM SUMS
      ALOGQ = ALOG((E - E0 - S/EY) * (EY/SY))
      ALOGS = ALOG(S/SY)
      SUM1 = SUM1 + ALOGQ
      SUM2 = SUM2 + ALOGS**2
      SUM3 = SUM3 + ALOGS
      SUM4 = SUM4 + ALOGQ * ALOGS
      M = M + 1.0
      GO TO 12
C EXIT FROM INPUT LOOP - COMPUTE PARAMETERS
123   DENOM = M * SUM2 - SUM3**2
      ALOGA = (SUM1*SUM2 - SUM3*SUM4) / DENOM
      A = EXP(ALOGA)
      N = (M*SUM4 - SUM3*SUM1) / DENOM
C WRITE RESULTS
      WRITE (6, 34) A, N
34    FORMAT (1X, 2F12.5)
      STOP
      END
```

Figure 7.11. *A program to carry out the fitting of a geometric curve to a portion of the data plotted in Figure 7.10.*

Summarizing the results of the entire process:
1. From the linear fit of the elastic region:

$$E = 27.46 \cdot 10^3 \text{ ksi}$$
$$\sigma_0 = 6.987 \text{ ksi}$$
$$\epsilon_0 = -0.000254$$

2. From the linear fit of the plastic region we get the parameters needed in the next step.

$$E_p = 0.0938 \cdot 10^3 \text{ ksi}$$
$$\sigma_p = 112.83 \text{ ksi}$$

3. From the intersection of the two linear fits, using (7.73):

$$\sigma_y = 113.1933 \text{ ksi}$$

4. From the Romberg-Osgood fit:

$$A = 4.219$$
$$n = 22.886$$

Looking at the details of the data given in Table 7.6, we should not expect the deviations to be uniformly small; the measurements are evidently not too precise, and the behavior in the plastic region is such that a small increase in stress produces a relatively large increase in strain. If it were necessary to produce a fit that was a good deal more accurate than this one, it would be necessary to run the experiment more times to provide more data points for the fitting process. The statistical fluctuations caused by the nature of the experiment would then tend to be somewhat smoothed out.

Naturally, the "tricks" employed here will not apply in just this way to other practical curve-fitting problems. We have presented this case study, not as a cookbook recipe that can be followed directly, but to show the *kinds* of things one can do.

Bibliographic Notes

An elegant and somewhat heuristic justification for the use of least squares may be found in Section 3.1 of Stiefel [9]. More detailed and more rigorous justifications are given in Section 8.19 of Carnahan et al. [20], Chapter 14 of Scarborough [17], and the footnote on page 165 of Arden and Astill [5].

Linear regression is discussed by Hamming [6] in Section 10.2, and in Barrodale et al. [1] in Section 4, Chapter 7. The latter is quite elementary and includes a flow chart. The notion of regressing upon either of the two variables, however, is not discussed in most texts. One notable exception is Spiegel [see below].

Quadratic regression is discussed on pages 166–168 of Arden and Astill [5] and in Section 8.16 of Stark [3]. The more general case of polynomial regression is discussed in most books. Some references are: Section 6.3 of Ralston [19], Section 10.3 of Hamming [6], Section 145 of Scarborough [17], pages 169–171 of Arden and Astill [5], and Section 7.1 of McCalla [8]. The last two also contain flow charts and Fortran programs. Carnahan et al. [20] has not only a flow chart and Fortran program but also a computer generated plot of the second- and fourth-order regression equations in Example 8.5.

Nonlinear functions are discussed in much the same way as they are in this text by McCalla [8] in Section 7.2. Hamming [6] discusses an algorithm to solve the nonlinear problem directly in Section 10.6. Both Scarborough [17] in Section 147 and Pennington [10] in Sections 11.42 and 11.43 start with a first approximation to the parameters of a nonlinear equation and obtain corrections to these approximations through linearization (see also Exercises 40 and 41 of this text).

Fourier approximations are discussed by Ralston [19] in Section 6.8, Scarborough [17] in Chapter 17, Nielsen [2] on pages 313–320, and Arden and Astill [5] on pages 188–195. The last of these includes a Fortran program.

Multiple regression is discussed quite concisely by Carnahan et al. [20] in Section 8.20. Ralston and Wilf [25] contains a discussion that includes a flow chart and estimates of the errors in the regression coefficients in Chapter 17 of Volume 1. Numerical problems in least squares computations are covered quite well by Arden and Astill [5] on pages 172–174.

Smoothing of data is discussed by Hildebrand [18] in Section 7.13, Ralston [19] in Section 6.7, and Scarborough [17] in Section 149a. (See also Exercise 29 of the present text.)

An elementary and quite readable general reference to least squares is:

Murray R. Spiegel, *Theory and Problems in Statistics*, Chapter 13, "Schaum's Outline Series" (New York: McGraw-Hill, 1961)

An elementary discussion that covers linear regression, parabolic regression, multiple linear regression, nonlinear equations that can be reduced to linear form, and time series forecasts. Does *not* contain flow charts or computer programs. This one chapter alone contains 42 solved exercises.

Exercises

*1 Given two data points

x	y
2	3
3	2

find the equations of *three* lines such that the sum of the deviations (7.2) is zero. All three lines pass through one point. What point is that?

2 Show that (7.15) and (7.16) comprise a solution of the normal equations (7.13) and (7.14).

*3 Show that

$$m \sum x_i^2 - \left(\sum x_i \right)^2 = 0$$

only if all the x_i are equal.

Hint: Compute

$$m \sum (x_i - \mu)^2$$

where μ is the mean of the x_i, that is,

$$\mu = \frac{\sum x_i}{m}$$

4 Show that if $m = 2$, then (7.15) and (7.16) produce the line passing through the two points (x_1, y_1) and (x_2, y_2).

*5 Show that the linear regression line of y on x passes through the point that is the mean of the x and y values, that is,

$$\left(\frac{\sum x_i}{m}, \frac{\sum y_i}{m} \right)$$

6 Show that the linear regression line of x on y passes through the point that is the mean of the x and y values (see Exercise 5).

7 Compute the slopes, x intercepts and y intercepts of the linear regressions of y on x and of x on y for the data shown in Table 7.1. These regressions are given in (7.19) and (7.27). Compute the percentage change in the slopes and the intercepts.

8 Show that the method of least squares applied to the relation

$$y = a$$

yields an expression for the arithmetic mean of the y values.

9 Assume that the specific heat of water is a quadratic function of temperature. Using the data in Table 7.5, compute the least squares quadratic approximation. Compare your results with those in Case Study 11.

10 Show that if we try to fit a quadratic to two points the normal equations will have an infinite number of solutions, corresponding to the fact that an infinite number of quadratics can be passed through two points.

*11 Suppose that the x values in a data set are just the integers from 1 to N. Devise simplified normal equations for fitting a straight line to the points, in which the left-hand sides require no summations.

12 Fit the following data

x	y
−8	30
−6	10
−4	9
−2	6
0	5
2	4
4	4

a. Using the form (7.38).
b. Using the form (7.39).
c. Compare the results of (a) and (b).

13 Using (7.39) find a and b that fit the data

x	y
0	3
0.5	4
1	6
1.5	9
2	12
2.5	17
3	24
3.5	33
4	48

Answer should be "close" to $y = 3 \cdot 2^x$.

14 Using (7.40) find a and b that fit the data

x	y
-1	5
0	0
1	-4
2	-30
3	-110

Answer should be "close" to $y = -4x^3$.

15 Using the normal equations (7.50) with $\omega = 1$ find a_0, a_1, a_2, b_1, and b_2 that fit the following data:

x	y
0	2.
0.3	3.8
0.6	5.1
0.9	5.4
1.2	4.5
1.5	2.5
1.8	0.1
2.1	-2.1
2.4	-3.5
2.7	-3.8
3.0	-2.8
3.3	-1.0
3.6	1.0
3.9	2.5
4.2	3.1
4.5	2.7
4.8	1.6
5.1	0.4
5.4	-0.5
5.7	-0.5
6.0	0.5

Answer should be "close" to

$$y = 1 + 2 \cos x - \cos 2x + 3 \sin 2x$$

16a Derive the three normal equations for the least squares solution of

$$y = a_0 + a_1 \cos x + b_1 \sin x$$

This is a special case of (7.42) with $n = 1$ and $\omega = 1$.

b Find the coefficients a_0, a_1, and b_1 from part (a) that best fit the following data, including that at top of next page:

x	y
0	3.0
0.4	2.1
0.8	1.3
1.2	0.5

x	y
1.6	0
2.0	−0.2
2.4	0
2.8	0.3
3.2	1.1
3.6	2.0
4.0	2.9
4.4	3.5
4.8	4.0
5.2	4.2
5.6	4.0
6.0	3.5

Answer should be "close" to

$$y = 2 + \cos x - 2 \sin x$$

*17 Suppose we wish to find a and b so that (7.7) is a minimum where

$$y = \sqrt{a + bx}$$

a. Show how this approximation can be linearized.
b. Write the normal equations for the solution.

18 Find normal equations for fitting a curve of the form

$$y = y_0 e^{-h^2 x^2}$$

19 Find normal equations for fitting a curve of the form

$$y = a + \frac{b}{x} + \frac{c}{x^2}$$

It is possible to choose the quantities to be summed so that the normal equations are linear.

20 Find normal equations for fitting a curve of the form

$$y = a\sqrt{1 + bx^2}$$

Can you solve them?

*21 Find the normal equations for the multiple linear regression of x on y and z where

$$x = ay + bz + c$$

22a Using the 42 data points in Table 6.1 of Chapter 6, find the linear regression plane of equivalent still air temperature, S, on the actual temperature, T, and the wind velocity, V.
b Use the multiple linear regression equation obtained in part (a) to estimate the still air temperature equivalent to the following:

Temperature, °F	Wind Velocity (mph)
5	15
20	20
15	20

Compare these with the results obtained in Case Study 10 (Section 6.13) and with the exact results, which are $-25°$, $-9°$, and $-17°$, respectively.

23a Using the 25 data points in Exercise 23 of Chapter 6, find the linear regression plane of the ammonia equilibrium constant, K_p, on temperature, T, and pressure, p.

b Use the multiple linear regression line obtained in part (a) to compute K_p for $T = 473$ °C and $p = 217$ atm. Compare the result with the result of Exercise 23 of Chapter 6.

*24 Write a program to compute the coefficients on the left side of the normal equations (7.37) for $n = 5$ when $x_i = i/m$ for any m. Run the program for $m = 10$, 100, and 1000.

25 Write a program to compute the coefficients on the left side of the normal equations (7.37) for $n = 10$ where $x_i = i/m$ for any m. Run the program for $m = 10$, 100, and 1000.

26 Define

$$\Omega = \frac{\sum (y_i - \bar{y}_i)^2}{n - m}$$

where y_i = an experimental value
$\bar{y}_i$ = a value computed from a least squares fit
n = the number of x-y pairs
m = the number of parameters in the relation

Then the *Gauss criterion of goodness of fit* states that the best fit is the one that minimizes Ω.

Given the following data:

x	y
0	0
1	20
2	40
3	50
4	70

By the Gauss criterion, does a linear or a quadratic relation give a better fit?

*27 Using the values for E, σ_y and ϵ_0 given in Case Study 12, that is, $E = 27.46 \cdot 10^3$ ksi, $\sigma_y = 113.1933$ ksi, $\epsilon_0 = -0.254 \cdot 10^{-3}$:

a. Estimate A and n in (7.64) by using the 15 points numbered 16 through 30 in (7.67) to (7.70).

b. Estimate A and n in (7.64) by using the 17 points numbered 14 through 30 in (7.67) to (7.70).

*28 Use the first 15 data points of Table 7.6 to perform a linear regression to estimate E and σ_0. Use the last 12 data points (numbered 19 through 30) to perform a linear regression to estimate E_p and σ_1. Then use the last 15 points for the nonlinear regression to estimate A and n.

29 Rather than finding a least square curve that fits a set of experimental data, it is sometimes preferable to *smooth* the data to reduce the effect of statistical errors. One common method of smoothing is to replace each piece of data with the average of that piece of data itself and its two neighbors.

Suppose again we have a table of values $x_1, \ldots, x_m$ and corresponding values $y_1, \ldots, y_m$ where the y_i contain statistical errors. Then we let

$$\bar{y}_i = \frac{y_{i-1} + y_i + y_{i+1}}{3}$$

for $i = 2, \ldots, m - 1$. At the end points

$$\bar{y}_1 = \frac{y_1 + y_2}{2}$$

$$\bar{y}_m = \frac{y_{m-1} + y_m}{2}$$

We now have values $\bar{y}_1, \bar{y}_2, \ldots, \bar{y}_m$, which correspond to $x_1, x_2, \ldots, x_m$.

a. Use this smoothing technique on the specific heat data given in Table 7.5.

b. Use quadratic interpolation on this smoothed table to approximate the specific heat, c_p, for a temperature of 42 °C.

c. Compare the results of part (b) with the specific heat calculated from the quadratic regression given in Section 7.5 for $T = 42$.

30a Use the smoothing technique described in Exercise 29 on both the stress and the strain in Table 7.4.

b Perform a linear regression of stress on strain using the smoothed table. Compare the result with

$$\sigma = (27.46 \cdot 10^3)\epsilon + 6.987$$

given in Example 2 of Section 7.3.

c Graph the line obtained in part (b) together with the original data (Figure 7.7) and the least squares result given by the equations in part (b).

31 The following table lists the number of motor vehicle accidents in the United States in some years from 1950 to 1968.

Year	No. of Accidents (in thousands)	Accidents per 10,000 Vehicles
1950	8,300	1,688
1955	9,900	1,577
1960	10,400	1,397
1965	13,200	1,439
1966	13,600	1,418
1967	13,700	1,385
1968	14,600	1,415

Source: *Accident Facts*, National Safety Council, Chicago, Ill., annual report.

a. Compute the linear regression of the number of accidents on time. Use it to predict the number of accidents in 1980. This is called a *time series* analysis since it is a regression on time and is used for forecasting into the future.

b. Compute a quadratic regression of the number of accidents per 10,000 vehicles on time. Use this to predict the number of accidents per 10,000 vehicles in 1980.

c. Compare the results of part (a) and (b). Which would you be more likely to believe?

In any time-series work involving contemporary dates, it is a good idea to subtract off the starting date before forming the summations; this will materially reduce roundoff problems. For instance, instead of using x values of 1950, 1955, 1960, 1965, 1966, and 1967, we would use 0, 5, 10, 15, 16, and 17.

32 The following table shows the total value (in millions of dollars) of new construction put in place from 1950 to 1969 in the United States.

Year	Value of New Construction (in $ million)
1950	33,525
1955	46,519
1960	53,941
1965	72,319
1966	75,120
1967	76,160
1968	84,690
1969	90,866

Source: *Construction Reports,* Department of Commerce, Bureau of the Census, Series C30.

a. Perform a linear regression of the value of new construction on time. Use the result to predict the value of new construction in 1975, 1985, and 1995.

b. The data given above exclude Alaska and Hawaii prior to 1960. What could you do to obtain a predictive equation (linear time series) that is not influenced by this bias? (Assume there is no way to collect more data.)

33 The table at the top of the next page lists the indices of industrial production in the United States for all manufacturing, machinery, printing and publishing, and foods and beverages. In all cases the indices are based on a 1957–1959 average, that is, the average production from 1957 to 1959 is set equal to 100.

a. By plotting the data decide which type of regression would fit each of these, that is, polynomial (if so what degree), exponential, geometric, and so forth.

b. From your conclusion in part (a) perform a regression of the all manufacturing index on time using the appropriate approxi-

Year	All Manufacturing	Machinery	Printing and Publishing	Foods and Beverages
1950	76	73	79	83
1955	97	97	93	94
1960	109	111	110	107
1965	145	161	130	124
1966	159	184	142	129
1967	160	183	149	133
1968	167	184	150	136
1969	174	196	156	141

Source: *Industrial Production, 1957–59 Base,* Board of Governors of the Federal Reserve System.

mations. Use your result to predict the index of manufacturing in 1975 and 1985.

c. Same as (b) for machinery.

d. Same as (b) for printing and publishing.

e. Same as (b) for foods and beverages.

34 The table below lists the Gross National Product (GNP) in constant dollars and current dollars. Constant dollars represent the GNP based on the value of the dollar in 1958. Current dollars are simply the dollar value with no adjustment for inflation.

Year	GNP (Current Dollars, $ millions)	GNP (Constant Dollars, $ millions)
1950	284.8	355.3
1955	398.0	438.0
1960	503.7	487.7
1965	684.9	617.8
1966	749.9	658.1
1967	793.5	674.6
1968	865.7	707.6

Source: Executive Office of the President, Council of Economic Advisors.

a. Find a geometric regression (7.40) of each of the GNPs on time.

b. Use the results of part (a) to predict the two GNPs in 1975 and 1985.

c. What do the results of part (b) tell you about the rate of inflation in 1975 and 1985?

35 The table on the next page lists the purchasing power of the U.S. dollar based on a 1957–1959 average, that is, the average purchasing price of a dollar averaged over 1957 to 1959 is $1.00.

Year	Purchasing Power (based on consumer prices)
1940	$2.048
1945	$1.595
1950	$1.194
1955	$1.071
1960	$0.971
1965	$0.910
1969	$0.782

Source: Department of Labor, Bureau of Labor Statistics.

a. Find an exponential regression (7.39) of the purchasing power on time.

b. Use the results of part (a) to predict the purchasing power of the dollar in 1975 and 1985.

c. Compare what part (b) tells you about inflation with the results of part (c) of Exercise 34.

36 The following table lists the total water usage in the United States in billions of gallons per day.

Year	Water Use
1930	110.5
1940	136.43
1950	202.70
1960	322.90
1970	411.20

Source: *Water Use in the United States, 1900–1980,* Department of Commerce, Business and Defense Services Administration.

a. Find an exponential regression (7.39) of the water consumption on time.

b. Use the results of part (a) to predict the water consumption in 1975 and 1980.

c. Compare your results of the Department of Commerce's predictions of 449.7 for 1975 and 494.1 for 1980. Explain any differences.

37 One model of population growth, due to Verhulst, is that the population, P, grows in time according to the differential equation

$$\frac{dP}{dt} = (A - BP)P$$

The parameter A is the geometric rate of growth for relatively small populations. However, as the population grows, there is a retarding or braking effect caused by consumption of the food supply, pollution of the environment, and so forth. This braking effect is represented by the parameter B.

The solution of this differential equation is

$$P = \frac{A}{B + Ce^{-At}}$$

where C is the constant of integration and can be determined from the initial population at $t = 0$. To find the parameters A and B requires a regression of the type that we indicated at the close of Section 7.6 that could not be linearized. However, suppose we approximate dP/dt by

$$\frac{dP}{dt} \cong \frac{P_{k+1} - P_k}{\Delta t}$$

where P_k is the population at the end of the kth time period, that is,

$$P_k = P(k\Delta t)$$

Then the differential equation becomes

$$P_{k+1} = (1 + A\Delta t - BP_k\Delta t)P_k \qquad \text{(i)}$$

a. Using the United States census data for the 48 contiguous states given below for P_k and $\Delta t = 10$, find a linear regression of P_{k+1} on P_k.

Year	Census (in millions)
1890	62.947
1900	75.995
1910	91.972
1920	105.711
1930	122.775
1940	131.669
1950	150.697
1960	178.474
1970	199.308

Source: Department of Commerce, Bureau of the Census.

b. Use the values of A and B found in part (a) and (i), to predict the population of the United States in 1980 and 1990.

c. Use A and B and (i) to predict the population of the United States in 2550, 2600, and 2650. What do you conclude from the results?

38 The table on the following page lists the data for the critical temperature, T_c (°K) and critical pressure P_c (atm) for eight organic compounds.

Find the coefficients of the least squares fit of a quadratic, giving T_c as a function of P_c. Do the same for a seventh-degree polynomial, which will require the use of double precision or some other technique to get numerically meaningful results. Then use these fits to predict T_c for methyl ether ($P_c = 53$). The actual experimental value is 400.1. Discuss your results.

*39 Suppose, as suggested in Section 7.3, that both x and y contain inherent statistical errors, and that we do not wish to regress upon just one of the variables but upon both of them. We choose then

Compound	T_c	P_c
Acetaldehyde	461	44
Acetic acid	594.8	57.1
Acetone	508.7	46.6
Butanol	560	48.4
Ethyl alcohol	516	63
Ethyl ether	467	35.6
Ethylene oxide	369	71
Methyl alcohol	513.2	78.5

not to minimize the sum of the squares of the vertical distance $(y_i - \bar{y}_i)^2$ nor the squares of the horizontal distance $(x_i - \bar{x}_i)^2$. Rather we minimize the sum of the squares of the distances *perpendicular* to the least squares line. Those distances are shown in Figure 7.12 where the heavy dots are the data points.

a. Show that the perpendicular distance from the point (x_i, y_i) to the line whose algebraic representation is

$$Ax_i + By = 1$$

is given by

$$d_i = \frac{Ax_i + By_i - 1}{\sqrt{A^2 + B^2}}$$

b. Show that the normal equations that A and B must satisfy if Σd_i^2 is to be a minimum are

$$\left(\sum x_i^2\right) AB^2 + \left(\sum x_i y_i\right) B(B^2 - A^2) - \left(\sum y_i^2\right) AB^2$$
$$+ \left(\sum x_i\right)(A^2 - B^2) + \left(\sum y_i\right) 2AB = mA \tag{a}$$

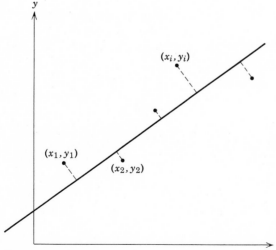

Figure 7.12. *Geometrical representation of the curve fitting technique of Exercise 39.*

$$-\left(\sum x_i\right)^2 A^2 B + \left(\sum x_i y_i\right) A(A^2 - B^2) + \left(\sum y_i^2\right) A^2 B$$

$$+ \left(\sum x_i\right) 2AB + \left(\sum y_i\right)(B^2 - A^2) = mB \qquad \text{(b)}$$

Notice that these are highly nonlinear.

c. By multiplying (a) by A and (b) by B and adding the two resulting equations, show that A and B must satisfy the *linear* equation

$$\left(\sum x_i\right) A + \left(\sum y_i\right) B = m \qquad \text{(c)}$$

d. Outline an algorithm for computing A and B from these equations.

*40 Suppose we wish to perform a regression of y on x where the relationship between the two variables is given by (7.51), that is,

$$y = ax^b + c$$

As we noted in Section 7.6, this cannot be linearized. However, suppose we have obtained "good" approximations to a, b, and c, for example, by plotting the points and "guessing" at the values. Call these approximations a_0, b_0, and c_0. By "good" we mean we can write

$$a = a_0 + \alpha$$
$$b = b_0 + \beta$$
$$c = c_0 + \gamma$$

where α, β, and γ are very small compared with a_0, b_0, and c_0. Thus we neglect terms in the squares and products of α, β, and γ. The deviations are

$$d_i = y_i - (a_0 + \alpha)x^{(b_0 + \beta)} - c_0 - \gamma$$

Using the fact that terms in α^2, β^2, γ^2, and so on, can be neglected, determine linear normal equations for choosing α, β, and γ which minimize Σd_i^2.

[Hint: Use Taylor's theorem to write

$$x^\beta = x^0 + (x \log x)\beta + \text{terms in } \beta^2, \beta^3, \ldots$$

so

$$x^\beta \cong 1 + (x \log x)\beta]$$

41 Suppose we wish to perform a regression of y on x where the relationship between the two variables is

$$y = ab^x + c$$

As noted in Section 7.6, this cannot be linearized. Suppose, however, we have "good" approximations a_0, b_0, and c_0 to a, b, and c in the following sense:

$$a = a_0 + \alpha$$
$$b = b_0 + \beta$$
$$c = c_0 + \gamma$$

where α, β, and γ are small, that is, we can neglect squares and products of α, β, and γ.

Show that the values of α, β, and γ which minimize the deviations of the y_i from $ab^{x_i} + c$ satisfy the normal equations

$$\left(\sum b_0^{2x_i}\right)\alpha + \left(\sum x_i b_0^{2x_i-1}\right)\beta + \left(\sum b_0^{x_i}\right)\gamma = \sum r_i b_0^{x_i}$$

$$\left(\sum x_i b_0^{2x_i-1}\right)\alpha + \left(\sum x_i^2 b_0^{2x_i-2}\right)\beta + \left(\sum x_i b_0^{x_i-1}\right)\gamma = \sum r_i x_i b_0^{x_i-1}$$

$$\left(\sum b_0^{x_i}\right)\alpha + \left(\sum x_i b_0^{x_i-1}\right)\beta + m\gamma = \sum r_i$$

where

$$r_i = y_i - (a_0 b_0^{x_i} + c_0)$$

42 Suppose we use the quadratic

$$y = 2 + 4x + x^2$$

to generate the data points

x	y
1	7
2	14
3	23
4	34
5	47

When an IBM System 360 was used to fit various polynomials to these points, using single precision, the results were

$$y = 2.000199 + 3.999820x + 1.000031x^2$$
$$y = 2.000087 + 3.999869x + 1.000054x^2 - 0.000006x^3$$
$$y = 1.943557 + 4.105430x + 0.936406x^2 + 0.015268x^3 - 0.001264x^4$$
$$y = 3.613389 + 0.406432x + 3.868546x^2 - 1.054154x^3$$
$$+ 0.181423x^4 - 0.011833x^5$$

Write a program to evaluate these polynomials at the five values of x and at some intermediate points, to show that, although some of the coefficients are rather different from those of the polynomial that generated the data, the deviations at the given x values are not too bad. Comment on the fact that, although there are infinitely many fifth-degree polynomials that pass through five points, which should lead to a breakdown in solving the normal equations by Gaussian elimination, we seem to have arrived at a fairly respectable result.

Write a program to do the fits in double precision and compare the results. If you are using a machine with a word structure different from that of the 360, you will discover that even in single precision the results will be quite different from those stated, showing the great dependence of roundoff problems on the details of word length and floating point normalization methods.

8 Ordinary Differential Equations

Equations involving the derivative of a function of one variable occur in many branches of applied mathematics. Broadly speaking, any situation that concerns the rate of change of one variable with respect to another leads to a differential equation, and such situations are clearly very common.

For a simple example, suppose that the rate of change of y with respect to x is proportional to y:

$$\frac{dy}{dx} = y \tag{8.1}$$

(We shall often use a prime to denote differentiation and thus write this equation: $y' = y$.) Elementary techniques lead to the classical solution

$$y = ae^x$$

where a is an arbitrary constant. Different values of a lead to a family of curves, all of which satisfy the given differential equation (8.1), which is simply a statement that at each point on the curve the value of the function and the value of its derivative are equal. If in addition to the differential equation we are given a value of y for some x, the constant a can be determined. It might be specified, for instance, that the solution to (8.1) is to pass through the point $x = 0$, $y = 1$, which we would ordinarily write

$$y(0) = 1 \tag{8.2}$$

360

Then we find easily that $a = 1$ and that the particular curve from the general family is

$$y = e^x$$

Many techniques exist for finding the solutions to differential equations in terms of elementary functions or in terms of special functions, such as Bessel functions. We would not wish to minimize the importance of this basic field of mathematics, but it should nevertheless be realized that often practical problems either cannot be solved at all by the classical methods or lead to solutions that are so difficult to obtain or so cumbersome to evaluate that they are not worth the trouble. For instance, the simple-appearing equation

$$y' = x^2 + y^2$$

has no elementary solution. In a great many instances of practical work some of the coefficients or functions in a differential equation are strongly nonlinear or are given only as a tabulated set of experimental data, the latter ruling out a classical solution from the outset.

Thus, for a variety of reasons we are led to search for methods of solution that apply when the classical methods are of no help to us. We should emphasize once again, however, that the existence of problems that cannot conveniently be solved by classical methods does not mean that the modern student should overlook the classical methods. The numerical approaches we shall discuss do not relieve the analyst of the responsibility of formulating the equation properly; they do not relieve him of the responsibility of recognizing an equation that has a reasonable solution in terms of special functions, some of which are widely used; and they do not change the fact that an informed analyst can frequently improve the initial formulation of a problem. *Numerical methods are no excuse for poor analysis.*

In this chapter we shall concentrate on the methods of solving a single first-order ordinary (no partial derivatives) differential equation with one initial condition:

$$y' = f(x,y) \tag{8.3}$$
$$y(x_0) = y_0 \tag{8.4}$$

The methods we shall consider are easily generalized to handle systems of simultaneous first-order equations. (See, for instance, Case Study 13 of Section 8.14.) Moreover, higher-order equations may be reduced to a system of simultaneous first-order equations. For instance, the second-order equation

$$y'' = g(y',y,x)$$

can be rewritten

$$z' = g(z,y,x)$$
$$y' = z$$

where z is a new dependent variable defined by the second equation. These are now two simultaneous equations in y and z; their solution gives both the function and its derivative. The methods we shall study will therefore have considerably broader application than the simplicity of the fundamental equation might suggest.

Let us consider what we mean by a solution to (8.3) and (8.4) and by a numerical solution. Equation (8.3) is a relation that may be viewed as a partial definition of a curve in the x-y plane. At each point on the curve we are told the value of its derivative in terms of x and y. There will in general be a family of curves that satisfy (8.3); (8.4) specifies the particular curve that passes through a given point. For example, (8.1) leads to a family of curves, some of which are shown in Figure 8.1; (8.2) picks out the one identified in the figure.

A solution is an expression for y in terms of x. To find numerical values of the function, we simply substitute particular values of x into the expression and compute the corresponding values of y.

In broad outline a numerical solution is obtained as follows. The differential equation gives the slope of the curve at any point as a function of x and y; at the outset we know only one point through which the curve passes, namely, x_0, y_0. We therefore begin there. We compute the slope of the curve at $x = x_0$ and proceed a small distance along the corresponding tangent. If the increment in x is called h, as we shall do, we arrive at a new point $x_1 = x_0 + h$, and from the slope of the tangent, obtained from the differential equation, we get a new value of y. We call this new value y_1. Continuing in this way, we get a sequence of short line segments which, we hope, approximates sufficiently accurately the true curve that is the solution.

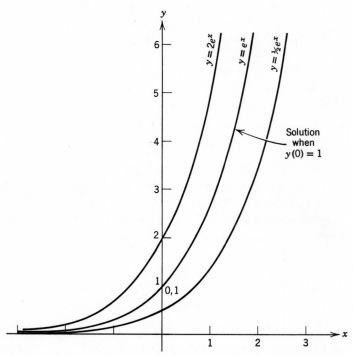

Figure 8.1. *Three members of the family of curves represented by the differential equation* $y' = y$. *The initial condition* $y(0) = 1$ *picks out a particular member of the family.*

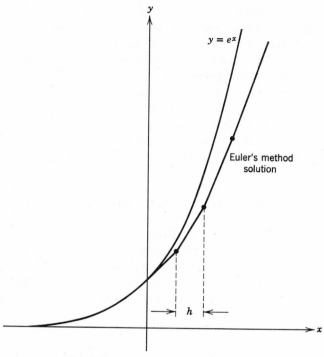

Figure 8.2. *Graphical representation of the meaning of a numerical solution of a differential equation. The process, described in the text, is essentially Euler's method.*

Obviously there are pitfalls in this simplest approach to numerical solution (which, as we shall see, is known as Euler's method). We are approximating a *curve* by a sequence of *line segments;* such a practice suggests difficulties at the outset. It can easily enough happen that the sequence of line segments deviates considerably from the true curve, as suggested in Figure 8.2. This is the problem of *stability*, to which we shall devote considerable attention.

Clearly, we must find some way to take into account the curvature of the true solution rather than simply approximating it by a sequence of line segments, as in Euler's method. We are led to two basic categories of methods.

1. One-step methods, in which we use information about the curve at one point and do not iterate the solution. A Taylor-series solution provides a fundamental method of this type; we base much of our analysis on this theoretical method, but, as we shall see, it is not usually practical. Practical techniques of this type, of which there are many, include the Runge-Kutta methods. We shall see that they are *direct* methods (no iteration), which seems to imply less effort, but they do in practical cases require more evaluations of the function. Furthermore, they have the serious disadvantage that it is difficult to estimate the error.

2. Multistep methods, in which the next point on the curve can be estimated with fewer evaluations of the function, but which require iteration to arrive at a sufficiently accurate value. Most methods of this type are called *predictor-corrector*. Offsetting the effort of the iteration and

a certain problem in getting the solution "started" is the fact that an estimate of the error is obtained as a by-product of the calculation.

As we have seen in many other situations, these contrasting methods have their strengths and weaknesses, and, as before, we shall be led to a judicious combination of the two.

There are a great many methods in both categories; the numerical solution of differential equations has received intensive study, especially in recent years. The methods we shall present will include approaches that the reader may use in solving practical problems and that will serve to introduce the basic ideas of most other current methods.

8.2 Taylor Series Solution

We begin our study with a method that theoretically provides a solution to any differential equation but is of little practical computational value. Its importance to us lies in the fact that it is a basis for evaluating and comparing the methods that are of considerable practical worth.

Suppose we have computed by some means an approximation to $y(x)$ for $x_0 \leq x \leq x_m$. Just how we can get to this point will become clear at the end of this section. In any case we use Taylor's Theorem, expanding $y(x)$ about the point $x = x_m$.

$$y(x) = y_m + y'_m(x - x_m) + \frac{y''_m}{2}(x - x_m)^2 + \cdots$$

$$+ \frac{y_m^{(j)}}{j!}(x - x_m)^j + \frac{y^{(j+1)}(\xi)}{(j + 1)!}(x - x_m)^{j+1} \quad (8.5)$$

where $y_m^{(j)}$ is the jth derivative of $y(x)$ evaluated at $x = x_m$. Recall that ξ in the last term is bounded by

$$x_m \leq \xi \leq x$$

where we have assumed $x > x_m$, although this assumption is not essential to the argument.

We can use (8.5) to approximate the solution $y(x)$ at $x = x_{m+1} = x_m + h$ by replacing x by $x_m + h$. Thus

$$y_{m+1} = y_m + hy'_m + \frac{h^2}{2}y''_m + \cdots + \frac{y_m^{(j)}}{j!}h^j + \frac{y^{(j+1)}(\xi)}{(j + 1)!}h^{j+1} \quad (8.6)$$

Generally we shall neglect the last term, thereby giving rise to a truncation error. The larger the value of j, the better the approximation will be. In any case, it is necessary to evaluate several derivatives of y. From (8.3)

$$y'_m = f(x_m, y_m) \quad (8.7)$$

Differentiating (8.3) with respect to x,

$$y'' = \frac{\partial}{\partial x}f(x,y) + f(x,y)\frac{\partial}{\partial y}f(x,y) \quad (8.8)$$

so that

$$y''_m = f_x + ff_y \quad (8.9)$$

where the letter subscripts denote partial derivatives with respect to the variable given by the subscript:

$$f_x = \frac{\partial f}{\partial x}$$

It is assumed that all functions and derivatives are evaluated at $x = x_m$, $y = y_m$.

Suppose we let $j = 2$ in (8.6). Then we get

$$y_{m+1} = y_m + hy'_m + \frac{h^2}{2} y''_m + \frac{y'''(\xi)}{6} h^3$$

From (8.7) and (8.9)

$$y_{m+1} = y_m + h\left[f + \frac{h}{2}(f_x + ff_y) \right] + \frac{y'''(\xi)}{6} h^3 \tag{8.10}$$

We neglect the last term and compute y_{m+1} from

$$y_{m+1} = y_m + h\left[f + \frac{h}{2}(f_x + ff_y) \right] \tag{8.11}$$

The truncation error is

$$e_t = \frac{y'''(\xi)}{6} h^3$$

If the third derivative is reasonably constant, we can say

$$e_t = \cong Kh^3 \tag{8.12}$$

where K is some constant.

It should now be clear how we can construct an approximate solution to (8.3) and (8.4). Letting $m = 0$ in (8.11) we compute y_1. This approximates the solution at $x = x_0 + h$. Then with this value of y_1 and $x_1 = x_0 + h$ we let $m = 1$ in (8.11) and compute y_2. Continuing in this way we compute $y_3, y_4, \ldots, y_m, y_{m+1}, \ldots$. The truncation errors (8.12) accumulate with each step. We must look for methods in which this accumulation is not too severe. We return to this problem of error accumulation repeatedly in the ensuing discussion.

The Taylor series solution is classified as a one-step method because finding y_{m+1} requires the information at only one preceding point, x_m, y_m.

The practical difficulty of this method is that it may be hard—in fact, in some cases impossible—to find f_x and f_y. Moreover, if we wish to get a better approximation, that is, with a smaller truncation error, we need to evaluate y'''_m, which is

$$y'''_m = f_{xx} + 2ff_{xy} + f^2 f_{yy} + f_x f_y + ff_y^2$$

Succeeding derivatives become even more complicated. Recall also that each of these partial derivatives of f must be re-evaluated first for $x = x_0$, $y = y_0$, then for $x = x_1$, $y = y_1$, and so on.

The method is therefore generally impractical from a computational point of view. However, as we now turn to methods that are practical, we have a yardstick for judging them: the extent to which they agree with the Taylor series expansion. Some methods will agree only as far as terms in h, others will agree through terms in h^4, and so forth. This way of judging a method will apply even though the methods of practical interest do not involve computing the value of any derivatives of $f(x,y)$.

8.3
Runge-
Kutta
Methods

Our study of practical computing methods begins with a broad class of techniques known as *Runge-Kutta methods*. As we might expect, the different methods in this category involve more or less computation and accordingly have more or less accuracy. To establish the pattern of the methods, we shall in fact consider one (Euler's method) that is seldom used but is of historical interest and, like the Taylor series solution, provides a necessary starting point for other discussions.

Runge-Kutta methods have three distinguishing properties:

1. They are one-step methods: To find y_{m+1}, we need only the information available at the preceding point, x_m, y_m.
2. They agree with the Taylor series through terms in h^p, where p is different for different methods and is called the *order* of the method.
3. They do not require the evaluation of any derivatives of $f(x,y)$, but only of the function f itself.

It is the third property that makes these methods more practical than the Taylor series. We should expect, however, that we shall have to evaluate $f(x,y)$ for more than one value of x and y. This is the price we pay for not having to evaluate the derivatives, but it is a price well worth paying.

Let us begin, as usual, by considering what we can learn from geometrical intuition, after which we shall justify the results analytically.

Suppose we have a solution y_m at the point $x = x_m$. We can draw the line with the slope

$$y'_m = f(x_m, y_m)$$

which passes through the point x_m, y_m. The situation is pictured in Figure 8.3, where the curve is the exact (but unknown, of course) solution and the line just described is identified as L_1. We can then let y_{m+1} be the point where L_1 intersects the ordinate erected at $x = x_{m+1} = x_m + h$.

The equation of the line L_1 is

$$y = y_m + y'_m(x - x_m)$$

but

$$y'_m = f(x_m, y_m)$$

and

$$x_{m+1} - x_m = h$$

so

$$y_{m+1} = y_m + hf(x_m, y_m) \qquad (8.13)$$

The error at $x = x_{m+1}$ is shown as e. Let us compare this with the Taylor series solution and thereby determine the truncation error and hence the order of the method (see point 2 above).

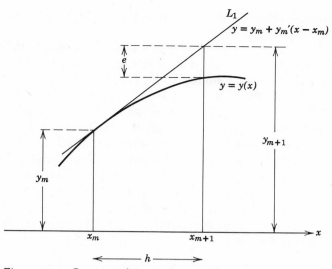

Figure 8.3. *Geometrical representation of Euler's method.*

From (8.6) with $j = 1$ we get

$$y_{m+1} = y_m + hy_m' + \frac{y''(\xi)}{2} h^2$$

where $x_m \leq \xi \leq x_{m+1}$. Comparing this with (8.13) and noting once more that $y_m' = f(x_m, y_m)$, we see that the truncation error in (8.13) is

$$e_T = \frac{y''(\xi)}{2} h^2$$

As we have become accustomed to doing, we assume that the second derivative does not vary too much over the range of interest, that is, $x_m \leq x \leq x_{m+1}$; and hence

$$e_T \cong K h^2$$

We should note that, although y_m is shown in Figure 8.3 as lying on the solution $y = y(x)$, in practice y_m is, of course, approximate and does not lie exactly on the curve.

Equation 8.13, which is Euler's method, is one of the oldest and best known numerical methods for integrating differential equations.

Besides having a relatively large truncation error, Euler's method is often unstable; that is, a small error—roundoff, truncation, or inherent— becomes magnified as the value of x increases. We shall, therefore, not discuss the method any further but pass on to more accurate approaches. We might note, however, that according to our definitions Euler's method is a Runge-Kutta method, specifically, one of the first order, since it agrees with the Taylor series through terms in h.

Euler's method uses only the slope at the point x_m, y_m in computing the value of y_{m+1}. The method can be improved in a number of ways. We shall investigate two, called the *improved Euler method* and the *modified Euler method,* and then show that they are but two of a family of second-order Runge-Kutta methods.

In the improved Euler method[1] we work with the average of the slopes at x_m, y_m and $x_m + h$, $y_m + hy'_m$. The latter point is the one we called x_{m+1}, y_{m+1} in Euler's method. Geometrically (see Figure 8.4), we use Euler's method to find the point $x_m + h$, $y_m + hy'_m$, which is on line L_1 in the diagram. At this point we compute the slope of the curve that represents the solution of (8.3) that passes through the point $(x_m + h, y_m + hy'_m)$. Ideally this latter curve would also represent the solution of the original problem, that is, pass through (x_0, y_0). It does not. Nevertheless, we compute the slope at the point $(x_m + h, y_m + hy'_m)$ simply by evaluating the function f there. This leads to the line L_2 in Figure 8.4. When we average the two slopes of L_1 and L_2, we get the dashed line $\bar{L}$. Finally, we draw a line L parallel to $\bar{L}$ through the point x_m, y_m. The point at which this line intersects the ordinate $x = x_{m+1} = x_m + h$ is taken to be the point x_{m+1}, y_{m+1}.

The slope of the line $\bar{L}$, and also that of the line L, is

$$\phi(x_m, y_m, h) = \tfrac{1}{2}[f(x_m, y_m) + f(x_m + h, y_m + hy'_m)] \tag{8.14}$$

where

$$y'_m = f(x_m, y_m) \tag{8.15}$$

The equation of L is then

$$y = y_m + (x - x_m)\phi(x_m, y_m, h)$$

so

$$y_{m+1} = y_m + h\, \phi(x_m, y_m, h) \tag{8.16}$$

Equations 8.14, 8.15, and 8.16 define the *improved Euler method.* We now turn to a discussion of the accuracy of this method.

First we recall from Taylor's Theorem for a function of two variables

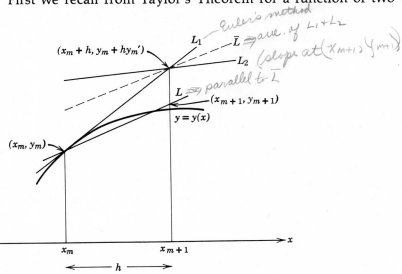

Figure 8.4. *Geometrical representation of the improved Euler method.*

[1] Also known as Heun's method.

that if $f(x,y)$ has continuous second-order partial derivatives

$$f(x,y) = f(x_m,y_m) + (x - x_m)f_x(x_m,y_m) + (y - y_m)f_y(x_m,y_m)$$
$$+ \tfrac{1}{2}[(x - x_m)^2 f_{xx}(\xi_0,\eta_0) + 2(x - x_m)(y - y_m)f_{xy}(\xi_0,\eta_0) \quad (8.17)$$
$$+ (y - y_m)^2 f_{yy}(\xi_0,\eta_0)]$$

where ξ_0 is in the interval bounded by x and x_m and η_0 is in the interval bounded by y and y_m.

If we let $x = x_m + h$ and $y = y_m + hy'_m$ and use (8.15) to replace y'_m we get

$$f(x_m + h, y_m + hy'_m) = f + hf_x + hff_y$$
$$+ \tfrac{1}{2}h^2[f_{xx}(\xi_0,\eta_0) + 2ff_{xy}(\xi_0,\eta_0) + f^2 f_{yy}(\xi_0,\eta_0)]$$

where again f and all its partial derivatives are evaluated at x_m,y_m unless otherwise noted. Substituting this result in (8.14) and then in (8.16), we arrive at

$$y_{m+1} = y_m + h\left[f + \frac{h}{2}(f_x + ff_y)\right] + \frac{h^3}{4}[f_{xx}(\xi_0,\eta_0)$$
$$+ 2ff_{xy}(\xi_0,\eta_0) + f^2 f_{yy}(\xi_0,\eta_0)]$$

where $x_m \le \xi_0 \le x_{m+1}$ and $y_m \le \eta_0 \le y_{m+1}$. (Here for convenience we have assumed $y_m \le y_{m+1}$.) Comparing this with (8.10) we see that the improved Euler method agrees with the Taylor series solution through terms in h^2; hence the improved Euler method is a second-order Runge-Kutta method. The truncation error is

$$e_T = h^3\left[\frac{y'''(\xi)}{6} - \frac{f_{xx}(\xi_0,\eta_0) + 2ff_{xy}(\xi_0,\eta_0) + f^2 f_{yy}(\xi_0,\eta_0)}{4}\right]$$

Assuming again that f_{xx}, f_{xy}, f_{yy}, and y''' are constant

$$e_T \cong Kh^3 \qquad (8.18)$$

In the improved Euler method we are required to evaluate $f(x,y)$ *twice* (at x_m,y_m and at $x_m + h$, $y_m + hy'_m$). As a comparison of the computational effort for the same order of accuracy, the Taylor series required three function evaluations: f, f_x, and f_y.

In the improved Euler method we averaged the *slopes* obtained from two different points. Another approach is to compute the slope at the average of two *points*. To do so we proceed as follows. In Figure 8.5 we start as before with the line L_1, which passes through x_m,y_m and has a slope given by $f(x_m,y_m)$. We proceed along this line only until its intersection with the ordinate erected at $x_m + h/2$, the average of x_m and x_{m+1}. This is the point P in the diagram, where $y = y_m + (h/2)y'_m$. We calculate the slope there:

$$\phi(x_m,y_m,h) = f\left(x_m + \frac{h}{2}, y_m + \frac{h}{2}y'_m\right) \qquad (8.19)$$

where

$$y'_m = f(x_m,y_m) \qquad (8.20)$$

The line through P with this slope is shown as L^*. We next draw a line parallel to L^* passing through x_m,y_m, which is shown as L_0. Now let y_{m+1}

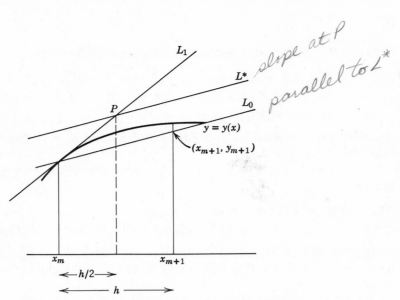

Figure 8.5. *Geometrical representation of the modified Euler method.*

be the intersection of L_0 with $x = x_m + h$. The equation of L_0 is

$$y = y_m + (x - x_m)\phi(x_m, y_m, h)$$

where ϕ is given by (8.19). Thus

$$y_{m+1} = y_m + h\,\phi(x_m, y_m, h) \tag{8.21}$$

Equations 8.19, 8.20, and 8.21 define what is known as the *modified Euler method* or the *improved polygon method*. We leave the reader to show that it agrees with the Taylor series (8.10) through terms in h^2 and is therefore another second-order Runge-Kutta method.

Since we now have two rather different second-order Runge-Kutta methods, it might be interesting to see what the two have in common and whether they can be generalized.

We note that both are given by an expression of the form

$$y_{m+1} = y_m + h\,\phi(x_m, y_m, h) \tag{8.22}$$

and that in both cases ϕ is of the form

$$\phi(x_m, y_m, h) = a_1 f(x_m, y_m) + a_2 f(x_m + b_1 h,\ y_m + b_2 h y'_m) \tag{8.23}$$

where

$$y'_m = f(x_m, y_m) \tag{8.24}$$

In particular, for the improved Euler method

$$a_1 = a_2 = \tfrac{1}{2}$$
$$b_1 = b_2 = 1$$

whereas for the modified Euler method

$$a_1 = 0 \qquad a_2 = 1$$
$$b_1 = b_2 = \tfrac{1}{2}$$

Now (8.22), (8.23), and (8.24) represent a formula of the Runge-Kutta type in that they require only the values of x_m and y_m and also in that they require only the function of itself to be evaluated, not the partial derivatives of f.

Let us see what order formula they can yield, at best, and what the permissible values for the parameters a_1, a_2, b_1, and b_2 are. To obtain agreement with the Taylor series through terms in h will in general require one parameter. To obtain agreement through terms in h^2 will require two more parameters, since there are the terms $h^2 f_x$ and $h^2 f f_y$ to consider. Because we have only four parameters at our disposal, and three of them will be used to approximate the Taylor series through terms in h^2, a second-order formula will be the best we can do. With four parameters available and only three conditions to be met, we should be able to derive many different second-order formulas, varying the one free parameter. This is indeed the case.

In the series expansion for $f(x,y)$ about x_m, y_m (8.17) let

$$x = x_m + b_1 h$$
$$y = y_m + b_2 hf$$

Then

$$f(x_m + b_1 h, y_m + b_2 hf) = f + b_1 h f_x + b_2 hf f_y + O(h^2)$$

where the functions on the right are evaluated at x_m, y_m and $O(h^2)$ indicates h^2 multiplied by the appropriate partial derivatives.[2] Then (8.22) can be expressed as

$$y_{m+1} = y_m + h(a_1 f + a_2 f + h\{a_2 b_1 f_x + a_2 b_2 ff_y\}) + O(h^3)$$

We compare this with the Taylor series (8.10). If terms in hf are to agree, then we require that

$$a_1 + a_2 = 1$$

From comparing terms in $h^2 f_x$, we require that

$$a_2 b_1 = \tfrac{1}{2}$$

And finally, from comparing terms in $h^2 ff_y$, we require that

$$a_2 b_2 = \tfrac{1}{2}$$

Since we have three equations in four parameters, we may choose one of the parameters arbitrarily, perhaps excluding zero, depending on which parameter is taken as the free one. For instance, let

$$a_2 = \omega \neq 0$$

Then

$$a_1 = 1 - \omega$$

$$b_1 = b_2 = \frac{1}{2\omega}$$

---

[2] Strictly speaking $O(h^2)$ means that as $h \to 0$ the term $O(h^2)$ divided by h^2 approaches a constant. This is clearly true in this case since we have assumed continuous second partial derivatives. We shall use $O(h^p)$ to indicate an expression that, when divided by h^p, approaches a constant as $h \to 0$.

and (8.22), (8.23), and (8.24) reduce to

$$
\begin{aligned}
y_{m+1} = y_m + h\bigg[(1 - \omega)f(x_m, y_m) \\
+ \omega f\bigg(x_m + \frac{h}{2\omega}, y_m + \frac{h}{2\omega}f(x_m, y_m)\bigg)\bigg] + O(h^3)
\end{aligned}
\qquad (8.25)
$$

This is the most general second-order Runge-Kutta method. For $\omega = \frac{1}{2}$ we get the improved Euler method (Heun's method). For $\omega = 1$ we get the modified Euler method. The truncation error for any nonzero choice of ω is

$$
e_T \cong Kh^3
\qquad (8.26)
$$

It is possible to obtain bounds on $|K|$. A paper by Ralston[3] shows that the smallest upper bound is obtained when $\omega = 2/3$.

Example

Before going on to higher-order Runge-Kutta methods, we pause to consider the simple example (8.1):

$$
y' = y
$$

with the initial condition

$$
y(0) = 1
$$

As pointed out earlier, the exact solution is

$$
y = e^x
$$

The second-order Runge-Kutta method, from (8.25) is

$$
y_{m+1} = y_m + h\bigg[(1 - \omega)y_m + \omega\bigg(y_m + \frac{h}{2\omega}y_m\bigg)\bigg]
$$

which, for any nonzero choice of ω at all, reduces to

$$
y_{m+1} = y_m\bigg(1 + h + \frac{h^2}{2}\bigg)
$$

It follows that

$$
y_{m+1} = \bigg(1 + h + \frac{h^2}{2}\bigg)^{m+1}
$$

The term in parentheses is the same as the first three terms of the Taylor series for e^h, and

$$
y_{m+1} \simeq e^{h(m+1)} = e^{x_{m+1}}
$$

as we should expect.

---

[3] Anthony Ralston, "Runge-Kutta Methods with Minimum Error Bounds," *Mathematics of Computation*, 16 (1962), 431–437. See also Anthony Ralston, *A First Course in Numerical Analysis*, New York, McGraw-Hill, 1965, chap. 5, exercises 40 and 42.

Table 8.1

i	x_i	y_i	Error
1	0.1	1.105	0.000
2	0.2	1.221	0.000
3	0.3	1.349	0.001
4	0.4	1.491	0.001
5	0.5	1.648	0.001
6	0.6	1.821	0.001
7	0.7	2.012	0.002
8	0.8	2.223	0.003
9	0.9	2.456	0.004
10	1.0	2.714	0.004

h = 0.1

If we let $h = 0.1$, the computed values of y are shown in Table 8.1, which also lists the errors, $e^{x_i} - y_i$. It is clear that the error grows as x increases. By the time $x = 2$ ($i = 20$), the error will have grown to 0.021. Notice that the error is always positive, since

$$1 + h + \frac{h^2}{2} < e^h \qquad \text{for } h > 0$$

Third- and fourth-order Runge-Kutta methods can be developed in ways that are entirely analogous to those we have used to get first- and second-order methods.[4] We shall not follow the derivations but content ourselves with stating the fourth-order formula, which is one of the most commonly used methods of integrating differential equations. (It is so widely used, in fact, that in the literature of numerical computation it is often referred to simply as "the Runge-Kutta method," without any qualification of the order or type.) This classical Runge-Kutta method can be defined by the following five equations:

4th order

$$y_{m+1} = y_m + \frac{h}{6}(k_1 + 2k_2 + 2k_3 + k_4) \tag{8.27}$$

where *Runge-Kutta*

$$k_1 = f(x_m, y_m) \tag{8.28}$$

$$k_2 = f\left(x_m + \frac{h}{2}, y_m + \frac{hk_1}{2}\right) \tag{8.29}$$

$$k_3 = f\left(x_m + \frac{h}{2}, y_m + \frac{hk_2}{2}\right) \tag{8.30}$$

$$k_4 = f(x_m + h, y_m + hk_3) \tag{8.31}$$

The truncation error here is

$$e_T \cong Kh^5$$

[4] See, for example, Ralston, "Runge-Kutta Methods with Minimum Error Bounds," *op. cit.*, Section 5.6–3.

so we have a fourth-order method. Bounds for K are given in the paper by Ralston referred to earlier, in which the fourth-order method that produces a minimum upper bound on K may also be found.

Notice that in this method the function must be evaluated *four* times. The estimate of the truncation error assumes that $f(x,y)$ has continuous fourth partial derivatives.

Example

Let us return again to the simple example

$$y' = y, \; y(0) = 1$$

Then (8.28) to (8.31) yield

$$k_1 = y_m$$

$$k_2 = y_m + \frac{h}{2} y_m$$

$$k_3 = y_m + \frac{h}{2}\left(y_m + \frac{h}{2} y_m\right)$$

$$k_4 = y_m + h\left[y_m + \frac{h}{2}\left(y_m + \frac{h}{2} y_m\right)\right]$$

Using these equations in (8.27), we get

$$y_{m+1} = \left(1 + h + \frac{h^2}{2} + \frac{h^3}{6} + \frac{h^4}{24}\right) y_m$$

The term in parentheses is now the same as the first *five* terms of the Taylor series of e^h. Recall that the second-order methods produces the first three terms in the Taylor series for e^h.

Again, with $h = 0.1$, the computed values for y together with the errors are shown in Table 8.2. Compare these results with Table 8.1 for a second-order method.

Table 8.2

i	x_i	y_i	Error
1	0.10	1.105171	0.00000008
2	0.20	1.221403	0.00000019
3	0.30	1.349858	0.00000031
4	0.40	1.491824	0.00000046
5	0.50	1.648721	0.00000063
6	0.60	1.822118	0.00000084
7	0.70	2.013752	0.00000108
8	0.80	2.225540	0.00000137
9	0.90	2.459601	0.00000170
10	1.00	2.718280	0.00000208

It will be interesting to compare a method that integrates a function of x and y with the methods we discussed in Chapter 5 for integrating a function of x alone. For this purpose let us suppose that f is a function of x only; that is

$$f(x,y) = F(x)$$

and

$$y(x) - y_0 = \int_{x_0}^{x} F(x)\, dx \tag{8.32}$$

recalling that $y(x_0) = y_0$.

Let

$$p = \frac{h}{2}$$

and define

$$F_j = F(x_0 + jp)$$

Now

$$y_m = y(x_0 + mh) = y(x_0 + 2mp)$$

We define

$$Y_j = y(x_0 + jp)$$

so that

$$y_m = Y_{2m}$$

Thus (8.27) becomes

$$Y_{2m+2} - Y_{2m} = \frac{p}{3}(F_{2m} + 4F_{2m+1} + F_{2m+2})$$

where we allow $m = 0, 1, 2, \ldots, n - 1$. Thus

$$Y_2 - Y_0 = \frac{p}{3}(F_0 + 4F_1 + F_2)$$

$$Y_4 - Y_2 = \frac{p}{3}(F_2 + 4F_3 + F_4)$$

$$\cdots \cdots \cdots \cdots \cdots \cdots$$

$$Y_{2n} - Y_{2n-2} = \frac{p}{3}(F_{2n-2} + 4F_{2n-1} + F_{2n})$$

Adding all these equations, we get

$$Y_{2n} - Y_0 = \frac{p}{3}(F_0 + 4F_1 + 2F_2 + 4F_2 + \cdots + 2F_{2n-2} + 4F_{2n-1} + F_{2n})$$

This is precisely Simpson's rule for the evaluation of (8.32), where $x = x_0 + 2nh$. (Notice that $y_0 = Y_0$.)

Thus the classical fourth-order Runge-Kutta method given by (8.27) to (8.31) is a generalization of Simpson's rule, the generalization being that we are not restricted to functions of x alone. For this reason the method is often referred to as the *Runge-Kutta-Simpson rule.*

**8.5
Truncation
Error in
Runge-
Kutta
Methods**

We have noted that the truncation error in a pth-order Runge-Kutta method is Kh^{p+1}, where K is some constant. Bounds on K for $p = 2, 3,$ and 4 are given in Ralston's paper (footnote 3). The derivation of these bounds is not a simple matter, and, moreover, their evaluation requires quantities that do not appear in (8.27) through (8.31). One of the serious drawbacks of Runge-Kutta methods is the lack of simple means for estimating the error. The methods of the following sections owe part of their attractiveness to the fact that error estimates are an easy by-product of the calculation of a new point.

Without some measure of the truncation error, it is difficult to choose the proper step size, h. A rough rule-of-thumb has been given by Collatz.[5] If

$$\left| \frac{k_2 - k_3}{k_1 - k_2} \right|$$

becomes large (more than a few hundredths), h should be decreased.[6]

Scraton[7] has shown that an estimate of the truncation error can be obtained at the expense of one additional evaluation of $f(x,y)$. This may be costly if $f(x,y)$ is at all complicated. The derivation of these results is beyond the scope of this text. However, we shall indicate how such an error estimate can be obtained by considering the simple case of a first-order Runge-Kutta method (Euler's method). Recall from the discussion in Section 8.3 that

$$y_{m+1} = y_m + hf(x_m, y_m) \tag{8.33}$$

is a first-order Runge-Kutta method and that the truncation error is

$$e_T = \frac{y''(\xi)}{2} h^2$$

From (8.8), however,

$$y'' = f_x + ff_y$$

Thus we can estimate the truncation error by

$$e_T \cong \frac{h^2}{2} (f_x + ff_y) \tag{8.34}$$

where f, f_x, and f_y now are evaluated at $x = x_m$ and $y = y_m$. Of course, the truncation error *should* be evaluated at $x = \xi$ and the corresponding value of y. Since we cannot even find ξ, much less perform the necessary function evaluations, we must be content with an *estimate* of the truncation error as indicated in (8.34).

Again using Taylor's Theorem for a function of two variables, see (8.17),

[5]Collatz, L., *Numerische Behandlung von Differentialgleichungen*, Berlin, Springer Verlag, 1951, p. 34.

[6]See also Anthony Ralston and Herbert S. Wilf (eds.), *Mathematical Methods for Digital Computers*, New York, Wiley, 1960, vol. 1, chap. 9.

[7]R. E. Scraton, "Estimation of the Truncation Error in Runge-Kutta and Allied Processes," *Computer Journal*, (October, 1964), pp. 246–248.

and letting $x = x_m + h$ and $y = y_m + hy'_m$

$$f(x_m + h, y_m + hy'_m) = f + hf_x + hff_y + O(h^2)$$

where the functions on the right are evaluated at $x = x_m$ and $y = y_m$, and where, as usual, $O(h^2)$ is a function that approaches a constant times h^2 as $h \to 0$.

From this last equation

$$\frac{h^2}{2}(f_x + ff_y) = \frac{h}{2}[f(x_m + h, y_m + hy'_m) - f(x_m, y_m)] + O(h^3)$$

Referring back to (8.34) then

$$e_T \cong \frac{h}{2}[f(x_m + h, y_m + hy'_m) - f(x_m, y_m)] \qquad (8.35)$$

Thus we can estimate the truncation error in Euler's method by evaluating $f(x,y)$ at $x = x_m + h$ and $y = y_m + hy'_m$. Euler's method itself required evaluating $f(x,y)$ at $x = x_m$ and $y = y_m$.

In summary: Euler's method requires one function evaluation. With one additional function evaluation we can estimate the truncation error. The observant reader will notice that if we add this truncation error estimate (8.35) to the right side of Euler's method (8.33), the result is the improved Euler method (8.14), (8.15), and (8.16).

In general one additional function evaluation produces an estimate of the truncation error for a Runge-Kutta method of any order. However, adding this truncation error estimate to the original formula does *not* always produce a higher-order Runge-Kutta method. Only in the first-order case shown above does this occur.

For further information see Mayers[8] or the paper by Scraton.[9]

A more precise estimate can be obtained at the expense of considerable extra effort by using Richardson's deferred approach to the limit, which we discussed in Chapter 5.

To do this, let Y_m be the "true" value of the solution at $x = x_0 + mh$. For the classical fourth-order method

$$Y_m = y_m^{(h)} + Kh^5 \qquad (8.36)$$

where the superscript (h) on y_m indicates that Y_m was calculated with a step size of h. We then recompute the solution with a step size of $h/2$, so that

$$Y_m = y_m^{(h/2)} + K\left(\frac{h}{2}\right)^5 \qquad (8.37)$$

Subtracting (8.36) from (8.37) we get

$$y_m^{(h)} - y_m^{(h/2)} = -\tfrac{31}{32}Kh^5$$

---

[8]D. F. Mayers, in L. Fox (ed.), *Numerical Solution of Ordinary and Partial Differential Equations,* Pergamon Press and Addison-Wesley, 1962, chap. 2, sec. 16.
[9]Scraton, *op. cit.*

and the truncation error is

$$e_T \cong Kh^5 = \tfrac{32}{31}[y_m^{(h/2)} - y_m^{(h)}] \tag{8.38}$$

If the fifth derivative of y is reasonably constant, we have a fairly good estimate. The problem, of course, is that the solution must be computed *twice.* The original computation of $y_m^{(h)}$ required $4m$ function evaluations (four for each step). The computation of $y_m^{(h/2)}$ requires an additional $8m$ function evaluations. The information obtained from (8.38) is, therefore, usually not worth the effort.

Similar results can be obtained with second-order Runge-Kutta methods, in which the truncation error is Kh^3.

**8.6
Partial
Instability**

Even if the truncation error is small, a Runge-Kutta method may produce extremely inaccurate results under unfavorable conditions. Such erroneous results can arise because small errors (roundoff or truncation) may become magnified as the solution is carried out for larger and larger x.

For example, consider the simple equation

$$y' = -10y$$

with the initial condition

$$y(0) = 1$$

The exact solution is

$$y = e^{-10x}$$

From an analysis completely analogous to that leading to Table 8.1, we find that any second-order method leads to

$$y_{m+1} = (1 - 10h + 50h^2)^m$$

But notice that the term in parentheses is greater than 1 if $h > 0.2$. For large m, therefore, y becomes indefinitely large. The exact solution, on the other hand, becomes small.

One might think that using a higher-order Runge-Kutta method would eliminate such problems. However, a higher-order method merely alleviates the problem in the sense that the trouble appears only when h gets much larger. Again by way of example for

$$y' = -10y$$
$$y(0) = 1$$

an argument analogous to that leading to Table 8.2 with a fourth-order method leads to

$$y_{m+1} = \left(1 - 10h + 50h^2 - \frac{500h^3}{3} + \frac{1250}{3}h^4\right)^m$$

The term in parentheses is greater than 1 if $h > 0.27853$. Hence with a fourth-order method we can use larger values of h than we can with a second-order method. Sooner or later, however, trouble still arises.

This phenomenon of a numerical solution that deviates markedly from the actual solution as we take more and more steps is called *partial* _instability_ by Mayers.[10] The word "instability" arises from the unstable nature of the numerical solutions. The instabilities we shall encounter in Section 8.10 depend upon the differential equation and upon the numerical algorithm. They will _not_ depend upon the step size h. Since the instability just discussed in this section _does_ depend upon the differential equation, the algorithm, _and the step size_, it is called "partial."

The reader is warned that such partial instability exists for Runge-Kutta methods even when the exact solution does not decay exponentially, as in the foregoing example.

8.7
Predictor-
Corrector
Methods

A distinguishing feature of Runge-Kutta methods is that in getting the next point, x_{m+1}, y_{m+1}, we use the information provided by x_m, y_m, but no prior points. In second-order or higher methods we have to evaluate the function at one or more additional points. This appears to be unreasonable on the face of it, for once the integration process has proceeded a few steps we already have available additional information without _any_ function evaluations, namely, the values of y at the prior points. The fact that Runge-Kutta methods do not use the readily available prior information, plus the lack of a convenient error estimate, makes us look for additional methods. We shall see, however, that these methods cannot "start" themselves, since they not only _use_ prior points but _demand_ them. Some other method must be used to get the new processes started or to change the step size. We shall be led, therefore, to a judicious combination of methods.

These methods, of which there are many variations, go by the name of _predictor-corrector_. As implied by the name, we first "predict" a value for y_{m+1}. We then use a different formula to "correct" this value. We may then, if it appears desirable, employ the corrector formula again to "re-correct" the value of y_{m+1}. This process can be iterated as many times as we wish, although we shall see that there are efficiency considerations that suggest choosing a step size that avoids going through a great many iterations.

Among the many possible formulas for the predictor and for the corrector, we shall choose an example of each that the reader will find applicable to many practical problems. With the basic ideas clearly understood, there will then be no difficulty in applying the many other methods found in the literature and the exercises at the close of the chapter.

For the predictor we shall use a second-order method:

$$y_{m+1}^{(0)} = y_{m-1} + 2hf(x_m, y_m) \tag{8.39}$$

where the superscript (0) indicates that this is our first "guess" at y_{m+1}—a predicted value. This suggests immediately that this method cannot be used to compute y_1, since to do so would require a point prior to the initial point x_0. A Runge-Kutta method is often used to start a predictor-corrector method, a matter to which we shall return later.

---

[10]Mayers, _op. cit._, chap. 4, sec. 7.

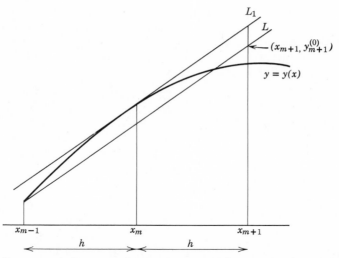

Figure 8.6. *Geometrical representation of the second-order predictor described in the text.*

One might think that this requirement for x_{m-1}, y_{m-1} could be avoided by using Euler's method. This turns out not to be practical because the truncation error in Euler's method is too large. It is this use of prior information without additional function evaluations that leads to the classification as *multistep* methods.

Geometrically (see Figure 8.6), the predictor amounts to finding the slope at x_m, y_m and drawing a line L_1 with that slope through x_m, y_m. We then draw a line L, parallel to L_1, through x_{m-1}, y_{m-1}. The point at which this line intersects the line $x = x_{m+1}$ is the predicted value, $y_{m+1}^{(0)}$.

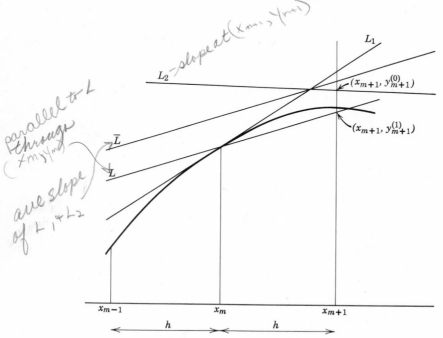

Figure 8.7. *Geometrical representation of the second-order corrector described in the text.*

We now need a method of improving our predicted value. Since we know y_{m+1} approximately, we can calculate an approximate slope at $x_{m+1}, y_{m+1}^{(0)}$. This is exhibited as the line L_2 in Figure 8.7. The line L_1 is the same as L_1 in Figure 8.6, having the slope given by $f(x_m, y_m)$. We now average the slopes of the lines L_1 and L_2, giving the line L. Finally, a line L is drawn parallel to $\bar{L}$ through the point x_m, y_m. Its intersection with the line $x = x_{m+1}$ yields a new approximation to y_{m+1}. We call this the *corrected* value $y_{m+1}^{(1)}$. It is given by

$$y_{m+1}^{(1)} = y_m + \frac{h}{2}\,[f(x_m, y_m) + f(x_{m+1}, y_{m+1}^{(0)})]$$

We can now get another and presumably better estimate of $f(x_{m+1}, y_{m+1})$ by using $y_{m+1}^{(1)}$ and recorrecting the value of y_{m+1}. Thus, in general, the ith approximation to y_{m+1} is given by[11]

predictor-corrector
$$\left(\quad y_{m+1}^{(i)} = y_m + \frac{h}{2}\,[f(x_m, y_m) + f(x_{m+1}, y_{m+1}^{(i-1)})] \quad \right) \qquad (8.40)$$

for $i = 1, 2, 3, \ldots$. The iterations are stopped when

$$|y_{m+1}^{(i+1)} - y_{m+1}^{(i)}| < \epsilon \qquad (8.41)$$

for a specified positive ϵ.

The observant reader will notice several things. First, there is a similarity between the predictor (8.39) and the modified Euler method given by (8.19), (8.20), and (8.21). This similarity is most easily seen by comparing Figures 8.5 and 8.6. One line, L_1 in Figure 8.5, is not seen in Figure 8.6. The line L_1 in Figure 8.6 corresponds to L^* in Figure 8.5.

Second, there is an even more striking similarity between the corrector (8.40) and the improved Euler method given by (8.14), (8.15), and (8.16). Once again this similarity is best observed by comparing Figures 8.4 and 8.7.

Finally, the essential difference in the corrector and the improved Euler method is that the latter was really used as a "predictor" and no iterations were performed. Here we use the more accurate (8.39) as a predictor and then use (8.40) only to improve the results.

The questions that naturally arise, and that we must answer are, will (8.41) ever be satisfied? And, if so, under what conditions? In other words, when does the predictor-corrector process converge?

To answer these crucial questions, we begin by noting that

$$y_{m+1}^{(i+1)} - y_{m+1}^{(i)} = \frac{h}{2}\,[f(x_{m+1}, y_{m+1}^{(i)}) - f(x_{m+1}, y_{m+1}^{(i-1)})]$$

Using the mean value theorem,

$$y_{m+1}^{(i+1)} - y_{m+1}^{(i)} = \frac{h}{2}\left(\frac{\partial f}{\partial y}\right)[y_{m+1}^{(i)} - y_{m+1}^{(i-1)}] \qquad (8.42)$$

---

[11] We emphasize that in (8.40) and in the remainder of this section the superscript (i) refers to the ith approximation to y in an iterative process, *not* to the ith derivative of y.

where $\partial f/\partial y$ is evaluated for $x = x_{m+1}$ and for some y between $y_{m+1}^{(i)}$ and $y_{m+1}^{(i+1)}$.

We now assume that $\partial f/\partial y$ is bounded; that is, that there is some M such that

$$\left| \frac{\partial f}{\partial y} \right| \leq M$$

It follows from (8.42) that

$$|y_{m+1}^{(i+1)} - y_{m+1}^{(i)}| \leq \frac{hM}{2} |y_{m+1}^{(i)} - y_{m+1}^{(i-1)}|$$

Similarly

$$|y_{m+1}^{(i)} - y_{m+1}^{(i-1)}| \leq \frac{hM}{2} |y_{m+1}^{(i-1)} - y_{m+1}^{(i-2)}|$$

Substituting this in the preceding inequality,

$$|y_{m+1}^{(i+1)} - y_{m+1}^{(i)}| \leq \left(\frac{hM}{2} \right)^2 |y_{m+1}^{(i-1)} - y_{m+1}^{(i-2)}|$$

Continuing in this way, we arrive finally at

$$|y_{m+1}^{(i+1)} - y_{m+1}^{(i)}| \leq \left(\frac{hM}{2} \right)^i |y_{m+1}^{(1)} - y_{m+1}^{(0)}|$$

Thus, if the step size h is chosen so that

$$h < \frac{2}{M} \tag{8.43}$$

the difference in the corrected values approaches zero and the process thus converges.

It should be clearly understood what we have just proved. Subject to the condition stated, the method has been shown to converge to *some* definite value, but not necessarily to the *true* solution. The difference between the two is the truncation error, which we consider in Section 8.9.

At the close of Section 8.9 we shall discuss how rapid the convergence should be. Obviously, the smaller h is, the more rapidly the process will converge.

We shall also discuss the question of stability in Section 8.10; that is to say, we shall investigate under what conditions small errors—inherent, roundoff, or truncation—are or are not amplified as we take more and more steps (x becomes large). It should be clear that we would prefer methods that (1) have a small truncation error, (2) converge in a few iterations and (3) do not amplify errors as x increases. We shall see that the predictor-corrector formulas (8.39) and (8.40) satisfy all three of these criteria to a large extent under rather lenient conditions.

In Section 8.4 we pointed out that the fourth-order Runge-Kutta method was a generalization of Simpson's rule. We saw that by looking at the special case

$$y' = F(x) \tag{8.44}$$

We now examine the application of the corrector formula (8.40) to this differential equation.

Integrating both sides of (8.44) from x_0 to x

$$y(x) - y_0 = \int_{x_0}^{x} F(x)\, dx \tag{8.45}$$

recalling that $y(x_0) = y_0$. If we drop the superscripts in (8.40) we get

$$y_{m+1} = y_m + \frac{h}{2}\, [F(x_m) + F(x_{m+1})]$$

Since y_{m+1} does not appear on the right, there is no need to iterate, and we are justified in dropping the superscripts that indicated the number of the iteration. Letting $m = 1, 2, \ldots, n$ and combining these results

$$y_n - y_0 = \frac{h}{2}\, [F(x_0) + 2F(x_1) + \cdots + 2F(x_{n-1}) + F(x_n)]$$

This is simply the trapezoidal rule (5.38) for the evaluation of (8.45), where $x = x_0 + nh$. The corrector formula is therefore a generalization of the trapezoidal rule, in the same sense that the classical Runge-Kutta method is a generalization of Simpson's rule. This naturally implies that the improved Euler method is also a generalization of the trapezoidal rule.

From our development of the trapezoidal rule in Chapter 5 it follows that the truncation error in the corrector formula (8.40) is $O(h^3)$. More precisely, from (5.48) and Exercise 6 of Chapter 6, the truncation error in (8.40) is

$$e_T^{(c)} = -\frac{h^3}{12}\, y'''(\eta)$$

where $x_{m-1} \leq \eta \leq x_{m+1}$.

8.9
Truncation
Errors in
Predictor-
Corrector
Methods

The analysis of errors and related matters in predictor-corrector methods can conveniently be broken into several distinct investigations. We shall first discuss the truncation errors in the predictor (8.39) and the corrector (8.40). The results will be expressed easily in terms of quantities already computed in getting the solution. We shall then discuss the proper choice of the step size h. Finally, in the next section, we shall consider the problem of stability: whether errors—inherent, roundoff, or truncation— grow as x increases.

To find the truncation error in the predictor (8.39), recall that Taylor's theorem states that when $y(x)$ is expanded about the point $x = x_m$

$$y(x) = y_m + y_m'(x - x_m) + \frac{y_m''}{2}(x - x_m)^2 + \frac{1}{6}(x - x_m)^3 y'''(\xi)$$

where ξ lies between x and x_m. Letting $x = x_{m+1}$, we get

$$y_{m+1} = y_m + hy'_m + \frac{h^2}{2}y''_m + \frac{h^3}{6}y'''(\xi_1), \quad x_m \le \xi_1 \le x_{m+1}$$

Similarly, letting $x = x_{m-1}$, we get

$$y_{m-1} = y_m - hy'_m + \frac{h^2}{2}y''_m - \frac{h^3}{6}y'''(\xi_2), \quad x_{m-1} \le \xi_2 \le x_m$$

If we subtract these two equations and note that from the intermediate value theorem

$$\frac{y'''(\xi_1) + y'''(\xi_2)}{2} = y'''(\xi), \quad x_{m-1} \le \xi \le x_{m+1}$$

it follows that

$$y_{m+1} = y_{m-1} + 2hy'_m + \frac{h^3}{3}y'''(\xi)$$

The truncation error is then

$$e_T^{(p)} = \frac{h^3}{3}y'''(\xi), \quad x_{m-1} \le \xi \le x_{m+1} \tag{8.46}$$

This verifies our claim in Section 8.7 that the predictor is a second-order method. [See the remark immediately preceding (8.39).]

We have already noted that the corrector (8.40) is a generalization of the trapezoidal rule. In the previous section we saw that the truncation error in (8.40) is

$$e_T^{(c)} = -\frac{h^3}{12}y'''(\eta), \quad x_{m-1} \le \eta \le x_{m+1} \tag{8.47}$$

The fact that the truncation errors in both predictor and corrector are of the same order allows us to develop a simple method of estimating y''', hence $e_T^{(c)}$. The technique is closely allied to the deferred approach to the limit used in Chapter 5 and in Section 8.5.

We let Y_m be the true value of the solution at $x = x_m$. Then from (8.46)

$$Y_m = y_m^{(0)} + \frac{h^3}{3}y'''(\xi)$$

and from (8.47)

$$Y_m = y_m^{(i)} - \frac{h^3}{12}y'''(\eta)$$

where $y_m^{(0)}$ and $y_m^{(i)}$ are given by (8.39) and (8.40) respectively. Subtracting these last two equations we get

$$0 = y_m^{(i)} - y_m^{(0)} - \frac{h^3}{12}[y'''(\eta) + 4y'''(\xi)]$$

If we assume that y''' is reasonably constant for $x_{m-1} \le x \le x_{m+1}$, then

$$\frac{5h^3}{12}y''' = y_m^{(i)} - y_m^{(0)}$$

and

$$e_T^{(c)} = -\frac{h^3}{12}\,y''' = \frac{1}{5}\,[y_m^{(0)} - y_m^{(i)}] \qquad (8.48)$$

The values needed for this estimate are already available from the calculation. Thus, in contrast to the Runge-Kutta methods, we have an easily computed estimate for the truncation error. Notice that the argument depended on both truncation errors being of the same order. It is therefore desirable that any predictor-corrector pair have this property.

We are now ready to discuss the choice of the step size h. There is no straightforward way to choose the initial value of h, with the possible exception of (8.43), which is usually not much help: M may be hard to estimate, and, if it varies over the interval of integration (8.43), will quite likely be unduly conservative at most points. Once the calculation has started, however, we can compute the truncation error from (8.48). If this number is too large, we decrease the step size (often by halving it). If the number is smaller than we need, we increase the step size (often by doubling it).

We can make one further remark on the choice of h. Recall from (8.43) that the method converges if

$$h < \frac{2}{M}$$

But, as we just noted, we usually do not know the value of M. However, the smaller h is, the more rapid the convergence will be. We thus have an economic choice. If we choose a small h, not many iterations will be required per point, but there will be many points. If we choose a larger h, there will be fewer points but more iterations per point. There is strong empirical evidence[12] to indicate that the most *efficient* number of iterations is usually *two*. (Here efficiency is used in the sense of minimum computation for a given accuracy.) In other words, if the step size is chosen so that the convergence criterion (8.41) is satisfied in two iterations, the total amount of computation will be minimized.

This approach is readily programmed. We count the iterations; if more than two iterations are required, we reduce the step size, but if one iteration is sufficient we increase it.

We have not yet discussed the actual process of changing the step size. It is clear that some thought must be given to the matter because once the step size is changed the predictor formula no longer applies directly. If the step size is to be doubled, it would theoretically be possible to go back *two* steps (in terms of the preceding step size) in order to get started with the larger interval, but in practice a more direct attack is quite adequate. What we actually do is to stop the calculation by the predictor-corrector method and take x_m, y_m to be a new starting point. The predictor-corrector method is then restarted with the new step size, using a Runge-Kutta method.

[12]T. E. Hull and A. L. Creemer, "Efficiency of Predictor-Corrector Procedures," J. Assn. for Computing Machinery, 10, (1963), 291–301.

We have seen that h must be chosen to satisfy (8.43) if the corrector iterations are to converge. We have also seen in Section 8.6 that in some cases an inappropriate choice of h can lead to instability of the numerical solution, that is, an increased and dramatic deviation of the numerical solution from the true solution. We now turn to a discussion of the error growth in the predictor-corrector process as m, the number of steps, increases. We would like this error growth to be "controlled" within some reasonable bounds no matter how large m becomes. If we can achieve this control, we say that the method is *stable*.

The error is governed by the corrector formula (8.40). Thus the final choice of y_{m+1} satisfies

$$y_{m+1} = y_m + \frac{h}{2} [f(x_m, y_m) + f(x_{m+1}, y_{m+1})] \tag{8.49}$$

apart from roundoff error. If Y_m is the exact solution, then

$$Y_{m+1} = Y_m + \frac{h}{2} [f(x_m, Y_m) + f(x_{m+1}, Y_{m+1})] + e_m \tag{8.50}$$

where e_m includes the truncation error and the roundoff error in (8.49). If we subtract (8.49) from (8.50) and let

$$\epsilon_i = Y_i - y_i$$

it follows that

$$\epsilon_{m+1} = \epsilon_m + \frac{h}{2} \{[f(x_m, Y_m) - f(x_m, y_m)]$$

$$+ [f(x_{m+1}, Y_{m+1}) - f(x_{m+1}, y_{m+1})]\} + e_m$$

From the mean value theorem

$$\epsilon_{m+1} = \epsilon_m + \frac{h}{2} [f_y(x_{m+1}, \xi_{m+1}) \cdot \epsilon_{m+1} + f_y(x_m, \xi_m) \cdot \epsilon_m] + e_m$$

where ξ_i lies between y_i and Y_i. Thus

$$\epsilon_{m+1} = \mu \epsilon_m + \delta \tag{8.51}$$

where

$$\mu = \frac{1 + \dfrac{h f_y}{2}}{1 - \dfrac{h f_y}{2}} \tag{8.52}$$

and

$$\delta = \frac{e_m}{1 - \dfrac{h f_y}{2}} \tag{8.53}$$

The arguments have been omitted from the f_y terms and we assume that e_m is independent of m.

Equation 8.51 is called a *difference equation*. We shall discuss its solution for ϵ_m shortly. First, recall that (8.43) required that

$$\left|\frac{hf_y}{2}\right| < 1 \tag{8.54}$$

for convergence. Suppose that

$$f_y < 0 \tag{8.55}$$

Then, if h satisfies (8.54), it follows that

$$0 < \mu < 1 \tag{8.56}$$

Thus the error ϵ_m in y_m is not magnified in ϵ_{m+1}. That is to say, the errors do not grow, and the method is therefore said to be *stable*, or, more precisely, it possesses absolute stability.[13]

On the other hand, if

$$f_y > 0$$

then

$$\mu > 1$$

and the method is unstable, but this does not mean that we cannot then use the method. We shall see that even in this case the *relative* errors do not grow.

Suppose, for the moment, that f_y is constant; that is, that the differential equation is

$$y' = Ay$$

where A is a constant. Then the exact solution is

$$Y = ae^{Ax}$$

and

$$Y_m = ae^{A(x_0+mh)} = be^{(hA)m} \tag{8.57}$$

where b is a new constant incorporating the constant factor e^{Ax_0}. If $A > 0$, then Y_m grows exponentially with m. Even if ϵ_m grows, the relative error (ϵ_m/Y_m) may not grow. In fact, it is unreasonable to ask that the absolute error remain bounded in this case.

In order to investigate the growth of the relative error, we note that the solution[14] of the difference equation (8.51) is

$$\epsilon_m = a_0\mu^m + \frac{\delta}{1 - \mu} \tag{8.58}$$

where a_0 is an arbitrary constant. The reader may verify this result by substituting (8.58) in (8.51).

Carrying out the division indicated in (8.52) and recalling that $f_y = A$,

[13] The absolute errors do not grow.
[14] For an elegant discussion of difference equations of this type and their solution see S. Goldberg, *Introduction to Difference Equations*, New York, Wiley, 1961, sec. 2.4.

$$\epsilon_{m+1} = \mu a_0 \mu^m + \frac{\mu\delta}{1-\mu} + \delta \qquad \qquad \delta - \mu\delta$$

$$\epsilon_{m+1} = a_0 \mu^{m+1} + \frac{\delta}{1-\mu}$$

we have

$$\mu = \left(1 + \frac{hA}{2}\right)\left[1 + \left(\frac{hA}{2}\right) + \left(\frac{hA}{2}\right)^2 + \left(\frac{hA}{2}\right)^3 + \cdots\right]$$

$$= 1 + hA + \frac{(hA)^2}{2} + \frac{(hA)^3}{4} + \cdots$$

a series that converges for $|hA| < 2$, which by happy coincidence is the condition of convergence (8.54) of the predictor-corrector method. Now

$$e^{hA} = 1 + hA + \frac{(hA)^2}{2} + \frac{(hA)^3}{6} + \cdots$$

so that

$$\mu = e^{hA} + O(h^3)$$

that is to say, $\mu = e^{hA}$ to the same accuracy as the truncation error in the method. Thus, from (8.58)

$$\epsilon_m \simeq a_0 e^{(hA)m} + \frac{\delta}{1 - e^{hA}} \tag{8.59}$$

The latter term is independent of m, and the first term dominates as m increases.

Comparing (8.57) and (8.59)

$$\frac{\epsilon_m}{Y_m} \simeq \frac{a_0}{b} = \text{constant}$$

and the relative error remains fixed.

Similarly for $A < 0$, e_m and Y both behave as e^{-hA}. Again the relative error does not grow.

We may say then that the method described in Section 8.7 has _relative stability_.

We must recall that the arguments leading to relative stability assumed that f_y was a constant. In any case of interest this is not true. However, there is strong empirical evidence to suggest that the relative errors do not—on the average—grow in a relatively stable process. The same may be said of the absolute errors in an absolutely stable process.

In summary, then, our simple predictor-corrector method (8.39) and (8.40) is a relatively stable process. Moreover, it is absolutely stable if $f_y < 0$.

We may make one final remark. Recall from (8.48) that

$$Y_m - y_m^{(i)} = E_T^{(c)} = \tfrac{1}{5}[y_m^{(0)} - y_m^{(i)}]$$

Thus, a more accurate solution may be found by making one final correction:

$$y_m = y_m^{(i)} + \tfrac{1}{5}[y_m^{(0)} - y_m^{(i)}] \tag{8.60}$$

We cannot give a detailed analysis of the effect of uncertainty in the parameters in the differential equation (8.3) or the initial condition (8.4) because of the wide variety of possible equations. We can, however, indicate the serious consequences of errors in data on the solution with a simple example.

Following Mayers,[15] we consider the differential equation

$$y' = y - x$$

For the initial condition

$$y(0) = 1$$

the solution is

$$y = x + 1$$

Suppose now that the error in the initial condition may be as great as 1%. The solution then may vary between

$$y^{(1)} = 0.01e^x + x + 1$$

and

$$y^{(2)} = -0.01e^x + x + 1$$

We see that at $x = 5$, y may be in error by as much as $0.01e^5$, or about 30%, as a result of a 1% error in the initial condition. The percentage error in the result grows rapidly with x.

No numerical method can produce a solution more accurate than 30% at $x = 5$ because this size error in inherent in the original problem. For this reason Mayers refers to this type of error growth as *inherent instability*.

We have in the course of our discussion encountered four types of instability: partial, absolute, relative, and inherent. We pause here to recapitulate the meanings of the terms.

First we repeat that a numerical solution is unstable if, as the algorithm progresses, the numerical values deviate more and more from the true solution. Sometimes a solution is unstable regardless of the numerical algorithm selected. The difficulty lies in the sensitivity of the differential equation itself. This is termed inherent instability. The term "inherent" is applied to a differential equation, not to a method of solution.

Other times the differential equation may be quite well behaved but a particular algorithm may be unstable. If the deviations themselves become large, then the algorithm is said to be absolutely unstable. If the ratio of the deviations to the true solution becomes large, then the algorithm is said to be relatively unstable. An algorithm may be absolutely unstable but relatively stable and vice versa. Notice that "absolute" and "relative" are applied to algorithms.

There are still other times when an algorithm is stable except for

[15] Mayers, *op. cit.*, chap. 4, sec. 6.

particular choices of the step size, h. In such cases the algorithm is partially unstable when applied to the differential equation in question. "Partial" is applied to a particular combination of algorithm, differential equation, and step size.

**8.13
Comparison of
Methods**

We have noted at various points in the preceding discussion the relative merits and deficiencies of one-step (Runge-Kutta) and multistep (predictor-corrector) methods. We summarize the results here and suggest an appropriate way to combine the two types of methods to take advantage of the strengths of each.

Runge-Kutta Methods

1. Since they do not use information from previously calculated points, Runge-Kutta methods are self-starting.
2. For the same reason, however, they require several evaluations of the function $f(x,y)$ and are therefore time-consuming.
3. Being self-starting, they permit an easy change in the step size.
4. They provide no easily obtainable information about truncation error.

Predictor-Corrector Methods

The characteristics are complementary to those of Runge-Kutta methods.

1. Since they do use information about prior points, they are not self-starting.
2. They substitute information about prior points for repeated evaluation of $f(x,y)$ and are therefore more efficient (unless, of course, the step size is so large that many iterations of the corrector formula are needed).
3. Except in special circumstances that are usually not of practical usefulness, a change in step size requires a temporary reversion to a Runge-Kutta method.
4. A good estimate of the truncation error flows naturally out of the computation.

The complementary nature of the two types of methods suggests immediately that a combination of the two will prove useful. We suggest the following course of action.

1. Start the solution with a Runge-Kutta method, such as (8.25), to find y_1.
2. Use the predictor-corrector pair (8.39) and (8.40) to compute succeeding y_m.
3. If more than two iterations of the corrector are needed to obtain the desired accuracy *or* if the truncation error given by (8.48) is too large, decrease the step size (see point 4 below). If, on the other hand, the truncation error is exceedingly small, the step size can be increased.

4. To change the step size, consider the last value of y_i that was sufficiently accurate to be an initial point. Restart the solution from that point, using a Runge-Kutta method as in 1 above.

5. In any case, when $y_m^{(i)}$ has been obtained from the corrector, use (8.60) to compute the final value of y_m. $y_m = y_m^{(i)} + \frac{1}{5}\left[y_m^{(0)} - y_m^{(i)}\right]$

Naturally, there are many other predictor-corrector formulas that give higher accuracies. They are catalogued in most texts on numerical analysis,[16] and some of them are sketched in the exercises. However, more accurate Runge-Kutta methods, such as (8.27) to (8.31), should be used to start them.

4
ase
udy 13:
olving the
fferential
quation of
rge De-
ections
a Beam

In this case study we consider a physical problem that leads to a nonlinear second-order differential equation. As we indicated in Section 8.1, a second-order equation can be reduced to a system of two first-order equations. We shall perform this reduction and then use the techniques developed in this chapter to find a numerical solution of the resulting two simultaneous first-order differential equations. Specifically we shall use the improved Euler method to get started and then the predictor-corrector method of Section 8.7 for succeeding calculations.

As with all of our case studies, a complete understanding of the physical problem is not necessary in order to follow the numerical procedures. Obviously the development will be more interesting and more meaningful to the reader who does comprehend the formulation of the differential equation. However, the reader unfamiliar with mechanics is advised to skip over the next few paragraphs and after looking at the differential equations, (8.61) and (8.64), to proceed to the numerical analysis starting with (8.66).

Consider a cantilever beam of length L subjected to a load P at its free end (see Figure 8.8). We let x be a distance measured along the axis of the beam with $x = 0$ at the built-in end. The variable y measures the deflection of the beam with the positive direction taken to be downward.

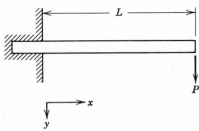

Figure 8.8. *The deflected beam studied in Case Study 13.*

---

[16]See, for instance, Peter Henrici, *Discrete Variable Methods in Ordinary Differential Equations,* Wiley, New York, 1962, chap. 5; or Richard W. Hamming, *Numerical Methods for Scientists and Engineers,* New York, McGraw-Hill, 1962, chap. 15.

(See the coordinates as shown in Figure 8.8.) If E is Young's modulus for the material and I is the moment of inertia of the cross section of the beam about a line through the center of mass of the cross section and perpendicular to both the x and y coordinates, then it can be shown[17] that the *elastic* deflections satisfy the differential equation

$$\frac{y''}{[1 + (y')^2]^{3/2}} = \frac{P(L - x)}{EI} \tag{8.61}$$

Since the beam is built-in at $x = 0$ both the deflection and its slope vanish there. Thus

$$y(0) = 0 \tag{8.62}$$
$$y'(0) = 0 \tag{8.63}$$

In many engineering applications, the slope, y', of the deflection is so small for all values of x that the square of y' may be neglected compared with 1. In such cases (8.61) reduces to the linear equation

$$y'' = \frac{P(L - x)}{EI} \tag{8.64}$$

with again the initial conditions (8.62) and (8.63). Equation 8.64 is often referred to as the Bernoulli-Euler law. From classical methods the solution of (8.64) with the initial conditions (8.62) and (8.63) is

$$y(x) = \frac{P}{6EI} x^2(3L - x) \tag{8.65}$$

This solution is valid provided the deflections are "small," that is, for relatively small loads P.

If P becomes large then both y and y' are large compared with unity, and we can no longer neglect the term $(y')^2$ in (8.61). In this case no analytic solution comparable to (8.65) exists, and we must have recourse to numerical techniques.

We proceed to the use of numerical techniques to solve (8.61) for various values of the load P. We shall compare the results with those provided by the solution (8.65) of the linear problem. In this way we can obtain some feeling for how small the deflections (or load) must be in order for the linearized solution to be valid. Of course, we must keep in mind that even the nonlinear equation (8.61) is only valid as long as the stresses in the entire beam remain in the elastic range (see Case Study 12 in Section 7.9). This will place an upper limit on the magnitude of the load P. We return to this question of the maximum allowable value of P later.

If in (8.61) we define a new function z to be the derivative of y, that is,

$$y' = z \tag{8.66}$$

then (8.61) becomes

$$z' = C(L - x)(1 + z^2)^{3/2} \tag{8.67}$$

---

[17] See, for example, Archie Higdon, Edward H. Ohlsen, William B. Stiles, and John A. Weese, *Mechanics of Materials* (2nd ed.), New York, Wiley, pp. 276–330.

where for convenience we have defined a new constant

$$C = P/EI \qquad (8.68)$$

The initial conditions (8.62) and (8.63) become

$$y(0) = 0 \qquad (8.69)$$
$$z(0) = 0 \qquad (8.70)$$

Thus we have two simultaneous first-order differential equations (8.66) and (8.67). To find a numerical solution we proceed as follows:

1. Let

$$F(x,z) = C(L - x)(1 + z^2)^{3/2} \qquad (8.71)$$

2. Use the improved Euler method to compute y_1 and z_1, recalling that $y_0 = z_0 = 0$.

$$y_1 = CLh^2/2 \qquad (8.72)$$

$$z_1 = \frac{h}{2}[CL + F(h,hCL)] \qquad (8.73)$$

3. For $m = 1, 2, 3, \ldots$, predict values of y_{m+1} and z_{m+1} from

$$y_{m+1}^{(0)} = y_{m-1} + 2hz_m \qquad (8.74)$$
$$z_{m+1}^{(0)} = z_{m-1} + 2hF(x_m, z_m) \qquad (8.75)$$

These are analogous to (8.39).

4. Correct the values of y_{m+1} and z_{m+1} from

$$y_{m+1}^{(i)} = y_m + \frac{h}{2}[z_m + z_{m+1}^{(i-1)}] \qquad (8.76)$$

$$z_{m+1}^{(i)} = z_m + \frac{h}{2}[F(x_m, z_m) + F(x_{m+1}, z_{m+1}^{(i-1)})] \qquad (8.77)$$

These are analogous to (8.40). Notice that (8.77) does not involve y_{m+1}. Hence we can solve (8.77) *alone* without reference to (8.76). Once the values of $z_{m+1}^{(i)}$ have converged, that is, once

$$|z_{m+1}^{(i)} - z_{m+1}^{(i-1)}| < \epsilon \qquad (8.78)$$

we stop the iteration. We shall return to the computation of y_{m+1} in point 6 below.

5. We make one final correction to z_{m+1} by estimating the truncation error from

$$e_T = \tfrac{1}{5}[z_m^{(0)} - z_m^{(i)}] \qquad (8.79)$$

and then letting

$$z_{m+1} = z_m^{(i)} + e_T = z_m^{(i)} + \tfrac{1}{5}[z_m^{(0)} - z_m^{(i)}] \qquad (8.80)$$

6. We return to (8.76) where we replace $z_{m+1}^{(i-1)}$ by the value of z_{m+1} just computed. Thus

$$y_{m+1} = y_m + \frac{h}{2}(z_m + z_{m+1}) \qquad (8.81)$$

Notice now that we no longer need the predictor (8.74) for $y_{m+1}^{(0)}$ since (8.81) computes y_{m+1} directly.

The entire process is summarized in the flow chart of Figure 8.9. The procedure should be clear from that flow chart, but we point out a few details that may not be entirely obvious. First, we have chosen to fix the beam length, L, Young's modulus, E, and the moment of inertia, I as program constants. On the other hand, we read values of the load, P, and the step size, h. We do this because of the use we intend to make of the Fortran program that will be constructed from the flow chart. We want to try different step sizes in order to observe the number of iterations required by the corrector for various step sizes. The smaller we make h, the fewer the number of iterations. But how many fewer? We also want to vary the load and observe the deviation of the nonlinear solution from the linear one as the load increases.

The program computes the solution for a given P and h and then reads another pair of values for P and h and recomputes a solution. This process continues until reading a zero or negative value for h. Obviously $h \leq 0$ would cause trouble with the algorithm so we wish to guard against such a blunder on the user's part anyway. It also provides us with a convenient stopping criterion. We need not be concerned with negative P since, in our model, this merely deflects the beam upward.

We have also inserted an iteration counter, ITN, in the corrector loop in order to make sure that the algorithm will terminate under any circumstances.

The flow chart calls for printing values of x (the dimension along the length of the beam) for $x = 0, h, 2h, \ldots, L$. For each value of x, the program prints the value of y that satisfies the nonlinear differential equation (8.61) and the value of y that satisfies the linear equation. The latter is computed from (8.65). For all but the first two values of x (0 and h), the *relative percentage* error in $z = y'$ and the number of iterations used are printed as well.

A program that follows this flow chart quite closely is shown in Figure 8.10. Notice that two function statements are used. The function statement FNCZ corresponds to $F(x,z)$ defined in (8.71). The function statement FSOL is the right-hand side of (8.65).

As an example we have chosen a beam of high-strength aluminum alloy with a rectangular cross section. The beam is 3 in. wide, 0.8 in. deep and 100 in. long. Then

$$L = 100 \text{ in.}$$
$$I = 0.128 \text{ in.}^4$$

and a typical value for Young's modulus is

$$E = 10 \times 10^6 \text{ psi}$$

In what follows we vary the load, P, and the step size, h. Recall that P is in lb and h is in inches.

The result of running this program for a load of 64 lb and using $h = 2$ in and $h = 4$ in is shown in Figures 8.11 and 8.12. The results vary little whether the smaller or larger step size is used. For $h = 2$ there were 149 evaluations of the function $F(x,z)$ given by (8.71), counting its

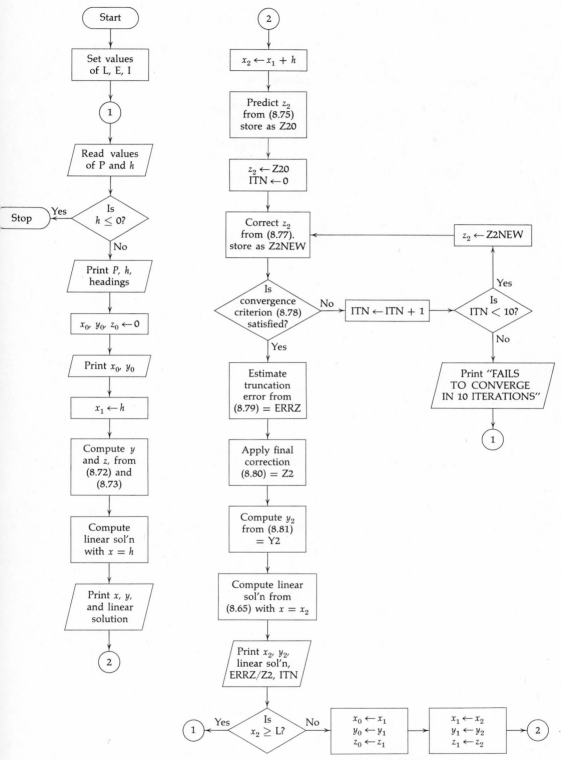

Figure 8.9. *Flow chart of the method of solution of the differential equation describing the deflection of the beam shown in Figure 8.8.*

```
C CASE STUDY 13
C SOLUTION OF THE DIFFERENTIAL EQUATION OF LARGE
C   DEFLECTIONS IN A BEAM BY A PREDICTOR-CORRECTOR METHOD
C
      REAL LINEAR
C DEFINE STATEMENT FUNCTIONS FOR LINEAR SOLUTION AND CORRECTOR
      FSOL(X) = (C*X*X/6.0) * (3.0*XL - X)
      FNCZ(X, Z) = C * (XL - X) * (1.0 + Z*Z) * SQRT(1.0 + Z*Z)
C SET VALUES OF LENGTH OF BEAM, YOUNG'S MODULUS, AND MOMENT OF INERTIA
      XL = 100.0
      XE = 1.0E7
      XI = 0.128
C READ VALUES OF LOAD AND STEP SIZE
100   READ (5, 1000) P, H
1000  FORMAT (2F10.0)
C STOP IF H IS NOT POSITIVE
      IF (H .LE. 0.0) STOP
C PRINT INPUT DATA AND COLUMN HEADINGS
      WRITE (6, 2000) P, H
2000  FORMAT (/'     LOAD',F10.4,'  LBS;  STEP SIZE',F10.4,'  INCHES'///
     1  6X,'DISTANCE    DEFLECTION   LINEAR SOLN',4X,
     2  '%ERROR    NO. ITERATIONS'/)
C INITIALIZE VALUES OF X, Y, AND Y' = Z
      X0 = 0.0
      Y0 = 0.0
      Z0 = 0.0
      WRITE (6, 4000) X0, Y0, Z0
4000  FORMAT (1X, 3F13.5)
      C = P / (XE*XI)
C COMPUTE Y(H), Y'(H) AND LINEAR SOLUTION AT X = H
      X1 = H
      ZZ = H * C * XL
      Y1 = 0.5 * H * ZZ
      Z1 = 0.5 * H * (C*XL + FNCZ(H, ZZ))
      LINEAR = FSOL(H)
      WRITE (6, 4000) X1, Y1, LINEAR
50    X2 = X1 + H
C PREDICT VALUE FOR Y'(M+1)
      Z20 = Z0 + 2.0 * H * FNCZ(X1, Z1)
      Z2 = Z20
      ITN = 1
C ITERATE TO CORRECT VALUE OF Y'(M+1)
40    Z2NEW = Z1 + 0.5 * H * (FNCZ(X1, Z1) + FNCZ(X2, Z2))
C IF CORRECTOR HAS NOT CONVERGED, INCREASE ITERATION COUNTER, CHECK
C   FOR LIMIT ON ITERATIONS, AND IF OK RETURN TO CORRECTOR LOOP
      IF (ABS(Z2 - Z2NEW) .LT. 1.0E-6) GO TO 20
      ITN = ITN + 1
      IF (ITN .GE. 10) GO TO 30
      Z2 = Z2NEW
      GO TO 40
30    WRITE (6, 5000)
5000  FORMAT (1X, 'FAILS TO CONVERGE IN 10 ITERATIONS')
      STOP
C WHEN Y'(M+1) CONVERGES, ESTIMATE TRUNCATION ERROR AND MAKE FINAL
C   CORRECTION
20    ERRZ = 0.2 * (Z20 - Z2NEW)
      Z2 = Z2NEW + ERRZ
C COMPUTE Y(M+1) AND LINEAR SOLUTION AT X(M+1)
      Y2 = Y1 + 0.5 * H * (Z1+Z2)
      LINEAR = FSOL(X2)
      PCT = (ERRZ/Z2)*100.0
      WRITE (6, 6000) X2, Y2, LINEAR, PCT, ITN
6000  FORMAT (1X, 4F13.5, I8)
C CHECK FOR END OF BEAM, X = XL, AND GO BACK FOR MORE DATA IF AT END
      IF (X2 .GE. XL) GO TO 100
C RESET VALUES OF X(M-1), ETC., AND X(M), ETC.
      X0 = X1
      Y0 = Y1
      Z0 = Z1
      X1 = X2
      Y1 = Y2
      Z1 = Z2
C RETURN TO INCREMENT X(M+1) BY H
      GO TO 50
      END
```

Figure 8.10. *A program to solve the differential equation of a deflected beam, corresponding to the flow chart of Figure 8.9.*

LOAD   64.0000 LBS; STEP SIZE   2.0000 INCHES

DISTANCE	DEFLECTION	LINEAR SOLN	%ERROR	NO. ITERATIONS
0.0	0.0	0.0		
2.00000	0.01000	0.00993		
4.00000	0.03950	0.03947	-0.00139	2
6.00000	0.08822	0.08820	-0.00061	1
8.00000	0.15576	0.15573	-0.00043	1
10.00000	0.24174	0.24167	-0.00030	1
12.00000	0.34579	0.34560	-0.00020	1
14.00000	0.46752	0.46713	-0.00015	1
16.00000	0.60655	0.60587	-0.00008	1
18.00000	0.76253	0.76140	-0.00006	1
20.00000	0.93507	0.93333	-0.00004	1
22.00000	1.12381	1.12127	-0.00001	1
24.00000	1.32838	1.32480	0.00001	1
26.00000	1.54840	1.54353	0.00002	1
28.00000	1.78351	1.77707	0.00003	1
30.00000	2.03334	2.02500	0.00003	1
32.00000	2.29752	2.28693	0.00004	1
34.00000	2.57568	2.56247	0.00005	1
36.00000	2.86743	2.85120	0.00005	1
38.00000	3.17242	3.15273	0.00006	1
40.00000	3.49026	3.46667	0.00006	1
42.00000	3.82058	3.79260	0.00006	1
44.00000	4.16299	4.13013	0.00005	1
46.00000	4.51712	4.47887	0.00006	1
48.00000	4.88257	4.83840	0.00006	1
50.00000	5.25897	5.20833	0.00006	1
52.00000	5.64592	5.58827	0.00006	1
54.00000	6.04302	5.97780	0.00007	1
56.00000	6.44989	6.37654	0.00006	1
58.00000	6.86612	6.78407	0.00006	1
60.00000	7.29131	7.20000	0.00006	1
62.00000	7.72507	7.62393	0.00005	1
64.00000	8.16697	8.05547	0.00006	1
66.00000	8.61662	8.49420	0.00005	1
68.00000	9.07360	8.93974	0.00006	1
70.00000	9.53750	9.39167	0.00005	2
72.00000	10.00789	9.84960	0.00006	1
74.00000	10.48436	10.31314	0.00004	1
76.00000	10.96648	10.78187	0.00004	1
78.00000	11.45383	11.25541	0.00004	1
80.00000	11.94599	11.73333	0.00004	1
82.00000	12.44251	12.21527	0.00004	1
84.00000	12.94298	12.70080	0.00003	1
86.00000	13.44695	13.18954	0.00003	1
88.00000	13.95400	13.68106	0.00003	1
90.00000	14.46368	14.17500	0.00002	1
92.00000	14.97556	14.67092	0.00002	1
94.00000	15.48920	15.16846	0.00002	1
96.00000	16.00415	15.66721	0.00001	1
98.00000	16.51999	16.16672	0.00001	1
100.00000	17.03627	16.66667	0.00000	1

Figure 8.11. *Output of the program of Figure 8.10, run with* h = 2.

use in the predictor (8.75) and its use in the corrector (8.77), the latter sometimes more than once. For h = 4 there were 114 evaluations of $F(x,z)$. Balancing off the extra evaluations and some other additional arithmetic for h = 2 are two things: (1) the solution obtained when h = 2 is more accurate (note the error in y) although not enough to justify the extra effort; and (2) we have the solution of the nonlinear equation at twice as many points. Of course, we could use the solution obtained when h = 4 and interpolate linearly to find, for example, the deflection at $x = 18$. On balance it appears that h = 4 is a good choice and we shall use it in our future computations. Notice that for h = 4 two iterations are required in

LOAD   64.0000 LBS; STEP SIZE   4.0000 INCHES

DISTANCE	DEFLECTION	LINEAR SOLN	%ERROR	NO. ITERATIONS
0.0	0.0	0.0		
4.00000	0.04000	0.03947		
8.00000	0.15607	0.15573	-0.00495	2
12.00000	0.34591	0.34560	-0.00178	2
16.00000	0.60650	0.60587	-0.00103	2
20.00000	0.93484	0.93333	-0.00046	2
24.00000	1.32796	1.32480	-0.00015	1
28.00000	1.78292	1.77707	0.00008	1
32.00000	2.29674	2.28693	0.00022	2
36.00000	2.86648	2.85120	0.00032	2
40.00000	3.48912	3.46667	0.00038	2
44.00000	4.16167	4.13013	0.00042	2
48.00000	4.88106	4.83840	0.00044	2
52.00000	5.64421	5.58827	0.00046	2
56.00000	6.44799	6.37654	0.00046	2
60.00000	7.28922	7.20000	0.00045	2
64.00000	8.16469	8.05547	0.00043	2
68.00000	9.07112	8.93974	0.00041	2
72.00000	10.00520	9.84960	0.00038	2
76.00000	10.96359	10.78187	0.00034	2
80.00000	11.94289	11.73333	0.00030	2
84.00000	12.93967	12.70080	0.00025	2
88.00000	13.95048	13.68106	0.00021	2
92.00000	14.97183	14.67092	0.00015	2
96.00000	16.00021	15.66721	0.00010	2
100.00000	17.03212	16.66667	0.00005	1

Figure 8.12. *Output of the program of Figure 8.10, run with* h = 4.

most steps. As we pointed out earlier, a step size requiring two iterations is usually a good choice. A more careful study would require trying several other values of h (say $h = 5$ and $h = 10$) and also several other loads before fixing on a choice of h (see Exercises 36 and 37).

We should point out that we could make the program in Figure 8.10 somewhat more efficient by noting that in statement 40 the value of FNCZ(X1,Z1) does not change during the iterations. Hence it could be computed once outside of the corrector loop. For example, just prior to statement 40 we could use

$$F1 = FNCZ(X1,Z1)$$

and then change statement 40 to read

$$40 \ Z2NEW = Z1 + .5*H* (F1 + FNCZ (X2, Z2))$$

The number of evaluations of $F(x,z)$ then becomes 93 for $h = 4$ and 148 for $h = 2$. Thus $h = 4$ still appears to be a better choice.

We now turn to the question: Did we really need to evaluate the nonlinear equation numerically or would the solution of the linear equation have done just as well?

If we draw a graph of the two deflection curves they will not appear to differ much unless we use a highly exaggerated scale along the y-axis. On the other hand, suppose we look at the percentage relative error in the deflection at the free end ($x = 100$) using the linear solution. This error is

$$e = \frac{17.036 - 16.667}{17.036} \times 100 = 2.16\% \tag{8.82}$$

We still cannot answer the question: Is the linear solution good enough? The answer to such a question depends upon the use to which we put the results of the computation. If those uses can tolerate an error of the magnitude shown in (8.82), then the linear solution is satisfactory and much easier to compute. On the other hand, if this size of error is not tolerable, then we must resort to the more tedious numerical solution of the nonlinear equation.

As one final variation on our theme, suppose we decide that a 4% error in the maximum deflection is acceptable. We then ask: How large can the load become before we must use the nonlinear solution?

To answer this question we run the program[18] several times for varying loads P. The results are:

Load	Nonlinear Deflection (inches)	Linear Deflection (inches)	Percentage Error
10	2.605	2.604	0.03
20	5.219	5.208	0.21
30	7.850	7.812	0.48
40	10.505	10.417	0.84
50	13.195	13.021	1.32
60	15.929	15.625	1.91
70	18.719	18.229	2.62
80	21.575	20.833	3.44
90	24.512	23.438	4.38
100	27.546	26.042	5.46
110	30.694	28.646	6.67
120	33.977	31.250	8.02
130	37.424	33.854	9.54
150	44.942	39.063	13.08
200	70.516	52.083	26.14

A graph of these results is shown in Figure 8.13. The graph for a different beam (different E, I, or L) would yield a curve with the same general shape but not the same numerical results. In this case, however, it appears that the linear solution is acceptable for loads less than 90 lb.

We should note that the results in the last several entries in the above table are meaningless. Recall that the basic equation (8.61) was an accurate model for the elastic deflections. At a load of 200 lb, part of the beam, notably near the fixed end, will have stresses in the plastic range. Hence the entire analysis breaks down. Indeed, for the aluminum alloy in question loads of more than 120 lb are likely to produce some plastic behavior. Of course, the differential equations—linear and nonlinear—still possess solutions, and we can compute those solutions. The point is: *Even though a solution exists and can be computed, it may be meaningless* because the differ-

[18] Actually an abbreviated version of the program was used since all we need are the linear and nonlinear deflections at $x = 100$ because the maximum deflection occurs there.

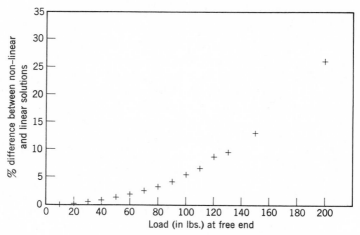

Figure 8.13. *The percentage error in the maximum beam deflection as a function of load.*

ential equation is not an accurate representation of the physical phenomenon. There is no way for the numerical analysis or the computer to tell us when this happens. The responsibility for determining the proper mathematical model rests with the analyst himself. Of course, in this case we could enter a maximum allowable stress (the yield stress) for the material, compute the maximum stress occurring in the beam, and then print a warning message if the actual stress exceeded the allowable stress. If this program were to be used by persons other than the writer of the program, such a safeguard might well be worth incorporating in the program. It does, of course, complicate not only the writing of the program but the use of the program as well; the user must now specify another piece of data—the maximum allowable stress.

Here is an example of a frequently encountered tradeoff—simplicity versus completeness. The simplest program does not check for excessive loads. A program to make such a check is more complex.

As another example of the simplicity–completeness tradeoff, consider the problem of automatic interval changes. We mentioned earlier that a program can be written so that the step size is automatically halved if too many iterations are required and doubled if there are too few. We have not done this here to avoid the complexity that a thorough program of this kind would need.

Some of the things that have to be considered if automatic step-size changing is employed are:

1. It could happen, unless suitably prevented, that the program would try to halve and to double at the same point; the two actions would put us back where we started, ready to do both of them over again—indefinitely.

2. Many differential equations have singularities, points at which a solution does not exist. On approaching such a point, an automatic interval-halving routine might halve indefinitely, never reaching the singularity. A counter would have to be provided to set a limit on the number of halvings.

3. It would be highly desirable to write the program so that automatic interval changing could be disabled. For instance, it might be necessary to plot a graph from the results, in which case it might be more important to have results at specified points than to save a little time. (This applies more to doubling.)

4. If halving should be called for the very first time the corrector is called into action, how far do we go back? If we accept the point computed from the improved Euler method, we have doubtful accuracy. If we return to the beginning, we have to think about the line of output already printed, based on the larger interval.

All of these problems can be solved; in some cases it is quite feasible to develop automatic interval changing. For our purposes it seems inappropriate.

Bibliographic Notes

Taylor series solutions are discussed in Sections 14.2 and 14.3 of Henrici [23], Section 6.2 of Carnahan et al. [20], and Section 7.3.1 of Redish [12]. Taylor series, referred to as the "extended Euler method," are also discussed by Stark [3] in Sections 7.6 and 7.7.

Excellent discussions of general Runge-Kutta methods are to be found in Section 5.6-3 of Ralston [19] and Chapter 2 of Fox [see below]. Another recommended source is Stark [3], Sections 7.14 and 7.15 where a Fortran program may also be found. In addition Runge-Kutta methods may be found in Sections 6.15 and 6.16 of Hildebrand [18], Section 6.33 of Stiefel [9], and Section 14.5 of Henrici [23]. The last of these is the most concise. A fifth-order method is given in Chapter 5, Section 32, of Milne [see below].

Euler's method as such is discussed by Stark [3] in Sections 7.4 and 7.5 where a Fortran program is given, Scarborough [17] in Section 84, and Carnahan et al. [20] in Section 6.3. The last of these includes a numerical example, an error discussion, and a Fortran program. One of the most complete and brilliant expositions of Euler's method is given in Chapter 1 of Henrici [see below] where the statistical distribution of the roundoff error is also to be found.

The general second order Runge-Kutta method is discussed by Hildebrand [18] in Section 6.15, Carnahan et al. [20] in Section 6.5 and Henrici [see below] in Section 2.1-2. The special case of the improved Euler method is found in Stiefel [9] in Section 6.32. Another special case, the modified Euler method, is discussed by Stark [3] in Sections 7.8 and 7.9 where a Fortran program may be found. Stark refers to the modified Euler method as a predictor-corrector but does not iterate with the corrector.

Truncation errors are discussed by Ralston [19] in Section 5.6-3-1, Carnahan et al. [20] in Section 6.6, and Henrici [see below] in Section 2.2. The Kutta-Merson method, which provides a direct estimate of the truncation error in the fourth-order method, is discussed in Chapter 2, Section 16, of Fox [see below] and in the paper by R. E. Scraton, "Estimation of the Truncation Error in Runge-Kutta and Allied Processes," *Com-*

puter Jour. (October 1964), pp. 246–248. This paper contains a discussion of additional ways for estimating the error in Runge-Kutta methods.

Partial instability of the Runge-Kutta methods is ignored in most texts. An excellent reference, however, is Sections 7 and 8 of Chapter 4 of Fox's book [see below]. Fox includes examples that do not have exponentially decaying solutions but that still exhibit this type of instability.

Predictor-corrector methods are covered in Sections 5.5–2 and 5.7 of Ralston [19], Section 8.3 of Hamming [6], Section 6.11 of Carnahan et al [20], Chapter 8 of Volume 1 of Ralston and Wilf [25], and Chapter 2, Section 6–8, of Milne [see below]. Perhaps the most thorough discussion of these methods is found in Chapter 15 of Hamming [22].

The convergence of the corrector formula is discussed by Ralston [19] in Section 5.5–1, Carnahan et al. [20] in Section 6.11, and Milne [see below] in Section 9, Chapter 2. Truncation errors are covered by Ralston [19] in Section 5.5–3, Hamming [6] in Section 8.5, and Carnahan et al. [20] in Section 6.12. Stability of predictor-corrector methods is described in Section 6.12 of Carnahan et al. [20], Sections 14.5 and 14.6 of Hamming [22], and Chapter 8, Section 2e, of Ralston and Wilf [25].

Inherent instability is neglected by most authors. Two exceptions are Carnahan et al. [20] in Section 6.6 and Fox [see below] in Section 6 of Chapter 4 and in Section 1 of Chapter 8.

Comparison of the various methods for solving ordinary differential equations is discussed quite well by Hildebrand [18] in Section 6.19.

There are four other highly recommended references concerned with the numerical solution of ordinary differential equations. They are:

William E. Boyce and Richard C. DiPrima. *Elementary Differential Equations and Boundary Value Problems.* New York: Wiley, 1965, Chapter 8.

> An elementary discussion at about the same level as the present text. Does *not* include flow charts or computer programs. Covers Euler's method, the improved Euler method, Taylor series, fourth-order Runge-Kutta method, predictor-corrector methods, and systems of equations. Discusses truncation error for Euler's method. Does not discuss numerical stability.

W. E. Milne. *Numerical Solution of Differential Equations.* New York: Wiley, 1953.

> This is a classic text in the numerical solution of differential equations. It covers both ordinary and partial differential equations and requires somewhat more mathematical sophistication than does the present text. It does *not* contain either flow charts or computer programs. Indeed, the numerical methods are, as the date of publication would indicate, desk-calculator oriented.
>
> Methods I and II introduced at the start are the predictor-corrector pair used in this text. Milne does discuss the convergence of this algorithm. The Taylor series solution as well as other predictor-corrector methods are discussed in some detail.
>
> Runge-Kutta methods are covered quite briefly. Both fourth-order and fifth-order Runge-Kutta methods are given. Systems of equations, higher-order equations, and boundary value problems are also discussed.

Peter Henrici. *Discrete Variable Methods in Ordinary Differential Equations.* New York: Wiley, 1962.

A thorough and complete treatment of ordinary differential equations. It requires much more mathematical sophistication than does the present text. Contains a few flow charts but *no* computer programs.

The book is divided into three parts: Runge-Kutta methods, predictor-corrector methods, and boundary value problems (see Exercises 20 and 38 of this chapter). The discussion also includes existence and uniqueness theorems for the differential equations under consideration. Henrici is the only text that treats roundoff errors from a probabilistic point of view and gives statistical estimates for roundoff errors together with numerical examples exhibiting the statistical distribution of roundoff.

Part I discusses Euler's method, Taylor series solution, the general second-order Runge-Kutta method and the usual fourth-order method. Systems of equations and equations of higher order than one are also covered. *The first chapter,* which deals with Euler's method and the statistical behavior of roundoff errors in that method, *is highly recommended even to the novice* in numerical analysis and/or differential equations.

Part II covers multistep (predictor-corrector) methods. The discussion starts with the interpolating polynomial and develops the Adams-Bashforth, Adams-Moulton, Nyström, and Milne-Simpson methods. Convergence and stability are discussed in great detail. There is also a discussion of some special second order equations.

L. Fox (ed.). *Numerical Solution of Ordinary and Partial Differential Equations.* New York: Pergamon Press and Addison-Wesley, 1962.

This is a reference more than a text. There are no exercises. It requires much more mathematical sophistication than the present text, but is very well written and contains a wealth of information. Does *not* contain flow charts or computer programs.

The book is in four parts, only the first of which deals with ordinary differential equations. Half of the ten chapters in this first part were written by the editor, L. Fox; the other five chapters were written by D. F. Mayers. The discussion of Runge-Kutta methods includes a derivation of a general third-order method and also a development of the so-called Kutta-Merson method, which provides an estimate of the truncation error in the fourth-order method. Predictor-corrector methods are discussed and several such methods are compared. Stability is covered in great depth and with equally great clarity. In addition to inherent and partial instabilities, strong, weak and induced instabilities are discussed. There is a chapter on boundary value problems (see Exercises 20 and 38 of this chapter), eigenvalue problems, and Chebyshev solutions of ordinary differential equations.

Exercises

1 Given that $y' = 0.04y$ and that $y(0) = 1000$,
   a. Compute $y(1)$, using Euler's method with $h = 1$.

b. Compute $y(1)$, using Euler's method with $h = 0.5$.

c. Compute $y(1)$, using Euler's method with $h = 0.25$.

d. Compute $y(1)$ from the solution to the equation $y = 1000e^{0.04t}$.

e. Interpret parts (a) to (d) in terms of a familiar banking operation.

*2 The rate of emission of radioactivity of a substance is proportional to the amount of the substance remaining. The differential equation is therefore $y' = -ky$, where the minus sign reflects the fact that the radioactivity decreases with time. Suppose that $k = 0.01$ and that there are 100 g of the material at $t = 0$; how much will remain when $t = 100$?

The solution of the equation is $y = 100e^{-kt}$; the exact answer is 36.788 g. Solve the equation numerically, using

a. Euler's method, $h = 25$;

b. Euler's method, $h = 10$;

c. Euler's method, $h = 5$;

d. Euler's method, $h = 1$;

e. Improved Euler method, $h = 20$;

f. Improved Euler method, $h = 10$;

g. Modified Euler method, $h = 20$;

h. Modified Euler method, $h = 10$;

i. Fourth-order Runge-Kutta method, $h = 100$;

j. Fourth-order Runge-Kutta method, $h = 50$;

k. Second-order predictor-corrector method in the text, with $h = 20$, given that $y(20) = 81.8731$ exactly;

l. Predictor-corrector, with $h = 10$, given that $y(10) = 90.4837$.

3 A body with an initial mass of 200 slugs is accelerated by a constant force of 2000 lb. The mass decreases at a rate of 1 slug/sec. If the body is at rest at $t = 0$, find its velocity at the end of 50 sec. The differential equation is $dV/dt = 2000/(200 - t)$; the solution is $V = 2000 \log [200/(200 - t)]$, so that $V(50) = 575.36$. Solve the equation numerically, using

a. Euler's method, $h = 10$;

b. Euler's method, $h = 5$;

c. Euler's method, $h = 2$;

d. Improved Euler method, $h = 10$;

e. Modified Euler method, $h = 10$;

f. Fourth-order Runge-Kutta method, $h = 10$;

g. Text predictor-corrector method, $h = 10$.

4 Suppose that the body described in Exercise 3 is subject to an air resistance equal to twice the velocity. The differential equation is now $dV/dt = (2000 - 2V)/(200 - t)$. If the body is at rest at $t = 0$, the solution is $V = 10t - t^2/40$, so that $V(50) = 437.5$. Solve the equation numerically, using

a. Euler's method, $h = 10$;

b. Improved Euler method, $h = 10$;

c. Modified Euler method, $h = 10$;

d. Fourth-order Runge-Kutta method, $h = 10$;

e. Text predictor-corrector method, $h = 10$.

5 Given $y' = 4 - 2x$, $y(0) = 2$, solve by the improved Euler method and the modified Euler method, using $h = 0.5$ and continuing to $x = 5$. Compare with the solution, $y = -x^2 + 4x + 2$. Would you expect Euler's method to be exact also? For what kind of equation would you expect Euler's method to be exact?

6 Given that $y' = -x/y$, $y(0) = 20$, evaluate $y(24)$ using
   a. Modified Euler method, $h = 2$;
   b. Fourth-order Runge-Kutta method, $h = 4$. What happens?

7 Given that $y' = (6y + 2x + 1)/x$, $y(1) = -17/30$, find $y(4)$, using the text predictor-corrector method with $h = 1$. Repeat with $y(1) = -16/30$.

8 Given that $y' = xy^2 + 3xy$, $y(0) = -0.5$, find $y(3)$, using the text predictor-corrector method with $h = 0.5$.

9 Given $y' = \cos x - \sin x - y$, $y(0) = 2$, solve by the text predictor-corrector with $h = 0.5$ to $x = 10$. Show that the solution possesses absolute stability. The analytic solution is $y = \cos x + e^{-x}$.

10 Given that $y' = 2y/x + x^2 e^x$, $y(1) = 0$. Solve by the text predictor-corrector with $h = 0.2$ to $x = 5$. Show that although the absolute error grows the relative error does not grow. The solution is $y = x^2(e^x - e)$.

11 Draw flow charts and write programs to solve differential equations by the methods of Euler, improved Euler, modified Euler, fourth-order Runge-Kutta, and the text predictor-corrector. Each program should have as its first statement an arithmetic statement function defining the differential equation; this can be changed to solve different equations. Each program should read a card containing values of x and y (the initial condition), h (the step size), and $xlast$ (the final value of x). The program for the predictor-corrector should use the fourth-order Runge-Kutta method to find the necessary second value of y; it should not modify the step size, but it should include an iteration counter to stop the program if convergence has not been achieved after ten iterations.

12 Extend the predictor-corrector program of Exercise 11 to provide a printout of the estimate of truncation error at each step.

13 Extend the predictor-corrector program of Exercise 11 to halve or to double the step size as dictated by the iteration counter.

14 Show that the second-order Runge-Kutta method (8.25), when applied to $y' = -y$, $y(0) = 1$, yields

$$y_m = \left(1 - h + \frac{h^2}{2}\right)^m \simeq e^{-x_m}$$

In using this approximation would you expect the error always to have the same sign?

15 For the equation $y' = ky$ the corrector formula (8.40) can be solved explicitly for y_{m+1}. (We may therefore drop the superscripts.) Show that the resulting expression agrees with the Taylor series through terms in h^2.

16 Consider the following predictor-corrector pair:

$$y^{(0)}_{m+1} = y_m + \frac{h}{2}[y'_m + f(x_m + h, y_m + hy'_m)]$$

and

$$y_{m+1}^{(i+1)} = y_m + \frac{h}{2}\left[y_m' + f(x_{m+1}, y_{m+1}^{(i)})\right] \qquad i = 0, 1, 2, \ldots$$

where $y_m' = f(x_m, y_m)$.
a. What is the name of this predictor?
b. What are the orders of the two formulas?
c. What advantage does this predictor have over (8.39)?
d. What is the disadvantage of using this predictor rather than (8.39)?

*17 Reduce $y'' + y = F(x)$ to a pair of first-order equations. Show that the right-hand member of each equation is independent of the differentiated variable on the left. Does this mean that no iterations of the corrector formula are required?

18 Reduce $y''' + a(x,y)y'' + b(x,y)y' = c(x,y)$ to a set of three first-order equations and describe a numerical method of solution.

19 If Euler's method is used as a predictor,

$$y_{m+1}^{(0)} = y_m + h\,f(x_m, y_m)$$

then an appropriate corrector is

$$y_{m+1}^{(i)} = y_m - h\,f[x_{m+1}, y_{m+1}^{(i-1)}]$$

a. Show that the truncation error in the predictor is

$$E_T^{(p)} = \frac{h^2}{2}y''(\xi) \qquad x_m \le \xi \le x_{m+1}$$

and in the corrector is

$$E_T^{(c)} = \frac{-h^2}{2}y''(\eta) \qquad x_m \le \eta \le x_{m+1}$$

Assuming that y'' is constant, find an estimate of $E_T^{(c)}$ in terms of $y_{m+1}^{(0)}$ and $y_{m+1}^{(i)}$. Derive a correction term that can be used to improve $y_{m+1}^{(i)}$.
b. Show that the corrector converges if $h < 1/M$, where

$$\left|\frac{\partial f}{\partial y}\right| < M$$

c. Show that the corrector possesses absolute and relative stability if $f_y > 0$ but that it is unstable—in both a relative and an absolute sense—if $f_y < 0$.

20 Consider the second-order equation $y'' + ay' + by = c$, where a, b, and c are functions of x. Suppose it is given that $y(0) = K_0$, $y(1) = K_1$. Propose a numerical method for finding $y(x)$ for $0 \le x \le 1$. *Hint.* Take a "guess" at $y(h)$ and see if this yields $y(1) = K_1$. If not, modify the "guess."

21 Show that the difference equation

$$\epsilon_{n+1} - 2a\epsilon_n - \epsilon_{n-1} = 0$$

has the solution

$$\epsilon_n = c_1\lambda_1^n + c_2\lambda_2^n$$

where
$$\lambda_1 = +a + \sqrt{a^2 + 1}$$
$$\lambda_2 = +a - \sqrt{a^2 + 1}$$

and c_1 and c_2 are arbitrary constants. By making use of these results, show that the predictor (8.39) is unstable.

*22 Consider the general predictor formula

$$y_{m+1} = A_0 y_m + A_1 y_{m-1} + h B_0 y'_m$$

This is usually referred to as a *Milne-type predictor*[19] and it is characterized by the fact that on the right there is one more value of y than of y'.

a. Determine the equations that A_0, A_1, and B_0 must satisfy if the predictor is to be exact for $y = 1$, $y = x$ and $y = x^2$.
b. Show that the solution of the equations above yields the predictor given by (8.39).
c. By using $y = x^3$ show that the truncation error is of order h^3.

23 Consider the predictor formula

$$y_{m+1} = A_0 y_m + h(B_0 y'_m + B_1 y'_{m-1})$$

This is called an *Adams-Bashforth-type predictor*,[20] characterized by the presence of one more value of y' on the right than of y.

a. Determine the equations that A_0, B_0, and B_1 must satisfy if the predictor is to be exact for $y = 1$, $y = x$, and $y = x^2$.
b. Show that the resulting predictor is

$$y_{m+1} = y_m + \frac{h}{2}(3y'_m - y'_{m-1})$$

c. By using $y = x^3$ show that the truncation error is of order h^3. This predictor may therefore be used with the corrector (8.40).

24 Consider the corrector formula

$$y_{m+1} = a_0 y_m + h(b_{-1} y'_{m+1} + b_0 y'_m)$$

a. Why is this a corrector formula and not a predictor?
b. Determine the equations that a_0, b_{-1}, and b_0 must satisfy if the formula is to be exact for $y = 1$, $y = x$, and $y = x^2$.
c. Show that the resulting formula is the corrector of (8.40).
d. Using $y = x^3$ show that the truncation error is of order h^3.

*25 Consider the predictor formula

$$y_{m+1} = A_0 y_m + A_1 y_{m-1} + A_2 y_{m-2} + h(B_0 y'_m + B_1 y'_{m-1})$$

a. Is this a Milne or an Adams-Bashforth type predictor? (See Exercises 22 and 23.)
b. Determine the equations that A_0, A_1, A_2, B_0, and B_1 must satisfy if the formula is to be exact for $y = 1$, $y = x$, $y = x^2$, $y = x^3$, and $y = x^4$.

---

[19] See Richard W. Hamming, *Numerical Methods for Scientists and Engineers*, New York, McGraw-Hill, 1962, sec. 15.6.
[20] See Hamming, *ibid.*, Section 15.7.

c. Show that the resulting formula is

$$y_{m+1} = -9y_m + 9y_{m-1} + y_{m-2} + 6h(y'_m + y'_{m-1})$$

d. What power of h appears in the truncation error terms?

26 Consider the predictor formula

$$y_{m+1} = A_0 y_m + A_1 y_{m-1} + h(B_0 y'_m + B_1 y'_{m-1} + B_2 y'_{m-2})$$

a. Is this a Milne or an Adams-Bashforth type predictor? (See Exercises 22 and 23.)

b. Determine the equations that A_0, A_1, B_0, B_1, and B_2 must satisfy if the formula is to be exact for $y = 1$, $y = x$, $y = x^2$, $y = x^3$, and $y = x^4$.

c. Solve these equations for A_0, A_1, B_0, B_1, and B_2.

d. By using $y = x^5$ show that the truncation error is of order h^5.

*27 Consider the corrector formula

$$y_{m+1} = a_0 y_m + a_1 y_{m-1} + h(b_{-1} y'_{m+1} + b_0 y'_m + b_1 y'_{m-1})$$

a. Is this an explicit or implicit formula?

b. Determine the equations that a_0, a_1, b_{-1}, b_0, and b_1 must satisfy if the formula is to be exact for $y = 1$, $y = x$, $y = x^2$, and $y = x^3$.

c. Why cannot these equations be solved for a_0, a_1, b_{-1}, b_0, and b_1?

d. Solve the system of four equations for a_0, b_{-1}, b_0, and b_1 in terms of a_1.

e. Show that the truncation error is of order h^4 if $a_1 \neq 1$.

f. Show that for $a_1 = 1$ the truncation error is of order h^5.

Note. Despite this result, $a_1 = 1$ is not the best choice even though it produces a smaller truncation error, since the choice of a_1 strongly affects the stability of the method. For certain differential equations it may be necessary to choose $a_1 \neq 1$ in order to achieve the desired stability.

*28 Consider the following differential equation

$$y' = -5y$$
$$y(0) = 1$$

a. Solve this equation using a *second-order* Runge-Kutta method and a step size $h = 0.5$.

b. Solve this equation using a *fourth-order* Runge-Kutta method and a step size $h = 0.5$.

c. How do you account for the difference in behavior of the two solutions?

*29 Solve the following differential equation

$$y' = -10y$$
$$y(0) = 1$$

using a second-order Runge-Kutta method and a step size of $h = 0.2$. What phenomenon do you observe?

30 Consider the following differential equation

$$y' = -y$$
$$y(0) = 1$$

Using the fourth-order Runge-Kutta method described in (8.27) through (8.31) show that the method is unstable for $h \geq 2.79$. This is the same partial instability referred to in Section 8.6.

31 Using the deferred approach to the limit show that the truncation error in a second-order Runge-Kutta method can be estimated by

$$E_T = \tfrac{8}{7}[y_m^{(h/2)} - y_m^{(h)}]$$

where $y_m^{(p)}$ is the value of y computed at $x = x_m$ using a step size of p.

32 Show that Euler's method, (8.13), when applied to a right-hand side that is a function of x alone, produces the rectangular integration rule of Exercise 26 in Chapter 5.

33a Show that the modified Euler method, (8.19) to (8.21) when applied to a right-hand side that is a function of x alone, produces the rectangular integration rule of Exercise 28 in Chapter 5.

 b Recall from Section 8.8 that the improved Euler method reduces to the trapezoidal rule when f is a function of x alone. What does this tell you about the truncation errors in the rectangular rule of Exercise 28 in Chapter 5, and the trapezoidal rule? (See Exercise 29 in Chapter 5.)

34 Investigate the stability, both absolute and relative, of Euler's method, (8.13).

35 Consider the following Runge-Kutta formula:

$$k_1 = h f(x_m, y_m)$$
$$k_2 = h f\left(x_m + \frac{h}{2}, y_m + \frac{k_1}{2}\right)$$
$$k_3 = h f(x_m + h, y_m + 2k_2 - k_1)$$
$$y_{m+1} = y_m + \tfrac{1}{6}(k_1 + 4k_2 + k_3)$$

a. Show that this is a third-order formula, that is, show that it agrees with the Taylor series through terms in h^3.

b. Show that if f is independent of y the formula reduces to Simpson's rule.

c. Explain why the fourth-order method given in (8.27) through (8.31) is the same as this formula for $f(x,y)$ independent of y.

*36 Run the program in Figure 8.10 for $P = 64$ and $h = 5$ and also $h = 10$. Count the total number of evaluations of $F(x,z)$ in both cases. Compare this with the number of iterations used for $h = 4$ in Case Study 13. Compare the numerical results obtained for the nonlinear deflection as well. Based on these comparisons, what value of h would you recommend for future computations?

37 Run the program in Figure 8.10 for $P = 80$ and $h = 2, 4, 5$, and 10. Compare the total number of evaluations of $F(x,z)$ and the accuracy of the results achieved for the nonlinear deflection in all four cases. Based on these comparisons what value of h would you recommend for future computations?

38 An initially straight, centrally loaded column of length L (see Figure 8.14) will remain straight as long as $P < P_{cr} = \pi^2 EI/(L)^2$ where E and I are constants depending on the material and the cross section

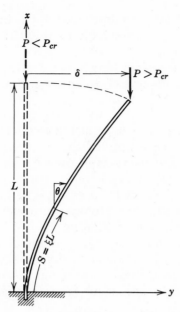

Figure 8.14. *The loaded column of Exercise 38.*

of the column. For $P > P_{cr}$ the column experiences a large lateral deformation that is governed by the differential equation[21]

$$\frac{d^2\theta}{d\xi^2} = -\frac{PL^2}{EI}\sin\theta \qquad \text{(a)}$$

where ξ is a dimensionless coordinate measured along the column and θ is the angular rotation from the vertical. The boundary conditions are

$$\theta(\xi = 0) = 0 \qquad \frac{d\theta}{d\xi}\bigg|_{\xi=1} = 0 \qquad \text{(b)}$$

Note that $dx/d\xi = -L\cos\theta$ and $dy/d\xi = L\sin\theta$.

a. Devise a numerical method to solve (i) subject to the boundary conditions (ii) that will calculate the deflected shape of the column $x(\xi)$, $y(\xi)$. (*Hint:* Refer to Exercise 20.)

b. Obtain sufficient results to plot P versus ξ for $1 \leq P/P_{cr} \leq 2$.

c. Plot the deflected shape of the column for $P/P_{cr} = 1.5$.

39 The numerical techniques presented in this chapter for the solution of differential equations provide a powerful tool for the analysis of networks that contain time-varying and nonlinear elements (as well as those that consist of the more usual time-invariant and linear ones.) As an example of a nonlinear situation that is very difficult to solve by convential (nonnumerical) techniques, but that is easy to solve by the methods presented in this chapter, consider the circuit shown

---

[21]See, for example, S. P. Timoshenko, and J. M. Gere, *Theory of Elastic Stability* (2nd ed.), New York, McGraw-Hill, 1961, pp. 76–82.

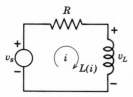

Figure 8.15. *The circuit of Exercise 39.*

in Figure 8.15 consisting of a voltage source with output voltage $v_s(t)$ in series with a resistor R and a nonlinear inductor in which the value of the inductance is a function of the current flowing through the inductor. Thus, we may write $L = L(i)$. If we apply Kirchhoff's voltage law to this circuit, we obtain

$$v_s(t) = Ri(t) + v_L(t) \qquad \text{(a)}$$

where $v_L(t)$ is the voltage across the inductor. In the nonlinear case this voltage is related to $i(t)$ by the expression

$$v_L(t) = \frac{d}{dt}[L(i)i(t)] = \frac{di}{dt}\left[L(i) + i(t)\frac{dL}{di}\right]$$

Inserting this result in (a) and solving for di/dt we obtain

$$\frac{di}{dt} = \frac{v_s(t) - Ri(t)}{L(i) + i(t)\dfrac{dL}{di}}$$

This is a first-order nonlinear differential equation. As such it may be solved by any of the numerical techniques given in this chapter. As an example, suppose that the inductance $L(i)$ is defined as

$$L(i) = 3 + e^{-2i} \qquad i > 0 \qquad \text{(b)}$$

This relation implies that for low values of $i(t)$ the inductance is higher than it is for higher values of the current. Such a phenomenon is called *saturation*. Let us also assume that the voltage source has an output consisting of a 10-v step of voltage starting at $t = 0$, that the initial condition on the inductor current is zero, and that it is desired to find the value of this current at $t = 1$ sec. Inserting the relation for the value of the inductance in (b) and with $R = 4$ we obtain the following equation:

$$\frac{di}{dt} = \frac{10 - 4i(t)}{3 + e^{-2i(t)} - 2e^{-2i(t)}i(t)}$$

Find $i(1)$, that is, the value of the inductor current at $t = 1$.

40 The methods presented in this chapter are readily applied to solve simultaneous sets of first-order differential equations. Such sets of equations arise frequently in connection with the analysis of electronic circuits. As an example of such a case, consider the circuit shown in Figure 8.16 in which a voltage source $v_s(t)$ is used to excite a circuit consisting of a series connection of a resistor, an inductor,

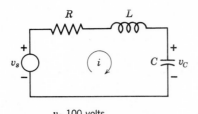

v_S 100 volts
R 1000 ohms
L 0.1 henry
C 1000 microfarads

Figure 8.16. *The circuit of Exercise 40.*

and a capacitor. Applying Kirchhoff's voltage law to this circuit, we obtain

$$v_s(t) = R\,i(t) + L\frac{di}{dt} + v_C(t) \tag{a}$$

where $i(t)$ is the mesh current and $v_C(t)$ is the voltage across the capacitor. This latter variable is related to the mesh current $i(t)$ by the expression

$$i(t) = C\frac{dv_C}{dt} \tag{b}$$

Rearranging the terms in the two relations given in (a) and (b) we obtain the following set of first-order matrix differential equations:

$$\frac{di}{dt} = \frac{v_s(t) - R\,i(t) - v_C(t)}{L} \tag{c}$$

$$\frac{dv_C}{dt} = \frac{i(t)}{C} \tag{d}$$

Thus we have a pair of equations that express the derivatives of the two variables $i(t)$ and $v_C(t)$ in terms of these variables and a specified function of time as given by $v_s(t)$. Such a set of variables are frequently referred to as *state variables*. The solution to such a set of equations, that is, finding the values of $i(t)$ and $v_C(t)$ at any specific value of t, is readily obtained.

As an example of such a problem, let the resistor, inductor, and capacitor have the values shown in Figure 8.16 and let $v_s(t)$ have a value of 100 v starting at $t = 0$, that is, $v_s(t) = 100$, $t > 0$. The equations of (c) and (d) now become

$$\frac{di}{dt} = 10 - 100i(t) - 0.1v_C(t)$$

$$\frac{dv_C}{dt} = 1000i(t)$$

These equations are readily solved to find $v_C(0.5)$ and $i(0.5)$, that is, the values of the capacitor voltage and the inductor current evaluated at $t = 0.5$ sec. Assume that $v_C(0) = i(0) = 0$.

*41 Consider the second-order differential equation

$$y'' = g(x, y, y')$$

where

$$y(0) = y_0$$
$$y'(0) = y_0'$$

Show that the *improved* Euler method when applied to this equation can be reduced to

$$k_1 = hg(x_m, y_m, y_m')$$
$$k_2 = hg(x_m + h, y_m + hy_m', y_m' + k_1)$$
$$y_{m+1} = y_m + hy_m' + \frac{h}{2} k_1$$
$$y_{m+1}' = y_m' + \tfrac{1}{2}(k_1 + k_2)$$

for $m = 0, 1, 2, \ldots$.

42 Consider the second-order differential equation

$$y'' = g(x, y, y')$$

where

$$y(0) = y_0$$
$$y'(0) = y_0'$$

Show that the *modified* Euler method when applied to this equation can be reduced to

$$k_1 = hg(x_m, y_m, y_m')$$
$$k_2 = hg\left(x_m + \frac{h}{2}, y_m + \frac{h}{2} y_m', y_m' + \frac{1}{2} k_1\right)$$
$$y_{m+1} = y_m + hy_m' + \frac{h}{2} k_1$$
$$y_{m+1}' = y_m' + k_2$$

$m = 0, 1, 2, \ldots$.

43 A fourth-order Runge-Kutta method for a second-order differential equation

$$y'' = g(x, y, y')$$

where

$$y(0) = y_0$$
$$y'(0) = y_0'$$

is

$$k_1 = hg(x_m, y_m, y_m')$$
$$k_2 = hg\left(x_m + \frac{h}{2}, y_m + \frac{h}{2} y_m' + \frac{h}{8} k_1, y_m' + \frac{k_1}{2}\right)$$
$$k_3 = hg\left(x_m + \frac{h}{2}, y_m + \frac{h}{2} y_m' + \frac{h}{8} k_1, y_m' + \frac{k_2}{2}\right)$$
$$k_4 = hg\left(x_m + h, y_m + hy_m' + \frac{h}{2} k_3, y_m' + k_3\right)$$

$$y_{m+1} = y_m + hy'_m + \frac{h}{6}(k_1 + k_2 + k_3)$$

$$y'_{m+1} = y'_m + \tfrac{1}{6}(k_1 + 2k_2 + 2k_3 + k_4)$$

for $m = 0, 1, 2, \ldots$.

Use this Runge-Kutta method on the second-order differential equation (8.61) for the elastic deflection of a beam given in Case Study 13 (Section 8.14). Use $h = 4$ and $h = 2$ and compare the numerical results with those obtained in the case study using the second-order predictor-corrector.

Note: This Runge-Kutta method is completely equivalent to applying the Runge-Kutta method for first-order equations to the system of two first-order equations

$$y' = z$$
$$z' = g(x,y,z)$$

For details see, for example, Section 6.16 of F. B. Hildebrand, *Introduction to Numerical Analysis,* and also Exercises 41 and 42.

Annotated Bibliography

Listed below are 25 text or reference books all of which are recommended to the reader who wishes to supplement the material in this text. The references marked with an asterisk (*) are especially recommended. In most cases the primary reason for the special commendation is shown in italics in the annotation. However, all eight of these asterisked texts are also well written and each has been of considerable value to the authors not only in preparing this text but in the past as well. There are additional special references listed at the close of some of the chapters under "Bibliographic Notes."

By and large, the books listed here are in ascending order of difficulty for the reader. That is to say, the most elementary from a mathematical point of view are listed first. However, we hasten to point out that the ordering is only partial and should not be taken too seriously. Indeed the ordering is meant only as a rough guide to the reader who is relatively unfamiliar with the field of numerical analysis.

*[1] Barrodale, Ian, Frank D. K. Roberts and Byron L. Ehle. *Elementary Computer Applications*. New York: Wiley, 1971.

Much more *elementary* than the present text and *extremely readable*. Contains flow charts but *no* computer programs. The first part of the book discusses roots of equations, systems of linear equations, and numerical integration. Of the topics covered in the present text, Barrodale *et al.* does *not* discuss numerical differentiation, interpolation, or ordinary differential equations. There is some discussion of elementary probability and statistics as well as linear programming. Last part of book deals with data processing.

[2] Nielsen, Kaj L. *Methods in Numerical Analysis* (2nd ed.). New York: Macmillan, 1964.

At about the same mathematical level as the present text. Contains *no* flow charts or computer programs. Heavy reliance on tables that are included in appendices of the book. Covers all of the topics in present text and includes some formal error analysis. Also covers partial differential equations and linear programming.

*[3] Stark, Peter A. *Introduction to Numerical Methods.* New York: Macmillan, 1970.

About the same level of difficulty as the present text. *Very readable by students.* Contains a considerable number of 1130 Fortran IV programs but *no* flow charts even for complicated algorithms, for example, Gaussian elimination. Computer output is from an IBM 1130. Covers all topics in present text except numerical differentiation. Also covers Chebyshev approximations and economization of power series. In general, however, all topics are covered in less depth than does the present text. First chapter discusses roundoff errors. However, roundoff errors are not considered to any significant extent in later discussions.

[4] McCracken, Daniel D., and William S. Dorn. *Numerical Methods and FORTRAN Programming.* New York: Wiley, 1964.

A predecessor to the present text and at the same level of difficulty. Includes instruction in Fortran II programming. Computer output is from an IBM 7094 computer. Of topics in present text, McCracken and Dorn covers roots of equations, systems of linear equations, numerical integration, and ordinary differential equations. McCracken and Dorn does *not* cover numerical differentiation, interpolation, nor least squares. It does cover Chebyshev polynomials and partial differential equations. Uses process graphs to analyze roundoff errors as does present text. Relies heavily on case studies, most of which are different from those in present text.

[5] Arden, Bruce W., and Kenneth N. Astill. *Numerical Algorithms: Origins and Applications.* New York: Addison-Wesley, 1970.

About the same level of difficulty as present text. Does contain flow charts and Fortran IV programs. Computer output is from IBM System 360. Covers all of the topics in present text and also covers eigenvalues and partial differential equations. First chapter discusses error analysis, but the analysis is not used much in succeeding chapters.

[6] Hamming, Richard W. *Introduction to Applied Numerical Analysis.* New York: McGraw-Hill, 1971.

About the same level of difficulty as the present text. Does *not* contain flow charts or computer programs. Covers all topics in present text except numerical differentiation. The discussions are generally more brief than the discussions in this text. In addition Hamming discusses

Chebyshev approximations, Fourier series, orthogonal functions, random number generators, and optimization. The latter is treated quite briefly and in broad terms. Error analysis consists primarily of specific examples rather than the detailed style of the present text. Contains very few exercises.

[7] Conte, S. D. *Elementary Numerical Analysis.* New York: McGraw-Hill, 1965.

About the same level of difficulty as the present text. Contains a few flow charts and computer programs (Fortran IV). Computer output is from an IBM 7090. Covers all of the topics in the present text except for least squares. Contains brief opening remarks about formal error analysis but does not use the analysis in subsequent developments. Also covers boundary value and eigenvalue problems.

[8] McCalla, Thomas Richard. *Introduction to Numerical Methods and FOR-TRAN Programming.* New York: Wiley, 1967.

About the same level of difficulty as the present text. Covers the same general topics: roots of equations, systems of linear algebraic equations, interpolation, numerical integration, least squares, and ordinary differential equations. Does *not* cover numerical differentiation. Contains many flow charts and Fortran IV programs. Treatment is generally more brief and concise than that of the present text. Covers a wider variety of methods but in less depth. Error analysis is entirely algebraic as opposed to the semigraphical technique used here. Includes a first chapter on instruction in Fortran IV programming itself but excludes such items as logical IF.

*[9] Stiefel, Eduard L. *An Introduction to Numerical Mathematics.* Werner C. Rheinboldt, trans. New York: Academic Press, 1963.

About the same level of difficulty as present text. Does *not* contain flow charts or computer programs. Stiefel covers all of the topics in the present text but with little or no error analysis. Also covers linear programming, partial differential equations, and eigenvalue problems. *Uses a rather novel approach* to the subject by basing many developments especially those in linear algebra on an "exchange-step" process.

[10] Pennington, Ralph H. *Introductory Computer Methods and Numerical Analysis* (2nd ed.). New York: Macmillan, 1970.

About the same level of difficulty as the present text. Does contain flow charts and Fortran programs. Some programs are terminal oriented and the computer programs and output reflect this, for example, INPUT statements are used. Covers all of the topics in the present text and Chebyshev and rational approximations and spline interpolation as well. Includes instruction in elementary Fortran programming but omits logical IF and certain format features generally available, for example, use of quote marks. Discusses error analysis quite thoroughly but from a different viewpoint than present text. Tendency is to use computer to compute error bounds.

[11] Grove, Wendell E. *Brief Numerical Methods.* New York: Prentice-Hall, 1966.

About the same level of difficulty as the present text. Contains a few flow charts but *no* computer programs. Covers most topics in present text but does *not* cover numerical differentiation and, quite surprisingly, systems of linear equations are also missing. Does *not* discuss roundoff or truncation errors except for brief comments at the close of the book.

*[12] Redish, K. A. *An Introduction to Computational Methods.* New York: Wiley, 1961.

About the same level of difficulty as present text. Does *not* contain flow charts or computer programs. Oriented toward hand or desk calculator computations. Covers all topics in present text except least squares. *Good discussion of inherent and truncation errors* but no discussion of roundoff errors.

*[13] Scheid, Francis. *Theory and Problems of Numerical Analysis. Schaum's Outline Series.* New York: McGraw-Hill, 1968.

A problem book and reference rather than a text. *Contains a wealth (775) of solved problems.* About the same level of difficulty as present text. Does *not* contain flow charts or computer programs. Covers all topics in present text and, in addition, covers Chebyshev and rational approximations, linear programming, boundary value problems, and Monte Carlo methods.

[14] Acton, Forman S. *Numerical Methods That* (Usually) *Work.* New York: Harper & Row, 1970.

Requires somewhat more mathematical background and maturity than does the present text. Does *not* contain flow charts or computer programs. Uses a circular approach, that is, discusses the same topic at several scattered places throughout the text. Of the topics in the present text, Acton covers roots of equations, simultaneous linear equations (as a part of the section on eigenvalues), numerical integration, interpolation, and ordinary differential equations. Does *not* cover numerical differentiation or least squares approximation. There is no formal error analysis. Acton also includes eigenvalues, partial differential equations, continued fractions, rational approximations, and optimization techniques. Replete with quotations from Seneca, Shaw, Shakespeare, etc.

[15] Jennings, Walter. *First Course in Numerical Methods.* New York: Macmillan, 1964.

Slightly more difficult than the present text. Does *not* contain flow charts or computer programs. Is written with hand or desk calculator calculations in mind. Covers all topics in the present text except numerical differentiation and least squares. Jennings also covers eigenvalues, boundary value problems, and Chebyshev approximations. Does not discuss roundoff errors and gives minimal treatment to truncation errors.

[16] Wendroff, Burton. *First Principles of Numerical Analysis: An Undergraduate Text.* New York: Addison-Wesley, 1969.

Requires somewhat more mathematical sophistication than present text. Much more rigorous mathematically than present text. Contains a few flow charts and ALGOL-like computer programs. Covers all topics in present text except numerical differentiation and least squares. Does not discuss roundoff errors. First chapter deals with internal computer representation of numbers and operation of a computer.

*[17] Scarborough, James B. *Numerical Mathematical Analysis* (4th ed.). Baltimore, Md.: Johns Hopkins Press, 1958.

This *classic text* was first published in 1930 and has been revised several times. Requires more mathematical sophistication than does the present text. Does *not* contain flow charts or computer programs. Covers all topics in present text and a wider variety of algorithms. All methods are based on hand or desk calculator calculations. Also covers integral equations, partial differential equations, and harmonic analysis. Relies heavily on difference calculus.

[18] Hildebrand, F. B. *Introduction to Numerical Analysis*. New York: McGraw-Hill, 1956.

A classic among numerical analysis texts. Requires much more mathematical sophistication than does the present text. Its publication date implies it is not computer oriented. Covers all of the topics in present text in more depth and with more rigor. Also includes Chebyshev approximations. Includes a wider variety of algorithms than does the present text. Heavy emphasis on the difference calculus. Does *not* discuss roundoff errors except for a brief discussion in the first chapter.

*[19] Ralston, Anthony. *A First Course in Numerical Analysis*. New York: McGraw-Hill, 1965.

Requires more mathematical sophistication than present text. Does *not* contain flow charts or computer programs. Covers all topics in present text and for each topic includes a greater variety of algorithms than does present text. In addition Ralston discusses Chebyshev and rational approximations, boundary value problems, and eigenvalues and eigenvectors of matrices. Has little error analysis. Contains *excellent bibliographic notes* with each chapter *and an exhaustive bibliography* (as of 1965). Solutions or hints are given for all of the *many exercises*.

*[20] Carnahan, Brice, H. A. Luther, and James O. Wilkes. *Applied Numerical Methods*. New York: Wiley, 1969.

Much more difficult to read and requires more mathematical maturity than does the present text. Does contain many flow charts and Fortran IV programs. Computer output is from IBM System 360. Covers all of the topics in present text at a more sophisticated level and with a wider variety of algorithms. Also covers partial differential equations and both descriptive and inferential statistics. *Replete with case studies and case-study type exercises.* An encyclopedia of numerical methods but not easy reading. Somewhat surprisingly, little attention is paid to roundoff error analysis.

[21] Wendroff, Burton. *Theoretical Numerical Analysis*. New York: Academic Press, 1966.

Requires more mathematical sophistication than the present text. Does *not* contain flow charts or computer programs. Covers all topics in present text except numerical differentiation and least squares. In addition Wendroff covers eigenvalues, Chebyshev approximations, and partial differential equations. Discusses roundoff errors in the chapter on linear equations.

[22] Hamming, Richard W. *Numerical Methods for Scientists and Engineers*. New York: McGraw-Hill, 1962.

Considerably more sophisticated mathematically than the present text. Contains a few general (not detailed) flow charts but *no* computer programs. Heavy emphasis on the "band limited function approach" that arises out of electrical engineering. Does not contain formal error analysis. Hamming covers all of the topics in the present text although from a different point of view and in a different order. Hamming also covers Chebyshev and rational approximations, Fourier series, eigenvalues, computer simulations, and Monte Carlo methods.

[23] Henrici, Peter. *Elements of Numerical Analysis*. New York: Wiley, 1964. Requires considerably more mathematical sophistication than present text. Contains *no* flow charts or computer programs. Of the topics in the present text, Henrici covers roots of equations, numerical differentiation and integration, interpolation, and ordinary differential equations. The book closes with a rather formidable discussion of error analysis including a statistical approach. Henrici does not cover least squares or solution of linear systems.

[24] Isaacson, Eugene, and Herbert B. Keller. *Analysis of Numerical Methods*. New York: Wiley, 1966.
Requires considerably more mathematical sophistication than present text. Does *not* contain flow charts or computer programs. This is a rigorous mathematical treatment of numerical analysis. Isaacson and Keller cover all of the topics in the present text in great depth. They also cover partial differential equations and boundary value problems. Does contain formal error analysis.

[25] Ralston, Anthony, and Herbert S. Wilf, (eds.). *Mathematical Methods for Digital Computers*. 2 vols. New York: Wiley, Vol. 1, 1960; Vol. 2, 1967.
A reference not a text. Requires considerably more mathematical sophistication than does the present text. Both volumes contain many flow charts. The second volume also contains Fortran programs.

Volume 1 covers roots of equations, systems of linear equations including eigenvalues, numerical integration, ordinary differential equations including boundary value problems, partial differential equations, linear programming, and generation of elementary functions.

Volume 2 covers roots of equations, systems of linear equations including eigenvalues, numerical integration, partial differential equations, Monte Carlo methods, and Chebyshev approximations. Volume 2 also contains an introductory chapter on the elements of Fortran and ALGOL.

Answers to Selected Exercises

1 -0.7071. No, because x near $+0.5$, $f'(x)$ is greater than 1.

4
$$x_{n+1} = x_n - \frac{x_n^3 - c}{3x_n^2} = \frac{2x_n^3 + c}{3x_n^2}$$

7   For the root of interest, $x \neq 0$, so divide through by it first to simplify: $0.1x - \log x = 0$. If we convert to natural logarithms to take the derivative, the iteration formula can be simplified to

$$x_{n+1} = x_n - \frac{x_n - 10 \log_{10} x_n}{1 - \frac{4.3429}{x_n}}$$

The root is $x = 1.3713$.

9 $1.100, \ -2.300, \ 2.673$

12 $x = 2.753; \ |\epsilon| \simeq 0.127$.

18   The successive iterates are, approximately,

$$2.3465 + 0.7942i$$
$$1.9696 + 0.8998i$$
$$2.0015 + 1.0072i$$
$$2.0000 + 1.000i$$

38 $x = 1.932, \ y = 0.517$. Yes.

Chapter 2

1 Write

$$e = iR$$

where e = volts

$\quad i$ = amperes

$\quad R$ = ohms

and let e_e, e_i, e_R be the respective absolute errors. Then from the problem data

$$e_R = 10\% \text{ of } 10 \text{ ohms} = \pm 1$$
$$e_i = \pm 0.1 \text{ amp}$$

Then

$$e_e = Re_i + ie_R$$
$$= 10 \cdot (\pm 0.1) + 2.0 \cdot (\pm 1)$$

and

$$|e_e| \leq 10 \cdot |\pm 0.1| + 2.0 \cdot |\pm 1| = 3 \text{ volts}$$

Therefore

$$e = 20 \pm 3 \text{ volts}$$

The relative error is

$$\left| \frac{e_e}{e} \right| \leq \left| \frac{\pm 3}{20} \right| = 0.15$$

Also

$$\left| \frac{e_e}{e} \right| \leq \left| \frac{e_i}{i} \right| + \left| \frac{e_R}{R} \right| = \left| \frac{0.1}{2} \right| + |\pm 10\%| = 0.05 + 0.10 = 0.15$$

5 $\quad u = a + a$

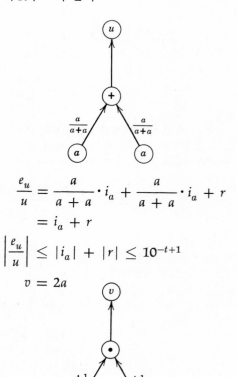

$$\frac{e_u}{u} = \frac{a}{a + a} \cdot i_a + \frac{a}{a + a} \cdot i_a + r$$
$$= i_a + r$$

$$\left| \frac{e_u}{u} \right| \leq |i_a| + |r| \leq 10^{-t+1}$$

$$v = 2a$$

$$\frac{e_v}{v} = +1 \cdot i_2 + 1 \cdot i_a + r$$

$$= +1 \cdot 0 + 1 \cdot i_a + r$$

$$\left| \frac{e_v}{v} \right| \leq |i_a| + |r| \leq 10^{-t+1}$$

6 $u = a + a + a$

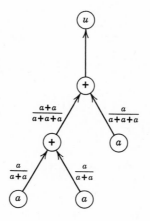

$$\frac{e_u}{u} = \frac{a + a}{a + a + a} \left(\frac{a}{a + a} \cdot i_a + \frac{a}{a + a} \cdot i_a + r_1 \right)$$

$$+ \frac{a}{a + a + a} i_a + r_2 = \frac{1}{3} i_a + \frac{1}{3} i_a + \frac{2}{3} r_1 + \frac{1}{3} i_a + r_2$$

$$\left| \frac{e_u}{u} \right| \leq |i_a| + \left| \frac{2}{3} r_1 \right| + |r_2| \leq \frac{8}{3} \cdot 5 \cdot 10^{-t}$$

$u = 3a$

$$\frac{e_v}{v} = +1 \cdot i_3 + 1 \cdot i_a + r$$

$$= +1 \cdot 0 + i_a + r$$

$$\left| \frac{e_v}{v} \right| \leq |i_a| + |r| \leq 2 \cdot 5 \cdot 10^{-t}$$

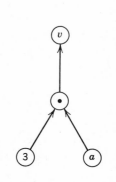

If $a = .6992$, $a + a = 1.3984$, which rounds to 1.398, $(a + a) + a = 2.0972$, which rounds to $2.097 = u$. $3a = 2.0976$, which rounds to $2.098 = v$.

8 $u = x \cdot (x \cdot (x \cdot x))$

$$\frac{e_u}{u} = i_x + i_x + r_1 + i_x + r_2 + i_x + r_3$$

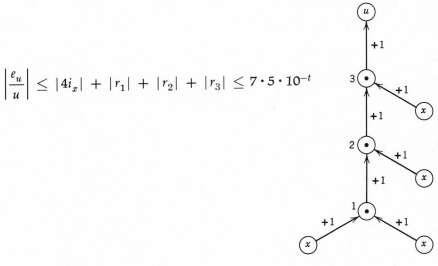

$$\left|\frac{e_u}{u}\right| \le |4i_x| + |r_1| + |r_2| + |r_3| \le 7 \cdot 5 \cdot 10^{-t}$$

$$v = (x^2)^2$$

$$\frac{e_v}{v} = i_x + i_x + r_1 + i_x + i_x + r_2 + r_3$$

$$\left|\frac{e_v}{v}\right| \le |4i_x| + |r_1| + |r_2| + |r_3| \le 7 \cdot 5 \cdot 10^{-t}$$

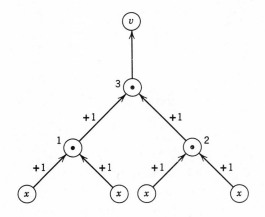

11 $u = ax + bx^2$

With all inherent errors taken to be zero,

$$\frac{e_u}{u} = \frac{bx^2}{ax + bx^2}(r_1 + r_2) + \frac{ax}{ax + bx^2} \cdot r_3 + r_4$$

$$\left|\frac{e_u}{u}\right| \le \left|\frac{a}{a + bx} \cdot r_3\right| + \left|\frac{bx}{a + bx} \cdot r_1\right| + \left|\frac{bx}{a + bx} \cdot r_2\right| + |r_4|$$

$$\le 5 \cdot 10^{-t} + \frac{bx}{a + bx} \cdot 5 \cdot 10^{-t} + 5 \cdot 10^{-t}$$

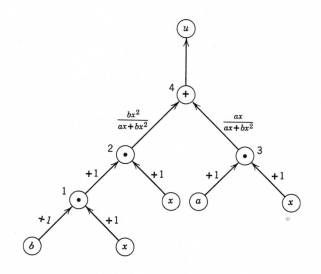

$$v = x \cdot (a + bx)$$

$$\frac{e_v}{v} = \frac{bx}{a + bx} \cdot r_1 + r_2 + r_3$$

$$\left| \frac{e_v}{v} \right| \leq \left| \frac{bx}{a + bx} \right| \cdot 5 \cdot 10^{-t} + 5 \cdot 10^{-t} + 5 \cdot 10^{-t}$$

Let the symbol $\simeq$ stand for the rounded result. Then

$$bx = 0.29885994 \simeq 0.2989$$
$$bx^2 = 0.12858678 \simeq 0.1286$$
$$ax = 0.32802750 \simeq 0.3280$$
$$ax + bx^2 = 0.4566 = u$$
$$a + bx = 1.0614 \simeq 0.1061 \cdot 10^1$$
$$x(a + bx) = 0.4564422 \simeq 0.4564 = v$$

The exact answer is 0.456597.

16

$$u = \frac{a - b}{c}$$

With all inherent errors taken to be zero,

$$\frac{e_u}{u} = r_1 + r_2$$

$$\left|\frac{e_u}{u}\right| = |r_1| + |r_2| \leq 10^{-t+1}$$

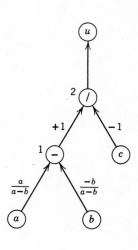

$$v = \frac{a}{c} - \frac{b}{c}$$

$$\frac{e_v}{v} = \frac{a/c}{a/c - b/c}\, r_1 - \frac{b/c}{a/c - b/c}\, r_2 + r_3$$

$$= \frac{a}{a - b}\, r_1 - \frac{b}{a - b}\, r_2 + r_3$$

$$\left|\frac{e_v}{v}\right| \leq \left|\frac{a}{a - b}\, r_1\right| + \left|\frac{b}{a - b}\, r_2\right| + |r_3|$$

If $a \simeq b$ this is approximately equal to

$$\frac{2a}{a - b} \cdot 5 \cdot 10^{-t} + 5 \cdot 10^{-t}$$

which can be very large if $a - b$ is small.

$$u = \frac{(a - b)}{c} = \frac{(0.41 - 0.36)}{0.70} = \frac{0.05}{0.70} = 0.071428 \simeq 0.71 \cdot 10^{-1}$$

$$v = \frac{a}{c} - \frac{b}{c} = \frac{0.41}{0.70} - \frac{0.36}{0.70} = 0.5857 - 0.51428 \simeq 0.59 - 0.51$$

$$= 0.80 \cdot 10^{-1}$$

18 $\quad x_1 = \dfrac{-b + \sqrt{b^2 - 4ac}}{2a} \qquad x_1' = \dfrac{-2c}{b + \sqrt{b^2 - 4ac}}$

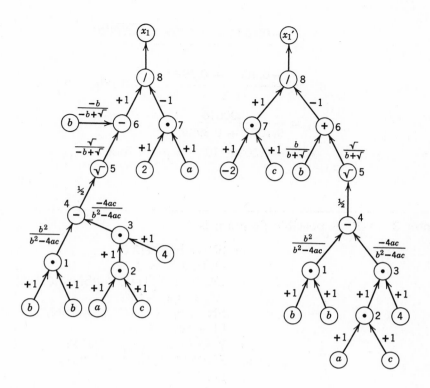

$$\frac{e_{x_1}}{x_1} = \frac{\sqrt{b^2 - 4ac}}{-b + \sqrt{b^2 - 4ac}}$$

$$\left[\frac{1}{2}\left(\frac{b^2}{b^2 - 4ac}r_1 - \frac{4ac}{b^2 - 4ac}(r_2 + r_3) + r_4\right) + r_5\right]$$

$$+ r_6 - r_7 + r_8$$

with $b^2 \gg 4ac$, this gives approximately

$$\left|\frac{e_{x_1}}{x_1}\right| \leq \frac{b}{-b + \sqrt{b^2 - 4ac}}\left(\frac{|r_1| + |r_4|}{2} + |r_5|\right)$$

which can be very large.

$$\frac{e'_{x_1}}{x'_1} = \frac{-\sqrt{b^2 - 4ac}}{b + \sqrt{b^2 - 4ac}}$$

$$\left[\frac{1}{2}\left(\frac{b^2}{b^2 - 4ac}r_1 - \frac{4ac}{b^2 - 4ac}(r_2 + r_3) + r_4\right) + r_5\right]$$

$$- r_6 + r_7 + r_8$$

with $b^2 \gg 4a$, this gives approximately

$$\left|\frac{e'_{x_1}}{x'_1}\right| \leq \frac{1}{2}\left[\frac{1}{2}(|r_1| + |r_4|) + |r_5|\right] + |r_6| + |r_7| + |r_8|$$

$$x_1 = \frac{-0.4002 + \sqrt{0.16016004 - 0.00032}}{2}$$

$$= \frac{-0.4002 + \sqrt{0.1602 - 0.0003}}{2}$$

$$= \frac{-0.4002 + 0.3999}{2} = -0.1500 \cdot 10^{-3}$$

$$x_1' = \frac{-0.00016}{0.4002 + 0.3999}$$

$$= -0.2000 \cdot 10^{-3} = \text{exact root}$$

Chapter 3   **2** A possible program is

```
        SN = SQRT(2.0)
        DO 20 N = 2, 25
        OC = SQRT(1.0 − (SN/2.0)**2)
        AC = 1.0 − OC
        SN = SQRT(AC**2 + (SN/2.0)**2)
        PI = SN*2.0**N
   20   WRITE (6, 40) N, SN, PI
   40   FORMAT (1X, I3, 1P2G14.6)
        END
```

The expressions collapse to

$$s_{2n} = \sqrt{\left[1 - \sqrt{1 - \left(\frac{s_n}{2}\right)^2}\right]^2 + \left(\frac{s_n}{2}\right)^2}$$

For n large, s_n becomes small and thus $1 - (s_n/2)^2$ is close to 1 as is the square root of that expression. Thus

$$\left[1 - \sqrt{1 - \left(\frac{s_n}{2}\right)^2}\right]^2 \tag{a}$$

is very close to zero and the algorithm is approximately

$$s_{2n} \cong \sqrt{\left(\frac{s_n}{2}\right)^2} \tag{b}$$

This uses the first term in the series (3.14). Thus the algorithm as given in this exercise is approximately one term in the Taylor series solution. For n large, one term is sufficient to produce quite accurate results. Notice that subtractive cancellation still takes place; see (a) above. However, the term that remains in (b) dominates the loss of accuracy in subtractive cancellation. The first term lost in the subtraction is a constant times s_n^4.

4 Andree's method eliminates subtraction of nearly equal numbers, $\sqrt{1 + x}$ and $\sqrt{1 - x}$, and is much easier to derive and to use in computation than the Taylor series method. However Andree's method cannot be used on

$$\sqrt[3]{1 + x} - \sqrt{1 - x}$$

5 (a)

```
4   READ (5,5)X
5   FORMAT (F10.0)
    Y = (1.0 + X)**(1.0/3.0) − SQRT(1.0 − X)
    WRITE (6,6) X, Y
6   FORMAT (1X, 1P2G14.6)
    GO TO 4
    END
```

(b)

```
4   READ (5,5) X
5   FORMAT (F10.0)
    AK = X/3.0
    BK = −X/2.0
    TCK = AK − BK
    DO 10 K = 1, 12
    AK = (3.0*K − 1.0)/(3.0*(K + 1.0))*AK*X
    BK = (2.0*K − 1.)/(2.0*(K + 1.0))*BK*X
10  TCK = TCK + AK − BK
    WRITE (6,6) X, TCK
6   FORMAT (1X, 1P2G14.6)
    GO TO 4
    END
```

12 $I_m = 0$, so

$$I_{m-1} = \frac{1}{m}$$

$$I_{m-2} = \frac{1}{m-1}\left(1 - \frac{1}{m}\right) = \frac{1}{m-1} - \frac{1}{(m-1)m}$$

$$I_{m-3} = \frac{1}{m-2} - \frac{1}{(m-2)(m-1)} + \frac{1}{(m-2)(m-1)m}$$

and so on until

$$I_1 = \frac{1}{2} - \frac{1}{2\cdot 3} + \frac{1}{2\cdot 3\cdot 4} + \cdots + (-1)^m \frac{1}{m!} \qquad (a)$$

Now

$$e^x = \sum_{n=0}^{\infty} \frac{x^n}{n!}$$

For $x = -1$ then

$$\frac{1}{e} = \sum_{n=0}^{\infty} \frac{(-1)^n}{n!} = +1 - 1 + \sum_{n=2}^{\infty} \frac{(-1)^n}{n!} = \sum_{n=2}^{\infty} \frac{(-1)^n}{n!}$$

Thus (a) is the first $m - 1$ terms of the last infinite series and hence is $m + 1$ terms of the Taylor series for $1/e$. (The first two terms, $+1$ and -1, sum to zero.)

16 The mean of the y_i is, from the definition (3.38),

$$\mu_y = \frac{\Sigma y_i}{n} = \frac{\Sigma(x_i - m)}{n} = \mu_x - m$$

where μ_x is the mean of the x_i.

The variance of y is, from the definition (3.39),

$$V_y = \frac{\Sigma(y_i - \mu_y)^2}{n}$$

$$= \frac{\Sigma[(x_i - m) - (\mu_x - m)]^2}{n}$$

$$= \frac{\Sigma(x_i - \mu_x)^2}{n}$$

but this is, by definition, the variance of x.

Chapter 4

1 $x = 3$, $y = 6$, $z = -1$.

3 $x = 3.000$, $y = -2.000$, $z = 6.000$.

6 $x = 1 + i$, $y = 2 - i$.

8 Without row interchanges, $x = -1.400$, $y = 0.7406$. With row interchanges, $x = -1.590$, $y = 0.7409$.

14 $x = 2.222$, $y = 3.333$, $z = 4.444$.

17 Without interchanges, $\delta_x = 1.5 \cdot 10^{-2}$, $\delta_y = 1 \cdot 10^{-2}$. With interchanges, $\delta_x = 2.5 \cdot 10^{-2}$, $\delta_y = 1 \cdot 10^{-2}$. The difference reflects the fact that these are bounds; the actual error can be less than the bound. These are clearly not *minimum* bounds, which would be much more powerful.

18 (a) $\delta_x = 3.1 \cdot 10^{-2}$ $\delta_y = 1.8 \cdot 10^{-2}$ $\delta_z = 0.8 \cdot 10^{-2}$

    (b) $\delta_x = 28.4 \cdot 10^{-2}$ $\delta_y = 16.3 \cdot 10^{-2}$ $\delta_z = 7.6 \cdot 10^{-2}$

    (c) $\delta_x = 31.5 \cdot 10^{-2}$ $\delta_y = 18.1 \cdot 10^{-2}$ $\delta_z = 8.4 \cdot 10^{-2}$

    (d) $\delta_x = 12.0$ $\delta_y = 6.9$ $\delta_z = 3.2$

20 $x = 1.003$, $y = -2.990$, $z = 3.994$.

34 The solution, starting with $x_0 = y_0 = 0$, is $x = 0.4$, $y = 1.2$. This solution can be found in six iterations using $\omega = 0.939$, although the convergence does depend on the word length of the computer used so that seven iterations may be needed in some machines. Without acceleration, 12 iterations are needed.

43 Arts and Sciences: $3227.70 per student
Engineering: $8705.91 per student
Business: $3691.65 per student

Chapter 5

4 For $h = 0.1$, $f''(1) = 2.72$.
For $h = 0.01$, $f''(1) = 2$.
In the expressions for the truncation errors (5.11) and (5.12), if the third and fourth derivatives are approximately the same, as they are here, then the truncation error in the second derivative is twice as large as the corresponding error in the first derivative.

7 (a) 0.27.   (b) 0.06.

17 (a) 1.00018

(b) 1.08193

(c) 1.00491

(d) 1.58190

For high accuracy, it is better to integrate backward to reduce round-off error.

18 (a)

```
        GAUSS = 5.0 * EXP(−5.0) *
     1  (0.1713245*(EXP(5.0*0.9324695) + EXP(−5.0*0.9324695))
     2  + 0.3607616*(EXP(5.0*0.6612094) + EXP(−5.0*0.6612094))
     3  + 0.4679139*(EXP(5.0*0.2386192) + EXP(−5.0*0.2386192)))
```

(b)

```
        I = 1
        SUM = EXP(−10.0)
     23 X = I
        SUM = SUM + 2.0*EXP(−10.0 + X)
        I = I + 1
        IF (I .LT. 10) GO TO 23
        TRAP = 0.5*(SUM + 1.0)
```

(c)

```
        I = 1
        SUM = EXP(−10.0)
     23 X = I
        SUM = SUM + 4.0*EXP(−10.0 + X)
        SUM = SUM + 2.0*EXP(−9.0 + X)
        I = I + 2
        IF (I .LT. 9) GO TO 23
        SIMP = 0.3333333*(1.0 + (SUM + 4.0*EXP(−1.0)))
```

(d)

```
        I = 0
        RECT = 0.0
     23 X = I
        RECT = RECT + EXP(−10.0 + X)
        I = I + 1
        IF (I .LT. 11) GO TO 23
```

21 In Figure 5.10 replace statements 32–61 with the following:

```
     32 ENDA = F(A)
        ENDB = F(B)
        BMH = F(B − H)
        SIMP = 64.77*(H/3.0)*(4.0*(SUM4 + BMH) + 2.0*SUM2
     1       + ENDA + ENDB)/T**4
        TRAP = 64.77*(H/2.0)*(2.0*(SUM4 + SUM2 + BMH)
     1       + ENDA + ENDB)/T**4
        WRITE (6, 61)T, SIMP, TRAP
     61 FORMAT (1X, 1P3E15.6)
```

37 (a) 13, 47.

(b) 7, 30, 53.

(c) 4, 20, 40, 56.

Chapter 6 **1** From (6.23)

$$P(x) = f(x_0 - h_1) \left(\frac{(x - x_0)(x - (x_0 + h_2))}{(-h_1)(-h_1 - h_2)} \right)$$

$$+ f(x_0) \left(\frac{(x - (x_0 - h_1))(x - (x_0 + h_2))}{(+h_1)(-h_2)} \right)$$

$$+ f(x_0 + h_2) \left(\frac{(x - (x_0 - h_1))(x - x_0)}{(h_2 + h_1)(h_2)} \right)$$

$$= f(x_0 - h_1) \left(\frac{x^2 - (2x_0 + h_2)x + x_0(x_0 + h_2)}{h_1(h_1 + h_2)} \right)$$

$$- f(x_0) \left(\frac{x^2 - (2x_0 + h_2 - h_1)x + (x_0 - h_1)(x_0 + h_2)}{+h_1 h_2} \right)$$

$$+ f(x_0 + h_2) \left(\frac{x^2 - (2x_0 - h_1)x + x_0(x_0 - h_1)}{h_2(h_1 + h_2)} \right)$$

Differentiating:

$$P'(x) = f(x_0 - h_1) \left(\frac{2x - 2x_0 - h_2}{h_1(h_1 + h_2)} \right)$$

$$- f(x_0) \left(\frac{2x - 2x_0 - h_2 + h_1}{h_1 h_2} \right)$$

$$+ f(x_0 + h_2) \left(\frac{2x - 2x_0 + h_1}{h_2(h_1 + h_2)} \right)$$

$$P'(x_0) = \frac{-h_2^2 f(x_0 - h_1) + (h_2^2 - h_1^2)f(x_0) + h_1^2 f(x_0 + h_2)}{h_1 h_2(h_1 + h_2)}$$

Differentiating again:

$$P''(x) = f(x_0 - h_1) \frac{2}{h_1(h_1 + h_2)}$$

$$- f(x_0) \frac{2}{h_1 h_2}$$

$$+ f(x_0 + h_2) \frac{2}{h_2(h_1 + h_2)}$$

$$\boxed{P''(x) = \frac{2[h_2 f(x_0 - h_1) - (h_1 + h_2)f(x_0) + h_1 f(x_0 + h_2)]}{[h_1 h_2(h_1 + h_2)]}}$$

For $h_1 = h_2 = h$

$$P''(x) = \frac{f(x_0 - h) - 2f(x_0) + f(x_0 + h)}{h^2}.$$

5

$$\int_{x_k}^{x_{k+1}} y \, dx = \int_{x_k}^{x_{k+1}} y_k + \left(\frac{x - x_k}{x_{k+1} - x_k}\right)(y_{k+1} - y_k) \, dx$$

$$= y_k(x_{k+1} - x_k) + \left(\frac{x_{k+1}^2 - x_k^2}{2}\right)\left(\frac{y_{k+1} - y_k}{x_{k+1} - x_k}\right)$$

$$\qquad - (x_{k+1} - x_k)\frac{x_k}{x_{k+1} - x_k}(y_{k+1} - y_k)$$

$$= y_k(x_{k+1} - x_k) + \frac{1}{2}(x_{k+1} + x_k)(y_{k+1} - y_k)$$

$$\qquad - x_k(y_{k+1} - y_k)$$

$$= y_k(x_{k+1} - x_k) + \frac{1}{2}(x_{k+1} - x_k)(y_{k+1} - y_k)$$

$$= \frac{1}{2}(y_{k+1} + y_k)(x_{k+1} - x_k)$$

If $h = x_{k+1} - x_k$, the trapezoidal rule given in Section 5.8 results.

6 The truncation error in the trapezoidal rule from Exercise 5 and (6.8) is

$$e_T = \int_{x_k}^{x_{k+1}} \frac{f''(\xi)}{2}(x - x_k)(x - x_{k+1}) \, dx$$

Now $(x - x_k)(x - x_{k+1}) < 0$ for $x_k < x < x_{k+1}$. From the first mean value theorem for integrals then

$$e_T = \frac{1}{2}f''(\rho)\int_{x_k}^{x_{k+1}}(x - x_k)(x - x_{k+1}) \, dx$$

for $x_k \le \rho \le x_{k+1}$. But

$$\int_{x_k}^{x_{k+1}}(x - x_k)(x - x_{k+1}) \, dx = \frac{1}{6}(x_k - x_{k+1})^3$$

so

$$e_T = \frac{1}{12}(x_k - x_{k+1})^3 f''(\rho)$$

Letting $x_{k+1} - x_k = h$ and adding up all n intervals

$$e_T = -\frac{h^3}{12}[f''(\rho_1) + \cdots + f''(\rho_k) + \cdots + f''(\rho_n)]$$

If $f''(x)$ is continuous then by the intermediate value theorem for some ρ such that $a \le \rho \le b$

$$f''(\rho_1) + \cdots + f''(\rho_k) + \cdots + f''(\rho_n) = nf''(\rho)$$

so

$$e_T = -\frac{h^3}{12} nf''(\rho)$$

But $(b - a)/n = h$ so

$$e_T = -\frac{h^2}{12}(b - a)f''(\rho)$$

Since

$$|f''(\rho)| \le M$$

it follows that

$$|e_T| \le \frac{h^2}{12}(b - a)M$$

10 (a) Since $f(x) = x^2$ then $f''(x) = 2$ so the truncation error is

$$E_T = \frac{2}{2}(x - x_k)(x - x_{k+1})$$

Now $E_T \le 0$, so $|E_T|$ will be a maximum where E_T is a minimum. Since

$$\frac{dE_T}{dx} = 2x - (x_{k+1} + x_k)$$

and

$$\frac{d^2 E_T}{dx^2} = 2$$

The maximum value of $|E_T|$ occurs when

$$x = \frac{x_{k+1} + x_k}{2}$$

Thus

$$\text{Max } |E_T| = \frac{(x_{k+1} - x_k)^2}{4} = .25$$

(b) Again

$$E_T = (x - x_k)(x - x_{k+1})$$

Now, however, $E_T \ge 0$ so $|E_T|$ is a maximum where x is a maximum, i.e., $x = 40$. Since $x_k = 31$ and $x_{k+1} = 32$

$$|E_T| \le 72$$

14 (6.23) Uses the values for $k = 4, 5,$ and 6 while (6.48) etc. uses the values for $k = 5, 6,$ and 7.

16 Each product requires $2(n - 1)$ additions, $(n - 1)$ divisions, and $(n - 2)$ multiplications. There are n such products. The sum requires n multiplications and $n - 1$ additions. Then there are $(2n + 1)(n - 1)$ additions, $n(n - 1)$ multiplications, and $n(n - 1)$ divisions. The total number of operations is $(4n + 1)(n - 1)$.

18 $-72°$.

19 (a) and (b) both produce $-40.96°$.

434   Answers to Selected Exercises

1 There are infinitely many solutions, all of which pass through $x = 5/2$ and $y = 5/2$. Three possible lines are: $y = 5 - x$; $y = x$; $y = -(5/2) + 2x$.

3 $\Sigma(x_i - \mu)^2$ is a sum of squares and is therefore positive and nonzero unless all $x_i = \mu$. But

$$m\Sigma(x_i - \mu)^2 = m\Sigma x_i^2 - (\Sigma x_i)^2$$

Therefore the right-hand number is zero only if all x_i are equal.

5 Using (7.17) with $x = \Sigma x_i/m$ and with a_0 and a_1 replaced by (7.15) and (7.16)

$$
\begin{aligned}
y &= \frac{m\Sigma x_i y_i - \Sigma x_i \Sigma y_i}{m\Sigma x_i^2 - (\Sigma x_i)^2} \cdot \frac{\Sigma x_i}{m} + \frac{\Sigma y_i \Sigma x_i^2 - \Sigma x_i \Sigma x_i y_i}{m\Sigma x_i^2 - (\Sigma x_i)^2} \\
&= \frac{\Sigma x_i y_i \Sigma x_i - (\Sigma x_i)^2(\Sigma y_i/m) + m\Sigma x_i^2(\Sigma y_i/m) - \Sigma x_i \Sigma x_i y_i}{m\Sigma x_i^2 - (\Sigma x_i)^2} \\
&= \frac{(\Sigma y_i/m)(-(\Sigma x_i)^2 + m\Sigma x_i^2)}{m\Sigma x_i^2 - (\Sigma x_i)^2} = \frac{\Sigma y_i}{m}
\end{aligned}
$$

11 Since

$$\sum_{i=1}^{N} i = \frac{N(N + 1)}{2}$$

and

$$\sum_{i=1}^{N} i^2 = \frac{N(N + 1)(2N + 1)}{6}$$

we get

$$Na_0 + \frac{N(N + 1)}{2} a_1 = \Sigma y$$

$$\frac{N(N + 1)}{2} a_0 + \frac{N(N + 1)(2N + 1)}{6} a_1 = \Sigma xy$$

17 (a) Squaring both sides and letting $z = y^2$

$$z = a + bx$$

(b) The normal equations for m data points are

$$ma + (\Sigma x_i)b = \Sigma y_i^2$$
$$(\Sigma x_i)a + (\Sigma x_i^2)b = \Sigma x_i y_i^2$$

where the sums extend from 1 to m.

21

$$mc + (\Sigma y_i)a + (\Sigma z_i)b = \Sigma x_i$$
$$(\Sigma y_i)c + (\Sigma y_i^2)a + (\Sigma y_i z_i)b = \Sigma y_i x_i$$
$$(\Sigma z_i)c + (\Sigma z_i y_i)a + (\Sigma z_i^2)c = \Sigma z_i x_i$$

24 The following program computes the sums required for the normal equations. The left column contains k and in the right

$$\sum_{i=1}^{m} x_i^k$$

```
        DIMENSION S(10)
5       READ (5, 100) M
100     FORMAT (I4)
        XM = M
        DO 10 I = 1, 10
10      S(I) = 0
        DO 20 J = 1, M
        XJ = J
        DO 20 I = 1, 10
20      S(I) = S(I) + (XJ/XM)**I
        DO 30 I = 1, 10
30      WRITE (6, 200) I, S(I)
200     FORMAT (1X, I3, F12.4)
        GO TO 5
        END
```

For $m = 10$

1	5.5000
2	3.8500
3	3.0250
4	2.5333
5	2.2082
6	1.9784
7	1.8080
8	1.6773
9	1.5743
10	1.4914

For $m = 100$

1	50.4996
2	33.8348
3	25.5024
4	20.5033
5	17.1708
6	14.7907
7	13.0058
8	11.6178
9	10.5075
10	9.5992

For $m = 1000$

1	500.4612
2	333.8184
3	250.4964
4	200.4974
5	167.1644
6	143.3554
7	125.4987
8	111.6100
9	100.4993
10	91.4086

27   (a) $A = 4.305$ $n = 22.737$
       (b) $A = 4.531$ $n = 19.881$

28    $E = 25.36 \cdot 10^3$ ksi
       $\sigma_0 = 9.69$ ksi
       $\epsilon_0 = -0.382 \cdot 10^{-3}$
       $E_p = 0.1159 \cdot 10^3$ ksi
       $\sigma_p = 111.652$ ksi
       $\sigma_y = 112.12$ ksi
       $A = 3.122$
       $n = 23.457$

39   (i) The slope of $Ax + By = 1$ is $-A/B$. Thus the slope of a line perpendicular to that line is B/A. A line with this latter slope and passing through (x_i, y_i) has the equation

$$-Bx + Ay = Ay_i - Bx_i$$

The intersection of this line with $Ax + By = 1$ is at

$$x_0 = \frac{A - ABy_i + B^2x_i}{A^2 + B^2}$$

$$y_0 = \frac{B + A^2y_i - ABx_i}{A^2 + B^2}$$

The distance from (x_i, y_i) to (x_0, y_0) is

$$d_i = \sqrt{(x_i - x_0)^2 + (y_i - y_0)^2}$$

which becomes, upon simplification,

$$d_i = \frac{Ax_i + By_i - 1}{\sqrt{A^2 + B^2}}$$

(ii) We wish to minimize

$$S = \Sigma \frac{(Ax_i + By_i - 1)^2}{A^2 + B^2}$$

The two partial derivatives of S with respect to A and B when set equal to zero produce (a) and (b) respectively.

(iii) Observe that the procedure outlined to combine equations makes the coefficients of Σx_i^2, $\Sigma x_i y_i$, and Σy_i^2 vanish.

(iv) One fairly simple procedure is to solve (c) for B, i.e.,

$$B = \frac{m - (\Sigma x_i)A}{(\Sigma y_i)}$$

Use this to replace B in either (a) or (b). The result is a cubic equation in A. A cubic equation has at least one real root. All three roots must be found if they are real. For each of the real roots, B is evaluated from the last equation above. All possible pairs of values of A and B must be checked to see which pair really minimizes Σd_i^2.

40

$$d_i = y_i - (a_0 x_i^{b_0} + c_0) - [x_i^{b_0}\alpha + a_0 x_i^{b_0}(\log x_i)\beta + \gamma]$$

Letting

$$r_i = y_i - (a_0 x_i^{b_0} + c_0)$$

and taking partial derivatives of Σd_i^2 with respect to α, β, and γ

$$(\Sigma x_i^{2b_0})\alpha + a_0(\Sigma x_i^{2b_0}\log x_i)\beta + (\Sigma x_i^{b_0})\gamma = \Sigma r_i x_i^{b_0}$$
$$(\Sigma x_i^{2b_0}\log x_i)\alpha + a_0[\Sigma x_i^{2b_0}(\log x_i)^2]\beta + (\Sigma x_i^{b_0}\log x_i)\gamma = \Sigma r_i x_i^{b_0}\log x_i$$
$$(\Sigma x_i^{b_0})\alpha + (\Sigma x_i^{b_0}\log x_i)\beta + m\gamma = \Sigma r_i$$

These are three linear equations for α, β, and γ.

Chapter 8 **2** (a) 31.64
(b) 34.87
(c) 35.85
(d) 36.64
(e) 37.07
(f) 36.85
(g) 37.07
(h) 36.85
(i) 37.50
(j) 36.82
(k) 36.69
(l) 36.76

17 Let $z = y'$. Then

$$z' = F(x) - y$$
$$y' = z$$

Iterations of the corrector are still required because the y-value on the right of the first equation is a result produced by the predictor and is no more accurate than the z-value.

22 (a) $A_0 + A_1 = 1$
$-A_1 + B_0 = 1$
$A_1 \quad = 1$

25 (a) Milne.
(b) $A_0 + A_1 + A_2 \quad = 1$
$-A_1 - 2A_2 + B_0 + B_1 = 1$
$A_1 + 4A_2 - 2B_1 \quad = 1$

$$-A_1 - 8A_2 + 3B_1 = 1$$
$$A_1 + 16A_2 - 4B_1 = 1$$

(d) Fifth.

27 (a) Implicit.

(b)
$$a_0 + a_1 = 1$$
$$-a_1 + b_{-1} + b_0 + b_1 = 1$$
$$a_1 + 2b_{-1} - 2b_1 = 1$$
$$-a_1 + 3b_{-1} + 3b_1 = 1$$

(c) Because there are four equations in five unknowns, and thus infinitely many solutions.

(d) $a_0 = 1 - a_1$

$$b_{-1} = \frac{5 - a_1}{12}$$

$$b_0 = \frac{2a_1 + 2}{3}$$

$$b_1 = \frac{5a_1 - 1}{12}$$

28 The solution is $y = e^{-5x}$.
(a) A second-order Runge-Kutta method produces poor results while (b) a fourth-order method is quite accurate. (c) A second-order method is unstable for $h > 0.4$ whereas a fourth-order method is not, i.e., partial instability accounts for the difference in the solutions.

29 Partial instability.

36 For $h = 5$, 96 evaluations are required, and for $h = 10$, 44. The number of evaluations continues to decrease for larger step sizes. The decision on step size would ordinarily depend more on the accuracy required and such considerations as whether values are needed at points suitable for plotting. If these factors are of no importance, the answer to the question would be "as large as possible."

41 Let $y' = z$
$$z' = g(x, y, z)$$
Applying the improved Euler method to this system of equations

$$y_{m+1} = y_m + \frac{h}{2}(2z_m + hz'_m) \tag{a}$$

$$z_{m+1} = z_m + \frac{h}{2}[g(x_m, y_m, z_m) + g(x_m + h, y_m + hy'_m, z_m + hz'_m)]$$

The latter becomes, upon replacing z by y',

$$y'_{m+1} = y'_m + \frac{1}{2}(k_1 + k_2)$$

where

$$k_1 = hg(x_m, y_m, z_m)$$
$$k_2 = hg(x_m + h, y_m + hy'_m, y'_m + k_1)$$

Then (a) becomes

$$y_{m+1} = y_m + hz_m + \frac{h^2}{2} g(x_m, y_m, y'_m)$$

$$= y_m + hy'_m + \frac{h}{2} k_1$$

Index

This index was prepared using a
Fortran program that was run on
the time-sharing facilities of
National CSS, Inc.